The Practice of
Collective Bargaining

THE IRWIN SERIES IN ECONOMICS

Consulting Editor
LLOYD G. REYNOLDS   *Yale University*

The Practice of Collective Bargaining

EDWIN F. BEAL
University of Oregon

EDWARD D. WICKERSHAM
Late of the University of Detroit

PHILIP K. KIENAST
University of Washington

 Fifth Edition   1976

RICHARD D. IRWIN, INC.   Homewood, Illinois   60430

Irwin-Dorsey Limited   Georgetown, Ontario   L7G 4B3

Fifth Edition

First Printing, April 1976
Second Printing, November 1976

ISBN 0-256-01821-9
Library of Congress Catalog Card No. 75-35098
Printed in the United States of America

Preface

INSTRUCTORS adopting this textbook for the first time, students new to the field, and those who have used the book in the past, all are undoubtedly aware that in a field of study as active as collective bargaining, a textbook that is not from time to time updated falls behind the pace of events. But they will want assurance, too, that enduring aspects of the subject have not been cast aside for the interests of the moment. We have tried in this revision to meet both sets of expectations.

We have updated factual material, including tables and statistics. Our text brings forward into the present the chronicle of development in unionism, labor-management relations, labor relations law and administration, and public sector bargaining. We present a completely revised and contemporary annotated bibliography, probably the most extensive and authoritative in any comparable textbook. Users of this fifth edition can be confident that in adopting it they are keeping up to date.

We have preserved the integrity of treatment of theory and principles underlying practice that was so well received in preceding editions, but have improved, we think, the order of presentation of the topics and the clarity and readability of the chapters treating them.

In this edition we have added a new chapter on unions of professional and white collar workers (Chapter 14) and dropped one chapter of the three that formerly treated the wage and effort bargain, combining what was relevant in it with the revised chapter on pay levels (Chapter 10). We offer a much strengthened, completely rewritten chapter on management organization for collective bargaining (Chapter 4) that takes account of recent contributions from organization theory.

We have retained the appendixes that reproduce the text of current federal labor relations law, a feature much appreciated in the past by both students and instructors. We have cut down on the number of cases in the book but have provided a diversified selection, retaining from past editions those that have proved to be most useful and adding new ones.

To sum up, we think we have made an already well accepted textbook even more useful to those involved in teaching and in learning about collective bargaining in the United States today.

Our goal in this fifth edition of our book, as it was in the fourth and earlier editions, has been to take another step forward in our attempts to analyze the practice of collective bargaining in the United States. Our viewpoints are set in perspective against developments in the theory of collective bargaining, the ongoing research of behavioral scientists, and the onward march of economic and social progress. The probable effects of recent and anticipated changes in the structure of employment in the United States on collective bargaining are analyzed.

The conclusions set forth in these pages have come out of the experience of the authors as teachers, consultants, arbitrators, and representatives in collective bargaining situations in the United States and Europe. Most of the material presented here has been used by the authors in the college classroom and special refresher courses for management and union representatives. Teachers and students who have used this material have been most helpful in suggesting ways of clarifying the issues and improving the presentation of materials.

Some of the explanations and interpretations given by the authors may be found, like other writings in this far-from-settled field, to be controversial. The authors take full responsibility for all such statements of position and for errors or omissions that have eluded them in preparing the material for the press.

ACKNOWLEDGMENTS

We are grateful to many people for their constructive criticism and helpful suggestions. Our greatest debt is to Lloyd G. Reynolds of Yale University for reading the first edition manuscript and for his valuable and helpful comments then and since. Dale S. Beach of Rensselaer Polytechnic Institute provided constructive criticism and valuable suggestions that were important to the revised edition. Thomas W. Gavett, West Virginia University, Dalton E. McFarland, Michigan State University, Thomas H. Patten, Jr., University of Detroit, Dell Bush Johannesen, University of North Carolina, and George W. Buckingham, Jr., provided valuable comments that helped improve, successively, the third and fourth, and this fifth edition.

Many publishers generously granted permission to reproduce copyrighted material. Special thanks are due to the Bureau of National Affairs, Inc., for the use of cases in Part Five of the book. As the publisher of *Labor Arbitration Reports* they provided the material used in Cases 1, 3 through 5, and 10 through 18. Credit to the arbitrator in these and other cases is given in the introduction to the cases themselves.

Thanks are also due to the American Arbitration Association; the

American Management Association; the Bureau of National Affairs, Inc.; Commerce Clearing House; the Committee for Economic Development; the Economic Research Department of the Chamber of Commerce of the United States; the Foundation on Employee Health, Medical Care and Welfare, Inc.; *Harvard Business Review;* Division of Research, Graduate School of Business Administration, Harvard University; *Industrial and Labor Relations Review; Industrial Management Review;* Industrial Relations Counselors, Inc.; New York State School of Industrial and Labor Relations at Cornell University; National Industrial Conference Board; Prentice-Hall, Inc., Public Affairs Press; George Strauss of the University of California; John Wiley & Sons, Inc.; and AFL–CIO and governmental sources. Appropriate credit is given at the places where the material is used.

We are grateful to Peter Feuille, State University of New York at Buffalo, for updating and improving the annotated topic bibliographies; Mildred Carmack, University of Oregon Law School, for the material on Title VII of the Civil Rights Act of 1964 in Chapter 5; Donald W. Brodie, University of Oregon Law School, for the notes on court decisions in the appendixes to Chapter 5, 6, 7, and 13; and to James W. Mitchum, of the University of Oregon Industrial and Labor Relations Institute, for help in updating charts and tables.

For this edition Philip K. Kienast revised Chapters 15 and 16 that make up Part Five, The Public Sector. The rest of the book remains the responsibility of the senior author, Edwin F. Beal.

March 1976   EDWIN F. BEAL
                                                               PHILIP K. KIENAST

Contents

part one

Organizing for Collective Bargaining

Part One of this book explores the nature of the collective bargaining system in the United States and the parties who have a vital interest in the operation of the system. It deals primarily with formal organizations designed to represent the interests of employers, workers, and the general public, and presents historical background on the unions and collective bargaining.

1 The Collective Bargaining System

COLLECTIVE BARGAINING centers in the enterprise, where workers and managers meet. From there, it has to look outward and upward into the international unions and union federations, the employer organizations, the government agencies concerned with labor relations. It also has to look inward and downward to the departments that make up the enterprise, the work groups in the departments, the cliques and factions in the local union. The point of view remains that of the enterprise; for the enterprise—not the industry, not the state or nation—is the highest autonomous unit of economic activity in capitalist society. The enterprise and the local union: these are what take up the foreground of the field of view in the study of collective bargaining; and collective bargaining is the only study that takes them both in and concentrates on their relationship. Collective bargaining is the formal and institutionalized interaction of representatives of workers and management to regulate relations at the work place during the working day and establish wages and work standards.

It is quite true, as later chapters in this book will show, that there is a trend toward carrying the practice of collective bargaining to higher levels, above the individual enterprise. Many of today's labor agreements are reached by unions and associations of employers rather than, in the first instance, between a local union and its enterprise. That is, in fact, and has long been the rule in an important segment of the economy, the construction industry, but it is still the exception in mass-production industry. Even so, that does not take collective bargaining out of the enterprise. The rules laid down in the master agreement reach into the enterprise. They almost always have to leave important questions to be settled specifically and in detail at enterprise level. Local agreements supplement the master agreements and apply their terms to the local situation. Furthermore, administering and enforcing agreement terms is always an enterprise responsibility: management's and the local union's. One field of enormous present importance deals almost exclusively with enterprise incidents and issues: that is industrial arbitration.

This book makes no apologies for centering the study of collective bargaining in the enterprise, and on the relations between its management and the members and officers of the local union. It is from this vantage point that the entire system can best be seen in meaningful perspective. But enterprises differ from each other. So do unions; and so, consequently, do the relations between them. No single enterprise is more than a unit—often an inconsiderable one—of the total economy whose markets bind together the whole system of production and exchange of goods and services. In the same way, collective bargaining, which is specific and particular in the enterprise, goes on there as a part and extension of an entire system, the industrial relations system. This is a subsystem of the general social system, and collective bargaining is one of the forms it takes.

The concept of the industrial relations system as a subsystem of the enveloping social system comes from the work of John T. Dunlop, a Harvard professor who, before he became Secretary of Labor in 1975, was one of the scholars who attempted to explain collective bargaining in a theoretical setting in the present day.

What follows in this chapter states Dunlop's position in summary form. Dunlop is a prolific writer on economics and on many specific issues of collective bargaining. He brought together some of his ideas on collective bargaining theory, considering the matter as a whole, in a single book, *Industrial Relations Systems*, published in 1958.

It is hard to still further compress ideas already stated in concentrated form, but the main points can be outlined. The writers of this book accept the general framework Dunlop laid down, borrow from it, and acknowledge their debt to him, but do not follow him exactly. What we present here is a paraphrase and not a reproduction of Dunlop's thoughts; it rearranges the order of his presentation, but sticks to the line of argument he laid down and builds upon the base he laid.

THE INDUSTRIAL RELATIONS SYSTEM

Dunlop sees the industrial relations system as a set of relationships between people in society which take place under particular conditions. This can be studied—abstracted—in exactly the way economists study market relations, and political scientists study power relations. The industrial relations system, like the economic system and the political system, is a subsystem of the general social system. All three of these subsystems overlap in part and interact with the others. The industrial relations system, Dunlop says, may be studied in terms of what he calls three contexts. These are the market context; the context of technology at the workplace; and the context of power relations of the enveloping society, as reflected in the workplace.

The Three Contexts

Every enterprise or organization lives and grows (or withers and dies) by satisfying (or failing to satisfy) some human need and effective market demand, whether this be for cigarette lighters or for child welfare services. This is true for the private enterprise, and it is just as true for the governmental agency or nonprofit private organization, where the "market" consists of the budgetary limitations within which the agency must operate. In the long run, no enterprise can put more into its operation than it gets out of the market. Thus in any given period the market context limits the possibilities open to any given enterprise. The market therefore has a hand in determining the technology of the workplace, which is the second limiting context of the industrial relations system. For example, the mass market for cars at prices buyers are willing to pay practically dictates the technology of mass production and pushes the manufacturers toward automation. Relations between workers and managers in a Detroit factory today take shape in these contexts.

In turn, the technology of the workplace (or work flow, and the kind of jobs created at individual stations along the work flow) determines the kind of people brought into the production process in any given enterprise, and their relations with each other. The sizable remnant of handicraft technology upon which the construction industry still depends brings into that industry the skilled building trades worker who has served a trade apprenticeship and mastered a craft. Mass-production industry, on the other hand, calls mainly for semiskilled workers who get their training on the job. Such jobs consist of simple and usually repetitive tasks, easily learned and leading to no comprehensive mastery of a complex set of skills. In this way both the qualifications of the individual employees and their relations to the work, to those who manage and direct their efforts, and to each other grow out of the technology of the workplace, and work flows.

It may be worthwhile at this point to make clear the concept of workplace technology, as seen by the authors of this book. There are, as they see it, three technologies: handicraft, mass production, and automation.

In *handicraft* production, the goods produced or services rendered and sold by the employer are turned out directly by the labor of skilled craftsmen, working with their hands and with hand tools. These skilled people may have nonskilled helpers, but it is what the skilled people do that transforms the raw materials into the finished product. Thus there may be those who haul bricks and mortar to a construction site, but each brick is placed in the wall, by hand, by a bricklayer who has spent years learning that trade. Neither the contractor nor the construction supervisor needs to tell this person *how* to do the job; all they need to communicate is *what* they want done.

In *mass-production* manufacturing the employer's product is turned out directly by nonskilled operators, working with their hands or with machines, assisted by a few skilled workers. In an automobile assembly plant, for example, the employee working at any station along the line does only a simple, small part of what it takes to put a car together. This employee comes on the job without knowing either what to do or how to do it. Management trains the worker on the job, may even rigidly prescribe the exact bodily motions to complete the operation cycle. The movement of the conveyor paces the speed of the work. This is a semiskilled worker. Others more skilled may help, by making the tools and dies, or the jigs and fixtures, or they may set up or repair and maintain the machines; but it is the semiskilled who turn out the product. (Some employers are experimenting with "job enrichment" to help relieve this boring routine. See Chapter 10.) There is a wide range of semiskills, from almost completely unskilled work to tasks requiring the highest degree of expertise. The difference between expertise and skill in this context is that the expert is a specialist, the skilled worker a generalist at a trade. Later chapters in this book will deal with the question more fully.

Under the technology of *automation*, the product is literally turned out by machines without direct human labor, skilled or nonskilled. Technicians program the work, which the machines perform otherwise unaided. Skilled craftsmen maintain and repair the machines. Semiskilled workers "supervise" the machines; that is, they see that the machines are kept supplied, that nothing occurs that might cause a malfunction, and they turn the machines on and off as necessary or when directed.

These are the three technologies, in their historical order. Mass production displaced handicraft technology in manufacturing wherever there was a mass market. It proved capable of bringing products into common use, like airplanes and refrigerators, that were beyond the practical reach of handicraft technology. It did not exterminate the handicrafts: they flourish today in local and luxury or specialty markets. Automation now seems to be displacing mass production in many areas, but not in all. Automation depends to an even greater degree on mass markets. It cannot completely drive out either mass production or the handicrafts. The three technologies will serve different sectors of the market, different consumer needs.

The three technologies show most clearly in manufacturing, but have their application in the extractive, distributive, and service industries. This will be examined in later chapters. Also, the three general technologies described in principle above take on reality and concrete form in application to various industries, and, within an industry, to an enterprise. Each workplace may be said to have its own technology. This consists of the application of one or more of the three basic technologies, objectified in actual machines and equipment arranged in a specific layout of work stations, designed to carry out the processes of the particular enterprise.

The third of Dunlop's contexts is that of power relations in the enveloping social system, as reflected in the enterprise. Management writers today define power as a relationship, the reciprocal of which is dependence; they call this the power/dependence relationship. An employer or manager who has unrestricted authority to hire and fire, to grant or withhold a raise or privilege, has power over an employee, but only to the extent that the employee is dependent on the job, the raise, or (emotionally, perhaps, through the ego) on the privilege or distinction. Let the degree of dependence diminish—as when a labor agreement puts conditions on the exercise of management authority—and the power diminishes with it. Employer and employee now stand in a new power/dependence relationship.

This is not to say that power is the only—or even the essential—element of labor-management relations. There may be mutual esteem, affection, confidence, and respect. To cite an analogy: Parents have power over their children, but the stronger bond between them may be fully reciprocated love. When the children grow up and gain their independence the parental power is gone, but the love may remain. For that matter, an employer is as completely dependent on employees as they are on the employer. The difference is that while the employer depends on them collectively, as a work force, their dependence—that is, on the jobs they hold—is individual. The employer may be quite independent of any one of them and therefore, practically speaking, of all of them, unless they act together as a work force. Thus when employees organize in an "outside" union, they alter the power context inside the enterprise. The act of organizing is itself a reflection of the power relations of the enveloping social system, which must be such as to tolerate or encourage union organization.

The Contexts Are Dynamic

It should be noted at this point, and never forgotten, that the three contexts are not static elements but dynamic forces. They change; they interact. A context stands as given only for a single period, or point of time, in a particular analysis, not for eternity.

In a given market context, for instance, changes in technology can generate forces that change the market which, in turn, encourages the spread of that technology. Thus at the time of the Industrial Revolution, a growing, but still only potential, mass market welcomed the developing technology of mass production, initially of textiles but subsequently of other factory-made goods. The availability of cheap and highly functional factory products in turn strengthened the market and swept competing handicraft products off the counter.

The United States provides another example drawn from the early years of this century. An existing demand for means of local transportation was met through the local manufacture, by handicraft methods, of horse-drawn buggies and wagons. The earliest automobiles were also custom built by handicraft methods and sold in a luxury market—rich people to whom the mechanical buggies were a new toy and a visible symbol of their wealth. Then Henry Ford adapted the technology of mass production to the new product and began the serialized manufacture of a cheap and practical car, the famous Model T. The Model T welded the scattered local markets of the carriage makers into a national mass market for gas-powered vehicles. Anyone wanting now to serve this market had to compete with Henry Ford and had to adopt mass-production technology.

It ought not to be necessary to multiply examples to underscore the interdependence and interaction of the contexts.

These three contexts make up one of the theoretical concepts Dunlop offers. Another constitutes his identification of what he calls the actors. Who are the actors?

The Actors

Dunlop uses the word "actors" to refer to the participants or parties to industrial relations activity. There seems to be no good reason not to follow his terminology. There are three actors: (1) managers and their hierarchy both within the enterprise and in employer associations at levels above the enterprise; (2) workers and their hierarchy of organized representatives within the enterprise and above or beyond it; and (3) "regulators," agents of government who play specific roles in the industrial relations system, plus nongovernmental agents and agencies (such as, for example, arbitrators) called into being by the other actors.

The actors, as identified by Dunlop, are groups of individuals or organizations. It would be well at the outset to consider what brings individuals into the following groupings: (1) the worker and the enterprise, (2) the worker and the local union, and (3) the local union with other union organizations. In a free society, each of these relationships must be based on a degree of mutual consent—a mutually beneficial exchange.

The potential work force of a modern enterprise consists of individuals who are free to contract for their own labor. Of their own free will they may decline a particular offer of employment; but they are driven by individual needs to accept *some* offer, for without a job most people cannot live except on charity. The needs of the individual and the needs of the enterprise are reciprocal. Every individual needs to find a job, and to hold a job or jobs, and to earn a decent living at acceptable levels of effort. The reciprocal needs of the enterprise are to find suitable employees, to hold an appropriate work force, and to get competitive productivity from that work force. The relationship of the worker to the enterprise is explored in greater detail in Chapter 3.

Workers join and remain members of a union either because they consider it to be to their advantage or because they believe that the disadvantages of nonmembership outweigh the disadvantages of membership. They may want to belong to a union because they believe that this membership will raise wages, or give status, or provide an opportunity for pleasant social contacts, or they may accept union membership only because they feel that this is less onerous than losing jobs or enduring social ostracism from co-workers.

Union affiliation usually goes beyond simple membership in an autonomous local union. Union associations beyond the individual and autonomous enterprises of the local unions are, in part, a rational recognition of market and political forces beyond the enterprise, which if not met in a unified way may seriously impede the effectiveness of the autonomous units. Thus it is reasonable to expect that individual and autonomous unions of Chrysler, Ford, and General Motors workers would have certain market interests in common and would form a supralocal union to deal with these problems. On the political scene, a federation of 15 million members would be a more influential spokesman than 75,000 autonomous but unconnected locals representing the same membership.

Managers. Managers are the primary actors because they establish the enterprise, set its goals, exercise initiative in choosing the technology to be employed, and ultimately are accountable for the success or failure of the enterprise. Managers create and control the institution which provides employment opportunities. Chapter 4 discusses the problems confronting managers in creating an organization for effective employee relations. The discussion in Chapter 4 will deal with the nature of its organizational structure for effective employee relations.

Employee Organizations. This book argues that there are two "model" types of employee representative organizations, craft unions and industrial unions, and a third that combines some of the attributes of both, amalgamated unions. Since references to the models will occur throughout the book, it would be well to introduce them now. Chapter 3 compares the models in the course of a discussion of union organizational structure.

The Craft Union Model. Handicraft technology is the technological context in which craft unions appear. The building construction industry is the most prominent example of handicraft technology in modern American industry. Handicraft industry consists of enterprises in which the employer sells a product or service which is turned out directly by the hands of craftsmen. These craftsmen are workers who have served an apprenticeship or have learned by long experience an entire recognized trade, such as plumbing, carpentry, sheet metal work, or electricity.

Skilled labor here is a *direct* factor of production. Without the skilled labor of trained craftsmen, working with hand or power tools, the employer would have no product or service to sell. Not finding skilled workers, there would be no business, for it takes time to train skilled workers; indeed, it takes years. If the skilled workers were lost, production would stop, for there is no substitute for their skill.

The construction industry depends upon and uses to this day the handicraft method of production. Its product market is local. Construction work is carried out on the spot by skilled workers, who bring their efforts to bear on the building as it grows in place. Nonskilled workers may haul bricks to a construction site, but the brick is laid in the wall by qualified bricklayers who have served trade apprenticeships and are skilled craftsmen.

Job content in any given area of skill is the same; one carpenter performs the same kind of work as another carpenter; one roofer does the same job as another. Every skilled worker must at various times perform each of a range of tasks associated with the trade. In any given craft the worker qualifications are the same. Each worker must command a certain range of knowledge and of manual skills, common and traditional to the craft. The consequence is that in the handicrafts, for any given craft or trade, labor is homogeneous. It is not entirely surprising, then, to find workers organized according to their particular skills into separate craft unions.

"One skill, one union" might well be the slogan of craft unions. The local craft union takes in all the craftsmen of its trade in any particular locality, and no others. (This may include, however, helpers and apprentices.) When these skilled workers go on the job the employer does not have to tell them or show them *how* to do the work. They know how. They need only be told *what* they are to do. They take it from there.

While it may not be surprising to find craft unions organized along lines of skill, it is still necessary to explain why they actually do so organize. A general contractor employs not only carpenters but masons, bricklayers, plumbers, plasterers—an entire array of skills. Why should not all of these be organized in a single union to bargain for them all with their common employer? Again the context of technology supplies the answer.

Erecting a building calls for the use of skills *in sequence*. At one time the only work performed at a building site is clearing the land and excavation. This is pick and shovel work for unskilled laborers, or for the semiskilled tractor and bulldozer operators who have replaced them. Next, there is the rough carpentry work in the construction of forms for pouring concrete foundations; and work for masons, eventually for bricklayers, perhaps for ironworkers, certainly for carpenters. The plasterers, the painters, the sheet metal workers, the roofers, and many other crafts do not come on the job until later. By the time the electrician has wired the building, for instance, there is usually no further need for masonry workers.

Thus the personnel, the skills involved, and the actual crews employed are seldom the same from one week to the next. There is much overlap; but any given construction project, if surveyed at different points in time, will show a different composition of the work force.

The labor market reflects this technological need of the construction industry. For efficient operation it is necessary to have pools of all the various skills, from which any given construction project may draw at just the time such skills are needed on the job. It is also necessary that those employed when their skills are needed should be released when the need is over, so that they may go on to another project at a different stage of development. The employer needs to have the skills held separate, and administered separately, in order to have them available only when needed. No contractor could afford to keep a crew of painters on the payroll from the time of ground breaking just to paint the finished structure, nor retain the operators of the ground-moving equipment after the foundations had been laid.

The result of these necessary conditions, established by the context of the product market and the context of technology, is to bring into being as an actor, opposite the enterpriser, an entire galaxy of local unions organized by skills: craft unions. The fact of unionization introduces a new element in the context of power relations which influence the workplace rules and give rise to craft union practices.

At heart, craft unions are conservative. They guard and hoard an ancient skill and tradition that goes back to the medieval guilds. Though not direct descendants of the guilds, craft unions are their counterparts in today's changed situation and perform for our society the handicraft services the guilds performed for theirs. They are fraternities, entered by initiation and apprenticeship, practicing—as the guilds did—a "mystery," the secrets of the trade.

They make their bargains over wages by a strategy of bidding a restricted supply against what they conceive to be a fixed or relatively fixed demand. The essentially economic nature of their activity gives them a "lump of work" mentality that is hard to alter. That is, they see only so much work available (so many buildings to be erected, for example, during a given construction season), hence the need for only so many workers of a craft or trade. This contrasts with the outlook of indefinite—almost infinite—production in a factory.

Scarcity of work, scarcity of skills, scarcity of product (always, of course, in relative terms) are the concepts in which craft unions deal in a scarcity sector—the handicraft sector—of the economy. They more often resist than welcome innovation; they more often resist than gladly adopt devices (such as skill-saving machinery) that would change the ways and habits of the craft.

A society moving restlessly and relentlessly forward into the abundance and the potentially limitless production made possible by factory methods puts craft unions on the defensive. The defensive position is a strong one wherever handicraft methods still prevail. Well-entrenched craft unions have even held their own in places where technology has conquered some of the problems of their craft. Craft unions and craft-union bargaining will be with us for a long time.

The Industrial Union Model. Mass-production technology carries even further the *division of labor* by the breakdown of a set of what were formerly skilled operations into a series of simple tasks. No individual is the craftsman of the product turned out by a factory. Instead, the entire factory becomes a composite, or collective, craftsman. Its few skilled workers do not turn out the production; all they do is help the other workers, by preparing work for them, repairing, or setting up their machines. The bulk of the employees are nonskilled. They have come to be called *semiskilled* workers.

Unlike the craftsman, the semiskilled operator has not spent years of apprenticeship or mastered a recognized trade. He or she learns on the job, while working, coming to the job without any knowledge of its tasks. Training does not take long. The jobs are easily learned, and each of the workers specializes in a very minor part of the total process. This specialization may in some cases reach the point of a very high degree of *expertise*. It differs from the skill of a craftsman in that it is specialized rather than general, and often not applicable to anything but the particular processes of the workplace where it is exercised.

Perhaps a simple illustration will make clear the distinction we draw in this book between skill and expertise.

The secretary to a business executive comes on the job with the basic skills of shorthand and typing, backed up by knowledge that rests on a certain level of general education and special training. The boss would not expect to teach a secretary any of the skills and in fact would probably not possess them. The on-the-job training which could not have been learned in secretarial school is how the particular organization works, its rules, procedures, and its people, and how to handle the affairs of a particular executive's unique position in the organization. The secretary becomes more valuable to the boss the longer employed, not because of mere skills, but because of special knowledge and expertise.

If the secretary should quit, the boss would feel lost. A replacement would have all the skills, but not the expertise, and would need time to acquire it. On the other hand, the ex-secretary could take those skills to a new job, but a new boss in another organization would have no use for the expertise that made the secretary so valuable before. The worker would have to start all over again, acquiring new expertise.

In this book, therefore, what is meant by *skill* is the range of knowledge, ability, manual dexterity, and performance capability that is mastered through an apprenticeship in one of the recognized trades.[1]

What is meant by *expertise* is expertness, deftness, ability, or knowledge of some specialized task or group of tasks, such as can be acquired only through experience at that task, or on the job which groups those tasks.

Job content, under mass-production technology, consists of a variety of

---

[1] Some readers may appropriately comment that the authors are putting too great emphasis on a formal apprenticeship and that many journeymen members of craft union locals have not served a formal apprenticeship. Such a criticism is sound and based on solid facts. The authors would respond to this criticism only by arguing that the existence of a formal apprenticeship program does establish the content of a trade and that the apprenticeship program is recognized as the best method of receiving the training necessary to master the trade. Those journeymen who have acquired membership in the union without serving the apprenticeship typically have very long experience working in most if not all of the specialized segments of the trade.

semiskills, up to the highest degree of expertise. Worker qualifications to meet this job content are, initially, simple aptitudes. With training and experience, aptitude turns into ability to perform one particular task or a small group of related semiskills—into expertise.

While there is labor turnover in the factory, and movement in and out of the work force, the factory is a stable organization. That is, it replaces individuals from time to time, but there is not much displacement of jobs. The shoe factory must always and simultaneously have people who cut out soles, who stitch uppers, who sew or glue liners, who pack the finished pairs. The automobile assembly plants need workers at every designated station along the line, all the time, each doing different tasks which are coordinated by the production plans and layout to build the car. The result of this is that the appropriate organization for employees cannot be based on any given skill, for these are not skilled jobs. Organization has to be based on the entire coordinated process in the workplace; workplace unionism or industrial unionism.

The slogan of the industrial union might well be "one shop, one union." In the industrial union all the employees working for a given enterprise at a given workplace belong to the same local union without regard for what they do in the plant. The industrial union local takes in not only the semiskilled who directly turn out the product but such skilled workers also as may play an auxiliary part in the production process. It takes in, too, the completely unskilled, such as janitors or a yard gang—if there be any in the plant.

At the workplace the factory employee must accept direction, supervision, discipline, that inevitably looks upon each worker as a "replaceable part." Each is a unit in an integrated whole, highly differentiated in its parts, subdivided into specialties and groups of specialties, variable in magnitude up to the factory employing tens of thousands. It is necessary for every one of them, as workers in this vast complex, to be at their machine or station at the minute when all the others are at theirs, to work while they work, at a set pace, and to quit when they quit work for the day. They move in crowds as they enter and leave the gate, and at the noon-hour break.

They never see the shareholders who own the factory; rarely see the manager who runs it. Management, to them, is a supervisor who is a hired hand like themselves, and has a boss who has a boss in an upward chain of command reaching to a shining but far-distant pinnacle. The three simple upward steps in status from apprentice to journeyman to master that stand clear before the craftsman have given way to a dizzy stairway of many steps that leads up out of sight. There is no longer any personal warmth or friendly contact between employer and employee. Orders come down from on high, to be obeyed; no visible means exists for sending comment and questions back up the line.

The workers who make their living in a factory have lost the status that skill gives the craftsman. They have lost independence and become dependent. They never learned the craftsman's satisfaction in work as a creative act. What have they gained?

They have gained money wages that outdistance what they could earn elsewhere as an unskilled laborer. They have begun to earn without serving an apprenticeship, at a real wage that is enough to live on. As they gain practice in a specialty they may, under an incentive system, take home pay that compares favorably with the craftsman's earnings.

Their union does not fight the technology of the factory, does not object to new machines, new processes. Instead, it seeks to master them. Above all, it strives to secure for its own members, through seniority rights and the right to retraining, the new opportunities technology creates.

Internally, it practices democracy and suffers from ills that beset democratic institutions with a heterogeneous citizenry: the pulling and hauling of special interest groups; the seesaw of ins and outs, and controversy over policy and tactics; membership indifference and inaction when there are no pressing issues in the air. Today, the threat of mass displacement as a result of technological change puts the industrial union under a strain. Fewer and fewer of the overriding issues can be settled in the shop; only a rear-guard action can be fought there against mass displacement. The interests of threatened members can be furthered only by such broad social action as government can take. At the same time, concrete adjustment to the new technology has to be made where it appears: on the shop floor.

Industrial union leadership, with a generation of experience behind it now, is wary, and conscious of the dangers facing it. It is ready to cooperate, but ready still, if necessary, to fight.

The Amalgamated Union Model. This variant combines certain features of both basic models. It is not common, but important where it occurs. The garment industries provide an example.

The skill of the tailor turns cloth, thread, and other materials into a completed garment made to the customer's measure. Tailors have plied their craft since people began to wear clothes. The factory system with its division of labor broke down the process into a set of subskills, resulting in a product that is not a perfect fit but a nearfit: ready-made clothes in standard sizes that with minor alterations can be made to fit most normal wearers. For various reasons, however, the economics and technology of the industry did not jump from the single craftsman sitting cross-legged on a bench to the full scale factory. The putting-out, or homework system, a stage of the early Industrial Revolution, persisted longer than in other manufactures, and turned into a system of subcontracting. This brought into being many small, independent entrepreneurs, each of whose workshops carried the garment one stage further toward completion and sale. A workshop tended to employ people who had acquired one or another of the subskills of the tailor's trade. When they unionized, they formed what might be considered truncated craft unions of the various subcrafts. In structure and behavior they followed the craft union model.

Eventually, large-scale factory production evolved, particularly in men's clothing, where changes in style are comparatively slow. Big companies like Hart, Schaffner & Marx and Hickey-Freeman, reassembled, as it were, the complete range of tailoring skills under a single roof and management. The separate craft unions now found it desirable to amalgamate, and deal with their factory employer as if they were an industrial union. Through a joint board, with representatives of all the crafts, they negotiate a single agreement for the factory work force. At the same time, they retain their autonomy, because subcontracting still prevails in the industry and is likely to continue. Changes in style, especially in the women's garment industry, often favor—at least temporarily—the producer whose investment is minimal.

The amalgamated union thus meets a dual challenge: the necessity of dealing with the industry's giants in the factory, where the industrial union model applies, and the need for dealing with the small shops where the craft model is appropriate. Amalgamated unions are thus both models in one, depending on the employer with whom they deal.

Government.   The third actor, or regulator, in the collective bargaining system is mainly, but not solely, the government. The role of government in American collective bargaining is largely permissive. Nevertheless, the state is the ultimate source of power and order in any economic system. In other countries, the state plays a more important role in setting the conditions of employment than is true in the United States. In some countries the state itself carries out activities which are performed by unions in the United States. The rules for rule-making which the United States government establishes are of interest to the general public and vital to the two main actors in the collective bargaining system.

Employer and union organizations designed to influence the formulation of rules for rule-making are discussed in Chapters 3 and 4. Chapter 5 is devoted to a discussion of the public interest in collective bargaining and the current status of the rules for rule making in the United States. Other important legislative and judicial matters are dealt with elsewhere in the book.

The result of the interaction of the actors, according to Dunlop, is the establishment in a given industrial relations system of rules, and rules for rule-making. The word "rules," in the sense intended here, must be given a very broad interpretation. The rules cover a wide range of regulatory arrangements, from a national labor relations law (a rule for rule-making) down to something as detailed and specific as, for example, an agreed vacation schedule in a labor-management agreement. As used in this book "rules for rule-making" generally mean laws.

The Rules

Although Dunlop points out that the actors interact with the aim and purpose of establishing substantive rules to govern their relationship in day-to-day operations, he stops short of specifying what they make rules about, what issues the rules deal with and try to resolve, what functions they fill that need to be provided for. He does not expound or try to analyze the rules for rule-making, either in the American industrial relations system or, by comparative analysis, in the systems of other countries. Instead, in the remaining chapters of his book he presents a number of unanalyzed examples of labor-management agreements drawn from the practice of collective bargaining in various countries, leaving it up to his readers to make sense of them. Until someone analyzes the rules and explains their purpose and how they work, the theoretical framework remains incomplete.

Without criticizing Dunlop for what he didn't do—when what he did do is so helpful—the authors of this book have found it necessary to complete the framework by analyzing the rules and by outlining the rules for rule-making in at least one country, the United States.

Chapter 5 presents the laws and institutional arrangements that underlie the rules for rule-making in the United States. Other countries have different systems of law, custom, and procedure. In all systems, regardless of differences from country to country, the substantive issues recur, and the actors have to make substantive rules resolving these recurring issues. Figure 1–1 presents these issues in outline form, while Chapter 8 on the nature of the labor agreement discusses them in greater detail.

The Rules under Nonunion Conditions. Every free employment relationship centers on the wage and effort bargain. It is an exchange of the worker's ability and time for compensation provided by the employer. This exchange requires a consideration of: (1) pay for time worked, (2) the effort bargain (production standards), (3) premium pay, (4) pay for time not worked, e.g., paid holidays, vacations, and (5) contingent benefits, e.g., Blue Cross and Blue Shield, and pensions. Nonunion employers, regardless of size or industry attachment, must consider these five elements in establishing the conditions of employment. Nonunion workers weigh the value of various employers' "packages" against other employment opportunities or the value of leisure. The wage and effort bargain also provides the base for all collective bargaining agreements.

The larger the scale of an enterprise, the more complex its employee relations problems. Perhaps out of fear of unionization, some medium- and large-scale enterprises have established what under collective bargaining would be called individual security measures. Individual security measures must meet: (1) the individual workers' relative claim to available work and (2) the worker's claim to fair treatment on the job, or the establishment of a system of due process. A relative claim to available work raises such questions as: (1) Who gets laid off? (2) Who gets recalled from layoff when work becomes available? (3) Who gets promoted? and (4) Who gets overtime work and overtime pay when it is available? Due process deals with such questions as the fairness of disciplinary rules and the right of an employee to a day in court on disciplinary actions.[2]

Under nonunion conditions, the employer unilaterally establishes the rules on the wage and effort bargain and, perhaps, individual security measures. If workers will accept these unilaterally established rules, the employer operates without interference, except the veto power always available to a free worker of quitting employment, or the ability of employees to force change in conditions of employment by restriction of output.

The Rules under Collective Bargaining. While under nonunion conditions the rules may be largely implicit, under collective bargaining the rules are typically written down in explicit terms. Once a union wins recognition, management has to negotiate the rules with the union; as a result, the coverage of the rules becomes broader, and the rules themselves change in substance. In a collective bargaining relationship the written *labor-management agreement* is the basic rules system.

In their agreement, management and the union establish substantive rules in the fundamental area already mentioned: the *wage and effort bargain*, and in the other area referred to: *individual security*. Besides making rules in these two areas, they set up their own rules for rule-making under the heading of *union security and management rights*, and provide for joint *administration* in matters touching the substantive rules.

Of these four functions, the two last mentioned are found only in labor-management agreements; never under nonunion conditions. Union security and management rights, or the local rules for rule-making, consist of answers to the following four questions: (1) who speaks for whom? (2) with what authority? (3) for how long? and (4) with what exceptions? Administration deals with problems of making the written agreement an operational document in day-to-day activities. It provides a system of on-the-job representation for workers and establishes the procedures by which persons not employed by the enterprise will act if they are called in as neutrals to interpret the collective bargaining agreement. Chapter 13 discusses problems in agreement administration in some detail. The authors of this book hold that individual security is unique to the collective bargaining agreement on the assumption that no unilateral system of individual security would be genuinely binding on the employer who created it.

Figure 1–1 provides a preliminary summary of the rules under collective

---

[2] The existence of individual security measures in such diverse organizations as the Roman Catholic clergy, the military establishment, and the civil service must be noted as evidence that the need for a system of individual security is more basic than an employer fear of unionization. On the other hand, individual security measures which are unilaterally established and not subject to an impartial outside interpretation can hardly be considered to have the potency of identical measures which have been negotiated by collective bargaining. Cf. William G. Scott, *The Management of Conflict: Appeal Systems in Organizations* (Homewood, Ill.: Richard D. Irwin, Inc., and the Dorsey Press, 1965).

FIGURE 1-1

The Rules under Collective Bargaining

Rule	Scope
Union Security and Management Rights	Who speaks for whom? With what authority? For how long? Except in what conditions?
The Wage and Effort Bargain	Pay for time worked The effort bargain (Standards) Premium pay Pay for time not worked Contingent benefits
Individual Security	Relative claim to available work Absolute claim for fair treatment
Administration	On-the-job representation Arbitration

This presentation is taken from an article by Edwin F. Beal which appeared in the September/October 1962, issue of *Personnel,* journal of the American Management Association, by permission of the copyright owner. This presentation is expanded upon in Chapter 8 and Figure 8-1.

bargaining. Chapter 8 provides a more comprehensive tool for the analysis of labor agreements and contrasts the practices of craft unions, industrial unions, and professional associations in establishing the basic rules of employment. Chapters 10-13 treat the rules in America in some detail.

Levels of Application of the Rules. The object of the rules in the long run is to regulate relations at work, in the workplace during the working day, between the two main actors, managers and workers. Every workplace evolves or adopts a body of substantive rules. When the workers are organized in a union, these rules result from collective bargaining; but even without bargaining and without a union, there are always rules, no matter how one-sided. These substantive rules emerge out of procedures, or policies, or customs, or laws that may be called the rules for rule-making.

This book distinguishes three levels at which rules and rules for rule-making appear. They are the national level, the enterprise level, and various points between, which may be lumped together as an "intermediate" level.

National Level. Governmental action through laws, decrees, administrative and judicial decisions normally provides rules for rule-making. During a national emergency, as in wartime, the government may intervene directly in the affairs of individual enterprises; but ordinarily it acts in a general and not a specific way. The rules for rule-making that are laid down by government cut across industry lines and regional and state boundaries. They affect the entire industrial relations system. Of this nature, for instance, is labor relations law, such as the Taft-Hartley Act.

Enterprise Level. Here is where the substantive rules are made by the actors under rules for rule-making that come down from higher levels or that are elaborated on the spot—"ground rules"—by these same direct actors. The substantive rules cover, at a minimum, the wage and effort bargain (money for work) that is the root of the employment relationship. Under collective bargaining conditions they almost always deal with other issues in addition. This book will have a great deal more to say about the substantive rules.

Intermediate Level. Above the level of the enterprise but below the national level, interaction between the actors on industrial relations problems takes many forms designated here as "intermediate." Perhaps the most common intermediate form in the craft unions is bargaining at regional level and in the industrial unions, at the industry level. A greater proportion of the activity is private and voluntary (rather than government-sponsored) at intermediate levels.

Collective bargaining characteristically starts at enterprise level, but the trend seems to be toward progression and expansion, by agreement of the actors, to regional or industry level. A common example of regional bargaining is the building trades union's agreement with an employer association for an entire metropolitan area, or a county, or a whole state. A striking example of the industry trend comes from the steel mills whose managers negotiate an industry agreement with the steelworkers' union.

COLLECTIVE BARGAINING: A DEFINITION

Let's wind up this introductory chapter with a working definition of the subject this book deals with in all the chapters to follow: collective bargaining. While we titled our introduction "The Collective Bargaining *System*," it would be more accurate to say that collective bargaining is a set of activities *within* the larger industrial relations system; it is one form of interaction of the actors. Even more specifically, collective bargaining is the interaction of the actors when one main actor (Dunlop's worker hierarchy) organizes in a union or unions. In other words, you can have an industrial relations system whether unions are present or not, but you can't have collective bargaining without unions. Consultation, yes; contact, communication between the actors—even conflict—yes again; collective bargaining, no.

Collective bargaining therefore consists of interaction between *unions* and managers. It takes place within limits set by formal rules, accepted practices, laws, and conventions. It has the purpose and result of regulating relations between an organization under management, and its workers.

The actors in this particular manifestation of the industrial relations system aim at establishing and maintaining mutually acceptable, mutually beneficial substantive rules and practices to guide their conduct in day-to-day operations and in their work-related mutual and reciprocal claims and obligations.

Collective bargaining, then, is *behavior*—a set of activities—and also a *relationship*. It occurs when *unions* enter the industrial relations system.

SUMMARY

This book takes for the center of its field of view the practice of collective bargaining in the enterprise. It looks outward from time to time to the macroeconomic scene, backward into history, forward to the march of technological and social progress, and inward to the psychological and social aspects of the work group in the enterprise and the local union. Chiefly it concerns itself, however, with the enterprise as a whole in its dealings with the union that speaks for the employees there. None of the established disciplines of the social or behavioral sciences has taken, or can take, quite this point of view.

The approach to the practice of collective bargaining will be descriptive, analytical, and theoretical. The main theoretical concept is of collective bargaining as an aspect of the industrial relations system, a subsystem of the social system, linked with and overlapping the economic and political subsystems of the same social system.

The industrial relations system, both at enterprise level and above the level of the enterprise, takes shape in three *contexts*. They are the market context, or budgetary limitations; the technology context, as applied in the workplace; the power relations context of the enveloping social system, as reflected in the workplace.

Within these contexts, the industrial relations system evolves by interaction of the *actors*. They are managers and their hierarchy inside and above the enterprise; workers and their hierarchy of representatives; agents of government, or private agents activated by the other two actors.

The result of the interaction of the actors in the industrial relations system is a body of *rules*. They include rules for rule-making, and substantive rules.

These rules take force at various *levels*. These may be classified as: national level, enterprise level, and intermediate levels.

QUESTIONS FOR DISCUSSION

1. Show how Dunlop's concept of the *Industrial Relations System* requires an interdisciplinary approach to the study of collective bargaining.

2. An hourly wage certainly is an important "rule." Show how this rule might be applied at the national level, the enterprise level, and the intermediate level.

3. How does the prevailing technology of a society influence power relations in that society?

4. Can individual security, as discussed in this chapter, exist without unionism? Besides unionism, what institutions might provide security?

2 Unions in America: The Heritage

MANAGEMENT organizations of all kinds—business, government, private nonprofit enterprises—came first in the industrial relations system. Unions sprang up much later; centuries later. But collective bargaining begins only with the appearance of unions. Managers engage in collective bargaining only as a *response* to unions. We therefore start our treatment of the actors, here in Chapters 2 and 3 with the unions. We go on from there to the other main actor, management (Chapter 4) and complete the presentation with a look at the principal third actor, government—the regulator (Chapter 5). Once the three actors are on stage, we can observe the way they interact and the results of their behavior.

We divide this treatment of unions into two chapters: Chapter 2 deals with union history, Chapter 3, with unions of the present day. Some readers may want to skip the historical chapter and plunge at once into the contemporary scene. We urge any such to bear with what may seem to be an irrelevant digression into a past that is no more, and to read the chapter, or at least scan the chronology that accompanies it. Yesterday's unions, after all, brought today's unions into existence. They changed the world we live in. Anyone who is dealing with, or representing, or merely trying to understand labor today will have a blind spot in those perceptions if ignorant of at least the broad outlines of labor history. It is a significant, though largely neglected, part of our national heritage and history.

THE UNION TRADITION

Americans cherish traditions and honor some typical folk heroes: the frontier settlers, the cowboy and Indian-fighter, the Paul Bunyan logger. We seem never to tire of watching their dramatized portrayal in the movies or on TV, or reading about them in the paperbacks. We cheer the good guys and rejoice when, against odds, they lick the bad guys. Just as colorful a tradition, with real-life figures of heroic stature struggling against overwhelming odds, lies half-forgotten in the saga of union organizing. Perhaps one reason these dramatic stories haven't reached the television screen is that, depending on our point of view, we can't all agree on who are the good guys, who the bad. Was labor leader Terence V. Powderly the hero, and financier Jay Gould the villain of the Wabash strikes, or was it the other way around? The audience watching a western can tolerate a *crooked* banker as the villain, but in that simple sense Jay Gould was not a crook. Nonetheless conflict, suspense, and drama were all there in that first successful railway strike and in its sequel, one year later, when the railroaders lost everything they had gained. And those who like the spice of violence in their entertainment will find it in plenty in the labor story; mostly sporadic on one side, systematic on the other, full of blood and thunder: the Molly Maguires, Haymarket Square, the Steel and Coal Police, gunfighting in the Colorado mines.

For until not much more than a generation ago the workers of America, thought by some to be affluent today, were an oppressed class, struggling to be free. They were poor and comparatively uneducated. They faced the power of the political state with its police, its courts, even sometimes its army; and the economic power of capital: factory-owners, bankers, big business. Two great reforms we take for granted and regard as elements of American democracy today came in response to labor pressure in the 19th century: universal suffrage, and free and compulsory public education. They were, of course, not won in direct collective bargaining, but put forward as part of the political and social program of the unions.

Though today labor seems to have won all its important battles, and though some now see it as a conservative—even a reactionary—force, its days of heroic struggle are not over. Cesar Chavez, for example, whose migrants do stoop labor for the agri-business combines in the California fields, is not a freak of circumstance, but the authentic spiritual heir to a tradition that produced earlier crusaders; and some martyrs; and some secular saints. Eugene Debs, the steadfast leader of the Pullman strike; Wesley Everest, lynched, mutilated, and then hung by a mob of small-town Legionnaires, while nameless hundreds of fellow Wobblies went to jail in free-speech fights aimed at maintaining civil liberties; Joe Hill, executed on a charge of armed robbery and murder, but quite probably framed, whose labor songs have entered into the folk music of our culture; Mary Harris Jones ("Mother Jones") who spoke on behalf of workers from New York to Idaho and at the age of 93 was working among the miners of West Virginia.

If the nostalgia, drama, and romance of labor history leave the reader cold, consider just the rise in living standards workers have experienced over the past half century, the result in part, at least, of union activity. If you had been a factory worker in the 1920s you would have been well paid if you earned $20 for a 48-hour week. No income tax or social security deductions, true; but also no paid holidays, no vacations, no income during layoffs, no pension at retirement; and no recourse against arbitrary acts of supervisors. The dollar, you may say, was worth more then. Yes, but not *that* much more. And if you didn't like it, you could lump it.

In any case, we have to live with the consequences of change that has already taken place. It is conceivable that there are some who deplore the rise in the worker's standard of living and enhanced security, as, for example, through seniority rights. Indeed, at a time when other countries have pretty well caught up with American technology, a high-wage economy may have some disadvantages for the nation; though these may prove temporary. Try cutting wages, though, now that the unions are here! The past, the present, and the future are not separate time compartments, but a continuum; we live in a present that is forever slipping away into the past. Anyone wanting to shape the future would do well to learn whence we came as well as where we're heading.

Skip if you must, then, this historical chapter; but if you skip, don't think your understanding of today's unions and collective bargaining will ever be complete.

THE TWO HISTORIES OF COLLECTIVE BARGAINING IN AMERICA

Collective bargaining between managers of handicraft enterprises and representatives of craft unions has been going on in the United States almost since the nation won its independence, or for nearly two centuries. It still goes on, for the same ends and in much the same form, in the restricted sector of the economy where handicraft methods prevail. The outstanding example today is the construction industry, with its building-trades unions of skilled craftsmen.

Collective bargaining between industrial unions and the managers of mass-production manufacturing plants, and kindred enterprises mainly employing nonskilled labor, is much newer. It has been going on for less than half a century, although factory methods and mass production began to replace handicraft shops at least a century ago.

Not until after the year 1933 did unions succeed in establishing permanent organizations of factory workers, except in the garment trades which were by no means solidly organized. The only sizable industrial union was not in manufacturing but in the coal mines, and seemed then to be struggling against disintegration. The drive to organize the unorganized, which began to gather headway in 1935, built up the weak existing unions to a commanding position in their industries and created new unions where none had been before, as in the automobile and steel industries.

The story of collective bargaining thus becomes, in reality, two stories: a long and consistent, but somewhat discontinuous, tale of craft unions bargaining with handicraft employers in a relatively diminishing sector of the economy; and a brief, spectacular drama of industrial-union bargaining in mass-production industry, whose enterprises make up the vital and decisive elements of the economy today.

CRAFT-UNION PREHISTORY IN COLONIAL AMERICA

At the beginning of the colonial period there was no industry; by the end of the period there was still very little. Agriculture, plus a growing trade and commerce, dominated the economy. Manufacturing was in the handicraft stage and largely done at home.

Skilled craftsmen began early to establish a few small shops in the seaboard cities. As their "front room" enterprises grew they took apprentices, and some eventually began to employ wandering journeymen. Their trade was strictly local: village blacksmiths, shoemakers, and menders; tailors, carpenters, printers, tanners.

Not all workers were free laborers; some were slaves, indentured servants, or bound apprentices. Qualifications tended to cluster at the two extremes: a worker was either skilled in a trade that had to be learned by serving an apprenticeship, or, whether free or bond, was an unskilled field hand or common laborer.

There could be no question of union organization of bond laborers. The free laborers worked only singly, or if they were skilled, in small "family" groups, often actually living in the master workman's house and supping at his table.

Wages were high by the standards of those days. From the beginning of settlement in North America there was a chronic shortage of labor, and its price reflected the excess of demand over supply. Attempts to set maximum wages by law all failed, because the need for labor—skilled or unskilled—was so great that the employers themselves broke the law in bidding for labor. Individual, face-to-face bargaining, was the rule.

The Labor Market

Labor is not a commodity in the usual sense, but the price of labor, like commodity prices, may be subject to the fluctuations of supply and demand in the *labor market*. This was particularly true under the conditions that prevailed in the colonies in the early days. Communities were practically isolated from each other, except by water. The main influx of new workers was by ships that came from Europe, and the frontier drained a steady outflow to the west. Thus there would be a certain number of jobs and potential job openings at any given time, and a certain number of workers. A worker on foot could canvass and personally interview all prospective employers.

The Unskilled Worker. Wages paid for unskilled labor might vary slightly with the physical fitness or the willingness or persuasiveness of the individual, but tended to reach a general level at some point between two extremes: (*a*) In good times, employers seeking labor when it was scarce, bid wages up to the limit of what they could afford to pay and still make a profit. (*b*) In bad times, workers seeking jobs when jobs were scarce bid wages down to the limit of what they could afford to accept and still keep body and soul together—gain their subsistence.

Normally in the colonies there were more jobs or potential jobs than workers, and wages were nearer the upper than the lower limit. As time went on, after the colonial period, steady streams of immigration changed this picture, and the closing of the frontier finally reversed it. There came to be many more people than jobs, and wages dropped to near the lower limit.

Skilled Labor.   Just as there was a limit to the number of common laborers available for hire, and free to hire themselves out, there was an absolute limit at a given time to the number who possessed a skill—any particular skill. The same forces that acted on wage levels for common labor in the labor market acted upon wage levels in the smaller labor markets for each skill. Skilled labor was in special demand. A journeyman who had served time as an apprentice could not "name his own price," but could bargain within the limits described above, and do it face to face with the prospective employer. Being free to quit a job, a worker could get a raise when times were good by further bargaining with the employer.

When individual bargaining worked as well as has been outlined here—and this was the condition in the colonies through a good part of the 18th century—there was little need for collective bargaining; besides, the number of workers employed by one employer was usually small. Many economic and psychological factors also worked against the combination of workers into unions. Land was cheap and easy to get if you wanted it, and in the growing towns it was easy to make a living and get ahead. Class distinctions, left behind in Europe, had not jelled again too firmly. Society was fluid; most young men expected to rise in the world. So far as the records show, there were no unions, but as time went on there came to be certain kinds of worker organizations.

Worker Organizations

In some of the seaboard cities workers of the same skill or craft founded social clubs, like the clubs of merchants and professionals. Also like the associations of their colonial "betters," these clubs gave status to their members, who were several steps above the immigrant common laborers, bondmen, and slaves. Life insurance was unavailable in those days and there were no workmen's compensation laws, so it is not surprising that some of these clubs turned to establishing mutual funds out of which they paid death benefits to widows and orphans of deceased members, and gave relief to the sick or injured.

Embryo Unions. Members of craftsmen's clubs and mutual benefit so-cieties would not have been human if they had not indulged in "shop talk," and part of shop talk is wages, hours, and working conditions. Members were unwilling to have their wages and conditions undermined by compe-tition from itinerant workers, or "half-baked" craftsmen who would de-preciate the standards of workmanship and water down their skill. They found three ways of handling the problem:

The Closed Shop. One method of reducing potential competition was to subsidize itinerant brothers of the craft until they found a job or moved on. This was often done by boarding them around in the homes of mem-bers. Another way, more drastic, was to refuse to work with "foreigners," particularly if they had not served their time and mastered the trade. An employer faced with a "turnout" of dependable local workers would find hiring a floater or an ill-trained worker expensive. The result was the in-formal beginnings of the "closed shop"—the shop that was closed to any-one not a member of the union.

Apprenticeship. In those days youths were bound out for periods of from four to seven years to master workmen, who were the employers. The youngsters learned the tricks of the trade from their employer and other old hands in the shop.

The employers as a group could have relieved the scarcity of skill in the labor market if they had been able to train enough apprentices, but each apprentice during the learning years was a drain on the individual em-ployer, and besides, the already skilled workers did not favor training so many replacements that they would create potential competition for them-selves. Since the employers needed the cooperation of the skilled hands to train the replacements, the result was usually a compromise in which the skilled workers, as a group, got a voice in setting the number of appren-tices. This gave them a large measure of control over the right of access to the trade, and kept their skill scarce in the labor market.

Wages and Output. Finally, there was the question of the speed, or tempo, of the work. Since the craftsmen performed this manually, they could control it, but the employer was naturally anxious to encourage the one who worked the fastest, and to hold the others up to that standard. To avoid this, organized members of local groups agreed upon shop rules, either among themselves or with the employers. Once a standard of daily output had been established, it was logical to insist upon a standard daily wage, and this the group negotiated with the employers.

A *Craft-Union Program.* All this adds up to a full-fledged program of craft unionism, valid and practiced (with some additions) to this day. Little of it shows in the records and documents that have come down, for most of it was done by word of mouth, but it can be fairly inferred from what there is in print.

The basic strategy behind it was to control a scarce and vital element of production—skill. Keeping it scarce by limiting the number who possessed it and regulating the terms on which they offered it kept its price up in the labor market.

Any organization with fortunes tied so closely to the labor and product market is bound to suffer with the fluctuations of the economy. Craft unions flourished in a boom, languished when the bust came; appeared, disappeared, reappeared. The story of craft unions up to the Civil War, and after, is one of ebb and flow; it need not be followed in detail. If cats have nine lives, craft unions were like cats. Tied in a sack and drowned during a depression, they came scratching at the employer's door again as soon as times improved. They are still around.

INDUSTRIAL UNIONISM IN EMBRYO: RISE AND DECLINE OF THE KNIGHTS OF LABOR

The independence of the young republic had made possible expansion and activity that colonial status discouraged. Trade with Europe increased, particularly after the Napoleonic wars which ended in 1815. The government encouraged native industry and manufacture, which grew in importance to the economy, though methods of production remained primitive and did not change radically at first. Roads and canals and later, railroads, linked the cities and connected them with the hinterland. The market for goods ceased to be local and became national. Shoes and guns and yard goods made in New England sold in Michigan and Missouri. The labor market, too, ceased to be narrowly local (though it is never as "national" as the market for wheat or automobiles). Immigration increased greatly. Cities grew in size. Bankers extended their financial operations, and with the increased interdependence of the national economy, national panics and depressions made their periodic appearances.

The Factory System

England's Industrial Revolution took a generation to cross the Atlantic. American industry felt its influence after about 1840. It brought the factory system. Craft unions continued to grow, because the economy was growing, and handicrafts with it, but factory production began to displace handicraft manufacturing and spread to new areas of enterprise.

The Civil War, 1861–65, gave the factory system an enormous boost. The government, with armies in the field, became an insatiable cash customer for products in quantities such as only mass-production methods could supply. After the war there was a long depression, which brought about the usual eclipse of craft unions and shut down factories; but the factories had come to stay. With the return of prosperity the factories reopened. Craft unions revived in the handicraft shops and occupations that were still active, but the craft unions never succeeded in organizing the factories.

In 1869 a small group of custom tailors in Philadelphia formed a craft union which they called the Knights of Labor. Unlike other organizations of handicraft workers, it did not confine its membership to workers in a single trade, but spread, first as a multicraft federation, then as a general order of working men. By 1878 it had become a national organization. Unknowingly, it contained the embryo of industrial unionism. Though it did not reach the stage of collective bargaining in the factories, it did succeed temporarily on the railways, and it laid the foundations for an industrial union of miners.

What made the factory such a hard nut to crack?

Difficulties of Organizing. The traditional basis of organization was lacking in the factory. Unions could not control entrance to the "trade" because semiskilled work was not a trade and required no apprenticeship. Even apprenticeship for the regular trades slipped from union control in the factory, for factories were big enough to train their own apprentices for replacements. They did not need and did not ask for union help.

Skill itself was no longer vital. Skilled workers made up only a small minority of total factory payroll. The factory easily hired the small number of skilled workers it needed away from union control because it could offer union pay and conditions, or better, plus the inducement of steady work. A 10 percent raise for the toolmakers or maintenance workers might not increase the total wage bill by as much as 1 percent; thus a factory could pamper its few skilled workers. If pampering did not work and the skilled workers responded to a union call, the factory could get along without them, for a while at least, because the factory did not depend upon their output as a *direct* element of production. They made tools and dies for the production workers, or repaired machines; they did not turn out the factory's product. That was the job of the majority, the semiskilled.

The Semiskilled Worker. Semiskilled workers, trained in a few days or weeks in the factory, were dependent on the job in the factory that trained them. Alternate employment opportunities were at best restricted. Often the work they did was unique to the factory where they worked. If they wanted a job anywhere else, they would have to start as an unskilled trainee. Furthermore, they were easily replaceable—another raw hand could with the same few days or weeks of training, easily take their place.

Lack of Union Tradition. Semiskilled workers ordinarily had had no contact with or experience of unionism, perhaps having come from the farm, or from a peasant holding in a foreign country. They could hardly feel any solidarity with the skilled workers who held themselves above the common herd. Semiskilled workers came from every country in Europe, from the rural areas and from the towns, in all ages, shapes, and colors, in both sexes. Often they could not, literally, speak the same language.

A Living Wage. The semiskilled worker did not make as much money as the skilled worker, but made good money in relation to the learning time invested. The skilled worker must have put in four or more years of practically unpaid labor learning a trade. The semiskilled worker showed up on the job with no training at all, learned it in a matter of days or weeks, and got paid in the process. It was always enough to live on. (Except in certain depressed industries, like textiles, or during times of depression, as in the early 1930s, the factory in America has always paid a living wage.) The worker who came from any European country had a higher standard of living at the lowest wage earned in America than the majority of compatriots in the Old Country. What is more, the worker could sometimes increase earnings by hard work under a piecework plan, or qualify for higher graded jobs with higher pay. These employees were not tied, as the skilled worker is, to a single hourly rate for the life of a contract. All these things made it hard to organize them.

Employer Opposition.   Factory employers were more powerful than their handicraft counterparts had been. The factory represents a larger concentration of capital and economic power than the handicraft shop, and factory employers were richer and more influential, individually and as a group, than employers of a previous day. They controlled more job openings, exercised greater community leadership, and had more money to spend on lobbying or campaigning for political favors than predecessors. Many of the early employers smothered potential opposition with kindness, through "paternalism"—providing special benefits and care to their workers. Sometimes this was resented rather than appreciated, but it attracted the loyalty of a part at least of the working force.

The Knights of Labor

The Knights of Labor never squarely met the factory challenge, never fully comprehended it. They did not gain their victories in manufacturing, but they brought factory organization and collective bargaining into the workers' ken and made them part of their aims. The Knights established the first truly national union movement in America. They wrote a picturesque and honorable page of American labor history.

The Structure of the Knights of Labor.   At the height of their development, the Knights showed an organizational structure of three levels and had three kinds of local assemblies.

Levels of Organization.   The basic unit of the Knights was the local assembly. A dozen or more local assemblies, geographically close to each other, made up a district assembly. All the district assemblies, taken together, made up the national assembly, headed by a Grand Master Workman and an executive board.

Kinds of Local Assemblies.   The Knights recognized two kinds of local assembly. It is possible today to recognize three.

1. Craft Assembly.   The first local assembly of the Knights was composed exclusively of journeymen tailors; the second, of ship carpenters.

In the course of time many other local assemblies composed entirely of skilled practitioners of a single craft received charters.

2. Mixed Assembly. The Knights differed from previous labor organizations in accepting for membership any and all who worked for a living, regardless of their skill or lack of it. (In fact, they excluded only tavern keepers, professional gamblers, persons of ill repute, and lawyers. They did not exclude employers, though it does not appear that many big employers joined the Knights.) The advance of the factory system produced a category of nonskilled worker called semiskilled. The craft unions had always kept such people out; the Knights took them in. A community with only one local assembly of the Knights would have a mixed assembly. After enough craftsmen "swarmed" to found new craft assemblies, those who remained would still constitute a mixed assembly.

3. Industrial Assembly. In any locality where there was only one employer, what the Knights called a mixed assembly would turn out to be what now may be called an industrial assembly. This condition occurred in such places as textile towns with a single large mill, in the coal "patches" and railroad towns, and by chance in other places here and there. Such assemblies were mixed in the sense that they showed a mixture of various skills and degrees of skill, but they were homogeneous in terms of the industry from which the members came and the identity of their common employer. They were an embryo form of the industrial union local whose slogan is: One shop, one union.

Activities of Local Assemblies. The craft assemblies of the Knights engaged in collective bargaining exactly as the preceding—and succeeding—craft unions did, and with the same results, depending on the condition of the labor market and the scarcity of skill.

The industrial assemblies provided local and sporadic examples of collective bargaining, notably in railroad strikes in 1885. Local assemblies of miners also won some battles, but in manufacturing there is no record of success either in conducting strikes or collective bargaining.

The mixed assemblies probably could not do much collective bargaining (the record is blank on this) because it is hard to represent *all* employees in a locality with *all* employers.

Decline of the Knights. The program of the Knights was more ambitious than it lay within their power to attain. They multiplied the number of craft assemblies, but brought nothing new to craft unionism. Eventually they lost their craft assemblies to a rival federation of craft unions willing to concentrate on craft problems and let the semiskilled and unskilled workers go by the board.

Neither did the Knights succeed in working out a consistent program of industrial unionism. For one thing, they did not recognize the problem in their "mixed" assemblies, and for another, change was too rapid and factories were growing too lustily to be unionized.

The very grandeur of the Knights' conception of uniting all labor under a single banner helped seal the doom of the Order. It raised too many hopes, roused too many fears. Quite to its own surprise, the Order found itself fighting too many wars on too many fronts. In the first Wabash strike, it won a victory far in advance of the times. This was the first collective bargaining agreement of the industrial-union type. It provided for recognition of local committees and the adjustment of grievances. But when exuberant members tried to repeat and spread the victory, they lost, just one year later, all they had gained, and more. (See the chronology in the appendix to this chapter for details.)

An organization that was content with partial gains, on behalf of only part of the working population, in a part of the economy—and a relatively shrinking part at that—took over where the Knights had nobly failed. That organization was the American Federation of Labor. The AFL fully succeeded, in a humdrum, pragmatic way, in carrying out part of what had been the grandiose total program of the "Noble and Holy Order of the Knights of Labor."

LABOR'S RETREAT, INDUSTRY'S ADVANCE: THE RISE OF THE AMERICAN FEDERATION OF LABOR

The AFL represented what may be called the "production model" of craft unionism, the result of a century of unconscious experimentation in union forms and activities. It discarded the excess weight of the unskilled and semiskilled, and by concentration on the skilled worker, adopted the features of unions that—up to that time—worked. They still work today, but in a restricted sector of the national economy.

The craft-union tradition was almost as old as the nation, but the history was broken, discontinuous, and regional. That is, craft unions had sprung up, died, and sprung up again. They were confined before 1860 largely to the eastern seaboard cities. Even though some of them had united in national federations, they had few locals west of the Alleghenies. It was from one of these craft federations, the Cigar Makers' International Union, that Samuel Gompers came to lead the AFL.

The Knights of Labor gave *craft unionism* a tremendous boost in numbers by organizing *craft assemblies* throughout the land, all the way to the Pacific coast. Still, the older national craft unions retained their identity and held on to their locals, because craft unionism worked regardless of the label, and there was no room in the structure of the Knights for anything but local assemblies. In other words, the Knights did the *new* organizing in the field, the federations held on to the old.

The Craft-Union Strategy

In relation to the Knights, Samuel Gompers seems to have had two leading ideas: (1) to keep the already organized craft federations from losing their identity in the vague, mixed structure of the Knights, and (2) to capture the new membership represented in the craft assemblies of the Knights. He and his associates succeeded in both aims. Gompers brought off the coup with two brilliant strokes.

The Strike for the Eight-Hour Day. In 1881 a number of national craft unions came together in the National Federation of Organized Trades and Labor Unions, with Gompers as president. The member unions stuck to winning craft gains while the Knights stood forth as the champions of all labor; yet craft gains attracted the craft assemblies of the Knights.

In 1886 Gompers sent out a call for a nationwide strike on May 1 in favor of a popular demand: the eight-hour day in the building trades. He publicly sought the endorsement of Terence V. Powderly, Grand Master Workman of the Knights, but Powderly declined. He was wary of strikes in general after the spectacular defeat of the "second Wabash" strike earlier in 1886, which had damaged his organization; and he was wary in particular of Samuel Gompers and his craft unions.

But craft assemblies in the Knights wanted the eight-hour day as ardently as any of Gompers' National Federation men, and joined the strike. Then Powderly had a stroke of bad luck.

During a meeting at Chicago's Haymarket Square called by the Knights to protest violence against strikers, someone (possibly anarchists, possibly police provocateurs) exploded a bomb which killed several people. The Knights of Labor, who had sponsored the meeting, illogically and unjustly were blamed for the bombing, because anarchists charged with the crime were found to have been members of the Knights.

This incident accelerated the disintegration of the Knights. It gave Gompers a further opportunity.

The Breakaway of the Craft Assemblies. The trades and labor unions federation now proposed that the craft assemblies of the Knights affiliate with their appropriate national craft unions, and that the Federation then affiliate with the Knights in a body. This proposal would have taken the skilled workers in the craft assemblies away from their direct affiliation with the Knights and concentrated them, with their brethren of the Organized Trades and Labor Unions, in a virtually independent separate division. To this craft division the Knights might lend their celebrated name, but they could hardly expect to exercise much control over it. Powderly refused, but the craft assemblies proved more receptive to the invitation. It was by now commonly felt that the Knights were on the decline. As one after another of the craft assemblies went over to the Federation's national craft affiliates, the Order began to lose ground. The skilled workers had been a cohesive force in the Knights. For them, collective bargaining worked and brought results; without them, the nonskilled industrial workers failed to maintain the Order and it gradually fell apart.

Gompers picked up the pieces. Not all the pieces; just the pieces he wanted—the craft assemblies. He put them together in a pattern that has lasted to the present day.

Those left out of the new Federation, which reorganized in 1886 as the AFL, found the factory and mass-production industry an even stronger fortress against the assault of unionism, as a result of developments that call for attention at this point.

Scientific Management

The movement that came to be known as "scientific management" dates from the same decade that saw the almost simultaneous dissolution of the Knights of Labor and establishment of the AFL. Scientific management accompanied, and must be regarded as part of and an adjustment to, a series of technological achievements so advanced that they have been called by some a "new" and essentially "American" industrial revolution. It was marked by new inventions and the application of new sources of power: the telephone, the electric light, the internal-combustion engine, the electric motor, and many others. It also brought new methods of production. Henry Ford carried to its ultimate, logical development the serialized production of a complex mechanical product, the automobile, built out of interchangeable parts.

Aided by scientific management, the American industrial revolution brought sweeping changes in society and in the work relationship between employer and employee. The factory became the dominant unit of production in the economy, and in the factory the engineers had all but licked the problems of shortage of skill. They created instead the place of the semiskilled worker, and in so doing:

a.   They cut the ground from under craft unionism in the factory.
b.   They nullified, in manufacturing, the labor-market basis of bargaining for skill as a scarce and vital element of production.
c.   They increased productivity, built living standards, and made it possible for the untrained worker to come in and earn a living wage, after a few days' factory training.
d.   They made the jobs so simple that the worker was just as much an interchangeable and replaceable part as the product worked on.

All these developments made the factory impregnable to unionism of the old kind. If factories were going to be organized, new ways would have to be found.

It was no use looking to the AFL for the new ways. At the very time when the factory system quickened its advance on a broad technological and managerial front, the AFL beat its historic retreat into the handicrafts, not to move out again for nearly 50 years.

If it could be established that Gompers and his AFL colleagues foresaw, however dimly, what that half century would bring, the retreat might deserve to be called "strategic." The evidence available does not justify using the term in its full conscious implications, but students of the labor movement see in it today at least the strategy of elementary survival: He who simply runs away will live to fight another day.

PREINDUSTRIAL UNIONISM OF THE LEFT

The tangible assets left behind by the Knights of Labor—the craft assemblies—went to the AFL. The spiritual heritage passed to the radicals in and around the labor movement: the political socialists and the nonpolitical syndicalists. The syndicalists, in particular, who in 1905 founded the Industrial Workers of the World (IWW) built on the grand conception of the Knights, which was a single, all-embracing Order of those who worked for a living. The "Wobblies" (IWW) reached out to organize those working men and women to whom the AFL was closed, because they had no skill—the industrial workers. The Wobblies preached their gospel with a fervor that had not been felt since the great days of the Knights.

The Industrial Workers of the World (IWW)

In 1912 there was a spontaneous walkout of textile workers in some big factories in Lawrence and Lowell, Massachusetts, in protest against wage cuts and unadjusted grievances. The Wobblies, who had members in the mills, assumed the leadership of the strike and led the workers to victory: restoration of the wage cuts, adjustment of grievances. In the face of considerable provocation, they avoided violence, though an attempt was made to blame them for an explosion in the mills that was later discovered to have been set off by one of the factory managers.

This victory was as electrifying for its day as the Knights' victory in the first Wabash strike, but the success was short-lived. The following year the IWW lost an equally important strike in the silk mills of Paterson and Passaic, N.J. Taught by the experience of their Massachusetts brethren, the New Jersey mill owners did not wait for a pretext for violent action against the strikers, but turned unremitting violence against them at the plant gate from the very start.

Even if the IWW had won both strikes, there is a question whether they could have built a permanent organization or achieved settled collective bargaining. Their radical ideology opposed the very thought of making "peace with the exploiters." They did not know how to establish a permanent living relationship with management. To be fair, it ought probably to be said that management was no more reconciled than the IWW to the idea of peace and collective bargaining. Industrial workers *had* to strike to get a hearing. The Wobblies showed that such strikes could be won.

Lessons of the IWW Strikes

The IWW experiences in the textile mills showed that the factory was a single, unified, coordinated organism. It had to be organized totally, and all at once; it could not be organized piecemeal. The individual was too easy to replace. The entire force had to walk out to stop production.

This called for a *mass movement* of the workers. Mass movements were possible only under unusual conditions, when all the workers were stirred up at once. Spontaneous walkouts against wage cuts or widespread grievances provided the union's best opportunity of organizing.

Once workers were on strike, it became necessary for the union to control *physical access to the plant*. This was for the purpose of keeping not only outside replacements but wavering union members from going to work.

Any strike brings economic pressure to bear on the strikers. Craft unions, which rarely had more than a fraction of their members out on strike at one time, could ease the pressure by paying direct strike benefits. An industrial union that tried to pay benefits to keep strikers from going back would simply go broke, and even if it were possible, that would not keep the employer from hiring outside replacements. Thus the strategy of industrial unionism depended upon control of the plant gate. As long as moral persuasion or appeals to solidarity kept the gate closed, well and good. If these should fail, militants on the picket line had to keep out the timid by threats or violence. Violence on one side evokes it on the other.

Failure of Radical Industrial Unionism

Early industrial unionists had little experience to go on. To many, their theories seemed impractical. Industrial unionism had, indeed, existed in the mines since the 1890s, but mining is not manufacturing and has problems that are peculiar to the industry. Radical leadership of industrial unionism failed for several reasons.

It clashed with AFL vested interests. The AFL craft unions claimed jurisdiction over all members of their crafts, including those who worked in factories, even though they were unable to organize the factory craftsmen. They also opposed "dual unionism." Thus they opposed any attempt to organize dual factory unions that would deprive them of their jurisdictional rights.

Radical sponsorship was a liability. The socialists, syndicalists, anarchists, and others who had a program for organizing the factories also had things in their programs that many workers would not swallow. The Wobblies for instance, who were syndicalists, drew a large proportion of their members from itinerant workers—hoboes—whose mentality and view of life differed sharply from that of the stay-at-home factory workers with roofs over their heads. The anarchists preached and practiced violence.

The IWW experiment in preindustrial unionism was not the last attempt carried out by leftist elements. After the First World War the newly founded Communist Party led some strikes, all of which were lost. The communists in the AFL formed a "Trade Union Education League" to propagandize for industrial unionism, but were rebuffed and expelled, whereupon they changed the name of their organization to Trade Union Unity League and organized "dual" industrial unions. None of these made any headway toward collective bargaining.

PREINDUSTRIAL UNIONISM OF THE RIGHT

Although there were some further, ineffectual efforts from the left to form industrial unions after the war, the war year 1917 may be taken as the year of its defeat. The same year marked the start of a new development that evolved into industrial unionism "of the right."

The First World War, 1914–18

Factory production expanded tremendously, mostly in the metal-working industries, under stimulus of the war. For the first time since the appearance of large-scale factory production in America there was an *absolute* shortage of labor in all categories. A supervisor could no longer keep a worker in line by pointing to the crowd of job applicants at the gate. There wasn't anybody at the gate any more.

Old ways of doing things had to be discarded. Many supervisors were hastily promoted workers unaccustomed to the ways of supervision. Supervisors who had formerly, for instance, done the hiring of new employees could not spare the time to do it any more. Centralized hiring, centralized training, centralized handling of wages and raises, under newly established personnel departments, became the rule.

Wages skyrocketed as employers bid against each other for the available labor supply. Turnover became a major problem of management as workers shopped around for higher wages. The government had to resort to wage-freeze and job-freeze methods.

The Unions and the War. Gompers and the AFL stoutly supported the war effort. They gave a no-strike pledge for the duration and volunteered their services in war bond drives and other win-the-war activities. As has been seen, they did not have many members in the factories, where the bulk of war production was going on, but now there began to be an AFL influx to the factories.

Boom times are the traditional times of craft-union expansion, for the labor-market situation favors their bargaining power. Union members got jobs in factories, and skilled workers in the factories joined unions. Employers had to bargain with the AFL unions in order to keep their work force. This did not solve all the employers' problems. They had problems with *all* their workers, and dealing with craft unions could, at best, only solve part of the problems. An employer who might be willing to deal with a craft union on day-to-day problems, as a temporizing measure, did not relish the idea of permanent *recognition* of an organization—or cluster of organizations—that could not solve the problems.

The National War Labor Board. When in the First World War (as in the Second), the government froze wages and jobs it had to provide a substitute for the mechanisms of the market that had been abandoned. Labor relations and the regulation of labor resources became emergency problems. The government put these problems in the hands of a National War Labor Board, which had authority to determine questions of wages and representation on a plant-by-plant basis, as trouble developed or threatened.

A device the NWLB tried out to solve labor relations problems in war industry factories was the "works council." This was a plan that permitted employees to select representatives, by departments, and required employers to meet to deal with these repesentatives on grievances and matters of wages, hours, and working conditions. The program worked so well that it was applied to factory after factory, not only where trouble had broken out, but even in cases where trouble merely threatened. The works councils gave management and employees a way of settling current emergency problems, while side-stepping two issues considered important by management and by the AFL unions, respectively:

Recognition. Management did not have to recognize the unions, but only the elected representatives of their own employees.

Jurisdiction. The works councils, which were not membership organizations, did not challenge the jurisdictional claims of the established unions.

Postwar Industry

The war created larger factories and more of them. The labor shortage vanished when peace returned. This was the result of the loss of war orders, and it was augmented as time went on by reconversion cutbacks and widespread rationalization of plant and equipment.

Experience with Labor Relations. A number of factory managements got their first taste of dealing with employee representatives during wartime. Their experience seems to have taught them that craft unionism provided no constuctive answer to the problems involved in running a factory in which craftsmen are a minority, semiskilled workers the majority. The experience with works councils was favorable, or at least neutral. At their best, the works councils helped solve grievances and problems of upward communication, and they gave workers a sense of participation in the effort for production that the entire factory was making.

The Works Councils. When the NWLB disbanded at the end of the war, the legal and official sanctions that had sustained the works councils expired. This left it up to each individual employer to choose whether to continue them under company sponsorship.

Some employers dissolved their works councils, but a good many continued them. They did so because they had proved to be a good device for grievance adjustment and for securing employee cooperation, and were a hedge against unions, since they performed certain union functions without having either a membership base or outside affiliations.

As time went on, the works-council idea spread in the form of "Employee Representation Plans" or ERPs. This was partly the result of favorable experience of individual employers with the ERPs and partly on recommendation of employer organizations which made studies of them.

It is noteworthy that the ERPs, while not actually unions, had two important characteristics that go along with industrial unionism. "One shop, one ERP" might be a companion slogan to the industrial union slogan, "One shop, one union." Representation was by department, not by skill or status.

The committees set up by the plans closely correspond to industrial union shop-steward systems.

The Employee Representation Plan Committees. During the years 1919–28, Employee Representation Plans increased from a total of 196 to 869, and the number of workers covered from 403,765 to 1,547,766.[1] During the same period union and AFL membership declined from 4,124,200 to 3,479,800.[2]

The AFL called these plans "company unionism," and condemned them one and all. Looking ahead for a moment to the decade of the 1930s, it might be noted here that several of the Congress of Industrial Organizations (CIO) unions (steel and autos for example) got a good part of their start by capturing these company unions. They were, in fact, industrial unionism "of the right," created by management. They needed only to build their management-sponsored representation into a membership base, and gain a union affiliation, to emerge as full-fledged industrial unions.

This brings to an end the prehistory of industrial unionism and industrial-union bargaining in America. Labor gained experience in the ways and workings of the factory; management found that worker consent to factory conditions made for productive operations. The point implicitly at issue between labor and management was not whether there should be factory organizations of workers but whether these organizations should "belong" to management or to the unions.

The answer came in 1933.

THE TRIUMPH OF INDUSTRIAL UNIONISM

The Great Depression of the 1930s was the backdrop for the drama of the rise of industrial unionism. Never before had unions succeeded in es-

---

[1] Harry A. Millis and Royal E. Montgomery, *Organized Labor* (New York: McGraw–Hill, 1945), p. 835.
[2] Ibid., p. 837.

tablishing themselves in the factories; never since have they been driven out or lost appreciable ground.

The Great Depression, 1929–40

The tremendous number of persons thrown out of work or into part-time employment by the depression (estimated at up to one third of the working force, with others on reduced pay) had never been equaled, but this is only one measure of the impact of the event. It was a blow to management prestige and confidence. Herbert Hoover had been elected President in 1928 as a "great engineer." With the deepening of the depression, the prestige that had surrounded engineers and managers in the prosperous 1920s disappeared. Not only did the worker lose confidence in the ability of management to solve the problems of depression, but managers lost confidence in themselves. An appreciable number broke with traditional attitudes of independence to ask for help from the government.

The depression brought a growth of radicalism. As has been true whenever economic hardships threatened the workers' subsistence, they turned to radical political solutions. Demonstrations of the unemployed, "bonus marches," "hunger marches," armed skirmishes of farmers against tax sales, and similar instances of direct action took place. The Democratic victory in 1932 was largely a negative anti-Hoover vote. The New Deal program channeled the discontent into positive support for thorough-going measures of reform.

As has been brought out, company unions and Employee Representation Plans followed the wartime works councils into the factories. Management-sponsored and controlled, these organizations performed grievance-handling functions and were a medium of communication with the working force. Raises and benefits that had accompanied prosperity were passed on to employees through the ERPs. When wage cuts took the place of raises, workers lost faith in the efficacy of management-sponsored ERPs.

Effect on the AFL. The AFL, which had been shrinking in numbers through the preceding decade of prosperity, further lost members and influence as the depression advanced. The industries on which it depended, such as construction, went into stagnation. The AFL leaders turned to political lobbying for public works, and for such measures as the Davis-Bacon Act requiring payment of "prevailing wages" on government work. Prevailing wages, where the unions had any strength at all, meant the union scale.

NRA and the Unions. The NRA came at a time when the AFL was at its lowest ebb, and did not immediately help it recover. (The NRA, in fact, did not bring actual recovery, though it gave that illusion; genuine recovery came only when the war in Europe began to stimulate American industry with orders.) NRA developments affected the international unions making up the AFL in different ways:

The Craft Unions. Construction work, the mainstay of the craft unions, was slow to recover. Union members found part-time employment on public works, where they drew (under Bacon-Davis Act provisions) union wages for each hour worked, but shared the hours to spread employment. Craft-union activity waned in the private sector of the economy to concentrate on "pressure-group" tactics with the big employer of the day, the government. Full-scale recovery, when it came, put them back in the business of negotiating with private employers, but this was simply a return to what they had been doing before; depression did not change them.

The Mine Workers. The only true industrial union in the AFL was John L. Lewis's United Mine Workers. This union came to vigorous life, out of a slump, under the influence of the NRA. It rapidly completed the organization of the independently owned mines, but failed to make headway in the "captive" mines owned by the steel companies. Company unions had employer recognition in the captive mines. These included some of the largest and most productive, and the steel companies were constantly extending their mine holdings. Unless he could sign up the workers in the captive mines, Lewis's hold on the independents was threatened. This constituted pressure—pressure from the right—to organize the steel mills. The Homestead strike of 1892 had taught the lesson that the steel mills could only be organized industrially.

The Garment Unions. Two sizable "quasi-industrial" unions operated in the twin fields of men's and women's clothing: the Amalgamated Clothing Workers (ACW) and the International Ladies' Garment Workers Union (ILGWU). Each was a collection of craft unions amalgamated or fused into a single top-level organization, with joint boards at membership level to knit the locals together for united action. Under the NRA these garment unions made strides in organizing the many small shops that make up the production units of their industry, the bulk of which was centered in New York. They looked around for other fields to conquer. A special problem for them was the "runaway shops" that moved out of New York to escape the union. In addition, a large proportion of the members were foreign-born, from eastern European and Mediterranean countries. In this group a small but influential core of communists, surrounded by their sympathizers, strove to take away the leadership of the unions from the conservative socialists who headed them. Thus for ideological reasons—pressure from the left—the garment unions pressed for industrial organization of the factories throughout the land. This was a long-standing goal of the radical left in the labor movement.

Conflict of Interests and Personalities. It is in the interest of craft unionists to organize all who practice their craft, and no one who does not. To take in others, not qualified, is to water down their greatest asset, skill. Looking at the factories, craft-union leaders saw a minority of skilled workers whom they could accept as members, surrounded by a majority whom they would not. The easiest thing to do—and the most practical—was to let the factories alone, but if someone did organize the factories, the craft unions wanted these skilled people. They wanted them for the job opportunities they represented, and to extend their control over the right to learn the trade. That demand ran counter to a fundamental tenet of industrial unionism: One shop, one union; and only industrial unions could organize the factories.

Tradition also plays a part in any organization, and the tradition of the AFL was to stay out of the factories. Gompers taught them not to dilute their crafts but to concentrate on the skilled trades. They got their fingers burned every time they touched the factories.

Personalities. Human passions and ambition play their part in history. John L. Lewis was an able and ambitious man, with bitter enemies as well as powerful support in the top councils of the labor movement. Sidney Hillman was a dedicated man, a "reasonable" and practical labor diplomat and strategist, but nonetheless an old Socialist. Others were on the way up in the labor movement, too, impatient for power and unwilling to wait for the entrenched old guard labor leaders (who, like old soldiers, never die), to move out and make room for them. No vested interests, no sentimental memories, no hallowed traditions held them to the AFL; they stood to gain more by striking out on their own. Personal factors like this helped bring the CIO into being.

The Factory Workers. Leaders do not entirely determine the direction of events; the "masses"—people, public opinion, in this case, workers— have a share. Most of the new members who flocked spontaneously into the NRA unions were semiskilled workers with no previous experience in unionism. Their working lives had been spent in a factory environment; they thought in terms of "the shop," not any particular skill. They saw no place for their kind in the old-style craft union, and they resented craft-union attempts to split their ranks by taking out the members they prized the most—their own collection of skilled workers. (In Akron, for example, after federal locals were organized in the rubber factories, the AFL tried to put maintenance people from the shops into their corresponding building-trades locals. The answer was open revolt, and the rubber workers joined the CIO. The skilled factory workers themselves showed that their first loyalty was not to their craft, but with the shop.) Wherever the NRA called new unions into life, the pressure of the rank and file was practically unanimous for the industrial form of organization.

The Rise of the CIO (Congress of Industrial Organizations)

The moves and countermoves in labor's civil war are listed in the chronology, and the conflicting interests and motives of the contestants have been noted above. Here it is proposed to concentrate on the direction taken by the rebel branch of the labor movement, and the results achieved.

A brief reminder of the lessons taught by the IWW strikes in the textile mills is first in order. That experience showed that there were two essential conditions for success in organizing the mass-production factories: (1) organization must be total and simultaneous; and (2) the union must be able to control physical access to the plant.

Ideally, all of the workers of the factory must join the union at the same time. Practically, a good majority (or even, on occasion, a determined minority, provided they had the sympathy of the rest) would be enough, and they would have to join not at the same instant but in a very short time—a few days at most. That was to prevent the factory from hiring replacements, as could easily be done if organization were piecemeal and stretched over time.

Once organized, the union must be able to shut the plant gate by means of a picket line, and keep the plant gate closed. It might not have to do so, but that was the ultimate test of its ability to survive. Again, this was to prevent replacement.

The CIO organizing drive went through three phases, the first of which directly confirms the conditions set forth above. The two later phases do not contradict them, but reflect the modification of the situation that resulted from the Supreme Court's upholding of the Wagner Act.

The Phase of Mass Organization (1933–35). From the inception of the NRA to the defeat of the bitter strikes in Little Steel, workers literally poured into the new factory unions. It was a mass movement, like water flooding out of a broken dam. It took place during the period when the validity of the Wagner Act was still in doubt and while employer challenges against it were still pending before the Supreme Court which had declared the NRA unconstitutional. Some of the mass movement manifestations were the following:

Spontaneous Organization of "NRA Unions." Some of these unions died as quickly as they were born. Others, as noted, found places in the internationals such as the mine workers' and the garment workers' unions, that were ready to receive them. Still others, as in autos and rubber, made a nucleus around which new internationals were formed. Few of these latter unions came into being as the result of any concerted outside organizing drive; they were real instances of "spontaneous generation."

Capture of Company Unions. At least two of today's mightiest industrial unions, the Steelworkers and the Autoworkers, got their start by capturing the councils management had set up in the factories to give employees representation. The members of these ERP councils had been elected by their co-workers; they were the natural leaders. Depression experiences had shown many of them the futility of trying to get important results for their constituents when they were dependent upon management. Now, by going over in a body to the CIO, a General Motors or United States Steel ERP council could quickly convert its electorate into *a membership.* Membership support made a council independent of management. The issuance of a CIO charter, furthermore, ended the isolation of the individual plants and linked their workers up with others in the industry. The auto locals had to fight to keep their independence. In big steel, the companies signed up without a fight. In either case, there was a mass shift from company-union status to the CIO.

The Sit-down Strikes. Control of the plant gate is all very well, but when you control physical access to the very machine you work at, only physical violence can get you out to make room for a replacement. There is something hysterical and primitive about this notion, but the sit-downs were not festivals of pure reason: they were direct, emotional reactions to the mass movement of the day. They worked, though even their most ardent advocates knew they would not work forever. Either the emotional outburst that lay behind them would die down, or would develop into the most destructive violence in labor history. To the eternal credit of the then Governor Murphy of Michigan, the most critical of the sit-down strikes were settled without violence.

The Wagner Act Phase (1935–37). The Wagner (or Wagner-Connery) Act signalled a fundamental change in public policy and hence in power relations at the work place. It gave government, as regulator, a direct role in labor relations. Industry did not feel the impact of this law immediately, though its purport was plain enough. Whereas Section 7a of the National Industrial Recovery Act (NIRA) had declared that workers had the right to organize, and warned employers not to interfere with the exercise of that right, many employers had with impunity ignored the warning, because the law contained no provisions for enforcement: no "teeth." The Wagner Act had teeth, but many employers were convinced the teeth would never bite. They had just seen the Supreme Court declare the NIRA, with its Section 7a, unconstitutional; they felt sure the same principle, rewritten into the Wagner Act, would suffer the same fate. Not until 1937, when the same Supreme Court that had thrown out the NIRA upheld the constitutionality of the Wagner Act, did employers really comply with the new law's provisions.

What happened in between these two historic court decisions? For one thing, the sit-down strikes, which alarmed the nation. For another, the national elections of 1936, which returned President Franklin D. Roosevelt to the White House by the greatest majority ever—up to that time. Critics of the conservative Supreme Court of that era had called its members, contemptuously, "nine old men." Now they allowed that it consisted of nine old men who read the election returns.

The Wagner Act modified the situation in several important ways. The issue in the early CIO clashes with industrial management was recognition: Recognition always has to be the first issue in labor-management relations. The Wagner Act provided legal ways of getting recognition, and required employers to bargain "in good faith" with the unions that had recognition. It was no longer necessary to shut the shop gate; only to win a majority in a Labor Board election.

Union Jurisdiction and the "Appropriate Unit." The Wagner Act ignored the traditional AFL claim to determine "jurisdiction," with its corollary of "no dual unionism." Regardless of craft claims or industrial ideologies, the Labor Board had the power to determine the appropriate unit. To clinch this even further, the Board gave the union winning recognition an absolute right—a kind of monopoly—to bargain for that unit for a reasonable period of time, without disturbance from rival labor unions. In practice, the Board made the factory the appropriate unit in cases where factory organization was at issue. This was not done just to please the industrial unionists. Management preferred dealing with one union to having the headaches, well known in the building trades, of jurisdictional disputes, rivalry, and strikes between fractional or competing unions.

At first the AFL contested this arrangement, but the Board paid no attention to craft claims unless the contesting craft unions could show a previous history of collective bargaining with the company for the craftsmen in the plant.This, of course, they could not do, for the craft unions had never cracked the factories. Later the Board modified its position (the "Globe doctrine") and permitted small craft units to be carved out of the factories, provided the workers in the smaller unit desired it. This neither harmed the industrial unions very greatly nor very much benefited the craft unions. The AFL did not succeed in stopping the CIO steamroller until the AFL Internationals decided to reverse their tactics. Old craft unions like the International Association of Machinists and the International Brotherhood of Electrical Workers copied the CIO and started organizing unskilled and semiskilled, as well as skilled workers, in the factories. Only when they began to do this was the decline of the AFL checked. A dose of industrial unionism was the medicine that brought recovery.

Company unions flourished alongside the affiliated unions under the NRA. The Wagner Act outlawed company unions and effectively prevented employers from discriminating against workers for joining or being active in a union. This would seem to make the first of the essential conditions mentioned above—simultaneous and total unionization of the factory—no longer essential. Piecemeal organization now seemed possible. The difficulty for the union lay in proving that when a company fired a union member it was because of union activity. At first the unions won many cases, because employer habits were strong and methods direct, but as managers refined their tactics it became harder to get the evidence. (At the same time, real management conformity to the law increased.) An unfair labor-practice charge, at best, was not enough to organize a factory, and brought efforts in that direction to a standstill while the case was pending. If the Board's verdict went against the union, previous gains could easily be lost. Workers had never known the kind of protection the act guaranteed. They had to see results before they trusted it.

The company unions also proved harder to deal with than had been expected. Where management gave its support openly, the case was easily proved and the company union disestablished and dissolved. Where the support was secret, or subtly given, it was harder to draw the line between a company union and a genuine independent. It was the experience of most CIO organizers that the company union, except in its most obvious form, was their hardest nut to crack; harder by far than the AFL, until the AFL took up industrial-union tactics.

The Wagner Act phase was by no means a setback for the CIO but it was a period of slower going in organization. The mass movement days were over. A union had to make its way now by winning an election. It had to convince the worker to vote for the union.

The Collective Bargaining Phase (1937–41). The third phase of CIO growth overlapped the second phase in time, but shifted the emphasis from organizing to collective bargaining. Organizing still went on, but it was based on reaching the individual worker by "doorbell-ringing" methods of individual approach, either at home or at the factory. Mass media—handbills, shopgate meetings, loudspeaker appeals—became a supplement to, and not the mainstay of, organizing techniques. Reaching the individual worker, in tens of thousands, called for inner-union organization. This naturally took the form of departmentalization, after the pattern of the departments in the shop, since it is in the department that the workers meet their fellows and know them best.

Parallel with this development came grievance handling by the union as a service to its members. Local unions set up grievance machinery in the newly negotiated contracts, and set about gaining experience in settling grievances by contact with their equally inexperienced managements. The departmental organization was a natural for that, too. The inner-union organization that is active in the shop during the working day is the shop-steward system. It would seem that in the steward system, or shop committee, unions in mass-production manufacturing found the organ that enables them to operate effectively in the factories. In doing so they have solved, quite incidentally, some of management's problems in the field of grievance handling and communications. They have given workers a vital feeling of participation. The stewards make up a complete and flexible on-the-job medium for mutual accommodation and understanding between union and company. How well this medium works for both depends upon their attitudes, their trust in each other, their training and skill in dealing with each other, and the stresses and strains their over-all relationship exposes them to. If stewards were to disappear tomorrow from the factories, management would probably have to call them back in some form.

Subsequent Developments

The situation has not basically changed since the CIO unions reached the third phase of development described above. The process has continued; the parties have matured. It is necessary merely to mention four big incidents in this development:

The Second World War. The demands of national unity in the face of the emergency brought management and labor together for practical cooperation under the sponsorship of government. The two branches of the labor movement also dropped their rivalry for the duration. Both gave a "no-strike" pledge, and in return were given the means of adjusting grievances and disputes with management by representation on the tripartite National War Labor Board. In contrast to the First World War, the labor members now had a membership base, and agreements in the plants whose problems reached the Board. The unions could help with implementing, as well as making, Board decisions. They did much to "sell" the idea of unrestricted output to the war workers in the shops. These workers found that being in a union meant representation on the body that had power over their wages, hours, and working conditions. Union growth, as a consequence, continued and accelerated during the war.

The Strikes of 1946 and the Taft-Hartley Law. Just as the reconversion to peacetime production brought a wave of strikes in 1919, in the course of which management shook off the hold the unions had briefly gotten in the plants, a wave of strikes took place in 1946 after the Second World War. This time the unions were industrial unions, and they held their place. While wages, with prices, had been frozen, labor and management had to make their mutual accommodations during wartime mostly at the fringe. After the war, now, pensions and fringe benefits came to the fore along with the traditional issue of wages.

Public reaction against the magnitude of the postwar strike wave created an atmosphere favorable to the passage in 1947 of a law Sen. Robert A. Taft had been pushing for some time. Technically an amendment to the Wagner Act, the Taft-Hartley law reaffirmed its basic principles, but with some changes. It aimed at restoring balance by weighting the management side of the scale which, Taft contended, had been empty in contrast to the heavy concessions to labor. It is enough to say here that the new law worked out not so badly as labor leaders predicted nor so well as management people hoped.

The AFL–CIO Merger. It has been shown above that the issue of principle between the craft and industrial unionists, so bitterly contested in labor's civil war, ceased to separate the practice of the parties after the AFL adopted industrial-union forms in addition to its old craft forms. To bring this about it had been necessary to split the labor movement. Once the principle was accepted, there was no reason for the split to continue.

Still, the two labor federations did not come together very quickly. Reasons for their reluctance were various. The left-wing unions in the CIO feared any move that would put them under the domination of the outspokenly anti-Communist AFL. That problem the CIO solved by ex-pelling the left-wing unions and issuing new charters to absorb their former members. Personal rivalries, particularly after the death of Phillip Murray, president of the CIO, also played a part. But logic, and the Taft-Hartley law, inevitably pushed the AFL and the CIO toward a reconciliation.

Why it came exactly when it did, and in the form it did, is a matter for detailed study, but it was bound to come some way, sometime. It finally took place in 1955. The two organizations merged first at the top. The merger worked its way slowly down through state organizations to regional and city councils.

It did not bring about much realignment of international union jurisdictions. While it cut down on interunion rivalry and raiding within its ranks, it did not solve the problems of dual unionism, for some important unions failed to join and others left the ranks. "A rope of sand" was John L. Lewis's characterization of the newly formed federation. The two separate but intertwining strands of labor organization, craft and industrial, seemed again to be untwisting, as they had throughout the history of labor in the United States.

Chavez, the Teamsters, and the Agricultural Workers

Specifically excluded from the protection of labor relations law, farm workers organized in unions and began fighting for recognition in the 1960s in the California fields. They acted partly as a response to the civil rights movement that swept the country in that decade, for they were mostly of Mexican and Spanish-American origin, calling themselves "Chicanos," an oppressed minority. Out of their ranks came a charismatic leader, Cesar Chavez, president of the United Farm Workers union chartered by the AFL–CIO. Chavez organized strikes, demonstrations, and boycotts against the agribusiness farm employers who refused to recognize or bargain with the union. Just as these tactics were beginning to bring success in 1972–73, the Brotherhood of Teamsters, independent since its expulsion from the AFL–CIO, signed a "sweetheart agreement" with the growers, who recognized the Teamsters as the bargaining agent for the field workers Chavez claimed, as well as for the truckers who hauled the produce to market. Thus the growers reenacted the employer role long since outlawed in the rest of industry as contrary to public policy and democratic rights for employees.

In 1975 the California legislature took action bringing farm workers under the protection of the state equivalent of federal labor relations law. It remained to be seen whether, in free elections, Chavez and the AFL–CIO union still retained the loyalty of the workers, or whether the Teamsters had won them over. At any rate, the employer could no longer call the tune; and the California example might well spread to other areas of agribusiness enterprise.

Public Employee Bargaining

Without any doubt, the most significant development in collective bargaining today is the emergence of large-scale, vigorous unionization of public employees: federal, state, and local. Some have organized in craft unions or craftlike professional associations. The bulk of them belong to organizations of the industrial union type.

This extension of collective bargaining to government agencies and jurisdictions employing some nine million people would be a big event in terms of numbers alone. Besides that, it raises new issues with far-reaching implications. For example, government employees almost without exception have been forbidden by law to strike and most of them still are forbidden —yet they do strike, or have begun to do so recently. A strike of public employees takes effect in direct proportion to the essentiality of the services the strike denies. When 200,000 postal workers walked out for about a week in early 1970, they gave lawmakers and executive branch administrators some problems to solve that went far beyond the simple restoration of postal services or rise in postal rates. How do you deal with massive disobedience to law, particularly when the illegal act—the strike—would be legal if the employer were not the government? What follows if you deal with the leaders of the employees who are taking the illegal action? What follows if you *don't* deal with them?

The right of public employees to strike is a troublesome issue, but only one of many raised by unionization of this hitherto inactive group. Since government workers have shown they *can* strike even though they *may* not, is there a substitute for the strike over substantive issues? And if one can be found—thus far none has—will the substitute also apply in the private sector, where labor and management are at present free to resort to the strike or the lockout?

Unionized public employees thus seem to have chosen to follow the collective bargaining path towards altering and defining their relations with public employers. Because of the importance of this development, the authors of this book defer discussion at this point. Instead, they devote two later chapters to the subject, Chapters 15 and 16, which make up Part Four; and have included several cases on public employee bargaining in Part Five.

SUMMARY

Collective bargaining in America takes two forms: craft-union bargaining in handicraft industry, and industrial-union bargaining in mass-production industry.

Craft-union bargaining took shape early. It survives today, in the restricted sector of the economy still ruled by handicraft methods, not much changed from its original form.

Industrial-union bargaining did not become a practical reality until long after the rise of the factory system and the development of mass-production methods, which created the conditions for its eventual emergence. The history of the past century is therefore the story of a quest; a search—groping and tentative at first, confident and sure at last—for answers to the social and organizational problems raised by mass-production industry.

It is the story of the industrial worker's fight for something that would give them the kind of say in determining their conditions that craft unions give their members, as the semiskilled workers struggled to create organizations that would win them the right to engage in collective bargaining with their employers.

It is also the story of the industrial employers' fight to stay clear of the restraints of collective bargaining in the exercise of their function as enterprisers in a growing economy. Factory methods and machinery freed employers from the craft union's control in the first place, and they easily defeated every attempt at forcing them to bargain craft-union style. Industrial unionism in its embryo form posed a stronger challenge, but they defeated that, too, though it sometimes took bloody battles at the plant gate.

But the growth of enterprises, first in mere size, then in the increasing complexity of their internal organization and interdependence in a changing world, created needs—management needs—that in the end only industrial unionism and collective bargaining could answer.

The answers found to date are not final, but as this book has tried to show, they work. They raise new questions, but their study points, perhaps, to solutions that may serve society even better in the future.

QUESTIONS FOR DISCUSSION

1. Craft unions came early on the scene; industrial unions, late. Why did the industrial form not make the craft form obsolete and drive it out of existence? What has, in fact, made many craft unions obsolete? What keeps others alive?

2. How do you account for the success of the Knights of Labor? For its eventual failure?

3. Both the radical Industrial Workers of the World and the conservative Employee Representation Plans were, in contrast to the AFL, oriented towards factory conditions at a time when factory production had become dominant in the economy. How do you account for the fact that the craft-oriented AFL outlived them both?

4. What historical conditions favored the rise and ultimate success of the CIO? How did these differ from the conditions favoring the establishment of the AFL?

5. What made it possible for the AFL and CIO to drop their rivalry and merge in the AFL-CIO? Why did the merger not come a decade sooner? A decade later?

APPENDIX: CHRONOLOGY OF EVENTS IN THE HISTORY OF COLLECTIVE BARGAINING IN THE UNITED STATES, 1786–1960.

1786   First recorded strike, called by Philadelphia Journeymen Printers, against a wage cut.

1799   First recorded attempt at collective bargaining by Philadelphia Journeymen Cordwainers (shoemakers) was answered by the employers with a lockout and followed by a negotiated settlement between the union and the employer association.

1806   First criminal conspiracy case against Cordwainers in Philadelphia. Defendants found guilty of a combination to raise wages.

1820   A depression year. Unions died out or became inactive.

1824   With return of prosperity unions became active again. Numerous strikes in the larger cities.

1825   Boston House Carpenters struck for the 10-hour day; lost.

1827   Building-trades workers, striking in Philadelphia for the 10-hour day, formed the first City Central organization of local unions, the Mechanics' Union of Trade Associations. (This in turn established the first political party of labor, the Working Men's Party, which, like other labor parties of the 19th century, suffered defeat but left an imprint on the established political parties by causing them to woo workers with planks in the platform such as: free and compulsory public education, abolition of imprisonment for debt, and other reforms demanded by the labor parties.)

1831   New England Association of Farmers, Mechanics and Other Working Men formed in Providence, R.I., spread throughout New England. Seen by some as the first industrial union, but was more a political than a union movement. Agitated for the 10-hour day in textile mills and factories. Died out after 1834.

1833–37 During these years the workingmen's benevolent societies turned into genuine unions of craftsmen. City centrals were established in many cities; there were many strikes for wage demands. Some specific developments during this period were as follows:

1834   First attempt at forming a national organization of Labor: a federation of City Centrals called the National Trades' Union. Disappeared in 1837.

1835   In the Geneva Cordwainers case, and a similar case involving Tailors in 1836, New York courts upheld a law based on the conspiracy doctrine, making concerted activity to get a raise in wages illegal.

1836   Employer Association activity became marked in response to union activity. Fought closed-shop demands by attempting to refuse to employ union members. Turned with greater frequency to court action against unions under the conspiracy doctrine and existing legal precedent.

First national federation of local unions of a single craft was organized: the National Cooperative Association of Journeymen Cordwainers. Printers also federated, and other crafts followed in succeeding years.

1837   Depression year. Dropoff of union activity.

1842   In the case of *Commonwealth* v. *Hunt*, the very influential Massachusetts Supreme Court overturned the conspiracy doctrine and declared unions not illegal.

1840–60   Gradual (though intermittent) increase in volume of union activity along lines already followed: local union bargaining with local employer associations; activity of City Centrals; formation and growth of national federations of the various crafts.

Industrial Revolution influence increasingly felt: Bessemer process for steelmaking introduced to U.S.; greater mechanization; intensification of factory methods and invasion of many handicraft fields by the factories. Unions find little success in penetrating factories.

1861–65   The Civil War intensified the trends mentioned above.

1866   National Labor Union, a federation of national craft federations, established under leadership of William H. Sylvis, head of the Iron Moulders' Union. Lasted until 1872.

1869   Knights of Labor founded in Philadelphia by a group of journeymen tailors. Began as a secret society and spread slowly at first among skilled-worker groups; but under the influence of Uriah H. Stephens, a member who had started out to become a Baptist minister, it opened its ranks to all who belonged to the "Brotherhood of Toil."

1873   Financial panic, followed by a long depression.

1877   Strikes against pay cuts on the railways broke out on lines east of the Mississippi, with violent clashes between strikers and federal troops in Baltimore and Pittsburgh. More than 100 killed. Troops finally put down the strikes.

1878   Knights of Labor organized nationally. Stephens, first Grand Master Workman, succeeded by Terence V. Powderly.

Period of recovery from depression began.

1881   Delegates of craft unions met in Pittsburgh to form the Federation of Organized Trades and Labor Unions (the forerunner of the AFL).

1882   After negotiations between Powderly and Cardinal Gibbons of Baltimore, the Knights of Labor renounced secrecy and revised its ritual, and the Roman Catholic church withdrew its ban on membership in the Knights.

Strike of railway workers on the West Coast against wage cuts, led by members of the Knights of Labor, resulted in rescinding of cuts.

1883   Depression year.

1885   Railway workers on the "Southwest System" controlled by Jay Gould, New York financier, struck against wage cuts. Organized into the Knights of Labor after the strike broke out spontaneously, the workers kept the trains from moving until Gould met and signed an agreement in New York with Terence V. Powderly: first "Wabash strike."

Frederick W. Taylor started experiments at the Midvale and Bethlehem steel plants that led to the discoveries of "scientific management."

1886   A "big year" in labor history.

A strike which started as a "wildcat" on the Gould-controlled MKT line was decisively defeated. The Knights lost prestige and members as a result. (Second "Wabash strike.")

The Federation of Organized Trades and Labor Unions, led by Samuel Gompers, called a nationwide strike for the eight-hour day, to start May 1. Powderly refused to give the move the official support of the Knights, but many Local Assemblies of the Knights answered the strike call. Chicago police killed four strikers at the McCormick Reaper works. At a meeting in Haymarket Square called to protest these killings, a bomb was thrown that killed several police officers. The Knights of Labor became unjustly associated in the public mind with violence. This caused further loss of prestige and shrinking of membership.

Later in the year the Federation of Organized Trades and Labor Unions (craft unions) proposed a merger with the Knights which would give them control in the affairs of the Craft Assemblies of the Knights. Powderly turned down the merger offer. The Federation then sent out its own call for a convention and met in Columbus, Ohio, late that year to form the American Federation of Labor.

The American Federation of Labor elected Gompers president. As the Knights of Labor began to disintegrate, the AFL picked up most of its Craft Assemblies.

1892   Homestead Steel strike, led by AFL Amalgamated Association of Iron, Steel, and Tin Workers, led to violence between strikers and armed Pinkerton men. The strikers defeated the Pinkertons but were subdued by troops. After the strike only about 800 out of some 4,000 workers were taken back, all others being replaced by nonstrikers from outside.

1894   Pullman strike, put down by federal troops, Eugene V. Debs, Socialist and railway union leader, emerged to national prominence.

Frederick W. Taylor read a paper entitled "A Piece Work System" to the American Society of Mechanical Engineers: his first appearance before them, followed by others which gave him great influence. National Association of Manufacturers organized.

1905   Industrial Workers of the World (IWW) organized in Chicago. "Big Bill" Hayward one of its leaders.

1908   Section 10 of the Erdman Act applying to railroad employees, whereby the "yellow dog" contract was outlawed and an employer was forbidden to discharge a worker for union membership, was declared unconstitutional *(U.S. v. Adair)*.

A boycott by the United Hatters of Danbury, Conn., against D. E. Loewe and Co. was held to be in restraint of trade under the Sherman Anti-Trust Act of 1890. The individual union members were held responsible for the union's acts and assessed damages and costs totaling $252,000.

1911   A congressional committee conducting hearings on legislation for government-operated arsenals and navy yards heard testimony from Taylor and his associates. At these hearings Louis Brandeis, later to become a Supreme Court Justice, coined the term "scientific management," and helped publicize the achievements of the Taylor group, but Congress outlawed the use of the stopwatch and "efficiency" methods in arsenals and navy yards.

1912   Strikes against wage cut and "stretchout" in textile mills in Lawrence and Lowell, Mass., broke out spontaneously and striking workers were quickly organized by the IWW. The industrial form of organization, the well-conducted relief activities, and the nonviolent tactics the IWW employed in this strike resulted in a victory for the strikers, who got wage increases, revision of the stretchout program, and adjustment of grievances.

1913   Strikes in the silk mills of Paterson and Passaic, N.J., led by the IWW, were met by stern police measures, and failed.

1914   Clayton Act approved. It exempted unions from the provisions of the Sherman Act, limited the use of injunctions in labor disputes, and provided that picketing and other union activities were not to be considered unlawful. (Later judicial interpretation reversed the apparent prolabor provisions.)

1914–19 A war-boom period, characterized by labor shortages, rapid expansion of factory production, shifts in the labor force. The AFL under Gompers supported the Allied war effort and pledged cooperation with employers to win the war. AFL membership increased in the factories, but employers were reluctant to recognize unions, while unions were jealous of jurisdictional lines. To resolve these difficulties the National War Labor Board, created by Congress as an emergency measure, ordered the establishment in many factories of "works councils" consisting of elected representatives of workers in the various departments. These councils side-stepped the question of recognition and of jurisdiction, and carried on collective bargaining and grievance-adjusting activities with factory managements.

1917   The Supreme Court upheld the "yellow dog" contract and declared that union efforts to organize workers subject to such contracts were unlawful (*Hitchman Coal and Coke Company* v. *Mitchell*).

1919   Strike wave in steel and other industries, as industry reconverted and employers withdrew such recognition as they had accorded unions during wartime. Unions of the AFL lost their foothold in the factories. Legislation creating the National War Labor Board lapsed and works councils created by NWLB lost specific legal sanction, but many companies retained the councils as consultative bodies and for grievance adjustments.

National Industrial Conference Board started a series of studies of the works councils, and Employee Representation Plans that developed from them, and ended by recommending the idea to manufacturing employers.

1920–29 General trends: craft unions were ousted from the factories where they had gained a foothold during the war—"open shop" prevailed in manufacturing with many large companies establishing employee-representation plans; widespread adoption of the lessons of the scientific management movement; mounting prosperity up to crash of 1929.

1926   Railway Labor Act. Established collective bargaining for the railways to guard against stoppages in vital national transportation system. Outlawed "company unions," provided grievance procedure and arbitration machinery.

1929   Stock-market crash signaled the beginning of depression and large-scale unemployment.

1932   Norris-La Guardia Act. Outlawed the yellow dog contract and made the use of the injunction in labor disputes difficult.

1933   A turning-point year for industrial unionism.

Inauguration of Franklin D. Roosevelt as President ushers in the "New Deal" administration.

NRA. Section 7a of the National Industrial Recovery Act gives workers the "right to bargain collectively through representatives of their own choosing without interference, coercion or restraint on the part of the employer."

Unions receive big impetus from Section 7a. This includes company unions as well as the AFL.

AFL Convention votes to hold a Conference to devise ways of organizing industrial workers.

1934   AFL Conference advocates federal locals for the factories; sidesteps question of craft-union jurisdiction over workers in these locals.

"Labor's Civil War" begins at AFL San Francisco convention between craft and industrial unionists; first result a compromise.

1935   Supreme Court declares NRA unconstitutional.

Congress reenacts the substance of Section 7a in the form of the Wagner Act; outlaws company unions; establishes the National Labor Relations Board.

Clash at AFL Atlantic City convention ends with victory of craft unionists. Industrial-union advocates meet in November to form the "Committee for Industrial Organization," CIO.

1936   AFL Executive Council calls on AFL-affiliated unions to sever connection with CIO; few comply.

Sit-down strikes in auto factories in December.

1937   AFL expels unions connected with the CIO.

Auto Workers (UAW-CIO) sign contract with General Motors in February, Chrysler in April; Steelworkers (SWOC) sign with Carnegie-Illinois, U.S. Steel, Jones & Laughlin.

Strikes in "Little Steel" result in union defeats.

Supreme Court upholds constitutionality of Wagner Act.

1938   CIO organizes on permanent basis as "Congress of Industrial Organizations," with John L. Lewis as its first president.

1940   Lewis resigns as president of CIO; Phillip Murray elected in his place.

1941   United States declares war on the Axis powers; gets a "no-strike" pledge from labor; sets up tripartite (labor-management-public) National War Labor Board to deal with wartime disputes.

Ford Motor Co. Signs first contract with UAW-CIO.

1946   Postwar strike wave, most extensive to date in U.S. history. As after World War I, recognition at stake in some of the strikes. Unions succeed in winning new agreements.

1947   Taft-Hartley law.

1955   AFL-CIO merger.

1957   Teamsters Union expelled from AFL-CIO on grounds of alleged racketeering associations.

1959   Landrum-Griffin Act.

1962   Civil rights campaign starts in southern states with boycott of segregated buses in Montgomery, Alabama, led by the Rev. Martin Luther King.

1962   President John F. Kennedy issues Executive Order 10988 authorizing collective bargaining in the federal services.

1968   UAW withdraws from AFL-CIO, forms an "alliance" with Teamsters, later formalized (1969) as Alliance for Labor Action (ALA) joined by a few other AFL-CIO and independent unions. ALA now defunct. Strikes of teachers, sanitation workers, other public employees in New York, Baltimore, other cities and school districts.
Martin Luther King assassinated while leading support activities for striking sanitation workers in Memphis, Tennessee.
Sen. Robert F. Kennedy, campaigning for Democratic presidential nomination, assassinated in Los Angeles, where he appeared with Cesar Chavez, agricultural labor leader, in support of efforts to organize grape pickers.

1969   Strikes in transportation: railways and airlines. Merger of four large Railway Brotherhoods into United Transportation Union, with 270,000 members.
Civil rights militants demand jobs for blacks in construction industry; hold "Black Mondays" demonstrations in Pittsburgh, Chicago, and elsewhere. U.S. government offers "Philadelphia Plan" to open apprenticeship to minority workers; AFL–CIO opposes it.
President Nixon supersedes Executive Order 10988 with Executive Order 11491, mainly confirming and clarifying the previous order.

1970   Wildcat strike of postal workers spreads throughout U.S. Postmaster calls for troops to handle mail, but negotiates settlement with strikers. Walter Reuther dies in plane crash: Leonard Woodcock succeeds him in presidency of UAW, directs negotiations with auto companies for new agreement.

1972   Farm worker union led by Chavez wins recognition from some growers, sets up union hiring halls, but loses these gains when growers sign agreements instead with Teamsters union. Interunion clashes occur in the fields, but AFL–CIO intensifies its support of Chavez forces.

1974   Congress amends LMRA (Taft-Hartley) to bring employees in non-profit hospitals as well as other health care employees under NLRB jurisdiction; some restrictions on the right to strike.

1975   California legislature brings farm workers under protection of state labor relations law which provides for recognition by vote of workers in secret ballot election.
New York City medical internes strike for shorter work week; later,

M.D.s form first local union of medical doctors, affiliate with Service Employees union, AFL-CIO.

United Mine Workers Union president, W. R. "Tony" Boyle, convicted of conspiring to murder his defeated rival for the presidency, Joseph Yablonski, and members of his family. In Labor Department-supervised election, control of UMWA passes into hands of reform group.

James Hoffa, forced out of Teamster union presidency in 1969 on his conviction for jury tampering and pardoned in 1974 by President Nixon before serving full term in prison, disappears under mysterious circumstances.

Executive Order 11838 further extends and clarifies collective bargaining rules in federal service.

SELECTED ANNOTATED BIBLIOGRAPHY

BERNSTEIN, IRVING. *The Lean Years: A History of the American Worker 1920–1933;* and *Turbulent Years: A History of the American Worker 1933–1941.* Boston: Houghton Mifflin, 1960 and 1969.

Two detailed, insightful, and readable accounts of two decades of U.S. labor history, with the first book concentrating on the worker and the second on the unions.

BLOCH, HERMAN D. *The Circle of Discrimination: An Economic and Social Study of the Black Man in New York.* New York: New York University Press, 1969.

A thorough and scholarly treatment of the status and struggles of Afro-Americans from colonial days to the present in the populous and strategic state of New York, including a full discussion of the black worker and the unions.

CARPENTER, JESSE T. *Competition and Collective Bargaining in the Needle Trades, 1910–1967.* Ithaca: New York State School of Industrial and Labor Relations, 1972.

A very detailed examination of the development of collective bargaining in the clothing industries, with attention focused on the role of bargaining in regulating the cutthroat competition in these industries.

CHRISTIE, ROBERT. *Empire in Wood: A History of the Carpenters Union.* Ithaca: New York State School of Industrial and Labor Relations, 1956.

A well-done analysis of the conflict between the ideologies of social reform and pure and simple unionism as illustrated by the early growth and development of the carpenters union. Christie notes the emergence of the role of the business agent as the key event which led to the demise of the reform-oriented segment of the union led by the international union's founding father, Peter J. McGuire.

COMMONS, JOHN R., and ASSOCIATES. *History of Labour in the United States, 1896–1932.* 4 vols. New York: The Macmillan Co., 6th printing, 1951.

The classic University of Wisconsin study of American labor history, comprising: Volumes I and II by

COMMONS, JOHN R.; SAPOSS, DAVID J.; SUMNER, HELEN L.; MITTELMAN, E. B.; HOAGLUND, H. E.; ANDREWS, JOHN B.; and PERLMAN, SELIG.
Volume III, *Labor Movements*, by SELIG PERLMAN and PHILIP TAFT.
Volume IV, *Working Conditions and Labor Legislation,* by DON D. LESCOHIER and ELIZABETH BRANDEIS.

CORMIER, FRANK, and EATON, WILLIAM J.   *Reuther.* Englewood Cliffs, N.J.: Prentice–Hall, 1971.
A detailed biography of one of the most prominent and progressive figures in the American labor movement.

DUBORSKY, MELVIN.   *We Shall Be All.* Chicago: Quadrangle Books, 1969.
A thorough treatment, from a sympathetic point of view, of the IWW. Captures some of the spirit and mentality of the Wobblies, their day and generation.

FINK, GARY E.   "The Rejection of Voluntarism," *Industrial and Labor Relations Review,* vol. 26, no. 2 (January 1973).
A historian shows that the old AFL's rhetoric about "voluntarism" and opposition to governmental assistance in employment relations was espoused by national union officials but was opposed by union officers and members at the local level.

FINLEY, JOSEPH E.   *The Corrupt Kingdom: The Rise and Fall of the United Mine Workers.* New York: Simon and Shuster, 1972.
An examination of the development of the UMW as an organization from its early days to the present, with an emphasis upon the leadership and legacy of John L. Lewis.

GALENSON, WALTER.   *The CIO Challenge to the AFL: A History of the American Labor Movement, 1935–1941.* Wertheim Publications in Industrial Relations. Cambridge, Mass.: Harvard University Press, 1960.
A descriptive history of labor developments in the steel, auto, coal mining, electrical, rubber, clothing, textile, meat, lumber, petroleum, and maritime industries, as well as those affected by the teamster, machinist, building trades, printing and publishing, and railroad unions. Author relies heavily on hitherto unavailable AFL Executive Council and CIO Executive Board minutes.

HARDMAN, J. B. S., ed.   *American Labor Dynamics.* New York: Harcourt, Brace & Co., 1928.
Thirty-two labor leaders, teachers, editors, and technicians discuss the problems of organized labor during the bleak 1920s. Readers will find here a realistic statement of the problems of organizing the unorganized as they existed in the pre-New Deal era.

JAMES, RALPH, and JAMES, ESTELLE.   *Hoffa and the Teamsters: A Study of Union Power.* Princeton: D. Van Nostrand, 1965.
An exceptionally insightful analysis of the emergence of one of the most controversial figures in American union history, with special emphasis on Hoffa's sources and uses of power.

LITWACK, LEON.   *The American Labor Movement.* Englewood Cliffs, N.J.: Prentice–Hall, 1962.
A stimulating collection of documents placed in historical sequence that gives the reader a richer experience of the development of American labor.

Documents ranging from the preamble of the IWW constitution to the eloquent defense by Clarence S. Darrow of the union shop.

MACDONALD, ROBERT M. "Collective Bargaining in the Postwar Period," *Industrial and Labor Relations Review*, vol. 20 (1968).

An excellent brief account of the changing structure and issues of collective bargaining since the end of World War II. Relates these changes to developments both in the external environment and the attitudes and beliefs of the parties themselves.

MILLIS, HARRY A., research director. *How Collective Bargaining Works*. New York: Twentieth Century Fund, 1942.

This volume is a comprehensive statement of collective bargaining processes in 16 industries with notes on 13 more industries up to 1940. The contents are:

TAFT, PHILIP. "Organized Labor and the New Deal."

BURNS, ROBERT K. "Daily Newspapers."

BROWN, EMILY CLARK. "Book and Job Printing."

HABER, WILLIAM. "Building Construction."

FISHER, WALDO E. "Bituminous Coal."

———. "Anthracite."

WOLF, HARRY D. "Railroads."

MYERS, ROBERT J., and BLOCH, JOSEPH W. "Men's Clothing."

TAYLOR, GEORGE W. "Hosiery."

HARBISON, FREDERICK H. "Steel."

McPHERSON, W. H. "Automobiles."

ANTHONY, DONALD. "Rubber Products."

DERBER, MILTON. "Glass."

———. "Electrical Products."

CHRISTENSON, C. LAURENCE. "Chicago Service Trades."

TAFT, PHILIP. "Collective Bargaining Before the New Deal."

———. "Brief Review of Other Industries."

PELLING, HENRY. *American Labor*. Chicago: University of Chicago Press, 1960.

An excellent short history of the American labor movement.

PERLMAN, SELIG. *A History of Trade Unionism in the United States*. New York: The Macmillan Co., 1922.

Part I is a summary of the first two volumes of the *History of Labor in the United States* by J. R. Commons and associates. Part II carries the history down to 1923. In Part III the author begins to develop his own theory of the American labor movement, stressing that the attempt to improve the bargaining position ("job control") of the worker and not the desire for a revolutionary transformation of society "is the key to the conduct of organized labor in America."

PIERSON, FRANK C. *Unions in Postwar America: An Economic Assessment*. New York: Random House, 1967.

A brief but comprehensive view of the relation of union policy and practices to the American economic system.

RASKIN, A. H. "The Labor Movement Must Start Moving," *Harvard Business Review*, vol. 48 (January–February 1970).

An assessment of the institutional hardening of the arteries that is currently troubling the American labor movement, by the labor editor of the *New York Times*.

SLICHTER, SUMNER H.; HEALY, JAMES J.; and LIVERNASH, E. ROBERT. *The Impact of Collective Bargaining on Management*. Washington, D.C.: Brookings Institution, 1960.

A comprehensive treatment of contemporary American collective bargaining practices ranging from such specific topics as control of evaluated rate structures, hiring, and concepts of seniority to such general questions as the importance of line and staff cooperation. Authors resist developing an explicit theory of collective bargaining, but do provide some generalizations regarding the emerging characteristics of collective bargaining. In part, an updating of Slichter's *Union Policies and Industrial Management*.

TAYLOR, FREDERICK WINSLOW. *Scientific Management, Comprising Shop Management, The Principles of Scientific Management, Testimony before the Special House Committee*. New York: Harper & Bros., 1947.

The father of Scientific Management explains its principles to the American Society of Mechanical Engineers in 1903, the general public, and a special committee of the House of Representatives in the winter of 1911–12.

ULMAN, LLOYD. *The Rise of the National Trade Union*. Cambridge, Mass.: Harvard University Press, 1955.

A functional and historical analysis of the reasons for the emergence of national unions as the key power centers in the U.S. trade union movement.

WEBB, SIDNEY, and WEBB, BEATRICE. *The History of Trade Unionism*. New York: Longmans, Green & Co.; first published 1894, latest ed., 1920.

A classic history of trade unions in Great Britain. After rejecting the guild theory of the origin of unions and suggesting that unions arose only after "the great bulk of workers ceased to be independent producers," it traces the development of British trade unions from the latter part of the seventeenth century through the first two decades of the twentieth.

WITTE, EDWIN E. *The Evolution of Managerial Ideas in Industrial Relations*. Ithaca, N.Y.: New York State School of Industrial and Labor Relations Bulletin no. 27, 1954.

A leading authority on industrial relations traces the changes in American management's view of industrial relations in the 20th century.

3 Union Organization for Collective Bargaining

In any organization, each employee has a separate employment contract with the employer; but work is social. An enterprise of even moderate size organizes and integrates its tasks so closely that every job is interdependent, to some degree, with all the others. Thus an individual cannot bargain personally for job changes or conditions of employment without affecting others more or less directly, so that individual bargaining is ineffective. Even if it could be effective, it would be disruptive. Changes in individual employment contracts thus depend on a *general* review of the conditions of employment, and when workers feel the need for this they can obtain it only by *collective* pressure on the employer. To exert this pressure, workers form unions. In factories and other large-scale organizations with a high degree of job specialization, they form industrial unions. In other kinds of industry, including those in which skilled craftsmen perform substantially the same work and bring to their tasks the same qualifications, it seems natural to seek the same employment bargain for all who possess the same skills. Again the means of doing so is to form a union, and for skilled workers in the handicraft trades, a craft union.

Doctors, lawyers, engineers, and other professional people often form professional associations. Typically, these associations do not engage in collective bargaining and shun the label "union," but typically, also, they seek by other means many of the same ends as unions. Some professional associations do engage in collective bargaining and in this respect behave exactly like unions.

In this chapter we shall examine union structure, and observe both the similarities and differences between the craft and industrial forms. We start with what is conventionally called the manual or blue-collar segment of the labor movement as found in private industry, for it was the manual workers, skilled and nonskilled, who first formed unions and engaged employers in collective bargaining. By their interaction these original actors shaped the framework of labor law and custom, whereas white-collar and professional

61

people did not get into the act until much later. It would only confuse the picture if we dealt with these late-comers now. We therefore defer discussion of white-collar and professional unions until we have given an account of the background and present-day structure of the traditional, blue-collar participants in the activities that make up collective bargaining.

UNIONS TODAY

The preceding chapter explains how unions started in the United States and how they grew and developed in patterns that confront us today. Hardly a town in America remains untouched by union activity. City-dwellers, of course, belong to unions by the thousands and tens of thousands. Many country villages that used to have an all-farming population now consist to a noticeable degree of people who drive daily from their rural homes or small acreages to work in a nearby mill or factory, where they are members of an industrial union. Even in what would seem to be pure farming territory there is bound to be at least a building trades council at the county seat, while unionized truckers haul the farmer's harvest from feedlot or grain elevator to the unionized processing plants. No one can escape the unions any more by moving to a "bedroom" suburb inhabited exclusively by business executives and professional people: the mail carrier will be a union member, and probably the teachers in the public schools. The campus is no refuge, either: university professors have let the unions into their jealously-guarded ivory towers.

What are unions like? What do they want? How do they go about getting what they want? How does this affect society?

In Chapter 4 we shall make clear that business organizations pursue goals that reflect the values—that is, the needs, desires, and aspirations—of the people who set them up. We might expect unions to do the same, and indeed, for the most part, they do. They are *service* organizations. They produce no tangible product, but charge dues, fees, and assessments in return for the services they provide the members. Profit, the goal of the business enterprise, is not a goal of the union organization, though in a figurative sense members may believe they profit—that is, benefit—from the union's activities. We might sum up union goals, and union operating objectives, as follows:

1. *Goal:* to secure, and if possible, improve the living standards and economic status of their members. *Objective:* to establish wage and effort bargains that meet worker needs and are congruent with current or developing social norms and standards.
2. *Goal:* to enhance, and if possible, guarantee individual security against threats and contingencies that might result from market fluctuations, technological change, or management decisions. *Objective:* to establish

rules providing tenure and job rights and a system of due process, or justice at the work place.

3. *Goal:* to influence power relations in the enveloping social system in ways that favor and do not threaten union gains and goals. *Objective:* to shape rules for rule-making, or labor relations laws, that facilitate collective bargaining for acceptable substantive rules at the work place.

4. *Goal:* to advance the welfare of all who work for a living, whether union members or not. *Objective:* to promote social legislation and public policy leading towards a stable economy and a more equitable society in which unions can thrive.

Unions pursue the first two of these sets of goals and objectives by collective bargaining; the second pair, by political activity. That is, towards the collective bargaining ends, they mobilize the united efforts of their members in the *employee* role; towards the political ends, in their role as *citizen and voter.*

Most fairminded people would accept these goals as worthy ones, but many would be doubtful that they actually hold good in practice, and some would be cynical. There is, indeed, room for doubt. If union members always sanctioned the goals by democratic vote, and union officials unswervingly followed the objectives, only those people could object whose personal interests brought them in conflict with the unions. We need not join the cynics when we admit that unions often fall far short of the ideal. We need not cast aside all doubt when we say, also, that the statements do hold true much—perhaps most—of the time.

Like other organizations, unions concentrate money and power in the hands of a few leaders, and these few have to be allowed some discretion in discharging the responsibilities union members charge them with. They rarely fall down on their collective bargaining obligations, which serve the goals of most immediate concern to the members: a decent living, with some measure of security. Even outsiders—the public, people who are not union members—accept this kind of activity as right and proper for the union leader role.

The general public isn't quite as ready to approve union activities in the political arena. Here unions come up against competing and conflicting interests in a pluralistic society. Here they face issues that are more complicated than shop rules.

Out of the rough and tumble of labor organizing, striking, picketing, and hard bargaining, and the twists and turns of inner-union politics, strong and sometimes unscrupulous leaders emerge. Because of membership support, they wield power and influence that is felt beyond the union and the industry. They don't always act wisely or considerately; sometimes not even honestly. And in the huge and complicated union structures that have grown up, they are hard to call to account, even by their own members. An international union of half a million or a million members is a long way from town-hall democracy.[1]

The leaders might be brought under greater restraint if it were not for the apathy of the rank and file. A great many union members take little interest in union affairs as long as the union gets them a raise in pay from time to time and processes their personal grievances. These members pay their dues and expect a return for their money. Like stockholders who don't care how a corporation is run as long as it pays dividends, they are indifferent to union activities beyond the work group and the shop. It speaks well for the integrity of the bulk of labor leaders that abuse of union-based power is the exception and not the rule. The international unions and their federation speak out consistently on behalf of all workers, not just the unionized. They work hard for socially progressive legislation. They help organize the unorganized. It should not be forgotten that even though the Teamsters signed a "sweetheart" contract with the California growers, the rest of labor (including many Teamster members and local officials) stood by Cesar Chavez in his struggle for a decent living for the "working poor." And while it's true that some unions have come under gangster control, so have some industries, and some communities. Higher union bodies have not only never condoned gangster rule, but helped exploited members carry out perilous battles against it.

UNION DEMOCRACY

Union democracy takes on significance for the general public when we consider the traditional presumptions, embedded in law and ideology, that unions are *voluntary* and *private* institutions. If only those who want to join a union have to, and anyone who wants to leave a union may, then unions are voluntary. If unions seek no public subsidy and wield no public power, they are private. Anyone accepting these two propositions would have to conclude that union internal affairs are nobody else's business. Labor leaders would like to hold to this conclusion, but it would be hard for any of them to uphold the premises today.

A democratic society can tolerate even the most autocratically-managed private and voluntary organizations as long as they conform to law and custom in their dealings with the enveloping social order. Business enterprises, for example, are administered autocratically, from the top; so are some churches, though not all. If unions are indeed voluntary and private associations, then the members "own" the union and the will of the members must be paramount in all union activities. Thus authority must flow upward in unions from the owner-members to the elected officers. Majority rule and

---

[1] In his classic study of radical *Political Parties* and working-class movements, Robert Michels concludes that every system of leadership is incompatible with the most essential postulate of democracy.

town hall democracy provide the foundation upon which unions must be built. The individual member's inherent right to withdraw from the union provides a constant check on any undemocratic practices of the union leadership. If oligarchy develops, it has been approved through the apathy of the membership. In theory at least, the membership always possesses an absolute veto on any action of the leadership.

The private side of the assumption gives unions great discretion in the means they adopt to achieve their ends. So long as unions do not exceed the freedoms guaranteed to individual citizens, they would be free to engage in all sorts of fraternal and political activities, just as a lodge could endorse a political candidate or contribute to campaign expenses. Carried to the extreme, as private organizations unions could even become political parties.

Students of the labor movement have argued the relative merits of "bread-and-butter" unionism versus "utopian" unionism for almost a century now. Within the labor movement itself considerable controversy has raged over the obligation of unions to act as the protectors and advocates of the down-trodden in the society. It probably is not an exaggeration to say that the principle which split the labor movement in the formation of the CIO in 1935 was the question of the obligation of the labor movement to bring the benefits of unionism to unorganized workers. If one firmly supports the voluntary and private assumption, the question of organizing the unorganized beyond the immediate jurisdiction of existing unions is largely irrelevant. Certainly the voluntary and private assumption excludes any necessity for action seeking to modify the existing politico-economic structure of society. Today it is fashionable to criticize the failure of American unions to organize the real victims of poverty in the United States, and the authors of this book have frequently joined this lament. However, if the voluntary and private assumption were completely accepted, there would be little justification for this criticism. Under the voluntary and private assumption, union activity in organizing the victims of poverty could be judged a failure only if unorganized poverty-stricken workers posed a threat to the prosperity of the present members of unions.

Although the voluntary and private institution assumption about unions is helpful in explaining union activity and is deeply imbedded in tradition, it must be abandoned today simply because *it is contrary to fact.* Under current law, unions are obligated to represent *all* the workers under an NLRB certification whether they are union members or not. Thus American unions have become instrumentalities of the state at least to some degree. The significance of the quasi-public nature of unionism is discussed in Chapter 5.

Quite apart from the legal obligation to represent some nonmember workers, American unionism has interests which go beyond the simple representation of present members. These interests are dictated by the market context and the broader ideological objectives of *some* unions. Market conditions dictating union activity beyond the representation of present members are fairly noncontroversial. Low-wage, nonunion textile plants pose an obvious threat to the jobs and wages of unionized textile workers; the interests of the members of textile unions can be protected only by organizing the nonunion workers or raising their wages to union levels by law. On the other hand, the obligation of unions to represent the downtrodden in the society is a highly controversial question which ultimately is decided on the ethical standards of the discussants. In the discussion which follows, consideration will be given to the organizational elements best suited for serving these broader representational interests.

Probably the greatest deterrent to town hall democracy in unions is the apathy of rank and file. A good many union members have little interest in union affairs so long as the union is effective in negotiating wage increases and processing their personal grievances. These members pay their dues and expect the union to do a job for them, just as they may hire a neighborhood youth to mow the lawn. As long as the grass gets cut they are satisfied, and they couldn't care less about who cuts it or what methods are used to do the job.

Union democracy is hard to define. Two dimensions of the meaning of union democracy are suggested by a substantial body of scholarly literature. The legalistic dimension of union democracy is the existence of procedures for fair and regular elections, reasonable trial procedures in applying union discipline, and guarantees that members of the union have a right to express reasoned dissent from union policy.[2] Another, more humanistic, dimension of union democracy deals with the extent to which individual members of unions feel that they are capable of influencing union policy, and their satisfaction with the policies established.[3] It seems fair to say that rank-and-file apathy, the ambition of powerful leaders, and centralization of union decision-making power at levels above the local tend to dilute union democracy in both the legalistic and humanistic dimensions.

The wage and effort bargain and systems of individual security always originate at the level of the enterprise and the local union. Political activity more frequently is conducted at higher levels of union organization than the local.

ELEMENTS OF UNION ORGANIZATIONAL STRUCTURE

The basic elements of union organizational structure in the United States are: (1) the local union, (2) the international union, and (3) the federation, or AFL–CIO. Auxiliary elements of union structure which are directly engaged in the negotiation and administration of collective bargaining agreements include: (1) districts, (2) joint boards, (3) conference boards, and

---

[2] For example, see Philip Taft, *The Structure and Government of Labor Unions* (Cambridge, Mass.: Harvard University Press, 1954).

[3] A classic human relations study is Leonard R. Sayles and George Strauss, *The Local Union* (New York: Harper & Bros., 1953).

(4) trade councils. Auxiliary elements of union structure which are engaged primarily in representational or political activity are: (1) city centrals, (2) state centrals, and (3) COPE, the political arm. Each of these elements of union structure will be considered separately and then integrated with the general structure of the American labor movement.

THE TWO KINDS OF LOCAL UNIONS

As the preceding chapters brought out, there are two kinds of local unions: craft locals and industrial locals. They differ in a number of ways— basis of membership, bargaining strategy, strike tactics, contract adminis- tration, and other characteristics—but before emphasizing the differences, let's consider some of the attributes they share.

The local union is a voluntary association of workers who, as free citi- zens with economic interests in common, have banded together for mutual advantage. The members of the local work for an employer or for several or many employers, but the union exists as an organization independently of any employer, under the constitutional guarantee of freedom of assembly.

The members "own" the local and control it by majority vote: one vote per member. They elect officers and an executive board to act for them between meetings. They hold their meetings, ordinarily, at intervals of a month or less, and conduct them by the rules of order of democratic deliber- ative assemblies.

The membership meeting is the highest authority of the local union. All members in good standing have voice and vote there. A member maintains good standing by paying dues and assessments and observing the discipline of the union as laid down in the local constitution and bylaws, and in deci- sions of the local at membership meetings. New members gain admission to the union by complying with the conditions and qualifications of the con- stitution, paying the required initiation fee, and, if the constitution requires it, receiving the affirmative vote of the members.

In structure and the routine conduct of its business a local union resem- bles countless other private and independent organizations to which Ameri- cans belong: clubs, lodges, church groups, recreational, educational, and service associations. The difference is in the aims the local union sets itself and the functions it carries out.

The primary aim of the local union is to represent its members in relation to their employer or employers. Like any other membership association it also carries on social and subsidiary activities, but in pursuit of its primary aim, the most important functions it performs with employers are collective bargaining and grievance handling.

As independent entities, the local union and the employer of its members negotiate through authorized agents for an agreement defining the terms of the individual work contracts of the employee-members. Negotiation takes place at the policy-making level of the two organizations involved. In the local union, the membership meeting makes policy and selects agents to negotiate on policy with policy makers in management.

Corollary to the process of negotiating the agreement is grievance handling or administration of the agreement. The local union provides employees with a channel for complaints arising under the agreement and for solving problems not foreseen in the negotiations. An administrative organ of the local union sees to the application and enforcement of agreement terms.

Both craft locals and industrial locals devote their main efforts to influencing the wage and effort bargain and establishing systems of individual security at the workplace. Because their membership base is relatively small, they are capable of exerting only insignificant political influence on either the rules for rule making or power in the state.[4]

The Craft Local. "One craft, one union" is the slogan of the craft union. Craft unions dominate the building construction industry and also play an important role in printing and publishing and in the barbering trade. The "tie that binds" a craft union local is the mastery by its members of an entire recognized trade, such as plumbing, lithography, or barbering.

A worker typically masters a trade by serving an apprenticeship consisting of classroom instruction and on-the-job training of several years' duration. Approximately 800 detailed trades and occupations or crafts are recognized by government, unions, and employers as eligible to participate in the national and state apprenticeship programs. Figure 3–1 lists some apprenticeable trades in various industries and indicates the normal duration of the apprenticeships.

A craft union local typically seeks to enroll in its membership all practitioners of its trade in the immediate geographic vicinity regardless of who the employers of its members are. That is, a typical Carpenters' local would seek to organize all the carpenters in Peoria, Illinois, or in Tompkins County, New York. Journeymen carpenters who had served an apprenticeship or acquired journeyman status by long experience would be joined by apprentices in training and carpenter helpers in a single local union. One of the major functions of this local might be joint administration of an apprenticeship program with employers of carpenters in the area. An exception to this general rule might occur when a single employer had a large regular force of craftsmen, for example, a local of the International Brotherhood of Electrical Workers composed solely of skilled electrical workers employed by a power and light company.

The key person in a craft union is the business agent, who is a full-time paid employee of the local union and plays a critical role in the negotiation of the collective bargaining agreement and in its administration.

---

[4] Although some local unions are truly massive organizations and politicians eagerly seek their endorsements, single locals are typically inundated even in city elections. For example, the 40,000 members of Ford Local number 600 of the UAW are lost in a metropolitan Detroit electorate approaching 1 million.

FIGURE 3–1

Some Apprenticeable Trades and the Duration of Apprenticeship

Representative Trades in the Building Construction Industry

Bricklayer	3 years	Painter and decorator	2–4 years
Carpenter	4 years	Plasterer	3–4 years
Cement mason	3 years	Plumber-pipefitter	4–5 years
Electrical worker	4–5 years	Rigger	2 years
Ironworker	2–4 years	Roofer	2–3 years
Lather	2–3 years	Sheet-metal worker	3–4 years
Millwright	4 years	Stonemason	3 years
Operating engineer	3–4 years	Tile setter	3 years

Representative Trades in Printing and Publishing Industry

Electrotyper	5–6 years	Printer	5–6 years
Engraver	4–5 years	Printing pressman	5–6 years
Lithographer	4–5 years	Rotogravure engraver	5–6 years
Mailer	4–5 years	Stereotyper	5–6 years
Photoengraver	5–6 years		

Representative Trades in Service Industries

Arborist	3–4 years	Cosmetician	2 years
Barber	2 years	Photographer	3 years
Cook	3 years	Telephone worker	4 years

Representative Trades in Manufacturing Industry

Aircraft fabricator	3–4 years	Machinist	4 years
Brewer	2–3 years	Metal polisher and buffer	3–4 years
Butcher-meat cutter	3 years	Model maker	4 years
Candy maker	3–4 years	Pattern maker (foundry)	5 years
Drafter-designer	3–5 years	Pottery worker	3 years
Fabric cutter	3–4 years	Tool- and die-maker	4–5 years
Furrier	3–4 years	Upholsterer	3–4 years

Source: U.S. Department of Labor, Manpower Administration, *The National Apprenticeship Program*, 1965, pp. 9–27.

Bargaining Activities of Craft Locals. The business agent is influential in both the *policy-making* and *policy-enforcement* phases of collective bargaining. Policy making consists of negotiating a collective bargaining agreement with the employers of the local's members. Policy enforcement consists of checking on employer compliance with the terms of the agreement after it has been negotiated.

The business agent typically is the chief negotiator for the craft union local. The agent and other officers of the local meet with the representatives of the employer association and hammer out a basic collective bargaining agreement. This agreement is then presented to a general membership meeting of the local where it is ratified or rejected by a vote of the membership. Once ratified, this agreement becomes the policy of the signatory employers and the union.

Labor agreements negotiated by craft unions and internal craft union procedures fulfill the four basic functions of: (1) union security and management rights, (2) the wage and effort bargain, (3) individual security, and (4) administration. Typically, union security is achieved by a clause in the agreement which obligates the employers to go to the business agent when they seek to hire additional hands. The wage and effort bargain is settled by establishment of a standard union scale of wages and the tradesman's traditional control over the tempo of work. Individual security may be defined by the incorporation into the agreement of rules for employee conduct and by union practices in distributing available work among its members. Administration of the agreement is provided for by a system of on-the-job representation and the arbitration of unresolved grievances. The contents of a typical craft-union agreement are discussed in detail in Chapter 8.

The fact that some carpenter employers in the vicinity may not be members of the employer association imposes an additional negotiation responsibility on the business agent. After the basic agreement is printed, the agent then visits nonassociation member employers and insists that they sign a document identical to the basic agreement.

On-the-Job Representation in Craft Locals. An agreement setting forth wages, hours, and working conditions has been signed between the local and all the contractors employing carpenters in a given city. In response to the request of one of these contractors, the business agent of the local sends union members to work on a construction project. The first person hired customarily acts as "steward" for the Carpenters' union and is chosen by being sent out first. Or, if the policy of the local is to refer members to jobs on a strict seniority basis, the steward is the most senior member of the local who happens to be looking for work. The craft union job steward is chosen, then, either by the business agent or by seniority.

On the job, the steward's duty is to make sure that the contractor lives up to the union agreement in pay and treatment of the carpenters. If the steward observes a violation of the agreement (a copy of which the business agent has provided), the steward calls it to the attention of the supervisor in charge of the carpenters. If the supervisor does not correct the violation, the steward reports the matter to the business agent, who takes it up with the contractor. The business agent is often empowered to call the carpenters off the job if the contractor does not adjust the grievance, and keep them off until the dispute is settled.

This system constitutes a simple and effective machinery for enforcing the agreement. It gives the business agent, an administrative official of the union, a live contact with every one of the many jobs on which members of the local are working, getting information from them, and passing out information to the members through them. Several points about this system deserve notice.

Stewards representing different unions on a construction job have no official contact with each other, but only with the business agent of their own local: carpenters with the Carpenters' union, bricklayers with the Bricklayers, and so on. This need not prevent informal consultation between stewards of different unions, but there is little point in such contact since the members of each union work under a separate agreement. There is no one body of union representatives, or channel of communication, for all the workers employed on the construction project in dealings with their common employer. This will appear as one of the significant differences between craft and industrial unions.

All the stewards representing any one union—again the Carpenters, for instance—on all the projects where members are employed make up a potential "council." That is, they could be called together without calling a meeting of the local and provide contact with all the working carpenters in town. Calling them together would have little point, however, because each works for a different employer. The only things they would have in common are matters internal to the union; and for the purpose of considering internal union matters a meeting of the local would serve the same purpose and would have what the steward body would lack—power to take action affecting policy. This will appear as another of the significant differences between craft and industrial unions.

Craft union stewards, furthermore, do not represent the members on the job. They represent the business agent, who is responsible for enforcing the agreement. The steward personnel is constantly changing as the work on one project comes to an end and the members shift to other jobs in new and random groupings.

The practical consequence of all this is that the craft union stewards, as a group, do not constitute a separate, functioning organization within the structure of the local union and are not a continuing body. They are simply an extension of the authority of the business agent; an extension, in fact, of that person—being eyes and ears on the jobs where the members are employed. They do not influence the nature of collective bargaining.

Craft-union locals seldom find it necessary to take unresolved grievances to arbitration. Business agents and employers in handicraft industry share the tradition of the craft and settle their differences among themselves. The business agent, as the sole supplier of the employer's critically needed tradesmen, often holds the ace of trumps in these discussions.

The major activities of both craft and industrial local unions are influencing the wage and effort bargain and establishing a system of individual security. However, their bargains and systems are quite different from each other, as are their organizational structures for achieving these ends.

The Industrial Local. "One shop, one union" is the slogan of the industrial union. Industrial unions dominate manufacturing industry and also play important roles in trade, transportation, finance, and mining. It seems reasonable to expect that industrial unions will play an increasing role in government employment. The "tie that binds" an industrial local union is the workplace and the workers' common employer. In the industrial union all the employees working for a given enterprise at a given workplace belong to the same local union without regard for what they do in the plant.

An industrial local union typically seeks to enroll in its membership all production and maintenance workers at the place of employment, with the legally imposed exceptions of supervisors and guards. Although many industrial local unions would very much like to obtain representation rights for white-collar workers employed at their plants, such efforts have been largely unsuccessful to date.

Industrial local unions, unless very large, typically do not employ full-time business agents. Instead the major activities of the union are handled by elected officers who also are working employees at the plant. A full-time professional union person who helps an industrial local usually is an international representative, a full-time employee of the international union, not the local.

Bargaining Activities of Industrial Locals. Perhaps with the assistance of an international representative, the officers of the industrial local and a bargaining committee negotiate an agreement with the management of an enterprise. This agreement is then presented to a general membership meeting of the local where it is ratified or rejected by a vote of the membership. Once ratified, this agreement becomes the policy of the employer and the union.

Industrial union collective bargaining agreements are much more comprehensive and complex than craft union agreements, although they fulfill the same four functions as craft bargains, as will be discussed in detail in Chapter 8. Industrial unions achieve union security by a clause in the agreement requiring the employees of the enterprise to pay union dues. The agreement may also contain a lengthy section describing management rights or managerial prerogatives. Industrial unions find it necessary to negotiate an entire structure of wages, perhaps with as many as 50 different wage rates for a wide variety of jobs in contrast to less than half a dozen wage rates found in the typical craft union agreement. While a craft union agreement may make no reference whatsoever to work tempo, an industrial union agreement may contain several pages of principles and rules by which production standards are established and modified. Industrial union agreements invariably contain long sections on seniority and due process designed to provide the industrial worker with the individual security which a craft unionist receives from the internal operating procedures of the local union. The industrial union agreement also contains detailed provisions for on-the-job representation and the arbitration of certain unresolved grievances.

For the purpose of enforcing or administering its collective bargaining agreement the industrial local union makes use of a steward system and a grievance committee. The steward system, sometimes called a shop committee, provides on-the-job representation to the members of the union and sometimes assumes the character of a "union within the union."

On-the-Job Representation in Industrial Locals. Shop stewards in an industrial union are elected by the union members in the departments where they work. The term of office is usually six months or a year, but most unions permit a department to depose its steward by majority vote and elect a new one. (This seldom happens, but the fact that it can is supposed to keep the steward alert.) The steward's election may be a very informal affair, done by a show of hands at a department meeting held on the shop floor during noon hour, or it may be by a solemn secret ballot vote at the union head-quarters. A steward may be reelected indefinitely.

1. *The department steward.* The steward is the eyes and ears of the union in the shop, and its voice as well, and its strong right arm. The stewards as a group provide a two-way flow of communication, information, instructions, sentiment, and advice between the union and the members working in the plant, to its remotest reaches. They enforce not only the union agreement, which is company policy, but union discipline. If there is not yet a "union shop" clause in the agreement, requiring all workers to join the union as a condition of employment, the stewards are the union's organizers, all day and every day in the departments, striving to get nonmembers to join the union or to "make 'em wish they had." If there is no checkoff, the stewards collect dues from the union members and turn the money over to the local. For their trouble, they usually receive a small percentage of what they collect: five or ten cents on the dollar.

Each steward has a personal constituency, knowing the people who elected him or her and being known by them. They see each other every working day. The steward provides leadership and in case of strike is a rally-ing point as their picket captain. There could hardly be more direct or per-sonal contact, or greater confidence, between leader and followers. Unlike the supervisor, who works for management, the steward is one of the gang. Other workers see the steward as "on our side."

2. *The steward council and the chief steward.* The steward council brings together and coordinates the efforts of these natural, elected leaders of the working force. It provides the local with a "line organization" in the shop that is (or can be) as efficient, and more cohesive, than the company's own management hierarchy. It ties the local organically to the workers in the shop and to shop operations in a dynamic, reciprocal relationship.

Typically—or at any rate, ideally—the union elects a steward wherever members work under the direction of a first-line supervisor. The stewards then elect a chief steward from among their ranks. In a shop where there are several echelons of management, such as, for instance, division superinten-dents under a works manager and over groups of department (first-line) foremen, the stewards of a division may select a "chief division steward." If there is a night shift, the night shift stewards will have a chief night steward. All of these smaller "chiefs" are subordinate to *the* chief steward. The union's aim is to place a representative opposite every member of line man-agement—to parallel the line organization of the enterprise. The chief stew-ard—and thus the local union—has "line" channels exactly similar and equivalent to management's, which lead into every part of the enterprise where members of the union work under supervision.

The chief steward's election by the department stewards has to be ratified by a majority vote of the members of the local at a union meeting. That is because this person is an *ex officio* member of the grievance committee, a highly important committee of the local which deals centrally with the personnel department (or equivalent authority) on matters of administration of the labor agreement. Ratification of the chief steward's election by the membership also asserts the local's discretion and authority over those who are to represent it in official dealings with management, and is a token of the subordination of the stewards to the local union.

All of the stewards, including the chief steward, are and remain full-time working employees of the company. Their election to the job gives them certain special rights and duties, which the union agreement defines. They get their authority, therefore, from the union's agreement with the company, and exercise it within prescribed limits.

3. *The steward in grievance adjustment.* The person who wears the badge of a department steward is entitled to take time off the company job without loss of pay, under most agreements, in order to investigate, discuss, and adjust grievances. The steward's name goes to the top of the seniority list in the department, regardless of actual length of service, so that he or she is the last person in the department to be laid off if work gets slack. This is called "superseniority." Elected officers of the union also get superseniority in most agreements. The aim is to keep the union administrative apparatus in the shop intact, despite fluctuations in the level of operations, just as the company keeps intact its management cadres. Of course, an individual loses that superseniority when ceasing to be a steward or if not reelected to union office.

Grievance adjustment, for which the steward is given paid time off, is the primary function stewards perform in the shop. Most grievances consist of claims that the company has failed to live up to the terms of the agreement in its dealings with an individual or a group of workers. The steward is the union watchdog over contract compliance at the department level. For this purpose—and this purpose only—the steward is the equal of the company foreman who supervises the group of that stewardship; in all other aspects being merely one of the foreman's subordinates, like any other worker in the department.

It has been shown, but may be repeated here, that the union's agreement with the company has the effect of setting *company* policy in the areas it touches. Foremen and supervisors do not *make* policy for the company. They exercise delegated management authority in directing operations in accordance with company policy. Because they hold this delegated authority, workers under their supervision are bound to carry out their instructions and accept their decisions, but if—through error, ignorance, or other causes—these run counter to policy as set forth in the agreement, the union steward files a grievance.

Filing a grievance means that the steward formally requests the supervisor to reverse some action taken, or do something not done, or alter some action or decision affecting workers supervised. The supervisor, whose challenged action stands until it is altered, personally or by a higher authority, then has to decide whether the steward's demand is justified, and should be granted; or unjustified, and should be rejected. If the supervisor says yes, that settles the grievance. If no, the steward has the choice of dropping the demand, and thereby accepting that determination of the issue, or sending the case up to the grievance committee.

There may be stages or grievance-procedure "steps" at intermediate levels between the department steward and the grievance committee, but these are relatively unimportant. The number of these intermediate (and often superfluous) steps depends on the size of the enterprise and the extent to which management desires to give its various echelons a chance to "get in on the act," and slow down the process. The two really vital steps are the *first*, in the department where the grievance originated, and the one that puts the issue before the executive responsible for *centralized* administration of personnel policy for the enterprise as a whole, usually the personnel director.

If a grievance remains unsettled after it has been appealed to the central personnel department, it goes to the local union, and the stewards drop out of the case. They do not have the power to make policy decisions. The local union, which has the power, must decide whether to accept the company's determination of the issue or carry the case up another step to the policy-making level of management and thereafter—or directly—to arbitration or a strike.

Grievance handling is a duty the steward carries out as much for the benefit of the company as for the employees. Its aim is to ensure compliance with company policy. That is the reason most companies pay the union steward for time spent in grievance activity. The steward has other duties for which the company does not pay; duties the union demands as part of the job as steward.

4. *The steward and the local union.* Under the chairmanship of the chief steward, the department stewards meet together, either on call, or more commonly at regular intervals, to discuss problems that arise in the course of their grievance activity, and other problems bearing upon the union's relation with the company, and the union's internal affairs. There is often a danger that the steward council will encroach upon, or even usurp, the powers of the local union. Attendance at the council meetings is sometimes better than at membership meetings of the local, and the council is by its nature representative of the whole plant. Whether the steward council tail will wag the union dog depends on the strength of leadership of the officers of the local, who are entitled to attend steward council meetings. Most of them are graduates of the council, and having reached leadership in the chartered local by way of experience as a steward or chief steward, know how to keep the council in its place.

At council meetings, members report on events and developments in the shop. A steward whose supervisor has rejected a grievance may bring the problem to the council for advice. The chief steward reports on the activities of the grievance committee, and may ask the council to endorse a recommendation to the local union on a grievance case unsolved at the last session with the company's personnel department. Officers of the local explain union policies or outline union programs which the stewards are to support in the shop. As the time for renewing the union agreement rolls around, there is discussion of that. The stewards make suggestions for improving the terms or wording over the old one. After the new agreement is signed, the stewards receive an explanation of its provisions and of the union's interpretation of the way it should be understood. They ask questions about it and plan strategy towards issues that it raises.

The union-linked steward system in industrial relations is unique to the American (U.S. and Canadian) labor movements. Other industrial countries have shop committees operating in the enterprises, but the relation of these committees both to the unions and the workers differs from the steward system. Their existence seems to prove only that some kind of shop committee is a necessity of modern manufacturing and the large enterprise.

The foregoing discussion of craft and industrial local unions strongly suggests that unaffiliated and totally independent local unions could influence the wage and effort bargain and negotiate systems of individual security with employers. And, indeed, they can and do. Current membership in such unaffiliated and independent local unions has been estimated to be as high as 500,000 workers.[5] If unaffiliated, independent local unions exist and operate, why do most local unions affiliate with an international union?

The International Union

The typical local union is a part of an international union. A few present-day local unions may originally have joined with other locals in forming the international union of which they are now a part. Most present-day locals, however, were themselves organized and established by the international union with which they are affiliated. Even in those instances where a local took part in the founding of the international, the local, in so doing, gave up its original identity and took on a new identity by receiving a charter from the international, like any other local. This charter recognizes, and in a sense *creates*, the local union.

The international union is a federation of local unions, usually in the same trade (such as carpentry) or industry (such as steel). The international union stands as "parent" to the local union, which it creates by issuing a charter. An individual worker does not hold membership directly in the international union, but in the local union. The local union is a member of

---

[5] U.S. Department of Labor, Bureau of Labor Statistics, *Directory of National and International Labor unions in the United States 1967*. Bulletin No. 1596, 1969.

the international. It supports the international financially by contributing a fixed proportion of the dues paid, or per capita. The amount of per capita is set by the international constitution.

The international union is much like a local union on a grander scale. Its highest policy-making body is the convention, called together annually, biennially, or periodically at some other interval according to the provisions of the international constitution. Delegates elected from the locals, usually with voting rights proportional to the local membership, take part in the convention and transact its business. They elect officers and an executive board to act for them between conventions in accordance with policies and instructions laid down by majority vote in the convention.

Craft, Industrial, and Mixed International Unions.   The fundamental tie between a local and an international *should* be based on services rendered. An international union composed of craft locals renders somewhat different services to its constituent locals than the services rendered by an industrial international to its locals. Today many international unions have both craft and industrial locals, a situation which puts considerable stress on their structure or results in the neglect of the needs of the minority group of locals. In this discussion, international unions composed of significant numbers of both craft and industrial locals will be referred to as "mixed" internationals. Internationals composed primarily of craft locals will be referred to as craft internationals, while the term industrial international will be applied to internationals composed primarily of locals organized on the basis of workplace.

There are approximately 180 international unions in the United States, ranging in size from less than 1,000 affiliated workers to giants claiming over 1 million dues-paying members. Figure 3–2 attempts to classify some of the

FIGURE 3–2
Selected International Unions: Number of Locals, Claimed Membership, 1970

Organizations	*Locals*	*Membership*
Craft		
In manufacturing industry		
Lithographers and Photoengravers (AFL–CIO)	140	60,000
Printing Pressmen (AFL–CIO)	711	127,887
Typographical Union (AFL–CIO)	713	111,583
In government*		
Fire Fighters (AFL–CIO)	1,603	146,090
Teachers (AFL–CIO)	826	205,323
In service industries		
Barbers, Hairdressers, Cosmetologists (AFL–CIO)	775	63,000
Musicians (AFL–CIO)	670	300,000
In transportation industries		
Locomotive Engineers (Ind.)	817	37,900
Railway Carmen (AFL–CIO)	705	63,000
In construction industry		
Boilermakers, Iron Shipbuilders, Blacksmiths (AFL–CIO) ...	425	138,000
Bricklayers, Masons, and Plasterers (AFL–CIO)	862	142,751

FIGURE 3–2 *(continued)*

Organizations	Locals	Membership
Carpenters and Joiners (AFL–CIO)	2,435	820,000
Engineers, Operating (AFL–CIO)	279	392,783
Electrical, Radio, and Machine Workers (AFL–CIO)	627	300,000
Ironworkers, Bridge, Structural and Ornamental (AFL–CIO)	320	177,857
Laborers (AFL–CIO)	900	580,000
Painters, Decorators, and Paperhangers (AFL–CIO)[1]	1,000	210,000
Plumbing and Pipefitting (AFL–CIO)	680	311,550
Sheet Metal Workers (AFL–CIO)	...	120,000
Industrial		
In manufacturing industry		
Automobile Workers (Ind.)	1,550	1,485,609
Clothing Workers (AFL–CIO)	795	386,000
Electrical, Radio, and Machine Workers (Ind.)	180	163,000
Garment Workers, Ladies' (AFL–CIO)	...	442,333
Meat Cutters (AFL–CIO)	650	493,827
Mine Workers, District 50 (Ind.)[2]	1,475	210,000
Oil, Chemical, and Atomic Workers (AFL–CIO)	602	175,324
Pulp, Sulphite, and Paper Mill Workers (AFL–CIO)	770	193,174
Rubber, Cork, Linoleum, and Plastic Workers (AFL–CIO)	549	216,259
Steelworkers (AFL–CIO)	4,200	1,200,000
Textile Workers (AFL–CIO)	103	24,000
In trade		
Retail Clerks International Association (AFL–CIO)	220	605,202
In government		
Government Employees (AFL–CIO)	1,467	324,989
Letter Carriers (AFL–CIO)	6,258	214,877
Postal Clerks (AFL–CIO)[3]	...	.....
In service industries		
Building Service Employees (AFL–CIO)[4]	357	435,000
Hotel and Restaurant Employees (AFL–CIO)	460	461,373
In transportation and public utilities		
Communications Workers (AFL–CIO)	867	421,570
Maintenance of Way Employees (AFL–CIO)	1,240	126,000
Railway and Steamship Clerks (AFL–CIO)[5]	1,500	275,000
Teamsters (Ind.)	807	1,828,548
Transit Union (AFL–CIO)	316	132,000
Transport Workers (AFL–CIO)	107	150,000
Mixed		
Electrical Workers, International Brotherhood of (AFL–CIO)	1,677	921,722
Machinists, International Association of (AFL–CIO)	1,985	865,490

Statistics based on dues-paying membership or membership in good standing or members carried on the rolls for 1969 and 1970; and the number of locals in operation at the end of 1970.

[1] Painters, Decorators & Paperhangers changed to Painters and Allied Trades, International Brotherhood of.

[2] Mine Workers District 50 (Ind.) changed to Allied and Technical Workers of U.S. and Canada, International Union of.

[3] Postal Clerks merged with:
   a. National Association of Special Delivery Messengers (AFL–CIO);
   b. National Association of Post Office and General Service Maintenance Employees (AFL–CIO);
   c. National Federation of Post Office Motor Vehicle Employees (AFL–CIO);
   d. United Federation of Postal Clerks (AFL–CIO);
   e. National Postal Union (Ind.);
   to form (on July 1, 1971): American Postal Workers Union (AFL–CIO).

[4] Building Service Employees changed to Service Employees International Union.

[5] Railway and Steamship Clerks changed to Railway and Steamship Clerks, Freight Handlers, Express and Station Employees, Brotherhood of.

Source: U.S. Department of Labor, Bureau of Labor Statistics, *Directory of National and International Labor Unions in the United States, 1971*, Bulletin No. 1750 (1970), pp. 19–49.

larger international unions according to the primary organizational units of their constituent locals: craft, industrial, and mixed. The *sole* criterion for the classification of internationals shown in Figure 3–2 is the organizational unit of the majority of their constituent locals. Thus, the United Automobile Workers and the United Steelworkers are classified as *industrial* internationals, despite the fact that both organizations have locals in many industries and a few locals composed of workers who possess an apprenticeable trade. Although the Carpenters' International has a few locals composed as assembly-line workers engaged in the manufacture of furniture, it is classified as a *craft* international because of the predominant role played by its craft affiliates in the building construction industry. The International Brotherhood of Electrical Workers is classified as a "mixed" international because of its extensive apprenticeship orientation in the construction industry paralleled with substantial industrial organization units in the field of public utilities.

Before attempting to differentiate the services provided by craft and industrial internationals, it is well to discuss the general services which either international might provide to its constituent locals. To a substantial degree, the difference in services rendered is a matter of the blend of services required by the constituent locals.

Services Performed by International Unions. The most important service rendered by any international union is organizing the unorganized workers within its jurisdiction. Most local unions formed in the United States since the 1940s have been organized by the initial expenditure of effort and funds of some parent international union. This means that the international has assigned organizers to the community or place of employment of the potential members, sought to enroll workers in the union, and, frequently, conducted the negotiations with the employers and NLRB prior to obtaining the local's first collective bargaining agreement. As will be discussed in Chapter 6, this can be a long, difficult, and expensive process. The price that a newly formed local pays for this service is affiliation with the international union.

Suppose that a local had been organized by an international in 1942. Why is organizing the unorganized important to that local in 1976? It really is not very important to the local or its members *if* the product market served by the employer of the local's members is fully unionized. On the other hand, any significant number of nonunion competitors poses a threat to the conditions of employment that can be established by collective bargaining in unionized enterprises. Even in highly organized industries like automobiles and steel, the international unions spend large sums of money every year for the purpose of maintaining and consolidating a high degree of unionization. If organization is permitted to crumble, locals will be undercut in their negotiations.

Many international unions also provide a variety of expert research, negotiation, and educational services to their constituent locals. Complex issues such as pensions, health and welfare plans, and the legal intricacies of various hiring hall, strike, and picketing situations require professional research of a variety beyond the competence of the membership of a local union. International unions often provide this research and the services of a full-time professional negotiator to their locals as one of the benefits of affiliation.

One of the initial purposes of unionization in the days before the Wagner Act was the provision of insurance benefits for members at a time when insurance benefits were not readily available in the general market. Some international unions continue to provide these services as supplements to the more recently developed employer-financed insurance and pension arrangements or in the form of retirement homes for members or special union-supported medical centers.

The strike benefits provided by many international unions might be considered to be another form of insurance. Because of their huge membership base compared to the membership base of any local union, international unions provide a means of pooling the costs of strikes. A local union with even 5,000 members has at its disposal relatively insignificant funds for the financing of a strike compared to the taxing power of its parent international with perhaps several hundred thousand potential contributors.

International unions also may perform important political and representational services in behalf of their constituent locals and their members. Leonard Woodcock, speaking as the president of a 1-million member UAW, is likely to get more attention from a congressional committee on social security than a letter written by the president of a 500 member local union. Among the many political programs important to local unions and their members are campaigns for minimum wage legislation, social security, workmen's compensation, the income tax, unemployment compensation, and medicare. In many of these fields, the international can provide highly professional representational services at a fraction of the cost of less effective local efforts.

Services provided by the international are financed from the per capita revenues of the international. The more services provided, the higher the per capita tax must be, and the higher the per capita tax, the less autonomous the locals and the less influence rank-and-file members of the locals have on their own fates. Although the members of a local can properly feel reassured by the promise that the international may pay them substantial strike benefits, the price that must be paid for these benefits is international approval of their proposed strike.

Both craft and industrial internationals provide bargaining and representational services to their constituent locals. However, the blend of these services provided, and the degree of autonomy of the two kinds of locals, differs significantly.

Services Performed by Craft Internationals. Craft union locals tend to have greater autonomy and to receive fewer services from their internationals than industrial union locals. This tendency is attributable to the nature of the product market and the history of craft unionism.

As noted above, the business agent, a full-time paid employee of the local union, plays a key role in craft union bargaining. This role is conditioned by the fact that the product market of craft unions is typically local in nature. Craft unionists earn high hourly rates and pay high union dues which are kept by the local for the important purposes of negotiating and enforcing the agreement and organizing the unorganized in the community served by the union.

Craft unions have a longer history than industrial unions in the United States. Typically they organized at the local level first and then affiliated with their international organizations. They have been jealous of their local autonomy and have surrendered very little of it to their internationals.

Craft internationals provide important representational services to their locals by attempting to influence the rules for rule-making which have been particularly cumbersome for craft unions since the passage of the Taft-Hartley Act in 1947. Craft internationals also provide a militant voice for their constituent locals in the defense of jurisdictional claims within the AFL–CIO. Craft internationals also play an important role in the national apprenticeship program.

Services Performed by Industrial Internationals. The typical industrial international provides all the services discussed above for its local unions in substantial degree. Because of a tradition of "top down" organizing of industrial locals they typically possess less autonomy than their craft union counterparts.

International unions are completely autonomous bodies usually affiliated with the federation of international unions, the AFL–CIO. Both craft and industrial international unions are members of the AFL–CIO.

The AFL-CIO

The American Federation of Labor and Congress of Industrial Organizations, or the AFL–CIO, represents the interests of labor and its constituent international unions at the highest national level. The federation itself engages in no collective bargaining. It serves and advises the internationals which make it up. Membership by internationals is voluntary. The federation gets its support by per capita from its member internationals.

The formation of the merged AFL–CIO in 1955 modified the AFL's traditional policy of noninterference in the internal affairs of constituent internationals. Under the AFL-CIO constitution international unions can be tried and expelled from the federation if proven corrupt or communist dominated.

The Department of Organization of the AFL–CIO assists affiliated internationals in the organization of the unorganized. Besides this, various internationals have cooperated in seeking to organize nonunion areas and enterprises.

In addition to membership in the AFL–CIO itself, most affiliated international unions have elected to pay an additional per capita tax required for affiliation with one or more of the nine trade and industrial departments of the AFL–CIO: (1) Building and Construction Trades Department, (2) Industrial Union Department, (3) Maritime Trades Department, (4) Metal Trades Department, (5) Railway Employees' Department, (6) Union Label and Service Trade Department; and (7) Government Employees Council, (8) Scientific, Professional and Cultural Employees Council; and (9) Railway Labor Executives' Association. Internationals pay a department per capita tax according to the number of their members who fall within the particular department's jurisdiction.

Each department is free to manage and finance its own affairs. Between the merger of the CIO with the AFL in 1955 and the year 1969 the Industrial Union Department was probably the best-financed and most active department in the federation. It was, in fact, a federation within the federation, consisting as it did of most of the CIO Internationals that entered into the merger. In 1968 Walter Reuther, then president of the Industrial Union Department as well as of the Automobile Workers Union, resigned from the department, and soon thereafter the Auto Workers withdrew from the AFL–CIO. In 1969 they joined the other large independent union, the Teamsters, to establish the Alliance for Labor Action which subsequently drew into its ranks other independents, notably District 50 of the United Mine Workers.

The Alliance for Labor Action

The founders of the Alliance claimed that the AFL–CIO, under conservative leadership, had done too little to extend unionization to the unorganized agricultural workers, the "working poor," and white-collar workers. They vowed to extend the benefits of organization to these groups. Neither the promise nor the threat implicit in the formation of the Alliance came to reality. The farm workers were indeed organized, but by an AFL–CIO affiliated union, while the Alliance-founding Teamsters joined the growers in denying them the fruits of their organizing struggles. Perhaps if Reuther had not died in a plane crash in 1970 things might have been different. The Alliance is defunct today.

Auxiliary Bargaining Elements of Union Structure

Auxiliary elements of union structure which are directly engaged in the negotiation and administration of collective bargaining agreements include: (1) the district, (2) joint boards, (3) conference boards, and (4) trade councils. Although these units appear in only a few industries, they are of great importance in these specific cases.

The District. The district is an administrative division of the international union, usually defined on geographical lines. It has the same structure, on a smaller scale, as the international. Not all internationals subdivide into districts, but in some unions the district is a very important and powerful body. The Teamsters union is an example. Truck hauls on the highway are for the most part more than local but less than nationwide. Certain areas, such as New England, the West Coast, the Chicago area, and the areas around Detroit, Minneapolis, St. Louis, Nashville, and other cities, have well-defined trucking routes that radiate from rail and water terminals of long-distance freight hauling. Effective union control over trucking can best be exercised from the strategic points these terminals create, and must extend over the entire area they serve. Local unions, whose activities cover only a single city, would be impotent beyond their own city limits when trucks took to the road if they did not have the cooperation of other locals in the area. The district acts as the coordinator, and becomes thereby a center of union authority which is much stronger, of course, than any local; strong enough almost to be independent of the international. District leaders of this union become very powerful figures, as exemplified by Dave Beck, who came to the presidency of the International from the West Coast district, and James R. Hoffa of Detroit, who succeeded him.

Joint Boards. The joint board is an affiliation obligatory only in a certain kind of union, the "amalgamated" union. The best examples are the garment workers' unions. In these amalgamations, former separate craft unions have fused into an industrial union international without completely giving up their craft identity. In a given city where there are enterprises of the industry, the locals elect a joint board to carry on collective bargaining for all locals, since members of each local are employed in all the firms. The need here is for *joint action* on a common problem.

Joint boards are seldom formed, and never on an obligatory basis, by local industrial unions whose members work in separate enterprises with which the separate locals bargain. They have no need for joint action.

Sometimes local unions of the same craft form a joint board, but this is on a voluntary basis. It occurs in cities which, because of their size or for historical reasons (such as the affiliation of a former independent union in a body with the craft international), support not just one craft local in a given trade but several. The joint board in such cases is a substitute or makeshift for the normal situation of having only one local union of a craft in a locality and often is a prelude to the actual merger of the locals that made up the joint board.

Conference Boards. Local industrial unions belonging to the *same* international and bargaining with the *same* employer, as in a multiplant manufacturing company, form conference boards, under the auspices of the international, to centralize their collective bargaining. Two examples of this would be the General Motors Conference Board of the United Auto Workers and the Westinghouse Conference Board of the International Union of Electrical Workers. The locals elect delegates who meet before negotiations, draw up a proposed master agreement to cover all the plants of the enterprise, plan strategy, select representatives, and then carry out negotiations. After the master agreement has been ratified and signed, each local negotiates supplements applying the terms of the master agreement to its own separate plant. The conference board is not a permanent body, has no constitution or officers, gets no per capita, but usually establishes a permanent "secretariat" at the international headquarters, which is made the responsibility of a specific international officer or representative.

A variant on the conference board organizational element may be emerging in the electrical products industry. Several international industrial unions have collective bargaining relationships with the General Electric Company. In recent years these unions have found bargaining there to be extremely tough and have suspected that the company has played one union off against the others. In order to strengthen their bargaining position these unions, e.g., the International Union of Electrical Workers, the United Auto Workers, and the Machinists, have entered an informal "alliance" that no one union will settle with the company without the concurrence of the other unions.

Trade Councils. Local unions belonging to *different* internationals in the building construction industry frequently form locality councils. The local Building Trades Council groups together the locals of the construction industry for the purpose of coordinating their activities and controlling jurisdictional claims. Facing it, almost inevitably, is to be found an association of building trades employers with a name such as the General Contractors' Association which groups the construction enterprises of the same locality. These two organizations together initiate and oversee the bargaining for the separate trade agreements signed between the locals and the employer association. Administration of these separate agreements then devolves upon the separate locals, with the Council (and the Association) standing by to help the locals and the enterprises keep the wheels turning smoothly.

Districts, joint boards, conference boards, and trade councils are important auxiliary elements of union structure for collective bargaining activity. There are other auxiliary elements of union structure which emerge primarily in political activity.

Auxiliary Political Elements of Union Structure

The city central and state central are important political representatives for organized labor and engage in a wide variety of welfare activities.

The City Central. The city central is a federation of local unions in a given city or county. The AFL City Central traditionally called itself the "Central Trades and Labor Council," and its CIO counterpart, the "Industrial Union Council." Now they are merged as AFL–CIO City Councils.

The city central includes locals of all the internationals which have chartered locals in the area. It does no collective bargaining, but focuses and coordinates the activities of organized labor generally in relation to the community. Elected delegates of the various locals exchange information; engage in programs of mutual aid (such as "Buy Union" campaigns) or they help to organize boycotts of "unfair" firms; give aid to locals on strike; and carry on other cooperative activities. Elected officers of the city central represent labor in civic affairs, bring labor influence to bear on local governmental bodies and officials, and advise local unions on community problems. A political candidate who wants labor's endorsement for a campaign tries to get it from the city central. This in itself wins few votes, but opens the door to the affiliated locals, whose members' votes are being courted.

The city central holds its charter direct from the AFL–CIO and sends a delegate (or delegates) to the AFL–CIO Convention. Through its direct affiliation, it brings news and directives of the federation to the locals in its community.

It is customary for all AFL–CIO local unions to join their appropriate city central. The city central gets its financial means by a per capita tax on the member locals.

The State Central.   The state central is a "city central" on a state-wide scale. It is composed of delegates from local unions of all internationals, plus delegates from city centrals. Some local unions that maintain affiliation with their city central do not bother to affiliate with the state central, which seems more remote from them.

The main activity of the state central is to bring labor influence to bear on the state legislature and executive. This activity may be very important in connection with such matters as unemployment compensation, workmen's compensation, factory inspection codes, minimum wage legislation, and when the legislature is considering a "right-to-work" law.

COPE—Labor's Political Arm

While the federation and the state and city centrals spend part of their money, time, and effort on lobbying and other representational activities that could be called political, COPE, the political action arm of the AFL–CIO concentrates all its energies on politics. The name COPE is an acronym formed from Committee on Political Education. COPE came into existence in 1955 by merger of the CIO Political Action Committee with the AFL League for Political Education when the two federations merged to form the AFL–CIO.

COPE operates out of the AFL–CIO headquarters in Washington, D.C., and has an organization in each of the fifty states. The international unions have COPE departments, while local unions and city centrals set up COPE committees. Naturally, COPE is most active in election years and during election campaigns, but maintains an administrative staff in Washington and in some 18 strategic locations throughout the country.

Samuel Gompers long ago expressed labor's political policy as: Reward your friends and punish your enemies. COPE operates in this tradition.

Federal law forbids unions from contributing dues money to political candidates, but COPE raises funds by soliciting voluntary contributions, and has more to offer, anyway, than money. Candidates deemed to be friends of labor can get the doorbell-ringing, precinct-walking kind of help that is most valuable from COPE volunteers, union members.

THE STRUCTURE OF THE AMERICAN LABOR MOVEMENT

The American labor movement claims about 18 million members in approximately 75,000 local unions. About 85 percent of this total membership is claimed by the affiliates of the AFL–CIO. Probably somewhere between half and three quarters of all union members belong to industrial locals as defined in this chapter, with the remainder organized along craft or occupational lines.

Figure 3–3 is a schematic diagram of the structure of the American labor movement. Organizations shown in the middle and left of this diagram exert most of their efforts in collective bargaining activity, while the organizations shown to the right of the diagram are primarily concerned with representational and political activities.

In Figure 3–3 special attention is called to the membership figures on international and local unions not affiliated with the AFL–CIO.

Since the beginning, American unions and the American labor movement have concentrated their efforts on the problems of obtaining, keeping, and improving collective bargaining agreements which set the conditions of employment for their members. Representational and political activity has been regarded as a secondary and reenforcing means of achieving the basic objective of influencing the wage and effort bargain and establishing systems of justice at the workplace. In sharp contrast to the experience in other countries, the present-day AFL–CIO could hardly be called a "movement" dedicated to sweeping economic and political reconstruction of the whole society. The organizational structure which has evolved seems well suited to the achievement of these "bread-and-butter" objectives.

In what sectors of the economy does the labor movement exert direct influence on the conditions of employment and how powerful is the influence exerted? Unfortunately, this very basic question cannot be answered with much statistical authority because of the paucity of data.

Industrial Distribution of Union Membership

Over 40 percent of all American union members are employed in three major industry groups—metal and machinery, transportation, and construction. Other industry groups with at least 1 million members each are food and tobacco, clothing and leather, transportation equipment, and retail and wholesale trade.

The U.S. Bureau of Labor Statistics is unable to provide detailed data on

FIGURE 3–3

The Structure of the American Labor Movement

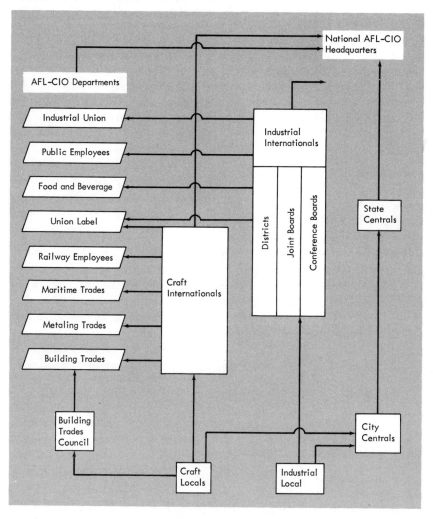

Some Important International Unions Not Affiliated with the American Federation of Labor and Congress of Industrial Organizations

Union	1974 Claimed Membership
Automobile Workers	1,500,000
Electrical, Radio, and Machine Workers	165,000
Locomotive Engineers	37,900
Longshoremen's and Warehousemen's Union	60,000
United Mine Workers Dist. 50	210,000
Teamsters	1,828,000

Source: *Encyclopedia of Associations*, vol. 1 (Detroit: Gale Recorder Co., 1975).

the extent of union membership by industry, e.g., that 90 percent of employment in over-the-road trucking is unionized. Instead, it is only able to list industry groupings in rank order of unionization as follows:

1. Transportation.
2. Transportation equipment.
3. Contract construction.
4. Food, beverages, tobacco.
5. Telephone and telegraph.
6. Mining and quarrying.
7. Electric and gas utilities.
8. Furniture, lumber, wood products, and paper.
9. Stone, clay, and glass.
10. Metals, machinery and equipment except transportation equipment.
11. Printing and publishing.
12. Petroleum, chemicals, and rubber.
13. Clothing, textiles, and leather products.
14. Federal government.
15. Trade.
16. Service industries.
17. State and local governments.
18. Finance and insurance.
19. Agriculture and fishing.

The Bureau further estimates that about one half of manufacturing employment is unionized, as compared with one fourth of nonmanufacturing and one seventh of government employment.[6] These estimates tend to understate substantially the significance of union influence because: (1) they are estimates of union membership while the coverage of collective bargaining agreements would be larger (unfortunately, it is impossible to say how much larger), (2) the divisor of each estimate includes employees whom unions do not seek to represent, e.g., managerial and salaried employees who frequently represent as much as 50 percent of an enterprise's employment,[7] and (3) some enterprises provide employment conditions parallel to unionized enterprises for the purposes of remaining nonunion.

Geographical Influence of the Labor Movement

The geographical distribution of union membership is important both as a measure of political influence and as an indication of the significance of organized labor in the economies of the several states. Union officials argue that certain areas, e.g., the South, are particularly hard to organize because of local custom.

Union membership is heavily concentrated in a few states having the

---

[6] U.S. Department of Labor, Bureau of Labor Statistics, *Directory of National and International Labor Unions in the United States, 1967,* Bulletin No. 1596 (1969), p. 62. (But see Chapters 15 and 16 on government employment, now near one-third unionized.)

[7] Unfortunately, no data are available on the extent of "organizable" employment within industries. A *crude* approximation could be made from the ratio of production employees to total employment. Such data are not available for transportation, telephone, and telegraph, government, services, finance and insurance, and agriculture and fishing. Of the other industries listed here, the percentages range from a low of 63 percent in printing and publishing to a high of 89 percent in clothing, textiles, and leather products.

largest number of workers in nonagricultural establishments. In 1967, six states, New York, California, Pennsylvania, Illinois, Ohio, and Michigan, accounted for 55 percent of the nation's total union membership.[8]

The top-ranking states in terms of total membership are not necessarily those in which unions have scored their greatest penetration among non-farm employees. As shown in Figure 3–4, New York ranked 9th, California

FIGURE 3–4

Union Membership as a Proportion of Nonagricultural Employment by States, 1971

Rank	State	Membership as a Percent of Employees in Nonagricultural Establishments
1	West Virginia	43.0%
2	Michigan	40.2
3	Washington	40.0
4	Pennsylvania	37.2
5	Ohio	36.3
6	Missouri	35.9
7	Illinois	35.7
8	Indiana	35.6
9	New York	35.6
10	Nevada*	32.8
11	Wisconsin	31.4
12	Oregon	30.7
13	California	30.5
14	Montana	29.9
15	New Jersey	29.5
16	Minnesota	28.9
17	Hawaii	28.1
18	Kentucky	27.3
19	Alaska	27.1
20	Rhode Island	26.1
21	Massachusetts	25.6
22	Connecticut	24.2
23	Maryland/D. C.	23.3
24	Delaware	22.6
25	Iowa*	21.1
26	Utah*	20.9
27	Tennessee*	20.6
28	Colorado	20.5
29	Alabama*	20.3
30	Idaho	18.5
31	Louisiana	18.4
32	Maine	18.4
33	Arkansas	17.9
34	Nebraska*	17.9
35	Wyoming*	17.7
36	Arizona*	17.6
37	New Hampshire	17.3
38	North Dakota*	17.2
39	Virginia*	16.7
40	Kansas*	16.6
41	Vermont	16.2
42	Georgia*	16.2
43	Oklahoma	16.1
44	New Mexico	14.8
45	Texas*	14.4
46	Florida*	13.9
47	Mississippi*	13.9
48	South Dakota*	11.9
49	South Carolina*	9.6
50	North Carolina*	7.8

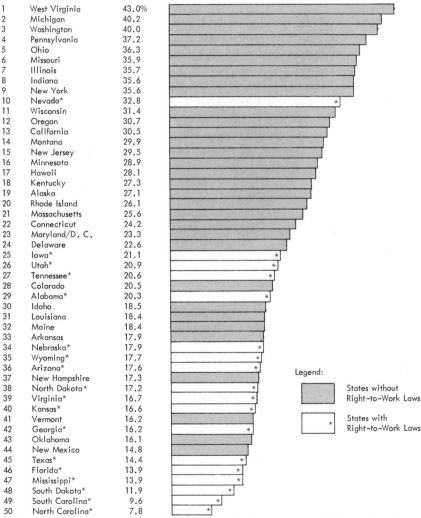

Legend:

States without Right-to-Work Laws

* States with Right-to-Work Laws

Source: U.S. Department of Labor, Bureau of Labor Statistics, *Directory of National International Labor Unions in the United States, 1971*, Bulletin No. 1750 (1972), p. 84.

[8] Ibid., p. 63.

13th, and Pennsylvania 4th in terms of the degree of union penetration. Highest proportions are recorded in West Virginia (a coal mining state) Michigan (heart of the auto industry) Washington (lumber and shipping) Pennsylvania (coal and steel) and then, in order, Ohio, Missouri, Indiana, and Illinois. Figure 3–4 graphically reveals the slight penetration of unionism into the still largely rural economy of the southern states, and in general, states having right-to-work laws.

SUMMARY

This chapter examined the structure of unions as instruments for achieving the goals of employees in collective bargaining. Craft union locals and industrial union locals have somewhat different objectives in collective bargaining and differ accordingly in their bargaining behavior and structure of organization.

At the local level union structure tends to parallel the structure of enterprises in particular industries. Industrial union locals need complex organizational structures to match the generally large employers with whom they bargain. Craft locals, on the other hand, organize to provide service to workers who have intermittent employment with a number of relatively small employers.

Above the local level, union structure is conglomerate. In general, industrial union internationals provide more services to their constituent locals and exert more control over them because they operate in national product markets, than craft internationals over their locals which serve in local product markets.

The political and representational interests of union members are served by the AFL–CIO national federation, the state federations, and city central organizations, and at every level by COPE, the political arm. None of these organizations is homogeneous in terms of either the occupational calling or industrial attachment of the workers who support and belong.

QUESTIONS FOR DISCUSSION

1. In the United States and Canada, union members belong directly to a local union. In some other countries, the individual worker affiliates directly with the international. What are the advantages of the U.S./Canadian way? The disadvantages?

2. In all western European nations there is some kind of a labor political party associated with the unions, but not in the United States? Should American unions form a labor party? What might they gain? Or lose?

3. Is union penetration of the southern states economy slight because of the right-to-work laws, or are the laws there because unionism is lacking?

4. If you were a candidate for president and wanted to line up union support for your election, would you rather have the building trades workers or the

auto workers campaigning for you? Why? What if you were running for governor in the state of Michigan? Pennsylvania? Arizona?

SELECTED ANNOTATED BIBLIOGRAPHY

ASHENFELTER, ORLEY, and PENCAVEL, JOHN H. "American Trade Union Growth, 1900–1960." *Quarterly Journal of Economics*, vol. 83 (August 1969).
An examination of the variables which contributed to union growth during this century.

BARBASH, JACK. *Labor's Grass Roots: A Study of the Local Union.* New York: Harper & Bros., 1961.
A description of the organization and functions of the local union, its scope and evolution, its formal constitutional foundations, and its relationships to the international union, other unions, and city and state labor federations. Membership characteristics and attitudes, duties and behavior of business agents, stewards, and other leaders; and internal conflict, controversy, and democracy in the local are studied.

————. *American Unions: Structure, Government and Politics.* New York: Random House, 1967.
A brief and insightful examination of how U.S. unions are organized and administered.

CADDY, DOUGLAS. *The Hundred Million Dollar Payoff.* New Rochelle, N.Y.: Arlington House, 1974.
An investigation of the political activities of U.S. unions designed to show that they wield political influence disproportionate to the number of members they represent, including a description of COPE (The AFL–CIO's Committee on Political Education) as the "nation's most powerful political machine."

ESTEY, MARTEN S. "The Strategic Alliance as a Factor in Union Growth." *Industrial and Labor Relations Review*, vol. 9 (October 1955), pp. 41–53.
A study of interunion alliances in the retail trades. Relates growth of retail union membership to the "strategic alliance" between weaker retail unions and unions having control over strategic positions such as truck drivers, warehouse workers, and retail butchers.

————. *The Unions, Structure, Development, and Management.* New York: Harcourt, Brace and World, Inc., 1967.
A good outline and overview of the design and operation of American unions. Emphasis is on management of unions as organizations striving to achieve a variety of objectives.

GALENSON, WALTER, ed. *Trade Union Monograph Series.* New York: John Wiley & Sons, 1962.
Each volume in this series describes the government of a major American trade union. The emphasis is on those aspects of government which may be said to further or retard internal democracy. The volumes in this series are:
HARRINGTON, MICHAEL. *The Retail Clerks.*
HOROWITZ, MORRIS A. *The Structure and Government of the Carpenters' Union.*
KRAMER, LEO. *Labor's Paradox—The American Federation of State, County, and Municipal Employees AFL–CIO.*

PERLMAN, MARK. *Democracy in the International Association of Machinists.*

ROMER, SAM. *The International Brotherhood of Teamsters: Its Government and Structure.*

ROTHBAUM, MELVIN. *The Government of the Oil, Chemical and Atomic Workers Union.*

SEIDMAN, JOEL. *The Brotherhood of Railroad Trainmen: The Internal Political Life of a National Union.*

STIEBER, JACK. *Governing the UAW.*

ULMAN, LLOYD. *The Government of the Steel Workers' Union.*

GREENSTONE, J. DAVID. *Labor in American Politics.* New York: Alfred A. Knopf, 1969.

The author examines U.S. unions' past and present involvement in politics at all levels of government, including an examination of COPE. A more dispassionate analysis than the Caddy book.

HARDMAN, J. B. S. *Labor at the Rubicon.* New York: New York University Press, 1972.

A journalistic look at internal democracy among U.S. unions, which the author finds too limited.

HUTCHINSON, JOHN. *The Imperfect Union: A History of Corruption in American Trade Unions.* New York: E. P. Dutton, 1970.

A well-researched analysis of nefarious practices in American unions, including the various kinds of corrupt union officials and practices, and the conditions which gave rise to corruption.

KENNEDY, VAN DUSEN. *Nonfactory Unionism and Labor Relations.* Berkeley: University of California. West Coast Collective Bargaining Systems Series, 1955.

A study of service-industry unions on the West Coast. Author emphasizes the differences between "factory" and "nonfactory" labor relations. Professor Kennedy's emphasis might be compared with the "industrial union" and "craft union" distinction drawn in this book.

MARSHALL, RAY. *The Negro and Organized Labor.* New York: John Wiley and Sons, 1965.

A comprehensive analysis of the discriminatory behavior of many American unions. Marshall says that remedial action is occurring but at a painstakingly slow pace.

MERGEN, RICHARD. "Blacksmiths and Welders: Identity and Phenomenal Change," *Industrial and Labor Relations Review*, vol. 25, no. 3 (April 1972).

An investigation of the reaction of blacksmiths and welders to technological and social change, which included the disappearance (via merger with the Boilermakers) of a separate Blacksmiths Union.

MILLIS, HARRY A., and MONTGOMERY, ROYAL E. *Organized Labor.* New York: McGraw-Hill Book Co., Inc., 1945.

Volume III of the authors' brilliant Economics of Labor series, this book covers labor history through the early 1940s, union government, structure, and policies. Reference to this volume should be one of the early steps in any research undertaking on American unionism.

SAYLES, LEONARD, and STRAUSS, GEORGE. *The Local Union.* New York: Harper & Bros., 1953.

Based on extensive field research, this volume presents a penetrating insight of the place of the local union in the industrial plant.

SHILS, EDWARD B. "Union Fragmentation: A Major Cause of Transportation Crises," *Industrial and Labor Relations Review*, vol. 25, no. 1 (October 1971).

The author examines the fragmented bargaining structures in the transportation industries where numerous unions compete with each other. He believes this fragmentation and resulting competition contributes to transportation strikes.

STRAUSS, GEORGE. *Unions in the Building Trades: A Case Study*. Buffalo, N.Y.: University of Buffalo Series no. 24, 1958.

A field study of building trades unions in a community of 400,000 population. Major emphasis is placed on the functions and attitudes of business agents.

TAFT, PHILIP. *The Structure and Government of Labor Unions*. Cambridge, Mass.: Harvard University Press, 1954.

An in-depth study of union elections, dues, discipline, and appeals. Essays on the internal procedures of the unlicensed seafaring unions, the Autoworkers, the Steelworkers, and the Teamsters.

U.S. DEPARTMENT OF LABOR, BUREAU OF LABOR STATISTICS. *Directory of National and International Labor Unions in the United States*. Washington, D.C.: U.S. Government Printing Office.

Issued biennially, this bulletin contains a detailed listing of international unions, officers, location, conventions, publications, and claimed membership of the approximately 200 unions headquartered in the United States.

ULMAN, LLOYD. "Multinational Unionism: Incentives, Barriers, and Alternatives," *Industrial Relations*, vol. 14, no. 1 (February 1975).

A comprehensive examination of the reasons why multinational or international collective bargaining mechanisms have not developed.

4 Employer Organization for Collective Bargaining

THIS CHAPTER presents the first of the actors in the industrial relations system: the employer or, in Dunlop's terms, the hierarchy of managers representing the employer. We shall examine the structure of American private enterprise and note some of the ways this structure has adapted to the rise of unions and how it responds to the demands of interaction with unions in collective bargaining.

CHANGING EMPLOYER-EMPLOYEE RELATIONS

Basic to an understanding of the management of people in an enterprise, whether unionized or not, is a clear perception of the employment relationship. The "employers" of antiquity (and the not too distant past) held their "employees" in a bond relation as slaves. Slaves were the personal property of the slaveowners. If they were wise and self-controlled they treated the "slaves" well and got good work from them by the standards of those days, but they did not have to take employees' wishes into account and could compel them by force to do the employer's will.

Today's employer cannot compel workers by any kind of force. They cannot fine them. The most severe disciplinary penalty they can impose is to dismiss them—terminate the employment contract—so that they cease to be employees. The employer's way of drawing workers, keeping them in service, and motivating them to be productive is to make them want to do the work. Older systems bound one party to the relation and benefited the other. The free labor system binds both parties but binds them only to their mutual benefit. The contract that so binds them lasts only as long as both receive benefit from it. It rests upon consent, and it confers reciprocal advantage.

ENTERPRISE GOALS AND OBJECTIVES

Why does anyone start and maintain a business enterprise? The pat answer to that used to be: to make a profit. Profits are indeed an accepted *goal* in a free-enterprise economy, but not all organizations are profit-making, and even those that are, cannot make profits in the abstract, for profits take form only in concrete dollars and cents. Before an enterprise can make a profit it must manufacture products and sell them, or provide services and get paid for them. Profits materialize as a kind of by-product, the result— by no means inevitable—of operations. Profits result only when an organization successfully carries out operations aimed at specific *objectives*. A pair of dogmatic statements will illustrate the difference between what we call goals, and operating objectives.

> The goal of a manufacturing company (General Motors, General Electric, the local bakery) may be to make a profit, but its operating objective *must be* to make a product or line of products (cars, electrical appliances, hot dog rolls) and sell them at prices above their costs.
>
> The goal of a service organization (Bell Telephone, the local dry-cleaning establishment) may be to make a profit, but the operating objective *must be* to provide a service (telecommunications, spot removal) and get paid at rates above cost.

Goals need not be rationally justifiable. They may spring from pure emotion: the love of humanity (an orphanage), or the fear of cancer (a research hospital), as well as the love of money and what money can buy. Goals arise out of values: personal values (enriching *me*), or social and cultural values (improving highways; educating the next generation). Operations aimed at attaining these goals cannot contradict cultural values or offend social norms. The profit-motivated entrepreneur whom our society tolerates—even glorifies—would not last long in Chairman Mao's China. Even in our own country a person seeking the culturally-acceptable goal of self-enrichment who organizes a heroin-pushing operation risks prison.

Much more directly than goals, operating objectives determine an organization's behavior. Emotions may sometimes intrude here, for they are an inevitable part of human life, but operations fail unless they are directed by reason: by perceptions of reality and probability, or what used to be called cause/effect relations. The manager of a factory, the contractor building a dam, the president of a bank, all seek the goal of profit, but each selects different objectives and needs different human and material resources to attain them; each has to deploy the work force in a different way to carry on the different kinds of operations. The head of any going organization has to give operating objectives top priority. Failure to meet them means failure to achieve the goals. This holds just as true for the many organizations such as government agencies, religious bodies, educational institutions, and the like, that do not take profit as their goal.

In any case, only those who draw the profits—owners or stockholders— can have profit-making as a primary motive. Others have career and personal goals of their own, based on their own values, and personal operating objectives, down to the simple objective of making a living. The organization has to accommodate all these goals. In order to succeed in its operations (and hence move toward its goals) an enterprise must provide scope for individuals who work for it, or buy from it, or deal with it, to meet their personal objectives. It is certainly not the goal of most business organizations simply to provide paid employment, and not ordinarily the goal of an employee just to perform taks, but to attain its objectives (and thus realize its goals) the enterprise has to employ people; and people, in order to get paid or to move toward career objectives, have to perform tasks; collectively, all the tasks that make up the company's operations.

With all this in mind, we can drop our consideration of goals, including the profit goal, and from now on speak in terms of objectives. General enterprise objectives set the framework for many subsidiary and contributory objectives, including those that have to do with people: the *personnel objectives*.

PERSONNEL MANAGEMENT OBJECTIVES OF THE ENTERPRISE

The personnel management objectives of any enterprise can be simply stated as: (1) to find suitable employees, (2) to maintain an adequate work force, and (3) to get competitive productivity from that work force. The achievement of these objectives is far from simple and the methods used for their achievement are diverse.

What are *suitable employees* and how can they be found? The answer to this question is provided in part by how management designs jobs. In mass-production industry, management has designed jobs in such a way that the bulk of suitable potential employees need little special prior experience or training, but even in mass-production industry there is a need for some employees possessing substantial experience or training, and these are sometimes in very short supply. In this situation the employer has to search for people possessing the needed skills or take the sometimes more difficult and costly route of training present employees to the skill level needed.

What is an *appropriate work force* and how can it be held? An appropriate work force is the number and kind of employees that management needs at the time that management needs them. Just as management needs enough workers, it also needs to be able to get rid of unneeded workers. Holding an appropriate work force boils down to making employment at a particular enterprise attractive to the kind of employees needed and insuring sufficient management flexibility to escape having unneeded or redundant employees.

The measure of *competitive productivity* is unit labor costs. Low wages give an enterprise a competitive edge only when those low wages are accompanied by output that equals that of higher wage competitors. In the same vein, high wages may mean a competitive advantage over a lower wage competitor if the high-wage firm achieves higher work-hour productivity.

In order to achieve objectives, the work to be done must be assigned to individuals who will perform it. This division of work, with the concomitant delegation of authority and assignment of responsibility, is the task of formal organization.

ORGANIZATION OF THE BUSINESS ENTERPRISE

Business enterprises (as well as other kinds of organizations) came into existence before unions. Many companies today still operate without unions. When the workers in a given enterprise do organize a union, as we all know, that doesn't destroy the enterprise; unions are not the *negation* of the enterprise. But when a union appears, power relations change, and the organization has to adapt to the change. Thus far, business enterprises have successfully adapted to this new kind of constraint, and continue to meet operating objectives (and make profits) without letup. Perhaps we ought to spend a little time examining the structure and dynamics of this remarkable phenomenon, the business organization. It meets society's demands for goods and services. It provides employment and a livelihood for most of the population. By the wealth it creates and the wages and salaries it pays, it directly or indirectly supports the government, the churches and charitable institutions, education, and the arts and sciences. And it has accommodated its activities to deal with another remarkable social phenomenon, the union.

Nowadays business schools in colleges and universities all over the country offer courses in organization theory, and encourage research in organizational behavior. We don't need to take time out to survey the whole field, but we ought to look briefly at the nature of organizations in order to see where personnel management fits in, and how collective bargaining fits into personnel management.

The Simplest Organization

A person with some disposable capital (even if it is borrowed capital) selects the personal goal, let's suppose, of making money, and finds that it is possible to profitably manufacture a certain line of products and sell them at prices that more than cover costs; this is an operating objective. The person who does so as an independent craftsman, working alone, has to reckon with the market, but is not part of an organization. The moment this person lays out any resources to hire one or more people to help, an organization comes into being. As a condition of paying the workers, the organizer contracts with them to perform prescribed tasks and supervises their work. From the status of an independent worker the entrepreneur has become an employer and the manager of an organization. As long as the organizer directly supervises employees and personally conducts all the activities of the small business—buys supplies, pays rent and taxes, meets payroll, keeps books, sells the output—all the functions of management are personally concentrated. This can be done because the organization is small and operations are simple.

Suppose now that with growing business the organizer decides to specialize in sales, and appoints one of the employees—or for that matter, hires a sister-in-law—to supervise manufacturing operations. In delegating authority to this supervisor, management's representative in charge of operations, the organizer brings into being a second level of management. Under the new arrangement each of the original employees continues to have a work contract with the owner; there are as many contracts as there are employees; but now another employee, the supervisor, directs the workers in operations. And now, for the first time in this still simple organization, we see that the employment relationship is *twofold* in nature. Let's call the employee's relationship with the supervisor *operational;* with the owner *contractual.* On one side the owner, who personifies the organization, and on the other the individual worker, who personifies only himself or herself, are still the contracting parties.

In order to keep operations going, the owner does not have to pass on to the supervisor any authority touching the organization's side of the contract; in fact, there are some responsibilities the owner can't delegate. Management must meet the payroll, for instance; wages for the work force don't come out of the supervisor's pocket. The owner may delegate some authority over contractual matters to the supervisor such as the power to hire and fire; that is, to create or terminate a worker's contract of employment with the organization. Even if the owner should delegate this authority—and the owner doesn't have to—the owner hasn't gotten free of contractual responsibilities. The owner merely accepts the supervisor's discretion *as if* it were his or her own; and can, if need be, reverse the supervisor's decision.

The point here is that the two aspects of the employment relationship—the contractual, and the operational—can be administered separately, though operations suffer if they are not coordinated. As long as the owner-manager supervised the work personally, it could be coordinated mentally. When the owner withdrew from direct supervision, the operational relationship *had* to be delegated to someone else.

Larger organizations than the small business we have been using as an example do, in fact, administer the two sets of relationships separately. Like an owner-manager, the president of a corporation personifies the organization. Though possibly having no personal ownership interest, the president acts for the owners (the stockholders) and exercises owner-like authority. In the employment relationship, or work contract, the president personifies one of the two contracting parties. The other is, again, the individual employee. Neither that employee's supervisor, nor any other manager below the chief executive, becomes a party to the contract. All that a supervisor does, at any level, is to see that subordinates carry out *their part* of the contract; that is, that they perform the tasks assigned to them in operations.

The operational relationship is what management literature, by tradition, calls a *line relation:* supervising people at work. The contractual one can be exercised by a line manager (as we saw in our owner-manager example) but when an organization grows beyond a certain size, the administration of this relationship splits off and becomes a *staff function*. We don't want to get lost in definitions, so we must make clear what we mean by the difference between a line relation and a line function, and between line functions and staff functions.

The Line Function

We hope no one will get confused now when we say that an organization's operating objectives are also twofold in nature. The enterprise must both *make* and *sell;* or it must both *serve,* and *be paid* for the services. Any manager in the organization's hierarchy who supervises people engaged in making the product or providing the services is carrying out what management writers traditionally call a *line* activity. So is any manager engaged in selling the product or service. Making and selling, then, selling and providing services, are the two *line functions*. In a manufacturing concern the factory manager is a line executive, and so is the company's sales manager. The president of a corporation, its chief executive, who is responsible for both of these functions, is the chief line manager.

The factory manager breaks down that function by delegating parts of the manufacturing process to subordinates: superintendents and supervisors. The sales manager appoints district managers to supervise the sales staff. The chief executive expects to get projected results through the direct efforts of these two line subordinates; but also needs other kinds of help, and so do they if they are to carry out their line responsibilities. The chief executive needs, for instance, someone who will recruit workers when needed, make detailed surveys and studies for setting up wage and salary schedules, and in a unionized firm, keep track of grievance handling under the terms of the labor agreement. In other words, someone to administer in detail, on a day-to-day basis, the organization's responsibilities for contractual relations with each and all of the employees. The chief executive consequently appoints a *personnel administrator*.

Now, the organization does not exist for the purpose of hiring people, or paying them, or dealing with a union (as it exists for the purpose of making products and selling them) but cannot carry out the purposes for which it does exist unless it also does just these things; and many more. Traditional management literature rather loosely classifies all non-line activities under the heading: *staff functions*. By this definition, the personnel administrator carries out a staff function. Writers on management are careful to point out that line *relations* can exist within an organized staff *function*, and we agree. The personnel administrator may appoint subordinates who work in a line relationship with the administrator, but to the rest of the organization, the personnel department is a staff department.

What the traditional (and even some of the most modern) writers on management fail to see—or if they do, fail to point out—is that in a large or even fair-sized organization there are three kinds of staff.

Staff Organizations

Staff departments advise and serve the line organization; they do detailed preliminary planning, and recommend policy; they carry out management controls and administer activities that support line operations. Colonel Lyndall F. Urwick makes a useful distinction between three kinds of staff: personal staff, special staff, and general staff.[1]

Personal staff consists of people who provide personal services which relieve the pressure on a manager's time. The secretary who takes oral dictation and types out letters the manager would otherwise have to write personally is an example of personal staff. Another example is the "assistant to" the manager. The contribution of these employees is direct personal services to a particular manager at any level in the organization.

Special staff consists of people who possess special knowledge or other qualifications which the manager whom they serve may be presumed not to have. The legal adviser, the engineer, the staff psychologist are special staff people. They give advice, which the manager weighs in making decisions to which the advice is pertinent. Thus, the manager who was not a lawyer would not know the legal alternatives available in deciding whether to defend, or settle, or make countersuit in a legal process directed against the company. Even a manager who was an electrical engineer, might still need advice on product or process from a chemical engineer or other specialist. The special staff contribution is expert advice and takes the form of *recommendations*, or the analysis of alternatives.

General staff consists of people who do part of the manager's own job but do it in greater detail. The top line manager, for instance, is responsible for the budget, but the controller (a general staff manager) must make sure the figures are correct down to the last decimal point. The line manager's judgment on the components of the budget ought to be as good or better than the controller's. The line manager is quite capable of sizing up the value of the controller's work (though not necessarily capable of judging the validity of a chemist's formula) but needs help in getting detailed proposals in order, coordinating them with all the departments affected, and putting them together in final form.

General staff also provides services, this time not to a specific individual manager but to the entire line organization (example: recruiting personnel for an entire factory, a general staff service of the personnel manager) and counsel to any manager who may ask for it. In addition, general staff carry

---

[1] Colonel Lyndall F. Urwick, *Organization in Business: An Address Given at the University of Virginia Graduate School of Business Administration, April 2, 1957*, Occasional Papers on Business Management, no. 2 (Charlottesville: University of Virginia Graduate School of Business Administration, 1958).

out routine managerial controls in their various staff fields: i.e., audits by the controller, inspection by the quality control staff, job analysis and evaluation by the personnel staff, and so on. In carrying out services and control, general staff act with organizational authority. They get this, just as any line manager does, by delegation from higher management. They use it on behalf of the whole organization or a division thereof under a particular line manager, but strictly within the bounds of their field of responsibility.

Line-Staff Relations

Both the line manager and the people in a personnel department ought to be able to see the difference in principle between their separate but complementary functions, yet often both find it hard to honor the principle in practice. One reason for this, perhaps, is that *every* line manager—not just the personnel administrator and personnel department subordinates—has to deal with people. As Lawrence A. Appley, past president of the American Management Association, used to like to put it: Management *is* personnel management. What he meant, of course, was that human effort—not the inert material resources of an organization—is what brings results. He was not trying to obscure the distinction between the operational and contractual aspects of the twofold employment relationship. Personnel department people are just as prone as line managers to overlook the distinction.

Consider, for example, work-place discipline. Suppose a supervisor, in a fit of anger, fires a troublesome worker. Keeping order in a department— that is, maintaining discipline—is certainly a supervisor's responsibility and part of the operational relationship with anyone who might disturb it. Firing the troublemaker is not simply operational; it is contractual, for it terminates the employee's work contract with the company. By an impulsive act the supervisor has interfered in the proper functions of the personnel department. They might, for instance, have found another place for the culprit. If there is a union, they will certainly have to respond to a union grievance and perhaps, by the terms of the labor agreement, reinstate the worker.

Suppose, however, that after due warning the supervisor sends a troublemaker home for a few days without pay, and again the union files a grievance. The personnel administrator who presumed to reduce, rescind, or increase the disciplinary penalty would be interfering in the operational relationship. Second-guessing the supervisor would undercut authority and weaken the supervisor's ability to maintain discipline in the department. No front-office expert can reasonably expect to keep order out on the shop floor with no personal contact.

Both sides in this situation could have avoided line-staff conflict by keeping the bounds of the other's responsibilities in mind. The supervisor has to know and follow the rules and procedures company policy and the labor agreement lay down. These usually consist of a series of warnings and graded penalties, culminating in discharge. And the procedures may actually work: the troublemaker heeds the warnings, ceases to cause trouble, and settles down to be a productive worker. Or they may fail. In that case, when all steps short of discharge have been taken, the supervisor has fulfilled any operational responsibilities and can turn the problem over to the personnel staff. Should they now decide that the miscreant might still be "saved" by transfer to another department, that does not disrupt, but reinforces, discipline in the old department, for the source of persistent trouble has been removed, while the department has no valid interest in what now happens to the departed member. If instead they decide the culprit should be fired, he or she is likely to stay fired. The supervisor's careful effort to correct disruptive behavior, and the record of that effort, strengthens the personnel administrator's hand in dealing with the union, even if the union should appeal the case to arbitration.

The personnel administrator and department aren't the only ones who may occasionally find themselves in conflict with line managers. The head of a line department may get into a fight with the controller over a budget allocation. For that matter, conflict can arise between line departments. The sales manager, for instance, may insist that the sales staff be allowed to promise customers speedy delivery, while the production manager wants to space out schedules to cut overtime costs. If the two fail to agree, their only recourse is to higher authority: their common boss, the chief executive.

Conflict can arise, then, whenever activities either of line or staff nature seem to compete. Clear definition of functions does not eliminate, but helps prevent such clashes. In personnel matters, both line managers and the personnel administrator deal with people, but (if they will only be aware of it) there is a dividing line between their separate, but complementary, responsibilities. It is the difference between the operational and contractual relation of employees with the organization. Line managers stand in an operational relationship with their immediate subordinates and (from the opposite point of view) with their superior. The personnel administrator does that part of the chief executive's *own job* that has to do with the contractual relations with each and all of the employees.

PERSONNEL MANAGEMENT AND THE CONTRACTUAL RELATION

A contract is an exchange. A contract always implies a set of reciprocal rights and obligations. What are these rights and obligations in the work contract, or contract of employment? Can we differentiate, count, and classify them?

Yes, we can: broadly and in a general sense; narrowly and in detail in particular cases. There is some "fine print" even in the apparently simple and straightforward work contract. Let's stay with the broad outlines.

Broadly speaking, the exchange is: work for pay. That is, the employee agrees to perform tasks (mental or physical, simple or complicated) under supervision, in a given set of surroundings or working conditions, in exchange for which the organization agrees to pay wages or salary, and other benefits. The employee discharges those obligations under the contract as a member of a work group engaged in operations. The company discharges its reciprocal obligations by paying wages or salary and providing other benefits. The company gains from the exchange by getting production; the worker, by earning income.

The "other benefits" that are part of the company's obligation and the worker's expectation can consist of a variety of nonmonetary items such as, for example, the promise of some measure of security on the job, such as a seniority plan; or protection, such as a grievance procedure, from arbitrary, one-sided management decisions.

By now the alert reader has probably become aware that the issues dealt with in an employee's work contract have already appeared in the outline entitled, "The Nature of the Labor Agreement" in Chapter 1 (Figure 1–1). As noted there, these same items receive fuller treatment in Chapter 8, while Part Three (Chapters 9–13) show that they can be elaborated into very fine print indeed in a union agreement. Explicitly, if there is a recognized union, implicitly if not, the personnel administrator deals from day to day and one year's end to another with precisely these issues. In each of these areas the personnel administrator helps shape company policy; also takes part in negotiating substantive rules (which become company policy) with the union. The substance these rules deal with is what collective bargaining is all about.

In saying this, we don't imply that collective bargaining is all there is to personnel management as a general staff function: by no means; by no means at all. For one thing, the number of employees in the bargaining unit represented by a union is always less than the total work force of an organization; often much less. For another, an organization's general personnel objectives usually look far beyond just the problem of coming to terms with a union and administering the resulting agreement. While an employee may only be concerned with a satisfactory work contract, the organization regards that not as an end, but as a means toward broader objectives. Collective bargaining is thus no more than a part—albeit an important part—of the range of responsibilities of a chief executive and the personnel administrator. Of even greater long-range importance to an organization may be such personnel management activities as management development, personnel planning, organizational design; and so on. This book does not pretend to deal with personnel management in all its ramifications, but in order to understand where collective bargaining belongs in the personnel function we need to see where personnel administration belongs in the total system of operations of an organization. Collective bargaining is clearly part of an organization's contractual relations with employees because the rules and arrangements that result from it set the *terms* of the work contracts of the employees represented by the union.

In the simplest organizations, such as an owner-managed small business, one person—the owner, or sole manager—carries out both line and staff functions; is responsible for both operational and contractual relations; and bargains with the union, if one is present.

In organizations with more than one level of management, the person who heads the enterprise delegates the conduct of operations to subordinate managers, but retains contractual responsibilities and ordinarily still does the bargaining with a union. When an enterprise grows beyond a certain critical size (which varies with the nature of operations and the inclinations of management) the chief executive designates a personnel administrator to take charge of the general staff personnel function, including collective bargaining. The person holding this position may do it all personally, but in a large organization breaks down the various activities and hands them over to subordinates. One of these personnel department subordinates (if there is a union) is bound to get the labor relations, or collective bargaining assignment, unless the personnel administrator does it. In very large organizations, even the labor relations function subdivides and becomes departmentalized.

Figure 4–1, which is a greatly abbreviated sketch of the corporate industrial relations staff of an enterprise employing well over 100,000 persons, provides only a hint of the problems inherent in the organization of the industrial relations department of a giant corporation. Note that this company has three industrial relations specialists bearing the title vice president and six directors of industrial relations subspecialties. As is the case in many large corporations, Figure 4–1 shows a divorce of functions for hourly and salaried personnel, the vice president–labor relations having major responsibility in the area of hourly personnel while the vice president–personnel and organization is primarily concerned with salaried personnel problems. Typically, hourly rated employees are represented by a union while salaried employees frequently are nonunion. The divorce of hourly and salaried personnel activities is significant in at least two respects: (1) the necessity for careful coordination of compensation and benefits lest the salaried people feel left out and (2) the rapidly increasing costs of providing tandem adjustments for salaried people as their number increases. Twenty years ago it was not uncommon for the salaried employee head count to represent less than 20 percent of corporate employment. Under these conditions, it was relatively inexpensive to give salaried employees a little something extra above and beyond what the union was able to negotiate for hourly rated employees. Today in many large corporations salaried employee head counts equal or surpass hourly employee head counts. The problem is further complicated by the fact that any benefits granted to salaried employees this year will certainly be demanded by the union for hourly employees the next time negotiations roll around.[2]

---

[2] Some of the problems of "tandem" adjustments for unionized and nonunion employees in a large corporation are discussed in Case No. 5 of this book.

FIGURE 4–1

Partial Organization Structure of Corporate Industrial Relations Staff Department: Multi-Industry, Multinational, Multiplant, Corporation

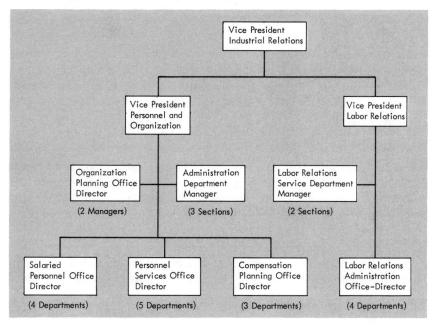

Examples of Advisory Service and Functional Authority Provided by Central Staff Organizations

1. In the personnel administration field, the director, salaried personnel office: provides *advisory service* such as:
    recommending recruitment, selection, and placement policies applicable to salaried personnel,
    recommending training and management development programs applicable to salaried personnel.
    exercises *functional authority* such as
    coordinating company-wide recruitment of college graduate trainees,
    conducting attitude surveys of salaried employees.
2. In the labor relations field, the director, labor relations administration office; provides *advisory service* such as:
    advising on local agreement negotiations,
    advising on content of labor relations training sessions for foremen,
    advising on grievances at steps below umpire appeal level.
    exercises *functional authority* such as:
    negotiating company-wide master agreements with international unions,
    researching present and future issues in collective bargaining,
    presenting grievance cases at the umpire appeal level.

THE LABOR RELATIONS FUNCTION

Now let's look at the job of the manager responsible for labor relations and collective bargaining with a union or unions. On behalf of the line management, what *results* does the organization expect from the labor relations manager? How does this person get the desired results?

Results expected.   An organization wants to be able to carry out its planned activities and attain its operating objectives without interference or obstruction from the union. What the line managers desire is labor peace, or at least, truce; perhaps even active cooperation. Some of these managers, perhaps, look back nostalgically to the free hand they had before unionization and would like to get rid of the union if they could; they are, of course, unrealistic if they expect this result. Short of that irrational dream, they probably want the labor relations manager to keep the union "out of their hair."

If a union is just beginning to organize the workers, a policy of trying to keep the union out is not unrealistic, but requires that managers handle themselves with care. An organization risks legal consequences if its agents —that is, its managers, down to first-line supervisors—try to counter the union drive with threats or discrimination or promises of benefits. At this stage, line managers expect the labor relations staff to give them guidance on how to confront the situation and to do everything legally permissible to keep the union from ever getting into their hair.

Once a union gains recognition and negotiations start, line managers want written into the agreement the kind of substantive rules that will allow them the flexibility they need to continue efficient operations. They look to the labor relations staff to assist in preparing for negotiations, and aid in arriving at satisfactory terms.

If negotiations get snagged and a strike threat looms, line management expects its labor relations staff to provide reliable assessments of alternatives and possibilities; and if the strike materializes, to do strategic planning and take tactical countermeasures. This holds true not just for an initial union agreement but for the periodic renewals as well.

Whether or not it takes a strike to reach agreement, the organization expects its labor relations staff to help line managers live with the agreement, and to themselves administer directly those activities (such as, for example, grievance adjustment on appeal) that affect the contractual, as distinct from the operational relationships. If cases go to arbitration, the chief line executive expects the labor relations manager to represent the organization and defend its interests.

Encompassing, but going beyond all these expectations are the long-term results an organization expects of all its managers, whatever their function: that they will look ahead continuously, foresee and forestall problems and complications and prepare for contingencies. For the labor relations manager, this means charting the organization's course in interaction with the other actors, in the particular contexts of the industrial relations system in which it operates.

This is a tall order. The general staff manager in charge of labor relations and collective bargaining takes on one of the most responsible and challenging roles in any organization.

The Labor Relations Role

We have just pointed out what the organization expects. What does this tell us about the kind of behavior and qualifications needed to produce the desired results?

To begin with, the labor relations manager needs to be or become an expert on the local union (or unions) dealt with, the international union with which it is affiliated, and unions in general. That is because the local union objectifies one of the main actors in the enterprise's industrial relations system. Because the labor relations manager represents and personifies the other main actor, that manager needs to become acquainted with the local union officers and business agent (if any) and size them up while transacting union-related business with them. The labor relations manager needs to know something about the international union, its mode of operation, the background of its development, its strengths and weaknesses in the industry and the community. From time to time as occasions arise to meet the international representative who services the local union, and perhaps some of the international's officers, they are evaluated too. And because union affiliations and connections do not stop at the plant gate, and may go beyond even the industry, it becomes important to know how the labor movement is put together and how it operates. A strike in a supplier's plant may affect operations in the enterprise almost as much as if the local union took the action; it might even be conceivable that the firm's own local, through its affiliations, could help solve a problem for the company in another company's plant. Then too, the labor climate in the community is part of the immediate environment in which the enterprise operates, so the labor relations manager must know the makeup and leadership of the city's labor council to which the company's own local belongs. And keep that knowledge up to date.

Labor relations managers must know the fundamentals of labor relations law: the rules for rule-making. This doesn't mean they have to be lawyers, though they may get to know this branch of law better than a lawyer who doesn't specialize in it. Lawyers in industry are special staff people; the labor relations officers are general staff managers. Unless the enterprise is huge, with its own permanent legal staff, they are likely to have to go outside, to a law firm, for legal advice, services, and when need be, representation. On behalf of the firm they may have occasion to hire a lawyer to appear in court, or even handle an arbitration hearing, but it's up to them, as managers, to weigh the import of legal advice before formulating company policy recommendations; and then, when it is approved, to put the policy in practice. The labor relations manager doesn't, we repeat, need to be a lawyer, but needs to know when to consult and how to talk to a lawyer and how to use this kind of professional service. Most of the time the labor relations manager will draw on a knowledge of labor relations law as an informed layperson, and a grasp of operating objectives as a manager, to guide and advise the line organization in day-to-day activities which labor law touches.

For their own enterprises people holding the labor relations job must know practically by heart, and thoroughly understand, the substantive rules governing the workplace. They find them in company policy and in the labor agreement; and help formulate new policy and, periodically, rewrite the agreement. They get to know the operations of the enterprise, so that they can shape substantive rules to promote and not retard progress toward organizational objectives. Day to day and in detail they administer those activities the rules give them in their labor relations role: grievance adjustments on appeal from the shop floor; research and investigation; preparation for arbitration and representation of enterprise interests at arbitration hearings; drafting of position papers in negotiation, and participation as company expert; and many other duties and responsibilities.

Although, as general staff managers they do not have authority to promulgate policy, they formulate policy proposals, generally in a form that the military services (and increasingly, management literature) call "completed staff work." That is, they put themselves imaginatively into the skin and skull of the chief executive and think through a problem *as if* they were actually in that busy person's place and could devote full time to labor relations. They consider what effect various alternatives would have on operations. They consult line managers and other general staff managers—colleagues—and draw on the skills and knowledge of special staff professionals. They listen to suggestions, try to anticipate and to meet objections, get the necessary clearances and endorsements. At the end of all this activity they draw up a document or written proposal *in final form*, ready to take effect as policy and to authorize activity that commits the organization to a course of action and perhaps the expenditure of funds. Examples? A pension plan; or a set of counterproposals to union demands; or a letter for the chief executive's signature requesting federal mediation in a labor dispute. None of these take effect until authorized: the big boss signs the letter, or initials the counterproposals, or signs the order instructing the controller to accept the bid of the insurance company underwriting the pension plan. This is completed staff work. To the extent that the labor relations manager wins the confidence of colleagues and boss, so that they see her or him not just as a specialist in a function but as an expert who can help them with theirs, approval will be won for completed staff work. Instead of throwing it back for revision, or picking it apart and dropping the tattered pieces in the wastebasket, they will adopt those recommendations confidently and put them into effect. For their part, the labor relations managers will have a role in implementation. One of them will receive the mediator when that official shows up, and fill the mediator in on the company's side of the dispute, brief the company negotiators, and perhaps present the company's counterproposals; and so on.

Line Manager Roles in Labor Relations

Every manager stands in an operational relationship with subordinates and a superior, but the only line managers whose positions give them a direct role in labor relations and collective bargaining are the chief executive, at the top of the management hierarchy, and first-line supervisors, at the bottom. The chief executive (usually relying on the kind of completed staff work just described) carries responsibility for and exercises authority over contractual relations with employees, and hence determines policy. First-line supervisors put the policy into practice. Collectively, they bear the brunt of day-to-day relations with the union. Managers at intermediate levels rarely have anything to do with labor relations.

We have presented the labor relations function as carried out centrally, at the top of the organization; let's shift now to what might be called the "worm's-eye" view of the same function from out on the shop floor. Here we find workers engaged in operations under a first-line supervisor.

The First-Line Supervisor's Critical Role in Employee Relations in the Large-Scale Enterprise

It is the first-line supervisor who must take the plans of the specialists in the production control department and translate them into units of product by the use of people. In doing so he or she must exactly conform to the personnel policies and rules laid down in the labor agreement and interpreted by the specialists in the personnel department. Any leeway for personal initiative and decision in both the technical and personnel aspects of the job has thus been narrowed; authority has shrunk with reduced responsibility, yet the first-line supervisor remains management's living link with the human element of production. This person is also management's living link with the union in action, facing a shop steward not once a year in negotiations nor once a fortnight in a grievance session, but all day every day, and feels the union's scrutiny and pressure in everything done. It is not always easy to keep relations with the union entirely impersonal.

The supervisor's task and problems indicate the kind of help and training higher management needs to provide. This phase of supervisory training belongs to the personnel department. Two important subjects make up the curriculum: the labor agreement and what may be loosely called human relations.

Supervisors and the Labor Agreement. First-line supervisors ought to know the agreement at least as well as a steward who stands opposite them. In addition, they must be drilled in the company's position on any unclear or controversial provisions. If the personnel department does not give the supervisor this understanding, they can only learn by the costly way of trial and error. They will meet with reversals of actions in grievance cases;

and that never adds to their prestige with the workers. Other managers above the first-line supervisor need to know the agreement, too, but none in such intimate and accurate detail, for none of them is as directly on the firing line as the supervisor is in front of the workers. The supervisor shares with the personnel department the most vital role in collective bargaining after the actual negotiation of the agreement—that is, living with the agreement.

The Supervisor and Work Group Interaction: Human Relations. What used to be called human relations in industry, or work-group behavior, is the other main subject in the curriculum. Over the past few decades, behavioral researchers have pretty well discredited the old, crude, negative motivators such as threats and punishment, and instead advocated positive appeals to the wellsprings of human nature. In any case, unions and the changed power relations unions bring about have muzzled most of the threats. Supervisors nowadays hear about such things as McGregor's Theory X and Theory Y, Maslow's hierarchy of needs, Herzberg's "hygiene" factors versus motivators, and the way to job enrichment. They go in for T-group training, "laboratory" exercises, management by objectives, and similar programs and approaches.[3]

It seems possible (but not likely) that the old whip-cracking, authoritarian style of supervision might have given way to the more positive behavioral approach without the advent of unions. Unions at least made the older approach less practical. When, as the labor agreement specifies, supervisors can punish only "for cause," and must be able to justify their actions, they can no longer hope to get positive results simply by saying: Do this . . . or else!

An increasing number of practitioners is helping an increasingly receptive corps of managers, including first-line supervisors, to assimilate and apply an increasing body of knowledge drawn from the findings of behavioral science research. At the lowest operational, as at the highest contractual level, those who carry on labor-management relations and collective bargaining are becoming more experienced, expert, and sophisticated.

THE ACTORS IN A DIFFERENT CONTEXT

After having presented the personnel function in enterprises of every size, from the owner-managed small business to the giant corporation, and at management levels from chief executive down to first-line supervisor, we have to admit that little of what we have said holds true in one important sector of the economy. That is the sector to which the craft union model applies. The same two actors appear: management, and labor as rep-

---

[3] Douglas McGregor, Abraham Maslow, and Frederick Herzberg are writers on motivation whose ideas have been widely disseminated in the business world. T-group and laboratory exercises and the like are varying techniques aimed at improving a supervisor's interpersonal skills.

resented by craft unions. Employers face the same three personnel management needs: to find suitable workers, to maintain an appropriate work
force, to get competitive productivity. But the contexts are different, the
needs are met in different ways, interaction of the actors leads to different
substantive rules. A general contractor, for example, may employ several
thousand people on a mammoth construction project such as a huge office
building, yet never feel the need to employ a full-time personnel administrator. For all practical purposes, *unions* take on the day-to-day personnel
function in this kind of situation.

A building contractor's work-place technology demands skilled workers. The labor market consists of dozens—perhaps scores—of labor pools of
each of the skills needed. Craft unions organize by skills; each of these labor
pools consists of members of a local craft union: carpenters, plumbers, roofers, electricians, and so on. Practically speaking, therefore, the only suitable workers the employer can find are those who report to the hiring hall
of their local union. The contractor doesn't have to search them out to recruit them, or to interview them, or test them, but simply picks up the
phone and calls the business agent of the local union. The business agent
sends the workers needed, selecting them from among the members registered and available for work at the local union hiring hall. An employer can
do the same for all of the skills the operation requires, and so assemble an
appropriate work force. As qualified journeymen, these workers are immediately productive; and competitively so, for they have learned to work at
the tempo and by the standards of their trade and will give the same pace
and quality, for the same price (the union scale) to any employer. And the
employer keeps the work force appropriate to the stage and scale of operations simply by letting go those workers whose skills are no longer needed.
There is no further obligation to them once they have been paid. They go
back to the hiring hall, ready for a call to another job.

The unions—not a personnel administrator, not an employment manager
in a personnel department—thus directly serve all three of the personnel
management needs of this kind of enterprise. They meet an employer's
short-run demands by maintaining pools of skilled labor and hiring halls.
They look after the long-run needs of the industry by participating, jointly
with government and *employer associations* in apprenticeship programs.
Through these programs they recruit and train young workers to replenish
the labor pools. And they negotiate substantive rules that govern relations
at the work place, not with any single employer, but again, with the employer association. The enterprises don't even do their own collective bar-
ganing; an employer association bargains for them all.

EMPLOYER ASSOCIATIONS

Business leaders organize for many reasons besides collective bargaining.
Only a minority of their associations do, in fact, directly engage in it.
Others, which do none of it themselves, carry out representational activities

(lobbying, public relations, and the like) that may affect the collective bargaining process generally, or they may give aid and advice to member firms involved in specific negotiations, strikes, or other relations with unions. The term "employer association" to designate management groups that directly engaged in collective bargaining, will differentiate this type of organization from other management associations.

Conditions for Association Bargaining

No employer association enters in directly when collective bargaining takes place between a single local union and a single employer, or between a number of locals and a single employer. Employer association bargaining takes place only in two situations:

The first is when a number of employers each hire workers who are members of the same local, or group of locals organized in a joint board or district of the same international. This occurs, for instance, in the trucking industry; not universally, but in those localities where employers have succeeded in forming an association. It occurs in the garment industry as a normal and regular thing. An untypical but outstanding instance of the same nature shows up in the coal mines. Regional and national employer associations bargain jointly with the United Mine Workers' International.

The unions in this picture are industrial unions, or industrial amalgamations of craft unions, as in the garment trade; and in every case a big union deals with a lot of small companies, all of which are in competition with each other. In all these industries except mining—mining is always an exception—labor costs are a high proportion of total costs. The effect of this industrial union type of multiemployer, or association, bargaining is to eliminate or reduce competition between companies based on wage differences.

The second situation occurs when a number of employers each hire workers who are members of different locals of as many different internationals. This is the characteristic situation in the construction industry. It is the craft-union type of association bargaining, which is not only multiemployer, but multiunion as well. The association negotiates and signs agreements with each of the locals, and these agreements bind all the members of the association in their dealings with each of the unions. The reason for this is that the employers need and use different kinds of labor at different stages of their construction projects, and so deal with the local representing that particular craft at the time when its members are on the job; and not before, and not after. Their association gives them the protection of a valid agreement with established rules and terms at the time they have need of that particular trade, or class of employee. It relieves all of the employers from having to negotiate separate agreements with each of the many craft unions.

Not to be confused with true association bargaining is employer *coop-*

eration. An example of this might be the agreement between New York City newspaper publishers that if any one of their papers is hit by a strike, all the others will suspend publication. This is certainly a strong pledge of support for an enterprise to get from its competitors, but the bargaining, and the agreements signed, are separate.

BARGAINING RELATIONSHIPS

Thus far, this chapter has discussed the employer's *internal* organization for collective bargaining. The *external* relationship with a union or unions may fall into a number of different patterns, depending on the nature of the industry and the unions. Here are the possible variations.

One Employer/One Local Union. This is the typical and most common pattern in manufacturing, with a local industrial union.

One Employer/More than One Local Union of a Single International. A large, multi-plant corporation may bargain with separate locals of the same international in a number of its plants. A typical example might be the Ford Motor Co., bargaining with locals of the United Auto Workers union. The typical pattern arising out of this relationship is *conference board bargaining.*

Certain issues (such as agree-on rules for rule-making, and some substantive rules with company-wide application, such as an "across the board" raise) can be settled at corporate level. Others can only be settled locally (such as crew sizes, conveyor speeds, or a seniority unit). The international union therefore sets up a conference board, to which the locals elect representatives. The conference board bargains with the corporation, centrally, for a master agreement. Once that is tentatively agreed to, the representatives go back to their locals and bargain with their local plant managers on the local issues. The press often calls these local issues "work rules," and failure to agree on them can hold up ratification of the master agreement.

One Employer/More than One Local, More than One International. Sometimes for historical reasons, sometimes because of diversity of product and operations, a single multi-plant employer faces in its separate plants local unions belonging to more than one international. This might happen after a corporate merger or in the formation of a conglomerate, or simply because competing internationals have won bargaining rights in different plants.

In this situation, management and the local unions may prefer to follow the simple one-plant/one union pattern; which they are free to do, since the bargaining unit is the plant. Or, the unions may prefer to get together and engage in *coalition bargaining.*

Coalition bargaining requires the cooperation of the international unions and not just the locals involved, but once the alliance is formed, it resembles conference board bargaining.

Employer Association/One Local Union. Unions and employers in the construction industry typically follow this pattern of bargaining. The association to which the contractors belong bargains for all of them with each of the building trades unions in turn; the type and model of craft union bargaining.

Employer Association/One International Union. In some industries, industrial union bargaining takes this form. Thus in coal mining and in the trucking industry, a number of small enterprises combine forces to deal with a union that would otherwise be overpoweringly larger than any of them. In steel manufacturing the enterprises are larger, but over the years have developed a relationship with the big steelworker union that takes this pattern. Since the locals in the mills of all the companies belong to the same international, this pattern resembles conference board bargaining on an industry-wide scale.

Employer Association/More than One International Union. Two or more competing international unions, making conflicting demands on the comparatively small employer units of a far-flung industry can bring this pattern into being as the employer response. Longshoremen and teamsters on the West Coast provide an example. These two unions assert jurisdictional claims that sometimes clash and overlap, but in the lumber industry— again on the West Coast—an employer association bargains with industrial union internationals (such as papermakers, woodworkers) whose jurisdictional claims do not conflict.

Problems of Association Bargaining

All bargaining involving more than one employer raises problems of representation. The National Labor Relations Board will, on request, designate by means of an election among workers, the union representation for a given group whether or not all workers in the unit belong to the union. Employers who bargain jointly must, on the other hand, do so by agreement among themselves and on a voluntary basis. A bargain made by the union is binding on all the workers in the bargaining unit, but a bargain struck by the organized employer group is in no way binding on other employers who are not members of the association. In any practically enforceable legal sense, it is not even very binding on association members.

The employer association has problems that parallel in several curious ways the problems of a union, and are often even more acute. Among the more troublesome are organizing, leadership, and the administration and policing of the labor agreement.

Organization. Employer associations are strictly voluntary since there is no law that compels an enterprise to abide by decisions of a body to which it does not belong. The first hard job in forming an association is to round up members. The next is to keep them in line.

Unions are also, technically, voluntary associations, but through arrangements worked out in collective bargaining (closed shop, union shop) they have found ways of making workers want to join the union—or at least, want not to *refrain from* joining—and to maintain their membership. In any case, a union that has won an election and gained recognition has the legal right to bind the nonunion minority in accordance with the decisions of the prounion majority.

Certain employers, in contrast, may have powerful motives rooted in competition for staying out of the association, or personal inclinations against risking a reduction of accustomed freedom of individual action. In particular, if it is the larger operators who want to play the lone wolf role, the holdouts can cripple the association's effectiveness. Concessions granted to the union by a nonmember can force the hand of the association.

The businessperson, more accustomed to competition than cooperation between enterprises—indeed, often dedicated by conviction to that view— is harder to organize than workers who are conditioned to cooperation on the job and accustomed to joint action and discipline.

Leadership.   Under a union constitution all employees are equal, but to paraphrase George Orwell's quip, some employers are "more equal" than others: that is, some enterprises are larger, or are under more vigorous management, or make a greater financial contribution to the employer association. Though they may temporarily sink their differences on matters that have to do with the union, they remain in competition with each other. An elected leadership may consequently be subject to distrust or jealousy, and with the necessity for consultation over decisions may hamper the speed and decisiveness of action.

As a remedy for these difficulties, many associations turn to the employment of professional labor relations experts to conduct the business of the association. The member firms set general policy and review the results of the neutral hired manager's activities. Assuming an able manager, this seems to be a satisfactory plan.

Administration.   It is sometimes easier to negotiate a joint agreement than to make sure of observance of its provisions by those who are party to it. In pursuance of this aim the employer association frequently gets help from the union, which has, perhaps, an even more direct interest than any employer in uniformity of performance and strict adherence to the agreed terms.

Greater difficulty arises when the union, instead of helping, hinders proper enforcement. It may attempt to take advantage of the separation of the enterprises to seek local gains or set precedents that can be used against other signatory employers. This is a variant of the old union game called "whipsawing." It sets the members of the association against each other.

Professional managers prove their worth in this kind of situation. Between negotiations they can devote a great deal of time to policing the agreement, advising and assisting member firms in the handling of grievance cases, and in many ways assuring uniform application of the agreement terms.

Another device associations also use is the employment, jointly and by agreement with the union, of an impartial umpire, or arbiter. To this person they submit disputes that arise during the life of the agreement, and both sides bind themselves in advance to abide by the decisions. The arbiter's role, which does not differ much whether the agreement is multilateral or bilateral, receives more detailed explanation in Chapter 13.

Essentials of Association Bargaining

Association activity of any sort in the labor relations field always follows the rise of unions and is a reaction against it. It is either a specific response to a need for united employer action to meet an immediate union threat, or a generalized answer to the growth of union influence in the community, state, or nation.

There would seem to be need for united action by employers whenever the union is bigger than the enterprises with which it deals. Now, when is the union "bigger"?

"Big" Unionism. The union is bigger than the employer when the union body with which an organization deals brings to bear, in the bargaining process, the bargaining power of members who work for all the employers in a given labor or product market. This is true when the union controls the pool from which they all draw their workers, so that labor could be withheld from one employer while competitors went on unhampered. Obviously, a craft union is in such a position in relation to its employers. An industrial union, ordinarily, is not, for the source of factory labor is open to all, and workers hired in the employment office do not come under union influence until they are part of the factory working force.

The union is also bigger when the union body with which employers make their bargain controls the supply of materials an enterprise needs, or the market to which it sells, or the channels of distribution to the market. A perfect example of this is the Teamsters, an industrial union, which can cut the channels of distribution or supply by refusing deliveries.

Either one of the two situations sketched out above cries out for employer organization. Unless employers facing such situations bargain through an association they are simply inviting exploitation by the union, and may lay the industry open to racketeering. The size of the employer association needs to be exactly proportioned to the size of what was called above the "union body."

This union body may be a local, as in the building trades. It may be a joint board of locals, as in the garment trades. It may be a district, as in the trucking industry. It may be an entire international, or a major part thereof, as in the coal mining industry.

Without the protection of an association, employers face the prospect of having the union "knock down" the individual enterprises of the industry one by one. The first bargain with the union may consist of seeing an organizer walk in with a printed agreement and say, "Sign here." If the employer signs, knowing that the penalty for not doing so would be a shutdown of business while competitors continued to operate, the next bargain might be: "Sign here. And slip a C-note into the papers when you hand them back: cash, no checks." Before long an entire industry could get into the hands of racketeers who used the employers to keep the workers in line and beat each of the employers over the head with the threat implied in control of all the others. Once such a condition arrives it is harder than ever for the employers to organize. Association bargaining balances the strength of the opposing forces.

Equality in Bargaining. Some see the union as always bigger than any employer because it organizes all the enterprises in an industry or all the practitioners of a single skilled trade whose craftsmen work for many employers.

The union is not bigger just because it has a million members while the enterprise employs only a thousand workers, if the enterprise bargains only with a local composed of its own thousand employees. The union's other members in other plants have managements of their own to bargain with; every enterprise in the industry could conceivably be evenly matched with its own segment of the union. That seems, in fact, to be generally the case in mass-production manufacturing. It is undoubtedly one of the reasons why association bargaining is rare in manufacturing outside the garment industries.

Even the "Big Three" auto companies, General Motors, Ford, and Chrysler, only began to approach joint and simultaneous bargaining as a thinkable but potentially dangerous possibility, in their dealings with the challenge of the United Auto Workers Union in 1958, the year the auto agreements expired without renewal and the plants operated without a contract. The Big Three companies would seem, offhand, well suited to engage in association bargaining. Together they produce more than 90 percent of the nation's cars. They face a common adversary in the big and powerful UAW. They maintain headquarters in the same city of Detroit, where the UAW International also has its offices, and the auto company top managers are personally acquainted and in frequent cordial social contact with each other. Time and again in the past the UAW played off one or another of the three companies against its two competitors to win important gains the others had to match; yet the Big Three held off.

They have held off, in part, perhaps, for fear of antitrust action, always a delicate subject in their circles. Another reason certainly must be competition for the new car market, in which the customer takes performance pretty much for granted and spends money for style and conveniences. Any one of the companies, convinced that its designers have come up with styling that will catch on with the public, meets an immediate union demand without too much regret, confident that whatever it gives the union, the union will make the other two grant in time. Thus it was, for instance, with the Supplemental Unemployment Benefits plan, first put to General Motors by the union, but first granted by Ford. The UAW is a big union, but the giant corporations of the auto industry are pretty big themselves and are confident and willing to take a chance. Why should they tie their own hands by being timid?

In spite of this, some observers claim to see a trend toward multi-employer bargaining on an industry-wide scale with industrial unions even in the largest enterprises. The logic of events would seem to favor this, but it will probably not come until the big employers are convinced the union really is bigger than they are. Certainly the unions have little to gain by pushing it; they have been doing very well without it. Would the UAW really welcome a united front of the Big Three auto companies against itself?

Despite this auto industry exception, the trend is certainly setting in the direction of association bargaining. Besides the industries already mentioned in this chapter, a number of others have engaged in it for years, while some have come to it comparatively recently. The garment unions have been doing it for a long time. The lumber industry, the shipping industry, the canneries on the West Coast, have been at it for two decades or more. In fact, association bargaining is prevalent as a regional phenomenon on the West Coast to an extent unknown as yet in the East or Middle West.

Most notable example of industry-wide bargaining is probably the steel industry negotiations. Technically, this is still only cooperative bargaining, in which the United Steelworkers discuss terms jointly and simultaneously with the huge steel employers; but one product of the 1962 contract was an *industry-wide* seniority pool from which all the firms would draw workers, these workers having gone into the pool as they were displaced from any of the firms by technological improvements.

The standard European practice from the start has favored association bargaining. It would appear that American practice tends in the same direction; but the process still has far to go. The greater portion of the mass-production and mass-distribution industries has not come to it yet.

OTHER MANAGEMENT ASSOCIATIONS

Unions engage not only in collective bargaining but in "representational" activities such as lobbying and public relations, and service activities such as workers' education and research. These kinds of activity, directly or indirectly, frequently supplement collective bargaining. They encourage helpful, or ward off harmful, legislation affecting the process. They promote a favorable climate of public opinion. They provide training for improved union leadership and functioning, and information useful to locals engaged in negotiations. The bulk of this representational activity goes on at levels above the local union (which is the primary collective bargaining organization) in any given international, and in the mixed bodies such as city centrals, state centrals, and the national union federation.

Similarly, certain management organizations specialize in representational and service activities for employers, and these are likely to be of greater than local scope and mixed in character. Those that unite enterprises of a single industry, unless formed for the express purpose of collective bargaining, are likely to center their attention on technological or marketing problems peculiar to the industry rather than on labor relations.

The National Association of Manufacturers

The employer counterpart of the AFL–CIO, the national union federation, is the National Association of Manufacturers, commonly called the "NAM." Of all employer groups engaged principally in representational activity the NAM takes the greatest interest in labor relations. It carries on the most vigorous and massive "pressure-group" activity—similar, but counter to, union pressure tactics—aimed at influencing the legislative and executive branches of government. It conducts the most extensive public relations work and does the most research in the labor relations field. Its network of affiliates throughout the country includes industry groups that contain employer associations for collective bargaining as well as mixed, nonbargaining associations of manufacturers and other industrialists organized on a geographical basis. This heightens the resemblance of the NAM to the organized labor movement opposite which it stands. The NAM structure is much looser than the unions', but the prestige, power, and financial resources of its employer members gives it great influence.

The Chambers of Commerce

Another important network of management associations is the Chamber of Commerce, or "C of C," units of which exist locally and affiliate on a state-wide and national scale. Throughout its structure the C of C is of mixed composition, and so does no bargaining. Local Chambers are largely service and promotional organizations, which are drawn into the representational type of activity that supplements collective bargaining only occasionally, by virtue of the stake and interest many of the member enterprises have in the field. Membership in the C of C, as in other management associations, is voluntary.

In addition to these two nationwide federations of employees, many local and unaffiliated associations, some of a quite informal nature, others well organized and enduring, bring together groups of employers for collective bargaining or representational and service functions. They may be considered analogous to unaffiliated local unions.

SUMMARY AND CONCLUSIONS

Previous systems for the management of labor have shown only two parties in the relationship: the "employer" (slaveowner, lord of the manor) and the "employee" (slave, serf). The present free-labor system shows in addition a third element, the union. The employer may be an individual or a company of people incorporated as an artificial "person," and acting through agents with delegated authority. The union is always an association of people, acting through representatives. Only the worker is always an individual, full-blooded person. Collectively, workers are the flesh-and-blood link between the company and the union.

The "Four Sets of Relations"

Between these three elements there are three sets of relations, and perhaps a fourth that encompasses them all:

1. *The company and the worker.* This is a freewill contract in which the worker exchanges work against wages, under conditions laid down by the employer and accepted by the worker, or agreed upon between them.
2. *The worker and the union.* Here the relationship is a free association between the worker as a member and the union to which the worker belongs. Technically, at least, it is a voluntary association and the right to enter it comes from the Bill of Rights of the Constitution.
3. *The union and the company.* The relation between the union and the company is usually thought of, and referred to, as a "contract," but it is more nearly analogous to a *treaty* between two sovereign powers. It is an exchange of pledges and promises that have to do with the contract between the company and each of its individual workers.
4. *The "encompassing fourth" relationship.* The company and the union are linked so intimately by the body of the workers, who are at the same time employees of the one and members of the other, that they may be thought of as a three-link chain, or perhaps more appropriately symbolized by overlapping circles.

The "Key" Element

The *key element* that brings the other two into association with it is the company. The *company* organizes the working force around its production processes. The union has to take the workers as it finds them in their relations with each other and with the company, their employer.

But labor-management relations, expressed in bargaining for agreements and in administering the agreements, is a process of interaction. Companies bring unions into existence by creating work groups for the union to organize. Unions act on the company, and the company registers their impact in terms of management organization structure and functioning. Internal change is the result, but there are also external effects. Union pressure on separate, independent enterprises forces them into united action and mutual dependence.

Multiemployer bargaining, which long ago reached maturity in the handicraft sector of the economy, spread into mass production and distribution with the growth of industrial unions. Industry-wide bargaining, not yet much developed, seems to be almost in sight, and, some say, sure to come.

Industry-wide bargaining involving the big and decisive mass-production and distribution units of the economy will surely affect management structure and functioning within the enterprise, and the relation of enterprises to the society they sustain with their products and services. The enerprise will no longer be as free and independent as before. The local union, which is a direct, responsive membership organization, will yield its rights and powers in collective bargaining to the international, which is a delegate organization remote from local control.

While these possibilities unfold, the enterprise remains the key element. It will hardly remain passive but will act as well as be acted upon. It is to be hoped that in association it will act as effectively as when it stood alone, to help sustain a vigorous economy and provide the material basis for a good society.

QUESTIONS FOR DISCUSSION

1. Supervisory training in human relations is a major development of the post-World War II period. Why?
2. What is the influence of the prevailing form of ownership of capital on management organization, objectives, and methods?
3. How do you explain the fact that there frequently is substantial friction between line and staff organizations in the handling of personnel matters in large-scale enterprises?
4. Compare and contrast management objectives and methods in handicraft industry and mass production.
5. In 1947 several proponents of the Taft-Hartley law favored outlawing multiemployer bargaining. Although this proposal continues to crop up occasionally, it is less frequently heard nowadays. What do you think of this proposal and why does it seem to have gone out of style?

SELECTED ANNOTATED BIBLIOGRAPHY

ALLEN, A. DALE, JR. "A Systems View of Labor Negotiations," *Personnel Journal* (February 1971), pp. 103–14.

   An attempt to develop a systems model for collective bargaining with a view to improving the goal setting, forecasting, and decision making of industrial relations executives. Allen stresses the flexibility of his model to various situations.

ANTHONY, PETER, and CRICHTON, ANNE. *Industrial Relations and the Personnel Specialists.* London: B. T. Batsford Ltd., 1969.

   An extensive reevaluation of the industrial relations process in light of recent findings in the field of organizational behavior, particularly socio-technical systems theory. Authors see a need to integrate the industrial relations process into line management.

BAKER, HELEN, and FRANCE, ROBERT R. *Centralization and Decentralization in Industrial Relations.* Princeton, N.J.: Industrial Relations Section, Princeton University, Research Report Series, no. 87, 1954.

Discusses management and union preferences for centralization and decentralization in industrial relations responsibility and authority in multiplant firms and the actual practice of centralization or decentralization in these companies.

BELCHER, A. L. "How Top Management Views the Industrial Relations Function," *Personnel,* vol. 34 (March–April 1958), pp. 65–70.

Results of a personnel director's survey of some 200 executives and university professors to determine the factors necessary for success as a personnel administrator.

BROWN, DOUGLASS V., and MYERS, CHARLES A. "The Changing Industrial Relations Philosophy of American Management," *Proceedings of the Ninth Annual Meeting of the Industrial Relations Research Association,* pp. 84–99. Madison, Wis.: The Association, 1957.

Discusses five forces causing changes in the approach of management to industrial relations in the preceding decade.

COPP, ROBERT. "The Labor Affairs Function in a Multinational Firm," *Labor Law Journal,* vol. 24, no. 8 (August 1973).

A Ford Motor Co. executive describes how Ford carries out the industrial relations function in its multinational operations.

CUTHBERT, N. H. and HAWKINS, K. H. eds. *Company Industrial Relations Policies: The Management of Industrial Relations in the 1970s.* London: Longman Group, 1973.

A collection of articles which examines selected industrial relations issues and their administration in Great Britain.

GUNTER, HANS, ed. *Transnational Industrial Relations: The Impact of Multi-National Corporations and Economic Regionalism on Industrial Relations.* New York: St. Martin's Press, 1972.

A collection of articles which deals with industrial relations in companies which span national boundaries, with emphasis on Europe.

HILL, LEE H., and HOOK, CHARLES L., JR. *Management at the Bargaining Table.* New York: McGraw-Hill Book Co., Inc., 1945.

A comprehensive review of the issues and practices of collective bargaining from a management viewpoint. Provides a penetrating insight into management thinking at the end of World War II.

KOCHAN, THOMAS A. *Resolving Internal Management Conflicts for Labor Negotiations.* Public Employee Relations Library series, no. 41. Chicago: International Personnel Management Association, 1973.

The author analyzes the nature of the organizational context in which city government collective bargaining takes place, the sources of conflict among management officials that arise over bargaining issues, and offers suggestions on how to resolve these conflicts.

LYNCH, EDITH. "The Personnel Man and His Job: An AMA Survey," *Personnel*, vol. 32 (May 1956), pp. 487–97.

A profile of "the average personnel man" derived from an American Management Association questionnaire survey of 450 participants in a personnel conference.

McFARLAND, DALTON E. The Labor Relations Consultant as Contract Negotiator," *Personnel*, vol. 34 (May–June 1958), pp. 44–51.

Discusses the advantages and disadvantages to a company in the use of outside consultant as contract negotiator. Interesting observations on the impact of this practice on internal management organization.

McGREGOR, DOUGLAS. *The Human Side of Enterprise*. New York: McGraw-Hill Book Co., Inc., 1960.

Argues for greater participation in decision making by subordinates in business enterprise.

McMURRAY, ROBERT N. "The Case for Benevolent Autocracy," *Harvard Business Review*, vol. 36 (January–February 1958), pp. 82–90.

A leading management consultant argues against participative management and in favor of his proposed "benevolent autocracy."

———. "War and Peace in Labor Relations," *Harvard Business Review*, vol. 33 (November–December, 1955), pp. 48–60.

A leading management consultant takes issue with the "philosophies" growing out of "causes-of-industrial-peace" type of thinking and advocates a preventive labor relations policy to maintain a balance of power between company and union.

METZGER, NORMAN and POINTER, DENNIS D. *Labor Management Relations in the Health Services Industry: Theory and Practice*. Washington, D.C.: The Science and Health Publications, 1972.

Written primarily for hospital and nursing home administrators, this book examines the development and content of health care labor relations, with emphasis on management's efforts to deal with the unions.

MYERS, CHARLES A., and TURNBULL, JOHN G. "Line and Staff in Industrial Relations," *Harvard Business Review*, vol. 34 (July–August 1956), pp. 113–24.

Professor Myers of M.I.T. and Professor Turnbull of the University of Minnesota survey the organizational placement of the industrial relations in management and propose methods of clarifying the relations between the industrial relations department and line management.

PATTEN, THOMAS H., JR. "Personnel Research: Status Key," *Management of Personnel Quarterly*, vol. 4 (Fall 1965), pp. 15–23.

Reviews the personnel research carried out by specific large corporations.

RYDER, MEYER S., REHMUS, CHARLES M., and COHEN, SANFORD. *Management Preparation for Collective Bargaining*. Homewood, Ill.: Dow Jones-Irwin Inc., 1966.

An analysis of personal interviews with approximately 100 officials from 40 companies about how they forge policy, strategy, and tactics for collective bargaining.

SCOTT, WILLIAM G. *The Management of Conflict: Appeal Systems in Organizations*. Homewood, Ill.: Richard D. Irwin, Inc., and the Dorsey Press, 1965.

Examines appeal systems in business and nonbusiness organizations without unions.

SLICHTER, SUMNER H.; HEALY, JAMES J.; and LIVERNASH, E. ROBERT. *The Impact of Collective Bargaining on Management*. Washington, D.C.: Brookings Institution, 1960.

See chapter 2, "Issues for Management in Industrial Relations" and chapter 29, "Line and Staff Cooperation and the Position of Foreman."

SOMERS, GERALD G. "Pressures on an Employers' Association in Collective Bargaining," *Industrial and Labor Relations Review*, vol. 6 (July 1953), pp. 557–69.

Compares experience under multiemployer bargaining in the bituminous-coal and flint-glass industries.

WALKER, CHARLES R.; GUEST, ROBERT H.; and TURNER, ARTHUR N. *The Foremen on the Assembly Line*. Cambridge, Mass.: Harvard University Press, 1956.

Examines the roles and points of view of supervisors in an automobile plant.

5 The Government and the Public Interest

IN THIS CHAPTER we encounter the third main actor in the industrial relations system, the government. In its three branches: legislative, executive, and judicial; and its three orders of magnitude: federal, state, and local, the government is the most potent *regulator*. It shapes and enforces the rules for rule-making. Although laws have influenced collective bargaining in America ever since colonial times, the first general nationwide labor relations law, the Norris–La Guardia Act, did not come to pass until 1932. The exercise of the judicial and executive powers of government in labor relations has a longer history, but today it appears to follow the guideposts set by the more recent legislation. This chapter examines the current status of legislative, executive, and judicial regulation of the actors and their interaction in collective bargaining.

Government may take many forms, from absolute monarchy to pure democracy. Regardless of its form, a government draws upon the resources of society and organizes the people in it by the exercise of moral authority and the possession of power. In a democracy, the moral authority of government derives from its efforts to represent what is called the public interest. The public interest may be conceived of as a delicate balancing of pluralistic private interests for the common good or as an overpowering, unified popular objective. In either case, a government claiming to promote the public interest cannot be neutral toward the private interests of management and unions or toward the activity in which they engage their separate, and often opposing, interests: collective bargaining.

In a democratic state, defining and interpreting the public interest is the responsibility of those representatives of the public who wield governmental power: legislators, executives, and judges. Every citizen has a right to a personal interpretation of the public interest and the right also to advocate that interpretation, but only the appropriate officials of government have the final say, so long as they retain their position of public trust. Thus at any particular time the public interest is what the legislators say it is when they pass a law, and what the executives say it is when they enforce the provisions of a law, and what the judges say it is when they rule on disputes under the law. The public interest, then, is not something eternal and unchanging. This chapter seeks to show that the public interest has, in fact, changed over the years. It will go on to explain how the present-day public interest, as reflected in present-day law and its enforcement, regulates unions and management. It will point out some areas in which controversy over different interpretations of the public interest has not yet settled down into a determination of law.

CONCEPTS OF THE PUBLIC INTEREST

At various times, different groups of people have viewed labor relations legislation as a vehicle for achieving one or more of the following social goals, which were conceived to be in the public interest: (1) preserving property rights; (2) advancing the civil rights of working people; (3) keeping the government out of economic affairs; (4) lessening or eliminating public inconvenience resulting from labor disputes; (5) controlling monopoly power; (6) controlling the business cycle; (7) equalizing bargaining power between conflicting private interests.

Although several of these goals conflict, each has found some expression in present-day labor relations legislation. A brief statement of each of these concepts will explain the thinking behind them and help evaluate their influence on law.

Preserving Property Rights

The right of an individual to hold property is enshrined in the Constitution; it is not the right that is in question here, but rather various interpretations of what constitutes its proper exercise in management. Some see it as an "inalienable" right not only to set prices and to determine what goods or services to produce and the way to produce them, but also to set wages and employee performance standards, to hire and fire at will and without challenge, to set rules and regulations governing the conduct of employees. So sweeping a view of the management prerogatives derived from property rights would naturally call for the elimination of collective bargaining and for laws prohibiting or severely limiting union activity.

Advancing the Civil Rights of Working People

In contrast to the above, an extreme view of the civil rights of working people would require their participation and consent in every act of management. A more moderate statement of this position would give employees the right to bargain collectively only over the conditions of their employment. Once collective bargaining becomes the method of establishing these conditions, a simple extension of the civil rights concept would insist that workers also have a right to full democratic participation in the affairs of their unions. Further, if racial or religious or age or sex discrimination violates civil rights, unions themselves must be clean of any taint and must open their membership rolls and activities without discrimination.

A twist to this civil rights concept is the "right to work"—the right of an individual to hold a job, whether or not he or she elects to join a union.

Keeping the Government out of Economic Affairs

Classical political economy makes out a very strong case for keeping the government from interfering with labor-management relations in a democratic state with a free enterprise economy. The presumption is that free employers and free unions know what is best for them and have a primary interest, which should not be disturbed, in settling their own affairs.

As a matter of fact, American law on collective bargaining today rather follows this concept and is largely *permissive*, both with regard to the terms and to the methods by which the parties reach agreement. The concept of governmental noninterference must not be confused with neutrality. In terms of the total effect of government policy at any given time, nonintervention in labor-management relations strengthens the hand of either management or the union.

Lessening Public Inconvenience

Most citizens have at one time or another been inconvenienced by a strike. Some strikes go beyond mere inconvenience and may imperil public health or jeopardize the national defense. Public policy, under this concept, looks toward preventing strikes; or if they occur, toward lessening their impact.

It is sometimes forgotten that the Wagner Act (seldom viewed as a strike control measure) virtually eliminated what had been, before its passage, the principal cause of strikes in the United States: the strike for union recognition. The Taft-Hartley law went further and tackled the problem of national emergency strikes. Experience has shown that the attempt was only moderately successful. The legislative quest continues for a solution to the problem of lessening public peril and inconvenience.

Controlling Monopoly Power

This concept has two contradictory aspects. On the one hand there are those who claim that the employer has monopoly—"monopsonistic"— power over job opportunities, so that the individual worker is helpless in bargaining. Collective bargaining restores the balance. Against this, on the other hand, there are those who see *unions* as the real monopolies and believe they should be broken up under the antitrust laws.

Controlling the Business Cycle

There is little doubt that the idea of increasing purchasing power as a step toward ending the Great Depression won many congressional votes for the passage of the Wagner Act in 1935. It has also been argued that the Taft-Hartley restraints on union power were aimed at controlling inflation in 1947. Both concepts hold that labor relations law is a proper field for countercyclical legislation.

Quite apart from law, government action taking such form as the Presidential "guidelines" of 1965 (withdrawn in 1967) which looked toward wage-price stability, went on the presumption that collective bargaining had a bearing on the health of the economy. The guidelines clearly stated the national objective to be noninflationary full employment and asked employers and unions to conduct their affairs in harmony with this objective. President Nixon's wage-price freeze of 1970 made an even more explicit move toward the same end.

Equalizing Bargaining Power

Probably the most venerated concept of the public interest in labor relations is the idea that government should equalize the "bargaining power" of management and unions. This concept implies that labor's interests conflict with management's; that they are bound to fight; and that the stronger will most likely win, to the detriment of broader interests. If, however, government backs up the weaker and thus makes them equal, they may settle their differences without a fight, and if they fail, at least the fight will be fair. Thus the Wagner Act prohibited unfair labor practices by employers, who at the time were felt to be stronger. The Taft-Hartley Act, some 12 years later, turned the same argument around to prohibit unfair labor practices by unions.

Another application of this argument, never enacted in law, holds that some big unions dealing with many employers should be broken into smaller units, just as business combines sometimes are required to divest themselves of their holdings. An example is the United Automobile Workers, which has members working for Chrysler, Ford, and General Motors. Public policy would oppose a merger of the Big Three; why should not the UAW, it is argued, break down into units that would equalize bargaining power?

These concepts of the public interest have had their partisans, and perhaps all have some validity, though taken together they would be hard to apply to any specific labor-management relationship, or even to any particular piece of legislation. Too frequently an individual's zeal for a particular principle, or an interest in a specific legislative proposal, blinds her or him to equally valid aspects of the public interest. Somewhere, sometime, the powers that be in government have to make a decision. It is rarely one-sided, but it is never—and it cannot be—completely neutral.

Before discussing the substantive regulation of the parties, it is well to identify the agencies of government currently active in the industrial relations field. In this brief survey of agencies, their major functions and their points of contact with the other actors will be emphasized.

GOVERNMENTAL AGENCIES ACTIVE IN THE INDUSTRIAL RELATIONS FIELD

American government is organized around the legislative, executive, and judicial functions at the federal, state, and local levels. Under the commerce clause of the Constitution, federal authority has emerged as the dominant force in the regulation of collective bargaining.

Legislative Agencies

Since 1932, the U.S. Congress has shown substantial interest in regulating the collective bargaining process. The basic federal law on collective bargaining today is incorporated in three statutes: the Norris–La Guardia Act of 1932; the Taft-Hartley Act of 1947 which amended the Wagner Act of 1935; and the Landrum-Griffin Act of 1959. The Norris–La Guardia Act deals with the use of injunctions in labor disputes. The Taft-Hartley Act provides procedures for establishing union recognition and preventing "unfair labor practices" by management and unions. The Landrum-Griffin Act regulates the internal affairs of unions and managements.

Beyond the direct regulation of the collective bargaining process, Congress has enacted a substantial body of federal legislation in the social security, wage and hour, taxation and tariff fields which is a legitimate concern of managements and unions. This legislation is considered in an Appendix to this book. Most recently, civil rights legislation has affected collective bargaining.

Congress is subjected to continuous pressures from management and labor organizations. Most major corporations maintain legislative liaison departments or offices in Washington and these voices are supplemented by such organizations as the U.S. Chamber of Commerce and the National Association of Manufacturers plus a multitude of associations concerned with the affairs of individual industries. The fact that 55 international unions maintain their headquarters in the city of Washington is some evidence of union interest in legislative affairs. Beyond the individual internationals, the AFL–CIO and its departments engage in lobbying activity at the federal level.

Under the police power, state legislatures have played a major role in the field of protective labor legislation—child labor, minimum wage, factory inspection, fair employment practices, protective hours limitations, wage payment and collection, time off for voting, and the regulation of private employment agencies. Although much of protective labor legislation is peripheral to the collective bargaining process, unions and managements have a vital interest in state unemployment compensation and workmen's compensation statutes and, where operative, state labor relations statutes regulating collective bargaining relations which are excluded from the coverage of federal law. Although the federal law is supreme in most collective bargaining areas, the Taft-Hartley law, in ceding jurisdiction to the states for laws restricting union security (so-called right-to-work laws), set the stage for some bitter legislative battles at the state level.

Lobbying at the state level finds local unions and the state federation representing organized labor, while enterprises speak for themselves or use the services of state-wide industry associations.

County commissions and city councils almost never regulate the collective bargaining process or the affairs of managements and unions, but they spend a good deal of money on building construction and they employ many civil servants. Enterprises and unions affected by their activities are engaged in attempting to influence their deliberations.

Executive Agencies

As chief executive, the president of the United States is concerned with all aspects of American life. The President's public pronouncements on labor relations carry great weight. Perhaps even more important is the influence which that office wields in behind-the-scenes conversations with the captains of industry and with labor leaders. Most presidents of the 20th century have used the power of their office in at least some labor-management crises.

Presidents Wilson, Roosevelt, Truman, Eisenhower, Kennedy, Johnson, and Nixon have all personally intervened in major labor disputes. Although their interventions have taken different forms and their personal philosophies of the desirability of intervention have differed, their actions have demonstrated the significant role which the president himself plays in labor-management relations. It seems that the times in which we live require at least some presidential participation in labor-management relations. The form that this intervention will take depends upon the personality of the incumbent of that office.

Presidents Wilson, Truman, Kennedy, and Johnson have used the authority of their office in attempts to reconcile the interests of labor organizations and management for the national welfare. President Wilson's first Industrial Conference in 1919 and President Truman's National Labor Management Conference in 1945 failed. The President's Advisory Council on Labor-Management Policy, established by President Kennedy and reactivated by President Johnson was not much more successful.

Three independent agencies of the executive branch of the federal government concern themselves directly with labor relations. They are: (1) the National Labor Relations Board, (2) the Federal Mediation and Conciliation Service, and (3) the Department of Labor.

The National Labor Relations Board.   First established by the passage of the Wagner Act in 1935, the National Labor Relations Board, its regional offices, and its General Counsel's office are responsible for administering the basic federal law of management-union relations. Many enterprises and unions find it desirable to use the facilities of the NLRB for resolving representation questions even before they negotiate their first collective bargaining agreement. The NLRB also possesses broad authority for investigating charges of noncompliance with the law, and enforcement. Every effort possible to secure voluntary compliance precedes formal action, but in case of controversy NLRB investigators gather evidence and Board lawyers prepare cases for a hearing before a trial examiner appointed by the Board or the Board itself.

The Federal Mediation and Conciliation Service.   Formally established as an independent agency by the Taft-Hartley Act of 1947, the Federal Mediation and Conciliation Service is the successor organization to the Labor Department's Conciliation Service which was established in 1913. The Federal Mediation and Conciliation Service works entirely through the voluntary cooperation of enterprises and unions. It has no power to prosecute anyone or to issue orders; it is even chary of comment and criticism. The function of the Federal Mediation and Conciliation Service is to assist managements and unions in reaching collective bargaining agreements, by the procedures of conciliation and mediation. For many years efforts at conciliation and mediation started only when labor or management were on the point of having a strike or even after a strike was on. Lately mediators have been called in to help much earlier in the game, even in the process of adjusting grievances. The role of mediators is discussed in Chapter 13.

United States Department of Labor.   Although the main activity of the U.S. Department of Labor lies in the protective legislation field and in research activities, it is the President's official liaison with organized labor and with employers in their collective bargaining capacity. The Landrum-Griffin Act of 1959 greatly expanded the functions of the Secretary of Labor in the new field of protecting inner-union democracy.

State Executive Agencies.   In the 15 states with labor relations statutes, these laws are administered by either the state labor department or a state labor relations board similar to the NLRB. Most states have an executive agency charged with responsibility for assisting in the mediation of labor disputes. Every state has an executive agency responsible for the administration of its unemployment compensation and workmen's compensation laws and, where applicable, the administration of factory inspection, minimum wage, child labor, and other protective legislation. Particularly serious intrastate strikes, either because of their impact on the state economy or the exceptionally rare violent strikes, often involve the governor of the state.

The Courts and Collective Bargaining.   Judges have at varying times been the villains, and alternately the heroes of the drama of collective bargaining in the eyes of both labor and management. The last word in interpretation of the law comes from the courts.

Before the passage of the Norris–La Guardia Act in 1932, the courts, through the interpretation of the common law, often "legislated" in the collective bargaining field. The subsequent passage of a substantial body of statutory law on collective bargaining has reduced the participation of the courts in labor relations. Today the courts have the very important function of ruling on the constitutionality of labor relations legislation and providing the final say on the interpretation of whatever legislation is enacted by the legislative branch of government and enforced by numerous executive agencies.

Managers and union leaders come in contact with a wide variety of governmental representatives who are responsible for the law of collective bargaining. What is the substance of that law?

FEDERAL LABOR RELATIONS LAW

All American labor relations law that has been written into the federal statutes dates from the 20th century. That part of it which remains currently valid is embodied in five laws: (1) the Railway Labor Act of 1926, as amended; (2) the Norris–La Guardia Act of 1932; (3) the Wagner–Connery Act of 1935; (4) the Taft-Hartley Act of 1947, as amended; and (5) the Landrum-Griffin Act of 1959.

Of these five laws, the first applies only in the privately owned but publicly franchised railways and airlines. All others in one way or another regulate collective bargaining in the private sector generally. Some authorities would expand this list to include as labor legislation the antitrust laws. We prefer not to. While it is true that in the early years of this century the courts applied some antitrust provisions to unions and collective bargaining—even though the framers of the legislation had not so intended—more recent Supreme Court rulings have restricted or thrown out these earlier judicial interpretations.

Some would also include laws such as the Davis-Bacon Act of 1931 and the Walsh-Healy Act of 1936, that set standards employers must adhere to when engaged on government contracts. Again we prefer not to. While the standards these laws set have an impact on the bargains reached, and are important where they apply, they do not regulate collective bargaining activity as such, and are of limited scope. Of much greater scope is the more recent civil rights legislation, with its accompanying administrative regulations and court interpretations, but again, the laws do not directly regulate collective bargaining. We would find it more logical to include the Executive Orders, or administrative laws, that govern labor relations in the federal service, but defer our discussion of them to Chapter 15, which deals with collective bargaining in the public sector. We deal with the civil rights laws and their impact on collective bargaining at appropriate places, and in particular in Chapter 13, which has to do with agreement administration.

We shall have more to say about the civil rights laws and their impact on collective bargaining later in this chapter. First we intend to outline the basic rules for rule-making in the American system, as laid down in law. An appendix to the book presents changes and additions to the rules, none fundamental but none insignificant, that have come out of further legislative action or judicial decision.

The discussion of labor relations law in this chapter focuses on several substantive areas of regulation. Figure 5–1 traces the emergence of American legislation on labor relations.

First Principles: The Railway Labor Act

A generation of Americans accustomed to going everywhere by car or, if time and distance press, by air, finds it hard to think back to a day when neither of these means of transportation was in comomn use. Outside city limits there were few paved roads. For a long time a booming auto industry made and sold cars faster than state highway departments could build or widen—or finance—hard-surfaced roads for cars to run on. Although today the trucking companies move an increasing share of the nation's freight, railroads still do the bulk of the long-distance overland hauling.

Railroads are a form of monopoly, subject to public regulation. They were an even more powerful monopoly in the days when neither goods nor passengers could move from place to place except over their fixed steel rails. Populist farmers of the Middle West, who saw the profits of their harvests vanish to make profits for the privately-owned railroads, waged their main battles against this monopoly power; and railway management fought back.

They fought the unions, too, when railway workers tried to organize. They refused recognition, hired spies and strikebreakers, set up company unions. In two great railway strikes (1877; and the 1894 Pullman strike) they got the federal government to intervene by sending troops against strikers, and blood was spilled. Nonetheless, in spite of bitter management resistance, over the years the unions gained strength. What were then called the Railway Brotherhoods, along with their allies in the shops, came out of World War I (a period of union growth) strong enough to vigorously resist management's postwar offensive. With transportation between cities utterly dependent on trains, a strike of railway workers could quickly turn into a regional or national emergency. Even today the government regards a railway strike as an emergency.

FIGURE 5–1

The Emerging Substance of American Labor Relations Law

Norris–La Guardia Act (1932)	Wagner–Connery Act (1935)	Taft–Hartley Act (1947)	Landrum–Griffin Act (1959)
1. "Yellow dog" contract made unenforceable at law.	Outlaws "yellow dog" contract (Sec. 8[B][3]).	No change.	No change.
2. Severely restricts use of injunctions in labor disputes.	No change.	President empowered to obtain injunctions: (a) in national emergency disputes (Sec. 208–210) and NLRB; (b) to prevent unfair labor practices (Sec. 10[E]–[M]).	No change.
	3. Established NLRB (Sec. 3–6)	Separated General Counsel functions from Board functions (Sec. 3–6).	Representation questions delegated to Regional Directors (Sec. 3).
	4. Empowers NLRB to resolve questions of representation (Sec. 9)*	Special treatment for foremen, guards, and professional employees (Sec. 9[B]).* Only one election per year (Sec. 9[C][3])*; decertification elections (Sec. 9[C][1]).*	No change.
	5. Prohibits management actions aimed at frustrating employee free choice of representatives and organizational efforts (Sec. 8[A]-[1]–[4]).	Employer "free speech" amendment (Sec. 8[C]).*	No change.
	6. Requires management to bargain with union (Sec. 8[A][5]).	No change.	No change.
		7. Requires union to bargain (Sec. 8–[B][3]).	No change.

FIGURE 5–1 *(continued)*

Norris–La Guardia Act (1932)	Wagner–Connery Act (1935)	Taft–Hartley Act (1947)	Landrum–Griffin Act (1959)
		8. Prohibits union actions aimed at frustrating employee free choice of representatives (Sec. 8[B][1]).	No change.
		9. Outlaws closed shop (Sec. 8[B]-[4]).‡	No change.
		10. Authorizes state "Right to Work" Laws (Sec. 14[B]).‡	No change.
		11. Outlaws secondary boycott (Sec. 8[B][4]).*	Outlaws "hot cargo" agreements except in garment and construction industries.
		12. Requires 60-day notice of contract termination (Sec. 8[D]).	No change.
		13. Created Federal Mediation and Conciliation Service (Sec. 202–205).†	No change.
		14. National Emergency Disputes procedures (Sec. 206–210).†	No change.
		15. Makes union subject to suits in federal courts (Sec. 301).	No change.
			16. "Bill of Rights" for union members (Title I).
			17. Responsibilities of union officers (Titles II, III, IV).
			18. Safeguards on union funds (Title V).

* Discussed in greater detail in Chapter 6.
† Discussed in greater detail in Chapter 7.
‡ Discussed in greater detail in Chapter 9.

This was the background of the Railway Labor Act of 1926. As monopolies, the railroads were already under federal regulation. A Congress that had the power to set the terms of the franchise system under which they operated naturally had the power to change those terms, and could do so without bringing into question the free enterprise ideology that prevailed, and still prevails, in the private sector of the economy.

The Railway Labor Act of 1926 curiously foreshadows the Wagner Act of 1935. The basic principles that later became public policy in the private sector were first laid down in the law intended to apply only to the monopolies.

The 1926 Act set up procedures for determining union recognition by vote of the workers. It forbade discrimination against union membership and activity and it outlawed company unions. It required management to meet with representatives of the employees to hear grievances, and it set up appeals procedures for arbitration of disputes not settled directly with the unions. These principles still underlie the law and animate current practice. When Senator Wagner, nine years later, drafted the law that bears his name, he merely applied the principles to the entire private sector of the economy. Ideological objections against this extension made no headway in 1935 because times had changed. The country was in the grip of what is still called the Great Depression.

And now the once limited and special Railway Labor Act has proved applicable, with modifications, in another area of franchised and regulated monopoly, the airlines. Airlines more nearly resemble railroads than might appear at first glance. Just as trains have to stop at stations not just for goods and passengers, but for fuel, servicing, and repairs, aircraft must touch ground at developed airports. For the long haul, the airlines now carry the passenger traffic; the railways, still, the freight. The same basic set of rules for rule-making fits them both.

Not all monopolies fall under the Railway Labor Act. Privately-owned utility companies, for instance, are subject to the same labor relations laws that hold for the rest of the private sector. So are other forms of transportation, such as the trucking industry and merchant shipping. The Railway Labor Act continues to have a limited application. Unions and managements to which its terms apply have to know it well and follow it with care; the rest of industry observes different rules.

This book stays in the mainstream. For most people likely to become involved on either side in collective bargaining it would be a distraction, and irrelevant, to go into detail about the Railway Labor Act. We accordingly return to the remaining body of American labor relations law.

Positive Nonintervention: The Norris–La Guardia Act

The Norris–La Guardia Act was a very modest piece of legislation. It created no new governmental agencies and had the net effect of reducing the work of the courts in labor relations matters. Although addressed only to restricting the use of injunctions in labor disputes and making the "yellow dog" contract unenforceable in the courts, the Norris–La Guardia Act did state a new policy for the United States on the employment relationship and freedom of contract.

Noting the protection given to property owners in the corporate form of enterprise and other ownership associations, the Norris–La Guardia Act stated:

> . . . the individual unorganized worker is commonly helpless to exercise actual liberty of contract and to protect his freedom of labor . . . though he should be free to decline to associate with his fellows, it is necessary that he have full freedom of association, self-organization, and designation of representatives of his own choosing, to negotiate the terms and conditions of his employment and that he shall be free from interference, restraint, or coercion of Employers of labor. . . .

The words "full freedom of association," "representatives of his own choosing," and "free from interference, restraint, and coercion" were to become the cornerstones of American public policy on labor relations.

The Norris–La Guardia Act made the question of representation a private matter between workers, employers, and the unions, not subject to intervention by the courts. It provided no penalties for employer actions seeking to prevent unionization, but it stripped such actions of all legal protection.

The act attacked two abuses that seemed to give management an unfair advantage in fighting unions: the "yellow dog" contract and the unrestricted use of injunctions in labor disputes. Neither of these management abuses had any basis in statutory law, but got their sanction from common law and judicial precedent; they were admittedly not crimes against the unions, only inequities. The act provided positive statute law which deprived these abuses of legal sanction.

The Yellow Dog Contract. Employers opposed to the unionization of their workers hit upon an ingenious idea, somewhere around the turn of the century, of making workers "take the pledge" against the union. As a condition of employment, employees had to sign a card in which they affirmed that they were not union members and would not join a union as long as they went on working for the company. They acknowledged that if they did join or became active on behalf of a union, they would have broken their contract with the company and given cause for terminating their employment. The worker forced to sign the pledge to hold his job, union people said, felt like a dog with its tail between its legs—a yellow dog, at that!

It seemed to many Americans outside the labor movement as well as in it that employers who required the yellow dog contract were forcing workers to waive a portion of their inalienable civil rights in order to make a living. This, they argued, deprived a citizen of freedom. The issue reached the courts and was tested in U.S. Supreme Court case of *Hitchman Coal and Coke* v. *Mitchell* (1917). The Supreme Court upheld the legality of the yellow dog contract. Since this decision rested on interpretation of the common law, the remedy was a specific statute—the Norris–La Guardia Act of 1932.

Section 3 of the Norris–La Guardia Act declared yellow dog contracts to be contrary to the public policy of the United States. The law simply stated that such contracts "shall not be enforceable in any court of the United States and shall not afford any basis for the granting of legal or equitable relief by any such court."

The Norris–La Guardia Act did *not* outlaw yellow dog contracts, it merely made them unenforceable at law. Under the Norris–La Guardia Act employers were still free to require yellow dog contracts and to fire any worker who joined a union. An official outlawing of the yellow dog contract had to wait until the Wagner Act of 1935 made it an unfair labor practice for an employer to discharge or discriminate against a worker because of his union activity.

Norris–La Guardia Restrictions on the Use of Injunctions. Injunctions are preventive court orders issued at the discretion of a judge *before* a case has been heard.

A judge issues an injunction to forestall some threatened or contemplated act that is not inherently illegal but that might cause "irreparable" harm. This allows time to examine the case in court by the due processes of law to determine whether the damage that is feared will indeed result if the act is carried out.

The judge may then either withdraw the injunction or make it permanent.

For example: A person might learn that a neighbor intends to cut down a shade tree on or near the unmarked dividing line between their properties. In discussion with the neighbor it might develop that each contends that the tree is growing on his own side of the line. One wants to cut it down because the roots are ruining a garden plot; the other wants to keep it for its shade and beauty. Supposing that they fail to settle the argument in reasonable fashion, and that the tree lover has reason to believe the neighbor intends, perhaps out of spite, to cut the tree down anyway; he could ask for an injunction to prevent it. This would restrain the neighbor (under pain of contempt of court) from using the ax until a resurvey of the boundary established ownership. If in truth it belonged to the neighbor, he would then be free to cut it down; but if he had done so before the survey, and the survey went against him, he would have done irreparable damage which would be hard to measure in money and which he could not replace; for it might take a century to grow a new tree.

Following similar reasoning, an employer threatened with strike action (before the Norris–La Guardia Act) would ask a judge for an injunction against the union, on the ground that the strike would do irreparable damage to the business. Or, with a strike actually in progress, the employer would allege that damage and disorder were imminent if picketing and other strike activity continued, and ask the judge to enjoin the complained-of activities. If the judge agreed—and judges seemed prone to agree on what often seemed very slight grounds—the strike was delayed, frustrated, or brought to a close as soon as police or sheriff's deputies moved to enforce the injunction.

Thus while strikes were not in themselves unlawful and could not legally be forbidden outright, the terms of an injunction could so hamstring the union's activities as to have the effect of outlawing the strike. It must be remembered that before the passage of the Wagner Act in 1935 a union could not ordinarily win recognition without a strike. In recognition strikes, timing is often a crucial element of failure or success. Even if after a hearing the injunction was withdrawn, the damage to the union's cause might have been done—irreparably—with union members demoralized and intimidated, the union weakened or destroyed.

As with the yellow dog contract, many citizens who were not themselves union members found the abuse of the injunction in labor disputes unfair. It seemed to pervert the law's wise provision for protecting a citizen against threatened harm to property or person by turning it into a tricky and oppressive device for depriving other citizens, the union members, of rights that were lawfully theirs under the Constitution.

The act did not outlaw the use of the injunction, even in labor disputes when necessary, but made the conditions for getting an injunction so stiff that the effect was almost the same.

Impact of the Norris–La Guardia Act.   Professor Charles O. Gregory sees the Norris–La Guardia as the culmination of the philosophy of laissez-faire in union-management relations.[1] Its meaning in the 70s is very different from what it was in the 30s.

The net impact of the Norris–La Guardia Act on the society and on unions and managements depends upon the legal and economic environment of the time in which it is evaluated. At the time of its passage in 1932, the impact of the Norris–La Guardia Act was little more than sweet talk to the unions. Even without a yellow dog contract, the employer's powers of persuasion (the perfectly lawful threat and exercise of discharge for union activity or membership) were indeed effective. In those very rare cases where unions were strong enough to force employers to recognize them, they were free to exert their full power. The Norris–La Guardia Act gave little direct help to unorganized workers and weak unions. In 1932 union membership was at an all-time low. If the Norris–La Guardia Act were to become the sole industrial relations statute in effect in the 70s the net effect of the law would be quite different. Many of the unions in America today

---

[1] Charles O. Gregory, *Labor and the Law,* rev. ed. (New York: W. W. Norton & Co., Inc., 1958), p. 185.

could defend themselves quite adequately in a fair fight with management. Under the Norris–La Guardia Act alone, the unions would have full use of the strike, boycott, and picketing. These weapons are very potent indeed when they are supported by a union membership in being, and when potential allies are available in the union movement. These weapons were substantially less effective when, as in 1932, the union membership existed only in the hopes of labor leaders.

Positive Protection of the Right to Organize: The Wagner Act of 1935

The Great Depression was three years old, and at its deepest, when Franklin Roosevelt took office in 1933. Almost his first official act was to close all the banks. For reasons fully understandable only to people who lived through those days, this ultimate gesture of economic collapse gave the nation its first breath of confidence. It seemed to wipe the slate clean for a fresh start, or, to use the imagery of those days, it called off all bets and broke out a new deck of cards. In quick succession other measures followed. Preeminent among these was the National Industrial Recovery Act, or NIRA, the predecessor of the Wagner Act of 1935.

The NIRA aimed to build public confidence by halting the decline of prices and encouraging production and jobs. It called upon industry to adopt codes of "fair competition," which were to be drawn up and administered by the participants, promulgated and policed by the government. To this end it authorized the formation of industry associations and suspended the antitrust laws. Minimum prices were part of the plan of fair competition and also minimum wages. As a means toward keeping wage levels up, and hence maintaining purchasing power, the act guaranteed to unions the right of collective bargaining. This was the famous Section 7a.

Worker response to Section 7a was overwhelming. Unions formed spontaneously in plant after plant, the internationals which mounted a vigorous organizing compaign (like the mine workers and the clothing workers) got an enthusiastic response. The newly formed CIO began its campaign to organize the unorganized in mass-production industry and met with unheard-of success.

In 1935, the Supreme Court declared the NIRA unconstitutional. Immediately, Sen. Robert Ferdinand Wagner of New York introduced a bill in Congress that reaffirmed, with amplifications, the substance of 7a.

The Wagner Act passed easily in Congress, but for two years its constitutionality remained in doubt, under challenge of litigation headed for the Supreme Court. This proved no check on the union drive. In 1936, the auto industry sit-down strikes broke out in the Detroit area.

As with the bank closings, one must have lived through this experience to understand fully the impression the sit-downs made on the public mind. American labor relations seemed to be rushing to the brink of violence—and who could be sure?—maybe revolution. In the relative calm of a "cease-fire" between the auto industry and the union, negotiated by the governor of Michigan, the same Supreme Court that had thrown out the NIRA upheld the constitutionality of the Wagner Act. Militant unionism abandoned the sit-down and, for its most pressing aim of recognition, turned to the ballot box in Labor Board elections. Since the Supreme Court's validation of the Wagner Act, industrial unions have fought their strikes out at the plant gate instead of on the factory floor.

The Wagner Act solved three hard problems that had been plaguing American labor relations for many years: union recognition, company unionism and discrimination against unionists, and company refusals to bargain. Because of the large sector of economic life covered by the Wagner Act and the need for flexibility in administration, the Wagner Act created the National Labor Relations Board to implement its provisions.

The National Labor Relations Board.   The National Labor Relations Board is an independent administrative agency. It is empowered to investigate, to hold hearings, and to issue decisions and orders. The orders and decisions of the Board are subject to court review for their final enforcement, but the courts have shown considerable reluctance in setting aside the orders of the NLRB. The NLRB can impose no penalties for the violation of the laws that it administers. The Board is empowered to prevent unfair labor practices by cease-and-desist orders and to require affirmative action to effectuate the law.

Although the Taft-Hartley law of 1947 and the Landrum-Griffin law of 1959 modified the organization of the Board and its jurisdiction, the present day NLRB is a direct lineal descendant of the organization created by the Wagner Act.

Jurisdiction of the NLRB.   Federal regulation of collective bargaining is based on the commerce clause in the Constitution. As the Supreme Court has interpreted the commerce clause, the federal government has very wide jurisdiction in regulating collective bargaining activities in enterprises of all sorts. This broad constitutional authority is limited by the statutory provisions governing the NLRB and minimum standards which the NLRB has established governing the volume of business that an enterprise must do before the NLRB will exercise its power over an enterprise.

Under Taft-Hartley and the Landrum-Griffin law, the following employers and employees are specifically *excluded* from the jurisdiction of the NLRB:

1. Employers:
    a. The U.S. government and the states or any political subdivision of either.
    b. Federal Reserve bank.
    c. Wholly owned government corporations.
    d. Nonprofit hospitals.[2]

---

[2] In 1975 employers and employees in the health care industry, including nonprofit hospitals, were brought under NLRB jurisdiction by an amendment to the Taft-Hartley law.

      e. Any employer who is subject to the terms of the Railway Labor Act.

2. Employees:
      a. Agricultural laborers.
      b. Domestic servants.
      c. Any person employed by parent or spouse.
      d. Any individual employed by an employer who is subject to the Railway Labor Act.
      e. Independent contractors.
      f. Supervisors.
      g. Government employees, federal or state, including government corporations and Federal Reserve banks.

Although the Board has legal jurisdiction over enterprises that affect commerce, it has, with the approval of Congress and the courts, limited the exercise of its jurisdiction to enterprises whose effect on commerce, in the opinion of the Board, is substantial. The Board's standards for determining those enterprises over which it will exercise jurisdiction are based on the total annual volume of sales or of purchases, and these standards are different for different kinds of business. In addition, the Board exercises jurisdiction over all enterprises that affect commerce when their operations have a substantial impact on national defense. The Board, in its discretion, may decline to exercise jurisdiction over any class or category of employees where a labor dispute involving such employees is not sufficiently substantial to warrant the exercise of jurisdiction. The Board has refused to exercise jurisdiction over hospitals operated for profit, or over racetracks, and real estate brokers.

Section 701 of the Landrum-Griffin Act gives to state labor relations agencies and courts full jurisdiction over any dispute which the NLRB declines to hear, and directs the NLRB to hear every case that was covered by its jurisdictional standards in effect on August 1, 1959. The NLRB is empowered to broaden its jurisdiction up to the full coverage of the law, but is forbidden from reducing its jurisdiction from the coverage in effect on August 1, 1959.

Organization of the NLRB. The Taft-Hartley Act divided the functions of the NLRB into a trial section and an investigative section headed respectively by a Board of five members and by a General Counsel—all appointed by the president. The Board makes decisions on cases which the General Counsel, who is not responsible to the Board, investigates and prepares for hearing. This separates the executive and judicial functions in the enforcement of national labor relations policy.

The work of the National Labor Relations Board consists of two parts: (1) representation cases and (2) unfair labor practices cases. Representation cases deal with the question of union recognition. The Wagner Act prohibited five unfair labor practices by management. Retaining the Wagner Act's unfair labor practices by management, the Taft-Hartley Act added six unfair labor practices by unions and the Landrum-Griffin Act added a seventh.

Union Recognition and Representation Issues.   The Wagner Act stated that "Representatives designated or selected . . . by the *majority* of the employees in a *unit appropriate* . . . (for collective bargaining), shall be the *exclusive representatives* for the purpose of collective bargaining." (Emphasis added.) Thus in representation cases, the Board has three problems to solve:

1. What is an appropriate unit?
2. What is the will of the majority of the employees in this unit?
3. How can a change in the will of the majority be accommodated?

These questions and the evolution of Board policies are discussed in some detail in Chapter 6.

The important things to note now about union recognition and representation issues are: (1) *employees* are the sole judges of whether or not they should be represented by a union; (2) a *majority* of the employees can commit what may be a very unhappy minority to representation by a particular union; and (3) it is the job of the NLRB to determine what the majority wants.

The Board may certify a union as the exclusive bargaining agent either by an election or by other means of determining the majority's will. In the early days of the Wagner Act, the Board often placed reliance on union dues books or authorization cards as a means of determining the majority's will. Elections, however, have since the very early days of the act been the principal method of determining the will of the majority. This democratic procedure greatly eased the unions' job of organizing the unorganized. Before the Wagner Act, union members usually had to strike to obtain union recognition. Under the Wagner Act and its successor legislation, all the union has to do is to convince a majority of the employees to vote for it in a secret ballot election conducted by the government. Once the union has won the election and been certified by the Board, the employer has no choice but to deal with the union.

"Ballot box organizing," initiated by the NLRB under the Wagner Act and continued to this day, is unique in the United States. This procedure, which Congress has seen fit to continue and strengthen through 35 years of industrial relations legislation, indicates a strong endorsement of the assumption that collective bargaining is in the public interest.

Unfair Labor Practices by Management.   The unfair labor practice section of the Wagner Act specifically protected only employees from interference, restraint, and coercion. The unfair labor practices prohibited by the Wagner Act were all *employer* actions. The Wagner Act sought to balance the position of employees and employers by restricting the activities of employers.

Section 8 of the Wagner Act prohibited five unfair labor practices by management. The prohibited practices were:

1. To interfere with or restrain or coerce employees in the exercise of their right to self-organization.
2. To dominate or interfere in the affairs of the union.
3. To discriminate in regard to hire or tenure or any condition of employment for the purpose of encouraging or discouraging union membership.
4. To discriminate against or discharge an employee who had filed charges or given testimony under the act.
5. To refuse to bargain with chosen representatives of employees.

The unfair labor practices section of the Wagner Act was one-sided in that it attacked excesses by management only. At the same time, it is very important to note what the Wagner Act did *not* do. First and foremost, it did *not* make the unfair labor practices a crime; that is, it did not impose any penalties or fines for violation of the act. The "teeth" in the Wagner Act became apparent only when the courts began to uphold NLRB orders instructing employers to reinstate *with back pay* employees who had been discharged in violation of the act. Second, the Wagner Act did *not* require an employer to concede to the demands of a union for higher pay or for anything of substance; but only required acceptance of the act of bargaining. Probably the most difficult problem confronting the NLRB even today is giving practical meaning to the obligation to bargain.

Redressing the Balance: The Taft-Hartley Act of 1947

Preserved in the Taft-Hartley law, as stated, are all the fundamental principles of the Wagner Act. To these the new law added some things that dismayed union leaders, pleased many management people, and kept the issue simmering just below the boiling point in politics from the day of passage almost to the present.

During the 12 years following the Wagner Act, unions enormously increased their strength. In advocating his bill to amend the Wagner Act, Senator Taft leaned implicitly on the concept of balancing bargaining power. The employer, he said, had now become the underdog. Union leaders promptly replied that his supposed equalizing measures put the employer on top again. There was probably exaggeration in both views.

The year of reconversion to civilian production following World War II brought on more strikes, and bigger ones, than any previous year in American history. In contrast to the strike wave following World War I when management shook off the slight hold unions had gained in the factories during the war, this time the unions, for the most part, won their strikes. They won them because they were organized industrially and because, on the crucial recognition issue, the law was on their side. That is, recognition was no longer at stake; the unions could hold concrete, attainable economic issues before the strikers' eyes.

But the American public, newly released from the pressures of war, did not take kindly to the strikes. Many people not hitherto opposed to unions became alarmed at the magnitude and duration of strikes which they saw the big industrial unions were capable of bringing about. In this climate of reaction against the spectacle of union power, the Taft-Hartley bill passed in Congress. President Truman vetoed it, but it passed again over his veto and became law.

What follows is a brief statement of the substance of the new law. Its fuller implications for managements and unions will be discussed in later chapters.

Changes in the Right to Union Representation.   Section 7 of the Wagner Act was explicitly amended to give a majority of the workers the protected right to *refrain* from union organization and collective bargaining. The Taft-Hartley law also contained new election procedures which were designed to permit workers to refrain from collective bargaining. In the case of supervisors, plant guards, and professional employees, the Taft-Hartley law defined specific permissible and nonpermissible forms of union recognition. Last but not least, the Taft-Hartley law gave employers a strong voice in influencing workers in their free choice of union representatives.

The Taft-Hartley law provided that the NLRB could hold only one election in any year for a single group of employees. Thus if a union lost an election or employees wanted to rid themselves of a nonrepresentative union, the *status quo* was frozen for one full year. Strikers who had been replaced were not eligible to vote in NLRB representation elections. The Taft-Hartley law created the decertification election by which employees could use the facilities of the NLRB to remove a union which was no longer representative.

Under the Taft-Hartley law, supervisors were denied all protection of the law in seeking union recognition. The NLRB was directed to allow plant guards to be represented only by unions composed exclusively of plant guards. Professional employees could be represented by plant unions only if a majority of the professional employees had voted for such representation.

Obviously, employers might very well have preferences about whether or not their employees were represented by a union and which union would represent them. The Wagner Act and NLRB interpretations of that law took the position that employer attempts to influence the outcome of NLRB elections were "interference, restraint, and coercion" of employees in the exercise of their guaranteed right to free choice of representatives. The Taft-Hartley law, Section 8(c), called the "free speech" amendment, stated:

> The expressing of any views, argument, or opinion, or the dissemination thereof, whether in written, printed, graphic, or visual form, shall not con-

stitute or be evidence of an unfair labor practice under any of the provisions of this Act, if such expression contains no threat of reprisal or force or promise of benefit.

This free speech amendment substantially increased the influence which employers could exert on the outcome of NLRB elections. We shall discuss the free speech problem in some detail in Chapter 6.

The net effect of the Taft-Hartley law in the area of union recognition was to encourage employees and employers who wanted to avoid collective bargaining. The right to collective bargaining was retained, but the implicit right to refrain from bargaining was made explicit in the words of our national industrial relations policy.

Unfair Labor Practices by Unions.   The Wagner Act defined and prohibited certain unfair labor practices *by management*. That was on the theory that employees and their unions were weaker and needed protection. The Taft-Hartley law extended the concept of unfair labor practices to *unions*, and brought them under the same sanctions and penalties for infractions as were applicable to management. The prohibitions on unfair labor practices by unions were designed to protect employees and employers.

Section 8(b) of the Taft-Hartley law enumerated six unfair labor practices by unions:

1. To restrain or coerce employees in the exercise of their guaranteed rights to engage in, or to refrain from, collective bargaining.
2. To cause an employer to discriminate against an employee who is not a member of a labor union for any reason other than failure to tender the periodic dues and initiation fees uniformly required as a condition of acquiring or retaining membership.
3. To refuse to bargain with an employer, provided the union is the representative of those employees.
4. To engage in or to induce employees to engage in strikes or concerted refusal to work or boycotts—refusal to use, process, or handle certain goods or materials—when an object of such action is:
    a.   forcing or requiring an employer or self-employed person to join any organization or forcing anyone to cease using the products of, or doing business with, any other person,
    b.   to force recognition by any other employer of a union unless certified by the NLRB,
    c.   to exert pressure against any employer to recognize a particular union when another union has been certified by the NLRB, and
    d.   economic pressure in a jurisdictional dispute.
5. To charge an excessive or discriminatory fee as a condition precedent to membership in a union under a union shop clause.
6. To cause or attempt to cause an employer to pay or deliver any money or other thing of value, in the nature of an exaction, for services which are not performed or not to be performed.

The prohibition on unfair labor practices by unions protected employees in several ways. First, employees were protected from union restraint and coercion, just as the Wagner Act had protected them from employer coercion. Employees were also protected from union pressure exerted through their employers—with the sole exception of the obligation to pay union dues under a valid union shop agreement. Section 8(b)(4) protected nonunion workers in nonunion firms from union pressure even if they had obtained business by undercutting the conditions that existed in unionized firms. Under the union shop, employees were also protected from excessive or discriminatory initiation fees and dues.

The protection given to employers by the Taft-Hartley Act was certainly as significant as the protection given to employees. Unions were stripped of their power to induce employers to discharge persons who were antiunion. Section 8(b)(4) gave nonunion employers very substantial new insulation from unions that sought to organize their employees through boycotts. Section 8(b)(3), which required unions to bargain, and Section 8(b)(6) which was aimed at eliminating featherbedding were not to prove as significant. The new obligation for unions to bargain was somewhat frivolous since a union's reason for being is to bargain. The prohibition against featherbedding proved to be too vague to be meaningfully interpreted by the NLRB and the courts.

Obligatory Bargaining Procedures. The Taft-Hartley law changed the definition of the obligation to bargain, which the NLRB and courts had formulated, in only one important way—it provided a cooling-off period in the termination of agreements. Section 8(d) requires the party intending to terminate or modify a collective agreement to serve a written notice of such intention on the other party to the agreement 60 days prior to the proposed date of termination or modification. Thirty days after the serving of a termination notice, the Federal Mediation and Conciliation Service and the state mediation agency must be notified of the existence of the dispute. A strike or a lockout before the expiration of this 60-day period or the termination date of the agreement, whichever occurs later, is an unfair labor practice. An employee who strikes in violation of this provision loses all protection of the law and may be discharged for this kind of union activity. We shall discuss the functions of the Federal Mediation and Conciliation Service later.

Regulating the Internal Affairs of Unions. Many of the legislators who supported the Taft-Hartley law were deeply concerned over Communist infiltration of labor unions, the misappropriation of union funds, the monopoly aspects of the closed shop, and undemocratic procedures in unions. These concerns provided a basis for a new legislative departure in regulating the internal affairs of unions.

The Taft-Hartley attack on Communist influence in unions made the services of the NLRB available only to internationals and locals whose officers swore out "non-Communist affidavits." This indirectly, for the first time, told unions how to run—or at least how *not* to run—their business. (The Landrum-Griffin law has gone further on this issue by a direct and positive prohibition and added a ban on racketeers.)

Congressional concern over the use of union funds was evidenced by the reporting requirements imposed on labor organizations and the prohibition on political expenditures by unions and corporations. Unions which failed to file annual reports on their finances with the Secretary of Labor were denied all access to the facilities of the NLRB. Violation of the ban on political expenditures was punishable by fines and imprisonment.

The Taft-Hartley ban on the closed shop deprived unions of the time-honored right to *effectively* set their own rules for admission to the union. Although the unions' rights to set their own admission standards were explicitly excepted from the union unfair labor practice of restraint and coercion of employees, the real power to set admission requirements ultimately resides in the ability to force the discharge from employment of the nonmember. In the closed shop ban and the Taft-Hartley's provisions for discharge only for nonpayment of dues, Congress severely restricted the power to set admission requirements. Even the question of "excessive and discriminatory" initiation fees came under the scrutiny of the NLRB. We shall have more to say about the importance of the ban on the closed shop and Section 14(b) which authorized state "right-to-work" laws in Chapter 13.

The Taft-Hartley Act's regulations of the internal affairs of unions were primarily aimed at the disclosure of union rules and procedures to governmental officers and the union membership. The Landrum-Griffin law goes beyond disclosure in prescribing affirmatively how unions shall operate.

National Emergency Strikes.   As defined in the Taft-Hartley Act, a national emergency dispute has two essential features: (1) it affects an entire industry or a substantial part thereof *and* (2) it imperils the national health and safety. In such a dispute, the president is empowered to appoint a board of inquiry to ascertain the causes and circumstances of the dispute. Upon receipt of the report of the board of inquiry, the president may direct the attorney general to petition any district court for an 80-day injunction against the strike or lockout. The district court will issue the injunction if the dispute has *both* of the features required. The board of inquiry is reconvened when the injunction is issued. If the dispute is not settled in the next 60 days, the board of inquiry reports the positions of the parties and the employer's last offer to the President who in turn makes the report public. The NLRB within the next 15 days conducts a secret ballot of the employees involved to determine if they wish to accept the employer's last offer. If no settlement is reached by the 80th day, the injunction is discharged. The president then reports to the Congress and *may* recommend legislation to deal with the dispute.

It needs to be emphasized here that after the 80-day injunction the union is free to strike and the management is free to lock out. *Neither* the president *nor* the board of inquiry is empowered to recommend terms of settlement. The procedure consists of an 80-day cooling-off period, extensive publicity to the positions of the parties (but no official judgment of the propriety of those positions), and the permission for presidential petition of Congress for ad hoc legislation if all else fails.

It is neither unfair nor premature to say that the Taft-Hartley provisions did not solve the problem of national emergency strikes. The Landrum-Griffin law did not amend the Taft-Hartley Act on national emergency disputes.

Remedies under the Taft-Hartley Act. Besides substantially increasing the scope of governmental regulation of collective bargaining, the Taft-Hartley law imposed new sanctions in addition to the remedies provided by the Wagner Act, on persons and organizations who violated its provisions. The new sanctions were: criminal penalties of fine and imprisonment, injunctions, and private suits for damages. The criminal penalties applied to violations of the ban on political contributions, false non-Communist affidavits, violations of the rules on checkoff and welfare funds, and willful interference with an agent of the Board. The Board was empowered to obtain injunctions to prevent the occurrence of unfair labor practices. In the case of boycotts, this injunction process was mandatory on the Board. Federal courts were empowered to hear private damage suits against labor unions for violations of collective bargaining agreements.

Just as the substance of the Taft-Hartley law was directed mostly against unions, the new remedies related primarily to union activity. It is important to note that the NLRB (*not* private parties) was empowered to get injunctions against unfair labor practices. The Norris–La Guardia Act was not repealed, it was merely amended, in that a specific governmental agency was empowered to use injunctive relief against specific unlawful acts. As has been indicated above, the injunction is a particularly potent weapon in labor relations. Congress very wisely limited the use of this weapon to a governmental agency.

The Taft-Hartley Act in Perspective. The Taft-Hartley law was passed in a climate of postwar reaction against the upsurge of union power. Time and experience have dissipated much of the emotion that enveloped earlier discussions of the Taft-Hartley Act. What is important about the law today is quite different from what appeared to be most important in the late 40s. The law's lasting impression on society and collective bargaining in the enterprise can be briefly summarized.

From the viewpoint of society, the Taft-Hartley Act leaves some unsolved problems as well as some clear failures and some clear progress. Experience with the Taft-Hartley law clearly illustrates the futility of trying to exactly balance the bargaining power of managements and unions in society as a whole. General remedies cannot provide the much sought balance between such diverse relationships as the small union against the giant corporation or the giant union against the tiny employer. Although the

Taft-Hartley's legislative recognition of the national emergency disputes probably served the public interest well, the remedies provided by the Taft-Hartley Act leave much to be desired. For better or for worse, the free speech amendment, the ban on secondary boycotts, and the regulation of union security both in the Act and in right-to-work states retarded the spread of unionism in nonunion areas and industries. The seed for the governmental regulation of the internal affairs of unions found in the Taft-Hartley Act sprouted in the Landrum-Griffin Act. It is still too soon to make firm predictions about exactly where the governmental regulation of internal affairs of unions will lead society. Probably the most significant conclusion that can be drawn from the operation of the Taft-Hartley Act is that unions have been recognized as a permanent institution in society.

From the viewpoint of bargaining in the enterprise, the impact of the Taft-Hartley Act was relatively slight. The total fabric of the Taft-Hartley law made organizing more difficult for unions in their formative stages than in earlier years. The Taft-Hartley prohibition on the closed shop in industries with casual and intermittent employment was so unrealistic that it encouraged widespread violation which had to be (at least partially) patched up in the Landrum-Griffin Act. The statutory bargaining procedures provided by the Taft-Hartley Act probably have been helpful to the parties in establishing a better plan for negotiations.

The Landrum-Griffin Act of 1959

When it was first enacted newspaper headline writers called this act the labor reform law. This reflected the hope of some of its sponsors and a large segment of the public that it would bring about inner-union democracy and honest leadership where these might be lacking or in danger. Other observers, not so confident, admitted at least that it put the means for doing this within the grasp of rank-and-file union members. Still others sardonically called it the lawyers' full employment act because of its precedent-shattering provisions, some of which were most obscurely and ambiguously drafted and seemed headed for years of test and challenge in the courts.

It will be helpful to look into the events that brought about its passage.

Background of the Act. The issue which split the AFL and called the CIO into being—the issue of industrial unionism—soon ceased to be a difference in practice. Unions of both federations organized industrial locals where that form was appropriate. Reunification of the labor movement thus became thinkable soon after the split, and unfriendly overtones in Taft-Hartley gave unions common cause to heal the breach. Before the merger in 1955, some leaders in both camps opposed reunification. Others who wanted it hesitated, because each side imputed to the other a tolerance of certain evils that were barriers to unity. These were: Communist leadership and influence in some CIO unions; and racketeering in some unions of the AFL.

Reunification, therefore, seemed to call for action on both these inner-union problems; and effective action proved difficult. Neither the AFL nor the CIO could step in to straighten out the internal affairs of an autonomous International. Expulsion, the strongest disciplinary measure available, merely drove out the per capita paying members as well as their offending officers, without accomplishing reform. Outside authority was needed.

From 1957 to 1959, a committee headed by Sen. John L. McClellan of Arkansas conducted hearings that uncovered evidence of crime, corruption, collusion, malpractices, and dubious dealings in a few old-line AFL unions, notably the Longshoremen (East Coast) and the Teamsters. It was at the height of public excitement over these revelations that the Landrum-Griffin Act became law.

What does it aim to do? How does it propose to do it?

Aims of the Law. The Landrum-Griffin law has two aims: *(a)* to set minimum standards of democratic procedure, responsibility, and honesty in the conduct of the internal affairs of unions and *(b)* to clarify congressional intent on basic labor relations policy as stated in the Taft-Hartley Act. The first six titles of the Landrum-Griffin Act, taken together, lay down a comprehensive program dealing with three problem areas of inner-union democracy: (1) the rights of union members; (2) responsibilities of union officers, and (3) safeguards on the use of union funds. Parenthetically it should be stated that Title II also requires employers to file reports on their financial relationships with union leaders and payments made to persons for the purpose of influencing employees in the exercise of their rights under the law. Title VII amends the Taft-Hartley Act by (1) tightening up the Taft-Hartley regulation of secondary boycotts and hot cargo agreements, (2) liberalizing the Taft-Hartley law on union security and the right of economic strikers to vote in NLRB elections, and (3) imposing additional restrictions on the rights of unions to picket for recognition.

Inner-Union Democracy and Responsibility. Before the passage of the Taft-Hartley Act, no agency except the courts was ever responsible for regulating the internal affairs of unions. It probably is not an exaggeration to say that, in general, unions were viewed as private clubs or fraternal organizations. Like college fraternities, they were free to set their own qualifications for membership and to exclude from membership anyone who violated their rules or incurred the indignation of the officers or the membership. In some unions, particularly the old-line craft unions, discrimination based on race and sex played a role in admission to membership. Most unions also took a very dim view of a member who crossed its picket lines. However, such discrimination in employment was perfectly legal in many states and even churches have been known to crack down on members who violate their rules.

Many persons both sympathetic and hostile to the labor movement were gravely concerned about civil liberties in labor unions. By 1947, many unions were powerful enough to negotiate agreements which made membership in the union a condition precedent to employment. Under a closed shop agreement, the union literally could deny a job to a worker. This concentration of power in the hands of the union could be viewed in three ways. First, it could be argued, as most union leaders did argue, that this power held by unions was no greater than the power held by any employer. This argument, if it carried, would result in no governmental regulation of unions' internal affairs. Second, it could be argued—and this argument carried in the Taft-Hartley Act—that no unions should be permitted to possess this power. The Taft-Hartley Act simply outlawed the closed shop. No matter how distasteful a worker might be to the union, the right to work could be upheld by an employer so long as the worker paid union dues. Third, it could be said that union members had a legitimate interest in who worked alongside them and that any legislation should be directed at the arbitrary, discriminatory, or antisocial exercise of the power that the closed shop created. Although supported by many public-spirited authorities on labor-management relations and civil liberties, the third argument has not been accepted in legislation. The Taft-Hartley law sought to protect workers from undemocratic unions by depriving all unions of effective control over the act of employment.

The Landrum-Griffin law carries the basic civil liberties rationale of the Taft-Hartley law one step further. It seeks to guarantee union members democratic procedures inside their unions. The Taft-Hartley law's protection of the worker who wants to refrain from membership in a union is unchanged.

a.   *Rights of Union Members.*   Title I of the Landrum-Griffin Act sets forth a bill of rights for members of labor organizations. These rights are summarized in Figure 5–2. Members are guaranteed the right to vote on union matters and to engage in political activity within the union. Union dues can be increased only by following a prescribed procedure. Members are given the right to sue the union and its officers in federal courts for deprivation of their guaranteed rights .Title VI makes it a criminal offense punishable by fines and/or imprisonment to use violence or the threat of violence to interfere with a member's exercise of guaranteed rights.

b.   *Responsibilities of Union Officers.*   The Landrum-Griffin Act extended the regulation of union officers started by the Taft-Hartley law and changed the method of applying congressional pressure on the unions. Taft-Hartley denied the use of the NLRB to *unions* whose officers refused to swear out non-Communist affidavits. The Landrum-Griffin Act imposed its penalty on the union *officer* who violated its provisions and repealed the Taft-Hartley's penalty on unions which had noncomplying officers. The Landrum-Griffin Act prohibited former Communists and felons from holding union office for five years after they left the Party or were convicted of crime, or were released from jail after conviction.[3] Labor organi-

---

[3] The Supreme Court in 1965 declared the anti-Communist ban unconstitutional. See the Appendix to this chapter.

FIGURE 5–2

The Landrum-Griffin "Bill of Rights" for Union Members

Under Title I, every member of a labor organization engaged in an industry affecting interstate commerce is to have the following rights and privileges:

1. *Equal rights* to nominate candidates for union elections, attend membership meetings, and vote on union business.
2. *Freedom of speech and assembly* in and out of union meetings, so long as such conduct does not interfere with the union's performance of its legal or contractual obligations.
3. *Dues and initiation fees* can be increased, and assessments can be levied, only as follows:
   a. by locals, by secret vote of the membership.
   b. by internationals,
      (1) by majority vote of the delegates to a convention, or
      (2) by majority vote of the members in good standing voting in a secret ballot referendum, or
      (3) between conventions, if authorized by the union constitution, by the majority of the executive board, but effective only until the next regular convention.
   c. The AFL-CIO and similar federations of unions are specifically excluded from these regulations.
4. *Members' right to sue.* Unions are prohibited from limiting the right of any member to bring a court action or administrative proceeding against the union. However, union members may be required to exhaust reasonable hearing procedures within the union (but not to exceed a four month lapse of time) before instituting a legal or administrative proceeding against the union or any of its officers.
5. *Procedural safeguards.* No member may be disciplined by a union or any of its officers, except for nonpayment of dues, without being served with written specific charges, given a reasonable time to prepare his defense, and afforded a full and fair hearing.
6. *Retention of existing rights.* Nothing in Title I limits the rights of any union member under any state or federal law or before any court or other tribunal, or under any union's constitution or bylaws.
7. *Right to copies of collective bargaining agreements.* Local unions must supply every member who requests it a copy of any agreement made by the local which directly affects his rights as an employee. International unions are required to supply their constituent units with copies of agreements directly affecting the constituent unit's membership.

Any person whose rights under Title I have been infringed may bring action for appropriate relief including an injunction in a United States District Court. Section 610 of the law states: "It shall be unlawful for any person through the use of force or violence, or threat of the use of force or violence, to restrain, coerce, or intimidate, or attempt to restrain, coerce, or intimidate any member of a labor organization for the purpose of interfering with or preventing the exercise of any right to which he is entitled under the provisions of this Act. Any person who willfully violates this section shall be fined not more than $1,000 or imprisoned for not more than one year, or both."

zations and their officers were charged with the responsibility of excluding such persons from union office. Persons who willfully violate this section of the Landrum-Griffin law are subject to fines of up to $10,000 and/or one year in prison.

Title IV of the Landrum-Griffin Act is devoted to the regulation of union elections and internal political campaigns. International unions are required to hold elections for officers at least every five years and more frequently if required by their constitutions. Such elections must be held by secret ballot among the members in good standing or at a convention of delegates chosen by secret ballot. Local unions must elect their officers not less often than once every three years by secret ballot among the members in good standing. If the secretary of labor finds that a union constitution does not contain adequate provisions for the removal of officers guilty of misconduct, any officers guilty of such misconduct may be removed, after notice and hearing, by a secret ballot of the membership. A member of the union is authorized to enlist the assistance of the secretary of labor and the courts in invalidating improper elections after the member has exhausted the remedies available to him within the union. Title IV also gives candidates for union office an opportunity to examine lists of eligible voters and prohibits the expenditure of the union's funds to support candidates for union office.

Many international constitutions permit the executive board of the convention to establish a "trusteeship" or provisional government over a local union or other subordinate union body. The power to create a trusteeship has been used in the past for such laudatory purposes as preserving a local's funds from embezzlement or to eliminate Communist or other officers who were undermining the legitimate activities of the local. The trustee device is also a powerful means of suppressing democracy within the local, or destroying opposition to the international officers at the grass roots level, or the milking of a local by the international officers. Title III of the Landrum-Griffin law brings the trustee device under statutory control. Trusteeship may be established only in accordance with the union's constitution for the purposes of: (a) correcting corruption or financial malpractice, (b) assuring the performance of collective bargaining agreements, (c) restoring democratic procedures, or (d) "otherwise carrying out the legitimate objects of such labor organization." During a trusteeship the votes of a local union may be counted in a convention or union election only if the delegates have been chosen by secret ballot in which all members of the local could vote. The funds of a local in trusteeship cannot be transferred to the international. The secretary of labor must be informed when a trusteeship is imposed and semiannual reports on the operation of the trusteeship must be submitted to him.

c.   *Safeguards on Union Funds.*   The officers, agents, shop stewards, and other representatives of a labor organization occupy positions of trust in relation to the union and its members as a group. Title V of the Landrum-Griffin law requires persons holding such positions to hold the union's money and property solely for the benefit of the union and its members. Persons holding offices in unions or employed by unions are prohibited from holding or acquiring any pecuniary or personal interests which conflict with the union's interests. Every union representative who handles union money must be bonded for at least 10 percent of the funds normally handled in a fiscal year, but need not be bonded for more than $500,000. Labor organizations may not loan any officer or employee more than $2,000. Unions may not pay the fines of their officers or employees convicted of violating the Landrum-Griffin Act. Theft or embezzlement of union funds is a federal crime subject to a fine of up to $10,000 and/or imprisonment for up to five years.

Before leaving the comprehensive code for the regulation of the internal affairs of unions, a word should be said about new powers and duties of the secretary of labor. The secretary of labor is not only required to receive a large number of reports of internal union affairs, but also is empowered to conduct investigations on a wide range of union affairs and to assist union members in court cases. Under the Landrum-Griffin Act, the Bureau of Labor-Management Reports of the Department of Labor has become a great depository of all kinds of information on the internal operations of labor unions. The files of the Bureau are a gold mine for persons interested in research on unionism. It is to be hoped that researchers will give us a much better understanding of union operations by taking full advantage of the Bureau's policy of encouraging scholarly research.

In addition to regulating the internal affairs of unions, the Landrum-Griffin Act carried forward the legislative intent of the Taft-Hartley law.

Taft-Hartley Amendments. Secondary boycotts, the rights of economic strikers to vote in NLRB elections, and recognition picketing were regulated by the Taft-Hartley Act. Apparently Congress was dissatisfied with the application of the Taft-Hartley provisions because it substantially amended the previous regulations in all three areas.

a. Secondary Boycotts and Hot Cargo Agreements. Section 8(b)(4)(A) of the Taft-Hartley Act was aimed at "secondary boycotts." Secondary boycotts are not easy to define, but in general they are attempts by a union to induce some other party (union members, consumers, or an employer) to cease doing business with someone. As the NLRB and the courts interpreted Section 8(b)(4)(A) several kinds of activities were not in violation of the Taft-Hartley law, e.g., (1) inducements of a *single* employee to strike or to refuse to handle goods; (2) inducements of employers directly, instead of through a strike of their employees; and (3) inducements of employees excluded from the definition of employees in the Taft-Hartley Act, i.e., railroad workers or municipal employees. The Landrum-Griffin Act amended Section 8(b)(4)(A) of the Taft-Hartley and closed the secondary boycott loopholes tight, by substituting the word "person" for "employees."

A *hot cargo clause* is an agreement between an employer and a union that the employees covered by the agreement will not be required to handle "unfair" goods, e.g., struck work or nonunion goods. The Landrum-Griffin Act outlawed hot cargo agreements except: (1) in the construction industry agreements relating to "the contracting or subcontracting of work to be done at the site of the construction, alteration, painting or repair of a building, structure or other work," and (2) "persons in the relation of a jobber, manufacturer, contractor or subcontractor working on the goods or premises of the jobber or manufacturer or performing parts of an integrated process of production in the apparel and clothing industry."

The Landrum-Griffin amendments on secondary boycotts and hot cargo restrict a union's power to make its strike effective. Under Landrum-Griffin a struck employer is free to transfer work to other plants and to subcontract the work that otherwise would be performed by the people on strike. The hot cargo ban restricts the power formerly held by the Teamsters' union to help strikers by cutting off the flow of goods and services to a struck plant. Although unions have some protected activity in advertising to their members and the general public the presence of unfair goods, they no longer are permitted to picket an employer who is selling unfair goods or who is performing operations on struck work.

  b. *Union Security and Economic Strikers.* There was very little in the Landrum-Griffin Act that could be termed prounion. Still, building trades union leaders could be heartened by the new union security provisions, garment union leaders could be encouraged by the exemption of their industry from the hot cargo and secondary boycott bans, and industrial unions could get some comfort from the revised right of economic strikers to vote in NLRB elections.

In 1947, the Taft-Hartley law outlawed the closed shop and thereby threatened to upset long-established ways of doing business in the construction industry. It is not inaccurate to say that the Taft-Hartley law failed to destroy the closed shop practice in many industries. Landrum-Griffin took a step backward toward the realities of life in the construction industry. A new Section 8(f) permits employers and unions primarily engaged in the building and construction industry to enter into agreements before workers are hired and to establish a seven-day union shop. The prehire contract coupled with the seven-day union shop certainly approximates the closed shop modus operandi in the construction industry.

Under the Taft-Hartley law strikers not eligible for reinstatement were denied the right to vote in NLRB decertification elections. Under this provision it was possible for an employer to provoke an economic strike, to replace the strikers, and then obtain an NLRB election in which the union members on strike could not vote. Obviously, the assured result of such an election would be the decertification of the striking union. Landrum-Griffin sought to remedy this unfair situation by providing that the NLRB was empowered to permit economic strikers who had been replaced to vote in an NLRB election held within 12 months after the beginning of the strike.

  c. *Organizational and Recognition Picketing.* The Landrum-Griffin Act adds a new Section 8(b)(7) to the National Labor Relations Act. This section makes it an unfair labor practice for a union to picket, or to threaten to picket, where an object is to gain recognition or promote organization of the employees, under three circumstances: (*a*) where the employer has recognized another labor organization; (*b*) for 12 months following a valid representation election lost by a union; and (*c*) where, apart from the foregoing circumstances, "such picketing has been conducted without a petition under section 9(c) being filed within a reasonable period of time, not to exceed 30 days." The circumstances described in (*c*) are qualified in two respects: (1) the union need not demonstrate "a showing of substantial interest" or claim recognition, and (2) picketing beyond the 30-day period, or other publicity addressed to the public and consumers, is permitted if the effect of the picketing is not to induce a disruption of services at the employer's place of business.

Although the primary aim of Section 8(b)(7) was probably to protect employers from harrassment picketing, this provision does enable a union to obtain a quick NLRB election by the method of picketing.

Section 602 of Landrum-Griffin outlaws extortionate picketing. Any person who carries on picketing for the purpose of personal profit or the enrichment of any other individual (except a bona fide increase in wages or other employee benefits) by taking or obtaining anything of value from an employer against its will is subject to a fine of up to $10,000 and/or imprisonment up to 20 years.

The Significance of the Landrum-Griffin Act.   When the Landrum-Griffin Act was passed in 1959, the meaning of many provisions of the Taft-Hartley Act of 1947 was still uncertain because of a lack of full judicial review. It is still too soon to state the impact of the Landrum-Griffin Act except in the most general terms.

The provisions of the Landrum-Griffin Act that strictly belong in the field of labor-management relations are relatively minor. They seek to plug up the loopholes in the Taft-Hartley ban on secondary boycotts; they prohibit hot cargo agreements of the Teamsters and others (but not the garment unions); they restrict organizational and recognition picketing. They potentially extend the jurisdiction of the states in making labor law and improve the speed of case handling by the NLRB. They also meet some long-standing union demands. Economic strikers get the right to vote in NLRB elections. The closed shop, for all practical purposes, is reauthorized in the construction industry.

More important to the future of collective bargaining than these changes in labor relations law is the fact of direct government intervention in the affairs of unions. Unions heretofore were private organizations. Normally they were democratic; sometimes not. In either case, government regulation touched only their relations with other organizations. As long as they kept within the laws of the surrounding democratic society, it was no business of anyone in government whether they were democratic or autocratic, honest or corrupt, run by the members or by self-perpetuating bosses, or, indeed, by thugs. The Taft-Hartley Act provided only minimal regulation of the internal affairs of unions.

The Landrum-Griffin Act changes all that. In the most positive fashion, under the threat of heavy penalties, it *directs*, specifically and in detail over a wide range of issues, that unions shall be democratically administered. Whether it succeeds or fails to reach its aim, there will be repercussions in the years to come not only in the union hall but at the bargaining table.

THE CIVIL RIGHTS ACT AND ITS TITLE VII[4]

In recent years another kind of federal legislation has become increasingly important in the field of labor relations. Civil rights laws affect the policies and practices of both employers and labor organizations. The experience of the last decade suggests that the influence of the new civil rights laws on labor relations will continue to grow.

The most significant federal civil rights legislation is the Equal Employment Opportunity Act, which was enacted as Title VII of the Civil Rights Act of 1964. In general, Title VII makes it unlawful for an employer or a labor organization to discriminate against individuals because of their race, color, religion, sex, or national origin. Title VII applies to virtually all labor organizations, and to all employers of fifteen or more persons, including state and local governments and their agencies. In addition to the requirements of Title VII, private employers who contract with the federal government are required, by executive order, to include a nondiscrimination clause in their government contracts. Failure to comply with the provisions of the clause may be grounds for cancellation of the contract, and may make the contractor ineligible for future government contracts. Although the federal government as an employer is not covered by Title VII, nondiscrimination in federal employment has been required by executive orders since 1965.

Title VII created the Equal Employment Opportunity Commission, a bipartisan body consisting of five members appointed by the president. The Commission has the power to receive or to initiate charges of discrimination in employment, to investigate such charges, and to engage in conciliation efforts. The Commission, however, has no power to issue orders to employers or labor organizations; binding enforcement of Title VII requires action in a federal court. The Commission itself may bring such an action or, under certain circumstances, it may refer a case to the Justice Department for legal action. If the Commission does not act on a complaint, the complaining party may choose to bring a private action in federal court.

Title VII does not prohibit only direct and overt discrimination; it also proscribes practices which, although neutral on their face, tend in practice to adversely affect individuals in their capacities as employees on prospective employees, on account of race, color, religion, sex, or national origin.

---

[4] The authors are indebted to Prof. Mildred Carmack of the University of Oregon Law School for this discussion of Title VII.

If, for example, an employer requires all employees to be high school graduates, certain racial groups may be disproportionately excluded from employment. If all applicants for a particular job are required to be six feet tall, most women will be excluded from that job. Such criteria may be attacked under Title VII and, if they are not shown to be reasonably related to the actual performance requirements of the job, the attack may be successful. The legality of many provisions of collective bargaining agreements may be called into question before the Commission and in the courts on similar grounds. If an agreement sanctions or requires an employment practice which is found to be unlawful under Title VII, neither the employer nor the labor organization may enforce it. Moreover, either or both may be held financially liable for damages on account of past compliance with such an illegal provision.

Soon after the passage of Title VII the federal courts were faced with charges of race and sex discrimination in the form of certain seniority rules, frequently embodied in collective bargaining contracts. One form of employment discrimination prior to the Civil Rights Act of 1964 was the reservation of desirable jobs for whites and/or males; other persons were hired only for less desirable departments or job classifications. Title VII clearly made such practices illegal. It was not always enough, however, for an employer to eliminate this kind of direct discrimination. Some employers, having put an end to discrimination in hiring, nevertheless retained "departmental" or "line" seniority rules under which an employee, regardless of the length of employment by the company, would have to forfeit all seniority and perhaps suffer a reduction in pay in order to transfer to a more advantageous job or department. The result was that minority employees hired before 1964 (or before actual hiring discrimination was eliminated by the employer) were, by virtue of the seniority system, "locked in" to the less desirable jobs and were effectively deprived of opportunities for advancement.

Title VII specifically provides that it is not unlawful for an employer to apply criteria established in accordance with a "bona fide" seniority system. However, in most of the Title VII cases involving a departmental seniority system, the federal courts have held that such a system is not "bona fide" if it operates to perpetuate the effects of past discrimination. Employers in such cases have been required to make transfers and advancements available on the basis of overall seniority to employees who had been the victims of earlier discrimination in hiring. The courts have also awarded back pay to employees who were deprived of advancement opportunities by such a system; the fact that the seniority system was embodied in a collective bargaining agreement has not been a defense. Moreover, labor organizations which agreed to the unlawful seniority systems have sometimes been held liable along with the employer for the payment of back wages.

Although the court decisions and settlements in these cases did interfere with advancement expectations to some extent, they were, on the whole, politically tolerable. Cash awards were paid by the employer, who had been responsible for the original discrimination, and in some instances by labor organizations which had failed to protect all of their members adequately. Innocent employees with greater departmental seniority but less plant seniority were forced to defer, temporarily, advancement or transfer, but suffered no other loss. While the country's economy was expanding, this type of remedy appeared to be not only tolerable but adequate. With the economic downturn in the 1970s, however, the necessity of extensive layoffs in many industries has raised a much more difficult problem under Title VII. If an employer discriminated against racial minorities or women in hiring prior to 1964, a plant-wide seniority system would not alleviate the effects of that discrimination when large numbers of employees had to be laid off. The widely-accepted principle of "last hired, first fired," applied in such situations, results in the layoff of disproportionate numbers of employees belonging to the very classes which Title VII was designed to protect. A number of cases involving this problem have been, and are now, in the federal courts. An equitable solution has proved difficult to devise. If minority employees are to be protected from disproportionate layoffs, the price will be paid not by the employer, who created the situation by past discrimination in hiring, but by employees with greater tenure who may have benefited from, but did not participate in, that discrimination. They will lose their incomes while more recently hired minority employees remain on the payroll. If, on the other hand, layoffs are handled on a straightforward seniority basis, the recently-hired minority employees will again suffer from the effects of the discrimination which Title VII made unlawful. The federal courts which have considered this problem have not agreed on its proper solution. It is likely that a final resolution will have to be sought in the Supreme Court.

Title VII covers many employment practices in addition to those relating to job security and advancement opportunities. Criteria for union membership, apprenticeship programs, and hiring hall procedures which effectively favor one racial group over another have been challenged in the courts—often successfully. Similar challenges to criteria and practices in these areas which tend to discriminate on the basis of sex may be expected. Sex discrimination in the provision of fringe benefits has been the subject of considerable dispute. Pension plans with different benefits for men and women, compulsory maternity leaves, and the exclusion of pregnancy-related disabilities from sick leave and income protection plans have had a mixed reception in the courts. Although the Equal Employment Opportunity Commission has published detailed guidelines for compliance with Title VII, the validity and application of the guidelines will eventually be worked out on a case-by-case basis in the courts. The influence of the civil rights laws in labor relations is certain to be both pervasive and controversial for some time to come.

SUMMARY

The third main actor in the collective bargaining system is the government, personified by many different elected officials and civil servants, each charged with some share of responsibility for protecting the public interest. On some issues, such as the obligation to bargain and the right of employees to representatives of their own choosing, the public interest has been clearly articulated by statutes and administrative rulings. In other areas, such as strikes, mediation, and noninflationary wage settlements, the public interest has not been so clearly defined. The public interest changes over time.

Statutory law on labor relations in the United States is largely permissive in nature. All of it dates from the twentieth century, starting with the restricted Railway Labor Act of 1926. The first labor relations law applicable to all interstate commerce, the Norris–La Guardia Act of 1932, restricted the issuance of injunctions in labor disputes and made the yellow dog contract unenforceable at law. The Wagner Act of 1935 created the National Labor Relations Board and gave it broad powers to formulate administrative law. The Wagner Act introduced the ballot box as the basic way of obtaining union recognition, and protected the right to organize by prohibiting unfair labor practices by management. The Taft-Hartley law of 1947 amended the Wagner Act by protecting the right of workers to refrain from joining unions, and redressed the balance of power between management and unions by prohibiting unfair labor practices by unions. The Landrum-Griffin Act of 1959 established a "bill of rights" for union members. It brought major innovations in labor relations law by providing for detailed regulation of the internal affairs of unions to insure fiscal responsibility and democratic practices.

The Civil Rights Act of 1964, Title VII, while not directed at collective bargaining issues, but against discrimination for reasons of race, religion, and sex, has turned out to have a strong impact on management and union practices, and on collective bargaining. Before Title VII it was possible to say (as previous editions of this book put it): "if a group of workers and an employer, in total ignorance of the law, were to sit down and bargain out an agreement, it is unlikely that they would agree to anything prohibited by existing laws." Since Title VII it has become clear that negotiated rules for hiring, for layoffs by seniority, and other matters are likely to run afoul of the law unless the negotiators know and respect its specific provisions. Thus a change in the rules for rule-making increasingly affects the substantive rules.

QUESTIONS FOR DISCUSSION

1. Since American labor relations law is largely permissive, why study it?
2. Show how the Norris–La Guardia Act, the Wagner Act, the Taft-Hartley

Act, and Landrum-Griffin Act succeeded or failed in "balancing" the bargaining power of management and unions.

3. Does *protective* labor legislation have any influence on collective bargaining?

4. By reference to specific pertinent provisions of the Wagner Act, Taft-Hartley Act, and Landrum-Griffin Act, trace changes in American public policy on the regulation of the internal affairs of unions. Have American unions become instrumentalities of the state?

5. The Railway Labor Act is noteworthy for the fact that it represented a consensus between management and unions. How might a consensus between managements and unions be developed for future collective bargaining legislation?

6. How can you justify taking away seniority rights, negotiated in good faith, because of a subsequently-passed law like Title VII?

APPENDIX: JUDICIAL INTERPRETATIONS OF LABOR RELATIONS LAW[5]

Norris–LaGuardia Act

The conditions for obtaining an injunction under the Norris–LaGuardia Act were very stringent. Many union contracts contain "no strike" provisions, which raised the question of whether the employer could specifically enforce the "no strike" provision or whether the employer would be forced to tolerate the strike and obtain enforcement of the "no strike" provision only by the collection of money damages for breach of contract. In a change of policy, the Supreme Court found that it was not inconsistent with Norris–LaGuardia to enforce the "no strike" clause by means of an injunction. The court, however, put strict conditions on the issuance of such an injunction. These conditions include a showing that there is a broad arbitration clause which covers the grievance giving rise to the strike threat, that the employer is willing to proceed to arbitration, and that there will be irreparable injury to the employer if the strike is allowed to proceed. (*Boys Market, Inc.* v. *Retail Clerks Union, Local 770*, 398 U.S. 235 (1970).)

Remedial Authority of the NLRB

The types of remedies used by the NLRB to remedy unfair labor practices has given both the courts and the NLRB difficult problems. Where a multi-employer association had negotiated and agreed to a contract on behalf of its employer members, one member refused to sign the agreement. The Supreme Court held that the NLRB had the authority to require the employer to sign the already negotiated agreement. (*NLRB* v. *Strong Roofing & Insulation Co.*, 393 U.S. 357 (1969).) However, where an employer refuses to agree to a contract provision, frustrating the making of a collective bargaining agreement, the NLRB is without the power to compel a company or union to agree to any

---

[5] The authors are indebted to Professor Donald W. Brodie of the University of Oregon Law School for material in this appendix.

specific substantive contractual provision. The NLRB has only the authority to require negotiations. (*H. K. Porter Company Inc.* v. *NLRB*, 397 U.S. 99 (1970).)

One of the most difficult questions concerns the appropriate remedy where an employer persistently refuses to bargain with the union after having been found to be in violation of the act on several different occasions for refusing to bargain. At issue is both the scope of the authority given by the statute to the NLRB as well as the willingness of the NLRB to exercise broad remedial authority, assuming it is granted. While no case is definitive on the point, a recent case is illustrative. Where the employer's continuing refusal to bargain with a certified union, despite prior NLRB orders, represents a clear, frivolous, and flagrant violation of the law, the NLRB may order remedies in addition to an order to bargain. The remedies may include giving the union reasonable access to the employer's bulletin boards to make postings, mailing notices to each employee, require the employer to provide up-to-date names and addresses of employees for a one-year period, reimbursement for litigation costs and expenses. (*Tiidee Products, Inc.*, 194 NLRB No. 198 (1972).)

8-a-3 Discrimination—Hiring Halls

Section 8-a-3 prohibits an employer from encouraging or discouraging membership by means of discrimination. It is likely that the hiring hall method of employee selection, where the union runs the hiring hall, has the effect of encouraging membership. Under these circumstances, the NLRB sought to put the operation of hiring halls under special rules. The Supreme Court overruled the NLRB. The Court acknowledged that a hiring hall might encourage membership, but found that the legislation prohibited encouragement or discouragement of membership only when it was accomplished by discrimination. Unless discrimination could be demonstrated as a matter of fact to exist, there could be no violation. (*International Brotherhood of Teamsters, Local 357* v. *NLRB*, 365 U.S. 667 (1961).)

Racial Discrimination

A lower Federal Court of Appeals has ruled that the NLRB cannot require the employer to bargain with a union that maintains a racially discriminatory policy. The full implications of this case are not yet clear. (*NLRB* v. *Mansion House Center Management Corp.*, 473 F.2d 471 (1973).)

Rights of Union Members

Section 102 LMRDA provides that a member may bring an action against a union which allegedly violated the members' rights in disciplinary proceedings. The courts, however, are not authorized to determine the scope of offenses for which a union may discipline its members. The union need only provide "some evidence" to support the charges made. The courts may determine the fairness of an internal union disciplinary proceeding. (*International Brotherhood of Boilermakers* v. *Hardeman*, 401 U.S. 233 (1971).)

Title IV of the LMRDA sets standards for candidates for union officers and provides that only the Secretary of Labor shall enforce that section. Union members cannot sue to enforce that section and violations of that section cannot be combined with violations under Title I, which can be enforced by suit by individual members. (*Calhoon* v. *Harvey*, 379 U.S. 134 (1964).)

A union member having a statutory right to complain to the Secretary of Labor about a union election is required to first exhaust internal union methods of redress before enlisting the aid of the Secretary. (*Hodgson* v. *Steelworkers Local 6799*, 403 U.S. 333 (1971).)

A restriction that limited eligibility for major elective offices in the union to union members who have previously held some elective office is unreasonable. The court noted that a member need not have held prior union office to be appointed to a vacancy in any office. (*Wirtz* v. *Hotel, Motel, & Club Employees Union*, Local 6, 391 U.S. 492 (1968).)

On removal of a union officer guilty of serious misconduct, *see* 29 CFR §417.1–417.25 (1974). In these regulations promulgated by the Secretary of Labor, provision is made for hearing and decision making processes to remove officers and provision for appropriate action where the union fails to act.

Union Discipline of Members

A union may not discipline a member for filing an unfair labor practice charge against the union without having exhausted the internal union procedures and remedies. (*NLRB* v. *Industrial Union of Marine and Shipbuilding Workers*, 391 U.S. 418 (1968).) However, a union may set a production ceiling rate and fine members who accept immediate payment for production in excess of the rate. The union may use the courts to enforce the fine. The court said a union is free to adopt rules which reflect a legitimate union interest, which impair no policy that Congress has adopted, and which is reasonably enforced against members. (*Scofield* v. *NLRB*, 394 U.S. 423 (1969).) A union may discipline a member for crossing a lawful picket line. (*NLRB* v. *Allis-Chalmers Manufacturing Co.*, 388 U.S. 175 (1967).)

Where the individual is no longer a member, the union's powers are limited. A union may not fine a person for strikebreaking where the individual resigned from membership prior to returning to work. (*NLRB* v. *Granite State Joint Board, Textile Workers*, 409 U.S. 213 (1972).) A union constitution may impose an obligation for members to refrain from strikebreaking. Once an individual resigns, the individual is not bound by the constitutional obligation and is beyond union discipline. (*Booster Lodge 405, Machinists* v. *NLRB*, 412 U.S. 84 (1973).)

Because Congress did not intend that the NLRB could examine internal union affairs, the NLRB cannot regulate the size of the union fine or establish standards with respect to a fine's reasonableness. (*NLRB* v. *Boeing Co.*, 412 U.S. 67 (1973).)

A union may fine or expel a supervisor-member for crossing a picket line and performing regular employee struck work during a lawful economic strike. (*Florida Power & Light Co.* v. *IBEW*, 416 U.S. 790 (1974).)

Restrictions on Office Holding

Section 504(a) of the LMRDA provided, among other things, that no person may be a union officer or employee for five years from the time of holding membership in the Communist Party. The Supreme Court held the provision was unconstitutional as a bill of attainder. (*United States* v. *Brown,* 380 U.S. 278 (1965).)

SELECTED ANNOTATED BIBLIOGRAPHY

AARON, BENJAMIN. "The Labor-Management Reporting and Disclosure Act of 1959," *Harvard Law Review,* vol. 73 (March–April 1960), pp. 851–907 and 1086–1127.

    An authoritative discussion of the Landrum-Griffin Act.

AARON, BENJAMIN, and MEYER, PAUL S. "Public Policy and Labor-Management Relations," in *A Review of Industrial Relations Research,* vol. 2. (Madison: Industrial Relations Research Association, 1971).

    The authors review some of the more important public labor policy developments and writings on those developments which occurred during the 1960s.

BAKKE, E. WRIGHT; KERR, CLARK; and ANROD, CHARLES W., eds. *Unions, Management and the Public,* 3d ed. New York: Harcourt, Brace & World, 1967.

    A classic book of readings on the role of unions, management, and the institution of free collective bargaining in the United States. Readings deal with the full spectrum of issues relating to collective bargaining.

CHERNISH, WILLIAM N. *Coalition Bargaining: A Study of Union Tactics and Public Policy.* Philadelphia: University of Pennsylvania Press, 1969.

    An analysis of one of the most controversial developments in collective bargaining. The study looks at union coalition behavior in several companies and industries including General Electric. Also contains a review of relevant NLRB and court decisions regarding coalition bargaining.

COHEN, SANFORD. "An Analytical Framework for Labor Relations Law," *Industrial and Labor Relations Review,* vol. 14 (April 1961), pp. 350–62.

    The author suggests that the timing and character of labor law can be regarded as a variable which is dependent upon the "resultant of the prevailing ideology of property rights and the degree of access to political power enjoyed by private power blocks." This two-variable framework is applied to an analysis of the American legal experience; the concept of "countervailing power" as an alternative explanation is also considered.

COX, ARCHIBALD. "The Duty to Bargain in Good Faith," *Harvard Law Review,* vol. 71 (June 1958), pp. 1401–42.

    Professor Cox analyzes NLRB decisions having the effect of enlarging the scope of substantive issues in collective bargaining.

CULLEN, DONALD E. *National Emergency Strikes.* ILR Paperback no. 7. Ithaca, N.Y.: New York State School of Industrial and Labor Relations, 1968.

    A comprehensive, definitive, and very readable examination of many years' experience with "emergency" strikes under the Taft-Hartley and Railway Labor Acts.

"Developments under the Landrum-Griffin Act: A Symposium," *Georgia Law Review,* vol. 5 (Summer 1971).

    This issue contains a collection of articles which review and evaluate the various effects of the Landrum-Griffin Act.

Gregory, Charles O. *Labor and the Law.* 2d rev. ed. New York: W. W. Norton & Co., Inc., 1958.

A scholarly and very readable account of American labor relations law with heavy emphasis on the common-law background.

Independent Study Group, Committee for Economic Development. *The Public Interest in National Labor Policy.* New York: CED, 1961.

Clark Kerr, Douglas V. Brown, David L. Cole, John T. Dunlop, William Y. Elliot, Albert Rees, Robert H. Solow, Philip Taft, and George W. Taylor compose the membership of the Study Group. George P. Shultz, Abraham Siegel, and David Burke compose the staff. Discussion of, and recommendations on: the public interest and private responsibilities; function and control of strikes and lockouts; collective bargaining, inflation and effective use of manpower; private power and its control; and individual rights in effective institutions.

McCulloch, Frank W., and Bornstein, Tim. *The National Labor Relations Board.* New York: Praeger, 1974.

A former NLRB chairman and staff member examine the development and substance of federal labor laws, the NLRB's duties and methods of operation, and assess the Board's impact.

Meltzer, Bernard D. "Labor Unions, Collective Bargaining, and the Antitrust Laws," *University of Chicago Law Review,* vol. 32 (Summer 1965).

One of the classic evaluations of the applications of antitrust laws to unions, written contemporaneously with the Supreme Court's landmark antitrust decisions in the *Pennington* and *Jewel Tea* cases.

Millis, Harry A., and Brown, Emily Clark. *From the Wagner Act to Taft-Hartley: A Study of National Labor Policy and Labor Relations.* Chicago: University of Chicago Press, 1950.

A landmark in labor legislation scholarship. Part I, The Wagner Act, by Professor Brown. Parts II and III, the Taft-Hartley Act, planned and partially written by the late Professor Millis, former Chairman of the National Labor Relations Board. Parts of this book provide a statement of Professor Millis's philosophy of industrial relations. The book includes detailed analyses of a number of the NLRB's major policies and their change over time.

Mitchell, Daniel J. B. "Phase II Wage Controls," *Industrial and Labor Relations Review,* vol. 27, no. 3 (April 1974).

The former chief economist of the Pay Board examines the wage standards used by the Board during Phase II of the Nixon Administration's wage-price controls and assesses their effectiveness.

Northrup, Herbert R. "The Railway Labor Act: A Critical Reappraisal," *Industrial and Labor Relations Review,* vol. 25, no. 1 (October 1971).

A very sharp critique of the Railway Labor Act, which the author claims hinders rather than promotes the settlement of collective bargaining disputes.

Oberer, Walter E., and Hanslowe, Kurt L. *Cases and Materials on Labor Law: Collective Bargaining in a Free Society.* St. Paul: West Publishing, 1972.

A recent and widely used legal casebook which covers the gamut of American labor relations law.

Ross, Philip. *The Government as a Source of Union Power.* Providence, R.I.: Brown University Press, 1965.

A landmark evaluation of the employer's mandatory duty to bargain in good faith with the union representing employees, including an analysis of the development of this governmentally-imposed requirement and an empirical examination of its impact.

Schmidt, Emerson P. *Union Power and the Public Interest.* Los Angeles: Nash Publishing, 1973.

An antiunion work written to show that unions serve no legitimate economic purpose and therefore should enjoy very little legal protection.

Shister, Joseph; Aaron, Benjamin; and Summers, Clyde W., eds. *Public Policy and Collective Bargaining.* New York: Harper & Row, 1962.

A volume published by the Industrial Relations Research Association. Specialists in industrial relations and law analyze the following: "An Historical Evolution of Public Policy in Labor Relations," by Douglass V. Brown and Charles A. Myers; "Employer Free Speech," by Benjamin Aaron; "The Obligation to Bargain in Good Faith," by Robben W. Fleming; "The Union Security Issue," by Paul E. Sultan; "Picketing and Boycotts," by Donald H. Wollett; "Collective Bargaining and the Antitrust Laws," by George H. Hildebrand; "Legal Regulation of Internal Union Affairs," by Joseph R. Grodin; and "A Comparison of U.S. and Canadian Experiences," by Harry D. Woods.

Smith, Russell A.; Merrifield, Leroy S.; and St. Antoine, Theodore J. *Labor Relations Law: Cases and Materials.* 5th ed. Indianapolis: Bobbs–Merrill, 1974.

Another recent and widely used legal casebook which covers the range of American labor relations law.

"The Taft-Hartley Law after Ten Years: A Symposium," *Industrial and Labor Relations Review,* vol. 11 (April 1958), pp. 327–412.

Seven experts discuss experience under the Taft-Hartley law. Contents:

Aaron, Benjamin. "Amending the Taft-Hartley Act: A Decade of Frustration."

Shister, Joseph. "The Impact of the Taft-Hartley Act on Union Strength and Collective Bargaining."

Taft, Philip. "Internal Affairs of Unions and the Taft-Hartley Act."

Abelow, Robert. "Management Experience under the Taft-Hartley Act."

Klaus, Ida. "The Taft-Hartley Experience in Separation of NLRB Functions."

Isaacson, William J. "Federal Preemption under the Taft-Hartley Act."

Summers, Clyde W. "A Summary Evaluation of the Taft-Hartley Act."

U.S. Department of Labor, Bureau of Labor Statistics. *Monthly Labor Review.*

Each issue contains a "Significant Decisions in Labor Cases" section which provides the layperson with a handy reference service to the more important developments in labor case law.

Weber, Arnold R. *In Pursuit of Price Stability: The Wage-Price Freeze of 1971.* Washington, D.C.: Brookings Institution, 1973.

The former director of the Cost of Living Council analyzes the 1971 wage-price freeze (or Phase I) portion of the Nixon Administration's wage-price controls program.

WELLINGTON, HARRY H. *Labor and the Legal Process.* New Haven: Yale University Press, 1968.

A comprehensive examination of the national policy toward labor-management relations and the role of law and legal institutions in accomplishing of that policy.

part two

Collective Bargaining Activities

Part Two of this book considers the activities of employers, workers, and government representatives in establishing the collective bargaining relationship, arriving at the collective bargaining agreement, and the nature of the collective bargaining agreement.

6 Establishing the Collective Bargaining Relationship

THE COLLECTIVE bargaining relationship always starts with the recognition of a union by the management of an enterprise. Recognition is preceded by a decision of some of the employees of an enterprise that they will seek union representation, or a union decision that a non-union enterprise must be organized, or a manager's decision that a unionized operation is the best way to run the newly established business. No matter whether employees, a union, or management takes the initiative in establishing the collective bargaining relationship, an "outside" agent, the union, appears on the scene and solicits members from the employees or prospective employees of the enterprise. What happens in this period *before* the first collective bargaining agreement is negotiated is of great importance to the managers, employees, and union(s) involved. These activities are regulated by law. Prenegotiation activities sometimes generate hostility which leaves a long-lasting scar on the collective bargaining relationship. This chapter describes how a collective bargaining relationship comes into being.

THE INITIATIVE IN ESTABLISHING THE COLLECTIVE BARGAINING RELATIONSHIP

Typically management is the initiating force in all employment activities and the preservation of the right of managerial initiative is generally considered to be essential to enterprise efficiency. The major exception to the rule of management initiative is the activity of establishing the collective bargaining relationship. With one small exception, in the contemplation of the law, the initiative in establishing a collective bargaining relationship belongs either to employees or to a union.

Employee Initiative

Every job holds some potential of real dissatisfactions for anyone who might hold it: the pay is too low, the boss is unfair, the pace is too fast, the job itself is insecure or potentially short-lived, the hours are too long, the working conditions aren't as good as they should be, or the co-workers aren't friendly. Each employee has a "boiling point" and an evaluation of the qualities of the job, but for some reason a group of employees becomes dissatisfied with the conditions of their employment and conclude that the only way they can get "justice" is to form a union. These employees call a union and an organizing drive begins.

Probably no two union organizing drives are exactly alike, but some general rules do seem to apply. At the early stages of the drive, organization is conducted in secret, the union contacting employees who might join the union through other employees who have shown interest in forming a union. Only after a fair number of employees have shown an active interest will the organization conduct its campaign for members in the open. The secrecy aspect protects the early joiners from management retaliation and gives the union an idea about the prospects of a successful organizing drive before overcommitting itself or its new members. Secrecy also has the advantage of preventing management from killing an incipient union with kindness.

When a group of employees has taken the initiative in calling in a union, the union's organizing job is simplified. The employees who took the initiative can supply the union with information about grievances in the enterprise and the names of employees who most likely would favor a union as well as the names of employees who should be avoided because of their loyalty to the enterprise and the probability that they would inform management that a union organization drive was under way. Employees sympathetic to the union cause also can supply information about the sometimes vital matter of enterprise organizational structure. As a rule, an industrial union seeks membership in all production departments of the enterprise. Most important of all, the employees who took the initiative in calling the union serve as union organizers in the shop.

Most union organizing drives are initiated by dissatisfied employees, but some union organizing drives are initiated by unions and managements.

Union Initiative

A union is an institution to some degree independent of both its members and the enterprise which provides jobs for its members. As an independent institution, the union has ambitions for growth and an important defensive strategy of organizing all enterprises which compete with enterprises that it has organized. A pure union initiative in an organizing drive springs from the growth motive or the defensive strategy of organizing the unorganized.

Most international unions keep an eye on developments in their industry. Two examples will suffice: The International Ladies' Garment Workers' Union and the Amalgamated Clothing Workers' Union operate in industries where it is very easy to open a small shop. Both unions expend a substantial portion of their resources on finding these new shops and organizing them.

A different kind of situation arises when a huge industrial combine like General Motors, General Electric, or United States Steel opens an entirely new facility. The unions which have collective bargaining relationships with the parent organization watch these developments closely and launch organizing drives as soon as they learn of the company's plans.

In all of these cases the motive to unionization is different from when employees take the initiative, but the techniques of organizing are similar. In a union initiated drive, the union looks for, or "manufactures" employee grievances, sells the advantages of union membership, and seeks to start an internal chain reaction among the employees of the enterprise.

Management Initiative

A management initiative in establishing a collective bargaining relationship is extremely rare and poses a serious problem at law. *Only* employers engaged "primarily in the building and construction industry" can take the initiative in establishing a collective bargaining relationship with reasonable immunity from an unfair labor practice charge of interference, restraint, coercion, or company domination of the union.

In the construction industry, new enterprises usually come into being when a unionized tradesman bids successfully for a subcontract. The natural thing for this new entrepreneur to do is to contact a union business agent as the source of potential employees. Under the Landrum-Griffin Act, except in states with general right-to-work laws, employers and unions in the building and construction industry are free to:

1. Make collective bargaining agreements *before* the majority status of the union is established under Section 9 of the law,
2. Require membership in the union as a condition of employment after the *seventh day* following employment or the effective date of the agreement, whichever is later,
3. Require the employer to notify the union of job opportunities or give the union an opportunity to refer qualified applicants for employment, and
4. Specify minimum training or experience qualifications for employment or establish priorities in opportunities for employment.

These provisions of the Landrum-Griffin Act are a substantial step toward reauthorizing long-established methods of doing business in the building trades. The prehire agreement and seven-day union shop are a close approximation of the old-time closed shop. Although the NLRB has ruled that the Landrum-Griffin prehire contract shall not stand as a bar to a petition for an NLRB certification,[1] employers in the building and construction industry have very substantial immunity under the law in taking the initiative in establishing a collective bargaining relationship.

---

[1] *Twenty-Sixth Annual Report of the National Labor Relations Board for Year Ended June 30, 1961*, p. 42.

Employers not engaged in the building and construction industry are well advised *not* to take the initiative in establishing a collective bargaining relationship. In the early days of the Wagner Act employers frequently sought out "responsible" and "cooperative" unions and entered into "sweetheart" agreements with them. When there is evidence of union and management collusion in the signing of a collective bargaining agreement, the NLRB voids the agreement and brings unfair labor practice charges against the management. Although employer initiatives in establishing collective bargaining relationships are on the outer fringe of lawful employer activity, it is likely that a few employers do take these actions and are able to do so within the bounds of the law or without getting caught. Because union representation is so vitally significant to enterprise welfare and the wide variety of unions which might organize a single employer, it seems fair to expect that many employers are sorely tempted to take the initiative in establishing the collective bargaining relationship even though such action is of questionable legality.

Regardless of whether employees, a union, or the employer takes the initiative in establishing the collective bargaining relationship and whether the union organization drive is conducted openly or in secret, eventually there must be a union and management confrontation on the question of union recognition. Today there are two methods by which union recognition may be established.

THE TWO METHODS OF ESTABLISHING UNION RECOGNITION

Before the passage of the Wagner Act in 1935, a union could obtain recognition only by persuading an employer to grant such recognition voluntarily. Although statistics are not available, it seems quite fair to say that most unions found it necessary to persuade employers through the use of strikes, picketing, and boycotts.

Today there are two methods by which a union may obtain recognition from an employer: (1) *without* governmental intervention, and (2) through the processes of the National Labor Relations Board. The law severely restricts the use of picketing by unions as a means of persuading employers to grant recognition. At the same time it provides orderly procedures for obtaining recognition. Governmental intervention is the rule of the day, but the law still protects the rights of the parties to settle their own problems without governmental intervention so long as those private settlements do not violate public policy.

Union Recognition without Governmental Intervention

If a majority of the employees in an enterprise want a certain union to represent them in collective bargaining and that union can satisfy the employer on this point, the employer may voluntarily recognize the union and bargain with it. In such cases, the union usually satisfies the employer by showing authorization cards or petitions signed by a majority of the employees in the unit. This method may be followed in any employee group whether or not the business affects commerce.

In those exceptional cases which are not subject to federal or state labor relations statutes, the union is free to strike, picket, and boycott to obtain recognition. For example, supervisors, agricultural workers, and independent contractors (none of whom are "employees" under the Landrum Griffin Act) are free to strike, picket, and boycott for recognition unless prohibited by state law.

Unions of employees who are covered by the Landrum-Griffin law are subject to restrictions on how they may persuade employers to grant recognition. These restrictions on picketing and jurisdictional disputes were designed to curb abuses of the past and to protect employers from conflicting claims for union representation.

Picketing for Recognition. Under the Landrum-Griffin Act, picketing by a union that is not recognized as bargaining agent and has not been certified by the NLRB, for the purpose of securing recognition or of forcing the employees to select it as bargaining agent, is sharply restricted. Organizational picketing is forbidden altogether where a valid NLRB election has been held within the previous 12 months or the employer lawfully recognizes another union. In such cases, an election petition will not be entertained by the NLRB. In other circumstances, e.g., a nonunion shop with no recent NLRB election, the picketing may not continue for more than 30 days without the filing of a petition for an NLRB election.

Union jurisdiction is a direct concern of the labor movement. Employers can assert only an indirect influence in the resolution of jurisdictional disputes. The old AFL attempted to control interunion competition by issuing mutually exclusive charters to international unions and deciding disputes between unions. When the CIO was born, all restraints on the issuance of overlapping charters lapsed. The high cost of jurisdictional warfare was a major inducement to the merger of the AFL and the CIO in 1955. Because of the high cost of jurisdictional warfare to union treasuries, many unions have entered into "no-raiding" agreements under the auspices of the AFL–CIO. Thus a new form of jurisdictional rights based on established collective bargaining relationships seems to be taking shape from the merger of the AFL and CIO.

The Taft-Hartley law imposes several restrictions on the freedom of unions to fight it out over jurisdictional claims. The law differentiates two types of jurisdictional strikes: (1) strikes for recognition and (2) work assignment disputes. The strike for recognition involves the attempt of a union to establish an initial collective bargaining relationship with the employer. The work assignment dispute is an attempt by a union already having a collective bargaining relationship with the employer to assert its control over certain jobs.

Jurisdictional Strikes for Recognition.   The Taft-Hartley law prohibits one union from calling a strike against an employer who is dealing with another union under an NLRB certification. It also prohibits a union from strike action against Employer A for the purpose of forcing Employer B to recognize or bargain with any union which has not been certified by the NLRB as the representative of the employees of Employer B.

The NLRB's interpretation of these provisions may be illustrated by three cases:

1. Employer A deals with Union A under an NLRB certification. Union B violates the law if it calls a strike of A's employees. Union B also violates the law if it pickets A's premises because this is an inducement to strike.
2. Employer A deals with Union A and purchases materials from Employer B. Employer B is nonunion or deals with Union B which has been certified by the NLRB. Union A violates the law if it strikes Employer A for the purpose of forcing Employer B to deal with any union other than Union B. Union A also violates the law if it proposes to call off the strike on the condition that Employer A refuses to place further orders with Employer B.
3. The Meat Cutters' Union represents meat buyers in a number of markets. The union wants to organize the meat sales staff of Packer A. The union violates the law if it instructs its meat buyer members not to purchase Packer A's products.

Work-Assignment Disputes.   Work-assignment disputes need not involve an employer's original refusal to recognize a union. After recognition has been achieved, two rival unions may both insist on the right of their members to perform a particular task. These disputes most frequently occur in industries like building construction, organized by craft unions. A classic example of this type of dispute is the disagreement between the carpenters and the concrete workers as to who should build the necessary wooden forms. The carpenters claimed the work because the forms were wood and constructed with carpenters' tools. The concrete workers insisted that the forms were incidental to concrete work and, therefore, were within their jurisdiction.

The Taft-Hartley law provides for ultimate NLRB determination of work-assignment disputes if the disputants fail to settle them by themselves. Section 8(b)(4) forbids a labor organization from engaging in or inducing strike action for the purpose of forcing any employer to assign particular work tasks "to employees in a particular labor organization or in a particular trade, craft, or class rather than to employees in another labor organization or in another trade, craft, or class, unless such employer is failing to conform to an order or certification of the Board determining the bargaining representative for employees performing such work."

The Board may not intervene in a work-assignment dispute until certain statutory requirements are fulfilled. Section 10(k) requires that the parties to a jurisdictional dispute be given 10 days, after notice of the filing of charges with the Board, to adjust their dispute. If at the end of that time they are unable to "submit to the Board satisfactory evidence that they have adjusted, or agreed upon methods for the voluntary adjustment of the dispute," the Board is empowered to hear and determine the dispute. Section 10(k) also provides that "upon compliance by the parties to the dispute with decision of the Board or upon such voluntary adjustment of the dispute," the charge shall be dismissed. A complaint issues only if there is a failure to comply with the Board's determination. Also, a complaint may be issued in a case of the failure of the method agreed upon to adjust the dispute.

Before the passage of the Taft-Hartley law, the American Federation of Labor had made several attempts to establish machinery for the adjustment of jurisdictional disputes within the "house of labor." At best, this machinery was able to survive only a short time.

The jurisdictional disputes provisions of the Taft-Hartley law were completely unacceptable to building trades unions. They motivated the formation of a National Joint Board of Adjustment in the Building Construction Industry. This Board is composed of equal numbers of labor and contractor representatives. Its major functions are the arbitration of local jurisdictional disputes and the negotiation of national jurisdictional agreements between unions in the construction industry. The chairman of the Board has a vote to break deadlocks, but has been extremely reluctant to use it, instead using influence as a mediator of disputes. Because of the reasonably successful operation of the Board, the NLRB has received only a very few construction-industry jurisdictional disputes for arbitration. It seems fair to say that the Taft-Hartley provisions have done a good job in forcing the building trades unions to settle their jurisdictional disputes without resort to extensive strike action.

Union Recognition through the NLRB

If an employer covered by the Landrum-Griffin Act refuses voluntary recognition of a union, and there is a question as to whether the union represents a majority of the employees in the unit, or if there is a dispute over the appropriateness of the unit, the matter can be settled by filing a representation petition with the Regional Office of the NLRB.

Filing a Representation Petition. A petition can be filed by an employee or group of employees or any person or union acting on behalf of a substantial number of employees. An employer who is presented by a union with a claim that it represents a majority of his employees, or with competing claims by two or more unions each seeking recognition, can file a petition to determine the question.

If a union is currently acting as bargaining representative, any employee or group of employees, or any person or union acting on their behalf, can file a petition asking that the current union be thrown out. This is called a "decertification" petition.

A representation petition contains: (1) description of the unit of employees in which an election is sought; (2) the approximate number of employees in the unit; and (3) the names of all unions that claim to represent the employees in the unit.

When a representation petition is filed at the Regional Office, a field examiner is assigned to get answers to determine the following questions of fact:

1. Are the employer's operations within NLRB jurisdictional standards?
2. Is the proposed unit appropriate for collective bargaining?
3. Is there a sufficient showing of employee interest?
4. Is the filing of the petition timely?

In answering these questions the field examiner applies the facts of the particular case to standards that have been established by the NLRB. For a discussion of NLRB jurisdictional standards and the coverage of federal industrial relations legislation see Chapter 5.

The Appropriate Unit for Collective Bargaining.   The law requires an employer to bargain with the employee representatives. In some instances all of the employees in a plant will want the same union to represent them because their interests are essentially the same. In other cases, different employees in a manufacturing plant may have different interests. For example, the clerical employees in an enterprise may have interests in collective bargaining substantially different from those of production employees in the same plant. In those situations each group of employees, called a "unit" for collective bargaining purposes, is entitled to have a different union represent the unit in bargaining with the employer. Acting through its Regional Director, the NLRB determines which employees should be included in the appropriate unit for collective bargaining.

The Importance of the Unit to Workers, Management, and Unions.   The bargaining unit is of considerable importance to employees, management, and the unions seeking representation rights. The wage concessions available to particular groups of employees can be influenced by the bargaining unit established. For example, a small group of skilled employees might be able to negotiate substantially larger wage concessions for themselves (at the expense of the larger less skilled group) in separate bargaining. Such a separate bargaining unit in a factory might be able to impose standard rates prevailing in less regular construction employment. This would not necessarily impose excessive costs on the enterprise, since it might be able to trim wage concessions to the larger group of semiskilled (and perhaps nonunion) employees.

The employer may favor small bargaining units in the hope of playing one unit off against the other and thereby minimize costs. Or the employer may favor large units, thereby avoiding the hazards of union "whipsawing" and the costs of multiple agreements and negotiations. The employer may have a particular interest in excluding a few key jobs from the bargaining unit feeling that such workers should be identified with management, e.g., the chef in a restaurant.

From the union viewpoint, the bargaining unit determination of the NLRB may have a decisive influence in deciding who (if anyone) wins representation rights. A craft union would almost certainly be doomed to failure in an election contest with an industrial union if the NLRB decided that the appropriate unit included all production and maintenance workers. The probable fate of an industrial union in a contest with a craft union over the representation of a small group of employees who had served a traditional apprenticeship is equally certain. Of course, union election units are also potentially subject to the gerrymandering game. The inclusion of groups of employees known to be antiunion in an appropriate unit would have an important influence on the outcome of the election, as for instance the lumping of office staff with manual employees.

Given these diverse interests, what criteria does the NLRB apply in carrying out its statutory obligation to determine the appropriate unit for collective bargaining? The Board is governed by limited statutory guidance and its own long experience in dealing with the unit question.

Statutory Limitations on the Appropriate Unit. The law directs the Board to establish the appropriate unit for collective bargaining "in order to assure to *employees* the fullest freedom in exercising the rights guaranteed by this Act." (Emphasis added.) Beyond this injunction that the *employees'* interest shall prevail over the interests of employers and unions, statutory law on the bargaining unit is sparse, dealing only with: (1) professional employees, (2) plant guards, (3) craft severance, and (4) extent of employee organization.

Section 9(b) of the Taft-Hartley law prohibits the NLRB from including professional employees in a bargaining unit with nonprofessional employees unless a majority of the professional employees vote for inclusion in such unit.

Individuals employed as guards to enforce rules against employees and other persons to protect property of the employer or to protect the safety of persons on the employer's premises may be included only in a unit composed exclusively of guards. No labor organization that admits nonguard employees to membership or is associated with a nonguard organization may be designated as a representative for a guard unit.

Section 9(b)(2) of the Taft-Hartley law governs "craft severance" cases. Aimed at restricting the Board's authority to include craft workers in an industrial unit, this section provides that the Board should not "decide that any craft unit is inappropriate . . . on the ground that a different unit has been established by a prior board determination, unless a majority of the employees in the proposed craft unit vote against separate representation."

The Board is also prohibited from giving controlling weight to the extent to which employees have organized in determining the appropriate unit. If during an organizing drive a union has enrolled in its membership production workers, craft workers, salesworkers, and office workers who have diverse interests, the NLRB is prohibited from ruling that a single unit is appropriate solely because workers in these different groups have all joined the same union.

Before leaving statutory limitations on the Board's authority to establish appropriate units, it should be recalled that certain workers are not "employees" under the law and are therefore excluded from appropriate units and the protection of the law. These excluded persons are supervisors, agricultural workers, and independent contractors.

The Board makes bargaining unit determinations in three types of situations: (1) It establishes new bargaining units when a representation issue arises for the first time; (2) It reconsiders the propriety of established units in "craft severance" cases; and (3) It establishes units for expedited elections in recognition and organizational picketing cases coming under Section 8(b)(7)(C) of the Landrum-Griffin Act. An adequate understanding of the complexity of the Board's problem in determining the appropriate unit can be acquired by a brief consideration of some of the criteria used by the Board in original unit cases and craft severance cases.

NLRB Criteria in Initial Unit Determinations. The Board customarily accepts units agreed to by unions and management, but it does not recognize such stipulations as establishing Board policy. Moreover, union-management agreements to exclude certain individuals from the unit have been set aside by the Board where it believed that the persons involved should properly be included in the unit.

In exercising its power to determine appropriate units, the Board strives to give meaning and practical effect to the actual day-to-day relationships among employees. This aim, the Board has stated, "is best served by giving controlling effect to the community of interest existing among employees." This "community of interest" criterion is certainly basic to any Board determination of the appropriate unit.

Besides the community of interest criterion, the Board has, in different cases, considered such criteria as: union organizational structure, management organizational structure, extent of union representation interest, methods of wage payment, and regularity of employment. Comment on the frequently used criteria of bargaining history, craft or departmental units, and multiemployer units may be helpful.

Bargaining history frequently is a major factor in the Board's considerations. The Board is primarily interested in the bargaining history of the employees directly involved in the petition, but the bargaining history of similar employees in the area or industry may be considered on occasion. In several cases the Board has listed as one factor militating against a single-plant unit the fact that such a unit did not conform in scope to the pattern of relationships for that type of business in the particular area.

The Board will establish craft or departmental units only when the petitioner can show that employees in the proposed unit are functionally distinct *and* that they can be represented effectively as a separate group.

The Board will not establish multiemployer units unless the employers have chosen to bargain jointly and have held themselves bound by the results of these joint negotiations. An employer may withdraw from multiemployer bargaining and thereby reestablish those employees in separate appropriate units. A single-employer unit will be deemed appropriate in such circumstances when the employer manifests an intention to withdraw from group bargaining and to pursue an individual course of action in labor relations. The Board has found separate single-employer units appropriate where, following a breakdown in association-wide negotiations, individual employers: (1) abandoned group bargaining, (2) did not pay dues or assessments to the association—resulting in automatic termination of membership under the association's bylaws, and (3) indicated their desire to pursue an individual course of action by executing contracts on a single-employer basis.

Craft Severance Cases.   Craft unions use the facilities of the Board in gaining recognition but often prefer the direct approach to the employer. When craft unions use the facilities of the Board, they usually are involved in craft severance cases. In these cases, the craft unions are asking the Board to upset an existing collective bargaining relationship between an employer and an industrial union. The Board's responsibility is to decide the issue in the best interests of the employees. In craft severance cases, the Board's problem is to decide which employees—all the employees or the craft employees—are benefited or hurt most by severance. The authors of the Taft-Hartley law sought to restrict the Board's authority to include craft workers in the industrial unit. Section 9(b)(2) stated that the Board should not "decide that any craft unit is inappropriate . . . on the ground that a different unit has been established by a prior Board determination, unless a majority of the employees in the proposed unit vote against separate representation." In the National Tube Company case,[2] the Board dismissed the petition of a group of steel industry bricklayers for separate representation. The Board reasoned that the only restriction imposed by the law was that a prior determination by the Board "may not be the sole ground upon which the Board may decide that a craft unit is inappropriate without an election."

In passing on petitions for either the establishment of craft units, or the severance of craft or craftlike groups from existing larger units, the Board applies the American Potash rules.[3] Under these rules: (1) A craft unit must

---

[2] 76 NLRB 1999.

[3] 107 NLRB 1418 (1954).

be composed of true craft employees having "a kind and degree of skill which is normally acquired only by undergoing a substantial period of apprenticeship or comparable training; (2) A noncraft group seeking to be severed must be functionally distinct and must consist of employees who, "though lacking the hallmark of craft skill," are "identified with traditional trades or occupations distinct from that of other employees . . . which have by tradition and practice acquired craftlike characteristics"; and (3) A union which seeks to sever a craft or quasi-craft group from a broader existing unit must have traditionally devoted itself to serving the special interests of the type of employees involved.

Craft severance poses a knotty problem for the Board, for employees, employers, and unions. The Taft-Hartley provisions on craft severance reflected a congressional suspicion that the NLRB has displayed a pro-CIO bias in unit determination. There can be little doubt that many skilled workers believed that they could get better terms of employment if they were represented by craft unions instead of being swallowed up in industrial unions. Many employers were seriously concerned about the prospects of craft severance upsetting long-established and effective collective bargaining relationships. Craft severance was a threat to industrial unions, a promise of new hunting ground for craft unions, and a potential trump card for dissident factions within industrial unions.

Experience with craft severance has been significantly less unsettling than expected. American Potash rules restrict the number of severance cases likely to arise. Both industrial unions and employers dealing with them have given more attention to the problems of quasi-craft workers covered by industrial union agreements. Newly formed craft unions drawing their membership from dissident factions in established industrial unions have had tough sledding.[4]

Last but not least, where craft severance has occurred, it has not disrupted stable labor relations to the extent feared; and, generally speaking, it has not seriously harmed the welfare of production workers.[5]

---

[4] An example of the problems confronting dissident factions was the 1958 experience in the automobile industry. Newly formed, independent craft unions petitioned for severance of certain skilled employees from individual plants of the General Motors Corporation. Over the years before the petition, the NLRB had established single-plant industrial units at GM. The NLRB dismissed the petition of the new unions on the grounds that individual-plant craft severances would disrupt long-established collective bargaining relationships. In making this decision, the Board disregarded the technicality that it had established plant units and based its decision on the reality of a corporate-wide bargaining unit which had been established by the practice of both the company and union. Simultaneously, the UAW changed its structure to give a greater voice to quasi-craft employees. Although a newly formed union probably could effectively organize on a plant-by-plant basis, such a union would have a hard time in a frontal assault on a corporate-wide unit.

[5] For a careful study of the empirical results of craft severance, see Dallas L. Jones, "Self-Determination vs. Stability in Labor Relations," 58 *Michigan Law Review* (January 1960), pp. 313–46.

After the NLRB field examiner has decided that the petition is within the jurisdiction of the NLRB and has made a tentative finding on the appropriate unit, the examiner seeks to ascertain if a substantial number of employees want the union to represent them and if the petition is timely.

Sufficient Showing of Interest.   This showing of interest is usually made by producing cards signed by employees authorizing the union to represent the signer-employee, or authorizing the petitioner to seek decertification. This evidence must be filed with the petition or submitted to the regional office investigator within 48 hours thereafter. Normally the petitioner must establish that at least 30 percent of the employees in the unit have designated the union as their representative.

If it is the employer who files the petition, the NLRB does not require this sort of a showing of interest. The Regional Director usually proceeds with the matter, provided one or more unions have made a demand on the employer for recognition. Such a demand need not be expressed in words but can be implied from union conduct.

Timeliness of the Petition.   The law provides that no election can be conducted in any bargaining unit (or any subdivision of one) in which a valid election has been held during the preceding 12-month period. This provision of the act guarantees to both the employer and employees for this period of time stability in their relations and freedom from disruptions that attend an election.

To further insure stability of industrial relations, the NLRB has established what is called the "contract bar" doctrine. The contract bar doctrine states that a valid collective bargaining agreement between an employer and a union representing employees will ordinarily prevent the holding of an election among the employees covered by the agreement. In general, the contract bar doctrine rules a petition untimely if it is filed during the term of an existing contract with a three-year maximum in the case of contracts that run for more than three years. Under the rules of the Board, a petition may be filed at least 60 days, but no more than 90 days, before the expiration of a contract. This filing period makes it possible to upset a contractual relationship at an appropriate time.

If the petition meets the Board's requirements on jurisdiction, the appropriate unit, a sufficient showing of interest, and timeliness, the Regional Director either issues a notice of formal hearing or approves a consent agreement made by the parties.

Consent Election Agreements.   A consent election agreement between the parties to a representation question includes: (*a*) a description of the appropriate unit; (*b*) the time and place of holding the election; and (*c*) a basis for determining who is eligible to vote. A consent election agreement, when approved by the Regional Director, eliminates the formal hearing prior to an election.

Formal Hearing on Representation.   The representation case hearing is a formal proceeding. It aims to obtain information which the Regional

Director needs in order to determine: (1) the appropriateness of the unit; (2) the adequacy of the showing of interest; (3) the timeliness of the petition; (4) the eligibility of employees to vote; and other pertinent matters. All parties who establish their interests are given full opportunity to produce facts to support their positions on the matters to be determined.

Following the hearing, the Regional Director determines the need for an election and the procedures to be followed if an election is directed. In some complex cases the record is furnished to the entire NLRB for consideration before ordering an election.

The Election. Section 9(c)(1) of the Taft-Hartley Act provides that if a question of representation exists, the NLRB must resolve it through an election by secret ballot. The election details are left to the Board. Many observers have cited Board-conducted elections as examples of the best operation of the democratic process. Before discussing the important, and frequently neglected, question of what an employer can do to influence the outcome of an election, it will be well to consider the election mechanics and the election environment.

Election Mechanics. The Board's rules on election mechanics are designed to encourage workers' participation in the election and to assure the integrity of the election process. The arrangements and voting procedure in all elections are the same, whether they are consent elections or elections directed by the Regional Director or the Board.

Under the *Excelsior Underwear* rule,[6] within seven days after the Regional Director has approved or ordered an election, the employer must supply the Board with a list of the names and addresses of all persons in the unit. The Board then gives this list to the union in order that both the union and the employer have equal access to persons eligible to vote in the election.

A regional office official will arrange for the posting of notices containing a sample ballot and information about the location of voting places, the timing of the voting and eligibility rules. The actual voting is always conducted and supervised by Board agents. Secrecy in voting is assured. Either the Board agents or the authorized observers of the parties may challenge for reasonable cause any employee who applies for a ballot. To be entitled to vote, an employee must have worked in the voting unit during the eligibility period and on the date of the election. Challenged employees may mark ballots, but their ballots are not counted until the challenges have been resolved.

Section 702 of the Landrum-Griffin Act states ,"Employees engaged in an economic strike who are not entitled to reinstatement shall be eligible to vote under such regulations as the Board shall find are consistent with the purposes and provisions of this Act in any election conducted within twelve months after the commencement of the strike." Generally the Board has ruled that an economic striker forfeits any right to vote under Section 702

---

[6] 61 *LRRM* 1217–22.

when he or she obtains permanent employment elsewhere before the election.

Ordinarily the Board directs that elections be held within 30 days from the date of direction of the election. However, where an immediate election would occur at a time when there is not a representative number of employees in the voting unit—because of such circumstances as a seasonal fluctuation in employment or a change in operations—a different date will be selected in order to accommodate voting to the peak or normal working force.

Important as the mechanics of an election are, it is obvious that the outcome of an election can be influenced by improper electioneering, threats of violence, or other environmental influences.

The Election Environment. The area of legitimate employer and union conduct during an election campaign is one of the most difficult problems confronting the NLRB. It seems obvious that an employer's opinion on the probable consequences if a union should win an election would not always be free of bias, but would carry great weight with the employees. This would be particularly true if the "opinion" was that widespread layoffs would result, or that it would be forced to close the plant permanently. The NLRB has the delicate task of protecting the employer's freedom of speech and at the same time protecting employees from undue interference, restraint, or coercion that the speech might exert on them as they express their choice about union representation. Although Section 8(c) of the Taft-Hartley Act, commonly called the "free speech provision," has broadened management's freedom to try to influence the outcome of an NLRB election, management participation in the election process is still limited by law and NLRB rulings.

For more than 30 years, the NLRB has walked this tightrope. An example of two NLRB rules, both now abandoned, may help to illustrate the Board's problem. At one time the NLRB held that a "captive audience" (employees required to listen to the employer's antiunion statements during working hours) was a cause to set aside an NLRB election. At a later time the Board held that a captive audience was legitimate if the employer paid employees for "equal time" while the union attempted to refute the speech.

Another recurring question is whether supervisors exert undue influence on the outcome of an election when they talk about it to individual employees and groups of employees. The Board has consistently set aside elections where the employer resorted to the technique of calling upon all or a majority of the employees in the unit individually, in the employer's office or at their homes, to urge them to vote against a proposed bargaining representative, regardless of whether the employer's remarks to the employees were coercive in character.

Under present rules of the Board, an election will be set aside if it is accompanied by conduct which, in the Board's view, creates an atmosphere of confusion or fear of reprisals and thus interferes with the employees' free choice of a representative guaranteed by the act. In determining whether specific conduct amounts to such interference, the Board does not attempt to assess its actual effect on the employees but concerns itself with whether it is reasonable to conclude that the conduct tended to prevent a free expression of the employees' choice.

Electioneering is vigorously controlled by NLRB rules and the provisions of the law. Under the *Peerless Plywood* rule, the Board prohibits election speeches on company time to massed assemblies of employees within 24 hours before the scheduled time for conducting an election. Electioneering near the polling places during the election is also prohibited. All participants in an election are prohibited from using any document purporting to be a copy of the Board's official ballot, unless the document is completely unaltered in form and content.

The Board will not police and censure the parties' election propaganda except to prevent fraud or coercion. However, in the *Mosler Safe Co.* case, the Board ruled "when one of the parties deliberately misstates material facts which are within its special knowledge, under such circumstances that the other party or parties cannot learn about them in time to point out the misstatements, the Board will find that the bounds of legitimate campaign propaganda have been exceeded and will set aside an election."[7]

Although the Board tolerates intemperate, abusive, and inaccurate statements made by the union during attempts to organize employees, it does not interpret the act as giving either party license to injure the other intentionally by circulating defamatory or insulting material known to be false. In *Linn* v. *Plant Guards Local 114*, the U.S. Supreme Court ruled on February 21, 1966, that a Federal District Court has jurisdiction of a civil action for alleged libel instituted under state law by an official of an employer subject to the Federal Labor-Management Relations Act for defamatory statements published by a union during an organizing drive if the employer's official pleads and proves that the statements were made with malice and injured the official.[8]

Many an employer has felt abused in the course of establishing the collective bargaining relationship. Typically employers find themselves in a surprised, passive, and defensive position when first confronted by a union demand for recognition and the processes of the NLRB. Instead of occupying the usual role of planner, decision maker, and allocator of the enterprise's resources, the employer frequently is swamped by the demands of "ungrateful" employees, the intrusion of "outsiders" who appear to threaten the future of the enterprise, and a governmental proceeding where the "shall nots" outnumber the "shalls" by 1,000 to 1. What can be done?

The Employer in the Rules for Establishing the Collective Bargaining Relationships. Although collective bargaining relationships have worked

---

[7] 129 NLRB 747.
[8] 61 *LRRM* 2345–53.

amazingly well in vast segments of the American economy, the typical employer undoubtedly would prefer to operate the business on a nonunion basis. Any manager who sought out a collective bargaining relationship would be considered a wild-eyed idealist by the most generous of colleagues. How does an employer go about staying nonunion, defeating the union in an NLRB election, or getting rid of an unwanted union after it has been certified?

Unions lose about 40 percent of the NLRB elections held each year. This fact means that some employers *can* and *do* launch effective programs against unionization. There is no easy sure-fire formula to beat the union in an NLRB election, but several possibilities are open to an intelligent and aggressive management. A successful program could be built around the following steps:

1. Long before there is a union organization threat, do a good job of managing personnel. This would include:
    a. Good wages, hours, and working conditions.
    b. A *genuine* "open door" on grievances and perhaps a formal grievance procedure, the latter being particularly important in a large-scale enterprise.
    c. Economic education of employees, not in the abstract, but realistically, in the problems and prospects of the specific enterprise and its industry.
    d. Effective supervision of the labor force with a heavy emphasis on *fair* treatment of employees in disciplinary cases especially.
    e. Effective *upward* communication in the enterprise, with management really listening for employee grievances and suggestions.
2. When the union enters, vigorous campaigning against the union in the election.
    a. This campaigning has to be based on the *substance* of the enterprise being a good place to work, e.g., wages *are* good, the treatment of employees *is* fair, and, in fact, there is little that the employees can gain from unionization. The big hazard of a "hard sell" on how good things are is that if the union wins, the items that management has sold them become the starting point of negotiations. In later negotiations, management cannot claim credit for what the employees had in the preunion period.
    b. Publication of the fact that unionism may mean lost paydays due to strikes and that union membership costs money in terms of dues, assessments, and initiation fees.
    c. Take advantage of any derogatory information about the union which has been revealed in investigations or publicity.
    d. Emphasize the idea that the union is an outsider or third party that comes between the employees and the enterprise management.
    e. Adopt and enforce a uniform rule against all solicitations during

working hours and in work areas. Prohibit the distribution of union literature in work areas.

    f. If union organizers can contact employees on public property near the plant, prohibit them from entering the company parking lot or the plant area.

3. Scrupulously *avoid* any actions that are contrary to law and would result in an invalidation of the election. A full list of the "dont's" would be very long indeed. The following items are examples only:

    a. Don't threaten to close the plant if the union wins.

    b. Don't raise wages or benefits prior to the election.

    c. Don't promise to increase wages or benefits on condition of the union losing the election.

    d. Don't reduce wages or benefits prior to the election.

Probably the most critical matter in the outcome of NLRB elections is timing. An election ordinarily will be held within about 30 days of the union's first filing with the NLRB. If the union's petition comes as a genuine surprise to the employer, and it frequently does, there really isn't much that can be done about putting things in order. In most cases, the employer has to stand or fall on the policies used *before* the union makes a formal appearance.

Turning a union out after it has won an NLRB certification election is usually much harder than beating the union in its initial organizing drive. NLRB union decertification procedures will be discussed below.

Certification of Election Results. Where a valid election has been held, the Regional Director or the Board will issue to the participants a certification of the results. If a union has been chosen by a majority of the employees in the unit, it will receive a certificate showing that it is the official bargaining representative of the employees in the unit. If a majority of the employees have voted that no union be designated as their bargaining representative, the certificate will so state. This certificate protects both the employer and the winning union from a trial by election for 12 months. If an agreement is negotiated, the agreement provides even larger protection under the NLRB's contract bar rules.

The foregoing is an enterprise view of the rules for establishing a collective bargaining relationship in the United States. It is now appropriate to make a few observations about the process from a national and public policy viewpoint.

THE NATIONAL EBB AND FLOW OF UNION RECOGNITION

As discussed above, union recognition may be won either by voluntary action of management or by an NLRB election. Union recognition is lost either through business mortality or an NLRB decertification election. The

35-year trend in industrial relations legislation is a steady upgrading of the importance of an NLRB election as the major method of obtaining union recognition.

Figure 6–1 summarizes the outcome of NLRB elections from 1936

FIGURE 6–1

Results of NLRB Representation Elections, 1936–70

Fiscal Year Ending	Number of Elections Held	Number of Employees Eligible to Vote	Percent of Eligible Employees Voting	Valid Votes Cast for Union Representation	Percent of Total Vote Cast for Union	Number of Employees in Units Selecting Union as Agent
6/30/36*	31	9,512	79.6	6,162	59.1	N.A.
6/30/37*	265	181,424	90.5	142,428	69.1	N.A.
6/30/38*	1,152	394,558	87.1	282,470	82.8	N.A.
6/30/39*	746	207,597	85.4	138,032	77.9	N.A.
6/30/40*	1,192	595,075	89.5	435,842	81.9	N.A.
6/30/41*	2,568	788,111	92.6	589,921	80.9	N.A.
6/30/42*	4,212	1,296,567	82.3	895,091	83.9	N.A.
6/30/43*	4,153	1,402,040	80.3	923,169	81.9	N.A.
6/30/44*	4,712	1,322,225	81.1	828,583	77.2	N.A.
6/30/45*	4,919	1,087,177	82.8	706,569	79.1	N.A.
6/30/46*	5,589	846,431	82.6	529,847	75.8	N.A.
6/30/47*	6,920	934,553	86.2	621,732	77.2	N.A.
6/30/48	3,222	384,565	86.8	256,935	77.0	N.A.
6/30/49	5,514	588,761	87.7	377,360	73.1	N.A.
6/30/50	5,619	890,374	87.8	649,432	83.1	753,598
6/30/51	6,432	666,556	88.2	442,066	75.2	505,322
6/30/52	6,765	771,346	86.6	503,143	75.3	584,030
6/30/53	6,050	737,998	86.7	497,286	77.7	584,450
6/30/54	4,663	511,430	87.9	314,701	70.0	343,092
6/30/55	4,215	515,995	87.9	335,393	74.0	378,962
6/30/56	4,946	462,712	89.6	268,531	64.8	291,292
6/30/57	4,729	458,904	89.5	261,762	63.7	264,920
6/30/58	4,337	351,217	89.8	190,558	60.4	196,334
6/30/59	5,428	430,023	89.7	247,867	64.2	257,028
6/30/60	6,380	483,964	90.2	280,140	64.1	286,048
6/30/61	6,354	450,930	89.4	239,693	59.4	229,283
6/30/62	7,355	536,047	89.8	299,547	62.1	305,976
6/30/63	6,871	489,365	90.3	264,727	59.9	265,747
6/30/64	7,309	538,019	90.4	281,483	57.9	286,897
6/30/65	7,576	531,971	90.3	300,144	62.5	325,698
6/30/66	8,103	582,212	90.1	305,891	51.0	334,998
6/30/67	7,882	611,006	88.0	332,950	54.5	349,406
6/30/68	7,618	550,610	89.5	205,642	57.8	276,499
6/30/69	7,700	570,990	90.0	273,157	52.0	287,557
6/30/70	7,773	588,214	82.1	296,637	50.1	307,104
6/30/71	7,961	565,429	87.8	274,887	55.4	264,747
6/30/72	8,472	570,846	87.8	287,684	57.4	286,365
6/30/73	8,916	521,438	88.8	235,022	50.7	223,961
6/30/74	8,368	519,634	88.7	223,906	48.6	190,038

° During some of the years before 1948, data were presented as a composite of election and payroll checks or cross checks by NLRB. After the passage of the Taft-Hartley Act in 1947, the NLRB was empowered to certify a union for collective bargaining only on the basis of an election.
Source: *Annual Reports* of the NLRB.

through 1974. Several observations on the experience with NLRB elections are in order:

1. Consistently, workers have shown great interest in NLRB elections. Note that in every year but one, over 80 percent of the workers eligible to vote in NLRB elections have chosen to exercise their right to vote.
2. Since 1955, between 350,000 and 611,000 workers have been eligible to vote in NLRB elections each year. NLRB election activity seems to have declined rather steadily since a high-water mark in the early 1940s.
3. Although union success in elections has been slipping since the mid-1950s, unions continue to poll about 60 percent of the valid votes cast each year. The percentage of votes cast for the unions would be the most accurate measure of the popularity of unions among workers where representation rights were sought. Note the close relationship between the numbers of votes cast for unions and the number of employees in units selecting a union as representative.
4. The number of employees in units selecting a union as agent is the most important figure for measuring the dynamics of union recognition. This figure shows how many additional workers come under the potential coverage of collective bargaining agreements each year. If a union wins an election by only one vote, it still wins the right to represent all workers in the unit .The number of workers in units selecting the union as a representative is the potential membership base won by the union.
5. Figure 6–1 shows that NLRB elections since 1955 have enabled unions to increase their potential coverage of collective bargaining agreements from less than 200,000 workers in the 1957–58 fiscal year to over 300,000 workers in 1965–70. Although unions could be encouraged by NLRB election trends since 1962, the 60s are a hollow shell of the period before 1955. Of course, any *actual* increase in collective bargaining agreement coverage would equal only this *potential* gain minus any losses due to business mortality, declines in employment in unionized firms, and the employment of firms where unions lost decertification elections.
6. The sharp dropoff in 1973–74 in percent of total votes cast for unions and number of employees brought under union representation may herald a trend, or prove to be a temporary phenomenon, as in the years 1970–71.

Union recognition is lost either by business mortality or an NLRB decertification election. Indices of business mortality do not include information on whether or not the business was unionized.

The authors of the Taft-Hartley Act wanted to provide a means by which employees could rid themselves of unwanted unions. The method provided was the NLRB decertification election. Figure 6–2 summarizes the outcome of NLRB decertification elections since 1947. It should be noted that decertification elections have released fewer than 12,000 workers per year.

FIGURE 6–2
Results of NLRB Decertification Elections, 1947–70

Fiscal Year Ending	Number of Elections Held	Number of Employees Eligible to Vote	Percent of Eligible Employees Voting	Valid Votes Cast against Unions	Percent of Valid Votes Cast against Representation	Number of Employees in Units Choosing Decertification
6/30/48	97	8,836	88.9	3,914	49.8	N.A.
6/30/49	132	18,773	91.0	7,262	42.5	N.A.
6/30/50	112	9,474	89.6	4,164	49.1	4,034
6/30/51	93	6,111	87.5	2,954	55.2	3,429
6/30/52	101	7,378	88.6	3,465	53.0	4,045
6/30/53	141	9,945	90.0	4,389	49.1	5,076
6/30/54	150	10,244	88.7	4,774	52.5	5,935
6/30/55	157	13,002	90.0	5,936	50.2	5,524
6/30/56	129	11,289	91.9	4,761	46.3	5,598
6/30/57	145	11,018	92.9	5,516	54.3	6,888
6/30/58	153	10,124	89.7	4,787	52.7	4,499
6/30/59	216	16,231	90.3	6,984	47.7	7,705
6/30/60	237	17,421	88.1	6,817	44.4	8,695
6/30/61	241	18,364	90.4	6,570	45.6	10,607
6/30/62	285	12,323	86.8	7,365	68.8	6,930
6/30/63	225	13,256	87.9	5,208	53.3	8,033
6/30/64	220	13,732	90.4	5,562	44.8	5,399
6/30/65	200	12,565	88.9	4,618	41.3	4,718
6/30/66	221	10,510	89.3	4,905	52.5	6,061
6/30/67	234	12,705	87.6	4,744	42.6	4,997
6/30/68	239	15,554	88.6	4,628	33.6	4,804
6/30/69	293	21,771	86.5	8,316	43.8	9,349
6/30/70	301	20,344	88.3	8,025	44.6	8,558
6/30/71	401	20,726	87.2	9,110	50.4	10,773
6/30/72	451	20,790	86.8	8,724	48.4	10,028
6/30/73	453	20,007	85.5	7,902	46.2	10,940
6/30/74	490	24,697	86.1	9,879	46.5	11,470

Source: *Annual Reports* of the NLRB.

Since 1955, American unions have been substantially less successful in extending union recognition than they were in early periods. At least part of this decline can be attributed to the high level of unionization already achieved in many segments of the economy. At the same time, since 1955, unions have usually won the right to represent about 250,000 new employees through NLRB elections each year, while losing the right to represent fewer than 12,000 each year through decertification elections.

A number of important public policy questions on the rules for establishing the collective bargaining relationships are unresolved.

UNRESOLVED PROBLEMS IN PUBLIC POLICY ON UNION RECOGNITION

By now it should be clear that in the United States the government sets the terms of union recognition. It does so by defining the bargaining unit and conducting elections. Although the role of government is firmly established, several unresolved problems remain to plague the Congress, the NLRB, and the courts. The solutions developed to these problems may well have an important long-range effect on the structure of collective bargaining in America. Four major problems deserve attention: (1) employees excluded from NLRB jurisdiction; (2) the peculiar problems of union recognition in industries characterized by casual and intermittent employment; (3) free speech; and (4) the sometimes conflicting objectives of self-determination, stability, and effectiveness in union recognition.

Employees Excluded from the Protection of the Law

In aggregate, a very large number of American workers are excluded from the law's protection of the right to union representation. The largest single group of workers excluded are agricultural employees. Also excluded are the employees of small interstate and all intrastate enterprises and persons in supervisory positions.

It is possible that some of the employees excluded from the protection of the law are the object of deep-seated political pressures which are unlikely to yield. In the case of governmental employment, the systems of union recognition are, of necessity, grafted on established procedures for protecting the employees' interests. In the case of small employers, the administrative costs of extending the protection of the law seem to be greater than the benefits which society would gain.

Government Employees. On January 17, 1962, President Kennedy issued Executive Order 10988, Employee-Management Co-operation in the Federal Service. This order extended to some 2 million employees of the executive branch of the government a unique form of the right to union representation.[9] President Nixon reaffirmed its principles in Executive Order 11491 in 1969. The problems of government unions are considered in Chapters 15 and 16, Part Four of this book.

Organizations seeking to represent governmental employees must: (1) disavow the right to strike against the government, (2) not advocate the overthrow of the government, (3) not discriminate with regard to the terms or conditions of membership because of race, color, creed, or national origin, and (4) be free of corrupt or undemocratic influences which are incon-

---

[9] U.S. Department of Labor, Bureau of Labor Statistics, *Directory of National and International Labor Unions in the United States, 1965*, Bulletin no. 1493, p. 55.

sistent with the purposes of the order. When an employee organization has been recognized as the exclusive representative of employees, it shall be entitled to negotiate agreements covering all employees in the unit and shall be responsible for representing the interests of all employees in the unit without discrimination and without regard to employee organization membership.

Union recognition under Executive Order 11491 is required to be consistent with the standards of the Civil Service Commission, the rights of veterans, and the rights available to an individual governmental employee in the absence of union recognition. Heads of agencies are empowered to deny union recognition where they decide that this order cannot be applied in a manner consistent with national security requirements and considerations.

Agriculture, Hospitals, Small Firms. It is probably fair to say that agricultural workers and the employees of very small firms usually work under employment conditions less advantageous than those found in most unionized industries. On a humanitarian basis, it might be argued that these employees *need* union representation more than other employees.

It might be argued that hospital employees should be asked to renounce the right to strike, as is required of governmental employees. Obviously, the health and safety of a community depends on the continuous operation of hospitals. On the other hand, hospital employees certainly have interests *as employees* which should be heard. The law, which used to exclude them, now grants them the right to bargain.

The exclusion of small employers and agricultural employees from the basic law of union recognition usually is justified on the basis of protecting employers who could not remain in business if they had to meet the demands of unions. The authors of this text, nevertheless, wholeheartedly agree with the recommendations of a distinguished independent study group,[10] working under the auspices of the Committee for Economic Development, that the self-determination principle should be extended to cover farm, and small firm employees.

One of the problems in drawing up agricultural labor legislation comes from the intermittent and casual nature of employment. This problem also arises in certain other industries.

Casual and Intermittent Employment and Union Recognition. From its very beginning, the NLRB has tried to establish fair rules for getting and keeping union recognition in industries characterized by casual and intermittent employment. The Taft-Hartley ban on union hiring halls and the closed shop aggravated the Board's problems. The Landrum-Griffin law

---

[10] Clark Kerr, Chairman; Douglas V. Brown, David L. Cole, John T. Dunlop, William T. Elliott, Albert Rees, Robert M. Solow, Philip Taft, George W. Taylor, Members; George P. Schultz, Staff Director, and Abraham Siegel, Associate Staff Director. See *The Public Interest in National Labor Policy* (New York: Committee for Economic Development, 1961), pp. 74–79, 84–85.

cleared the air a little by permitting prehire contracts in the building construction industry.

As a minimum, the authors of this book believe that the Landrum-Griffin prehire and seven-day union shop permission should be extended to all industries characterized by intermittent and casual employment. Given the extensive protection of the right to membership in unions which is guaranteed by Landrum-Griffin, it is most likely that the best solution to the problem of all industries characterized by casual and intermittent employment would be any hiring hall, closed shop, or other arrangement which employers and unions in those industries worked out together.

Free Speech.   The problem of guaranteed free speech at the same time that employees are protected from interference, restraint, and coercion has occupied the NLRB, the Congress, and students of labor relations for over 30 years.[11] Any policy on free speech influences the outcome of elections and the prevalence of collective bargaining in society. Individual members of congress and members of the NLRB have deep convictions about both free speech and the desirability of extending collective bargaining. Changes in policy probably reflect changes in the composition of Congress and the Board.

We believe that most of the argument about free speech can be summarized in the commonplace statement: "It's not only *what* you say, but *how* you say it." Such an interpretation requires that actions be considered in their frequently complex context. The context of election statements varies between regions of the country, the histories of particular enterprises, and the education and attitudes of particular groups of employees.

Free speech is an emotion-laden issue in public policy on labor relations. It probably will remain as an unresolved problem in public policy. This is as much a tribute to the institutions of freedom as it is a source of continued frustration to the parties to collective bargaining and to people of goodwill who are charged with the responsibility for maintaining an environment consistent with a fair election process.

Most of the remaining unresolved problems in public policy on union recognition have to do with the relative weight to be given to three sometimes conflicting objectives of labor policy: self-determination, stability, and effectiveness of representation.

The Objectives of Self-Determination, Stability, and Effectiveness

Probably the cornerstone of American public policy on union recognition is *self-determination* by employees (and, to a lesser degree, by employers) of the method of union recognition. Employees are given the right

---

[11] For a definitive statement of the history of this problem and observations on the propriety of various NLRB rulings, see Benjamin Aaron, "Employer Free Speech: The Search for a Policy," chap. 2 of Joseph Shister, Benjamin Aaron, and Clyde W. Summers, eds., *Public Policy and Collective Bargaining* (New York: Harper & Row, 1962), pp. 28–59.

to vote on what union, if any, will represent them. NLRB unit determination policy on multiemployer bargaining protects the right of individual employers to decide whether they wish to go it alone or be represented by an association. Decertification elections protect the right of employees to "run the rascals out" when they wish to reject a union which they had previously embraced. Craft severance and professional employee elections preserve the right of self-determination for particular groups of employees.

The objective of self-determination sometimes runs afoul of the objective of *stability* in labor relations. NLRB contract bar rules, the statutory 12-month limitation on elections, and NLRB criteria for craft severance are outgrowths of a desire for stability in labor relations. It is obvious that subjecting employees and employers to an election every time a dissident group could muster a following would spell chaos for the employment relationship. At the same time a 12-month ban on elections may deprive employees of the right to representation on a permanent basis. Occasionally unions have lost NLRB elections by a very small margin and have been unable to maintain a semblance of organization for 12 months after the election. The contract bar rules of the NLRB occasionally have enabled an unrepresentative union to maintain its position in a collective bargaining relationship.

The fundamental purpose of national labor policy is to minimize obstructions to the flow of commerce. This would imply an objective of *effectiveness* in labor-management relations. Effectiveness in employee and employer representation might very well dictate a substantial reduction in the freedom of self-determination granted to the parties. For example, one powerful corporate-wide union probably would be most effective in dealing with management, regardless of how poorly it treated the interests of skilled workers or professional employees. It is not altogether certain that management would find such an arrangement distasteful. In a similar vein, in highly competitive industries with many small employers, effectiveness in collective bargaining might be achieved by governmental policing of the membership of an employers' association. There have been numerous cases where both an employer association and the union(s) representing workers in the industry would welcome government support in keeping wayward employers in line. As a final example, few objective observers would argue that archaic lines of jurisdiction over work in the railroads, airlines, and building trades foster efficiency in representation.

The basic problem in union recognition is a delicate balancing of the interests of employees and employers in the pursuit of the objectives of self-determination, stability, and effectiveness in labor relations. Unfortunately, neither society nor the parties can have all their cakes and eat them, too.

QUESTIONS FOR DISCUSSION

1. "Ballot box organizing" is unique to the North American continent. Does ballot box organizing fulfill any particular needs of a politically democratic

private enterprise society? Does it pose any challenges to free institutions? What might be substituted for ballot box organizing?

2. The Landrum-Griffin Act permitted the NLRB to delegate more authority to its Regional Directors for the handling of representational issues. Do you think it would be a good idea to give the Regional Directors authority to rule on unfair labor practice charges? Justify your position.

3. Since employers have a real interest in the determination of bargaining units, is it fair to make the interests of employees the controlling factor? By the same token, why is the employer's interest considered to be controlling in multiemployer units?

4. "Employers and the general public are always the innocent victims in jurisdictional strikes." Discuss.

5. Attack or defend the proposal that the closed shop be authorized by law.

6. The text recognizes several unresolved problems in public policy on union recognition. What are these problems? How would you resolve them? Why?

APPENDIX: COURT ORDERS AND DECISIONS AFFECTING ESTABLISHMENT OF THE COLLECTIVE BARGAINING RELATIONSHIP[12]

Union Recognition without Election

A union may be recognized as a bargaining agent in a variety of ways, including winning an NLRB election, voluntary employer recognition of majority status, and as a remedial order of the NLRB arising from the employer's unfair labor practices. Recognition by means of a remedial order of the NLRB has undergone considerable development. It had been established that a bargaining order was appropriate where the employer set out to destroy the union by "pervasive" and "outrageous" unfair labor practices which would render the election process meaningless. The rule was less clear where the unfair labor practices were less severe until the Supreme Court decision in *Gissel*. The ruling was that if a union had a provable majority in a unit, and the employer engages in less than "pervasive" and "outrageous" unfair labor practices, a bargaining order is a proper remedy where the unfair labor practices undermine a provable majority status and impede the holding of a fair election. On the problem of proving that a majority status once existed, the Supreme Court found that authorization cards would be acceptable evidence and put a heavy burden on anyone who would challenge the validity of the cards. (*NLRB* v. *Gissel Packing Co.*, 395 U.S. 575 (1969).)

An employer is required to recognize a majority union, but questions arise as to how the employer knows the union has a majority. What is the employer's duty when the union offers to show majority strength by presenting authorization cards? The Supreme Court held that unless an employer has engaged in an unfair labor practice which impairs the electoral process, an employer can re-

---

12 For material in this Appendix, the authors are indebted to Professor Donald W. Brodie of the University of Oregon Law School.

fuse to recognize a union with authorization cards which purport to represent a majority of the employees. The employer is under no duty to recognize or ask for an election, rather the union will have the burden of taking the next step in invoking the Board's election procedure. (*Linden Lumber Division, Summer and Co., v. NLRB*, 95 Supreme Court 429 (1974).)

In a related decision, it was found to be an unfair labor practice for a union to offer to waive its initiation fees only for those employees who sign authorization cards prior to an election. It would allow the union to buy endorsements and paint a false portrait of employee support during the campaign. (*NLRB* v. *Savair Manufacturing*, 94 Supreme Court 495 (1973).)

Election Procedures

When conducting elections, it is the NLRB's goal to provide a laboratory in which an experiment may be conducted, under conditions as nearly ideal as possible, to determine the uninhibited desires of the employees. An election may be set aside either for appropriate unfair labor practices or for a violation of the laboratory conditions, even if they do not rise to the status of an unfair labor practice. (*General Shoe Corp.*, 77 NLRB 124 (1948).)

An employer must furnish to all participants in a Board election a list of the names and addresses of the employees who are eligible to vote (the "Excelsior Doctrine"). (*NLRB* v. *Wyman-Gordon Co.*, 394 U.S. 759 (1969).)

Employers and unions are prohibited from making election speeches on company time to massed assemblies of employees within twenty-four hours before the scheduled time for conducting an election. (*Peerless Plywood Co.*, 107 NLRB 427 (1953).)

Managerial Employees

Managerial employees are excluded from coverage of the NLRA. Two groups are thus excluded: (1) those susceptible to a conflict of interest if they organized, e.g., those whose work includes the employer's bargaining strategy, and (2) those who formulate and effectuate management policies by expressing and making the operative decisions of their employer, such as certain buyers (*NLRB* v. *Bell Aerospace Co.*, 94 Supreme Court 1757 (1974).)

Access to the Employer's Property during Organizational Campaign

The legislation gives rights to employees. It is silent on the rights of union organizers who are not employees. Access by nonemployees to the employer's property during the organizational campaign raises questions under both the NLRA and the Constitution. In one case, an employer sought to prevent access to a shopping center mall generally open to the public. The U.S. Supreme Court found the action to be a violation of the First and Fourteenth Amendment free-speech rights. The mall was considered to be the functional equivalent of the community business block. (*Amalgamated Food Employees Local 590* v. *Logan Valley Plaza, Inc.*, 391 U.S. 308 (1968).) Earlier, the Supreme Court had stated that an employer may post company property against nonemployee distribution of union literature if reasonable efforts by the union through other available channels of communications will enable it to reach the employees and if the employer's order does not discriminate against the union by allowing other distribution. (*NLRB* v. *Babcock & Wilcox*, 351 U.S. 105 (1956).)

In one recent case, a company prohibited union solicitation by nonemployees in the parking lots which surrounded the store and which were generally open to the public. The Supreme Court upheld the employer's rule unless it could be shown (under *Babcock & Wilcox*, supra) that there were no other available channels of communication. (*Central Hardware Co.* v. *NLRB*, 407 U.S. 539 (1972).)

In a related, but not a labor, case the Supreme Court prohibited distribution of anti-war literature in a privately owned shopping center where the distribution was unrelated to the shopping center's operations, and where alternative means of communication exist. The public's access to the shopping center did not alter its privately owned character. (*Lloyd Center Corp.* v. *Tanner*, 407 U.S. 551 (1972).)

Nonunion Activities

In addition to protecting union related activities, the NLRA also protects certain concerted activities by unrepresented employees. For example, where the employees were unrepresented and had previously complained about cold working conditions, the employer could not discharge the employees for quitting work in protest over the cold working conditions. The Supreme Court noted that the employee protest was not unlawful, not violent, not in breach of a contract, and not indefensible by all recognized standards of conduct. (*NLRB* v. *Washington Aluminum Co.*, 370 U.S. 9 (1962).)

Relationship of NLRB and the Courts

The Administrative Procedures Act strictly limited the courts from giving preliminary review to representation elections. The courts are primarily limited to judicial review of final unfair labor practice orders. A federal court may enjoin preliminary NLRB action only where the act is in clear excess of delegated powers and contrary to a specific prohibition in the Act. (*Leedom* v. *Kyne*, 358 U.S. 184 (1958).) This exception, however, is strictly limited and applicable only in extraordinary circumstances. (*Boire* v. *Greyhound Corp.*, 376 U.S. 473 (1964).)

When the federal Courts of Appeal review final orders of the NLRB on questions of fact, they are bound by the substantial evidence rule. Under this rule, the court must affirm the NLRB finding of fact when it is reasonable, even though the court might have found the facts to be different if they had made the finding of fact in the first instance. (*Universal Camera Corp.* v. *NLRB*, 340 U.S. 474 (1951).)

SELECTED ANNOTATED BIBLIOGRAPHY

ABODEELY, JOHN E. *The NLRB and the Appropriate Bargaining Unit.* Labor Relations and Public Policy Series, Report no. 3. Philadelphia: University of Pennsylvania, Industrial Research Unit, 1971.

The author examines in considerable detail the criteria the NLRB uses in making unit determinations and modifications, and is critical of many Board decisions.

ALEXANDER, KENNETH O.   "Conglomerate Mergers and Collective Bargaining," *Industrial and Labor Relations Review*, vol. 24, no. 3 (April 1971).

An examination of how corporate mergers may shift tactical bargaining power in management's favor by creating conglomerate firms with increased product and labor market powers.

BROOKS, GEORGE W., and THOMPSON, MARK.   "Multiplant Units: The NLRB's Withdrawal of Free Choice," *Industrial and Labor Relations Review*, vol. 20, no. 3 (April 1967).

The authors, by examining NLRB decisions, show that once multiplant negotiating units are established employees effectively are barred from withdrawing from those expanded units.

Collective Bargaining Today.   Proceedings of the Collective Bargaining Forum, 1969; sponsored by the Institute of Collective Bargaining and Group Relations. Washington, D.C.: The Bureau of National Affairs, Inc., 1970.

The first set of proceedings from a newly founded institute gives a panorama of views by prominent management and labor officials as to their current objectives in collective bargaining. These proceedings are to be published annually and will provide a continuing up-to-date compilation of attitudes toward collective bargaining by those actually practicing it.

JACKSON, LOUIS, and LEWIS, ROBERT, eds.   *Winning NLRB Elections: Management's Strategy and Preventive Programs.* New York: Practicing Law Institute, 1972.

This is a how-to-do-it manual on keeping the union out (see the Schlossberg and Sherman entry below).

PICHLER, JOSEPH A., and FITCH, GORDON H.   "And Women Must Weep: The NLRB as Film Critic," *Industrial and Labor Relations Review*, vol. 28, no. 3 (April 1975).

The authors examine NLRB rulings in election cases involving a controversial antiunion film, and present some empirical evidence regarding the film's impact.

ROSS, PHILIP.   "Origin of the Hiring Hall in Construction," *Industrial Relations*, vol. 11, no. 3 (October 1972).

An examination of some of the mechanisms by which the building trades unions have controlled the labor supply to employers in an industry where representation elections are rare.

SCHLOSSBERG, STEPHEN I., and SHERMAN, FREDERICK E.   *Organizing and the Law: A Handbook for Union Organizers.* Rev. ed. Washington, D.C.: Bureau of National Affairs, 1972.

This is a manual on the labor law that union organizers need to know in order to help them win organizing campaigns (see the Jackson and Lewis entry above).

SIRKIN, STUART A., and YEOMANS, GAYLE A.   "Effects of the NLRB's Unit Policies in the Retail Chain Store Industry," *Labor Law Journal*, vol. 23, no. 2 (February 1972).

The authors examine the impact upon unions, employers, and the bargaining process of the NLRB's 1962 decision to favor single store appropriate bargaining units in retail chains.

WEBER, ARNOLD R. "Stability and Change in the Structure of Collective Bargaining," in *The American Assembly, Challenges to Collective Bargaining.* Lloyd Ulman, ed. Englewood Cliffs, N.J.: Prentice-Hall, 1967.

Probably the best short piece available on the components and determinants of collective bargaining structures.

WEBER, ARNOLD, ed. *The Structure of Collective Bargaining.* New York: The Free Press of Glencoe, 1961.

A collection of essays dealing with the question of the size, scope, shape, and interrelationships of bargaining units. The essays are subdivided into four parts: theory, union and management interests, industry case studies, and finally questions of public policy.

WILLIAMS, ROBERT E.; JANUS, PETER A.; and HUHN, KENNETH C. *NLRB Regulation of Election Conduct.* Labor Relations and Public Policy Series, Report no. 8. Philadelphia: University of Pennsylvania, Industrial Research Unit, 1974.

A very detailed examination of NLRB standards for reviewing representation election appeals and of Board decisions to set aside challenged elections.

7 The Problem of Reaching Agreement

ONCE THE collective bargaining relationship is established, the actors must negotiate an agreement and learn to live with it; or rather, learn to live with each other under its terms. This chapter deals with the preparations and procedures for reaching agreement, including strikes as well as negotiations. Chapter 8 analyzes the nature of the agreement in terms of the functions served by the substantive rules. Chapter 13 discusses the problems of living with the agreement and administering the rules.

Today most labor-management negotiations are for the revision and renewal of existing agreements, which regularly expire at intervals usually ranging from one to three years, rather than for an initial agreement. Rare indeed is the agreement so carefully phrased and the labor-management relationship so nicely balanced that the parties renew it unchanged. One or the other, or both, almost always seek to adjust or improve it; and there was always the first time, when everything had to be considered. This chapter, therefore, treats negotiations as if they were for an initial agreement, though most of what is said applies to renewals as well. A strike can, of course, occur at any stage in a relationship if negotiations either for a new agreement or renewal of an old one break down.

NEGOTIATIONS

In negotiations the newly-certified union and newly-obligated management face the consequences and culmination of everything that has gone before: the organizing, the electioneering, the winning of recognition, the concentration of worker hopes and management fears. For the first time their representatives sit down, literally face to face, and formally engage in bargaining that sets the conditions that will govern their day-to-day relations for the year, or two or three, ahead. Each set of subsequent negotiations sums up their experiences together over that year or two or three, and marks a new beginning. In the whole range and gamut of the interaction that makes up a labor-management relationship, probably nothing is more concentrated and significant than negotiations.

Until fairly recently, few scholars had closely examined what goes on around the conference table during negotiations, or how the participants prepare for that crucial test. Less vital aspects of collective bargaining have drawn greater attention. Abitration, for example—an important, but still subsidiary activity, set in motion only if the negotiated agreement so specifies—has given rise to vast literature, with shelf after shelf of published awards and volume upon volume of commentary and critique.

This neglect of negotiations is not as surprising as it might seem. Negotiations usually take place in private. Until they crystallize in the final, formal agreement, they remain fluid, tentative, and usually informal. Once reached, the agreement captures attention and diverts interest from the preceding activity that produced it. Those whom it affects start thinking about what it will do to them in the future. All the time and talk and sweat that went into that final result becomes, except perhaps to the participants, as water over the dam: gone and forgotten; unimportant and overshadowed; of only what is called "academic" interest.

Only a little more than a decade ago two students of collective bargaining, Richard Walton and Robert McKersie, put labor negotiations under the microscope of academic scrutiny in a book entitled *A Behavioral Theory of Labor Negotiations*.[1] We cannot open a discussion of negotiations without a brief notice of their work.

The Walton-McKersie Models

In their study of bargaining strategy and tactics, Walton and McKersie adopt the model-building approach currently fashionable in the social sciences. They offer and elaborate upon four models, which they call: *distributive, integrative, attitudinal-structuring*, and *intra-institutional*.

Distributive bargaining, they say, is a zero-sum game; what one side gains the other loses; and concerns mainly (they seem to imply) the pay package. Integrative bargaining, on the other hand, gives both sides a chance to gain. These are their two direct bargaining models; the other two bear indirectly on the preparations for negotiations, and its outcome.

It is easy enough to visualize distributive bargaining as the familiar pie chart, where the amount to be bargained for is fixed and the size of one slice cannot be increased without decreasing the size of another. This puts it much too crudely, for the authors show that they are well aware that most wage bargaining is more complex than simply cutting up a pie. Again, one might think that an example of integrative bargaining would be bargaining over something like a seniority plan, which benefits both labor and management. Workers gain some measure of protection against layoffs, manage-

---

[1] Richard E. Walton and Robert B. McKersie, *A Behavioral Theory of Labor Negotiations* (New York: McGraw-Hill Book Co., Inc., 1965).

ment gets a stable work force. Walton and McKersie might accept this example, but it does not fully represent what they mean. They hold, for instance, that the *same* issue could be distributive if presented as a *demand*, integrative if presented as a *problem to be jointly solved*. This would make the distinction between distributive and integrative bargaining one of manner rather than matter. It becomes evident as one reads their book that Walton and McKersie are more concerned with the gamesmanship of bargaining than with the substance, or the substantive rules that result from the bargaining. They do indeed put the behavior of the negotiators under the microscope; their book is a real tour de force. Without ignoring—and certainly without disparaging—their insight and achievement, we shall try first to get an overview and grasp of the whole field of action, as it appears to the life-size participants.

Negotiations as Labor-Management "Diplomacy"

When managers and union representatives face each other across the bargaining table they approach the agreement they both want with separate and often conflicting objectives. Like diplomats, they generally behave courteously toward each other—at least at the start. They appeal to reason. They marshall facts and arguments (sometimes interspersed with emotional pleas) to promote their points of view. But each side brings to the encounter more than just a winning smile and a persuasive manner: they bring *power* to bear on the outcome. Behind the logic, the ritual, and the amenities, both sides are aware that the other has power, some of it evident and easy to calculate, some hidden and hard to estimate. Each tries to gauge the other's relative strength, and willingness to use it. The ultimate test of strength—or in this context, of the use of power—is the union's ability to strike, the company's ability to take a strike.

As was pointed out in Chapter 1, in the discussion of the power relations context, neither the union nor management needs to make power the only element in their calculations. They normally have much more in common than an outsider would expect. Both stand to gain something, not lose everything, from the rules they establish for the work place. They have always, inevitably, been interdependent, but the power latent in the work force side of their interdependency emerges only when the workers unionize and acquire the capability of taking concerted action. Bargaining power is basically standoff power; it is there in the background, looming over negotiations; but in the foreground, the actors engage in negotiations. They talk. They reason, and try to persuade.

The law requires employers to recognize and bargain "in good faith" with certified unions, but it does not force them to agree with the union. They are free to yield to the unions' persuasions, but they do not have to be persuaded; providing, always, that they give the unions an opportunity—in good faith—to persuade them.

The union's task is to persuade the employer to accept policies and administrative procedures the union wants. If the union's attempt succeeds, and the two parties reach agreement, then the law requires that, at the request of either party, they must reduce their agreement to writing. Since this requirement became a feature of the law, the universal practice has been to put the agreement in writing.

This written document, signed by the employer and by union representatives, is commonly referred to as a "contract," but as we shall see in Chapter 8, it is less a contract between union and company than an agreed-on code of rules that define the company's work contract with all—and each—of the employees in the bargaining unit. It specifies the conditions under which the employer offers work to the employees and it binds the company to abide by those conditions. It becomes, in effect, company policy and a pledge of company performance in all matters that it touches. If, for example, you were an assembly worker in a factory—or a toolmaker, or the operator of a fork-lift truck—you could find in the provisions of the labor agreement your appropriate range of pay, your seniority rights in relation to co-workers, your claim to paid vacation time or to various benefits, your right to present grievances and the procedure to go through; and so on. Just such items, and many more, become the issues to be settled in negotiations.

Labor and management work out the vast majority of collective bargaining agreements by what might be called peaceful "diplomacy" with no resort to force, or the overt use of power. Occasionally, agreement can be reached only by resort to force: a strike, or more rarely, a lockout. To paraphrase Clausewitz on war, strikes are the pursuit of the objectives of negotiations *by other means*. A strike is analogous to labor-management "war." During a strike the face-to-face negotiations may temporarily break off, but a strike cannot be settled without negotiations. Although the threat of strike almost inevitably hovers over negotiations, it would be well to consider negotiations first, and then the strike.

Under the heading of negotiations one should first meet the actors, or the people who do the bargaining, then the preparations they make, then the actual conduct of negotiations. After that, the always possible strike, and strike settlement.

The People Who Do the Bargaining

Preceding chapters have explored the various combinations of separate, and usually opposing, interests present in negotiations. But negotiating is an activity, carried out by people who meet at a definite point in time and space. These people stand in definite organizational relationships to the interests they represent, and perform definite functions. They come from the ranks of unions, enterprises, and, sometimes, from the government.

The Union Negotiating Committee.   There is no set rule about who is to negotiate with the company for the union.

It may be the committee that drew up the demands and saw them through to ratification. It may be a standing committee, such as the union's executive board, or, at the other extreme, a committee elected specially, and at large from the whole membership, expressly for the occasion. It almost always includes, in any case, certain ex officio members such as the president, one or more vice presidents, the secretary, the chief steward. If the local has a business agent, he or she will certainly accompany the negotiators.

Also accompanying the negotiators in most cases will be someone who is not a member of the local union: the international representative.

The International Representative. On the union side in negotiations sits an "outsider," the international representative. Of all the participants, often this is the only one who does not make a living by working for the company. The international representative does not work for the local union either, as a paid officer or business agent does, but only in its behalf and is answerable to the executive board of the international union.

Status of the International Representative. The representative is there in negotiations by request of the local union, to guide and counsel; usually, in fact, to act as spokesperson, strategist, and tactician for the union side. The company cannot keep the representative out, despite an outsider status, for the law permits workers to be represented by "agents of their own choosing."

The international representative is a professional negotiator, perhaps the only professional in a group whose business, and respective positions, require that they engage in collective bargaining, but only so rarely, and so incidentally to their other concerns, that in comparison they are amateurs. They meet each other to make these solemn agreements no more often than once a year; she or he engages in like activity, with other groups as well as this, day after day. For everyone else present, the outcome of negotiations will be felt as dollars-and-cents additions to income, or added production costs; the representative loses not a cent nor, for that matter, stands to gain a penny by what transpires, though success will be its own reward.

The representative may have entered the negotiations only when stepping in the door of the conference room, but more likely had been working with the local through all the stages or at least the later stages of preparations. The chances are he or she shared in shaping the demands and putting them in draft-agreement form, and it was through the representative that the research department of the international channeled information to aid in the negotiations.

The Role of International Representatives. These outsiders to the groups that meet for negotiations are, in a sense, the only full-time "insiders" to the collective bargaining process: it is their life and living. They have no authority except the prestige of position, but are the key people in negotiations, the professionals who really make collective bargaining work and keep it going. As will be seen, they are also the key people in strikes. In single-employer bargaining (which accounts for most of industrial union-ism) they have no regular counterpart on the employer side. In most nego-tiations they are the ones who call the signals and set the tone.

During discussions with the companies they give tactical leadership to the union committee. Their role varies with the circumstances and each rep-resentative's talents and personality. Sometimes they spearhead the attack on the company, perhaps with the aim—and frequently with the effect—of making the local's committee of company employees look reasonable and moderate to their employer, so that the company will offer concessions. Or, with a militant committee, they may seem moderate, receptive to "reason-able" offers of concessions, which they imply they will try to "sell" the committee in the recess that they then call.

A representative may be vain and stubborn, or smart or stupid, or sly or sincere—actually; or may only appear so. Often one has to be an actor, play-ing a role. Only after a number of encounters with a given management, getting to know them and be known, can one drop into a consistent natural pattern of behavior with them. The representative will usually then be found a shrewd and sensible person with a good deal of personal integrity, and pride—for it is a professional asset—on being "as good as one's word." Sometimes one becomes almost a mediator between company and union, who soothes ruffled feelings, saves people's faces, and harmlessly grounds dangerous emotional charges that have built up in a labor relations situation. Sometimes one serves the useful function of the scapegoat, who assumes the "sins" of the community—both sides—and carries them away, to leave the local people cleansed and reconciled for the next period of the life they have to live together.

There are negotiations in which not one but two or several outside repre-sentatives participate, either alternately or together. One may deliberately build up tension, concentrating company hostility, so that a colleague, blandly smiling, can walk in and, in the ensuing relief and atmosphere of cordiality, reach the settlement.

The Employer Representatives.   Union agreements set or affect com-pany policy. A line executive responsible for policy—president, vice presi-dent for industrial relations, or at the very least a works manager—sits in directly on this policy-making process, or designates someone with author-ity to act.

Single-Employer Bargaining.   In any single-company negotiations, then, the delegation of authority is a simple matter. The person exercising this authority and speaking for the company is usually a production person and line executive, but with staff advisers such as the personnel director, and perhaps a public relations expert, and a company lawyer. Of all these, the lawyer has least to contribute, in most cases, to the actual progress of negotiations.

In contrast to the union representatives, the negotiators for the employer are usually armed with full authority to conclude an agreement, though in some cases the Board of Directors may have to ratify results. There is a simple reason for this: in the company, authority flows downward; in the union, upward. At the policy-making level where negotiations take place, authority is already concentrated on the company side, while in the union there has to be a specific act of delegation, and the delegation is not complete but only provisional and temporary.

Multiemployer Bargaining. Multiemployer bargaining, as has been noted, is more common in the trades, with craft unions, than in manufacturing. There are some notable exceptions—perhaps enough to constitute another rule, and not just exceptions.

In the garment industries, for instance, employer associations bargain as a group both with the Amalgamated Clothing Workers and with the International Ladies' Garment Workers' Union. These two well-known and well-organized industrial unions are the composite modern form of older separate craft unions. Some of these crafts were once truly skilled—cutters, for instance, who are direct descendants of custom tailors—while others formed satellite unions of the unskilled—"floor boys," for example—and of the semiskilled, as new machines created specialties. This is a situation comparable in some ways to the construction unions where skilled workers and their unskilled satellites form a complex of closely related unions under the Building Trades Council. The garment workers did not stay separate; they fused; and now they act together just as if they were a single union, though they are still enrolled in locals based on craft and occupation, not on workplace.

Garment-industry employers, faced with the problem of dealing with the huge, fused union, followed the lead of other similar employers throughout history and organized. The producing units of their industry are small and many; together in an association they are somewhat like a counterpart of the union with which they deal. Member firms promise to abide by bargains the association makes with the union.

The small size of the enterprises seems to be a factor in bringing employers together, but an equally compelling one seems to be competition; competition in both the product market and the labor market. Labor costs are so high a percentage of total costs that once the bulk of the industry was unionized the organized firms found themselves sharing the union's own interest in fighting cutthroat nonunion competition based on lower wages. In this, again, they are like the building trades. They are also like highway transportation, for the pattern already clear in the garment industries appears to be spreading to the trucking industry which is also an area of small firms and a big union.

The Employer Association Representative. This kind of multiemployer bargaining—of "employer unionization"—has brought forth a type of person who may fairly be called the equivalent of the international representative. That is the labor relations adviser and negotiator on the employer side. One is not universally present in multiemployer bargaining, for many associations speak through respected senior member-firm executives; but the neutral expert is coming to the fore.

This person's title is likely to be executive secretary or labor relations director of the association; duties are analogous to those of an international representative, and so is the function in negotiations. The employer association representative organizes—gets firms to join the association, helps draw up employer counterproposals to union demands, directs or arranges for research to back up the proposals, and negotiates. He or she also inspects the member firms' administration of the agreement, helps take care of grievances and arbitration, and polices the rules of the association. Wherever they are active, they, like the international representative, are the key people.

(This is a field, incidentally, where the college graduate enamored of the labor relations "game" may find it possible to break in. The unions bring their representatives up from the ranks, while even in a medium-sized corporation it is a long way up from management trainee to industrial relations director. But the employer association often has room for a person from the outside who has had experience or training in labor relations work. Being from the outside is, in fact, an advantage. The future may see more professionals, on both sides of collective bargaining, as this trend continues. Even the unions may have to turn to the colleges for representatives as the employers "wise up" and as the union old-timers die off.)

The Government Representative.   As long as labor and management obey the law, the government regards collective bargaining between them as a private matter.

But it is not a matter of indifference to the government, nor to the public which government represents, particularly if a strike seems a prospect. In order, therefore, to assist the bargainers reach constructive results that are satisfactory to both, and compatible with the public interest, the government provides—*on a strictly voluntary basis*—the services of its Mediation and Conciliation Service.

The Mediator in Negotiations.   The interchangeable terms "conciliator" and "mediator"—not to be confused with *arbiter* or *arbitrator*—apply to anyone who seeks to bring labor and management to agreement in a dispute; but the field is passing to the professional. In some disputes a mayor or other public official, or even on occasion a presidentially appointed board, may step in with an offer of good offices. More likely, though, it will be an obscure and not overpaid civil servant, a state or federal employee, who makes a career of mediating and conciliating in labor disputes. The mediator comes at the call of either party, or even on personal initiative, but can do little without the consent of both parties, who must at least agree to talk. This person's job is to help them find a way out of their impasse.

As with negotiation itself, there are no set rules for conciliation and mediation. Much depends on circumstances, and the personalities involved, including the personality of the mediator. Wisest procedure usually seems to be for the mediator to meet with each side separately before attempting to get them both together. In that way he or she hears the uninhibited viewpoint of both sides, and gets a grasp of the problem.

The Mediator's Methods.   The mediator listens. The mediator is neutral, and can sympathize impartially with each disputant in turn while hearing the story of the iniquity and unreasonableness of the other. This makes it possible to size up the people, who are part of the problem, as well as the facts, and it undoubtedly has cathartic and therapeutic value for the complainants, who are often pretty well fed up with each other by the time the mediator arrives. The mediator acts as a lightning rod for charges of mutual hostility between them.

They have more to offer than emotional release, however, for like the "rep" they have had varied experience, and are pros. They can suggest ways out of what appear dead ends to the negotiators, because they have seen these ways work in analogous situations before. They have no emotional "blocks" that blind them, as the participants are sometimes blind to unconsidered possibilities. They talk the language of either side, and both. Mediators can help both sides "save face" when they have gotten into untenable positions.

Frequently it is the mediator who finds the magic formula that will resolve the dispute. If skillful, he or she will bring both sides around, unconsciously, to thinking it was their idea. Successful mediation can avert a strike or settle a strike when one has broken out, for mediation can occur at any stage. If the strike settlement happens to coincide with the formula the mediator suggested to avert strike, the mediator never says "I told you so." As smoke comes out of the factory smokestacks again and workers troop through the gates to start drawing paychecks once more, the person who did much to make it possible packs a battered briefcase and smilingly bids goodbye. A telegram has arrived, probably, calling the mediator on to another situation in which a company and local union are at loggerheads.

Good mediators, like union "reps" come from all kinds of varied backgrounds. Personal qualities count for more than formal qualifications. Some of the best are former union officials. Mediation is a form of government service open to college-trained men or women with a consuming interest, as well as background, in active labor relations work; but it is not for the person whose mind is made up in advance about labor's rights, or management's prerogatives. It is not for the show-off or know-it-all.

Skillful, patient mediation can do a lot toward preventing strikes, or settling strikes amicably once they have broken out.

PREPARATION FOR NEGOTIATIONS

The men and women who carry on labor-management negotiations shoulder a heavy responsibility. Their work sets policy. Its results are bound to affect the welfare, the earnings, the chances for promotion, the security, the job satisfaction of every member of the union, every employee of the company in the bargaining unit (and some outside it) for the next year, or two years, or even three or five. Equally affected are company profits, productivity, and competitive positions, as well as prices and production available to the public.

Negotiating the agreement is the very heart of collective bargaining. Proper discharge of the responsibilities it lays upon the bargainers calls for preparation.

The Union Initiative

Unions prepare more or less carefully for negotiations. Big national negotiations, such as those between the United Auto Workers and General Motors, have repercussions throughout the national economy and are carefully prepared for a year or more in advance, with full attention to public relations as well as to keeping the members informed. Many smaller local unions make little or no preparation other than to draw up demands.

Preparation for negotiations involves: (1) drawing up demands or formulating what the members want; (2) assembling information to support the demands; and (3) publicizing and explaining the demands. This last point usually means merely informing the members, and the workers in the plant, but often requires spreading the information to the public in the community at large.

Drawing up Demands. The union ordinarily initiates negotiations. To the union member the most important thing is what she or he, personally, will get out of the agreement. Sometimes workers have specific wants; at others, only that they want "more" than they have, but do not recognize it in concrete form until the union leaders formulate and explain it to them.

If they have had "nothing"—that is, if they have not worked under a union agreement before—then they want what workers in other shops and unions have already secured: such things as seniority, grievance procedure, a raise in wages, vacations with pay, and the like. If they are already working under a union agreement granting concessions of this sort, they want more of the same.

"New" Demands. Sometimes union demands appear to be new, but almost invariably they turn out, upon examination, to be merely novel forms and extensions of older ideas. The 1955 demand for a "guaranteed annual wage" worked out in practice, in the "S.U.B." plan of Supplementary Unemployment Benefits, as no more than a strengthening of the existing seniority system with increased pay (from private funds, to supplement public funds) for laid-off workers. The aim of the plan was to satisfy the worker's age-old demand for individual job security. Its proponents also hoped that it would promote steadier employment and cushion the impact of automation. The 1958 demand for profit sharing aimed at least in part to increase worker income by a supplement to wages. This is akin to many bonus schemes that preceded it. Ironically enough, the idea of giving work-

ers a share in profits is one that had often been advanced by management as an antidote to unionism!

A new demand once raised and won by a union in one enterprise, or the enterprises of one industry, gets copied by other unions trying to follow the leader—or better. Thus after the auto workers pioneered the S.U.B. plan the steelworkers took it up and secured even greater concessions based on the same idea. In neither case was the actual program a spontaneous creation that welled up, fully formed, out of the minds of the workers in the shops. In both cases, sophisticated professional labor leaders formulated proposals that appealed to the members' formless and inarticulate yearnings: the human desire to be secure in what one has, and to have a little more.

Spread of a Pattern.   The leaders exercise their foresight and inventiveness to devise plans and formulate demands that the members will recognize as corresponding to their needs. Political, and even personal, interunion rivalries spread first worker, and then company, acceptance of those demands that do successfully evoke worker response and support. The most recently organized local union therefore tends to adopt for its program of demands the schedule of gains registered, step by step, by others organized before it, just as a newly built factory gets the benefit of the latest technological progress.

There is no doubt that some union programs (S.U.B., for example) exert a far-reaching influence on the economy that may affect society in permanent and important ways, for good or ill. The worker and rank-and-file union member who thinks about this at all tends to minimize the question. This is only human, and on the order of the well-known fact that a flood in China drowning a whole province is a disaster that does not hit home quite as hard as a leaky pipe that floods one's own basement. In asking for a raise, the worker undoubtedly likes to believe that it is not sending the national economy into an inflationary spiral—and union leaders gladly oblige with the necessary assurance—but the question of whether the worker will get a raise in the next pay envelope is of more immediate interest to the worker, who tends to ignore the possible economic and social effects of an accumulation of separate union demands shaped to the same plan, paying attention chiefly to the special effects that flow from the local's direct action.

Restraints on the Demands.   Perhaps, in the back of the workers' mind, they look to the company to keep the situation from getting out of hand, just as they rely on the company to secure orders, maintain production, and pay wages. The workers regard the pressing of demands as a test of strength, and a necessary one, for it does not seem likely that they will get what they do not ask for, whereas they feel sure that the company will not give them more than it can truly afford. They are embarked, they feel, with management, on an enterprise making its way upon the vast and sometimes stormy economic sea. They do not want their own ship to sink under them or strike a rock, but they are convinced that those on the bridge want that no more than they do, and that management will not let it happen. They know there are profits to be made from the voyage and clamor for what they consider a just return for work, and a good living. And so they draw up demands, or adapt the demands others like them have drawn up, and present them; and, if need be, strike for them.

Some small companies and their unions, and some "sick" industries, have been forced to take a more careful look, and act more cooperatively toward union demands that would raise costs beyond the danger point. Higher wages and other concessions to the union in some situations could depress business and result in unemployment. Wage cuts, instead of wage raises, might even be in order.

Some Problems. This question has many ramifications. Should a union subsidize inefficiency in a small or backward company by permitting low wages and substandard conditions? Or should it force the small-scale, low-pay producer out of business to make way for more progressive enterprises? Can the union help the company increase efficiency by boosting worker productivity? Should the union fight against technological improvements that would throw members out of work?

A consideration of these questions, and others equally pertinent, would lead away from the problem of *drawing up* demands into the *content* of the demands. Such questions might, in a given case, condition the nature of the demands, but the union negotiator is more likely to have to deal with them as they come up during the course of negotiations.

Assembling Information. A strike threat frequently hangs over negotiations from the start. When this is so, the negotiations are a test of strength, and the end result may register not so much the merits of the case on either side as the relative strength of the parties.

But the parties carry on negotiations by discussion: they talk, they use arguments, they reason and try to convince. In spite of, as well as because of, the strike threat that lurks in the background, in the foreground people sit around a table and try to persuade each other.

They do persuade each other in many things. It is their function to reach an accommodation and reduce it to writing. Even when the general terms of their bargain reflect relative underlying strength rather than abstract objective judgment, these terms must at least be rationalized in wording acceptable to both sides. In order to reach common ground as well as to define their differences, the union and the company negotiators must exchange views and come to a meeting of the minds. Each side must show the logic of its position.

Both sides, therefore, build up information to support their arguments. The union negotiators want, basically, two kinds of information: (*a*) what might be called, by analogy with the military, "intelligence" that will help them gauge the company's strength and intentions, and (*b*) facts to back up arguments in favor of the union's specific demands. Under this heading would also come, of course, facts for rebuttal of possible company arguments.

"Intelligence." The union negotiators stand at a disadvantage unless they can find out something about matters on which the company already has a good deal of information: the state of the industry and the firm's position in the industry, competition, profits and sales, orders and prospects: in a word, economic and financial data. Some of these factors will indicate the company's ability to pay, others may give an inkling of the company's ability to withstand a strike, or willingness to make concessions. Such data remain confidential with the company, unless the company refuses union demands solely on the grounds of inability to pay. In such cases, the NLRB has ruled the company must open its books and show the union proof of its contention.

The international's research department provides most of the general economic information and financial data on the company. Experts and specialists employed by the international assemble and evaluate the information and make it available to the negotiators as part of the service provided local unions by the international. Local information along the same lines and word of specific innercompany developments may "leak" to the union from friendly office workers or sources in the community. The reports of shop stewards keep the negotiators abreast on actions taken by management in the various departments. These and other scraps of isolated information, fitted together and evaluated, may give clues to the company's intentions.

Ordinarily the company may be expected to know more about economic and financial prospects than union intelligence can unearth and correctly put together, but unions have steadily gotten better at the game. Through its international, a local draws on the services of economists, lawyers, and accountants no less expert in their fields than the company's own specialists.

Facts for Argument. Here again economic and financial data have a bearing, particularly when the costs of specific concessions are at issue, but a great deal of information comes from the shop itself. Experiences gained under the past agreement suggests changes in some of the provisions. The grievance records or other data drawn from practice provide facts for argument. The steward apparatus probably constitutes the main source of information in this category.

On the company side the assembling of information for negotiations shows the same twofold nature: the need to try to gauge the union's strength and determination; and the need for facts and figures to counter union arguments and support the company's position. Sources of information for the company are analogous: employer associations, which correspond to the union international, and the company's own supervisory apparatus and personnel department.

Publicizing and Explaining the Demands. Both sides have a public to which they appeal for understanding and support, and the most important segment of that public is the working force of the enterprise.

The union keeps its members informed by means of meetings, printed or mimeographed bulletins of various kinds distributed at the plant gate or circulated by union stewards, and, on occasion, mass media such as radio or television. The union also—and most importantly—"talks up" its information through its steward system and circulates it by word of mouth. The department stewards are in daily personal contact with the entire body of employees. They are elected representatives who have the confidence of their constituents. The workers turn to them for facts, advice, and direction as the negotiations proceed.

The wider public which consists of the community does not usually hear much about specific demands under negotiation unless there is a strike. Then both sides take to the newspapers with their versions of the issue and wage a propaganda battle to win, or at least neutralize, public sentiment.

THE EMPLOYER DEFENSE AND COUNTERINITIATIVE

It still seems to be the practice of some employers to wait until the union has presented its demands before getting ready for negotiations. This is a purely defensive strategy. There is some justification for it in that decisions go by default to the employer unless the union requests a part in making them, and that most changes that could be made represent concessions by the employer to the union. Why give the union, as it were, things the union does not first ask for? Why not just sit back, see what they want, and say "No"?

Active Preparation for Negotiations. Nonetheless more and more employers are finding it wise to prepare more carefully and to anticipate union demands or deflect them with proposals of their own. Some of these counterproposals may actually be things the union has not asked for! Employer preparation for negotiations gives management an active, instead of a passive, function.

The farsighted employer or employer association calculates in advance the cost and relative desirability of various alternatives and meets the union with concrete proposals rather than a monotonous, "No, no, no" followed, perhaps, by a reluctant "Yes" to an arrangement shaped entirely by union initiative. The General Electric Company has been a leader of this trend. It has come to be known as Boulewareism, after a former G.E. vice president who initiated it.[2]

This does not mean that the employer gives up the defensive position,

---

[2] On Oct. 28, 1969, the U.S. Circuit Court of Appeals in New York, acting in a legal process started in 1960, ruled that General Electric's "unbending patriarchal posture" violated the National Labor Relations Act. The company appealed the ruling to the U.S. Supreme Court, but lost.

The Circuit Court's decision came one day after the IUE and 12 other unions struck in General Electric plants all over the country. In 1966 the company had refused to engage in coordinated bargaining with the IUE and seven other unions. This form of bargaining—one large firm with a number of different unions acting jointly, or as a coalition—was held to be proper in an NLRB decision of Oct. 24, 1968, when the Board upheld a trial examiner's decision that GE had acted illegally in refusing to bargain.

which is a strong one despite some disadvantages. It means that the company plans its defense and supplements it with counteroffensive strategy that does not leave all the issues, or points of attack, entirely to the union.

The Area to Be Defended.   The area of company policy where employees usually desire changes are those defining the employees' individual work-contracts with the company. The standard phrase used to designate this area is "wages, hours, working conditions, and other conditions of employment." It does not normally include, for instance, company sales policy; it does include such policies as layoff order, and practices that have to do with conveyor speeds or the way time studies are taken.

The union's aim is to influence the terms of the individual work-contract the company has with each of its employees. In effect, what the union seeks is to get the employer to *promise* that certain agreed-on conditions affecting wages, hours, working conditions, and other conditions of employment, will become part of this work contract. When the union signs its eventual agreement with the company, that does not make the union itself a party to the individual employee's work contract. The individual still holds that with the company, and holds it directly, delivering work in exchange for wages at certain conditions. The amount of the wages and the nature of the conditions become those the company has promised the union it will pay and perform.

PRESENTING THE DEMANDS

The union starts by drawing up its draft demands and presenting them to the company.

The nature of this process varies between craft and industrial unions, and the demands themselves differ. What follows will describe the process in the typical industrial union situation of the single-union single-employer pattern.

Procedure in the Local Union

At a meeting of the local industrial union the members charge a committee, or a group of officers, with the task of drafting proposals for negotiation. In due course this group reports back to the membership with the draft demands they have drawn up. These demands are in the form of a proposed agreement that sets forth the terms the union wants the company to offer and incorporate in the individual work-contracts with each of its employees in the bargaining unit and to adopt as policy in its dealings with all of them. Influences that shape the content of these draft demands have been discussed earlier in this chapter.

The members of the local discuss the recommendations. They suggest additions, deletions, alterations, and improvements in the terms and wording. Following parliamentary procedure, they go over the document paragraph by paragraph and vote, first on its separate provisions, then on the document as a whole. When they are finished with this procedure they have ratified the demands. Once ratified, the draft agreement becomes the official union program of proposals for the forthcoming negotiations with the company, and the union's instructions to its negotiating committee.

In the case of a new union and an initial agreement, the draft demands usually take for their pattern a standard form recommended by the international union, or copy the model of some similar agreement known to the local union. The committee fills in specific items, such as wage rates or seniority rules, to make it applicable to local conditions.

In the case of an established union already working under an agreement, the deliberations center on proposed changes and improvements. Perhaps the history of grievance adjustment over the past year points out loopholes that need to be plugged, or too-rigid wording that needs to be relaxed to give the union some leeway. Experience may suggest the addition of new clauses, the deletion of inoperative or undesirable ones. Words may be weighed, punctuation revised. Generally, the agreement grows at least a little every year. Clauses that have stood the test of time remain; new ones, to cover previously unforeseen contingencies, are added. Eventually, the draft demands are ratified and ready for negotiation. The union sends or presents them to the company as a basis for discussion.

THE ACT OF NEGOTIATION

The union presents its demands and asks for a meeting. The employer, ready or not with counterproposals, designates the company's representative and agrees on a date. The two sides meet and start negotiating. They continue to meet until they have achieved some result.

The Context of Negotiations

The union may be newly organized, seeking its first agreement. Negotiations then are new, exceptional to the experience of both management and labor, surrounded with hopes, fears, and uncertainty. They may be charged with tension; there will certainly be a feeling of strangeness. Or, they may be routine renewal talks in an established and stable collective bargaining relationship; expected, understood, and taken very calmly. In any case the workers in the plant or bargaining unit follow them closely, and even the general public may take an interest.

If a strike is in prospect—and this threat lurks somewhere in the background in any negotiations—then union members, other employees of the company, their families, their creditors, and the community in which they live wait anxiously for the outcome. Stockholders of the company may, and the board of directors certainly will, be on the alert. The negotiators on both sides are bound to feel the pressure and to realize that what they do will have repercussions. Much is at stake for many, at the bargaining table.

Because of this interest from the outside, the negotiations sometimes attract a good deal of publicity. The sessions themselves almost invariably take place behind closed doors, but the union delegates have to report back to their members, and a union meeting—even a closed one—is no place to tell a secret. Reporters may try to question the participants on either side as they leave the bargaining sessions, or later, and this brings the temptation for the parties to carry their case to the newspapers.

So long as no confidence is violated, the propriety or the wisdom of such a course is a matter of judgment, but it has its dangers. There is, for instance, the danger of being misquoted, or the opposite one of being caught off guard and quoted all too accurately in a rash statement. There is the danger of taking a stand publicly from which it may be necessary later to retreat—publicly. But there are also occasions when a word to the press can become an effective tactical weapon in the bargaining. It all depends. The real negotiating still has to be done in the conference room.

THE CONDUCT OF NEGOTIATIONS

Negotiating is so personal an art, and its practice so dependent upon the mixture of personalities present, as well as the circumstances and issues, that little of a general nature can be said that would be valid in all cases. A few remarks may still be hazarded.

Privacy of the Negotiations

The presence of outsiders seems to inhibit fruitful negotiation, and so does the making of a written or taped record. Real human conflict takes place at the bargaining table, with moments of high suspense and drama. This is part of the process. When an audience is present, participants tend to speak for the effect they hope to make on the audience; that is, instead of making progress with each other, they spout propaganda. Sessions degenerate into ham acting, posing, clowning, or name-calling. Something of the same sort happens when there is a stenographer taking down what people say, or it is known that the proceedings are going on a sound track that may be played back someday. Under such circumstances, only a trial lawyer would feel at ease. Speeches "for the record" take the place of honest bargaining. Spontaneity, and the flexibility of give-and-take disappear; the people "freeze" and act unnaturally.

Informality and an atmosphere of freedom, on the other hand, seem to produce the best effect. People are then not afraid to express themselves; and more important, lest they be made to appear later as ridiculous, or wrong, to reverse themselves if necessary. It is much easier to eat one's words when they have been uttered in private, in the presence of opponents who may also have to eat a few ill-chosen words of their own.

Negotiation Strategies

As for negotiating strategy—that is, the narrow strategy of how to present or defend a case—that depends greatly on the counterstrategy it has to meet, but there are two typical approaches.

The Piecemeal Approach.   The first is the piecemeal, or step-by-step approach. This tries to settle the issues one by one in some order such as "easiest" first, or from the beginning to the end of the draft demands. It is the approach that comes naturally to the practical-minded worker, who knows that you do a job by finishing the first task before going on to the second, and so on to completion. Each item arises as a separate issue, is argued out, disposed of, and tucked away, while attention turns to the next.

The Total Approach.   The second is the "total" approach, or just the reverse of the piecemeal. This regards nothing as settled until everything is settled. Bargaining "points" are offered and discussed, then laid aside as others are brought forward; every question remains open until suddenly the whole complex is ready to crystallize into a total agreement. This is frequently the company approach. Legal fiction supports this concept of bargaining, for no part of an agreement is valid until the whole has been signed. Management people generally are accustomed to thinking in terms of a complex of interrelated factors, interdependent variables, no one of which can be fixed until its effects on all the others have been calculated.

Combining Strategies.   It can readily be seen that there must usually be something of both approaches in any given strategy. The company is understandably reluctant to tie itself down irrevocably on Point A until it sees how great a concession it has to make on Point X. The employees are prone to view with distrust a juggling of issues, as if they are colored balls flying through the air all at once and never coming to rest.

Here is where the easy-to-hard sequence often provides a middle way. The union gets the company fairly well tied down on minor matters, one by one, until there are only a few big issues "up in the air." This provides opportunity for serious efforts at compromise. Offers combining elements of the unsettled issues in different proportions are tried out, considered, rejected, reshuffled, and reworked until finally the mix is right. When that occurs, negotiations are almost over, and successful.

The final formula may be the result of some pretty tall horse trading at the end. Anticipating this, the union's demands and the company's counterproposals usually contain from the start a certain number of built-in bargaining points that are intended to be thrown away, or swapped for something else, at the last moment. Part of the problem for each side is to feel out the other to find out which "vital" demands have been put in just for trading purposes and which are really vital—so much so that they may take a strike to settle. Often these bargaining points are obvious "phonies," but there is enough difference between the outlook and mentality of both sides to lead to occasional serious miscalculations.

Personality in Negotiations

Negotiations are a contest, and like any contest put a strain on the participants. "The union" and "the company" are abstractions, but their representatives at the bargaining table are human beings. Human beings differ in knowledge, skill, attitudes, systems of values, temperament, endurance. It would be hard to overestimate the influence of individual personalities on negotiations.

Different people get their results in different ways. What are the personal characteristics of a good negotiator?

Patience, intelligence, stamina, a level head, an open mind, and integrity; these would seem to be minimal qualities for a good negotiator; and one must be able to express oneself well and convincingly. A sense of humor always helps.

Not all people have these qualities, and even those who have are subject, under strain, to emotional influences. Bargaining sessions coop negotiators up together and pit them against each other. Tempers wear thin. "Bargaining fatigue" resembles the combat hazard of battle fatigue.

Broadly speaking, here is where the international rep (or in multiemployer bargaining, as pointed out, a management counterpart, the employer association secretary) is at an advantage, like a professional athlete among amateurs. The outcome of the contest is never as deadly personal to these as to the others. It is all part of the day's work, and the stage of frustration and exhaustion may be the very moment one has been waiting for. Gone now is the time when to keep things moving one would crack a joke. Now the negotiations are not moving; they have stalled and show no immediate prospect of getting further. Ugly remarks have passed across the table. Nerves are raw.

At such a moment—always depending on the personalities involved—the rep may rub the raw nerves of an overstrained company official to the point of provoking anger. In anger many people lose their heads. Or, again depending on personalities, this may be the time when anger drives both sides to greater stubbornness, or exasperation threatens to undo all that has been accomplished. The rep calls a retreat—a recess or adjournment for a day or two—and takes his people outside to cool off and recuperate.

A CLIMAX IN NEGOTIATIONS

With or without conciliation and mediation, the negotiations have to run a course. Perhaps the parties come to an agreement. They put it down in writing, piecing the text together, perhaps, from parts of the original union draft, the company counterproposals, and notes made during the course of the argument. They initial it, or even sign it.

But sometimes they fail to agree, by contract expiration date or by some other deadline. What then?

Then there may be a strike.

Negotiations now break off, to be resumed under the new conditions and added pressure of strike action. Aside from this added pressure, there is no basic change in the process of negotiation, though the results reflect not just the reason and logic of the parties but the fortunes of the strike. Interest shifts, therefore, to what is going on *outside* the conference room, in the streets, at the plant gate.

THE DECISION TO STRIKE

Although the actual calling of a strike is the union's move, strikes result from decisions made independently by the employer, the union, and the workers involved in negotiations.[3] Management could always avoid a strike by giving in to the demands of the union and unions could avoid strikes by capitulating to management. In the end, it is the workers who must hit the bricks so their decision is also of great importance. Although some strikes are emotional outbursts, it seems likely that most strikes are the result of at least partially rational decisions made under conditions of uncertainty.

The Management Decision to "Take a Strike"

In negotiations, management seeks "reasonable" labor costs and the flexibility needed to run the enterprise in an efficient manner. If the union's demands represent what management considers to be reasonable labor costs and adequate freedom for unilateral management decisions, management signs up and there is no strike. But union demands are not drawn up for the purpose of being reasonable in management's eyes and they very seldom turn out that way. Methods of determining the costs of a union agreement will be discussed in Chapters 8 through 13.

Typically, then, management is confronted with the difficult choice between accepting "excessive" union demands or incurring the costs of a strike. While the cost of a strike to management depends entirely on the circumstances of the individual enterprise; nevertheless, most strikes at least threaten the loss of anticipated profits during the strike, continuing fixed costs of operation, shutdown and reopening costs, and permanent loss of customers. These costs can—to some degree—be minimized by building inventories in anticipation of a strike, continued operations during the strike, and profit pooling arrangements between employers when only some of them are struck. In turn, each of these methods of minimizing strike costs involves some additional costs of its own. These include interest and storage costs when building inventories, the costs of obtaining and maintaining replacements for strikers if operations are continued during the strike, and the "premium" on strike insurance or profit pooling arrangements.

---

[3] The authors are indebted to Prof. Thomas W. Gavett of West Virginia University for suggesting much of the material in this section.

The costs of taking a strike also depends on the *duration* of the strike. A stoppage of one week's duration might only be an inconvenience, while a 30-day stoppage might be catastrophic for the enterprise. Once started, neither management nor the union nor the workers can say for sure when the strike will end. To complicate matters further, the union may up the price of an agreement if it has been necessary to strike.

The Union's Decision to Strike

The leadership of the union is usually confronted with an unhappy choice similar to that confronting management: They can accept an agreement not wholly satisfactory to the membership (and a vociferous dissatisfied group is almost always present); or they can face the potentially high costs of a strike.

When a union strikes it risks some very heavy costs. The union's greatest risk is that the employer will replace the strikers or go out of business. If the strikers are replaced, the union is dead. Even if the employer makes no attempt to replace the strikers, a strike involves costs for the union in terms of strike benefits, administrative costs, and the possible dissatisfaction of its members if the strike lasts too long or isn't "won big."

The Worker's Decision to Support the Strike

Workers expect the collective bargaining process to provide high wages and an opportunity to participate in the decision making of the firm. They are mightily unimpressed by competitive conditions which may depress wages or any need for flexibility which interferes with the "right" to a job. Although accommodations are imperative, the worker's goal in collective bargaining appears directly contrary to the manager's objectives.

The worker's choice is probably the most difficult decision to be made by any of the decision makers. The decision to strike puts the worker's livelihood on the line, and few things are less willingly undertaken than personal hardship. All the decision makers in negotiations must rely on incomplete information, but the individual worker does not have even the full knowledge of what transpired in negotiations to base a decision on. At very best, that decision must be based on secondhand interpretations of the company's stand and the union's goals and resources. Part of the worker's choice comes when the strike actually begins.

The Strike Vote

At some time during negotiations, and very commonly at the outset, a union is likely to strengthen the hand of its negotiators by taking a strike vote. In many cases this is almost a ritual. Unless it sets a specific date and time, the strike vote taken early in the negotiations is almost always a maneuver: a mere threat, a psychological weapon, a "cold-war tactic." The threat may even be pure bluff.

Any bluff raises the danger of being called, but the strike threat, when it is a bluff, happens to be a fairly safe one just as long as it does not turn into action, because the company has no effective counterbluff. The threat of lockout, potent enough in the craft situation, does not usually fit the factory. All the company can do in the face of a strike threat is to tell the union, in effect, that if the threat turns into action, the company is ready to withstand the strike.

Purpose of the Strike Vote.   Taking a strike vote therefore does not inevitably mean that there will be a strike. It conjures up, in visible and dramatic form, the specter that hovers in the background anyway, and pointedly reminds the company (and incidentally, the union) of what may come if negotiations fail. It puts a sense of urgency into the effort to reach agreement.

It is doubtful whether agreements embodying many concessions would ever be reached if the strike threat did not hang over negotiations.

The strike threat does not need to be explicit. The coal miners, for instance, have a slogan that expresses a tradition of their union: "no contract, no work." Neither the mineowner nor union representative in negotiations ever need doubt that there will be a strike if they do not succeed in coming to agreement before the expiration of the current contract.

Other industrial unions have not developed such a binding tradition. With some notable exceptions, they bargain not on an industry-wide basis as the miners do, but enterprise by enterprise. The history and experience of a given local union and the labor relations policy and record of the company with which it deals have much to do with the union's militancy, its willingness to strike. The current level of activity in the enterprise, or highly local and temporary conditions, may affect a union's readiness, its ability to strike.

Effect of the Vote on Union Members.   The threat expressed in a strike vote does not bear solely against the company; it has its psychological effect on the minds of the union members, too. It reminds them of the price they may have to pay to get their demands and sometimes helps keep the demands within reason. A leadership doubtful of membership support in rough going may call for a strike vote early, when conflict seems far away and unlikely, in order to condition the members' minds to the idea, in case it later becomes necessary to mobilize them for strike action.

"Insurance" for the Committee.   Again, an early strike vote is a form of insurance for the committee. It puts responsibility back where the authority remains: in the members' hands. Most workers shrink from the perils and inconvenience a strike involves, unless pushed to it, or desperate. Once they have gone on record by a vote, the committee can take the position of urging acceptance of compromises from the original demands, as they develop in negotiations. This is frequently a sounder and more comfortable position

than that of having to try to cajole a reluctant membership to strike in support of the committee.

A Form of Referendum. Besides the initial strike vote, others may be taken at crucial points during the negotiations, according to (but sometimes against) the recommendations of the negotiators. They constitute a sort of referendum of member sentiment, registering the reaction of the workers to the course of negotiations. It can readily be seen that this can have a strong effect upon the negotiations themselves. A committee armed with a fresh and overwhelming vote of confidence returns to the bargaining table for the next session with new strength. There is nothing quite like it on the management side.

Because of the strength that comes from the unique, one-sided value of the strike threat (up to the point where it turns into strike action) union leaders set great store by the strike vote. It would not be to their advantage as negotiators to face the company with poor membership support, so they are careful not to take a strike vote that does not pass. When, on the other hand, they can feel fairly sure of an enthusiastic endorsement by an overwhelming vote, they have nothing to lose and everything to gain by staging a demonstration.

Effect of the Vote on Negotiations. A strike vote strengthens the union negotiators' hand as long as they are careful not to turn the threat into an ultimatum by setting a date when it will certainly turn into a strike. Much of the psychological value of a threat lies in its uncertainty. Once the term is set, the strike-threat pressure ceases to be directed solely against the company, but bears on the union committee too. Then they are under equal compulsion to come to agreement by the time stated—or else! Setting the term too early may unnecessarily harden the company's position so that it gives up nothing, short of actual "war." The strike threat requires flexibility in use and is ordinarily so phrased as to be an authorization to issue a strike call, not itself a call.

Timing. Choosing the time to strike (if strike should come) is a question of high strategic value to the union. Unless negotiations are for an initial agreement, the union of course does not have unrestricted freedom in this choice. The expiration date of the existing agreement is a sort of deadline, but even so the union has some flexibility of action. The old agreement can be extended, by mutual consent, for additional stated periods, or on an indefinite basis. In some cases the union can let the contract expire without an agreement to extend it, and thereby restore the conditions of an initial agreement. This, of course, involves risks for a union, which must go on a "war alert" footing, ready to strike; but the tension puts the company under pressure as well.

Retroactivity. In the past many companies and unions went on bargaining after the expiration date with the understanding that any agreements reached eventually would be retroactive. In more recent years company resistance to this practice has hardened. It relieved the union of all sense of urgency but left the company under pressure—increasing pressure! The trend, therefore, has been toward making the expiration date of the contract the probable date of a strike, *if* there is to be a strike. The strike threat, in negotiations, consists mainly of that "if."

Craft and industrial unions use similar methods in their negotiations with employers, but they seek different kinds of collective bargaining agreements and they strike in different ways to persuade employers to grant these concessions.

UNIONS ON STRIKE

In the conduct of their strikes, craft and industrial unions strike for different aims, follow different strategies, and employ different tactics.

Craft-Union Strikes

The craft union's aim is to get a favorable price for skilled labor and to maintain an acceptable economic supply-demand relation between job openings for workers in the craft and craftsmen seeking jobs. Thus carpenters will strike for a raise in hourly wages or against a cut. They will also strike against the employment of nonunion workers to do carpenters' jobs, usually on the ground that these nonunion workers are not qualified to do the work. This includes the jurisdictional strike in which some other skilled-worker union claims the right to do work which the carpenters consider "belongs" to them. An example might be the job of installing prefabricated windows. The glaziers claim them because they have glass panels; but so do the carpenters, because the frames are made of wood. In this case a decision either way expands the total demand for one kind of skilled labor and diminishes the demand for another kind. While jurisdictional strikes have fortunately become one of the less common kinds of strike, their incidence most clearly demonstrates the economic orientation of craft-union collective bargaining aims.

Strategy and Tactics.   Strategy in craft-union strikes springs from this supply-demand relation. It aims simply to withdraw a scarce element of production, skill, from the labor market and withhold it until the price is right. It has been pointed out before that craft unions flourish only where handicraft methods still prevail so that the product is directly turned out—as in the building trades—by a skilled craftsman. This craftsman is a person who has passed through an apprenticeship and taken several years to master a trade. An employer cannot replace qualified craftsmen with any Tom, Dick, or Harry. In the short run these craftsmen are irreplaceable. The more completely and the longer they withhold their skilled labor, the stronger grows the demand for it, until an offer of hourly wages is made that seems acceptable as the price of the labor to be supplied.

Tactics under this strategy can be quite simple. Basically, what the union members do is wait. If the strike is against a single employer, or a few out of many, and the others are complying with union terms, the business agent of the local finds jobs for the striking workers with these other firms. If there are not enough jobs to go around, the union pays individual cash benefits out of its strike fund to the members who are unemployed because of the strike. That is what the fund was built up for—to help the members wait it out.

Employer Answer.   Employers are not always willing to let the union pick them off one by one, as just described, but may answer the union's strike against one member firm of an association with a lockout by all the firms. That sharpens the struggle, but does not change the underlying basis of the union's fight. The waiting puts a heavier strain on the strike fund, but also puts a strain on all the member firms. Sooner or later the two sides resume negotiations and find a formula acceptable to both.

Picketing in craft-union strikes is token in nature and may even be done not by union members but by hired "sandwich" picketers. It is to advertise the fact that a given employer's union workers are on strike, so that a stranger recruited in another town will not make the mistake of accepting employment on a struck job. Such a mistake could be very costly to a craftsman; it could cost the worker's union card and any future opportunity to make a livelihood at that trade. And only an out-of-towner would be ignorant of the strike, for the craft-union local organizes all the craftsmen of a given skill in one community.

Instances where violence has flared on craft-union picket lines, are, like jurisdictional strikes today, both rare and illuminating. In most such cases it will be found that the fight is between local people and members of the same craft international from another locality. This underlines the fact that a strike of skilled workers can be broken only if other skilled workers of the same craft cross the picket line. This, of course, seldom happens. On the contrary, craft-union solidarity is generally so strong that members of one craft will not even cross the picket line of another craft. It takes no violence to restrain them; respect for picket lines is almost a "religion" to the craft unionist. The union member gives it to others when they are on strike, expects it (and gets it) in return when out. It can be said of craft unions: They win their strikes who only stand and wait.

Industrial-Union Strikes

Very different is the situation in the industrial-union strike. To stand and wait would be the surest way of losing a strike. The industrial union goes on strike for economic aims, but gets and holds them by methods that can only be called, for want of a better term, *political*, in the sense of power politics.

The Strike Objective.   The immediate strike objective of the industrial union in manufacturing is to control physical access to the workplace. This denies the employer the use of a productive plant until it is ransomed by making a satisfactory settlement. The industrial union in transportation aims to bring the employer's rolling stock to a standstill. Industrial unions in other fields have to select their strike objectives in the light of their particular circumstances, which vary. The underlying strategy in all of them is to prevent the replacement of individual strikers of many varieties and degrees of semiskill, by other individuals who can be taught the strikers' jobs.

Organization for Strike. The exact date and time of the strike may be set by vote of the members, or authorized by vote and set by call of the union officers or committee. Between internationals, and even locals of the same international, practices differ. The range is from a requirement in either the local or international constitution calling for a secret ballot of all the members, with a two-thirds or three-fourths majority in favor of strike necessary to carry, down to a simple majority of members present and voting at a meeting. The practice is likely to lie somewhere between these extremes, probably nearer the latter, or less rigorous, requirement.

In a factory union, mere prudence on the part of union leaders would indicate the desirability of taking a vote before calling a strike. The members are the union's army in the strike, as well as the union's citizenry. In a democracy, it takes a vote of the citizenry as represented in parliament—the local meeting—to mobilize the army. The secret-ballot, every-member method of authorizing a strike goes further yet: it submits the question to a referendum.

Opposing Interests within the Union. At the moment of taking the crucial strike vote, the interests of union leaders and union members may not quite coincide. The leaders are out in front, fighting for concessions the members say they want. The leaders are in direct contact with the company. They have presumably reached the conclusion that it will take more than mere arguments to win concessions, and that there are good chances of success through strike action. Conversely they fear the effect on the morale of the union members if they fail to win concessions by failing to strike. The leaders, therefore, want the strike vote to pass. The members (who may be egging their leaders on) want the concessions they have demanded, but hesitate as individuals to pay the price. That price, they know, means paydays missed, picket line duty, maybe a broken head. Even though reason may tell them they can only win by risking the strike, fear holds them back.

It may well be that at the crucial moment only a minority is actively in favor of strike. The rest—as is all too human—have gotten cold feet. But in a crowd situation a militant minority can get its way against a leaderless and wishy-washy majority. As will be shown shortly, it does not necessarily take a majority to close the factory: a militant minority can do it.

Role of the Shop Stewards. The stewards are a key group at a time like this; and indeed their support and activity are vital throughout the test that negotiations and the strike impose. They see the members in the shop from day to day. If properly informed and inspired, they are a flesh-and-blood, word-of-mouth link between the union leaders and the members. They campaign for the strike, and in the strike act as an officer corps to lead the workers.

Thus the strike vote is a critical test. In the typical, democratically organized factory union it cannot be sidestepped, because the citizen army may be mobilized by its own consent but not conscripted by decree; and yet, unless carefully handled, the conduct of the vote may expose the union to danger.

The Union's Forces. The forces at the union's disposal are the union members, a volunteer army often without experience; they make up the rank and file. Their officers are the shop stewards, who now serve as picket captains, and others who volunteer or are elected by their mates for special strike duties. This group makes up the line organization of the striking union.

The strike committee sets up subcommittees for staff and service functions, mostly service. Among the important activities that have to be carried on during a strike are the following: setting up a soup kitchen to feed the picketers; scrounging supplies and soliciting help from friendly sources in the community; publicity; transportation; a welfare center to provide relief in hardship cases; legal defense if trouble breaks out on the picket line; recreation, if the strike is long drawn out; and others. It is important to involve the strikers' wives or husbands in auxiliary strike activities.

Strike Headquarters. The union hall is the headquarters where the members meet, and serves as a base for most of the auxiliary activities mentioned in the last paragraph. In addition, the strikers set up a field headquarters near the plant, handy to the picket line. This may be a vacant store hired for the occasion, or a tent that also houses the soup kitchen, or even a public place like a café or saloon whose proprietor tolerates the strikers' presence (and gets their business), perhaps even making a back room available for their use. Here the picket captains report, and get encouragement, instructions, and advice from the rep and the strike committee. Pickets drop in between spells of sidewalk duty to drink a cup of coffee, warm their toes, and pick up gossip of the strike. To one who has seen service with front-line troops in combat, it is remarkable how much these other "front-line" headquarters reproduce the atmosphere of selflessness, shared perils, and camaraderie.

Allies. The striking local's allies are other locals of the international, and more immediately, other local unions in the town. The strikers' ambassador to the city central informs the other delegates of the union's plight, and the support that comes from the labor movement of the home community is almost always warm and often generous. After all, they are neighbors. Most of them can do no more than contribute to the strike fund, send fraternal delegations to the strike meetings, and pass resolutions of support in their own. Sometimes they can give active direct support, as when the Teamsters refuse to cross a strike picket line. But the Teamsters do not always respect picket lines of other unions, and when they do, or others join in a sympathy strike, the situation takes on a new significance beyond that of the situation being examined here, which is the simple strike of factory workers.

The Striking Worker. The plant gate channels a human stream, regular as the tide, set into motion daily during the week by the onset of the factory shift. The worker bound for the workplace who finds strike pickets at the familiar gate cannot help feeling an initial sense of shock. Not to walk through the open gate runs against habit and impulse. People are no creatures of blind instinct, and when the shop steward meets the workers at the gate and diverts them to picket duty, most of them will respond; but the unspent impulse is strong, and tautens nerves.

Emotionalism. That check to habit is the first of many emotional experiences of the strike. If the picket line keeps the workers from entering the plant the first day of the strike, and starts them on a new routine—the strike routine—the union has accomplished a great deal toward winning the campaign. It cannot always do this at the first try; if not, the task gets harder with each shift that does not see an empty plant. The union cannot always hold the lines after initial success, but that is another problem. The first task is to close down the plant.

This is not very difficult to do, nor does it necessarily take a majority to do it. A militant and determined minority is usually enough. Probably no more than a good handful assembly anyway, at dawn of the first day of strike, to get instructions and be posted at the gate or gates. They take their stations at all points where workers normally leave public property and step or drive onto the plant premises—parking lot entrances, street gates, and doors. As the first workers come—for habit is strong, and even those who know a strike is on cannot resist the pull of the current setting plantward at the onset of their shift—the strike leaders pass on the union's instructions. It may be to join the pickets and greet later comers with a bigger force. It may be to go to the union hall for a meeting, in cases where the strike leaders deem it desirable to keep the streets clear of crowds.

Those who act bold and confident carry the others along with them. The active ones are under leadership; the passive, leaderless, drift with the new tide. The mere sight from the head of the street of a crowd around the gate is enough to turn timid souls away. Discreetly they retire and go home (which they will find as strange, during working hours, as the deserted shop). From there, after a while, anxiety and curiosity may draw them to the union hall. At the union hall they are caught in the contagion of mass excitement and brought under organized leadership again. The factory worker, a disciplined person, responds to leadership, and in a day or two is taking a turn on the picket line.

The person who walks the picket line is not quite the same person who walked off the job the day before. After the strike, that worker will never be quite the same again.

There is no such type of factory worker as the "hardened striker," but one strike will usually "harden" a union. It gives the members a shared experience that changes their attitude toward management—not individually, but as a group, for striking is a social activity. They are like troops that have seen combat.

Lessons of the Strike Experience. For many, it is an illuminating—even exhilarating—experience to learn that they can collectively defy the authority that normally dominates their individual lives—and get away with it. This remains true even when they do not clearly win their strike, so long as they regain their places in the factory after it is over. What they have once dared they may do again. They feel a confidence they could not know before. They have learned caution, too, which tempers their boasts and threats but makes more meaningful, and to the company, ominous, those they do express. One strike is enough to last most factory workers—and factory managers—a long time. The strike transforms them both.

It changes them because, as has been shown above, a strike is a profoundly emotional experience. That does not mean that it is primarily an emotional outburst (strike causes run deeper than that), but it works strongly on the emotions of everyone involved. Most numerous of those involved, and most directly affected, are the workers.

The Picket Line. The aim of the strike is to deprive the company of production and make management sue for terms to get it rolling again.

The first step is to call the workers off their jobs. This is the formal meaning of the strike vote and is easily accomplished since workers leave the plant anyway at the end of the shift.

Shutting down the Plant. The second step is to shut down the plant, and this may be a little harder. Meeting-hall courage has been known to melt away overnight. A worker is not counted absent from work until failing to show up at the start of the next scheduled shift. The strike is not actually on until the shift fails to report. The union therefore must stop the shift from going on. As has been shown, that is not really difficult to do if there is any appreciable amount of strike sentiment and if adequate organizational measures are taken.

The third step, and the one that may be hardest in the long run, is to keep the workers, and strangers who might replace them, from going in to work. This is the aim that animates every move made by the union in the strike, the object of all its vigilance, the reason for any violence that may occur on either side. The way it is carried out is by means of a picket line.

A picket line consists of union members who walk back and forth in front of the plant gate or gates. They warn their fellows, and any others who might seek to enter the factory to work, not to cross the line. They do this by word of mouth and by carrying signs. If words are not enough, they may resort to deeds.

Blockading of the Gate. The picket line at the factory gate is not a siege of the factory. A besieging force is one trying to get into a defended place to which the gates are barred. The factory gate is open during a strike. People walk in and out of it: guards, executives, and supervisors, perhaps the entire office force; even a skeleton crew of maintenance people—union members—who keep the pipes from freezing or preserve other vital installations.

Picketing the plant is not a siege, it is a blockade. It cuts the plant off from a vital element of production: labor. It defends the approaches to the plant against the entrance of people who might provide the labor. Who are these people who might want to go in the open gate? Anybody and everybody, including union members who weaken.

This is an offensive, not a defensive, strategy. The union picketer does not have to wait until someone does something but must do something to make the potential replacement refrain from entering the gate, as the replacement has every legal right to do. The weapons available to the picketers for carrying out this offensive strategy are of two kinds: moral suasion and force.

Keeping the Line Solid.   Moral suasion appeals to some sentiment or belief such as worker solidarity, or sympathy, or shame. It may be powerful enough to overcome the desire to get a job by which one can make a living—at any rate, in that particular plant. It certainly will do so in most cases in a community where the mores contain a tradition of worker solidarity. It may not do so if the replacement is a "stranger," particularly if from a region (as, for instance, the South) where no such sentiments are common. It runs against the traditional belief that ours is a competitive society in which one person has as much right as another to take or refuse any job that is open and offered. Moral suasion can suffice, but it is more effective when it is supported by a powerful emotion, fear—fear of the use of force.

The force may be no more than jostling and getting in the way of a strikebreaker trying to enter the gate. No matter which way the strikebreaker turns, somebody is standing there and "accidentally" barring the way. This is sometimes called "belly-bumping" and requires a beefy physique. Force may go further than that, to manhandling and beatings.

Or force may be nonviolent with picketers standing in the way of a car headed into the company parking lot. The driver cannot get through the gate without running down the people and becoming liable for their injuries. Again, force may go further than that, to the point of rocking the car and rolling it over with its occupants inside.

The striker knows that the way to the workplace leads through the picketed gate. The striker who may not go in certainly does not want to see others go in, but the strikers' attitude toward these others depends upon whether they too have their "own" workplaces inside, or whether they are strangers, not fellow employees. If the person who goes through the gate is a fellow worker who has given in under the pressure, the picketer treats him with scorn for weakening; but if the strikebreaker is a stranger, the reaction may be fury. Any return to work of former employees and union members raises the prospect of having to settle for less than the desired terms, and possible individual victimization, but the advent of new workers threatens permanent displacement.

Where there is danger that many will try to enter the plant, the union's recourse is to the mass picket line. In fact, the mass picket line is the industrial union's natural and characteristic form of strike activity. It keeps the strikers busy and it keeps them together, so that they can keep an eye on the company and on each other all the time, and it assembles the force necessary to insure closing the gates.

Under the Taft-Hartley law mass picketing has been held to be illegal—an unfair labor practice—but someone has first to forbid it or disperse it: until then, it simply goes on.

Picket-Line Violence. Mass picketing, the industrial union's most effective way of blockading a plant, is probably the kind of picketing least likely to lead to physical violence unless interfered with. That is because the very size of the picket force discourages entry of strikebreakers. Nonviolent "living wall" tactics, in which the pickets lock arms and stand in the way, can keep out cars as well as people, and any overt violence has to come as an attack on the pickets. Of course, once a fight breaks out in a crowd of people already tense and with their livelihood at stake, there is no telling what may happen. The point is, it is not the strikers in such cases who are likely to start trouble.

But mass picketing, besides being effective, is illegal. A company can get a court order against it. With majestic impartiality (as pointed out earlier) the law prescribes for craft and industrial unions alike the uniform conditions of "peaceful picketing": 2 (or 4, or 6) pickets at each gate, spaced 10 (or 20, or 40) yards apart, showing signs to advertise the fact that there is a labor dispute, but not shouting, or calling, or jeering, or threatening any who "in their lawful purposes" may want to enter the plant. With variations, this is the stuff of a court order enjoining mass picketing.

The picketing becomes peaceful by legal definition but, ironically, whatever potential for violence the strike contains may actually build up in proportion to the reduction in the picketers' effectiveness in keeping the plant gate closed. If strikebreakers now feel safe in crossing the picket line, and enough of them do cross it, the union faces the uncomfortable but inescapable dilemma of losing the strike or breaking the law.

How many strikebreakers are "enough"? Only as many as it would take to raise the fear in the minds of the strikers that the company can replace them. If they are strangers that need be only a few, for every striker then feels threatened. If they are employees, perhaps union members, it might take more; but in either case the ones still on strike seek to halt the movement. Breaking the law then becomes one of the risks of battle. It is a risk the union leaders frequently, either out of pure heedless emotion or after due calculation, elect to take.

Financing the Strike.   A strike is financed in two ways. Basically, of course, the members support it by their self-denial in giving up their potential earnings for the period of the strike, and by the unpaid services they render on the picket line and in such related auxiliary activities as mentioned in the last section. Workers on strike are ineligible for unemployment compensation.

Strike Funds.   The other way is by drawing on strike funds accumulated by the union out of dues and assessments paid in while the members were working. All internationals have such funds, and most locals.

To get support from the international, a local must receive the international's approval before taking strike action. This must not be misunderstood to mean that the local always has to get permission to strike. As long as the strike does not violate an agreement with the company the local is usually free to make its own decision, but if it wants international money during the strike (and the help of an international representative) it has to notify the international beforehand.

Approval by the higher body is usually routine. It would be withheld only in unusual circumstances. Getting this approval is a step the local can use as part of its psychological war of nerves with the company in negotiations. In cases where a strike has been forced unexpectedly on a local, approval may still be gotten *ex post facto.*

The craft-union international, with its relatively fixed membership of skilled workers only a small proportion of whom are ever on strike at the same time or for very long, can afford to pay strike benefits to individuals out of a fund accumulated centrally. The industrial union international is in a different situation. Factory strikes often involve tens of thousands of workers, and sometimes last for months.

Strike funds in the industrial union come from a small percentage, rarely more than 10 percent, of the dues dollar; and dues in turn are a small percentage—perhaps 2 percent—of a worker's pay. To try to support a striker and family by paying directly even a fraction of a normal wage sufficient to live on, and to do this for all the workers who may be on strike, would soon deplete the treasury of the international.

Besides, the aim is not to help the worker wait it out in an industrial union strike; such conflicts are not won by waiting. The aim is to keep alive the striker's militancy; and while an empty stomach makes one abject, a half-filled belly whets the appetite and keeps one active. Strike benefits, when paid, are therefore nominal—perhaps $10 to $30 a week—just enough to keep a little change jingling in the striker's pocket for coffee, bus fare or a few gallons of gas, newspapers, cigarettes, and the most pressing personal expenses.

Most of the strike funds go to support general activities and to meet needs that are common to the union as a whole. They pay the rent of the field headquarters and purchase supplies for the soup kitchen where the striker can get a small meal. They provide hospital care for any strike casualties and buy bail and legal aid for prisoners arrested for activities on the picket line. Such portion of the strike funds as goes to individuals is given frankly as relief for the emergency. Of course the union's committee will eke out its own resources, if possible, by getting relief for needy cases from public or private welfare agencies, but this resource is not always available. In any case, not to take care of members facing real personal disaster through the strike (rather than mere belt-tightening austerity for a time) would hurt morale; and in a strike, which is a form of combat, morale is vital. A striker threatened with home eviction may be provided with rent money to stave off the landlord. A family with small children will get milk and groceries.

Besides the established strike funds of the local and international, contributions come in from other unions and from individuals in the form of cash and goods, particularly food. "Scrounging committees" solicit groceries from food stores and farmers. (The advent of the supermarket run by a hired manager is closing off this source of supply, but the trend toward part-time farming by industrial workers, and part-time work in industry by farmers, may have opened up another.) Every little bit helps: a few sacks of potatoes, a carton of eggs, perhaps a side of beef for the stew pot. In an extremity, the strike army "lives off the country" while it carries on its fight.

Employer Strike Strategy and Tactics

Strike action is by nature drastic in the original sense of the word. The company that permits a strike to occur and the union that calls one both expect to receive some hurt, but hope to win concessions by hurting the other side more. The things they are concerned about during a strike show curious parallels. Neither side wants the plant or equipment to suffer any permanent damage, else they will not be fit to turn out production and provide jobs again. Both hope for a short strike and for the return to work of the entire force. Both envisage, as the worst that could happen, complete replacement of the work force by new employees, but by the logic of their conflict both sides are compelled to act as if that worst were bound to come to pass. That is their main defense against its happening.

Strike Costs. A strike denies the company the use of its productive equipment, while overhead costs continue. In a sense that is by no means purely figurative, part of that productive equipment consists of the strikers. The most advanced techniques of personnel selection, placement, and training have gone into getting them together and fitting them into management's grand design that makes the factory as a whole a smooth, efficient apparatus of production. They represent the know-how that the company has developed over the years. The cost in money, time, and organizing efforts of replacing all of them at once would be staggering.

Employer Objectives. Obviously, the cheapest and most satisfactory way of getting the factory back in production calls for the return of all the workers—though there might be a few the management would prefer not to recall. This broadly coincides with the union aim of getting all its members—without any exception—back on the job. The only thing that prevents both sides from doing this at once is the thing that led them to take drastic action in the first place: disagreement over the terms at which workers resume their jobs. Until the strike, which hurts them both, hurts one side badly enough to make it give in to the other on these terms, they cannot do what they both fundamentally desire.

A factory in operation, making profits and providing good jobs, is their mutual aim and reason for existence, and even when they are locked in struggle neither side loses sight of this aim. The striking union gives "safe conduct" across the picket line to maintenance people assigned to protect vital plant installations. Strikers in a spiteful mood may commit malicious damage of the petty kind, such as breaking windows, but they will not blow up or set fire to the factory. Their own jobs would go up in the smoke.

If, then, the union wants to get all its people back to work, and the company wants them back, and only the terms of their return prevent this, why should not the company simply close down the plant, as in a craft employer lockout, and wait for the union to give in on terms?

The Lockout and the Factory Strike.   In general, the lockout is not the answer to the factory strike or to the demands of the industrial union.

That is not to say that the employer's cause is lost unless it tries from the very start, in a union-declared strike, to break the picket line around the plant. It will certainly want to keep the gate open at least long enough to make sure the union has been able to keep the work force from entering it; but acceptance of the fact that the plant is shut down, while negotiations continue, would be a sensible course in most cases for a time at least. Such action might have a tempering effect on the negotiations, which broke off, presumably, at white heat. It would give the union a chance to reflect on its course. Reopening the gate later, if initial reasonableness has failed of its purpose, might then have greater tactical effect than belligerence right from the start. A decision here depends on circumstances.

But keeping the gate closed indefinitely plays into the union's hands. Overhead costs continue to mount as long as a strike lasts, whether the gate is locked or left open. Locking the gate against an industrial union does not dispel the picket line, it simply makes the picketing job easier. If the employer has initiated the lockout to counter union demands, the workers may even be entitled to draw unemployment compensation while "on strike," which is not the case when the union calls the strike. Unless the terms are settled in negotiations, the pickets will be right back when the gate reopens. Meanwhile, a portion of the work force—and very likely, the best of it— may have dispersed, found other jobs and moved away. Keeping the gate open not only maintains pressure on the union to come to a settlement but concentrates the hopes as well as the fears of the strikers on the plant gate. The implied threat that one's job will be given to someone else seems to increase one's sense of proprietorship toward it. Instead of wandering off, one is more likely to stay and fight for it.

There may be unusual circumstances in which a lockout would be effective. In a one-factory town, for instance, strikers or potential strikers might be intimidated by the threat. A lockout would still be a dangerous move in any community not sufficiently isolated to be beyond an hour's drive from other employment opportunities. Shutting down the plant would almost certainly transfer to the company a share at least of the public opprobrium that would otherwise have been directed at the strikers. The lockout is a negative and passive answer to the union. Its use restricts more active possibilities open to the company.

Tactics. In most factory strikes the gate remains symbolically open all the time, watched from the inside by company guards, patrolled from the outside by union pickets. One of the first concerns of the company is the number of pickets at the gate or gates, and their conduct. If pickets are few and orderly, chances of getting nonstrikers to cross the line and enter the plant are enhanced. The Taft-Hartley law lists mass picketing as an unfair labor practice, but there is always the problem of determining how many pickets constitute mass picketing, and enforcing the ban against it. The responsibility for assuring legal and orderly picketing rests on the public authorities: city police or, outside city limits, the sheriff and deputies. It is sometimes necessary to apply for a court order enjoining mass picketing and prescribing the number of peaceful pickets.

Picketer Morale. With the number of pickets cut down to no more than a handful at each gate, it is possible to invite workers to return to their jobs. This is often done by mailing circular letters to all employees, sometimes reinforced by newspaper ads or radio announcements. Successful "infiltration" by a few emboldens others who would like to be at work again. Every person who responds "counts double," in the sense that each simultaneously augments the working force and diminishes the ranks of strikers. There may be little of a useful nature to do in the plant, but their presence there, with others who trickle in, undermines the morale of those still outside and tempts them back. They weigh the uncertainties of future settlement against present hardships and the invitation of the open gate, and perhaps the trickle turns to a gradually swelling stream. Eventually the balance may shift so far that the union either has to give in or resort to violence.

Violence at the Gate. Violence is double-edged; it may hurt the union, but it also hurts the company by checking the back-to-work flow. It takes effective law enforcement to minimize the likelihood of violent outbreaks and cope with them when they occur. Liaison with law-enforcement agencies, as well as skillful public relations work, has to be an important part of the company' activity during a factory strike.

Nowadays only the exceptional strike erupts into heavy and prolonged violence. For a strike to reach that stage, the issues must be practically insoluble, or else there must be an irreconcilable clash of powerful personalities in the leadership of company and union. The 10-year Kohler strike in Wisconsin seems to be an example of the latter. Both sides in the dispute became so deeply involved that neither could retreat and it developed into a "fight to the death." The strike moved on inexorably to the state that is "the worst that can happen": replacement of a decisive segment of the entire working force by new employees. This brought about the defeat of the local union and its disappearance as a viable organization in the plant. Had it not been for the massive and sustained intervention of one of the world's richest and most powerful international unions, the UAW, the local union and its members would have simply passed from the scene. Although the international union eventually won the largest back-pay settlement in NLRB history ($3 million plus $1,500,000 for restored pension rights), the lesson of the strike seems to be that a company determined not to give in can beat a local union in the field by replacing its members on the job; but the fight may be very long and the cost very high indeed.

The "Back-to-Work" Movement. The hope of destroying the union may often be present in the minds of management people during a strike— or indeed, at any time when managers feel the restrictions unions put on freedom of managerial action—yet rarely does a company really aim at unconditional surrender by the union. Rather, the company puts the union through its strike paces in the hope of softening the terms of a proposed agreement. A good healthy back-to-work movement will usually soften up the union, though failure of a move in this direction may have the opposite effect. Just how and when to do it are tactical problems that have to be solved in the circumstances of each specific strike. Several techniques have proved successful in certain cases.

During a strike, negotiations continue, mediation efforts increase. The atmosphere in which management and union people meet is even more highly charged than before. Emotional reactions often are transferred from the picket line and plant gate to the conference room. Management people have to hold particularly tight rein on their feelings at such times. A lost temper might prolong the strike, or lose it. The union rep they deal with is a cold-blooded professional. It is up to the company representatives to stay cool and keep their wits about them.

Military Analogies. To sum it up: The company's position in a factory strike, by analogy with the military, is defensive, and the defensive position is a strong one. The law is on the company's side in setting the conditions of the battle. The tension and emotionalism that grip the workers during a strike make the morale problem crucial. If the strikers lose their morale, the union loses the strike. Counteroffensive measures open to the company may undermine morale, and the most potent of such measures are those that persuade workers to return to their jobs without waiting for a strike settlement. This forces the union to give in or to resort to violence. Violence as such hurts the company, in most cases, as well as the union, but may be averted, sometimes, by careful coordination of efforts with law enforcement agencies.

If active measures fail to bring the strike to an end, and the company can afford it, waiting it out will eventually result in a settlement. Most industrial workers will have run through their savings and reserves in a few weeks, and each additional week subjects them and their families to greater hardship. Unless bitterness deep enough to offset the personal privations has been allowed to creep in, the strikers will eventually surrender.

Assuming that management has not launched a successful back-to-work movement, as the strike continues pressure on both sides mounts for a settlement. The strikers want to go back to work and to start drawing paychecks again. The management's fears of lost business are beginning to become reality as more and more customers look for more reliable sources of supply. The union's funds are running low and the membership is restive.

Negotiations are resumed, perhaps on the urgings of a mediator. Both sides have new facts to consider now and they weigh them with the intelligence of greater maturity that comes from combat. Eventually the negotiators come to an agreement. They initial it, or sign it provisionally, pending ratification.

CONSUMMATION OF THE AGREEMENT

The negotiators' agreement still remains tentative; it lacks validity until the members of the local, and perhaps also the international union's Executive Board and the company's Board of Directors have ratified it. The local does this in a meeting similar to the one at which the members ratified the draft demands. This time they vote on the agreement as a whole. They cannot ratify parts of it and reject other parts. If any parts of the agreement is so objectionable to the members that they will not swallow it, the whole agreement fails and the negotiators have to go back and try again. Their job is not complete until the whole of their work has met with membership approval.

The agreement is finally reached and ratified, the outsiders to the dispute (union professionals, mediators, and company consultants) leave the scene. The workers go back to work, the company resumes operations.

SUMMARY AND CONCLUSIONS

The process of reaching a labor agreement can be compared with the relations between two sovereign national powers. Negotiations are analogous to the conduct of international diplomacy. Strikes, like war, are the continuation of diplomacy (negotiations) *by other means.*

In negotiations, the union seeks benefits for its members which pose a serious challenge to management's need for reasonable costs and flexibility in the operation of the enterprise. Both parties arm themselves with whatever facts they have at their disposal, but the negotiations always involve decision making under conditions of uncertainty, and emotions are likely to prevent a purely rational approach to reaching an agreement.

The writers of this book hold that strikes are part of collective bargaining. They are not inevitable, but neither are they abnormal. Still, strikes bring loss to the participants, their dependents, and those who trade with them. They inconvenience, and may even endanger, nonparticipants. When of great magnitude or in a sensitive sector of industry, strikes can imperil the general health and welfare, and even national security. On the other hand, strikes are only one of many causes of economic waste, and by no means the major offender.

There can be no doubt that strikes can be eliminated by governmental action, but only at the expense of personal freedom and civil liberty, and with the danger of eventual violent revolt. To date, the American people have found the price too high, and are unwilling to assume the risks. The inconvenience, loss, and occasional danger incidental to strikes, and the waste they represent, are recognized as part of the price the public has to pay to maintain those free institutions of our society that go far beyond the strike situation and the industrial situation generally.

Unions go on strike when they cannot get an employer to agree with them on terms they feel are right, and are unwilling to accept the employer's terms. The strike thus becomes an additional argument—a direct and powerful one—to back up the stand the union has taken in negotiations. A strike aims to make it expensive and inconvenient for an employer *not* to agree.

Management may occasionally provoke a strike for basically the same reason to call a union bluff. If the union negotiators fail to get the members to respond to a strike call, or if the vote in favor of a strike is close and unenthusiastic, obviously the argument fails to impress; the strike threat not made good loses its force and softens up, rather than strengthens, the union bargainers.

Craft unions and industrial unions use essentially the same procedures in negotiations, although the agreements they seek are quite different, as will be discussed in Chapter 8. The strike strategy and tactics of craft and industrial unions differ radically.

Craft-union strike strategy consists of withdrawing a scarce skill from the market. Craft unions can win their strikes by merely waiting for supply and demand to come into balance at their desired price.

Industrial union strike strategy depends on closing the plant and keeping it shut *tight*. This is a power strategy, which gets no support from the law and may result in violence at the plant gate. The reason that plant gate violence does not occur more frequently is that most employers do not attempt to operate their plants during an industrial union strike.

Whether invoked by a confident union or provoked by a stubborn management, in either case it is the union that must assume the onus of calling the strike. A strike is the union's move.

Strategically speaking, the union is on the offensive during a strike, the employer on the defensive. The defensive position in a strike (as in classical, pre-H-bomb warfare) is strategically the stronger. An employer defensive, skillfully conducted, may turn into a counteroffensive that puts the union to rout; or the union may prevail, sufficiently (at least) to win an agreement more favorable than had been offered in the preceding negotiations.

The end product of negotiations (diplomacy) and strikes (war) is an agreement (treaty) which management, workers, and the union must try to live with.

QUESTIONS FOR DISCUSSION

1. If you were a plant manager of a firm employing 1,000 persons, would you want a first-line supervisor to sit in on negotiations? Why or why not? If you wanted one to sit in, what role should the supervisor play?
2. Assume that you are a mediator. How would you go about preparing for your role in a specific set of negotiations?
3. What happens if the local membership rejects the agreement after it has been negotiated?
4. Compare and contrast the strike strategy and tactics of craft and industrial unions.
5. Although craft and industrial unionists need to behave differently to accomplish their strike objectives, the law does not differentiate between them. Is this sound public policy?
6. An attorney for the UAW has proposed that all picketing be outlawed but that employers be prohibited from hiring new employees while a strike is in progress. Evaluate this proposal.
7. Does a strike deadline help or hinder the negotiation process?
8. Discuss the nonstoppage strike. (See Mangum in the bibliography.)

APPENDIX: JUDICIAL DECISIONS AFFECTING THE NEGOTIATIONS FOR COLLECTIVE BARGAINING AGREEMENTS, INCLUDING STRIKE ACTIVITIES[4]

Duty of Fair Representation

The duty of fair representation requires that unions fairly, without discrimination, represent all members of the unit in contract negotiations and administration. The duty of fair representation is a court created doctrine. (*Steele* v. *Louisville & Nashville Railroad Co.*, 323 U.S. 192 (1944).) Breach of the duty of fair representation may be an unfair labor practice. (*Ford Motor Co.* v. *Huffman*, 345 U.S. 330 (1953).)

Before a member of the unit may sue the union for breach of the duty, the person must show that the union acted in an arbitrary or discriminatory way, or in bad faith. It is not sufficient to show that the person's grievance was meritorious, but there must be a showing that the union acted improperly. The duty applies most strictly in grievance processes and less strictly in the bargaining

---

[4] The authors are indebted to Professor Donald W. Brodie of the University of Oregon Law School for material in this Appendix.

context. Before the employee can sue the employer for breach of contract under §301, the employee must show either that the employee exhausted the contractual remedies or that the employee was prevented from so doing by the union's improper action. (*Vaca* v. *Sipes*, 386 U.S. 171 (1967).)

Union Security

Section 14(b) allows states to regulate the union shop under so-called "right to work" legislation. The Supreme Court has ruled that an agency shop is the equivalent, for these purposes, of a union shop, even though the agency shop does not require membership. Accordingly, states are free to regulate the agency shop (*Retail Clerks, Local 1625* v. *Schermerhorn*, 373 U.S. 746 (1963).)

Subjects of Bargaining

The duty to bargain in good faith both in initial contract negotiations and during the life of a contract is limited to mandatory subjects. Mandatory subjects are those items encompassed in the phrase "rates of pay, wages, hours of employment, or other conditions of employment."

An employer may make unilateral changes without bargaining in contract terms involving permissive subjects. The benefits received by already retired employees are considered to be permissive subjects because retired employees are not within the NLRA definition of "employee" and cannot be considered to be part of the unit. (*Allied Chemical and Alkali Workers of America, Local 1* v. *Pittsburgh Plate Glass Co.*, 404 U.S. 157 (1971).)

If management insists that the union accept contract terms in a nonmandatory area, the company violates 8 (a) (5). (*NLRB* v. *Wooster Division of Borg-Warner Corp.*, 356 U.S. 342 (1958).) However, good faith insistence on a management rights clause to counterbalance union insistence on an arbitration clause does not violate 8 (a) (5). (*NLRB* v. *American National Insurance Co.*, 343 U.S. 395 (1952).)

Subcontracting of the employer's work with consequent loss of union jobs which is based upon economic considerations may be a subject of mandatory bargaining where there would be no alteration of the company's basic operation, the work was still performed in the plant, no capital investment was involved, and it involved merely the replacement of unit employees with nonunit employees to do the same work under similar conditions. An example would be subcontracting maintenance work. Where these factors are not present, the decision to subcontract may not be a mandatory subject. (*Fibreboard Paper Products Corp.* v. *NLRB*, 379 U.S. 203 (1964).)

Statutory Rights Waived by Contract

The NLRA protects both the right to engage in, as well as refrain from engaging in, union related activities. The union, as majority representative, cannot bargain away at least some of the rights of a minority of the employees. A contractual agreement prohibiting the distribution of union or antiunion literature during the employee's nonworking time, and other contractual restrictions on solicitation and distribution of union and antiunion information violates the protected rights of those who oppose the union. (*NLRB* v. *Magnavox Co.*, 94 Supreme Court 1099 (1974).)

Secondary Strike Activity

Reserved Gate. A union picketing an employer may not picket an entry gate reserved solely for and used exclusively by independent contractors where there is, in fact, a separate gate properly marked and set aside from other entry gates; where the work done by the independent contractor is unrelated to the normal operations of the employer; and where the work must be of a kind that would not, if done when the plant were engaged in its regular operations, necessitate curtailing those operations. Maintenance work can be an example. (*Local 761, International Union of Electrical, Radio & Machine Workers* v. *NLRB*, 366 U.S. 667 (1961).)

Struck Product or Consumer Picketing. A union may picket at the premises of a secondary employer for the purpose of attempting to persuade customers not to buy the product of a struck primary employer. It would violate the NLRA to seek to persuade the customers not to do business with the secondary employer in any fashion. For example, a union with a dispute with a fruit packer of apples may picket a grocery store for the purpose of requesting the consumer not to buy the "struck" apples. (*NLRB* v. *Fruit and Vegetable Packers, Local 760*, 377 U.S. 770 (1964).)

Will not Handle. Despite the broad language of Section 8(e) barring agreements to cease handling products of any other employer, a union may refuse to handle prefabricated doors at a construction where the contract so provides. Such an agreement seeks to preserve work traditionally done by the employees covered by the contract and does not have a prohibited secondary objective. Work preservation clauses are not hot cargo clauses. (*National Woodworkers Manufacturers Association* v. *NLRB*, 386 U.S. 612 (1967).)

Requests to Stop Doing Business. When the union has a dispute with a primary employer, it may request managerial personnel of a secondary employer to make a managerial decision not to handle the goods of the primary employer. The union may also accompany this request with a "threat" to distribute handbills to the public if the goods are handled. The court has distinguished between this type of request and the unlawful request to stop working for the secondary employer until that employer ceases doing business with the primary employer. (*NLRB* v. *Servette, Inc.*, 377 U.S. 46 (1964).)

Lockouts

The lockout is often considered to be the employer's equivalent of the union's strike. Unlike the strike, or picketing, there is no comprehensive mention of lockouts in the legislation. The NLRB had generally held lockouts to violate the act, as being destructive of the employees' rights to organize. The Supreme Court has taken a more generous but still restrictive view of lockouts. The court has permitted the "defensive" lockout, such as when the nonstruck members of a multiemployer bargaining association lockout their nonstriking employees as a defense against a strike by the common union against only one member of the multiemployer association. (*NLRB* v. *Truck Drivers Local Union No. 449*, 353 U.S. 87 (1957).) More recently, the court has permitted an "offensive" lockout so long as it is not discriminatory toward the union. An employer who bargains as a single entity may lockout the employees to bring economic—bargaining— pressure on the union after a legitimate bargaining impasse is reached. (*American Ship Building Co.* v. *NLRB*, 380 U.S. 300 (1965).)

Successor Employer Obligations

An employer has certain obligations toward a union representing the employees. When the employer sells the business, problems arise concerning whether the successor or new employer has any responsibilities toward the union or whether the new successor employer would begin completely anew. The Supreme Court has made several important rulings concerning successors.

Where the selling employer had a contract with the union, the purchasing-successor employer has an obligation to bargain with the same union when the bargaining unit remains unchanged and a majority of the old employees rehired by the new employer are represented by the union. The successor employer is not obligated to honor the collective bargaining agreement negotiated by the union and predecessor-selling employer. (*NLRB* v. *Burns International Security Services*, 406 U.S. 272 (1972).)

Where the successor did not hire a majority of the seller's employees, the successor was not bound by the seller's collective bargaining agreement to arbitrate grievances arising under the agreement for the discharge of the seller's employees. The employees remedy will lie against the selling employer. (*Howard Johnson Co.* v. *Detroit Local Joint Executive Board, Hotel and Restaurant Employees and Bartenders Union*, 94 S.Ct. 2236 (1974).)

A successor purchaser of a business, when there is no substantial change in business operations, may be required to abide by reinstatement and backpay remedies which were ordered by the NLRB as a remedy for the seller-predecessor's unfair labor practice. The successor is entitled to a hearing, before being ordered to make the remedy, on the questions of successorship and the buyer's knowledge of the pendency of the unfair labor practice charge. (*Golden State Bottling* v. *NLRB*, 94 Supreme Court 414 (1974).)

SELECTED ANNOTATED BIBLIOGRAPHY

This bibliography consists of two parts: (1) negotiations and (2) strikes.

1. Negotiations

BALKE, WALTER M.; HAMMOND, KENNETH R.; and MEYER, G. DALE. "An Alternate Approach to Labor-Management Relations," *Administrative Science Quarterly*, vol. 18, no. 3 (September 1973).

The authors reenacted a previous union-management set of negotiations with the original negotiators and report some mildly encouraging results from the application of an interactive computer device to help them reach agreement.

BURKE, DONALD R., and RUBIN, LESTER. "Is Contract Rejection a Major Collective Bargaining Problem?" *Industrial and Labor Relations Review*, vol. 26, no. 2 (January 1973).

The authors answer "no" to the above question by suggesting that rejection statistics may be inflated, that the phenomenon is not very widespread, and that it results primarily from poor communications.

DONNELLY, LAWRENCE. "Toward an Alliance between Research and Practice in Collective Bargaining," *Personnel Journal* (May 1971), pp. 372–99.

The author develops a frame of reference which he believes will help the practitioner make use of the vast but esoteric research being done on collective bargaining. A good succinct summary of insights that have come from academics.

DOUGLAS, ANN. *Industrial Peacemaking.* New York: Columbia University Press, 1962.

A penetrating psychological analysis of labor-management negotiations under mediation. An intensive study of six sets of negotiations.

HAMERMESH, DANIEL S. "Who 'Wins' in Wage Bargaining?" *Industrial and Labor Relations Review*, vol. 26, no. 4 (July 1973).

The author examines wage data from 43 public sector negotiations to see if the final wage outcome is closer to the employer's initial offer or the union's initial demand.

INDIK, BERNARD P.; GOLDSTEIN, BERNARD; CHERNICK, JACK; and BERKOWITZ, MONROE. *The Mediator: Background, Self-Image and Attitudes.* New Brunswick, N.J.: Research Program, Institute of Management and Labor Relations, Rutgers—The State University, 1966.

Reports on two surveys of the social background, employment conditions, attitudes, and opinions of state and federal mediators.

Labor Law Journal, July 1960. *Proceedings of the 1960 Spring Meeting of the Industrial Relations Research Association.*

The following papers all discuss the question of cooperation between employers in an industry in an attempt to meet an industry-wide union: "Mutual Aid in the Airlines," by MARK L. KAHN; "Cooperation among Auto Managements in Collective Bargaining," by WILLIAM H. MCPHERSON; "Company Cooperation in Collective Bargaining in the Basic Steel Industry," by JACK STIEBER; "Cooperation among Managements in Collective Bargaining," by FRANK C. PIERSON.

LEVINSON, HAROLD M. "Pattern Bargaining: A Case Study of the Automobile Workers," *Quarterly Journal of Economics*, vol. 74 (May 1960), pp. 296–317.

The essential points brought out by this analysis are that there has been a considerable degree of flexibility in union's approach; the most important variables affecting the union's wage policy were size of firm, relationship to industry, its financial condition, and the desires of unions to obtain "equitable" settlement; and that neither "economic" nor "political" hypothesis above provides an adequate frame of reference for understanding union's policies.

LIVERNASH, E. ROBERT. "Recent Developments in Bargaining Structure." ARNOLD W. WEBER, ed., *The Structure of Collective Bargaining: Problems and Perspectives,* pp. 33–55. New York: The Free Press of Glencoe, Inc., 1961.

Discusses the postwar growth of centralization in contract negotiation in the local and national product market structures of bargaining. Emphasizes the great diversity of bargaining structures in the United States.

MARTING, ELIZABETH, ed. *Understanding Collective Bargaining: The Executive's Guide*. New York: American Management Association, 1958.

Forty-six authors, most of them industrial relations executives, discuss bargaining and the company's future, getting ready to talk contract, bargaining procedures, the contract and its wording, the issues in collective bargaining, the use of mediation, strikes, and explaining management's position.

National Industrial Conference Board. *Preparing for Collective Bargaining*, Studies in Personnel Policy, nos. 172 and 182. The Board, 1959 and 1961.

A survey of hundreds of companies that reveals the similarities and differences in how enterprises plan and carry out contract negotiations. The report gives a comprehensive view of the complex set of interdependencies that make collective bargaining such a challenging event.

NORTHRUP, HERBERT R. "Boulwareism vs. Coalitionism in the 1966 GE Negotiations," *Management of Personnel Quarterly*, vol. 5 (Summer 1966), pp. 2–11.

Reviews Boulwareism in light of the attempt at coalition bargaining by a group of unions with G.E. in 1966.

ODEWAHN, CHARLES A., and KRISLOV, JOSEPH. "Contract Rejections: Testing the Explanatory Hypotheses," *Industrial Relations*, vol. 12, no. 3 (October 1973).

The authors examine numerous rejection cases and show that union member concern with economic factors is a far better explanation of rejections than social unrest, bargaining structures, or the Landrum-Griffin Act.

PILLSBURY, WILBUR F. *The Use of Corporate Financial Statements and Related Data by Organized Labor*. Bloomington: Indiana University, Bureau of Business Research, Report no. 18, 1954.

Discusses sources of corporate financial data for collective bargaining and the use of these data by union research departments. Suggests a series of financial statements which would prove most helpful in achieving factual collective bargaining.

SIMKIN, WILLIAM E. *Mediation and the Dynamics of Collective Bargaining*. Washington, D.C.: Bureau of National Affairs, 1971.

The former director of the Federal Mediation and Conciliation Service presents a detailed analysis of the dynamics of the negotiation and mediation processes.

SLICHTER, SUMNER H.; HEALY, JAMES J.; and LIVERNASH, E. ROBERT. *The Impact of Collective Bargaining on Management*. Washington, D.C.: Brookings Institution, 1960.

See chapter 30, "Negotiation of Union-Management Contracts."

STAGNER, ROSS, and ROSEN, HJALMAR. *Psychology of Union-Management Relations*. Belmont, Calif.: Wadsworth, 1965.

An interpretation of bargaining behavior and other aspects of industrial relations in light of modern psychological theories such as those dealing with perception and attitudes.

STEVENS, CARL M. *Strategy and Collective Bargaining Negotiations*. New York: McGraw-Hill Inc., 1963.

Stevens argues that the skill of the negotiator can dramatically enhance or diminish the power each party brings to the table. The book examines how various bargaining strategies affect bargaining power.

TAYLOR, GEORGE W., ed. *Industry-Wide Bargaining Series.* Philadelphia: University of Pennsylvania.

This series of monographs by experts in industrial relations provides the most comprehensive discussion of multiemployer bargaining available. The monographs in the series include:

KESSLER, SELMA, compiler. *Industry-Wide Bargaining: An Annotated Bibliography.*

TILOVE, ROBERT. *Collective Bargaining in the Steel Industry.*

FRIEDEN, JESSE. *The Taft-Hartley Law and Multi-Employer Bargaining.*

POLLAK, OTTO. *Social Implications of Industry-Wide Bargaining.*

BAHRS, GEORGE O. *The San Francisco Employers' Council.*

KERR, CLARK, and RANDALL, ROGER. *Collective Bargaining in the Pacific Coast Pulp and Paper Industry.*

PIERSON, FRANK C. *Multi-Employer Bargaining: Nature and Scope.*

FISHER, WALDO. *Collective Bargaining in the Bituminous Coal Industry.*

FEINSINGER, NATHAN. *Collective Bargaining in the Trucking Industry.*

KENNEDY, THOMAS. *The Significance of Wage Uniformity.*

GARRETT, SYLVESTER, and TRIPP, L. REED. *Management Problems Inherent in Multi-Employer Bargaining.*

TAYLOR, GEORGE W., ed. *Proceedings: Conference on Industry-Wide Collective Bargaining.*

ABERSOLD, JOHN R. *Problems of Hourly Wage Uniformity.*

LEVY, BERT W. *Multi-Employer Bargaining and the Anti-Trust Laws.*

SEYBOLD, JOHN W. *The Philadelphia Printing Industry: A Case Study.*

THOMSON, ARTHUR A., and WEINSTOCK, IRWIN. "Facing the Crisis in Collective Bargaining," *M.S.U. Business Topics* (Summer 1968), pp. 37–44.

Discusses the problems that are beginning to arise in bargaining attitudes and goals as managements begin to move more toward accepting McGregor's Theory Y assumptions while most labor unions continue to base their demands on Theory X assumptions about the worker.

TRACY, LANE. "The Influence of Noneconomic Factors on Negotiators," *Industrial and Labor Relations Review*, vol. 27, no. 2 (January 1974).

An empirical investigation of the correlation of selected noneconomic factors (such as the negotiators' desires for achievement or recognition) with negotiators' inclinations toward reaching agreement.

WALTON, RICHARD, and McKERSIE, ROBERT. *A Behavioral Theory of Labor Negotiations.* New York: McGraw-Hill Book Co., Inc., 1965.

The most ambitious attempt to date to explain bargaining activities by models adapted from social psychology and game theory.

2. Strikes

BAMBRICK, JAMES J., JR. Marquis of Queensbury Rules for Strikes," *Management Record*, vol. 18 (March 1956), pp. 85–87.

A Conference Board Study of 92 disputes shows that experienced managers and unionists tend to adhere to certain rules to be sure that the plant can re-open after a strike. Sometimes these rules appear in the contract, but they are more frequently only spoken agreements, sometimes made after the strike is under way.

BERNSTEIN, IRVING; ENARSON, H. L.; and FLEMING, R. W., eds. *Emergency Disputes and National Policy.* New York: Harper & Bros., 1955.

BIRD, MONROE M., and ROBINSON, JAMES W. "The Effectiveness of the Union Label and 'Buy Union' Campaigns," *Industrial and Labor Relations Review,* vol. 25, no. 4 (July 1972).

Although exhortations to consumers to "buy union" have been a union weapon for a century, these authors show that the 90 union labels in existence today have very little impact on consumers (including union members) and retailers.

BRIGGS, VERNON M., JR. "The Mutual Aid Pact of the Airline Industry," *Industrial and Labor Relations Review,* vol. 19 (October 1965), pp. 3–20.

Describes the establishment, principles, and effectiveness of the mutual assistance scheme adopted by a number of carriers to cope with the problem of whipsawing strikes.

BRINKER, PAUL A., and TAYLOR, BENJAMIN J. "Secondary Boycott Analysis by Industry," *Labor Law Journal,* vol. 24, no. 10 (October 1973).

The authors examine the unions and the causes involved in the NLRB's secondary boycott cases during the 1958–70 period.

CHAMBERLAIN, NEIL W., and SCHILLING, JANE METZGER. *The Impact of Strikes, Their Economic and Social Costs.* New York: Harper & Bros., 1954.

Discusses the impact of strikes in coal and railroad transportation.

———. *Social Responsibility and Strikes.* New York: Harper & Bros., 1953.

Discusses public opinion on strikes, direct and indirect sanctions in support of public opinion, the reliability of these sanctions, and strikes in a dominant firm and in a public utility.

CULLEN, DONALD E. *National Emergency Strikes.* ILR Paperback no. 7. Ithaca: New York State School of Industrial and Labor Relations, 1968.

A definitive account of experience with "emergency" strikes under the Taft-Hartley and Railway Labor Acts.

DUNLOP, JOHN T. "The Function of the Strike." In *Frontiers of Collective Bargaining,* John T. Dunlop and Neil W. Chamberlain, eds. New York: Harper and Row, 1967.

The author offers four functional classifications of strikes, analyzes the long-term decline of the use of the strike, and examines the use of the strike during the life of an agreement.

EATON, B. CURTIS. "The Worker and the Profitability of the Strike," *Industrial and Labor Relations Review,* vol. 26, no. 1 (October 1972).

The author uses cost-benefit analysis to measure the net returns to employees in a sample of strike situations.

EISELE, C. FREDERICK. "Organization Size, Technology, and Frequency of Strikes," *Industrial and Labor Relations Review,* vol. 27, no. 4 (July 1974).

After examining the 20-year strike record in 282 manufacturing plants, the author concludes that there is very little relationship between technology and strikes and a mixed relationship between plant size and strikes.

HAMMETT, RICHARD S.; SEIDMAN, JOEL; and LONDON, JACK. "The Slowdown as a Union Tactic," *Journal of Political Economy*, vol. 65 (April 1957), pp. 126–34.
Discusses the effectiveness of the slowdown as a union tactic and union members' attitudes toward its use.

HIRSH, JOHN S., JR. "Strike Insurance and Collective Bargaining," *Industrial and Labor Relations Review*, vol. 22 (April 1969), pp. 399–415.
Article describes impact of strike insurance on bargaining process, noting a probable increase in their use and their tendency to prolong strikes.

KARSH, BERNARD. *Diary of a Strike*. Urbana: University of Illinois Press, 1958.
Story of a strike's effects on individuals directly and indirectly involved, upon the company and entire community. Gives dramatic account of organizing campaign and strike.

KLINE, SHELDON M. "Strike Benefits of National Unions," *Monthly Labor Review*, vol. 98, no. 3 (March 1975).
A description of the financial support provided by U.S. unions to their members who are involved in work stoppages.

KORNHAUSER, ARTHUR; DUBLIN, ROBERT; and ROSS, ARTHUR M., eds. *Industrial Conflict*. New York: McGraw-Hill Book Co., Inc., 1954.
Experts on sociology, psychology, and economics make an interdisciplinary study of the causes and effects of industrial conflict. See especially the chapter by Clark Kerr and Abraham Siegel, "The Interindustry Propensity to Strike —An International Comparison."

McCALMONT, DAVID B. "The Semi-Strike," *Industrial and Labor Relations Review*, vol. 15 (January 1962), pp. 191–208.
Briefly notes the nature of, and objections to, several proposed non-stoppage strike plans which provide for uninterrupted production of goods and services while the parties to the dispute incur economic penalties, and develops own semistrike proposal.

MANGUM, GARTH L. "Taming Wildcat Strikes," *Harvard Business Review*, vol. 38 (May–April 1960), pp. 88–96.
Argues that "wildcat strikes are management's responsibility—they continue as long as the participants find them profitable; cease when management, through disciplinary action, makes them unrewarding." Experiences with six wildcat strikes are described.

PARNES, HERBERT S. *Union Strike Votes: Current Practices and Proposed Controls*. Princeton, N.J.: Industrial Relations Section, Princeton University, Research Report Series no. 92, 1956.
This study evaluates compulsory strike-vote legislation in terms of experience under such laws and describes the processes whereby strikes are authorized by American unions.

ROSS, ARTHUR M., and HARTMAN, PAUL T. *Changing Patterns of Industrial Conflict*. New York: John Wiley & Sons, Inc., 1960, p. 220.
An analysis of national trends and international differences in strike activity in 15 countries of North America, Europe, Asia, Africa, and Australia. An attempt to explain the "withering away" of the strike in most of the countries of Northern Europe. A discussion of the relation between national patterns of industrial conflict and certain features of the industrial relations system.

SCHULTZ, GEORGE P. "The Massachusetts Choice-of-Procedures Approach to

Emergency Disputes," *Industrial and Labor Relations Review,* vol. 10 (April 1957), pp. 359–74.

    Examines experience under the Slichter choice-of-procedures emergency strike law in Massachusetts.

SERRIN, WILLIAM. *The Company and the Union.* New York: Vintage Books, 1974.

    A Detroit reporter analyzes the "civilized" relationship between General Motors and the United Automobile Workers, with special attention to their 1970 strike.

SKEELS, JACK W. "Measures of U.S. Strike Activity," *Industrial and Labor Relations Review,* vol. 24, no. 4 (July 1971).

    The author examines the relationships among eight measures of strike activity and a variety of economic, social, and political variables.

SLICHTER, SUMNER H.; HEALEY, JAMES J.; and LIVERNASH, E. ROBERT. *The Impact of Collective Bargaining on Management.* Washington, D.C.: Brookings Institution, 1960.

    See chapter 22, "Wildcat Strikes and Union Pressure Tactics."

STAGNER, ROSS. *The Psychology of Industrial Conflict.* New York: John Wiley & Sons, Inc., 1956.

    A systematic and comprehensive application of psychological principles and concepts to an understanding of the dynamics of industrial relations.

THIEBLOT, ARMAND J., and COWIN, RONALD M. *Welfare and Strikes: The Use of Public Funds to Support Strikers.* Labor Relations and Public Policy Series, Report No. 6. Philadelphia: University of Pennsylvania, Industrial Research Unit, 1972.

    An analysis of how public funds are used to support strikers, with a recommendation that such benefits should not be available to workers on strike.

U.S. DEPARTMENT OF LABOR, BUREAU OF LABOR STATISTICS. *Monthly Labor Review,* vol. 96, no. 9 (September 1973).

    In a special section, "Exploring Alternatives to the Strike," 18 union, management, academic, and governmental authors examine the role of the strike in the public and private sectors and consider some alternatives.

8 The Nature of the Labor Agreement

"CONTRACT?" OR AGREEMENT

ANY COMPANY in the regular course of business enters into many contracts, written, verbal, or implied. The "union contract" would seem, at a casual glance, to be merely one of these contracts, much like all the others.

This is far from the case.

When a company purchases materials it enters into a contract with another company, the vendor, under which the vendor supplies the materials and receives money in return. But under the labor agreement the union supplies nothing tangible, receives no money from the company in return. The union does not "supply" labor; the workers supply that, and draw the wages for it. The union does not contract for the labor of its members. It does not own them. It could no more force them to deliver labor promised to the company than the company itself could exact forced labor from them.

When a company sells its products to a customer it makes a contract to deliver goods of specified quality and quantity for a specified price. But the union buys nothing from the company, pays nothing to it.

When a company engages a contractor (again by contract) to erect a building, or to do some hauling, or to manufacture a component part, it pays the contractor who pays the labor used on the job. The union does not pay its members for the work they do for the company, nor does the company pay its workers through the union as an intermediary.

It is because the union "contract" differs so markedly from ordinary business contracts that this text refers to it by preference as the "labor agreement," or "union agreement." Usage has made the other term so common, however, that it would be pedantic to condemn it and hopeless to try to suppress it. There is no harm in using the term "union contract" interchangeably with "labor agreement," so long as the user, or reader, understands how this special kind of agreement differs from other contracts. To do so it is necessary to get a firm understanding of the nature of the labor agreement.

The Contract with the Employee

The company does not contract for labor with the union, but with the company employees. They are the ones who supply something tangible, hours of labor or pieces of finished work, and who receive money wages in return. The company has a contract with each one of them—as many contracts as there are employees. This contract may or may not take form in writing; it may not even be explicitly expressed verbally, but is inherent in the company's offer of a job and the employee's acceptance of the job. This contract—work for wages—is enforceable at law, and so firmly recognized that a "mechanic's lien," or claim for wages due, takes precedence over the claims of all other creditors of an employer. It must be paid in full even though the other creditors get only partial payment.

The union is not a party to this contract, yet shapes it, under collective bargaining, by establishing its terms. The labor agreement negotiated by the union defines the *company's* offer of wages, hours, and working conditions that are to make up the employee's work contract. Any worker is free to accept or reject these terms. If one accepts them one enters into a contract *directly with the company*. One may terminate this contract at will, just by quitting. The company is also theoretically free to terminate it by dismissal, but part of the terms is usually a promise by the company not to exercise this right except under certain conditions: seniority, "just cause" for discharge, and other restrictions.

The Agreement with the Union

Without altering, therefore, the direct contractual nature of the employer-employee relationship, the labor agreement collectively sets the terms on which the company offers its individual work contracts to each of the employees in the bargaining unit. The labor agreement thus takes the place of company policy—*becomes* company policy—in all areas that it touches.

A great deal of the literature of collective bargaining consists of attempts to define these areas and their boundaries, and to list and classify them. Most factory agreements (in contrast to craft-union contracts) are bulky, complicated documents. Some of them, printed in handbook form in 8-point type, run to more than 100 pages. Attempts to make sense of the many articles and clauses, sections, subsections, paragraphs, and subparagraphs, are often as confusing as the ponderous and pseudolegal phraseology of the documents themselves.

As a working instrument, every labor agreement has to be studied, by those who live under its provisions, as carefully as a code of laws. Every agreement differs in some respect from every other; there is no standard, no pattern, no universal model; and this is particularly true of industrial union agreements, which tend to be long and complicated. What the student needs is a tool of analysis that will unlock the meaning of any agreement.

A Tool for Analysis

This chapter, with the points it makes, constitutes just such a tool. By its aid the bulkiest or most obscurely worded agreement yields its essential purport to analysis. Despite the dissimilarity in organization of topics and presentation of provisions that is found in different labor agreements, all are reducible to certain common denominators.

These are presented in Figure 8–1, and topics in the remaining part of the chapter are arranged to correspond with the chart. Part III, The Issues in Collective Bargaining, Chapters 9 through 13, follows the same format.

FIGURE 8–1
Functions of the Labor Agreement

Function	Category	Scope
I. Union Security and Management Rights	a. The bargaining unit	Who speaks for whom
	b. Form of recognition	With what authority
	c. Duration and renewal	For how long
	d. Management rights	Except in what conditions
II. The Wage and Effort Bargain	a. Pay for time worked	Day rates and base rates; job evaluation
	b. The effort bargain	Standards
	c. Premium pay	Hours: duration
	d. Pay for time not worked	Fixed labor costs
	e. Contingent benefits	Variable labor costs
III. Individual Security	a. Job Rights	Relative claim to available work; seniority
	b. Due process	Absolute claim to fair treatment; grievance procedures
IV. Administration	a. Internal	On-the-job representation; shop stewards
	b. External	Arbitration

This presentation is taken from an article by Edwin F. Beal which appeared in the September-October 1962, issue of *Personnel,* by permission of the copyright owner. Minor changes in terminology have been made in the version given here.

FUNCTIONS OF THE LABOR AGREEMENT

The function of a collective agreement as a whole is to set the terms and conditions of employment for the individual employees it covers.

In common usage, this collective agreement is called a contract, but the real contract is between the company and each of the employees in the bargaining unit, so that there are actually as many contracts as there are individuals. They individually do the work and draw the pay; the union agreement merely lays down rules under which each individual contract takes effect. These rules make up two of the four main sections shown on the chart—the Wage and Effort Bargain, and Individual Security. The other two—Union Security and Management Rights, and Administration—define the union's relationship with management, and provide for administration of the terms agreed to.

The four parts further break down into the 13 functional categories listed in Figure 8–1. Following is a detailed explanation of these various categories and what they cover:

I.   Union Security and Management Rights

Every labor agreement constitutes recognition by one party of the other, and defines their relationship—who speaks for whom, with what authority, for how long, and except in what conditions. In other words, the parties to the agreement set down their own rules for rule-making. The four categories appear in the table as:

a. The Bargaining Unit.   The bargaining unit is the people for whom the union speaks and for whom the company recognizes the union as speaker. At any given moment, these people could be listed as names on a payroll, but because people shift jobs, move on and off the payroll, it is customary to describe the unit in terms of jobs. This may be done positively, by listing jobs or job categories, or negatively, by listing exclusions. Or, as is usually the case, it can be done by both methods.

As Chapter 6 brought out, the parties themselves may have defined the unit, or had it imposed on them by the NLRB. In either case, the definition limits the application of any substantive rules that labor and management agree on to employees in the bargaining unit.

b. Form of Recognition.   The statutory form of recognition is sole and exclusive bargaining rights. Other, stronger forms of recognition are also legal, but go beyond the statutory minimum. Some items that will fall in this category are :

1.   Union hiring hall.
2.   Union participation in apprenticeship control.
3.   Provisions giving the union power over employment; that is, the individual's right to join and remain in the bargaining unit.

c. Duration and Renewal. The agreement must run some specific term, and usually contains provisions for renewal. Such, for example, are:

1. Notice of termination or negotiation.
2. "Openers" for wage adjustments during the contract period.

d. Management Rights. This balances union security. Many agreements do not contain management rights provisions, on the theory that all rights not specifically bargained away belong to management, but most companies find it more practical to insert reminders that certain specific areas of action and decision remain in management hands. What special rights does management most need to retain? Three stand out:

1. Freedom to select the business objectives of the company.
2. Freedom to determine the uses to which the material assets of the enterprise will be devoted.
3. Power to discipline for cause.

II. The Wage and Effort Bargain

This section, with the one that follows (III–Individual Security) lays down the substantive rules, and together they are the heart and soul of the agreement. With or without a union, there is always a wage and effort bargain, but when a union is present, the union helps shape and define it. The rules in this section tell the employer how much money it will cost to get desired performance and production. They tell the employee how much pay to expect in return for effort expended. Here we have five categories:

a. Pay for Time Worked. This means the hourly, weekly, monthly wage or salary paid for the job, by base rates or day rates. Determining the appropriate rates for the job is part of bargaining, but the technique most commonly used for establishing wage differentials, with or without bargaining, is standard job-evaluation procedure, including such considerations as:

1. Labor grades or classifications and rate ranges.
2. Pay steps within grade.
3. Expected average earnings under piecework systems.

b. The Effort Bargain. This part of the basic contract between the company and each of its employees does not always appear explicitly in the agreement, but it is always there, if only by implication. It is as important to management (for it determines costs) as the preceding item is to the employee (since that item determines income). The effort bargain, in a word, means standards for task performance.

Standards may take very concrete form, as in time studies, or they may be loose and undefined. If management is careless about standards, employees may set them by default. Standards determine the intensity of each hour worked—the "miles per hour," rather than distance traveled or hours on the road—the performance expected under the working conditions that surround the task. Incentive plans or piecework may permit variable earnings, but standards are firm. That is, once standards have been properly set, they ought to change only with changes in working conditions, technology, or other alterations in the task itself. The effort bargain makes stipulations such as:

1. Rules for setting standards or making time studies.
2. Crew sizes, manning tables.
3. Quotas.
4. Work rules, including safety rules applying to the task.

   c. Premium Pay.   This is what used to be called "penalty pay." Theoretically, it is money that would never be paid if no employee were asked to work outside regularly scheduled, normal daylight hours. Premium pay tends to limit the *duration* of work; that is, the length of the working day and working week, by making it more expensive for the company to operate beyond the scheduled hours. The most common types of premium pay are:

1. Overtime.
2. Call-in pay.
3. Shift differentials.

   d. Pay for Time Not Worked.   This item used to be lumped together with the following one, contingent benefits, under the general heading of "fringe benefits." Our outline separates them, putting in category II (*d*) payments that represent fixed labor costs, i.e., costs that are inescapable and predictable—the payments that all employees get such as:

1. Paid holidays and vacations.
2. Christmas or other bonuses.
3. Minor items, such as paid coffee breaks, washup time, and so forth.

   e. Contingent Benefits.   These are forms of insurance, the premiums being a cost to the company (and sometimes, also, to the employee) with benefits payable only to those who suffer a particular misfortune that affects earnings: i.e., layoff, accident or illness, untimely death, survival beyond retirement age. They differ from the preceding category in that not every employee gets all the benefits they offer; also, employees may contribute to the costs. Actuarial calculations will yield quite an accurate prediction as to the number of employees to whom these benefits will be paid, but the individual claims cannot, of course, be foreseen. Management must judge these items by their cost, whereas employees will judge them by their payoff in individual cases. The main types of contingent benefits are:

1. Death benefits.
2. Pensions.

3. Supplementary unemployment benefits.
4. Severance pay.
5. Health and welfare plans.

III. Individual Security

The wage and effort bargain, outlined above, is the fundamental contract offer the employee accepts when accepting the job. It obligates the company to pay one according to the terms set down. In turn, it obligates the employee to perform as specified in the agreement, or as directed by management in day-to-day operations. But it contains no guarantee of continuance. An employee who finds the bargain satisfactory wants some guarantee of continuity of employment. Broadly speaking, this attitude coincides with management interests, because the company does not want excessive turnover. Nevertheless, the company has to lay people off when work is slack; at times it needs to transfer people from one job to another; and it should have freedom to select good prospects for promotion. Thus, there has to be an accommodation of company and employee interests. The rules whereby the company, on the one hand, maintains a work force of the optimum quality and numbers, and employees, on the other, are assured of their individual security, fall into two categories:

a. Job Rights. Probably the most common job rights device is seniority. Other common forms are the closed shop or the union hiring hall. In the latter case, union practices or bylaws take care of individual claims to available work; they are then no concern of management. Seniority within the company, on the other hand, is a vast and complicated field of claims and counterclaims by individuals. Seniority is never absolute; it gives the individual only a relative claim to available work or other benefits flowing from the enterprise. Three types of seniority can be distinguished—protective, opportunity, and privilege—together with a special concept, the seniority unit, that has a bearing on all three.

To take the special concept first, the seniority unit usually consists of a list of employees' names ranked in order of their seniority. What is important here is the size of the list or lists in relation to the total work force in the bargaining unit. Criteria for compiling the list may range from simple job seniority on up through occupational, departmental, divisional, and plant-wide groupings to company-wide seniority. (The 1965 steel settlement even extended the concept to a "seniority pool" for the industry, thus cutting across company lines.)

Of the three main types of seniority, the first—protective seniority—applies in the case of layoffs: The most senior employee (within the specified unit) is the last to be let go and the first to be recalled when work picks up.

The second type, opportunity seniority, gives the most senior employee the first chance to get, or qualify for, a better job—or, in case of a cutback, to stay on the payroll. The "bid and bump" system exemplifies this type. Of course, the broader the seniority unit, the closer opportunity seniority comes to being the same thing as protective seniority, and in the plant or company-wide unit they become synonymous.

The third type, privilege seniority, is the employee's right to contingent benefits, such as pensions. This is probably the only completely noncontroversial kind of seniority, as evidenced by the fact that the unit is almost always company-wide, with pensions calculated according to total years of service.

But union agreements rarely make seniority the sole determinant of job rights. The broader the seniority unit, the more it is likely to be affected by . such factors as merit or ability to do the job, particularly in cases of opportunity seniority. Hence, in the job-rights category also fall such items as:

1. Superseniority for shop stewards.
2. Breaks in seniority.
3. Criteria other than seniority, such as merit, for individual advancement.

   b. Due Process.   This category covers the grievance-handling procedure (though not the machinery)—the rules that have been laid down for handling employee complaints of all types, including allegations of simple injustice as well as contract violations. This covers such items as:

1. Steps in the grievance procedure.
2. Time limits for replies to grievances.
3. Procedure for invoking arbitration.
4. No-strike, no-lockout pledges pending arbitration.
5. Warning notices and reprimands.
6. Disciplinary penalties and appeals.

IV.   Administration

This section covers the machinery that is set up to enforce agreement terms and put due process into effect, including the delegation of the requisite authority to specific individuals who have been given certain responsibilities in connection with the agreement. Part of this machinery is internal, in that it involves only employees of the company. Part is external, involving outsiders, such as union representatives, government officials, or private arbitrators. This gives us our two final categories:

   a. Internal: On-the-Job Representation.   Though union members may name their representatives, such as shop stewards, the election of those people does not confer authority upon them. They obtain their authority from the agreement, in which the special activities of shop stewards are recognized. Thus, this category covers such arrangements as:

1. Payment for time spent by stewards in handling grievances.
2. Permission for stewards to leave their workplace to confer with employees and with supervisors.

b. External: Arbitration. This category encompasses those sections of the agreement covering outsiders on whom it confers a certain authority. It includes such items as:

1. Grants of permission to union officials to visit workplaces during working hours, under certain conditions.
2. Composition of a board of arbitrators, or a disciplinary board, if this draws upon people from outside the company.
3. Duties and powers of the arbitrator and any limitations thereon.

DIVERSITY IN LABOR AGREEMENTS

This chapter purports to be a tool for the analysis of labor agreements. To show how this tool works, two labor agreements will be analyzed. This analysis will require consideration of long-established practices of the parties to an agreement as well as the written words. By noting the substantial diversity in the practices of craft and industrial unions, the basic unity of purpose of all collective bargaining agreements becomes apparent.

A Craft Union-Employer Association Agreement

The first agreement to be analyzed is 30 pages long and contains about 9,000 words. It covers the bricklayers in a major metropolitan area. Three employer associations and four local unions of the Bricklayers, Masons and Plasterers' International Union signed the agreement.

Union Security and Management Rights. To understand the union security provisions of this agreement it is necessary to look beyond the written words of the agreement. Such key words as "Union Security" and "Management Rights" appear nowhere in the agreement.

Bargaining Unit. The agreement contains no explicit reference to the "bargaining unit." However, the bargaining unit is defined in three other sections of the agreement: "Article XI: Scope of Work" (which deals with the nature of covered jobs), "Article XIV: Negotiations: Grievances" (which provides for the settlement of jurisdictional disputes), and "Article I" (which defines the relationships of individual employers to the three Associations who are signatories to the agreement).

Article XI: Scope of Work, reads as follows:

> The work covered by this Agreement is described as bricklaying masonry and shall consist of laying bricks, in, under and upon any structure or form of work where bricks are used, whether in the ground or over the surface, or beneath water, in commercial buildings, rolling mills, iron works, blast or smelting furnaces, lime or brick kilns, in mines or fortifications and in all underground work such as sewers, telegraph, electric and telephone conduits; all pointing and cutting of brick walls, fireproofing, block-arching, terra cotta cutting and setting, laying and cutting of all tile,

> plaster, mineralwool, cork blocks, cement and cinder blocks, glass brick, macotta and metalon, or any substitutes for the above materials where the trowel is used, and setting of all cut stone or artificial stone trimming on brick or stone buildings.

The work defines the jobs covered by the agreement which is the equivalent to the employee side of the bargaining unit question.

Because Article XI might come into conflict with bargaining units defined in other building and construction industry agreements, Article XIV provides for the local settlement of jurisdictional disputes or the ultimate referral of such disputes to the National Joint Board for the Settlement of Jurisdictional Disputes in the Building and Construction Industry.

"Article I" which has no descriptive title provides the answer to the question of what employers are covered by the agreement. The three associations which signed the agreement represent masonry contractors, general contractors who employ other tradesmen as well as bricklayers, and residential construction contractors. Article I states that the associations acted only as agents for their members in the negotiation of the contract and that the associations have an individual, but not joint, obligation to the terms of the contract. Article I also contains a "most favored nation" clause which binds the union not to negotiate more favorable contracts with other employers.

Form of Recognition.   The form of recognition or union security provisions of this agreement are contained in "Article VIII: Hiring Employees." The six sections of this article require the employers to notify the union of job vacancies and to give preference in employment to workers who have previously worked at the trade or to graduates or students in an approved apprenticeship training program. The union agrees to refer qualified workers to the employer for consideration. Workers who refuse to join the union within seven days after being hired must be discharged. All this boils down to either a "seven-day union shop" or a "modified closed shop"— neither of which terms can be found anywhere in the words of the agreement.

Duration and Renewal.   The provisions for duration and renewal are routine.

Management Rights.   The term "Management Rights" is also missing from the written agreement. Article XI, Section 1, states, "There shall be no limits or restrictions as to the amount of work performed by employees," but numerous other paragraphs provide that "No work shall be done which shall destroy the true principles of the trade." All this seems to indicate that management rights are defined by a tradition which places heavy emphasis on judgment of individual tradesmen.

The Wage and Effort Bargain.   The wage and effort bargain is the largest single section of the bricklayers' agreement. It covers almost 10 of the 30 pages of the agreement. Nevertheless, it is very brief and very simple compared to the typical industrial union agreement.

Pay for Time Worked. The wage scale contained in this agreement provides base wages for only *four* jobs: journeymen, subforemen, foremen, and apprentices. Foremen are paid 50 cents an hour more than journeymen and subforemen are paid 25 cents an hour more than journeymen. Apprentices receive a graduated percentage of the journeyman rate depending on how long they have served in the apprenticeship, e.g., 50 percent during the first six months of apprenticeship up to 80 percent in the seventh six months.

The Effort Bargain. The bricklayers' contract does not say much about the effort bargain as such. However, it contains quite detailed provisions on the types of scaffolds to be provided, the fact that supervisors must be "practical mechanics of the trade," limits on the work activity of supervisors, the obligation of workers to cooperate with one another, and workmanship standards which preserve "the true principles of the trade."

Premium Pay. Work in excess of eight hours per day is prohibited except for a few minutes of work in cases of necessity. Overtime work and work performed on Saturdays, Sundays, and holidays is paid at the rate of double time. Base wages on the second shift and third (or special) shift are 30 cents and 60 cents per hour higher than on the first shift. The "special shift" is any single shift when conditions make it impractical to work a shift wholly between the regular hours of 8 A.M. and 4:30 P.M.

Pay for Time Not Worked. Holiday pay is provided by the Bricklayers' Holiday Trust Fund which is supported by a 4 percent payroll contribution by the employers covered by the agreement. Washup time is limited to five minutes before lunch and before quitting time.

Contingent Benefits. The benefits provided by this agreement are described in a separate agreement which has been amended several times since its establishment. The basic agreement, however, provides for employer contributions of 4 percent of the base wages paid to the Bricklayers' Pension Trust Fund. Insurance is provided by the Construction Workers' Insurance Fund which is financed by employer payments of 15 cents per work-hour for all hours worked by employees. It should be noted that the Holiday Trust Fund, the Pension Fund, and the Insurance Fund are all multiemployer arrangements and that the worker is entitled to benefits by virtue of employment with any unionized employers in the industry rather than by continuous employment with a single enterprise.

Individual Security. Job rights, or the individual's relative claim to available work, is almost entirely absent from the agreement. Since the union refers workers to employment, *union* rules define the individual's job rights. However, if it becomes necessary to reduce the working force temporarily the supervisor is directed to divide the work equally among the crew, and no employee is to receive less than two hours' pay on any day on which the work force is reduced temporarily unless the supervisor sends the whole crew home for that day. The workers' absolute claim to fair treatment is described in the sections of the agreement dealing with supervisors. The agreement provides that supervisors shall be selected by the employer and shall represent the employer on the job. Another paragraph of the agreement states: "It shall be the duty of the foreman to abide by terms of this Agreement and he shall not be required as a condition of employment to violate any part of it." Although the agreement provides a method of wage payment for employees who may be discharged, the agreement lists no grounds for discharge and makes no reference whatsoever to disciplinary procedures.

Administration. Article VI of the agreement provides for a job steward on each job. The steward is a member of the union appointed by the business agent to act as steward. The steward and business agent may confer with employees during working hours.

The steward who is unable to settle a grievance with the foreman refers the grievance to the business agent. If the business agent is unable to settle the grievance with the employer, the grievance is referred to a Joint Arbitration Board consisting of equal numbers of union and employer representatives. If this Joint Board is unable to render a majority opinion on the grievance, the grievance is then referred to the international union. A representative of the international union and a representative of the associations then designate an umpire (arbitrator) who is empowered to render a final and binding decision.

The foregoing analysis of a craft union collective bargaining agreement shows: (1) the importance of unwritten practices in industries which have a long history of collective bargaining, (2) the omnipresence of the basic functions of the labor agreement, and (3) when compared to the following industrial union agreement, the great diversity in practice in the provisions of the labor agreement in different circumstances.

An Industrial Union–Single-Plant Agreement

The second agreement to be analyzed is 40 pages long and contains about 16,000 words. By industrial union standards, it is a short (many of them run to several hundred pages) and simple (one plant of a multiplant employer) agreement. Nevertheless, it will be obvious from the discussion that follows that this agreement is much more formal and complete than the typical craft union agreement.

Union Security and Management Rights. The industrial union agreement uses most of the terminology in Figure 8–1 in the form presented there.

Bargaining Unit. Article I—Recognition states that "The Company recognizes the Union as the exclusive bargaining agent with respect to wages, hours of employment or other conditions of employment for all production, maintenance and other factory employees, excepting office employees, office building janitors, time keepers, plant police, administrative employees, foremen, and clerks."

Form of Recognition. The form of recognition granted in this agreement is the agency shop, because the plant is located in a "right-to-work" state. The last paragraph of Article II provides that if the state right-to-work law is repealed the union shop clause will be reinstated in the agreement.

Article III of the agreement provides a voluntary and revocable check-off of union dues by the employer.

Duration and Renewal. The provisions for duration and renewal are routine.

Management Rights. Article IV of the agreement is entitled "Management of the Plant." Paragraph 4.0 reads as follows:

> The management of the plant and the direction of the working force, including the right to hire; discharge for just cause, suspend, discipline, promote, transfer; to decide the machine and tool equipment, the products, methods, schedules of production, processes of manufacturing and assembling together with all designs and engineering, and the control of raw materials, semimanufactured and finished parts which may be incorporated into the product, shall be vested exclusively in the Company.

Paragraph 4.1 provides that the rights of the company to discharge for just cause, suspend, discipline, to promote and transfer to jobs within the bargaining unit are subject to the provisions of the agreement and the grievance procedure.

The Wage and Effort Bargain. The wage and effort bargain provisions of this agreement cover approximately 15 of its 40 pages.

Pay for Time Worked. Appendix "A" lists the rates of pay for 124 different job descriptions falling into 13 labor grades. The lowest rate of pay is $2.43 per hour and the top rate is $3.22 per hour. New employees start at 10 cents per hour below regular rate and receive a 5-cent raise after 30 days on the job and another 5-cent raise after 90 days on the job.

The Effort Bargain. The agreement being analyzed here makes no reference to production standards as such, but its grievance procedure is sufficiently broad in coverage to make production standards subject to arbitration.

Premium Pay. Time and one half is provided for work in excess of 8 hours in a day, or 40 hours in a week, or for work on Saturdays. Double-time pay is provided for all work on Sundays and holidays. Fifteen cents per hour of premium pay is provided for workers of the second and third shifts. Four hours of call-in pay are provided.

Pay for Time Not Worked. Holiday pay is provided for eight holidays. Vacation pay of from one to three weeks is provided for workers having more than one year's seniority. A 10-minute clean-up period is provided for painters before the end of their work shift.

Contingent Benefits. The company provides Blue Cross and Blue Shield insurance coverage for all members of the bargaining unit. A separate pension agreement provides for company contributions to a pension fund which will permit the payment of a schedule of benefits for workers when they reach the normal retirement age of 65. The pension fund covers only the employees of the company at this one plant.

Individual Security.   Article VIII—Seniority describes the workers' relative claim to available work. The eight pages of Article VIII define the seniority unit, the applications of seniority, superseniority for stewards, and reasons for the revocation of seniority.

The workers' absolute claim to fair treatment is described in Article VIII —Discipline and Discharge. This article provides that all discipline shall be for "just cause." Article XIV provides that violation of company rules will provide a just cause for discipline. Appendix "B" lists 22 "Shop Rules and Regulations" and 10 "Safety Rules." Other provisions of the agreement outline the grievance handling procedure which terminates in arbitration.

Administration.   Article V provides for on-the-job representation by stewards to be elected by whatever method the union deems appropriate so long as stewards have at least one year's seniority with the company and the number of stewards is agreed to by the company and union. Stewards are paid by the company when engaged in handling grievances but they must be excused from work by their foremen and the company reserves the right to limit the discussion of a grievance to 15 minutes.

The powers of the arbitrator are very broad under this agreement because he is authorized to "rule on all disputes pertaining to the interpretation or application of this Agreement, provided, however, that he shall have no power to add to, nor subtract from, nor modify any terms of this Agreement." The arbitrator is to be selected by the parties from lists provided by the American Arbitration Association.

SUMMARY

Every employment relationship focuses on a wage and effort bargain. When the employment relationship becomes formalized through collective bargaining, the agreement expands to cover four basic functions: (1) Union Security and Management Rights, (2) The Wage and Effort Bargain, (3) Individual Security, and (4) Administration. These four functions are present in every collective bargaining agreement: sometimes the written agreement is quite explicit in defining these functions and sometimes it is necessary to look carefully at the practice of the parties to identify the functions.

This text has emphasized the diversity of the practice between industrial and craft unions. This diversity remains in the contents of their agreements, but the very diversity in these agreements is proof of the unifying significance of the four basic functions of every collective bargaining agreement.

QUESTIONS FOR DISCUSSION

1. Compare and contrast the union agreement with the "employment relation" entered into between a physician and patient or a lawyer and client. Com-

pare both of these relationships with the employment relation in a nonunion enterprise.

2. Would the "functions" discussed in this chapter be helpful in preparing for negotiations? Outline the desirable steps in detail.

SELECTED ANNOTATED BIBLIOGRAPHY

CHAMBERLAIN, NEIL W., and KUHN, JAMES W. *Collective Bargaining.* 2d ed. New York: McGraw-Hill, 1965.

See chapter 5, "The Nature of Collective Bargaining," for three useful conceptual interpretations of the collective bargaining agreement.

FELLER, DAVID E. "A General Theory of the Collective Bargaining Agreement," *California Law Review,* vol. 61, no. 3 (May 1973).

A long and complex legal discussion of the collective bargaining agreement, with a focus on the rights and obligations that unions, employers, and employees have under such agreements.

HEALY, JAMES J., ed. *Creative Collective Bargaining: Meeting Today's Challenge to Labor Management Relations.* Englewood Cliffs, N.J.: Prentice-Hall, 1965.

This book contains eleven case studies of collective bargaining which the editor believes illustrate fresh and creative approaches to collective bargaining. Some of the cases involve productivity bargaining.

U.S. DEPARTMENT OF LABOR, BUREAU OF LABOR STATISTICS. *Monthly Labor Review.*

Each issue contains a "Developments in Industrial Relations" section which is primarily (but not exclusively) devoted to descriptions of important or newsworthy collective bargaining settlements.

part three

The Issues in Collective Bargaining

Part Three of this book analyzes the issues in collective bargaining; the areas of accommodation and sometimes disagreement between employers, workers, and unions. The discussion follows the basic format proposed earlier for the analysis of collective bargaining agreements: union security and management rights; the wage and effort bargain; individual security; and administration. Management and union goals in matters of principle and cost are considered in the two "model" tyes of collective bargaining relationships. A final chapter analyzes unions of professionals and white collar workers.

9 Union Security and Management Rights

THE MANAGEMENT of an organization can assemble a work force, and that work force may remain nonunion, but a union—to be a union and not some other kind of association—cannot enroll members who are not actual or potential employees of an organization. To put this in specific terms: The X Manufacturing Co. can hire a thousand workers and bargain with each of them, legally, as single individuals; and go on dealing with them that way as long as the majority of them remain ununionized. Let the thousand—or even a small fraction of them, with the support of the majority—form a union, and under existing labor law the company must bargain with the union on the terms and conditions of employment of the thousand. Theoretically, these terms had hitherto been bargained with each individual, but management practically offered the terms on a take-it-or-leave-it basis. The union concentrates the bargaining power of all its members against the bargaining power of the company. Union security, or an assurance that the union will continue to exist and perform its bargaining function, thus becomes vital both to the union as an institution and to the members whose terms and conditions of employment it protects.

If the company had not put together a work force, there could have been no union. Now that the work force exists and is unionized, the union takes on an existence independent of the company. Labor relations law requires the company to recognize and bargain with it. The union often wants security that goes beyond (without contradicting) the law. Every collective bargaining agreement therefore confirms the recognition of the union by the employer of the work force the union represents, and defines the relationship of the parties.

Many collective bargaining agreements (though not all) contain sections clearly labeled "union security" and "management rights." Whether labeled and set apart or not, they specify who speaks for whom, with what authority, for how long, except in what conditions. They become a kind of enabling act that gives authority and binding effect to everything else in the agreement. They are rules for rule-making enacted by the parties them-selves.

UNION SECURITY

The union is not secure in its relationship with the employer if there is any doubt about (1) which employees the union does—and does not—rep-resent, (2) the form of recognition, or (3) the duration of the agreement and procedures for renewal or renegotiation.

The sections on union security aim to resolve these doubts.

The Bargaining Unit: Who Speaks for Whom

Rarely, if ever, does a union represent or even claim *all* the employees of a given employer. Often only a part, and not the whole of an employing enterprise or employer association, deals with a union. Who speaks for whom in any collective bargaining relationship appears in the definition of the bargaining unit.

The bargaining unit under existing labor law is a legally defined body or constituency empowered under certain circumstances to make, on behalf of both management and the employees contained in the unit, the crucial decision on recognition.[1]

The law does not leave this issue entirely up to bargaining between the parties but reserves to the government, acting through the NLRB, the right to define the bargaining unit. Public policy trusts neither management nor the union, separately or together, to make this determination in the public interest. When management had the power to make it, employers used their power to deny recognition and deprive employees of freedom of choice. When unions sought the power, they tried to assert jurisdictional claims that were often irrelevant to employer operations and contrary to employee wishes. Still, the bargaining unit is important both to the union and the com-pany—more directly important to them than to anyone else—so, when in a given situation they agree on a specific delimitation as appropriate, the NLRB will usually confirm their jointly-defined unit. If they cannot agree, the NLRB decides. The NLRB has shown itself reluctant to define the unit in ways that would interfere with operations. It will, indeed, "carve out" a craft or professional from an otherwise industrial unit, but only if the em-ployees in the carved-out unit vote for separation.

A bargaining unit is supposed to group together those employees who have common interests, and exclude those who do not share these interests. As a rule these groupings correspond to natural divisions brought about by workplace technology. Some commonly accepted units are: hourly paid production and maintenance workers; clerical employees; technicians or

---

[1] See Ch. 6, "Establishing the Collective Bargaining Relationship."

professionals; members of a recognized craft or trade. Guards may have a bargaining unit, but may not be represented by the same union as other employees.

The Form of Recognition

Before the passage of the Wagner Act in 1935 the forms of recognition and corresponding degrees of union security that unions won from management ranged all the way from "open shop"—no recognition, no security—to the maximum—closed shop (craft union)—and, in a few rare instances, union shop (industrial union). The range included intermediate forms such as recognition for members only or for specified purposes only—as for the presentation of complaints and grievances. This gamut carried through to the present day in public employment; for the federal service, Executive Order 11491 on collective negotiations still lists some graduated degrees of recognition. In private industry, labor relations law since 1935 has diminished the range.

Until the enactment of a law, actual union security could only be as great —regardless of the form of recognition—as union strength or company weakness made it. A company could refuse to recognize a union even though employees wanted it, or it could choose between rival unions without regard for employee preference, or start a company union and deal with it even though all but a few employees shunned it. To gain recognition from a reluctant company management, therefore, a union had first to lead the employees out on strike. The recognition strike was as much a regular feature of an industrial union's activity as the jurisdictional strike was of the craft union's.

One of the aims behind labor legislation was to eliminate strikes over recognition. The law accordingly gave *employees* the right to choose their own union representatives without interference either from management or from unions with rival jurisdictional claims. Employees do this by majority vote of all those eligible to vote in an appropriate bargaining unit in an NLRB election. Recognition follows automatically for the union that wins a majority. Legal recognition won in this fashion takes a *minimum* form that is already a strong guarantee of union security: exclusive bargaining rights. Stronger forms are permitted, though some of the strongest are limited or technically prohibited by federal or state law. Here, briefly, are some of the common forms.

Exclusive Bargaining Rights. This is the legal minimum. For a given bargaining unit, the employer recognizes one union, and that one only. Agreements reached with this union apply to all employees in the bargaining unit, whether or not they are union members. Nonmembers are not required to join the union, but the employer can make no deal with any of them that departs from the terms of the union agreement.

A union with exclusive bargaining rights is ordinarily secure from rival unions and from withdrawal of recognition for at least the duration of the agreement: a year or more.

Union Shop.   The phrase "union shop" is often loosely used to mean any unionized enterprise, even when the form of recognition is no stronger than exclusive bargaining rights. In this loose sense it merely means anything except a completely nonunion enterprise. Here, however—and throughout this book—union shop has a precise and technical meaning, the meaning recognized in labor law and collective bargaining practice. The union shop is the *maximum* form of security for an industrial union.

The union shop contains all the elements of exclusive bargaining rights and goes further. A union shop agreement requires the employer to make union membership a condition of employment for all employees in the bargaining unit. A new employee does not have to be a union member when hired, but within a specified time after hiring must join the union and remain a member in good standing or be discharged.

Because this requirement of the union shop works a hardship on people with religious scruples or strong personal convictions against union membership, the Taft-Hartley law of 1947 modified the forced-membership feature of the union shop: Employees need not actually join and be active in the union, provided they pay the equivalent of the union's initiation fee and regular dues just as if they were members. The minimum probation period before payments begin, under the same law, cannot be less than 30 days, but may be longer.

Agency Shop.   The union shop is unlawful in right-to-work states. What takes its place is a resourceful expedient devised to stay within the letter of state law, yet get the substance of union shop conditions. Under the agency shop form of recognition, employees are not required to join the union. Instead, the agreements make it a condition of employment that they pay the union the equivalent of initiation fees and dues as a kind of tax, or service charge, in return for the union's acting as their bargaining agent. This makes a rule out of the exception written into the Taft-Hartley law.

Closed Shop.   This is another maximum form, characteristic of craft unions, but also applicable wherever the conditions of the labor market favor operation of a union hiring hall. Such conditions tend to arise in industries that have traditionally depended on nonskilled, casual labor; notably, the maritime industry. Decasualization, or stabilization of employment for a restricted number of workers, is the union's aim in setting up a hiring hall as the central labor exchange. The employers on their side get a dependable labor pool to draw from at need. With the organization of pickers in the vineyards and row-crop farms of the Southwest, decasualization seems to be on the way in agriculture. The closed shop and the hiring hall thus fit the conditions and meet the needs of operations in industries drawing from the two extremes of the labor market: skilled craftsmen; and the unskilled.

The Taft-Hartley Act of 1947 outlawed the closed shop; but merely passing a law did not suppress it as an institution. It persisted without sanction of law in the industries mentioned, for more than a decade before the NLRB started proceedings to enforce the ban.

In 1959 the Landrum-Griffin Act rescued the closed shop and revived it—practically, or de facto, if not legally, or de jure—by exempting the construction industry from the Taft-Hartley 30-day probation period and substituting a 7-day minimum. Not many employers want to try to circumvent the union by hiring nonunion workers they will have to fire and replace in a week; it's easier to take union members out of the hiring hall right at the start. Thus unions and employing organizations in construction continue to sign agreements that may seem to have the form of the union shop but provide the substance of the closed shop, and closed-shop conditions.

The wording of an agreement that, while staying within the letter of the law provides closed-shop conditions, calls for the employer to apply first to the union for workers and to look elsewhere only when the union cannot meet demands. In effect, this means that a company may hire only workers who already belong to the union or who have a work permit from the union. When jobs are scarce, the union can reserve the openings for its members. When jobs are plentiful, the union still controls referrals to the job. It issues work permits to nonmembers—a sort of temporary membership without privileges—revocable at the union's pleasure. The union does not have to accept these temporary workers into permanent membership, but after the probationary period—7 days or 30 as the case may be—can require them to pay the equivalent of union dues. They will already have paid the equivalent of an initiation fee for the work permit.

Outsiders, such as college students working at unskilled jobs during vacations, often complain about the apparent injustice of this system. It was perhaps indignation at the supposed injustice that impelled Sen. Robert Taft to put the ban on the closed shop into his bill. But justice does not look the same to all. The worker depending for a living on an industry offering sporadic and temporary job opportunities sees no injustice in a device that gives one something like regular work and protects one from losing income to competitors who have no permanent attachment to the occupation.

Maintenance of Membership. This form of recognition seems to be dying out, but may be met occasionally. It occurs in industrial union agreements and falls somewhere between exclusive bargaining rights and the union shop; a compromise between the two.

Historically, maintenance of membership agreements first appeared in World War II. Unions had given a no-strike pledge. In return for renouncing the strike weapon, they accepted government mediation and, in those instances when they could not reach agreement with an employer, tripartite arbitration. This took place before the emergency National War Labor Board composed of representatives of labor, management, and "the public." Unions pushed, in their negotiations with employers, for union shop agreements. Some employers gave way, others resisted. The unions took this issue to the NWLB.

On the Board and its subsidiary panels, labor representatives naturally tended to side with the unions; employer representatives, with management. That gave the public representative the deciding vote. This third party, the public member, shrank equally from forcing the union shop on a reluctant employer and denying the union (which was honor-bound not to strike at a time when strikes would have been most effective) more than the minimal protection offered by exclusive bargaining rights.

The upshot (as might be expected) was a compromise. Under a maintenance of membership clause, all employees who are members of the union at a specified time after the signing of the agreement or who later join the union must continue to pay dues to the union for the duration of the agreement.

After the war, when unions were free again to strike for their demands, many of these agreements were renewed in the more clear-cut union shop form. Others reverted to the legal minimum of exclusive bargaining rights. Maintenance of membership today tends to be a transitional form, marking progress or retreat between the current extremes.

Maintenance of membership, like the closed shop, is illegal in right-to-work states.

Checkoff. The checkoff is really an administrative arrangement, not a form of recognition, since it may be associated with any of the forms. It most commonly accompanies the closed or union shop. It merely provides that the employer withhold union dues from union members' paychecks and transmit the money directly, in a lump sum, to the union. Under the Taft-Hartley Act, the checkoff is lawful only when each individual employee signs a checkoff declaration, which may continue indefinitely if not revoked, but may not be irrevocable for more than one year.

Duration and Renewal

Unions and managers customarily specify time limits to the labor agreements they sign. Managers benefit by being able to look ahead to a period of stability with predictable costs and assurance against disruption of operations. Unions get protection from rival union interference. The NLRB will not normally permit a rival union to challenge a certified union during the life of an existing agreement.

Craft unions started the tradition of signing agreements with one year's duration in the seasonal construction industry. The main issue at stake each season was the wage rate, with the union trying to estimate the new season's demand for labor against the supply. Industrial unions and their factory managements seldom had to reckon with this seasonal influence, but initially followed the same pattern when they signed their first agreements in the 1930s and began to gain experience in dealing with each other. With experience, growing confidence, and increasing security from rival attack, many unions and companies have settled down into relationships that look well beyond the single year ahead.

Today the bargaining partners quite commonly sign two-year, three-year, and even longer agreements. The steel industry and steelworkers' union, for a striking example, found in 1974 that their relationship had worked out so satisfactorily that they extended their agreements to the year 1980. The trend towards agreements of longer duration has worked back into the construction industry: in 1975 plumbers and steamfitters in the Northwest signed a five-year agreement (which contains a no-strike clause) with the contractors' association.

MANAGEMENT RIGHTS

Widespread interest in the proper formulation of management rights clauses in collective bargaining agreements developed after World War II, but the history of the controversy over rights is older. Two presidents of the United States convened well-publicized national conferences without getting management and labor to agree on principles of union security and management rights.

President Woodrow Wilson called the first industrial conference in the fall of 1919. His main purpose was to facilitate the orderly reconversion of the economy to a peacetime footing. Labor, management, and public representatives met but were unable to agree on principles to guide postwar labor-management relations. After 17 days of debate the conference collapsed. The stumbling block was union security. Labor representatives argued that employees should be entitled to representation by unions of their own choosing. Public representatives favored collective bargaining but thought that no employee should be denied the right to refrain from joining a union. Management representatives steadfastly insisted on the following statement of principles:

> There should be no denial of the right of an employer and his workers voluntarily to agree that their relation shall be that of the "closed union shop" or of the "closed nonunion shop." But the right of an employer and his men to continue their relations on the principle of the "open shop" should not be denied or questioned. No employer should be required to deal with men or groups of men who are not his employees or chosen from among them.[2]

As a practical matter, the principle advocated by management meant that unions could function only with the *consent* of management. This provided *no* union security. The failure of the conference resulted in a continuation of the status quo in collective bargaining and labor relation law. This status quo was the "closed nonunion shop" in mass-production industry in 1919. With no legislative protection of the right to organize, unions lost the footholds they had temporarily gained in the factories during the war.

---

[2] Department of Labor, *Proceedings of the First Industrial Conference (Called by the President) October 6 to 23, 1919* (Washington, D.C., U.S. Government Printing Office, 1920) p. 82.

Employers successfully extended the "closed nonunion shop" to most of American industry by 1930. Not until the passage of the Wagner Act in 1935 did the unions gain the means of achieving any real measure of union security.

President Harry S Truman called the second national industrial conference in 1945. Again the nation faced problems of harmonious reconversion to peacetime production. This time, with union security already written into law, management rights became the major issue. Again labor and management representatives found themselves unable to agree on principles. Management representatives stated their case this way:

> Labor members of the Committee on Management's Right to Manage have been unwilling to agree to any listing of specific management functions. Management members of the Committee conclude, therefore, that the labor members are convinced that the field of collective bargaining will, in all probability, continue to expand into the field of management.
>
> The only possible end of such a philosophy would be joint management of the enterprise. To this the management members naturally cannot agree. Management has functions that must not and cannot be compromised to the public interest. If labor disputes are to be minimized by "the genuine acceptance by organized labor of the functions and responsibilities of management to direct the operation of the enterprise," labor must agree that certain specific functions and responsibilities of management are not subject to collective bargaining.[3]

Labor's response was to reject the view that in the conduct of enterprise operations any given set of rights belonged inherently to management. According to union speakers, management rights were fluid and should be handled on a case-by-case basis by management and the union in each enterprise. They insisted:

> Because of the complexities of these [diverse union-management] relationships the labor members of the Committee think it unwise to specify and classify the functions and responsibilities of management. Because of the insistence by management for such specification the Committee was unable to agree upon a joint report. To do so might well restrict the flexibility so necessary to efficient operation.
>
> It would be extremely unwise to build a fence around the rights and responsibilities of management on the one hand and the unions on the other. The experience of many years shows that with the growth of mutual understanding the responsibilities of one of the parties today may well become the joint responsibility of both parties tomorrow.[4]

Two basic and opposed positions on management rights seem to emerge from these contrasting statements. The one put forward by management

---

[3] *President's National Labor Management Conference*, vol. 3, doc. 125 II/13 (November 29, 1945), p. 47.

[4] Ibid., vol. 3, doc. 120 II/11 (November 28, 1945), p. 45.

looks on the rights as inherent, but alienable; that is, that management may give some of them away. This formulation moves the management position a step back from holding that management rights and prerogatives are inalienable. Thus, though they may be alienable, managers still decline to give them away or to share their exercise with unions.

Labor's position in effect denies that management has any inherent rights and holds instead that management rights arise out of a definition of the relationship between management and labor in each particular enterprise.

To this day, both views have their adherents. One is an ideological approach and has been called the doctrine of the residual rights of management. The other is pragmatic. Before accepting either view, or rejecting both, it might be well to look at the logic of the respective positions.

The Residual Rights Doctrine

The residual rights approach starts from the premise that initially and inherently management possesses total freedom and discretion in ordering the affairs of an enterprise, and that union demands are an encroachment on this freedom or set of rights and prerogatives. It follows that every time a manager makes a concession to union demands, he gives away, and therefore loses, a part of the rights that inherently belong to management. What remains then are the *residual* rights not specifically renounced.

The personal experiences of many managers in their first encounters with unions seem to confirm, and originally may even have given rise to this line of thinking. In the early days of industrial union bargaining, employers often complained that unions were attempting to invade what they held to be the forbidden field of long-accepted management prerogatives. Before unionization, for example, managers had decided who might be allowed to stay and who would be laid off when business was slack. Now, instead, at union insistence they had to follow the seniority principle in layoffs and rehiring. Every time the company gave in to a demand of this sort, the argument ran, management surrendered some of its rights. By this interpretation, agreements signed with unions became, in every section, phrase, and clause, a record of lost management rights. One of the best-known early books on collective bargaining expresses in its very title this point of view: *The Union Challenge to Management Control.*[5]

It is not hard to understand and perhaps even sympathize with the outlook of managers who have seen power of this sort slip away. They feel they have lost something; something important personally and in the conduct of business. Suddenly one finds one cannot make decisions that were one's to make before: a countervailing and—it seems—inimical power opposes one's will. It is natural enough to believe that what one has lost the

---

[5] Neil W. Chamberlain, *The Union Challenge to Management Control* (New York: Harper, 1948).

union has gained. Carried to its logical extreme, this line of reasoning might well rouse the fear that unions are on their way to taking over *all* the rights and powers of management; getting ready (as the phrase goes) to tell an employer "how to run the business."

That nothing quite so dire has yet materialized does not dispose of the argument. Given the premises, the conclusion logically follows. What stops the unions, if they have indeed been stopped? What is to prevent union erosion of management rights from continuing until, of the residual rights, there is no further residue?

The error may lie not in the logic, but in the premises. What are these lost prerogatives, these threatened rights? At least one highly respected teacher and practitioner, Charles W. Killingsworth, says they are a myth; there are no management rights, and never have been. He gave his views in his inaugural address as president of the National Academy of Arbitrators in 1971.

The Pragmatic Approach

Killingsworth's attack on the residual rights doctrine draws its theme from his practice as an arbitrator and from certain important Supreme Court decisions affecting arbitration. Foremost among these is a 1960 set of three decisions on the arbitrability of issues not dealt with in specific terms in collective bargaining agreements. The companies in these three cases had stood on their residual rights in refusing to arbitrate certain issues, claiming unhampered freedom to take unilateral action. The Court rejected the companies' argument.

The outcome of this litigation, as decided by the Supreme Court, would seem to establish that there are no inherent management rights, even residual ones. That puts the matter much too baldly. Killingsworth does not argue from the legal decision alone, but draws on economic theory and practical experience to show that many constraints impinge on management's freedom to act—so many as to nullify any effective force or value to a set of management prerogatives. In general, he seems to agree with the views expressed in the above-quoted statement of labor representatives at President Truman's 1945 industrial conference: There are no management rights, only labor-management relationships; and the relationships are to be read in the aggregation of terms written into any given, specific collective bargaining agreement.

Yet labor agreements—many, though not all—continue to show specific provisions headed "Management Rights" and are likely to go on doing so.

A Synthesis of Opposing Views

The authors of this book take a position that differs from both extremes treated above, but that is not simply a compromise between them. We agree with those who hold that there are certain rights that belong to management, but we believe that union power had not diminished these management rights. Since they remain undiminished in our view, we can agree with the reasoning of those who hold that there has been no change, though not with the premise that they never existed. What has changed is the set of contexts—the climate or environment—in which management exercises its undiminished rights.

To call them rights rather than prerogatives already begins to strip away some of the mystique. Prerogatives—for instance, royal prerogatives—rise out of an ideology, but rest on political power. Thus, by the doctrine of divine right, rulers had prerogatives that went with succession to the crown. Those who were subject to the ruler's power respected the prerogatives. Should the monarchy give way to a republic, the ruler would retain prerogatives only in the minds of die-hard royalists. For republicans, the prerogatives go with the power.

Managers have never ruled by divine right nor, as managers, wielded political power; but owners of property under any regime have rights, property rights, defined and guaranteed by the prevailing political power. These property rights are no myth; they are real and enforceable. Owners of property can delegate their rights to managers. Since slavery was abolished, managers have never had any rights over people, only over property.

Property rights never have been absolute. An owner and appointed agents exercise the rights only under constraints and limitations which vary over the course of time and in different places and conditions. Managers of an enterprise exercise delegated ownership rights within the three contexts into which Dunlop's scheme analyzes the environment in which they operate.[6] When, as an enterprise, they have something to sell, they cannot compel but must persuade customers to buy. When they want to buy, they cannot force anyone to sell but must get the seller's consent and agreement on a price. This holds just as well for the labor market, in which the enterprise is a buyer, as for the product or services market which it enters as a seller.

As long as power relations in the enveloping society prevent or discourage people from organizing into unions, managers bidding for employees in the labor market can deal with them individually. Each work contract concluded and continued with an employee remains separate from the others, even though work is social and operations intricately coordinated. In slack times (to go back to the example already cited), a manager may decide to lay off or retain a particular employee according to a personal criterion: efficiency, or family obligations, or pure spite and favoritism, or, indeed, seniority. The choice is open. Nothing in the terms and conditions of the company's work contract with any one person ties the decision on what happens to him or her with what happens to anyone else. A separate contractual connection, terminable at will, ties each employed person with the em-

---

[6] See Ch. 1, the discussion of John T. Dunlop's theoretical framework.

ploying company and can be severed without reference to any of the others. The ability of the company to cut this connection at will is not a unique management right but the right of a contracting party to terminate a contract. Its counterpart is the right of the other contracting party, the employee, to quit a job. What makes it look like management's rights *over* the employee is that in slack times an employee does not usually want to quit a job and thereby lose the source of income.

When power relations in the enveloping social system permit and encourage collective bargaining, and employees unionize, workplace power relations reflect the change. Collectively, now, employees demand terms and conditions in *each* work contract that ties it to the others in some order; usually (for purposes of layoff and recall), an order of seniority. A single contractual thread still connects the company to each employee, but the company agrees that in slack times the threads will be released in certain sequence, and not at will or at caprice or in some other sequence or order.

Thus far in history power relations in the enveloping social system have not changed so radically that an employer is obliged by law to give in to a union's demands. The employer still retains the right to dispose of property and to lay out material resources, including money for wages, in the company's interests. Those interests may be better served in a given instance by accepting the union's demands or by fighting them; the choice is the employer's. Even when one accepts union demands (again, for example, in the matter of layoff and recall), workplace power relations do not deprive a company of the right to lay off people when their services are no longer required. One simply may not pick by name, but must lay off by category or by an individual's position on a previously-established seniority list. The same number of people go, the same number stay, but the names may differ. It is conceivable, though not inevitable, that the work force that is left will not be as efficient as would one that management might have picked; but it is equally conceivable that most of the time the senior employees are the efficient ones.

Over the years prices of goods and services have risen, and so have the costs incident to changes in the conditions of employment. Would any manager protest that a supplier's rise in prices was an attack on management rights? Why argue, then, that a rise in labor costs infringes on management prerogatives?

Perhaps what happens is that the old lord-of-the-manor, slaveholder mystique hangs on. The manager, pragmatic and clearheaded when dealing with physical limitations and with impersonal legal or economic constraints, responds emotionally to personal and human opposition to management's will. The manager seeks to rationalize the resultant feelings in an ideology. The pragmatic approach to management rights usually yields more practical results than ideology.

In Summary

The foregoing exposition of two views of management rights shows that the authors of this book take issue with the residual rights doctrine and favor the pragmatic approach. They agree with Killingsworth that management does not have—and never had—any rights inherent in the manager's role, but hold that in their role managers exercise the delegated property rights of ownership.

The residual school of thought maintains that management starts out with something like total freedom, total discretion; that managers have the ability as well as the right to order the affairs of an organization entirely at will; and that employees have the duty, and are bound, to conform to management's arrangements. By this view, management gives away part of the management rights it started out with each time it makes a concession to union demands. Whatever it does not concede and specifically renounce in the agreement remains as management's *residual* rights.

Given the premise, the conclusion logically follows. This book rejects the premise. Managers, like rulers, have no prerogatives except as they have power. Power is a relationship, with dependency as its reciprocal. Property rights confer power insofar as people are dependent on the material resources, including money wages, at the disposal of the property-owner. When the dependency ceases or declines—either absolutely or relative to the ability of wage earners to withhold their labor—so does the power decrease. Employees organized in unions are individually less dependent on the employer. The new *collective* bargains by which managers exchange material benefits—property—for human effort expended under specific terms and conditions, register the effect of present-day power relations as reflected in the enterprise. The bargaining is harder, the price is higher, but the exchange remains the same.

MANAGEMENT RIGHTS AS FUNCTIONS OF THE MANAGER'S ROLE

Management, then, has rights: delegated property rights; the right to dispose of, allocate, commit the material resources of the organization (including money) in order to carry on operations toward attaining the objectives of the enterprise. Rights alone do not make a manager; the actual owner (or owners, as in joint-stock companies) may, as a matter of fact, play no part in management. What makes a manager is managerial *use* of the delegated rights and the power and authority derived from them. In the total system of an organization, the rights *reinforce* the manager's role. A management rights clause in a union agreement makes practical sense when it takes the form of a definition of management's role instead of merely expressing an ideology.

An organization must have people who carry out operations. It must also have people who *plan* the operations, *organize* the work flows and work stations or jobs, who *direct* and *coordinate* activities, and *control* results. There are the accepted functions of the manager; their performance constitute's the manager's *role*. In performing this role, a manager at any level —and at all levels—acts for the organization, with and for and through the unit, however limited or however broad, for which he or she has accepted responsibility. Most likely, the manager is an employee too, and draws pay from the same source as the subordinates in the unit managed, but, organizationally speaking, acts for all. What must the manager be allowed to do as manager that other people playing the reciprocal nonmanager roles cannot do as part of their roles? What must they allow the manager in order that he or she may carry out the role?

As things stand in most enterprises today, in order to survive and meet the needs of members and owners, an organization must allow its managers some flexibility in three areas of activity: (1) discretion to organize, integrate, and coordinate operations; (2) discretion to deploy the work force and maintain discipline; and (3) discretion to deal with the outside world or environment, including (within an organization) other units of the organization.

Flexibility in Operations

Perhaps the most inflexible kind of operation would be an automated, serialized production line. The most flexible, most variable kind, perhaps, might be something like a band of strolling players at a tourist resort. Without going to this informal extreme, however, short-run job-lot production calls for flexibility in operations and might be kept in mind as a contrasting example. Management discretion in the design and layout of the automated line would have to precede operations, and would probably have to be pretty well unrestricted. In job-lot production, discretion has to enter in to daily operations.

At both these hypothetical extremes, the persons occupying management roles have to make decisions—organizational decisions—for others to carry out if the entire unit is to meet its objectives. At various points within the range there is bound to be an appropriate division of discretionary activity between managers and nonmanagers.

Operations integrate tasks. Operations concern people only as people are needed to carry out the tasks. Scientific management unflinchingly shouldered responsibility for ordering tasks and operations as management's role —and claimed it as a management prerogative. Present-day proponents of participative management see the same operations as an activity to be *shared* with nonmanagers.

Pragmatically speaking, collective bargaining makes operations neither a shared function nor a management right, but an activity in which managers and nonmanagers play separate but reciprocal roles. To the extent that both can contribute to a common aim, they parcel out areas of discretion. What has to be determined jointly in collective bargaining is the degree of discretion managers truly need, in a particular enterprise, in order to keep operations going for the good of all.

Flexibility in Deployment and Discipline

Decisions on deployment and discipline affect people rather than tasks; though tasks are carried out, of course, by people. Deployment involves assigning people to tasks and moving people around as operations demand. Discipline implies standards of performance, including task performance, and standards of behavior, including behavior toward other people.

A part of any manager's role is to deploy people to best advantage, but not as if they were inanimate objects. People have individual characteristics, career aims, perceptions of themselves and of others, desires, emotions, personal problems. They also acquire, through collective bargaining, job rights. Getting the best out of people, using their talents where they will do the most good, integrating the contribution of each with the joint efforts of all, would seem to be the very essence of the art of management.

No manager needs absolute power over the livelihood and career of any individual, but within limits needs discretion to fit employees into operations. No employee can fairly demand that the enterprise give one exactly what one wants, regardless of its needs or of the wants of others. A definition of job rights—always relative to the rights of others—gives the employee a measure of security against arbitrary acts of management. Beyond these stated job rights, management discretion rules. It takes effect not as a management right, but as a function of the manager's role in the organization.

When, for instance, it makes no difference to operations who stays on the job and who goes in a layoff, manager discretion need not extend to deciding, by name, who shall stay. When, as in promotion to or within management ranks, it does make a difference who gets the job, management can justify picking the person by name.

Discipline, too, bears upon people. Here the procedures of due process define employee rights. No manager needs the authority to discharge an employee, on the spot and without notice, even for cause, so long as one has authority to suspend, and after investigation make a decision. Every organization needs to be able to protect itself from those who thwart or hinder progress toward objectives, and must be able to discharge for cause. Due process protects the individual from arbitrary and unfair treatment, but need not—and in fact does not—prevent a management which observes procedures from following practices conducive to good discipline and countering harmful acts of individuals. Again the rights are individual, the role is management's.

Flexibility in Dealing with the Environment

Groups and collectives act as a unit towards other collectives by means of speakers, agents, and representatives. Through its managers an enterprise deals with buyers and suppliers, borrowers and lenders, government and the public, and indeed with unions. Within an enterprise, managers deal with other managers, with staff units, with technicians.

This area of management discretion is so clearly part of the manager's role that little attempt has yet been made by unions to enter it; in fact, they have shown little interest, at the level of the enterprise, except as management mistakes affect the equilibrium of the enterprise. Unions have sensibly perceived activities in this area as something managers are uniquely qualified to do and charged with doing. This does not make it an inherent management right. Unions are concerned, for instance, with the state of the market, but exert influence upon it, usually, at levels higher than the enterprise and through union organizations greater than the local union.

Management's Freedom to Perform Its Role

A study of the degree of management freedom and flexibility in the performance of its role in the enterprise helps show how things stand in some typical collective bargaining agreements. Although the researchers implicitly adopt the residual rights ideology, it is not necessary to adopt the ideology to grasp the significance of their findings. It makes sense as a record of actual arrangements that managers and unions have come to in defining the constraints and flexibility allowed the manager's role in a number of agreements.

In a study of union participation in decision making in 37 plants, Milton Derber, W. E. Chalmers, and Milton T. Edelman differentiated the *scope* and *depth* of union penetration of management rights.[7] *Scope* of union participation was measured by determining the number of important enterprise activities (e.g., contracting work out, product pricing, job evaluation, etc.) in which the union had a voice either through agreement negotiations or grievance settlement. The *depth* of union penetration was measured in terms of the agreement provision itself or the stage of a decision at which the union became involved. The measurement of *depth* of union penetration may be clarified by comparing two specific measures used by Derber, Chalmers, and Edelman: (1) Union security was judged solely on the terms of the agreement provision, i.e., sole bargaining rights, maintenance of membership, union shop, preferential hiring, or closed shop; (2) making major technological change was judged on the stage of a decision at which the

---

[7] Milton Derber, W. E. Chalmers, and Milton T. Edelman, "Union Participation in Plant Decision-Making," *Industrial and Labor Relations Review*, vol. 15 (October 1961), pp. 83–101.

union became involved, i.e., decision made without advance notice, advance notice given by management, management consults union, or changes require prior union agreement. Derber, Chalmers, and Edelman used this system of measurement for interfirm comparisons over time. Although individual enterprises might find it desirable to modify the specific measures used by Derber, Chalmers, and Edelman, the measures of *scope* and *depth* certainly are pertinent to the question of management rights. The framework for an analysis of the collective bargaining agreement outlined in Chapter 8 should be helpful in determining the *scope* and *depth* of union penetration of management rights in an enterprise.

How are management rights protected in the collective bargaining process? It seems to the authors of this book that management rights are most effectively preserved by effective and decisive management action in the overall operation of the business, in the negotiation of the whole collective bargaining agreement, and by the religious observance of the terms of the agreement negotiated. If a particular management runs a taut ship in all of its business relations, it will have little difficulty in determining what management rights it needs. With a clear objective in mind, the company's negotiators should be able to sell their position to the union. A good contract *adequately backed up with day-to-day supervisory practices* is within the grasp of any management worthy of its responsibilities.

Many management negotiators and the speakers for management organizations advocate the inclusion of management rights clauses in the collective bargaining agreement. These clauses may have an educational effect on the employees and the union over the years. When management action is in harmony with the management rights clause, the clause may also be helpful in arbitration hearings. Figure 9–1 contains illustrative management rights clauses.

SUMMARY

In order to serve its members, a union has to have *recognition* as their agent from the employer. The people for whom the union speaks make up a *bargaining unit;* and recognition takes the specific form of the union shop, exclusive bargaining rights, agency shop, or practically speaking (but not formally), the closed shop. Further, the union seeks continuity in its relationship. Management wants to define its areas of discretion in relations with employees.

The sections of a labor agreement on Union Security and Management Rights are a kind of enabling act that give authenticity and authority to the terms and conditions of employment the agreement defines. This answers the questions: Who speaks for whom? With what authority? For how long? With what exceptions?

The exceptions carry the label "Management Rights." Traditionally, managers have looked on their right to manage the affairs of an enterprise as

FIGURE 9-1
Illustrative Management Rights Clauses

Some employers prefer a long-form management rights clause like the Company Responsibility clause below. Other employers prefer a short-form clause like the Management Clause below. Employers favoring the short form feel that the enumeration of rights is dangerous, lest some rights be omitted.

Regardless of the form or content of the management rights clause, management functions may be given away, violated, or undermined by *other* clauses in the agreement or in company practices.

Company Responsibility

The Company retains the sole right to manage its business, including the rights to decide the number and location of plants, the machine and tool equipment, the products to be manufactured, the method of manufacturing, the schedules of production, the processes of manufacturing or assembling, together with all designing, engineering, and the control of raw materials, semimanufactured and finished parts which may be incorporated into the products manufactured; to maintain order and efficiency in its plants and operations; to hire, lay off, assign, transfer, and promote employees, and to determine the starting and quitting time and the number of hours to be worked; subject only to such regulations and restrictions governing the exercise of these rights as are expressly provided in this agreement.

Management Clause

The management of the business in all its phases and details shall remain vested in the Employer. The rights of the Employer and the employees shall be respected and the provisions of this contract for the orderly settlement of all questions regarding such rights shall be observed.

inherent in their status as managers and have regarded concessions made to a union as a dilution of management rights. By this line of thinking, any such rights not given away remained "residual" in management's hands. A more pragmatic approach that seems to be gaining ground concerns itself not so much with abstract rights as with the kinds of discretion management must exercise if the enterprise is to remain viable and employ the union members. These discretionary elements rise out of management's role. They have to do with ordering operations, deploying and disciplining the work force, and interacting with the environment. The terms of the agreement as a whole define the areas of management discretion and flexibility in action.

QUESTIONS FOR DISCUSSION

1. Maintenance of membership was a compromise form of union security suggested by the National War Labor Board during World War II. How do you account for this development at that time and its demise after the end of the war?

2. What are management rights? Why are they important? In a specific situation, how would you go about protecting them from union infringement?

3. Compared to unions in other countries, American unions are preoccupied with union security. Why? Does the law of collective bargaining have anything to do with this?

4. What is the "residual" theory of management rights? What changes in social, economic, and political conditions challenge the residual rights doctrine?

5. What rights (authority) seem most necessary for the exercise of the management role, and why? Do unions challenge these rights? Under what circumstances might they do so?

SELECTED ANNOTATED BIBLIOGRAPHY

CHAMBERLAIN, NEIL W. *The Union Challenge to Management Control.* New York: Harper & Bros., 1948.
   A landmark study of the impact of the union on the authority of management in the large corporation.

CULLEN, DONALD E., and GREENBAUM, MARCIA L. *Management Rights and Collective Bargaining: Can Both Survive?* Bulletin 58. Ithaca: New York State School of Industrial and Labor Relations, 1966.
   A readable account of the principle of management rights and the issues involved in determining the boundaries of management's freedom of action, with the prediction that "management rights" disputes will remain as salient as ever.

DEMPSEY, JOSEPH R., S.J. *The Operation of Right-to-Work Laws.* Milwaukee: Marquette University Press, 1961.
   Based on unreported court cases and interviews with jurists, employers, unions, and attorneys, this book compares the statements of state legislators on the meaning of right-to-work laws and the meaning of these laws as developed by the courts.

GINZBERG, ELI, and BERG, IVAR E. *Democratic Values and the Rights of Management.* New York: Columbia University Press, 1963.
   The authors examined numerous arbitration awards to see how the values of the broader society are implemented in the workplace via the grievance procedure.

GOLDBERG, ARTHUR. "Management's Reserved Rights: A Labor View," In *Management Rights and the Arbitration Process.* JEAN T. McKELVEY, ed. *Proceedings of the Ninth Annual Meeting of the National Academy of Arbitrators.* Washington, D.C.: Bureau of National Affairs, 1957, pp. 118–29.
   The then General Counsel of the United Steelworkers of America proposes some standards for the arbitration of management rights controversies.

JENNINGS, KEN. "Employee Abuse toward Supervision," *Arbitration Journal,* vol. 29, no. 4 (December 1974).
   The author examines numerous arbitration decisions to see how arbitrators handled cases where employees were disciplined for threatening or assaulting members of management.

KELLER, LEONARD A. *The Management Function: A Positive Approach to Labor Relations.* Washington, D.C.: Bureau of National Affairs, 1963.
   Defines a good labor policy, explores contracts in general, "management rights" clauses in particular, and gives model arbitration clauses which protect management rights. Suggests how to deal with labor attempts to restrict changes in methods, classifications, departments, and work schedules.

KILLINGSWORTH, CHARLES C. "Management Rights Revisited." In *Arbitration and Social Change*, GERALD G. SOMERS, ed. *Proceedings of the Twenty-Second Annual Meeting of the National Academy of Arbitrators*. Washington, D.C.: Bureau of National Affairs, 1970.

A distinguished arbitrator discusses the reserved rights doctrine under which management claims all rights of action not specifically abridged by the labor agreement.

PHELPS, JAMES C. "Management's Reserved Rights: An Industry View." In *Management Rights and the Arbitration Process*, JEAN T. McKELVEY, ed. *Proceedings of the Ninth Annual Meeting of the National Academy of Arbitrators*. Washington, D.C.: Bureau of National Affairs, 1957, pp. 102–17.

An executive of Bethlehem Steel Company proposes some standards for the arbitration of management rights controversies.

PRASOW, PAUL. "The Theory of Management Reserved Rights—Revisited." In *Proceedings of the Twenty-Sixth Annual Winter Meeting of the Industrial Relations Research Association*, GERALD G. SOMERS, ed. Madison: IRRA, 1973.

An arbitrator distinguishes between the theoretical doctrine of management reserved rights and the contractual management prerogatives clause, with special attention to the public sector.

SHISTER, JOSEPH; AARON, BENJAMIN; and SUMMERS, CLYDE W., eds. *Public Policy and Collective Bargaining*. New York: Harper & Row, 1962.

See "The Union Security Issue," by Paul E. Sultan.

SLICHTER, SUMNER; HEALEY, JAMES J.; and LIVERNASH, E. ROBERT. *The Impact of Collective Bargaining on Management*. Washington, D.C.: Brookings Institution, 1960.

See their chapters 8, 9, 10, 11 for a detailed examination of the impact of unions on management's ability to manage various aspects of their operations.

SMITH, RUSSELL A.; MERRIFIELD, LEROY S.; and ROTHSCHILD, DONALD P. *Collective Bargaining and Labor Arbitration*. Indianapolis: Bobbs-Merrill, 1970.

See their part three, chapter one, "Management Rights and Union Security," for an examination of various kinds of contractual language affecting these frequently opposing interests.

STONE, MORRIS. *Managerial Freedom and Job Security*. New York: Harper & Row, 1964.

A companion volume to the author's earlier *Labor-Management Contracts At Work*, this book addresses itself principally to job security issues, including the subcontracting of work; transfers of work outside the bargaining unit; attempts by the employer to change the content of a job; and out-of-classification assignments to solve special production problems.

SWIFT, ROBERT A. *The NLRB and Management Decision Making*. Labor Relations and Public Policy Series, Report No. 9. Philadelphia: University of Pennsylvania, Industrial Research Unit, 1974.

An analysis of NLRB decisions on subjects which directly involve management's ability to manage organizational resources, including such issues as subcontracting, plant relocation, plant closures, and automation.

WARNS, CARL A., JR. "Right of Management to Discipline for Refusal to Cross a Picket Line." In *Arbitration of Interest Disputes*, BARBARA D. DENNIS and

GERALD G. SOMERS, eds. *Proceedings of the Twenty-Sixth Annual Meeting of the National Academy of Arbitrators*. Washington, D.C.: Bureau of National Affairs, 1974.

The author examines management's ability to discipline its own employees who refuse to cross other employees' picket lines, including relevant contract language. See also the "Comments" by FRED W. ELARBEE, JR. and JEROME A. COOPER.

10 The Wage and Effort Bargain: Pay Levels

WITH OR WITHOUT a union, with or without collective bargaining, there is always a wage and effort bargain; it is the economic and legal substance of the employment relationship in our society. Every employee has a work contract with the employer; every employer has a work contract with each employee—as many work contracts as there are employees. The contract is: Work for pay. The employee applies physical and mental effort to the performance of tasks, in exchange for which the employer pays money wages or salary.

The wage and effort bargain costs the employer money, gives the employee income. The effort side costs the employee physical and mental exertion over set periods of time, gives the employer production. Thus the wage and effort bargain is a wealth-producing economic exchange that puts products and services on the market and provides people with a living. Its legal form distinguishes working relationships in our society from preceding bond systems. It rises out of the political reality of a population of free citizens legally competent to contract for their own labor: free to accept or reject an offer of employment or demand for work; free to quit or terminate the contract of employment.

The presence of a union and the practice of collective bargaining does not change either the economic or the legal basis of the relationship, but does affect the terms. Even though an agreement reached between a union and an employer is commonly called a "contract," the agreement does not bring a new contracting party into the old relationship. It merely sets new *terms* to the contract the employer offers and the employee accepts. The employee still exerts the effort and performs the work; the employer still pays the wage or salary.

THE WAGE AND EFFORT BARGAIN

Union members look on wage bargaining as the way to get a raise in pay; more money to spend. Employers weigh the outcome in terms of costs. The public worries about prices, which seem to rise with wages, whether this be cause or effect.

This chapter will not go into the economics of wages and wage policy. We leave that to the economist concerned with the gross national product or to the politician trying to frame a law or draft a program. What we propose to do is to observe the two main actors, managers and union representatives in a business enterprise, interacting with each other to devise substantive rules on wages and task standards (the effort bargain) and write them into an agreement.

Neither will we pay much attention in this chapter to what managers call the job structure; that is, the relationship between jobs in an enterprise or occupation that causes some to be valued more than others. This is a real relationship, based on job content. Any manager who doubts the reality of job stucture relationships might try paying engineers a janitor's wage and janitors the wage of an engineer. Though real, the relationship is not self-evident. Managers generally resort to the techniques of job evaluation to try to measure it, and usually welcome union inputs towards that end, for the job structure seems to reflect social norms and arises out of consensus. Pay for the different jobs in a job structure cannot violate the norms, but nothing intrinsically links any given job with a specific level or range of pay.

The job structure, in other words, is not bargainable; pay levels are. If you raise the janitor's pay you will eventually have to raise the pay of the engineer because the engineer's job is "worth more" than the janitor's; but nothing in either job tells you how much it's worth *in money*. The money measure is extrinsic, based on comparisons and calculations; alterable, and hence bargainable.

We propose in this chapter first to show that wage bargaining is normally *not* a zero-sum game in which one side's loss offsets the other's gain. We then go on to describe the typical industrial union wage demands and bargaining, with observations on the strategy and tactics involved. Then we look at the craft union model. We conclude with a review of the elements of the pay package and of the problems of substance posed by the various elements.

Distributive Bargaining

In Chapter 7 we took notice of the Walton-McKersie models, including their model of "distributive" bargaining. Whatever validity this model may have in the gamesmanship at the bargaining table, it rarely applies to a specific union and management engaged in setting the wage and effort bargain in a specific agreement. Wage bargaining is not simply a zero-sum game. It could be so only if the state of the market prevented employers from passing on any of their increased costs to the consumer, or if technology offered no means of increasing work-hour productivity and offsetting increased wages, or if power relations in the society absolutely stopped one side or the other from exerting any of the power that naturally flows from the interdependence of labor and management in the enterprise. Rarely are all three of these "ifs" present in a bargaining situation.

Consider first the market context. As will be brought out later in this chapter, the construction industry divides its projects into "big" work and "small" work. Big work would be a skyscraper office or apartment building, a hydroelectric dam or nuclear power plant; small work, construction and repair of single-family dwellings. Who is going to cancel a big-work project when it is half completed just because wages go up? Many contracts of this kind are, indeed, let out on a cost-plus basis. By analogy, the big-work manufacturer, such as an aircraft company working on missiles for the Pentagon, deals with cost overruns by renegotiating the government contracts, or even getting outright subsidies. Medium- to small-work manufacturers and small-work contractors may not be able to pass on added costs quite so easily, but they operate in the shadow of the rise in prices started by the big-work companies and find it easier to raise their own prices. Wages frequently follow rather than precede a rise in prices.

Pattern-setting bargaining also contradicts the zero-sum model. When for example the steel companies and steelworker union sit down to negotiate a new wage agreement, both sides know the outcome will have repercussions in the national economy. The press, the public, and the government watch the negotiations. The president may issue "guidelines" or engage in "jawboning" to persuade the parties to be moderate. The pattern that results from such negotiations turns out to be a pattern of prices as well as wages. Smaller companies and their unions, who follow the pattern-setters, adopt the price as well as the wages pattern.

Employers faced by wage demands can sometimes call upon technology to keep from being the loser in a zero-sum game. Partially in answer to rising pay rates, the Detroit auto factories turned to automation in the 1950s, starting a trend that has swept inexorably through manufacturing industry. It takes sharp cost accounting to sort out all the savings, but if an engineer can double, quadruple, or (as often happens) increase by a hundred or a thousandfold the output of a machine, the worker at the machine can get a raise without any reduction in the company's profits. This worker may not have to expend any extra effort on the new machine; may, in fact, expend less; but as we have already seen, there is no intrinsic connection between job content and the pay for a job.

Pattern-setting bargaining, big construction and manufacturing projects are beyond the scope of this book (as, indeed, they were of Walton and McKersie's). As we stated in the opening paragraph of the first chapter, we aim to present collective bargaining at the enterprise level, and our model is the local union, whose dynamics need to be understood before getting on to the national negotiations plane. We shall therefore proceed to describe wage and effort bargaining at the level of the individual enterprise and the local union.

PAY LEVELS

Pay levels, like prices, vary. For a business enterprise or other organization employing people, the pay level is the current price of hiring labor. This current price per unit of job worth will be unequally distributed over the different jobs in the job structure; but even when structures remain substantially unchanged over a period of time, pay levels vary. There is no *intrinsic* connection between pay level and job worth.

Pay levels vary from place to place, industry to industry, enterprise to enterprise as well as year to year. Company executives have always made more money than clerks, engineers than draftsmen, supervisors than laborers, and probably always will. Such differences arise from evaluated job worth: the *structure*. All of these jobs in the 1970s pay more than they did in the 1950s or the 1920s, pay more in some companies, industries, and regions than in others. These are differences in *pay levels*. Not all the increase over the years comes from inflation; real wages have risen, too.

The process of setting pay levels turns the algebraic x of job worth into a specific sum of money: concrete dollars-and-cents figures on the wage or salary check an employee cashes to meet weekly expenses or pay monthly bills. The amount on the face of the check is highly visible to the recipient, and strongly felt; it both confers and limits command over the range of goods and services money can buy. It directly measures a person's economic, and indirectly, social status in relation to the world outside the shop and after working hours. This is a *comparative* measure, and the comparison involves standards that are *external* to the enterprise.

Pay levels fluctuate—mostly upward—with changes in the labor and product markets and shifts in power relations. These outside forces generate pressures that make themselves felt within the enterprise, whether it be unionized or not. In a nonunion firm management has to estimate the pressures and act accordingly. In unionized firms, unions and their managements jointly negotiate the pay levels. From opposite sides of the table the bargainers apply—each according to their own outlook and interests—standards of *consistency*.

Consistency does not necessarily mean equality, or paying the average, or area, or industry rate. A given firm might, as a matter of policy, decide to pay consistently more; another, consistently less than the going rate. Most firms probably try to match what others pay in order not to be at a disadvantage in competing for labor. Unions try for consistency with the better, or above-average levels of pay.

External Consistency

Depending on the particular situation, managers and unions may favor either consistency in the labor market or consistency in the product market. While they appeal to the same abstract standard, they may actually be talking about two different things. A firm that sells its product nationally but manufactures in a low-wage region might argue for consistency with community rates; that is, consistency with rates in the local labor market from which most of the employees are recruited. The union, concerned about the jobs of members working for competing firms in high-wage areas, would be likely to argue just as aggressively for consistency with the product market. The union's aim is not simply to get raises for members in the lower-paid community, but to equalize labor costs between firms and take wages out of competition. In negotiations between firms and their unions in higher-paid areas, the bargainers often reverse themselves: The union argues for consistence with the local labor market, the firm for the industry or product-market rate. This sounds, and is, opportunistic. Both sides indulge in it. What they eventually agree on tends to affect pay levels both in the labor and product markets—the local community, and the industry—and in the long run tends toward equalizing labor costs.

A building trades union normally shows less concern about industry rates because its product and labor markets roughly coincide. When a craft union negotiates a master agreement with a contractors' association, the result equalizes labor costs for all contractors in the area and takes wages out of competition. The typical industrial union confronts a more complex problem because of the many variations in job content between employing enterprises and their geographic dispersal in areas of differing pay levels.

No matter from which angle it may be interpreted, does external consistency mean that all jobs are to receive rates consistent with the pay levels used as a standard of comparison? No. Only rarely are the jobs perfectly comparable or conditions identical; it still makes sense to arrive at a job structure by internal comparisons. Some jobs may prove to be hard to fill locally. Other factors of the particular situation may enter in. Complete consistency is unattainable. What is attainable is a rather rough approximation: consistency for most jobs most of the time; consistency with standards not entirely unacceptable either to management or the union.

Sources of Wage Data

The infomal, sporadic, and occasional exchange of wage information between employers has a long history. Impetus toward systematizing wage comparisons came from the policies of the National War Labor Board in the 1940s. In order to make sure that firms doing priority work for the wartime government could compete effectively for essential workers in the labor market without aggravating inflation, the NWLB required firms and unions requesting wage adjustments first to show that they had installed a formal job evaluation program and made careful wage surveys. Since World War II the quality of data gathered to compare interfirm wage rates has improved; the quantity available is still not overwhelming.

The major sources of wage rate information on individual jobs may be classified as follows:

1. Governmental wage surveys.
2. Employer association wage surveys.
3. Union wage surveys.
4. Individual company wage surveys.

We shall discuss each of these sources before discussing the problems of interpreting what limited data are available.

Governmental Wage Surveys. The Bureau of Labor Statistics gathers wage rates in two important series: Occupational Wage Surveys and the annual Union Wages and Hours surveys. In discussing wage structure problems, we are interested only in wage *rates*. Valuable as detailed *earnings* statistics may be for other purposes, they are irrelevant to questions of wage structure.

Occupational wage surveys are conducted regularly in a number of important industrial centers. In each area, data are obtained by personal visits of BLS field agents to representative firms within six broad industry divisions: manufacturing; transportation (excluding railroads); communication and other utilities; wholesale trade; retail trade; finance, insurance, and real estate; and services. Only firms employing 51 or more workers are surveyed. The surveys are conducted on a sample basis. A greater proportion of large than small establishments is studied. However, all establishments are given their appropriate weight in combining the data.

The occupations selected for study are common to a variety of manufacturing and nonmanufacturing industries. Occupational classification is based on a uniform set of job descriptions designed to take account of interestablishment variation in duties within the same job. A BLS Occupational Wage Survey job description for a tool-and-die maker is presented in Figure 10–1.

FIGURE 10–1
Job Description from BLS Occupational Wage Survey

Tool-and-Die Maker
(Diemaker; Jig Maker; Toolmaker; Fixture Maker; Gauge Maker)

Constructs and repairs machine-shop tools, gauges, jigs, fixtures or dies for forgings, punching, and other metal-forming work. Work involves *most of the following:* planning and laying out of work from models, blueprints, drawings, or other oral and written specifications; using a variety of tool-and-die maker's handtools and precision measuring instruments; understanding of the working properties of common metals and alloys; setting up and operating of machine tools and related equipment; making necessary shop computations relating to dimensions of work, speeds, feeds, and tooling of machines; heat-treating of metal parts during fabrication as well as of finished tools and dies to achieve required qualities; working to close tolerances; fitting and assembling of parts to prescribed tolerances and allowances; selecting appropriate materials, tools, and processes. In general, the tool-and-die maker's work requires a rounded training in machine-shop and toolroom practice usually acquired through a formal apprenticeship or equivalent training and experience.

For cross-industry wage study purposes, tool-and-die makers in tool-and-die jobbing shops are excluded from this classification.

Factory jobs surveyed are frequently limited to those in maintenance and power plant and custodial and material movement occupations.

Rate data exclude premium pay for overtime and for work on weekends, holidays, and late shifts. Nonproduction bonuses are excluded also, but cost-of-living bonuses and incentive earnings are included. Information is presented also on selected establishment practices and supplementary benefits as they relate to office and plant workers.

Several characteristics of Occupational Wage Surveys limit their usefulness for achieving external wage consistency:

1. They are conducted only in major industrial centers.
2. Surveys are conducted in specific areas only infrequently, e.g., every five years.
3. Frequently the group of jobs studied is small compared to the number of jobs in any particular firm.

We shall discuss the problem of job comparability as it applies to Occupational Wage Surveys later.

BLS conducts annual surveys of wage rates and scheduled hours of work for specified crafts or jobs as provided in labor-management agreements in four industries: building construction, printing, local transit, and local trucking. The studies present the wage rates in effect as of July 1 of each year as reported to the Bureau by the appropriate labor organizations in each of the cities.

Union scales are defined as the minimum wage scales or maximum schedules of hours. Rates in excess of the negotiated minimum are not included.

These surveys have the important advantage of frequency. For negotiations in noncovered industries, the rates on particular jobs might give a rough indication of the "going" rate in industries competing for the same skills. These surveys also provide bases for comparison between surveyed cities. The careful selection of a surveyed city might provide a rough guide for wage determination in nonsurveyed communities.

Employers' Associations. Employers' associations collect and distribute to their members vast quantities of wage-rate data. In 1952, Professors N. Arnold Tolles and Robert L. Raimon published the first general guide to nongovernmental wage surveys.[1] Tolles and Raimon present digests of surveys conducted by 120 associations, with 60,000 employer members, employing 10 million workers, surveying the wages of 4 million employees. Figure 10–2 shows the wage surveying associations that they uncovered in their research. It seems to be a safe guess that the coverage of wage surveys has increased rather than decreased since they made their study.

An area-oriented survey cuts across industry lines within a local labor

---

[1] N. Arnold Tolles and Robert L. Raimon, *Sources of Wage Information: Employer Associations*, Cornell Studies in Industrial and Labor Relations, vol. 3 (Ithaca, N.Y.: Cornell University, 1952), xvi.

FIGURE 10–2

Numbers of Associations Known to Conduct Wage
Surveys, by Industry or by Area Orientation

Association	Number
Industry-oriented associations	105
Food and kindred products	7
Textile mill products	6
Lumber, wood, furniture, fixtures	13
Paper and allied products	5
Chemicals and allied products	6
Products of petroleum and coal	2
Leather and leather products	3
Stone, clay, and glass products	7
Primary metal industries	7
Fabricated metal products	8
Machinery, electrical products	13
Miscellaneous manufacturing	2
Transportation	4
Trade: wholesale and retail	7
Finance, insurance, and real estate	3
Medical and health services	4
Miscellaneous nonmanufacturing	3
Area-oriented associations	61
Area employer associations	36
Chambers of commerce	25

Source: N. Arnold Tolles and Robert L. Raimon, *Sources of
Wage Information: Employer Associations* (Ithaca, N.Y.: Cornell
University, 1952), p. 233.

market. Employers seeking wage consistency in the locality need the data
supplied by an area-oriented survey. Employers can conduct their own individual surveys, as some large companies do, or they may utilize the
services of an employers' association. A well-managed association survey
provides detailed information at minimum cost. However, well-managed association surveys cost money and are most commonly available only in
metropolitan centers.

Figure 10–3 is a digest of one well-managed metropolitan wage survey.
This survey covers approximately 50 percent of the employment in the area
surveyed. Wage data are collected by job description instead of job title.
Rates are reported by four averages and a frequency table. This particular
survey does not report on fringe benefits. We shall return to this survey in
discussing the use of wage survey data.

As shown in Figure 10–2, the industry-oriented survey is more common
than the area-oriented survey. Perhaps the greater number of industry-
oriented surveys is a response to the needs of employers dealing with the
same union. Although no wage survey can compute comparative unit labor
costs, an industry-oriented survey offers a more fruitful opportunity for
speculation in this direction than does the area-oriented survey.

FIGURE 10–3
Digest of a Metropolitan Wage Survey

Coverage: 129 firms; 50 percent of local labor force; 30 industries (a cross section of area industry).

Jobs Surveyed: 81 jobs: Some jobs broken into as many as four difficulty levels.

Pay Period Covered: March 15, 1956.

Specimen Job Data:

Tool-and-Die Maker 1 (most difficult of four levels).

Plan and construct highly intricate tools, dies, fixtures, gauges, to extremely close tolerances. Considerable development work.

Highly skilled fitting, timing, and adjusting. Construct tools where no design is available. Select allowances, devise mechanism details, e.g., multistation progressive and deep forming dies, complex indexing fixtures, subpress dies for parts of delicate outline, optical gauges.

Straight Time		*Incentive*	
Number firms	23	Number firms	1
Number workers	1,010	Number workers	2
Average rate	2.89	Average rate	3.00
Weighted average	2.74	Weighted average	3.00

Firms reporting ranges, 17; Average minimum rate, 2.63; Average maximum rate, 2.87; Firms reporting males only, 24; Firms reporting females only, 0; Firms reporting both, 0.

Frequency Table: Straight Time

Rate	Number Workers	Rate	Number Workers	Rate	Number Workers
2.56	30	2.76	576	3.00	17
2.57	18	2.77	29	3.03	3
2.61	42	2.79	18	3.06	4
2.66	67	2.84	6	3.11	1
2.68	1	2.85	1	3.15	2
2.69	2	2.86	13	3.18	1
2.71	142	2.88	6	3.21	2
2.73	7	2.90	5	3.47	1
2.74	4	2.92	3	3.80	1
2.75	8				

Union Wage Surveys. Formal wage surveys conducted by unions are not available to employers. However, unions do have access to wage rates paid in companies having contractual relations with them. These data are sometimes introduced into negotiations in a union attempt to win a particular point. Unions probably would have the most detailed wage information on competitors that would be available from any other source. However, these data (like all data for collective bargaining) can be selectively edited. Thus both unions and managements are best advised to regard such data with some caution.

Individual Company Wage Surveys. Many large companies conduct their own wage surveys. Such surveys serve a particularly important function in small communities without other wage data collection agencies. Some companies prefer to conduct their own surveys because they can independently validate the data so collected. Finally a general wage survey is of limited value to a firm requiring highly specialized skills, e.g., certain oil refinery jobs, or in the case of women employed by public utilities companies.

Interpreting Wage Survey Data

Wage rate data are *not* generally available. Although we have emphasized the widespread wage survey work done by employers and unions, it is important to remember that these data are always considered at least partially *confidential* and available only to cooperating firms. Only under very exceptional circumstances would an association reveal wage data for a particular firm. The governmental data are available generally, but only with adequate safeguards to the identity of the individual firm.

Job Comparability. Figures 10–1, 10–2, and 10–3 should now be considered as a unit in attempting to resolve the problem of job comparability. Figures 10–2 and 10–3 are job descriptions for a tool maker's and a die maker's job in our hypothetical plant. Figure 10–1 is a tool-and-die maker's job description used in a BLS Occupational Wage Survey. Figure 10–3 includes the tool-and-die maker's job description used in a metropolitan wage survey. An employer confronted with this array of current wage rate information would be in an *extremely* fortunate position and would possess much more "comparative wage data" than is usual. However, one is confronted with a serious problem because of the obvious variations in job content between these four descriptions. If this difficulty seems minor, we need only remember that each of the job descriptions surveyed has been interpreted independently by each of the respondents to the survey. Only in that extremely rare situation when employers actually assign similar duties to workers in a single job is anything approaching real job comparability achieved.

Which Rate? Cheerfully assuming that we have resolved or ignored the problem of job comparability, we proceed now to the selection of a "going rate." Referring to Figure 10–3, which "average rate" do we want to use? The "weighted average" is the rate most nearly approximating the rate received by the "average employee" on the job. However, this rate would be inflated if a majority of the employees surveyed were at the top of the respective ranges for the job. This average is also heavily weighted by the largest employers in the area surveyed. Or we might select the "average rate." In this case a firm employing 1 tool-and-die maker is considered just as important as a firm employing 500 tool-and-die makers. The "average minimum rate" would be the impression of opportunities that a worker seeking employment would acquire from a careful job hunt. The "modal" rate can be determined by examining the frequency table. Here again, we are giving weight to the position of workers in the rate range.

Despite all the difficulties, management must decide that one of these rates *is* the "going rate." Wage decisions are then based on this choice. To the extent that both unions and management realize the shortcomings of the data available, the ultimate decision is probably improved.

Achieving and Maintaining External Consistency

External consistency and internal consistency may be opposing concepts in some situations. For example, the engineer shortage of the early 50s can be contrasted to the fear of an engineer glut in the immediate postwar period. Has the value of an engineer doing a particular job in a particular company *changed* because of these market pressures? More practically, just what can management do to assure itself of a reasonably contented and adequate supply of workers in a shortage calling? Should internal consistency be completely abandoned?

In his study of "Wage and Salary Administration in a Changing Labor Market," Prof. Preston P. LeBreton found that management was gravely concerned with the problem of maintaining both internal and external consistency. Wage and salary administrators referred to the problem as "frustrating" and "plagueing." At least eight alternative approaches are available to management in solving the problem. As shown in Figure 10–4, management has at least flirted with each of these approaches. In passing it should be noted that several of these approaches vitally affect nonwage

FIGURE 10–4

Management Approaches to Maintaining an Internally Consistent Wage Structure when Faced with Heavy Labor-Market Pressure

Approach	*Number of Companies Using This Approach**
Ignore market conditions and concentrate on maintaining internal consistency. Emphasize fringe benefits and other advantages rather than money rates	18
Bring new workers in at market price regardless of its relationship to company rates	17
Bring new workers in at market price unless it falls out of the established range for the job class	73
Deliberately evaluate the job higher than its objective worth	12
Eliminate the job by contracting out or distributing the work internally	6
Use outside agency help at the required rate (agency workers perform their duties on company premises)	11
Add work to job content thereby increasing its worth to the company	19
Raise the level of all wages in the company	18
Other approaches	23

* The total of the right-hand column does not correspond to the total number of participants because some of the correspondents selected several choices.

Source: Preston P. LeBreton, assisted by Thomas R. O'Donovan, *Wage and Salary Administration in a Changing Labor Market* (Detroit, Mich.: University of Detroit, March 1957), p. 2.

clauses in the collective bargaining agreement. For example, subcontracting and use of agency help would undoubtedly arouse substantial union opposition.

BARGAINING ON PAY LEVELS

Newspaper accounts of labor-management negotiations almost always emphasize wage demands and wage settlements. Reports of the outcome of almost any strike give prominence to the agreed-on pay package. Occasionally a strike continues even after agreement on the pay package, over what the papers refer to vaguely as "work rules." It is not always possible to tell from the newspaper accounts whether the work rules at issue are task standards; that is, the effort bargain; or other things such as seniority and kindred elements of individual security. In the popular view, at any rate, the pay package or pay level *is* the issue at stake in labor-management negotiations.

It is not as simple as all that. Pay level is always important, but does not by itself tell the whole story. It is directly and primarily important in craft union negotiations because effort is under the control of the skilled worker and individual security under the control of the union; productivity per hour is practically fixed, and can be taken for granted. Industrial unions have to be concerned with work rules as well as with the pay level. If these work rules were taken for granted or left to management, changes in work rules and procedures could practically nullify pay level gains.

Union Goals in Pay Level Bargaining

How does a union decide in a particular year that it will seek a 40-cent package raise in wages, and not a 20-cent or 60-cent package? And having decided that, how does it break the package down into general demands, wage inequity demands, demands for wage supplements such as medical care and pension improvements, or paid holidays, or longer paid vacations?

Or does the union build up a package by adding its minimum demands in each of these areas to arrive at a total? Does the union carefully apply economic formulas and estimates, or pull the figures out of thin air? Do the leaders have full and free discretion? Or do rank-and-filers, indirectly or directly, play a part in the decisions? What happens *inside* the union?

What happens inside the company? How does the management decide to counteroffer a 30-cent package, or meet the union's 40-cent demand, or even (in exchange, perhaps, for other concessions) exceed the union's wage demands?

Customarily, the union initiates collective bargaining by announcing and justifying its comprehensive demands. Management appears to play the purely defensive part of resisting; and, in some instances, this is probably the actual management policy. Increasingly, however, management tries to anticipate the union's moves and comes prepared with its own formulation of an offer that is not simply a counteroffer and reaction to the union initiative. Whether the company program be independently arrived at or only a defensive rejoinder to the union, what information, estimates, and hazards shape the management decision?

Both sides have to face certain economic facts of life, whatever their aims or desires. Some of these constraints and possible contingencies are known or can be forecast with reasonable assurance. Others are hidden, or dubious, or unpredictable; and in any case, they shift and change. Decision making under conditions of uncertainty is an old story to management; unions have had to learn to face the uncertain future, too. One of the elements of uncertainty for each is what the other will do. Whenever there is interaction between human beings, psychological and political and social motivations that are quite distinct from economic processes are bound to enter in. Union demands and management response thus take place in the contexts of both economics and power relations.

The Economic Context

Economic facts—Dunlop's market context—pertinent to the union and management positions have to do with the situation of the workers, the union itself, the company, the industry, and possibly the general state of the economy. Knowledge about these facts is never complete on either side, but in some matters the union may be better informed; in some, the company.

The Workers.   A worker tends to take primary interest in take-home pay and its purchasing power. Over the course of a year, take-home pay depends on whether the worker is laid off part of the time, and when working, how many hours worked. The cost of living thus has a bearing on the wage demand the worker deems appropriate—or indeed, essential.

Historically, money wages have tended to rise in periods of rising prices. For a number of years many unions followed the lead given by General Motors and the UAW in 1948 when they signed a long-term agreement containing an "escalator" clause. Escalator clauses provide for changes in wage rates to parallel changes in the Consumer Price Index. The Index, as everyone knows, has risen steadily, year by year. Although escalator clauses cover less than 25 percent of unionized workers, the national publicity given to such arrangements made many workers (and workers' wives) acutely conscious of the cost-of-living issue. Where escalators have not been negotiated, unions instead have asked for general wage adjustment aimed at catching up with—or, as management would say, anticipating—increases in the cost of living.

Nonetheless, tenure and continuity of employment outweigh the importance to a worker of the hourly real wage. If one suffers periods of layoff, or has only a part-time job of short work weeks, one will need high hourly wages while working in order to average out; yet widespread layoffs or short work weeks discourage hopes for higher hourly pay. Confronted with the *personal* and *certain* choice of low hourly wages, or no work, most workers could be expected to choose the low wage. In terms of income, workers do not live literally from day to day, but many live from week to week with little or nothing in reserve, often in debt, and with installment obligations. Few see the choice as certain, but the possible consequences of a fight for higher wages, if it should involve a strike, are always personal. The worker's perception of pay level issues includes an acute consciousness of a precarious financial situation.

The Union.   A union's ultimate weapon is the strike. A union's ability to strike successfully does not depend directly on the amount of money in the strike fund, but financial resources enter into the reckoning when a union formulates its *real* demands. In illustration of this point, we give the frank comments of a delegate to a Special Convention of the UAW.

> I work at a GM plant and am ready to hit the bricks for our demands, and I am sure the members of Local 645 are determined to get a much better contract than they have now.
>
> When we do hit the bricks, we want to have the money in the strike fund. The $16 million that will be raised by this dues increase will not be sufficient to carry on a successful strike this year.
>
> The book prepared by the financial secretary on strike assistance lists 350,000 GM workers and 200,000 auto parts workers who would be involved in a GM strike, thus taking 550,000 off the dues-paying list. This means a balance of only 650,000 dues-paying members not on strike.
>
> The dues from 650,000 workers will not carry the GM workers who are on strike. This book on strike assistance says it will cost $80 million plus to carry on an eleven week strike at GM, and $11,400,000 a week beginning with the twelfth week. If the strike lasts as long as 16 weeks, like the last one did, the cost would be more than $136 million.
>
> I think we should be realistic and have a strike fund that will take care of any trouble that comes up. A $25 million strike fund is too small, and any monies placed in the fund by this dues increase should stay there.
>
> Dues should be found to increase the amount to at least $50 million. I would like to see a fund of $80 million. Then we would have the power to back up our just demands.[2]

The arithmetic would be different for other unions or for the UAW at another time or under different circumstances. For example, if the union found it necessary to stike Chrysler, Ford, and GM at the same time, the delegate's $136 million would only be a drop in the bucket. Nevertheless, this kind of economic arithmetic problem must be worked out by any union as a part of the formulation of its final demands.

A striking union may receive economic support from other unions in the form of gifts or loans. These are probably less important in most cases than assurances or expectations of direct action by other unions to reinforce the strike. Refusal to transport goods across a picket line is worth more to a

---

[2] *Proceedings: Special Constitutional Convention, United Automobile, Aircraft and Agricultural Implement Workers of America, January 22–24, 1958*, p. 134.

striking union than any amount of money—and more visible to the strikers. Less visible, but equally welcome to the union would be another union's refusal to do work "farmed out" by the struck firm, or an effective boycott.

The Company.   Probably the most important economic facts about the firm for collective bargaining purposes are: (*a*) sales forecasts, (*b*) inventories and orders on hand at a probable strike date, (*c*) alternative methods of meeting customer demands during a strike, and (*d*) break-even points under different wage cost assumptions.

Sales Forecasts.   Sales forecasts are critical to sound managerial decision making. The economic concepts of elasticity of demand, expectation of profit yields, and competition in the product market are all reflected in the managerial sales forecast. Most sales forecasts also reflect management's general thinking about the short-run economic future. When management is producing a brand-name product with substantial customer loyalty for what appears to be an expanding market, management may conclude that it can pass any wage increase along to the customer in the form of a price increase. This interpretation of the facts is particularly final in cases where labor costs are a relatively small proportion of total costs of production. When a company has just experienced a record-making sales and profits year, the management often assumes that prosperity is here to stay.

Inventories and Orders on Hand.   Large inventories and few orders on hand tend to make management less receptive to union demands. Many unfilled orders and an empty warehouse have the opposite effect.

Sometimes the composition of inventories is as important as the size of inventories. Most manufacturing concerns produce a number of products. An inventory shortage of a product insignificant from the viewpoint of the company's total production may become the central issue in company thinking on the union's demands. For example, a very small order for an experimental product from a major customer accompanied by the prospect of large "add-on" orders may prove to be the union's strongest bargaining point without the union's even knowing it. Similar situations exist when the company is the sole source of supply to a major customer of some apparently insignificant bit of hardware. These situations take on even more gravity when they are enmeshed with a defense industry contracting and subcontracting structure.[3]

Alternative Methods of Meeting Customer Demands.   In a variety of

---

[3] Persons familiar with military procurement procedures are fully aware of the importance of inventory composition as a factor in collective bargaining strategy. In 1953, the U.S. Supreme Court ruled that a strike of some steelworkers at the Dunkirk, New York, plant of the American Locomotive Company was a "national-emergency" strike within the meaning of the Taft-Hartley law. This strike was only a part of a national steel strike which was *not* considered to be a national-emergency strike. The court ruled that the strikers in Dunkirk were closing a substantial part of an entire industry (the atomic reactor manufacturing industry) and that their strike imperiled or threatened to imperil the national health and safety. Not even all of the employees of the Dunkirk plant were engaged in work on the A.E.C. order.

situations, a strike imposes only minor inconvenience on the customers of the firm or industry struck. In these cases, management can put up stronger resistance to union demands because it runs a smaller chance of losing its regular customers as a result of failure to deliver during a strike.

In the petroleum industry, the interchange of products between competitors in various markets is a long-established practice aimed at reducing transshipment costs. This same system could be used to satisfy customer demand in the event of a strike against a single firm or refinery. Many firms produce their own brand-name products and have licensing arrangements with other firms. By careful management advanced planning, these licensing arrangements could enable the licensor to continue to supply brand-name customers almost indefinitely even though its own production facilities were closed down by a strike. Similar potential advantages are available to multiplant, single-product manufacturers who have different unions or contract expiration dates at different plants each one of which is fully integrated. In this case, the employer merely shifts orders from the strike-bound plant to plants which are operating during the strike.

In each of these situations management can be tough because the employer has insured itself against the *long-range* cost of actually losing customers to competitors.

Break-even Points under Different Wage Cost Assumptions. Break-even analysis under different wage cost assumptions is primarily important for the economic long run. In the short run, a management may minimize its losses by continuing to produce even though the revenue per unit sold is less than the average total cost of producing that unit. In the short run, management is "stuck" with its fixed costs, e.g., plant and equipment depreciation, property taxes, inventories of materials on hand, etc. As a result, it is good business to incur variable costs, e.g., wages, sales promotion expenses, etc., so long as the product can be sold at a price which exceeds these variable costs. In such a situation, the management may incur substantial losses, but these losses are *less* than the losses that would be incurred if the management chose not to produce. In the economic long run, however, a management will not continue to operate unless it anticipates that sales income from its product will exceed the total (variable plus fixed) costs of production. This is true because in the long run, management has the opportunity of eliminating fixed costs through sale of plant and equipment or simply not replacing plant and equipment as it wears out.

Break-even analysis brings together all business judgment about sales expectations and cost expectations. If it is believed that prices can be raised without adverse effects on the volume of sales, the break-even point is lowered and the promise of profits is enhanced. If it is believed that prices can be raised without adverse effect on the volume of sales, wages can also be increased with a minimum reduction of profits. On the other hand, if prices can't be raised because of the elasticity of demand or competition in the product market or a general business slump, wages can be increased only at the expense of profits. At the same time, there is always the possibility that such wage increases will cause management to discontinue certain lines of production or actually liquidate the business in its entirety. Or management might find it advisable to change the worker-machine mix in such a way as to provide substantially less employment. To be sure, as wages rise, the vital *relative* cost of laborsaving machines certainly declines.

This situation is further complicated by the fact that many costs of production are really matters of accounting *judgment*. Two examples, depreciation expense and cost of materials used, will suffice as illustrations. When management purchases a machine for the price of $100,000 it is merely converting cash into another form of asset. The $100,000 becomes a cost only as it is charged against production in the future. If the machine is *judged* to have no scrap value and a life of 10 years or for a total production of 100,000 units, it may be charged off as an expense at the rate of $10,000 per year or $1 per unit produced. In the first year, only 1,000 units are produced because of a general business slump. If the accountant charges the machine off on a straight-line annual depreciation basis, each unit contains $10 of machine cost (as compared to $1 per unit using a unit-produced accounting method). These two possibilities represent only a very small portion of the many variations which give radically different results and are all within the limits of conventional accounting practice. Similar problems arise in *estimating* the cost of materials used in production. No one *really* knows what the cost of materials or machine time is until such time as the business is totally liquidated. Important as it is to know what costs really are, they are impossible to determine with finality as long as the business continues to operate. Obviously, the curiosity of management and the union stop short of wanting to liquidate the business in order to get the full truth. Accounting methods do become a point of dispute, however, when management pleads inability to pay higher wages.

The Power Relations Context

While corporations are by no means immune from internal political power struggles that affect external relations, economic considerations would appear to take precedence, in most companies, over political aims. Industrial unions, on the other hand, are basically political organizations. They seek economic ends by political means. Union leaders approach negotiations under political pressures of at least four kinds: (*a*) rival union gains, (*b*) opposition within the union, (*c*) demand for uniformity within the international union's jurisdiction, and (*d*) the strike temper of the rank and file.

Rival Union Gains.   Union members look to their leaders to make gains for them and evaluate their leaders on the basis of how the gains won compare with those of other unions. What makes an acceptable bargain in the eyes of the union members?

The answer to that question depends partly on how the new rates compare with former earnings, and partly on what members of other unions have gained. If I. W. Abel of the United Steelworkers of America gets a sizable increase from the steel companies in wage negotiations, auto workers will expect their Leonard Woodcock to do at least as well for them when he bargains with the Big Three. Steelworker gains pose no threat of secession of UAW Locals to join the USA, but do put pressure on the UAW leaders. In another year, the pressure may bear in the opposite direction, with Mr. Abel expected by his members to match Mr. Woodcock's performance. A union leader cannot fall short of expectations too many times, and continue to hold the top job.

Rival union gains also strongly influence the contents of the package. In times of business recession, some unions tend to place greater stress on wage supplements than straight wages. In part, this may be attributed to the necessity of matching rival union gains even when wage increases are very hard to come by. For example, a very modest wage increase *plus* "sweeping improvements in pensions, S.U.B., seniority, etc. costing seventy cents per hour according to union estimates" might give the impression of a great victory to the rank and file without involving any substantial and immediate increase in labor costs for the company if spread out over several years. At some particular times, worker insurance and income-continuity benefits can be substantially liberalized with little or no cost to management. This situation sometimes enables a union leader to accept a moderate increase and to save face with rank and file by selling the great importance of the improved wage supplements. Cents-per-hour can be *easily* compared between unions by members of the rank and file; some forms of wage supplements are not so easily compared.

Opposition within the Union. The less secure the political future of a union negotiator, the more likely one is to insist on excessive wage demands. This situation is illustrated by the preference, frequently expressed by managers, for dealing with international officers rather than local officers. The typical international officer is quite secure in office through control of appointive jobs and in the frequent practice of electing international officers by convention roll call votes. As a result, one can afford the political luxury of responsibility in dealing with employers. A local officer who becomes too "responsible" also tends to become an ex-officer. Even international officers do face occasional opposition at the polls and when they are confronted with this prospect they usually become somewhat less responsible in the eyes of the managements with which they deal.

Need for Uniformity within the Jurisdiction of the Union. A union leader who negotiates substantially different wages for members doing similar work for different employers within the same industry is asking for political trouble. "Equal pay for equal work" has an almost universal political appeal. The application of this principle may force a union leader to bargain for less than the full amount that could be obtained from the richest employer within the union's jurisdiction. If this absolute maximum victory were attained, the union leader who could not follow through with other employers might be in a very unfavorable political position.

Strike Temper of the Rank and File. The union leader's ultimate weapon is the strike. The strike is also a crucial political test. In the strike, workers play for the stake of their most valued economic asset—their jobs. Workers pay union dues with little protest and *vote* to strike almost automatically, but when they strike on a union call they show the absolute maximum of faith in the union leadership. If they return to work before a settlement is negotiated, they are casting the most telling "no-confidence" vote that any union leader can ever receive. True wildcat strikes are also no-confidence votes. The leader who is to survive as a political leader must be closely attuned to the willingness (and in some cases, eagerness) of the rank and file to strike. This willingness on the part of the rank and file is undoubtedly the most significant political influence on the union side in the formulation of demands. At the same time that the union leader is the victim of the rank and file willingness to strike, the leader is also a force in determining that willingness. No one wants to lead a reluctant army. It is the union leader's job to make sure that the desire of the union rank and file for higher wages or other improvements in their agreement with the company equals their willingness to hit the bricks.

Formulating Strategy for Wage Level Bargaining

The foregoing discussion has touched on some of the economic and political elements of the situation management and the union face as they begin to draw up their demands, counterproposals, and bargaining positions. Each has imperfect knowledge of the facts. Management is likely to know the economic facts about the situation of the workers and the union almost as well as the union leaders, and economic facts about the company's position much better; but may find the political considerations harder to gauge. Union leaders are in a position to take meaningful, frequent soundings of the political situation, but may not be able to estimate with much accuracy the management's economic resources or its weaknesses.

Major employers maintain large industrial relations research staffs to make continuous studies on trends in union demands, the cost of living, employee attitudes, and other questions that might have weight in bargaining strategy decisions. International unions also maintain research staffs to do what amounts to the same thing from an opposite point of view. The final company position before entering negotiations appears usually to be the decision of the top management (president, board of directors) after consultation with senior officers of the enterprise, e.g., vice presidents of industrial relations, finance, production, and sales. Shifts or changes in position during negotiations—in particular, the decision on whether or not to accept the challenge of a strike—probably require the same procedures. By this time company negotiators may come to feel that they have a solid knowledge of what the union will really accept in the way of a wage settlement.

Management people tend to be reticent about how they come to their strategic and tactical decisions, although public and private utterances often contain some clues. One student of management bargaining behavior makes the following inferences:

> The factors which move the more influential segments of industrial management to a wage decision are: (a) the compulsion to maintain production, (b) the need to maintain a feasible price, and (c) the sine qua non profit.
> My theme is simple: *production, price, profit, and the greatest of these is production.*[4]

Obviously, production is important to management. If there are to be sales, there has to be production. There are times, however, when production gets out of balance with sales. This occurs from time to time in the auto industry, as in the years of bulging dealer inventories, when cars are slow to move off the sales floors. At such times the industry is under no urgent pressure to produce more cars. New model tooling during the summer months must, of course, go on uninterrupted, but production of cars is of slight significance. Dealers would, in fact, welcome a stoppage of production. Other years, when cars are selling like hot cakes, both tooling and production are imperative.

Unions are probably equally concerned with production as the key to strategy. They prefer to press their wage demands when management's need for production is high, because the potency of a strike is its ability to stop production. They tend to soft-pedal when the need for production eases. The union position on entering negotiations is undoubtedly less of a top-level decision than management's; rank-and-filers, and their stike temper, have to be much more of a consideration. During negotiations, in fact, rank and file response to the reports of union negotiators bears directly on the efforts of the negotiating team. In the last analysis, *any* increase in general wage levels is a gain for the union members, but the amount of the raise is not as important for either the members or the leaders as its consistency with expectations and comparisons with what other unions get.

Negotiations

No matter how economically sound the union's demands, they must be sold to the members and to employers before an agreement can be made.

---

[4] Leland Hazard, "What Economists Don't Know about Wages," *Harvard Business Review*, vol. 35 (January–February 1957), p. 49. See also Hazard, "Wage Theory: A Management View." In *New Concepts in Wage Determination*, edited by George W. Taylor and Frank C. Pierson. (New York: McGraw-Hill Book Co., Inc., 1957), pp. 32–50.

Management, in turn, must sell its position to the employees and the union before an agreement can be made. Most collective bargaining negotiations are private affairs between the union and the management. In pattern-making bargaining, the union and/or management sometimes seek public support for its position. We shall discuss this public bargaining after we have dealt with the semiprivate negotiation process.

Special Problems of the Union. As goods-producing or services-rendering organizations, most private enterprises are primarily units of the economic system, but they are subject to political constraints. One of these —and probably the most immediate—is the union, possessing as it does the power to shut down operations with a strike. The union is primarily a po-litical organization (in the power-political sense) subject to economic constraints of which undoubtedly the most immediate is the company's mar-ket and financial position. A company facing a particular set of negotia-tions, not surprisingly, determines its strategy largely on the basis of calcu-lations from economic estimates and data, on which (as has been brought out) it usually has better information than the union. What it seeks in nego-tiations is a political settlement consistent with its economic prospects.

In pay level bargaining the union leaders seek an economic settlement consistent with political relationships in the union. By formulating and pre-senting demands they have aroused expectations in the members' minds. The expectations are not always rational; but rational or not, they must be reckoned with. Union leaders usually have a better "feel" than the company for what the members want and how far they are willing to go to get it.

High expectations flow, for one source, from the union movement's own propaganda—usually called "educational activity." Year in, year out, union journals and union-leader oratory call attention to firms which make excess profits, to the rising cost of living, to the social need for strong, sustained, consumer purchasing power. Rival union gains may also raise the members' expectations. The common strategy of asking for more than you expect to get may fix the members' hopes on high demands and trap the leaders when the time comes to climb down.

At such times—and at other times when a company's sales or competitive or financial position puts limits on possible economic gains—high expecta-tions meet with disappointment. Members lose faith in their leaders; for faith, by definition, is not rational. Union leaders very often have to face the hard political problem and dilemma of rousing and holding firm support for high demands that it may take a strike to win, or getting members to accept a settlement that shatters their high hopes. Or both, in succession.

At the same time, clever leaders can often pick up political support for an otherwise moderate settlement in the negotiation of the wage supplements. Pensions are clearly something extra for the older, high-seniority workers. Unemployment benefits appeal to those low on the seniority lists, subject to frequent layoffs. Special pay concessions for strategic groups such as skilled workers who, if dissatisfied, might disrupt a settlement, can sometimes sweeten an otherwise disappointing flat cents-per-hour raise such as is typical of industrial union bargaining. Flat raises are the rule because at union meetings the least-skilled member's vote carries as much weight as that of the most highly skilled; and there are more nonskilled members.

Presenting Demands.   In presenting union demands to an employer, union negotiators use both positive and negative arguments. On the positive side, there is the moral argument: The union's demands are *right*.

Most employers, especially pattern-setting employers, want to do what's right by their employees. They may differ with the union over what *is* right, but there is little ground for cynicism about their motives. (After all, who willfully wants to do *wrong?*) But profits from missionary work are at best illusory. The same union leader who has argued fervently for some pioneering concession, and convinced a not-unwilling employer, may prove to be quite capable of going back to the members with a story of how hard he had to wrestle with the devil to convert the heathen boss. Pioneering employers have discovered that initial gains quickly evaporate; before long the novel concessions, copied in other agreements, become commonplace. Memories are short. Unions and union leaders change with the passage of time, and the "good guy" employer's past performance will not protect one from the "bad guy" image some time in the future.

Union Arguments.   There are also some positive economic arguments. One often advanced is that the union will impose the same conditions on competitors. To the degree that an employer finds this assurance credible, it carries weight. In general, managers feel confident of their ability to compete successfully if they are not handicapped by excessive costs.

The stumbling block is credibility. Big industrial unions like those in steel, autos, and the needle trades can virtually guarantee approximate pay-level equality in domestic industry, but they cannot control foreign competition. Nor can they exert much influence over the total market. A rise in the price of cars might make some people, who in the past have traded for a new car every other year, decide to drive the old car for a year or two longer and spend the money saved on other things instead. Buyers can also substitute one product for another. Steel competes with wood, aluminum, and plastics for certain uses: an increase in the cost of making steel could mean a worsening in some degree of the *industry's* competitive position, even if labor costs were equal throughout.

Other positive arguments appeal to management's concern with the effort part of the bargain: higher morale as a result of higher pay; readier cooperation; increased productivity. Management has to treat all such persuasions with a certain amount of skepticism. Undoubedly, the union's most telling arguments are of the negative sort.

On the negative side the union can hint at—or point out in so many words—the undesirable consequences of the company's *not* agreeing to the union's demands: a strike, the cost of idle plant and equipment, loss of sales and customers, employee dissatisfaction, ill will, and hostility. Workers in the plant sometimes reinforce the bargaining table arguments with well-orchestrated slowdowns, errors, lapses from quality standards, all of which are costly, and hint at costlier things to come.

If management has done its homework in preparation for the negotiations, it has estimated strike costs and is aware of possible consequences. It does not take much imagination for the company negotiators to clothe the union's veiled or open threats with a clear notion of what might happen. The union cannot guarantee a more productive work force in return for higher wages, but it is within the union's power to lighten a manager's fear of organized obstruction.

Employer Arguments.   Employers, too, can offer both positive and negative arguments. The most telling negative argument is a clear showing —or success in giving the impression—of readiness to endure a strike, even a prolonged strike. This threatens workers with loss of income, and the union with a heavy drain on its strike fund, perhaps with the depletion of its financial resources. If coupled with a reasonable company counteroffer, it puts before union leaders the prospect of perhaps having to send their members back, after prolonged hardship and sacrifice, on terms they could have settled for without a strike. Management's threat gains credibility and force if union leaders know, or can be brought to believe, that the company could hold its customers by farming out work, or transferring operations, or resuming production with nonunion labor.

The company's best positive argument is often the proposal (or counterproposal) itself: wage rates that are in step with raises won by other unions, and the prospect of uninterrupted and continued employment for the union members.

Pattern Setting.   Union and company negotiators often start their bargaining with a tacitly accepted pattern to guide them. (Of course, in key negotiations like basic steel or the auto industry, there is no previous pattern: They are themselves the pattern setters.) Information on terms reached in key agreements nationally is available to both sides from governmental sources, private reporting agencies (such as the Bureau of National Affairs, Commerce Clearing House, Prentice-Hall), and many trade associations. Employers frequently supplement such data with information which they get directly from competitors, while unions draw on other locals or other unions, including those dealing with competing firms.

The bargainers may, however, disagree over which pattern to apply. Food processors in coal-mining towns, for example, may encounter demands paralleling the national coal settlement from noncoal unions. Even when there is no dispute over the appropriate pattern, both sides will ordinarily seek modifications to fit local conditions. Management is more likely to break from the pattern; a less-than-pattern settlement would favor the company's interests. The union finds it harder to deviate from pattern terms: It cannot gracefully demand the pattern which it is holding up to the company as a model to follow, and at the same time deny it by trying to better its terms.

Management finds many arguments for deviating from the pattern. They are not all consistent with each other, but can be selected to fit the particular situation. Here are a few: Community labor market rates are lower than pattern rates; company wages compare with or exceed wages paid for comparable work in competing firms; company nonwage benefits (pay for time not worked, and contingent benefits) are better than the pattern, or than those offered by competitors, or than those prevalent in the community; competitors have lower nonwage costs, such as transportation; the company has had financial losses and profits are down; or even, the company is operating in the red.

Companies using these or kindred arguments have to bear two things in mind: First, they must be sure of their facts and able to document them, or the argument backfires; Second, each point, if accepted, tends to become a long-term commitment. Thus if the company pleads financial straits in a year when profits are down and gains concessions from the union for that reason, it must expect above-pattern demands in a year when profits are up. Similar long-term commitments grow out of wage-rate, fringe benefit, and productivity comparisons.

Just as the union may reinforce verbal efforts at the bargaining table with carefully coordinated action on the shop floor, management supplements negotiations by direct and indirect appeals to the employees. Most large companies carry on regular, often extensive, information and education programs. Company periodicals are not backward about reminding employees of the benefits they receive, and presenting the company's point of view, however baldly or however subtly, on issues that arise in labor-management relations. Special letters may go out on special occasions—and negotiating the agreement is a special occasion. Communications aimed at employees sometimes take the form of a direct appeal to accept the company's offer in collective bargaining. The company presents its proposals as generous, "final," and in the best interests of employees. If union leaders reject the offer (the message may suggest), employees will suffer layoffs or permanent loss of jobs, or loss of earnings through a futile strike that nobody wants.

Boulewareism. Just how far a management will go in making an offer directly to employees seems to depend on management philosophy and the state of business. The management philosophy expressing an extreme use of this approach, Boulewareism—for many years the General Electric policy— has been declared an unfair labor practice: refusal to bargain "collectively and in good faith." The NLRB and court decisions that struck down Boulewareism seem to draw a distinction between management's legitimate right to speak freely to employees, and a policy that would base bargaining strategy entirely on a direct appeal to each employee, and bypass collective bargaining with the union. Such an approach, the agencies finally concluded, was an attempt to circumvent public policy and the law.

Companies that make direct presentations to employees on a year-around basis seem to believe that little can be accomplished at the bargaining table without also getting the company's message across to employees over the heads of the union leaders. Special appeals seem to multiply in periods of poor business, probably on the presumption that from fear of unemployment, employees at such times will be more "reasonable" than their representatives. In all these special appeals, management tries to bring to bear on the leaders the kind of membership pressures that will favor the company position.

Appeals for support from the public, beyond the bargaining table and beyond the union, almost always accompany pattern-setting bargaining. Both sides make an effort to get public approval for their respective positions.

Enlisting Public Support.   To the extent that people who make up the entity vaguely called "the public" take an interest in labor-management negotiations, they start by thinking of themselves as consumers. That puts the public, at the outset, squarely on management's side. To say this is not to imply that the public is antiunion. Unionists and their families make up, in fact, a sizeable part of the public; but every consumer wants lower prices, and no one welcomes the inconveniences that sometimes accompany a strike. Naturally, management plays this advantage for all it's worth.

The union has a trickier public relations problem. It has to convince the public that higher wages will not boost prices, or that, even if prices rise, the needs of the workers involved justify the cost or the inconvenience to the public. Failing either of these, the union tries to divert resentment and put the blame on management. Post office workers, for example, took action that in 1971 raised the price of sending a letter—something everybody does, and often—from 6 to 8 cents, or a 33⅓ percent raise, yet escaped the public wrath and even the stigma of blame. At a time of rising living costs they pictured the people who move the mail as having been underpaid for years, and the public responded with sympathy. Other unionists making the same appeal might not be able to succeed as well, perhaps, because the public would not regard them as underpaid. The public half suspects—with or without adequate grounds for the belief—that union-negotiated wage increases are not caused by, but cause, increases in the cost of living.

Another union appeal for public support is to point to the rise in labor productivity. Credit for higher productivity over the course of the years properly belongs to technological innovation; the individual worker has not, in the main, increased effort. A case can still be made for cutting the worker in on a share of the higher productivity. This shades into the purchasing-power argument: the more money workers earn, the more they will buy, and the better business will be for everyone.

Still another union appeal tries to direct public attention away from wages to high profits. The figures cited need not be those that appear on a company's financial statements, though drawn from them. Profits may be recalculated by using accounting procedures that make them look as big as possible: percentage return on investment, perhaps, instead of sales; or more "realistic" calculations of depreciation. If these interpretations show gains that much exceed 10 percent, the union will argue that the industry is exploiting the consumer and could easily meet union demands out of the excess profits.

Management counters with its own public relations claims. It tries to create and maintain the image of acting as representative of the public and guardian of the public interest. By fighting against excessive wage demands, the industry people say or imply, they are trying to keep costs, and hence prices, reasonable; they are also fighting inflation, which hits everybody's pocketbook. The public relations specialist who coined the phrase, "wage inflation," and fixed it in the public mind, gave management a potent slogan of persuasion.

In this rivalry for favorable public opinion, what are the stakes for management and the union? After all, the public has no seat at the bargaining table, no voice in negotiations, no veto over the outcome.

It is not so much the general public, but government as the executor of public policy, that the parties have their eyes on. Government is always more or less responsive to public opinion. If government should intervene "in the public interest" as it does sometimes when a strike threatens or breaks out, each wants, if possible, to prevent its coming in on the other's side. It also seems probable that a good part of management's appeal, while ostensibly directed at the public, is really meant to reach employees; and the union's appeal is meant to hearten and rally the members.

SUMMARY SO FAR

Union-management negotiations reach their greatest intensity when wage adjustments are discussed. Although the nature of the wage question differs in the handicraft and manufacturing segments of the economy, it is a major issue in strikes in both segments.

Successful collective bargaining is based on facts. In this chapter we have reviewed the major sources of economic data for collective bargaining. Management possesses most of the vital economic facts that are needed for bargaining. What economic data employers refuse to supply, unions try to obtain by other methods. Economic data for collective bargaining are not cut and dried figures; they are sometimes vague and almost always subject to diverse interpretations.

Unions and managements, as organizations, must cope with certain internal and external pressures on their wage decisions. These economic, political, and social pressures vary from firm to firm, industry to industry, and union to union. The final agreement on general wage adjustments reflects these pressures.

In times of emergency, such as war, the decision-making power in wage controversies may be taken over by the government. Under these conditions, the interest of the consumer receives greater *conscious* consideration than when wages are set through the market pressures of collective bargaining. However, there is little evidence to prove that governmental wage decisions are actually better for the community at large than decisions which emerge from rough-and-tumble collective bargaining.

CRAFT-UNION WAGE BARGAINING

When a craft union bargains with an employer, the wage agreement is the essence of simplicity. Worker characteristics and the work to be done are clearly established prior to bargaining by the training of the skilled craftsmen. For example, carpenters perform a variety of operations on wood. The typical agreement with a carpenters' union assigns all wood work to the carpenters' union. Through union rules (written and unwritten) every carpenter knows the content of a "fair day's work" and performs only that amount of work because craftsmen control the tempo of work with their own hands. The only collective bargaining wage problem confronting the skilled craftsman and employer is what the rate shall be for a known quantity and quality of workmanship. After this problem is handled the auxiliary problems of rates for apprentices and helpers remain. Most employers of craftsmen are specialists employing only one or a few crafts. An employer of several crafts obtains a wage structure which relates the rates of various jobs only after having carried on several separate negotiations with different unions representing the different crafts. Thus craft-union wage negotiations deal almost exclusively with problems of general wage adjustments.

Collective bargaining in the building trades is an important example of craft-union bargaining. We shall discuss the structure of building-trades bargaining, factors creating a solid community of interest between craft unions and building-trades employers, and the points of disagreement between unions and managements in building-trades wage negotiations.

Structure of Building-Trades Bargaining

Building-trades unions and employers bargain on a local level. Because the product market is local, there is little need for, or benefit to be derived from, bargaining on an area or national basis.[5] Customarily, the collective

---

[5] An important exception to this general rule must be noted in the relations between the Associated General Contractors of Northern California and California Building Trades Unions. Here a master contract covering a broad geographic area has been negotiated. This arrangement seems to be a natural outgrowth of the technology of the California construction industry, where general contractors bid on jobs over a wide area, move heavy equipment from job to job over this area, and recruit labor from the area where the particular job is performed. See Gordon W. Bertram and Sherman J. Maisel, *Industrial Relations in the Construction Industry* (Berkeley: University of California, Institute of Industrial Relations, West Coast Collective Bargaining Systems, 1955); and its sequel, Gordon W. Bertram's *Consolidated Bargaining in California Construction: An Appraisal of Twenty-Five Years' Experience* (Los Angeles: Institute of Industrial Relations, University of California, 1966).

bargaining agreement covers many employers and the members of a single local union composed of workers of the same craft, e.g., carpenters, electricians, or plumbers. General contractors have contracts with many unions, while an occasional specialty contractor will have only one contract with one union.

Frequently employers in the same line of business bargain as a group through an employer's association. This employer's association usually includes the largest and most influential firms in the local industry. Very often smaller employers and even a few large employers are not members of the association and, as a result, do not have a direct voice in determining the terms of the master agreement. After negotiations are completed with the employer's association, the nonmember employers usually voluntarily accept the terms of the master agreement or the union forces acceptance of the agreement through strike action. Occasionally, the union permits deviations from the master agreement in the case of nonsignatory employers as an organizational device.

Each craft local union customarily bargains for itself, but it expects, and usually gets, substantial strike support from the local unions in other crafts. Craft international unions usually allow their locals to go their own way on general wage adjustments but may exert powerful influence on working rules and the protection of the union's jurisdictional claims. In those unusual cases where craft international unions have tried to influence wage negotiations, they have met with only very limited success.

Community of Interest between Local Unions and the Construction Industry

In many ways the industry is like one big family. The nature of their work throws construction men into close interaction with each other. Not only are there close social ties among members of a given trade, but the industry as a whole stands apart from the rest of the community.

The class line between employer and employee, supervisor and worker is quite thin. Most contractors and superintendents are former workers. Many still hold union cards. Only a small proportion of the supervisors have had college educations. The social gap which separates management and labor in mass-production industry seems to be lacking. In general they see problems from the same point of view.

As a consequence, relationships are highly personal (in the words of Max Weber, they are particularistic rather than universalistic). Friendships and feuds flourish. To the outsider disputes seem irrational and overemotional.[6]

The community of interest between building-trades unions and contractors is rooted in both social and economic institutions. The local nature

---

[6] George Strauss, *Unions in the Building Trades: A Case Study* (Buffalo, N.Y.: The University of Buffalo Series, vol. 24, no. 2, June 1958), p. 69.

of the product market dictates local day-to-day bargaining. The worker's control of work tempo and the high percentage of labor cost to total cost forces the employers, workers, and union to be cost conscious (at least in these segments of the product market where demand is price elastic). Since a significant part of sales in most markets is to governmental agencies or performed under conditions prescribed by the government, the employer and unions are frequently political allies. Because entry to the industry sometimes involves only a small capital outlay, the unions and present employers share an interest in policing the activities of new firms, be they outsiders trying to invade the local market or individual tradesmen who may undersell the union rate.

Even in the knotty problem of union jurisdiction, there may be a community of interest between employers and the union. Like the tradesmen, many employers are specialists in the use of certain materials and thus share an interest in maintaining a demand for their particular type of construction and materials.

Although tradesmen, unions, and employers in the building trades have much in common, they tend to separate on the central issue in craft union bargaining—the "standard rate." Even here, their disagreement is usually over the interpretation of the same facts. Occasionally the union leadership and management are in agreement, with the workers dissenting.

The Wage Dispute

Wages are the central, and frequently the *only*, issue in building-trades bargaining. Union security, production standards, seniority, and other major issues have been settled for so long in most communities that they aren't even discussed in negotiations. Usually these nonwage matters have merely been entrusted to the union's care and negotiations start with the closed shop, union working rules, and jurisdictional claims as settled issues. This normal situation may be upset by new governmental rules or some new union rule or new materials or methods, but such occurrences are exceptional. We turn now to the goals of unions and managements in craft-industry wage bargaining.

Craft-Union Wage Goals. Typically, craft unions seek to increase only the standard rate. Recently many craft unions have shown increased interest in the multitude of wage supplements, such as pensions, health and welfare benefits, and insurance which the industrial unions have pioneered, but primary emphasis continues to be placed on the basic wage rate. Because of the irregularity of employment in the building trades, these programs are administered on a market-wide basis with eligibility for benefits based on continuous employment in the industry which usually means continuity of union membership. As a result, when a union seeks a package it really means so many cents for wage increases and so many cents for welfare benefits. Because of the worker's control over tempo, the employer can almost convert this package into a unit labor cost increase. The entire bargain can be stated as income to the worker versus costs to the employer.

How much of an increase will a building-trades local union demand and strike for in a given year? What factors influence the determination of the union's demands?[7]

Like managers, college professors, and farmers, rank-and-file members of building-trades unions seem to have an insatiable desire for more money. They exert a rather constant pressure on the union leadership to get more. They become particularly insistent when business is good, the cost of living is rising, or other unions have negotiated substantial wage increases. The craft unionist feels entitled to as large a wage increase as other unionists get and frequently expects the union to get an even larger increase because of painstakingly acquired skill. On the other hand, the building-trades unionist probably knows more about the general state of business in that industry. This greater industry consciousness can be traced to the building-trades unionist's visits to the union hall for work and employment on different jobs during the course of the year. Because of this industry consciousness, craft unionists as a group may exhibit some concern over the employment effects of their wage demands.

A building-trades business agent who enters negotiations with employers is representing the interests of a more or less fixed number of union members. The agent's job is to get the best possible bargain for those members. Most of the members have a substantial investment in an apprenticeship and can earn a return on that investment only through employment in the building trades. When all members are working, the business agent usually presses for a very substantial wage increase. When many members are out of work, the agent tends to be much more conservative in wage demands. Several students[8] of building-trades wage bargaining have suggested that business agents tend to differentiate "big work" and "small work" in their thinking on wages. For big work such as large buildings and roads, business agents tend to believe that cost has little influence on the decision to build or not to build. In this case, the business agent would show little regard for the employment effect of wage demands. In the case of small work, such as residential construction and renovation, business agents may believe that cost is a major determinant of the decision to build. Thus, business agents might show greater restraint in increasing the wage paid on small work than on big work especially in periods when many unionists were unemployed. If this distinction does enter the thinking of building-trades business agents, it is clear that they tend to view the best bargain as consisting of both a

---

[7] Our discussion of some of these factors will be abbreviated in this section. Fuller discussion of some of these factors, especially the cost of living, will be found in the discussion of industrial-union bargaining.

[8] William G. Hosking, "Wage Decisions of Building Trades Unions in Central New York." *ILR Research*, vol. 2 (December 1955), pp. 2–5, and Strauss, *Unions in the Building Trades*.

wage and an employment component. It should be noted that Strauss indicates that although the business agents he studied seemed to be worried about the employment effect, he could not discover a single case where they had reduced wage demands because of fear of loss of employment.[9]

Undoubtedly the major consideration in building-trades demand formulation is the business agent's perception of the willingness and ability of the employers to meet demands. If the contract comes up for negotiation at the height of a very busy season with lots of work started and more on the drawing boards, the business agent is very likely to make substantial demands. Under these circumstances, even a short strike will hurt the contractors and they will be in a conciliatory frame of mind. If business is slow and no great pickup is expected in the near future, the business agent will probably go slow on wage demands. In this case, a strike threat loses much of its persuasive power. We turn now to the interests of the building contractors in wage bargaining.

Contractors' Bargaining Goals.   From the foregoing discussion it becomes clear that craft-union wage bargaining concentrates on wage *levels*, or pay for time worked. The effort side of the bargain may not even receive mention. The reason for this apparent oversight is that effort is under the control of the worker, who thus sets tempo; and the employer can do little about it.

Workers who have served a trade apprenticeship learn, among other things, how fast to work to maintain traditional standards of quality and quantity. They will not slacken their pace, but are not easily driven to quicken it. A bricklayer, for instance, will on the average lay so many bricks per hour and per day, and not many more or many less. From this known rate (which has varied over the years and may vary from one locality to another), a contractor can estimate quite accurately how much it will cost to put up a wall containing a given number of bricks: the unit labor cost per brick. In order to reduce this unit labor cost the contractor must either persuade the bricklayers to take a pay cut while continuing to work at the same tempo, or, without cutting pay, to speed up the work. Neither wage cuts nor speedups are popular with unionized craftsmen. Although muscle-saving machinery has made its way into the technology of the construction industry and lowered total costs, skill-saving devices and machinery have met adamant opposition from the craft unions. Unit labor costs for tasks requiring the work of skilled hands remain tied to the pace or work tempo of the craftsmen who apply the effort.

Other elements of the five-point package follow almost automatically from the outcome of the bargaining on pay for time worked. Premium pay simply applies time-and-a-half or double-time to the agreed hourly rates. Pay for time not worked, the fourth item, was not traditionally a part of the craft union bargain. A holiday was a layoff day; now it may be paid, or

---

[9] Strauss, *Unions in the Building Trades*, p. 76.

worked at premium rates. Contingent benefits, if any, came not from the employer but from the union or, after the passage of the social security laws, from the government. Craft workers typically are temporary employees. In successive seasons, or even a single season, they work for many employers. Now that industrial unions have won contingent benefits, craft unions negotiate agreements that call for employer contributions—so much per hour worked—to an industry fund administered by the union or jointly by the union and representatives of the employer association.

Setting the wage level, therefore, sets unit labor costs uniformly for the industry in a given locality, and gives no one employer a competitive wage advantage over another. Each contractor tries instead to cut total costs by finding more efficient methods of carrying out unskilled operations, such as materials handling. They look outward to the structure and economic health of the industry, and support measures that encourage the expansion of business generally. Large contractors usually have an influential voice in the decisions of the employers' association. Sometimes smaller employees don't bother to belong to the association because they fear being outvoted by their larger associates or believe that their interests will be represented even if they don't pay their dues.

Typically the union and the employers' association work closely together to police the industry for compliance with the master agreement. This is a service to the employers in that it protects each employer who abides by the agreement from being underbid by some employer who uses nonunion labor or who shades the prevailing wage scale by other methods. Although each employer probably would like to bid on projects with a personal wage cost advantage, the best interest of all employers is served by eliminating such advantages. The activity of the employers' association and the union, if effective, guarantees an equality of competition in the industry as far as labor costs go.

When building activity is slow, employers naturally start a serious search for methods of generating new business. One means of generating new business is to increase governmental building. Here the employers and unions are complete allies. Another way of stimulating new business that is likely to occur to the contractors is a "bargain sale." Since all building construction is on a made-to-measure basis, the employers seek ways of reducing their costs, by greater use of precut materials and gentle urging of the craftsman to pay less attention to unimportant details.

When building is booming the contractor is likely to be quite generous in wage bargaining. After all, customers are waiting at the door and they only frown when a price is quoted. The contractor and the customer both bemoan the high prices but the customer buys and the contractor adds on the customary profit (which is sometimes figured as a percentage of cost). Like the business agent, the employer may worry about the sales effect of high prices, but in periods of good business is unlikely to do anything about them.

Although the building-trades unions represent the elite of American unionists and compose a substantial portion of the labor movement, the typical building-trades contract is negotiated with little public notice or concern because of the local nature of bargaining. Once the contractors and the unions in a locality have made their peace, the contract goes into open operation and exerts practically no influence whatever on bargaining in other segments of the economy.

THE PAY PACKAGE

We are now back to the pay package and the five components of the wage and effort bargain, as set forth in detail in Chapter 8. As a reminder, here they are again: (1) pay for time worked, (2) the effort bargain, (3) premium pay, (4) pay for time not worked, and (5) contingent benefits, or worker insurance and income-continuity programs.

Managers and union representatives negotiate new levels of *pay for time worked*, and fix the new levels for stated periods such as the year ahead. They may also explicitly regulate standards of task performance—part of *the effort bargain*—as, for example, by setting crew sizes, or implicitly provide for it by specifying how standards are to be set or challenged. These two items—pay for time worked, and the effort bargain—are fundamental.

Premium pay (time-and-a-half for overtime, or double-time for work done on holidays) really aims at regulating hours, not pay, but the length of the work day and work week, if uncontrolled, would have a bearing on effort.

Many writers on collective bargaining throw together under the heading "fringe benefits" the two items, *pay for time not worked*, and *contingent benefits*. Contingent benefits have become such an important part of the pay package that we devote the entire next chapter to them. We conclude this chapter by discussing special aspects of the other four components.

Pay for Time Worked

We have already amply discussed *pay level* and *job structure*, which together establish the pay for time worked, but have said nothing about *method of wage payment*.

Method of Payment.   There are two basic ways of paying wages or salary: (1) time wages, or pay by the hour, day, month, or year, without specifying the amount of work to be done; (2) production wages, or pay related to the amount of work the individual or group performs, more or less disregarding the time involved in its performance. In fact, however, the time element cannot be effectively separated from production nor production from time. No employer would want to pay people for an hour of work without having some idea of the amount of work to expect in return. No employee would care to receive production pay, or pay based entirely on output, without some expectation of being able to earn an average wage appropriate to the type of work, that is, to the kind of tasks that made up the job. Production wages are often referred to as piecework. The rates paid for piecework depend upon standards which are often set by time study. In setting these rates, however, there must be some presumption about average expected earnings. It can be seen, then, that time and output are really inseparable, but that for purposes of calculating payment two opposite approaches may be made to this problem.

It now becomes possible to define pay for time worked in the sense intended by the category under the wage and effort bargain. Pay for time worked is the *level*, expressed in concrete dollars and cents terms, of the wage or salary paid for a given job within the job structure of an enterprise; or it is the *expected average earnings* for the same job, even though the method of payment may not consist of straight time wage but of piece rates or production wages.

The Effort Bargain

Pay for time worked, or pay for the job, always appears in concrete dollars and cents form. The effort bargain, on the other hand, is not always so easily identified. It consists of the amount of work expected or required during a given period of time. Another way of saying this is: The effort bargain is the standard or norm expected on a given task. Thus, the effort bargain is always measured in terms of the task. If the entire job consists of a single task endlessly repeated, measuring the time required for that one task in a sense sets the effort bargain on that job. If the job consists of a variety of tasks, then the effort bargain is the sum or composite of the work expected on each and all of the tasks making up the job.

The most obvious and observable way of setting the effort bargain is through time study. At this point only a few important matters need to be noted. The first of these is that the effort bargain implies the working conditions of the phrase: "wages, hours, and *working conditions*." That is, under one set of conditions the output expected may differ from that under an entirely different set of conditions, even though the productive task, and the finished work turned out, may be the same.

Premium Pay

Premium pay consists of rates, or formulas for determining rates, which are to be paid for extra work performed outside the normally scheduled daylight working hours, or at other personal inconvenience to the employee. Under this heading fall such matters as overtime pay (usually calculated at time and one half) after 40 hours in any 1 week or 8 hours in any 1 day; night-shift differentials; and call-in pay.

Theoretically, this is money the enterprise would never have to pay if it did not work its employees outside the scheduled daylight hours. It used to be called "penalty pay," because it was intended to punish the employer who made extra demands on employees and encourage scheduling of operations more carefully. A supervisor ought to know at the end of one shift if there will be work for a particular employee at the beginning of the next shift on the following day. If she knows, and fails to tell the worker; or if, through poor planning at that level or higher, the supervisor does not know, the worker may come in to work as usual, find no work waiting, and have to be sent home. Without a provision for call-in pay, the worker would have lost not only the day's pay but the free time which she might have used for herself—even if only to watch TV. A union agreement requiring that the company either notify the day before, or give at least four hours' work or four hours' pay, serves as a powerful reminder to the supervisor not to neglect giving appropriate advance notice when an employee is *not* going to be needed.

In practice, overtime pay has come to be regarded as "gravy" which many workers are eager to get. Some companies have even used overtime pay, systematically scheduled, as a means of raising take-home pay for their employees without disturbing the pay rates. Premium pay provisions still remain, basically, a means of regulating not the income to the worker or the cost to the company but the hours worked. This is true whether the maximum (before overtime) is set by law or by union agreement.

Pay for Time Not Worked

At least four common types of payment for time not worked appear in labor agreements today: (1) vacation pay, (2) paid holidays, (3) paid rest periods, lunch hours, travel time, washup time, coffee breaks, and (4) special allowances such as Christmas bonuses. All of these are costs to the employer and income to the employee, and all are implicit when the employee enjoying them, usually a white-collar worker, is paid a fixed salary. The hourly-paid worker has had to ask for them in explicit terms. They don't so much add to the hourly worker's pay as cancel out former deductions. Thus the factory worker who used to get Labor Day Monday off, but lost the day's pay, now gets the same holiday off, but is not docked for it. And every other worker in the factory gets the same holiday, and pay for the time not worked. By spread of the union example, these items have become part of the costs of employing labor for the nonunion employer as well.

When the bargainers do get down to specific terms as they try to write the explicit subtantive rules in this area, they face many complex questions. The problem of defining a vacation and holiday policy provides an example.

Vacations

An adequate agreement on vacation pay must deal with the following problems:

1. Scheduling Vacations. Will the plant shut down for a stated period to allow all workers to take their vacation at the same time or will vacations be staggered over the year? If the plant shuts down for vacations and some workers will be needed during the shutdown, which workers will be required to work and what will be their rate of compensation? If some workers are required to work during the vacation period, will they be given an opportunity for a vacation at another time during the year? If management wishes to operate the plant, due to a backlog of orders, during the vacation period, what compensation will be given in lieu of vacations? If vacations are to be staggered through the year, what method is used in determining when an individual takes vacation? If vacations are staggered, may a worker use vacation pay during an illness?

2. Eligibility for Vacations. How much seniority must an employee have before being eligible for a paid vacation? Is a worker on temporary layoff eligible for vacation pay? Are part-time workers eligible for vacation pay? Are paid holidays falling within a vacation period a basis for extra compensation? Does an unauthorized absence immediately before or after the vacation period disqualify a worker for vacation pay?

3. Duration of Vacation Pay. The length of paid vacation time to which an employee is entitled is frequently related to length of service, e.g., 1 week for 6 months' seniority; 2 weeks for a year's seniority; 3 weeks for 10 years' seniority; and so on. In computing the amount of vacation pay entitlement, what consideration is given to breaks in seniority? Are there any requirements that long vacations must be taken at the convenience of the company or that they must be split so as to minimize interference with production?

4. Computation of Vacation Pay. Does the vacation pay computation include overtime premium, shift premium, incentive earnings, and personal rates above the base rate for the employee's job? Sometimes vacation pay is computed as a percentage of the previous year's earnings, e.g., 2 percent of the previous year's earnings would equal one week's vacation pay. This percentage method includes overtime premiums paid, incentive earnings, holiday pay, etc., but tends to reduce the vacation entitlement of workers who have had substantial layoffs or absences in the previous year.

5. Vacation Pay for Workers Temporarily or Permanently Separated. Is a worker on temporary layoff at the vacation period entitled to vacation pay? If a worker quits or dies does the worker or the family have a vested right to "earned" vacation time? Is a worker discharged for cause entitled to "earned" vacation time at the time of discharge?

The foregoing list of vacation bargaining issues emphasizes the cost element of vacations. This is not an altogether fair emphasis, because some of this cost may be offset by improved employee morale or a saving of unemployment compensation costs. At the same time, it seems logical that the individual employer's gain in employee morale from granting generous vacations has been significantly diluted by almost universal adoption of the practice.

Holidays

Paid holidays vie with vacations as being the most expensive form of pay for time not worked. Five paid holidays per year would cost about 2 percent of the annual payroll. One day of holiday pay usually costs the employer more than one day of vacation because holiday pay frequently applies to everyone on the payroll regardless of seniority. Like vacations, paid holidays have become so common that the individual employer only succeeds in avoiding poor morale by granting them.

An adequate agreement on holiday pay must deal with the following problems:

1. Eligibility for Holiday Pay. How long must an employee be on the payroll before becoming eligible for holiday pay? Is an employee eligible for holiday pay if absent on a scheduled shift immediately before or following the holiday?

2. Work on Holidays. Are workers obligated to report to work on holidays if advanced notice is given? What rates of pay will prevail for workers required to work on holidays?

3. Holidays Falling on Nonwork Days. If a paid holiday falls on a nonwork day, is the holiday celebrated on the next or preceding work shift or is holiday pay disregarded in this case?

4. What Compensation Will Be Given for Holiday Pay? Is shift premium, incentive pay, and normal overtime included in the pay given for holiday?

5. What Days Will Be Observed as Holidays? The rather striking increase in the number of paid holidays in recent years has pretty well exhausted the list of national holidays available, e.g., Independence Day, New Year's Day, Labor Day, Memorial Day, etc. As a result an increasing number of religious holidays are being added to the list. This poses a problem where members of the labor force are adherents of different religious faiths.

SPECIAL COLLECTIVE BARGAINING PROBLEMS ON WAGES

Job evaluation, production standards, and, to a lesser degree, incentive wages are integral parts of the operation of a factory. The most militant union cannot realistically expect to turn back the clock by eliminating these basic tools of industrial management. Because of the vitality of these techniques and their impact on employee welfare, issues related to them are a permanent part of the collective bargaining process. Future bargaining on these issues may take any number of possible directions. We shall briefly discuss four illustrations of possible future trends: (1) guaranteeing personal rates against job restudy, (2) wage structures as a cause of internal industrial union stresses, (3) automation and wage structures, and (4) job enlargement, sometimes called job enrichment.

Job Restudy

The problem of job restudy can be a major problem to a union. The chief union negotiator for a firm confronted with an adverse industry outlook sees the problem like this: "We are opposed to the job evaluation system in principle, but we are living with it. . . . In good times there's no pressure for job reevaluation because the labor market in our industry is too tight. . . . In a slack period like this, if the company brings its job evaluation system to bear in a plant where technological changes have gone ahead faster than reevaluation of jobs, wage rates could be cut drastically." The union answer to this problem was to concentrate on the company's job evaluation program instead of pressing wage increase demands in negotiations. The union's demand was that all workers on specific jobs for six months prior to negotiations be "red-circled" and their rates be unchanged even if the job were downgraded after evaluation. The union also sought to protect certain job rates by urging greater emphasis on certain factors in the job evaluation system.[10]

Industrial Union Internal Stresses

The wage structure problem is almost exclusively the problem of the factory-type employer and the industrial union. One of the major problems of job evaluation is fitting the comparatively small number of skilled jobs into a wage structure which is dominated by the many semiskills of the factory. Skilled workers in a factory are usually represented by an industrial union in which they are only a small political minority. Because of the need for the militant support of the vast majority of the membership, industrial unions tend to negotiate across-the-board wage increases which reduce the skilled-unskilled wage differential. Many of the wage supplements initiated by industrial union bargaining also tend to reduce or conceal the skilled-unskilled wage differential.

The skilled worker in the factory may have a different type of employment relationship than a counterpart represented by a craft union. Factory employment is not subject to some of the severe seasonal fluctuations in such craft-union industries as building construction. The factory employer tends to retain skilled craftsmen as long as economically feasible in adverse business conditions because of the difficulty of replacing them in periods of business upturn. Many skilled factory workers have acquired their skills at their employer's expense in specialized training programs.

Nevertheless, the wage scales negotiated by craft unions look quite attractive to the skilled factory worker. Also, in periods of booming business activity, most factory skilled workers could find other jobs at higher rates

---

[10] "UAW Pratt & Whitney Local Seeks Wage Stability Instead of Boosts," *The Wall Street Journal* (Chicago ed.), Thursday, October 10, 1957, p. 24.

of pay, in job shops or elsewhere. Thus market pressures exert powerful in-influences on the factory wage structure. Skilled factory workers become restless and begin to believe that they are the "forgotten workers" of the industrial unions. They talk about secession from their union and pose a very serious problem for the union leadership.

Wildcat strikes of skilled tradesmen belonging to the UAW plagued the automobile industry for several weeks in 1955 and delayed the ratification of the UAW agreements with General Motors, Ford, and Chrysler. This dissension plus the formation of a dual union, the Society of Skilled Trades, resulted in the UAW giving skilled workers a greater degree of representation in bargaining than they had possessed previously. It is quite certain that the problem of compensation for skilled workers will plague both employers and industrial unions for some years to come.

Automation and Job Evaluation

The exact impact of automation on job assignments in different plants is impossible to predict. However, in almost all cases, automation results in very large increases in work-hour productivity, a greater emphasis on rapid machine maintenance, and a reduction of the physical exertion and an improvement in physical working conditions. Such radical changes undoubtedly will change much of our conventional thinking about job evaluation.

Two trends are already discernible. First, unions are advocating greater emphasis on certain "compensable factors" or the introduction of entirely new factors. In an attempt to justify substantially higher rates for automated jobs such factors as "monotony," "visual effort," and a myriad of others are cropping up in negotiation sessions. It seems likely that these or other factors will be recognized by management as a moderate cost for union acceptance of radical new production methods. Second, several cases of negotiation on automated jobs have resulted in a radical reduction in the number of different jobs and job rates. In one case, several hundred different jobs were eliminated for two new jobs: "automation tender" and "automation equipment maintenance technician." This bargain meant very substantial wage increases for all of the workers in the automated plant. From management's viewpoint, such a bargain provided for maximum flexibility in the assignment of workers in the plant.

Job Enrichment

Industrial managers for many years have believed that maximum output could be achieved at minimum cost by breaking jobs down into the smallest possible tasks. Recent experience, especially during and since World War II, has radically changed this traditional thinking. "Job enrichment," i.e., the combination of several tasks for a single worker, is receiving increasing attention. This new trend is supported by two factors: (1) extreme job simplification actually reduces total output because of monotony and (2) the need for varied skills in certain maintenance jobs. In the case of maintenance work, "down time" on machinery can be extremely costly and waiting for a skilled worker in a particular classification can prevent other maintenance workers from finishing their part of the repair work. Whichever motivating factor is present, job enlargement changes job content (almost always in the direction of increased complexity) and necessitates reevaluation of the job. When two jobs are combined, should the rate for the new job be equal to the rate of the more complex element? Or an average of the two elements? Or even higher than the sum of the two elements?

SUMMARY

Employer and employee come together in our society under no compulsion, but in a voluntary, mutually beneficial relationship that finds expression in a wage and effort bargain.

The employer pays wages and salaries, which are *costs of operation*, and gets work—*production*—in return. The employee performs *tasks* by expending physical and mental effort, and gets income—*a livelihood*—in return. The essence of the bargain at any given moment is the *amount* of pay agreed on as acceptable for the *amount and kind* of effort that goes into the performance of the *tasks* that make up the employee's *job*.

Craft unions concentrate on bargaining for a standard rate of pay; that is, on the *pay level*. That is because skilled workers control their own work tempo—the effort side of the bargain—and members of the same craft do substantially the same job.

Industrial unions and the employers with whom they deal face more complicated problems. Management tends to control work tempo by such devices as the worker-machine mix, conveyor-line speed, schedules, layout, and production controls. Semiskilled employees work at jobs that are nonstandard and unequal. Thus labor and management have to establish a *job structure* relating different jobs in terms of their comparative *job worth*, and set up procedures for measuring and comparing different *kinds* and *degrees* of physical and mental effort required. Agreement on pay levels cannot precede, but must accompany or follow resolution of these other issues.

Managers have turned to various methods of *job evaluation* as a means of establishing a job structure, often (but not always) with union participation. Managers and unions alike have found that job evaluation systematizes the job structure and simplifies bargaining on pay levels.

Managers also attempt to prescribe and control the effort bargain by various means, of which the most evident and best known is probably time study. Unions thus have to bargain on effort day by day and task by task, resorting to the grievance procedure or, on occasion, to the traditional strike, to set the effort bargain. At enterprise level, therefore, an industrial union is likely to be more directly concerned with the effort bargain than with the absolute pay level. This does not mean that pay level means nothing to industrial unions and their members, or that the problem of determining the level is not difficult and complex.

Union-management negotiations reach their greatest intensity when wage adjustments are discussed. Although the nature of the wage question differs in the handicraft and manufacturing segments of the economy, it is a major issue in strikes in both segments.

Successful collective bargaining is based on facts. In this chapter we have reviewed the major sources of economic data for collective bargaining. Management possesses most of the vital economic facts that are needed for bargaining. What economic data employers refuse to supply, unions try to obtain by other methods. Economic data for collective bargaining are not cut and dried figures; they are sometimes vague and almost always subject to diverse interpretations.

Unions and managements, as organizations, must cope with certain internal and external pressures on their wage decisions. These economic, political, and social pressures vary from firm to firm, industry to industry, and union to union. The final agreement on general wage adjustments reflects these pressures.

In times of emergency, such as war, the decision-making power in wage controversies may be taken over by the government. Under these conditions, the interest of the consumer receives greater *conscious* consideration than when wages are set through the market pressures or collective bargaining. However, there is little evidence to prove that governmental wage decisions are actually better for the community at large than decisions which emerge from rough-and-tumble collective bargaining.

QUESTIONS FOR DISCUSSION

1. What elements of the "pay package" have unions added to the fundamental wage and effort bargain? To what extent, if any, does the trend in this direction seem irreversible?
2. Why are craft unions primarily interested in the pay level? Is the same thing true and to the same extent of industrial unions? Why?
3. As a principle of equitable compensation, in what way can the slogan, "Equal pay for equal work," justify wage differentials?
4. How do job evaluation techniques lend themselves to assuring equity through different rates of pay for different jobs?
5. As a manager, would you want the union to take part in a job evaluation study and help administer the program? Why? As a union leader, would you want to participate? Why?
6. Does time study primarily affect pay levels, or the effort bargain?

SELECTED ANNOTATED BIBLIOGRAPHY

BAMBRICK, JAMES J., JR., and BLUM, ALBERT A. "Comparative Wage Data in Collective Bargaining," *Management Record*, vol. 19 (February 1957), pp. 38–41, 69–76.

    Discusses gathering and use of area and industry wage rates and wage supplements for employee information and collective bargaining negotiations.

BAUMBACK, CLIFFORD M. *Structural Wage Issues in Collective Bargaining.* Lexington, Mass.: D. C. Heath, 1971.

    An analysis of numerous arbitration awards dealing with such wage-related issues as job classification, rate ranges, promotion and progression, wage standards and incentive pay.

BEHREND, HILDE. "The Effort Bargain," *Industrial and Labor Relations Review*, vol. 10 (July 1957), pp. 503–15.

    Through interviews with (British) management and union representatives, the author examines the underlying assumptions of wage incentive systems in the context of labor-management relations.

BELCHER, DAVID W. *Compensation Administration.* Englewood Cliffs, N.J.: Prentice-Hall, 1974.

    A comprehensive text on the establishment and administration of compensation systems. See especially parts III ("Rewards") and IV ("The Comparison Process"). See chapters 4, 5, 6, 7 for an examination of the content, uses and impacts of job evaluation plans.

DANKERT, CLYDE E.; MANN, FLOYD C.; and NORTHRUP, HERBERT R., eds. *Hours of Work.* Industrial Relations Research Association, vol. 14. New York: Harper & Row, 1965.

    Contents include:

NORTHRUP, HERBERT R. "The Reduction in Hours."

MARSHALL, RAY. "The Influence of Legislation on Hours."

DYMOND, W. R., and SAUNDERS, GEORGE. "Hours of Work in Canada."

MOTT, PAUL E. "Hours of Work and Moonlighting."

MEYERS, FREDERICK. "The Economics of Overtime."

MANN, FLOYD C. "Shift Work and the Shorter Work Week."

BERRY, DEAN F. "Automation, Rationalization and Urbanization: Hours of Work in the Office."

BROWN, DAVID G. "Hours and Output."

DANKERT, CLYDE E. "Automation, Unemployment and Shorter Hours."

DAVID, LILY MARY, and SHIEFER, VICTOR J. "Estimating the Cost of Collective Bargaining Settlements," *Monthly Labor Review*, vol. 92 (May 1969), pp. 16–26.

    The article describes the BLS method of estimating the cost of the economic package. Includes a sample worksheet for calculation plus examples.

DOERINGER, PETER B., and PIORE, MICHAEL J. *Internal Labor Markets and Manpower Analysis.* Lexington, Mass.: D. C. Heath, 1971.

    The standard treatment of the origins and functioning of labor markets within the employing organization, with major attention focused on how wages are set and people allocated to jobs.

DUNLOP, JOHN T. *Wage Determination Under Trade Unionism.* Oxford: Basil Blackwell, 1950 ed.

Establishes a model for union behavior which encompasses union wage policies, bargaining power and intermarket relations, and the impact of the business cycle on wages. A landmark in wage theory.

FOSTER, HOWARD G. "Wages in Construction: Examining the Arguments" and D. Q. MILLS, "Construction Wage Stabilization: A Historic Perspective," *Industrial Relations,* vol. 11, no. 3 (October 1972).

Foster examines the reasons why construction wages rose so rapidly in the late 1960s and early 1970s, and Mills examines the federal government's attempts to deal with strikes and rapidly escalating wages. See also the articles on other aspects of construction industrial relations in the same journal issue.

HENLE, PETER. "Reverse Collective Bargaining? A Look at Some Union Concession Situations," *Industrial and Labor Relations Review,* vol. 26, no. 3 (April 1973).

The author examines the dynamics and results of a dozen situations in which company economics forced collective bargaining agreements to be renegotiated on terms less favorable to employees (usually involving pay cuts).

HOWARD, WILLIAM A., and TOLLES, N. ARNOLD. "Wage Determination in Key Manufacturing Industries, 1950–70," *Industrial and Labor Relations Review,* vol. 27, no. 4 (July 1974).

The authors examine negotiated wage changes in eight highly unionized groups of manufacturing industries to see what variables are associated with these wage changes.

HOROWITZ, MORRIS A. *Manpower Utilization in the Railroad Industry: An Analysis of Working Rules and Practices.* Boston: Northeastern University, Bureau of Business and Economic Research, 1960.

An analysis of the complex web of working rules that have developed in American railroads over the past four decades. The author presents an objective definition of "featherbedding" and "make-work," and examines working rules to see which have and do not have make-work or featherbed effects. He has selected for close examination the rules and practices that are considered to have the effect of restricting the economic utilization of manpower.

JURIS, HERVEY A. "Union Crisis Wage Decisions," *Industrial Relations,* vol. 8, no. 3 (May 1969).

An analysis of the responses of unions in the meatpacking industry to hard choices between wage cuts or loss of jobs at various plants.

KILBRIDGE, M. C. "The Effort Bargain in Industrial Society," *Journal of Business* (January 1960), pp. 10–20.

Discussion of factors that influence determination of industrial effort. Shows that bargaining enters at both general pace level and level of specific output requirements. Automation and process-paced work are turning discussions of work loads more toward manning assignments, less on output requirements.

LAWLER, EDWARD E., III. *Pay and Organizational Effectiveness: A Psychological View.* New York: McGraw-Hill, 1971.

An organizational psychologist presents research findings which show how pay can be related to performance, satisfaction, absenteeism, etc.

LESIEUR, FREDERICK G., ed. *The Scanlon Plan: A Frontier in Labor-Management Cooperation.* A publication of the Industrial Relations Section, Massachusetts Institute of Technology. New York: John Wiley & Sons, Inc., 1958.

Presents and evaluates a plan for labor-management cooperation in increasing productivity worked out by a man who had been a steel union official and a member of the Industrial Relations Section at M.I.T. The plan includes a formula for dividing the benefits of increased productivity.

LEVINSON, HAROLD M. *Determining Forces in Collective Wage Bargaining.* New York: John Wiley & Sons, 1966.

An empirical investigation of the operation of economic, union political, and "pure power" variables in six unionized industries to see how these factors affected economic collective bargaining outcomes.

LEWIS, H. GREGG. *Unionism and Relative Wages in the United States.* Chicago: University of Chicago Press, 1963.

The classic study of the impact of unions on relative wage differentials among groups of labor.

McKERSIE, ROBERT B., and HUNTER, LAURENCE C. *Pay, Productivity and Collective Bargaining.* New York: St. Martin's Press, 1973.

The authors examine numerous productivity agreements and assess their impact, with special attention focussed on the transformation of workplace labor relations.

MILLS, DANIEL QUINN. *Industrial Relations and Manpower in Construction.* Cambridge, Mass.: M.I.T. Press, 1972.

The author analyzes the collective bargaining, wage determination, and manpower utilization processes in the construction industry, with emphasis on the unionized sector.

MITCHELL, DANIEL J. B. "Union Wage Policies: The Ross-Dunlop Debate Reopened," *Industrial Relations*, vol. 11, no. 1 (February 1972).

The author attempts to resolve the conceptual conflict between the political approach to unionized wage determination (Ross) and the economic approach (Dunlop) with the concept of employer resistance to union demands.

NUNN, HENRY L. *Partners in Production: A New Role for Management and Labor.* Englewood Cliffs, N.J.: Prentice-Hall, Inc., 1961.

Outlines the Nunn-Bush Shoe Company's program for labor-management amity and cooperation. Describes the share-of-production plan, how it works, how it compares with the generally accepted plans of compensation, and how it differs from the Rucker and Scanlon plans.

REES, ALBERT. *The Economics of Trade Unions.* Chicago: University of Chicago Press, 1962.

A short and very insightful analysis of the goals, sources of power, and economic impacts of U.S. trade unions.

ROSS, ARTHUR M. *Trade Union Wage Policy.* Berkeley, Calif.: University of California Press, 1953 ed.

Major topics include: the trade union as a wage-fixing institution, the dynamics of wage determination under collective bargaining, responsible union wage policy, union-management relations and wage bargaining, and the influence of unions on earnings. A landmark in wage theory.

RYSCAVAGE, PAUL M. "Measuring Union-Nonunion Earnings Differences," *Monthly Labor Review*, vol. 97, no. 12 (December 1974).

His analysis of new data suggests a larger differential between union and nonunion earnings than had been indicated in previous studies.

SHAFRITZ, JAY M. *Position Classification: A Behavioral Analysis for the Public Service*. New York: Praeger Publishers, 1973.

The author evaluates and strongly criticizes the job evaluation methods that are widespread in public organizations.

SLICHTER, SUMNER H.; HEALY, JAMES J.; and LIVERNASH, E. ROBERT. *The Impact of Collective Bargaining on Management*. Washington, D.C.: Brookings Institution, 1960.

Special attention is invited to the following chapters: 17, "Wage Incentives"; 18, "Measured Day Work"; 19, "Evaluated Rate Structures"; and 20, "Wage Structure Considerations."

TAYLOR, GEORGE W., and PIERSON, FRANK C., eds. *New Concepts in Wage Determination*. New York: McGraw-Hill Book Co., Inc., 1957.

Twelve authorities (GEORGE W. TAYLOR, FRANK C. PIERSON, LELAND HAZARD, NATHANIEL GOLDFINGER, EVERETT M. KASSALOW, JOHN T. DUNLOP, E. ROBERT LIVERNASH, ARTHUR M. ROSS, RICHARD A. LESTER, LLOYD G. REYNOLDS, CLARK KERR, and MELVIN ROTHBAUM) discuss recent developments in wage theory and the influences of collective bargaining on wage determination.

WHYTE, WILLIAM FOOTE. *Money and Motivation*. New York: Harper & Bros., 1955.

A comprehensive analysis of the impact of financial incentives in the factory. The author has drawn on the works of MELVILLE DALTON, DONALD ROY, LEONARD SAYLES, ORVIS COLLINS, FRANK MILLER, GEORGE STRAUSS, FRIEDRICH FUERSTENBERG, and ALEX BAVELAS.

WOLF, WILLIAM B. *Wage Incentives as a Managerial Tool*. New York: Columbia University Press, 1957.

Discusses the nature of wage incentives, impact of wage incentives on manufacturing costs, the theory and logic of wage incentives, and understanding the use of wage incentives.

11 The Wage and Effort Bargain: Contingent Benefits

CONTINGENT benefits are payments made to an employee who suffers some particular misfortune: layoff or permanent separation from a job; illness or accident; early or untimely death; superannuation. Each of these is an income-threatening hazard or contingency to be feared by anyone whose lifeline is the wage or salary earned by working at a job. Contingent benefits provide safeguards against them. Previous editions of this book referred to them by the accurate but unwieldy term, "worker insurance and income-continuity programs." Perhaps "contingent benefits" is no better, but it is shorter.

Like wages, contingent benefits are costs to the employer, but unlike wages, they are not in the usual sense income to the employee. Only those who run afoul of the specified contingency—who suffer the misfortune—draw the benefits; others do not. Thus, for example, an unlucky worker who runs a hand into a buzz saw and loses a thumb cannot get the thumb back but is entitled to medical care and financial compensation for the permanent disability. Fellow workers who were luckier or more cautious get no compensation, but still have their thumbs. Similarly, a worker who lives beyond retirement age gets social security and perhaps a private pension, which he or she would never have drawn if they had died young. If a worker dies young, the spouse may claim death benefits. If there is no surviving mate or dependent children, only the undertaker benefits. Everyone knows that death is inevitable, but old age is not; and no one knows when death may come. A worker wants protection against the consequences of either contingency and against other hazards of a working life.

Actuaries can predict for a given population the number of claims that will be made for benefits, hence, calculate the probable costs, but cannot tell in advance who will make claims. Neither can the eventual claimants. Starting from estimated costs, a company providing contingent benefits spreads the risk over the whole work force that is exposed to the hazards and specifies conditions under which an individual will be entitled to receive benefits.

333

The work force covered by a plan may, in fact, share the costs—another difference between contingent benefits and wages—though almost always the employer, when it does not carry the full load, pays the larger share.

Life is full of hazards and those that threaten to cut the income lifeline do not by any means exhaust the list. At various times in the past, right up to the present day, people have coped with the uncertainties and dangers of the future—and more specifically, the economic future—in one or more of three basic ways: (*a*) reliance on personal resources, family assistance, or charity; (*b*) governmental action; and, more recently (*c*) collective bargaining.

Personal Resources, Family Assistance, and Charity.   All men are mortal (Socrates said) and some die when they are young and vigorous; some linger into senility and decrepitude. Some people live out their years in health; some fall prey to accident, illness, or disease. These things happen to rich and poor alike as fate decrees, but there is one hazard that does not threaten the person of means: unemployment. Other dangers are as old as human life; unemployment is modern, a plague of industrial society. It threatens all who are dependent on a wage or salary; and, most acutely, it threatens the manual worker.

Against the contingency of becoming unemployed (as against other hazards), the moralist of a century ago counseled workers to "save for a rainy day." The theory was that out of savings put aside from earnings the worker would accumulate reserves to tide over a period of unemployment. This was, in fact, pretty much what the skilled worker did, or tried to do: worked at high wages during the season, then tightened the belt a bit, and waited out the lean days until the following season.

Factory workers of early times found it hard to keep body and soul together even when working and quickly dropped to the starvation level if they lost their jobs. Today, when factory wages are high, the new moralists —merchant and advertiser—urge workers to buy to the limit of their credit and make it easy for them to do so by selling on the installment plan. They tell workers not to save, but to go into debt.

Results of the two opposed moralities are about the same. A spell of unemployment soon depletes a worker's personal resources and exhausts credit; the goods indebted for, and used but never owned, are repossessed. Where then can the worker turn?

And how about other misfortunes: accidents, illness, old age? The traditional recourse was—and still is—the family. Children went back to stay with the old folks; old folks might go to live with their grown-up children. Beyond the family (in disasters exceeding family means), the recourse was help from friends and neighbors, or help from a church or fraternal order— beyond that, public charity.

This system worked quite well in the early American agricultural and handicraft economy. It has not died out even today, though the forms have changed. Putting a few extra pennies in the sock has developed into bank savings, private insurance policies, shares in mutual funds (perhaps bought, like a car or refrigerator, on the installment plan), and kindred schemes. There are echoes of the old-time neighborhood mutual help in the present-day United Fund or Community Chest. Overtones of the old morality still animate debates over welfare and public assistance. It seems to be a rather generally held belief that a person *should* assume primary responsibility for personal and family security.

Governmental Action.   As the economic system grew more complex and interdependent and as individuals found their livelihood more closely tied to the prosperity of particular business enterprises—particularly factories—they began to turn to the government to provide security. This trend, which began in the 19th century led to the enactment, early in the 20th, of factory inspection and workmen's compensation laws in a number of the states. It culminated in the New Deal social security programs, enacted at federal level in the 1930s. Subsequent legislation has updated and improved the programs, but has not added much that is really new.

The principle that justifies governmental action to provide safeguards against the hazards of a working life seems to be that for individuals overtaken by misfortune a complex industrial society should do what they cannot any longer do for themselves. There are some indications that the public has accepted a broadening of this principle to embrace those things government can do better or less expensively than the individual. Government programs offer two advantages: (1) They increase the number of people covered; that is, the statistical population, thus making risks more predictable and lessening the costs of insuring against the hazards; and (2) They tend to levy the taxes that support the programs (which are analogous to insurance premiums) on a progressive basis, so that low-income wage earners pay less for what they get than more prosperous individuals or business enterprises.

The federal social security programs, integrated with and supplementing the various state systems, now offer workers a measure of protection against unemployment (Unemployment Compensation); against old age and untimely death (Retirement, Survivors, and Disability Insurance); against job-connected accidents or industrial diseases (Workmen's Compensation); and now, more recently, ill health in general after age 65 (Medicare). Many nonunion enterprises, and even more unionized ones, augment these governmental programs with supplementary private plans.

Collective Bargaining.   As described in Chapter 2, early-day craft unions actually grew out of the "friendly benefit" societies, that people who worked together in the same trade formed for mutual insurance. Widows and orphans and disabled fellow-craftsmen received help from those funds. After the evolution of the societies into craft unions, the tradition continued. These early union programs were by no means comprehensive. A worker's main source of personal security continued to be skill, and union efforts went toward keeping the skill scarce and in demand.

Strategy suitable to craftsmen did not fit the situation of the semiskilled worker in the rapidly expanding factory system. Factory workers did not become unionized in any large numbers until the 1930s. New Deal legislation in that decade gave them not only social security but a collective bargaining law, the Wagner act, which protected their right to organize in unions. The industrial unions did not immediately demand contingent benefits. Instead, they concentrated on wage raises and work rules, and pay for time not worked. Paid holidays and vacations had hitherto been practically unheard-of for blue-collar workers.

Collective bargaining for contingent benefits really began only after the United States entered World War II, in the decade of the 1940s. War times are boom times. Factories work full-blast and still cannot keep pace with orders. Qualified workers are scarce, and employers eager to bid for their services. But a wartime economy, unless controlled, leads to inflation.

Aware of the threat of inflation, the wartime government enacted wage and price controls. Labor and management gave reciprocal no-strike, no-lockout pledges. Unions which would gladly have negotiated raises, and employers who would gladly have met or exceeded union wage demands found themselves restricted in what the government would allow them to do. Contingent benefits, hitherto unknown to collective bargaining agreements, were not wages, and did not fall under the strictures of the wage freeze. In most cases, besides, actual payment of benefits could be deferred. Pensions agreed on today, for example, become payable some time in a perhaps far-off tomorrow. Not surprisingly, therefore, unions and managements which found themselves unable to bargain on current wage rates turned to bargaining on promises redeemable in the future.

The bargains reached, in general, *supplemented* governmental programs. Pensions augmented or complemented social security; health and welfare programs extended protection to family members as well as to the already-protected wage earner. Unemployment was no problem at this time; but later, after the war, it became an important issue. Unions succeeded in getting privately financed supplementary unemployment benefits, severance pay, and other forms of protection.

Some employers made efforts after the war to remove contingent benefits from the range of issues subject to collective bargaining; but they were unsuccessful. The NLRB and the courts ruled that benefits are bargainable issues. They remain part of the pay package—an ever growing part—and are a prime topic of collective bargaining negotiations.

THE HAZARDS OF A WORKING CAREER

In the course of a lifetime, any person dependent on wages or a salary faces four main threats to a livelihood: (1) unemployment; (2) accident, pregnancy, or ill health; (3) permanent total disability, or untimely death; or (4) old age. Measures to deal with these four kinds of hazard have to take account of the differences in the nature of the threat and the consequences of the misfortune, but also must recognize some characteristics the four hold in common.

All of them *cost* money; so there are problems of funding and finance. All of them *pay out* money—not to every person covered, but to those who fall victim to the contingency—so there are problems of benefits, eligibility, and claims. All of them are costs to the employer and some, also, to the individuals covered. Thus those who pay for the programs and those who get the protection have a common stake in them, but often opposing interests. So there are problems of policy—management policy, union policy—and problems of administration. Finally, there are problems of social concern that go beyond the particular unions and enterprises. The magnitude and widespread incidence of the plans, their impact on the economy, their relationship to governmental programs and to matters of public policy, need to be assessed.

These last-mentioned social implications of collectively bargained contingent benefits had best be considered last, after the programs have been examined. Isues that grow out of the problems common to all four categories of hazard ought to precede discussion of the hazards themselves. The plan of presentation, therefore, is as follows:

1. Principles and policy.
2. Administration.
3. Benefits, eligibility, and claims.
4. Funding and finance.
5. The four hazards.
6. Social implications.

Principles and Policy

An organization ordinarily formulates policy in terms of its interests and objectives, in the light of principles perceived—rightly or wrongly—to govern the outcome of action toward objectives. By analogy, an individual might work toward the personal objective of financial security in any one or more of many possible ways. One might purchase stocks and securities, start a savings account, buy land, or, indeed, bury valuables in a hole in the ground. Any of these policies—even the last-mentioned, during a war or revolution—might succeed. Any of them could lead to disaster—even the first-mentioned—as investors found out at the time of the stock market crash. The future is always uncertain and full of change, yet one principle holds true. Benjamin Franklin expressed it most succinctly in *Poor Richard's Almanac:* "Save and Have." It is a more reliable guide to policy aimed at security objectives than its opposite: "Let tomorrow take care of itself." One thing is sure: Set nothing aside, and there will be nothing left.

Policy in bargaining for contingent benefits similarly grows from interests and objectives of the bargainers and rests on principles which they perceive as applicable. It would be surprising if unions and management did not have different, often opposing interests and objectives, though it does not follow that these must needs be irreconcilable. It might even happen that unions and management would take different and perhaps opposing views about relevant principles. Certainly principles derived from clashing ideologies could put them in conflict. Just as likely, however, unions and management may find that they accept the same principles and differ only on objectives. Sometimes they will agree both on principles and objectives.

Whether they like it or not, both have to accept one general principle that public policy has laid down as binding upon them; that is, that workers are entitled to protection from the consequences of misfortunes not their own fault or under their control, which destroy or diminish their ability to make a living. Governmental programs provide a start in this direction in the private sector of the economy, and tax private enterprises and individuals to support them.

Not yet a part of public policy is an extension to this principle—that an employer *must* assume the added financial burden of supplementing the governmental programs, but that one *may* do so and thereby win esteem, has become clear. It is part of the accepted perception of the employer's role in our society. It may become a practical necessity if one is to continue to attract and hold a work force. While not required to do it, then, or condemned if one does not, an employer can no longer refuse *on principle* (as some employers did, on ideological grounds) to bargain with a recognized union on contingent benefits.

Bargaining then proceeds on other principles: those that apply to the general nature and specific demands of worker insurance and income-continuity programs, regardless of the particular form they take. The most important principles affecting policy in contingent benefits bargaining seem to center around the following issues; (a) noninterference with operations; (b) adequate benefits; (c) actuarial soundness; and (d) appropriate allocation of the financial burden.

Noninterference with Operations.   A business enterprise does not exist for the purpose of providing benefits, though it may have to provide them to carry out its operations and achieve its purposes. Operations are a first priority.

Sickness, for instance—real sickness—interferes with operations. It causes absenteeism, disrupts schedules, often means working short-handed. Granting paid leave to a sick employee does not solve the immediate operating problem the absence creates, but alleviates the personal misfortune and by providing timely care may bring a sick employee back to productive work sooner. A sick leave plan so overgenerous as to encourage a person with a slight headache or hangover to stay home rather than report for work would be of dubious benefit to the individual and interfere needlessly with operations. So would a benefits program so ill-considered or so costly as to tie up a major portion of a company's working capital.

A company is not, and cannot afford to be, a philanthropic institution. To stay in competition, it has to remain solvent and operate efficiently. Few people would expect contingent benefits to *directly* increase efficiency of operations, but at least they must not seriously interfere. The same could be said, of course, of any provision of a union agreement, but is especially true of benefits bargaining, where the negotiators often tend to lose sight of operational effects. Benefit programs seem to the bargainers to be remote from operations and in a separate compartment. Managers might be expected to be more alert to this danger, but they sometimes disregard it. They tend to reckon the impact only in dollar costs, not in effects on operations. Money saved by refusing paid sick leave, for instance, could be lost many times over, not in cash, but in lowered productivity.

Adequate Benefits.   That careless worker of a few pages back who lost a thumb in an industrial accident in the state of Connecticut would have received in compensation for it (in the late 1960s) not less than $3000; in the state of Oregon, $600. Who is to say which of the two amounts is adequate—or inadequate—or overadequate? How much is a human thumb worth? To the worker who loses it, moreover, it is not *a* thumb, but *my* thumb.

Measures of adequacy emerge somewhat more definitely in establishing pensions. A company pension of $10 a month to supplement social security would add more to the bitterness than to the means of a retired couple, in the face of rising costs of living. Under inflation and despite past increases, social security is already—and remains chronically—inadequate. Barring future inflation, a pension equal to full pay at retirement date would be *more* than adequate. But with inflation, how long will even so overgenerous a provision for retirement (far in excess of current practice) remains adequate? Unions naturally judge adequacy from the point of view of the recipient of benefits. Management tends to judge by the level adequate to gain acceptance for the agreement as a whole.

The same issue of adequacy arises in all four areas of contingent benefits. Various standards of adequacy have been tried in each of them, and will be discussed under the specific categories of hazard. Whatever the category, benefits bargaining starts from the principle of adequacy; though notions of what is adequate may differ.

Actuarial Soundness.   A program of inadequate benefits could be actuarily sound, and so could a program offering more-than-adequate benefits. No program can be actuarily sound, whatever the level of benefits, if it does not generate enough funds and maintain sufficient reserves to pay off on its promises. Actuarial soundness is a *calculation*. It matches anticipated payoffs, which are an estimate and forecast of the future, against necessary contributions to be set aside in the present. The future is always uncertain. Predictions of the future are never exact, but have to be expressed in probabilities. Within the range of probability, over the long run, costs must support the expected benefits, payoff must not exceed reserves.

Devising plans that are actuarily sound demands the professional services of actuaries, who are experts. Bargainers absorbed with immediate problems often feel tempted to ignore long-run possibilities, and just take a chance. (Even on an actuary's predictions they take a chance, but it is a calculated chance.) A program that is actuarily sound is more likely to meet employee expectations of benefits and employer expectations of cost. This holds true in any category of hazard.

There are many ways to implement the principle of actuarial soundness. Issues of policy that most frequently come up under this heading are whether a program is *funded* or *nonfunded*, and if nonfunded, whether it it insured or pay-as-you-go.

Appropriate Allocation of the Financial Burden. The main issue here is whether the plan should be *contributory* or *noncontributory;* that is, whether employees who are to benefit from the protection shall share part of the cost (contributory) or whether the enterprise shall carry it all (noncontributory).

Governmental programs presently in effect are of both kinds. Social security (RSDI) is contributory; workmen's compensation (in most states), noncontributory. Private supplements do not have to copy the governmental pattern. Many private pension plans are noncontributory, entirely paid for by the employer, though the social security pensions they supplement are contributory. Family health and hospitalization plans such as, for instance, Blue Cross, are usually contributory. The employer's contribution consists of so much per enrolled employee, with the employee making up the rest of a variable total based on family size. In some programs, such as certain forms of group life insurance, employees pay the full premium, but get the insurance more cheaply by virtue of their attachment to the employing organization.

Unions and management often hold different views of principle over the contributory/noncontributory issue. Arguing from the principle of individual responsibility, managers contend that employees should share the burden of providing for their own personal security. This seems to be part of the conventional morality of our culture. Practical considerations reinforce the principle: For the same level of benefits, a contributory plan will cost the employer less. Besides, many employers believe that their employees will appreciate the benefits more if they have to pay for them, and that an awareness of their own contribution will make them more aware of (and perhaps, more grateful for) the employer's.

While union negotiators may explicitly accept the principle of individual responsibility, they tend to take a more pragmatic approach. Their members expect *both* raises and contingent benefits. A contributory program reduces the apparent amount of the raise; noncontributory benefits increase it. Implicit and unrecognized, perhaps, behind the union approach there also stands a counter-principle: Provide for contingencies at the *source* of security, the enterprise. Enterprise operations, in which all engage, produce the wealth that is the source of security for all.

A subsidiary issue in allocating the financial burden is the relation of the privately financed benefits to governmental programs; that is, whether the governmental programs (obligatory, and supported by a form of payroll tax) are to carry a greater or lesser share of the total burden for various items of the benefits package. This is the *costs* side of the issue already encountered in its *payoff* form under the heading of adequate benefits.

Administration

A retirement fund can build up over the years to a temptingly large sum of money. Even a fairly small company can accumulate reserves for this and other purposes that run into the millions of dollars, and larger companies into the tens—indeed, the hundreds—of millions. It does *not*, unfortunately, go without saying that those who administer the funds will always be honest, and able, and will take a trusteeship view of their responsibilities. The law (specifically, the Landrum-Griffin act of 1959) had to spell out rules of conduct and standards of administration to safeguard the interests of those for whom such funds are built up: the workers. Certain union leaders, and others, are serving time in prison today for mishandling funds that had been entrusted to them. Even more serious losses to supposed beneficiaries of funded programs may come not from dishonesty so much as inexperience and ineptitude of those who administer them.

Safeguarding the integrity of administration thus becomes part of the responsibility of the bargainers. One issue they have to face is: *Who* will administer the program? Four answers to this question have been found: (1) the employer; (2) the union; (3) the employer and the union jointly; and (4) neutral outsiders such as a bank, an insurance company, or a foundation.

Employers. They are accustomed to administering financial affairs and have an interest in both the honesty and efficiency of administration. At the same time, as employers they have a partisan interest in many questions that could arise and that might possibly run counter to the interests of the beneficiaries. An objection to employer administration, then, is possible conflict of interest.

Union Administration. Subject to the same objection as employer administration, unions have gotten a bad name as sole administrators, chiefly because of a few well-publicized cases of embezzlement and shady dealing. Yet, in some circumstances, unions are the logical administrators. When one large union deals with many small employers, as in construction or the coal mines or the needle trades, the union would seem to be the natural agent of administration. Not as strong a case can be made when a single local union deals with a single employer.

Joint Administration. This is a common arrangement. Issues of principle and practical arrangements having been taken care of in collective bargaining, both sides presumably have a common interest in effective administration.

Outsider Administration.   Finally, a solution that minimizes influence from either side and takes administrative decisions out of the hands of both parties is administration by an outsider. It makes use of the experience and expertise of a financial institution such as a bank or insurance company, but also subjects administration to the conservatism and sometimes excessive caution of these organizations. A compromise between this way and direct joint administration sometimes takes the form of establishing a foundation. Management and the union name representatives to the board, which also draws from banks or other outside institutions.

Issues arising from administration of a program (whatever the form chosen) have to do with such matters as: investments; standards of eligibility for benefits and level of benefits paid (when this is discretionary, or depends on the amount of reserves); mergers, acquisitions, dissolutions of employing companies; and many other matters. On investment policy, for example, management usually thinks first about the safety of the investment and the expected earnings. Union policy may favor investment in socially desirable projects such as low-cost housing, which may not be as profitable as other possibilities but provide, as the union sees it, a double benefit.

Generally speaking, issues arising in the course of administration are less important both to the union and the company than provisions for responsible trusteeship and efficient operation.

Benefits, Eligibility, and Claims

A worker who gets a union-negotiated wage raise can spend the extra money at once; but to be able to comprehend the gains from an improvement in contingent benefits, has to make an effort of imagination. A young worker, for instance, rarely looks far enough ahead to appreciate the value of a pension plan. If the plan is contributory, the young may resent having to pay into a fund just for the benefit (as they see it) of a few broken-down old-timers. The old-timers look on it differently. Yet neither they nor the youngsters ever give a thought to what it would cost out of pocket or paycheck as individuals, if they had to buy the protection that this or any other benefits plan provides from a private insurance company.

The worker's eye is not on costs but on benefits: the dollar amount of the pension, the number of days of free hospitalization in case of accident or illness, the sum of money to be paid survivors if "anything should happen" to the breadwinner. Consequently, union negotiators also approach benefits bargaining with an eye on benefits, the best possible benefits, or at least such as the members will perceive as adequate. It is the manager who worries about costs. The union may, indeed, publicize the costs as part of a package raise, but convinces members to accept the benefits instead of a higher cash raise, in terms of the potential payoff. Adequacy of benefits is one thing that unions and management bargain over. Eligibility is another.

Eligibility.   This has to be established by or for an individual in advance of drawing the benefits and requires careful definition. No one can expect to collect damages for an automobile accident by insuring the car after it has crashed. Defining eligibility for various kinds of benefits opens up many complicated questions.

How many years of service, for example, entitle an employee to a pension? Are periods of layoff to count against this, or be ignored? Is retirement at, say, age 65 to be compulsory or discretionary; and, if the latter, at whose discretion? The worker's or the company's?

Or: How close must the relationship be to entitle a person to medical care under a family health plan? A spouse, of course; but children to what age? And how about dependent parents or other kin? Must they be living under the family roof? May they be in a nursing home?

Each of the four hazard categories poses problems in defining eligibility. It is not hard to see how important the definitions are both to the company and the union. In multiemployer bargaining, eligibility for benefits may be independent of any continuing relationship with a single company. Employers naturally want assurance that they are not going to have to support people who, directly or indirectly, have no proper claim on them.

This raises the related, important eligibility issue of whether benefits are *vested*.

Vesting. Vesting means giving the individual a right to the benefit independently of a continuing relationship with the employer. All governmental programs are vested. A worker who leaves one employer and goes to another takes social security rights with him or her. Each successive employer adds to the account credited to the worker's number and makes payroll deductions of the worker's own contributions. The worker who becomes eligible for benefits in accordance with legally established standards draws against the accumulated total.

Some privately financed benefits programs, like the governmental, are vested; most of them are not. Because workers often change jobs and employers in some industries, multiemployer plans to fit them practically have to be vested; single-employer plans do not. A trend toward vesting of private plans seems to be setting in, but has by no means swept all before it. Many companies still find it to their advantage to offer plans, as a matter of policy, that are nonvested.

A company with a nonvested pension plan (for example) pays pensions only to eligible employees who at retirement age are still in its employ. Anyone who quits, is fired, or otherwise becomes separated from the company loses whatever pension rights have been accumulated. If the plan is contributory, departing employees may draw the amount of contributions, often with nominal interest, but lose the company's matching contribution for which they would otherwise have become eligible.

A nonvested plan of this sort acts as a brake on worker mobility, and for that reason may fit in with an employer's objective of reducing turnover. It gives long-service employees an increasingly strong incentive to stay with the company. It builds a stable though perhaps aging work force, if that is what the company wants. If not, a vested plan might be the better policy.

Claims. Benefit claims depend on eligibility standards, but present some problems of their own. Of those not purely administrative, fraud and malingering are among the touchiest. The number of cases is relatively slight, but investigation is embarrassing and control difficult and costly. Partly to avoid the bother of dealing with fraudulent claims, the auto companies tied the administration of their privately financed S.U.B. plans (to be discussed) to the public unemployment compensation agencies. A laid-off worker otherwise might all too easily have gone on drawing a check from the company while working at another job.

Malingering (or feigning injury or illness in order to claim compensation) may arise in connection with industrial accidents where public agencies play a part and help evaluate and control; or disabilities not job connected that are wholly covered by a private plan. As between paying for medical care or granting paid sick leave, most employers would probably prefer to spend their money for medical care. They reason that medical care would be more likely to promote health and fitness in the work force, less likely to reward and hence encourage idleness. In addition, they undoubtedly presume it would be harder for a malingering worker to fool a doctor with fictitious symptoms than to "call in sick" and fool the supervisor. Paid sick leave is more commonly granted to salaried workers.

Funding and Finance

Essentially, benefits bargaining is bargaining over promises. The money to redeem the promises must be available when the specific contingency arises, or the promise might just as well not have been given. If an insurance company, for example, could not or would not pay a policyholder's claim for a wrecked car, one might just as well not have taken out collision insurance. The insurance company meets claims by collecting and investing the premiums paid by its many policyholders in order to compensate the statistically predictable few who are victims of accident. For given levels of compensation, actuarial calculations determine the premiums; but having the money ready to pay out is a matter of funding and financial management.

Taken for granted actuarial soundness (or setting it aside for the moment as irrelevant), there are two basic approaches to financing benefits: (1) *funded* or *trusteed* plans and (2) *nonfunded*, that is, *insured* or *pay-as-you-go* plans.

Funding. Governmental programs are funded; so are many—but by no means all private plans.

Funding means setting aside money in a fund that may not be touched except to pay the promised benefits and administer the program. A prime example is the social security system, which has accumulated vast reserves in the treasury of the United States out of taxes and contributions. This money may be spent only for meeting the obligations of the law to eligible beneficiaries and for administering the system. No other agency of government may draw on these funds, nor may they be diverted to any other purpose. Money needed for carrying out other intentions of government has to be raised from other sources, such as taxation and borrowing, not from the social security fund.

The government could quite conceivably provide social security benefits on a nonfunded basis, in the form of promises to meet claims out of future income. The Nixon administration, in fact, proposed exactly that in 1971. Acting on the recommendations of the 1971 Advisory Council on Social Security, the Secretary of Health, Education, and Welfare asked Congress to replace the current conservative, funded method of financing with a pay-as-you-go plan. Whether the change will be made, and if so, when, cannot at present be foreseen, but the funding method will not be without defenders. To them, the danger is that an administration unsympathetic to social security, or short of funds, might fail to carry out the promises made over the years to contributors and claimants. The personal stake in the existing fund that all now have who hold social security numbers tends toward conservatism. The existence of the fund makes people feel secure; it takes much of the terror and anxiety out of the hazards of an uncertain future.

A privately financed program can also be funded and provide the same kind of assurance, yet many are not and still offer protection. The difference is somewhat analogous to that between making purchases only with money already saved and in the bank, and buying the same thing on the installment plan; or again, between building for one's heirs a personal estate consisting of a portfolio of stocks and securities, and buying life insurance, for the same beneficiaries, out of earnings. The analogy is not complete, but indicative of the different ways of financing benefits. For some purposes, in some situations, management will prefer one approach, the union another; or they may agree on different methods of finance for different programs.

Nonfunded Plans. From the point of view of an enterprise engaged in benefits bargaining, nonfunded plans tend to fall into two categories: insured and pay-as-you-go.

Insured Plans. As the name implies, these plans finance the promised benefits by purchasing insurance from an insurance company.

Pay-as-You-Go Plans. They are like self-insurance. The company promises to make benefit payments out of its earnings and general resources as occasion arises.

Risks are easier to calculate for some categories of hazard than for others, and the financial arrangements for meeting them differ accordingly. Thus, pensions are usually easier to foresee and plan for than unemployment, which may result from economic forces quite beyond the control of the enterprise. Risks differ, too, in the seriousness of possible consequences. Plans for financing any program of contingent benefits have to consider the hazards.

THE FOUR MAIN HAZARDS OF A WORKING LIFE

Anyone who works for a living, no matter in what capacity or degree, spends on the job between a fourth and a third of all the time fate allots humankind. The income that makes the rest of the time livable, and more or less agreeable, comes from the job; so do most of the hazards that can cut it short or threaten it, or make it disagreeable and precarious. These hazards can be classified, as already noted, in four categories, for each of which there is a governmental program and each of which provides scope for collectively bargained contingent benefits.

The exposition that follows takes the four categories in this order: (1) unemployment; (2) illness and accident; (3) death and disability; and (4) old age.

The treatment of each hazard starts with: (*a*) the governmental program. It goes on to present, (*b*) collective bargained supplemental or complementary programs. It then discusses (*c*) special issues, trends, and tendencies.

Following the presentation of the four hazards is a brief discussion of their economic, political, and social impact on present-day society, and some implications for the future.

Unemployment

The unpleasant contingency that wage and salary earners fear the most and can personally do the least about is probably unemployment. No matter how much a worker may dislike the job, it is preferable to not having any job at all. The worker is most likely to lose it when others are losing theirs and when, consequently, jobs are hardest to find and competition the keenest. The older one gets, the slighter one's chances of opening up new opportunities and the more catastrophic the consequences of being without a job. If such fears lurk in the background of a worker's mind today, consider what they must have been before the federal government, in 1938, enacted its program of Unemployment Compensation.

Unemployment Compensation. Unemployment Compensation is a federal-state program providing a degree of income security to unemployed workers. Within a federal framework, each state is free to work out its own eligibility standards, benefit structure, and financing methods. At present about 80 percent of American wage and salary workers are covered by Unemployment Compensation. Several of its characteristics should be noted:

1. Unemployment Compensation is *noncontributory*. This means that U.C. taxes are assessed against the employer. (There is substantial ques-

tion about who ultimately pays for U.C. benefits. Some authorities argue that the employer passes U.C. costs along to the consumer in the form of price increases. Others argue that the employer must absorb this cost. Still others maintain that employees pay the cost because only so much is available for total labor costs. It seems likely that in competitive industries employers can pass on only the average cost of U.C. in price increases. Employers with very irregular employment probably are forced to absorb their extra U.C. costs under experience rating discussed below.)

2. Unemployment compensation is *funded*. Because future needs for unemployment compensation benefits cannot be predicted with a high degree of accuracy, funding of U.C. is not actuarially sound.

3. Most states use *"experience rating"* in assessing U.C. taxes against the individual enterprise. This means that an employer pays a higher tax rate when it has irregular employment than when it has stable employment.

4. The cost of U.C. fluctuates rather sharply between a minimum tax rate as low as zero in a few states to relatively high maximum rates.

5. Benefits vary widely between the states.

Collective Bargaining on Unemployment. No single enterprise can expect to find measures effective against cyclical unemployment; only the government has resources sufficient to cope with that. Even the existing governmental plan would be no more than a buffer if there should again be a large-scale, w100dpread, long-lasting depression of national or international scope. More amenable to control at company levels are periods of temporary unemployment such as result from seasonal fluctuations, model changeover and retooling, or variations in market demand; and to some extent, adjustment to technological change. The hazard remains unpredictable. There is not yet a *unified* national program of unemployment compensation, retraining, and relocation. Although unemployment occurs at the enterprise, absolute control is beyond the enterprise's power. A few managements and unions have nevertheless developed schemes for cushioning the impact of unemployment, and most labor agreements establish seniority rights that give individuals *relative* protection against layoff in terms of their length of service.

Some of the devices that have found their way into labor-management agreements as measures against unemployment are the following: (1) work sharing; (2) seniority; (3) severance pay; (4) retraining, relocation, early retirement, and other combinations; (5) guaranteed annual wage plans; and (6) supplemental unemployment benefits.

Work Sharing. "Sharing the misery" is what some cynics have called the plans that call for shorter work weeks when there is not enough work to keep everyone employed. It was a common device during the depression of the 1930s, and occasionally finds application in high-wage occupations, as when painters or carpenters adopt a "30-hour" rule. This spreads the work and pay over a larger number of union members during temporary slack periods. When unemployment compensation became available, and particularly after the spread of supplemental unemployment benefits, work sharing lost much of its already dubious attraction. No worker could see the point of spreading the work until wages dropped to, or near, the level of unemployment compensation.

Seniority. Like work sharing, seniority can hardly be classed as an unemployment benefit, but is rather a device for giving individuals a measure of security against layoff in terms of their relative position on a seniority list. A person low on the list expects to be laid off in slack times while those with more seniority stay on the job and also to be recalled when business picks up. Over the years one climbs the rungs of the seniority ladder and may reach a point that is safe against all but the most catastrophic reduction in force.

Severance Pay. This is a true contingent benefit for those who are to be permanently separated from employment with a company. Technology, in making jobs obsolete, makes the workers on those jobs redundant if they cannot qualify for new jobs or if the reduction in force made possible by technological advance cuts too deep. A lump-sum payment to the technologically displaced worker is compensation for the permanent loss of a job.

Most severance pay agreements require that an employee have a specified minimum length of service to be eligible. Benefits are graduated upward on the basis of length of service in the company. A fairly common arrangement is one week's pay for each year of service.

Unions prominent in negotiating severance pay plans include the Steelworkers, Autoworkers, Communications Workers, Ladies' Garment Workers, Electrical Workers (IBEW), and lately, the Railway Workers. A number of companies have extended severance pay plans to their nonunion white-collar employees, equally threatened by technological change.

Severance pay plans are seldom funded. This puts an unpredictable and theoretically unlimited liability on the employer, and hence may be presumed to encourage companies to be conservative in planning for technological change that will displace many of their employees. Some severance pay plans have been grafted onto supplemental unemployment benefit plans, which are funded.

Retraining, Relocation, Early Retirement. The railway strikes of 1971 and the years immediately preceeding made most people aware of the work rules that modern technology have rendered obsolete. A day's run for a train crew is no longer, realistically, 100 miles, but nearer 300. The rule that a train must change crews every 8 hours or 100 miles no longer accords with the industry's technology, but the problem remains of what to do about the redundant crews. In another instance, cargo for ships at sea no longer consists of miscellaneous boxes, barrels, and sacks, but arrives on the dock in containers, which are quicker and easier to load, with modern equipment that has taken the place of the old donkey engines, nets, and slings.

In an agreement with the powerful longshoremen's union providing a benefit fund (initially $29 million, built up over five and a half years), the longshore employers of the West Coast obtained freedom to introduce the labor-saving devices. The benefit fund finances guaranteed annual wages and early retirement benefits for a limited number of *registered* longshoremen, excluding a group of workers whose attachment to the industry was still more or less casual.[1]

The railways met the same problem of reducing the numbers employed while providing for those who were to be permanently separated from railway employment by a combination of measures: attrition (or not replacing those who quit, withdraw, die, or retire); displacement allowances (or early retirement) and severance pay; retraining; and preferential hiring.[2]

Guaranteed Annual Wage Plans. A true guaranteed annual wage would provide income for 12 months of the year regardless of how many or how few of the 2080 potential hours an employee might actually work. Salaried white-collar workers have traditionally enjoyed the security and convenience of regular pay throughout the year while manual workers, paid by the hour and only for hours worked, endured unpredictable fluctuations of income. Union demands for a guaranteed annual wage (G.A.W.) are therefore understandable and not surprising. One big industrial union, the United Auto Workers, made a historic breakthrough in October 1967 by getting a guaranteed wage as part of its agreement with the Ford Motor Company. The steel workers have had comparable successes.

Employers should not have found the union demand surprising, but when it was first raised they did consider it unreasonable. They had been treating their white-collar salaried and blue-collar hourly workers differently not just because of custom or on ideological grounds, but because of real constraints rooted in economics and work-place technology. The work done by white-collar workers affects and is affected only indirectly by production work. It can and often must go on whether or not the machines are

---

[1] For a discussion of this agreement, the factors leading up to its negotiation, and its probable long-term effects, see Charles C. Killingsworth, "The Modernization of West Coast Longshore Work Rules," *Industrial and Labor Relations Review*, vol. 15 (April 1962), pp. 295–306.

[2] Developments in the railways over the past decade have followed fairly closely the recommendations of the Presidential Railroad Commission, agreed to by the carriers and labor organization in the fall of 1960. Anyone interested in the general problems of unemployment, and technological unemployment in particular, will find the Commission's report rewarding. See *The Report of the Presidential Railroad Commission* (Washington, D.C.: U.S. Government Printing Office, February 1962), 327 pp. This volume is supplemented by four Appendix Volumes: I, Index-Digest to the Record of the Commission's Hearings; II, Pay Structure Study, Railroad Operating Employees; III, Studies Relating to Railroad Operating Employees; and IV, Studies Related to Collective Bargaining Agreements and Practices Outside the Railroad Industry.

running. It is a kind of overhead, a fixed charge against total costs, in contrast to production-worker wages, a variable cost.

Consider this extreme case: A cannery, operating only three months a year during the harvest season, needs few more clerical employees—if any —during the rush period than during the slack time. Operations in the busy season, on the other hand, call for a large temporary work force which the company could not afford to support during nine months of idleness. At most, it keeps together a small maintenance gang and warehouse crew when the factory is not working.

Other industries have a more stable pattern. At the opposite extreme, a public utility or perhaps an oil refinery might well be able to guarantee its relatively small force of manual workers the kind of regular income over the year that the much larger salaried group enjoys. In fact, that is what often happens even without a written guarantee. The collective bargaining problems connected with demands for the guaranteed annual wage come up between the two extremes.

Employers are finding that production-worker wages can no longer be considered a simple variable cost. In their growth and spread, contingent benefits and pay for time not worked (taken together, the "fringe") have made wages much more an item of fixed cost, or overhead, than in the past. At least for an essential core of the blue-collar work force of many enterprises (as perhaps for that maintenance gang and warehouse crew in the cannery) and for high-seniority employees, guaranteed annual wages are within reach. The union's "G.A.W." demand is no longer as unreasonable as it once seemed.

On their side, unions may have to give up work-rules arrangements they once cherished in order to give management the flexibility it needs in assigning the permanent force to whatever work may be available. Penalties for overtime work may have to be reduced. Younger and newer employees may have to wait for the protection until they have acquired seniority and developed versatility to qualify for the guarantees. There may even have to be, eventually, some changes in the laws with employees presently nonexempt from the maximum hours provisions of the wage and hour law moving into the exempt category. Spread of the programs may be slow, but seems to be on the way. Such programs may require the establishment of funds or reserves, though the more stable industries may operate them on a pay-as-you-go basis.

True G.A.W. plans—those which provide the full 52-week, 40-hour guarantee of work or pay—are still rare. The most famous of the early plans, i.e., Nunn-Bush, Procter and Gamble, and Hormel, contain limitations on eligibility and allow overtime offsets. The Hormel plan, for example, takes advantage of a provision of the wage and hour law permitting enterprises in a seasonal industry, by agreement with a bona fide union, to waive the overtime requirements of the law so long as employees do not work more than 1,040 hours in any six months or (according to the agreement reached) 2,080 hours in a year. Meat packing is a year-round industry with seasonal peaks. Its raw material, farm animals, reaches the market somewhat sporadically, when the farmers decide to sell, and consequently the company's stockyards are sometimes empty and sometimes overcrowded. Live animals lose weight unless watered and fed, and feeding before slaughter raises the cost. The company therefore worked out with its union a plan to pay employees a regular wage whether they were idle or working overtime (up to the legal limit). In return, they got a flexible work force, standing by when the yards were empty, able to work the production lines when the pens were full.

Though not a "true" plan, the Hormel program showed what unions and management can do to adapt the G.A.W. principle to a particular industry or enterprise. The Teamsters Union, fairly early in the game, negotiated some true G.A.W. plans. What may perhaps be expected is that industries which adopted plans for supplementary unemployment benefits (S.U.B.) will tend as time goes on to transform their S.U.B. programs into G.A.W. plans. The auto industry and union have, in fact, taken the lead in this as they did in S.U.B. A brief summary of the UAW-General Motors plan follows.

The General Motors Plan. The 1970 General Motors agreement with the United Auto Workers does not guarantee hourly paid workers the equivalent of a regular salary (as would a true guaranteed annual wage plan) but is a step in that direction, and greatly increases a worker's protection against fluctuations in employment and income. It amends the S.U.B. plan already in effect.

The S.U.B. plan eased the hardships of unemployment for laid-off workers; the amendment supplements the income of workers not laid off, but working short time.

Hourly paid employees under the new plan accumulate Guaranteed Annual Income credits (just as they build up S.U.B. credits) to be applied against short work weeks. Thus an eligible worker not laid off, but called in for less than 40 hours of work in any one week, automatically get a supplement of 80 percent of base pay for the hours *not* worked, just as if they had been worked. One can, of course, exhaust one's credits if there are too many short work weeks; thus it is not a true guaranteed annual wage; but management has a strong cost-saving incentive to smooth out production schedules so that not many short work weeks occur. As a result, the hourly paid worker can look forward to a more stable level of income. Practically speaking, the skilled workers and high-seniority semiskilled workers get a guaranteed annual wage.

The plan is funded, and nonvested.

Supplemental Unemployment Benefits. In 1955–56 the automobile and steel industries negotiated Supplemental Unemployment Benefits, or S.U.B. plans. By 1970 the coverage of various forms of S.U.B. extended to approximately two million workers represented primarily by the United Automobile Workers, the United Steelworkers, the National Maritime Union, the United Rubber Workers, and the International Ladies' Garment Workers' Union. Although these plans proved to be efficient in operation and not prohibitively costly, their coverage seems to have stabilized with little additional growth to be expected. Extension to workers in other firms and industries of the kind of protection offered seems likely to take the more outright G.A.W. form discussed above. It is still desirable to take a look at the S.U.B. arrangement.

S.U.B. plans start from a presumption that unemployment compensation (U.C.) is inadequate to the needs of workers displaced from jobs in high-wage industries. These plans do not aim to make up the difference between "rockin' chair money" and full pay, but up to as much as but generally not more than 75 percent of gross pay for 40 hours of work per week of unemployment. Beneficiaries may in some cases continue to draw S.U.B. pay for as long as 52 weeks even when, under state laws, their U.C. expires after 26 weeks.

An employee eligible for U.C. becomes eligible, in addition, for S.U.B. This tieup of S.U.B. with the governmental program probably explains why no troublesome problems have arisen in administering the plans. The Ford Motor Company, for example, had to add only five extra people to establish its original plan covering 140,000 employees.[3]

The typical S.U.B. plan is funded by employer contributions up to a Maximum Trust Fund Position, established at the start by agreement with the union on the basis of the company's unemployment experience record. Once Maximum position is reached, the employer replenishes the fund as claims are made on it. This follows the experience rating principle of U.C. and is intended to encourage an employer to stabilize employment.

Experience generally with S.U.B. revealed little interference with operations, but some influence on the wage and benefits differential between skilled and nonskilled workers. The worker most likely to become unemployed, and hence to draw from the fund, is the nonskilled, low-seniority worker. The skilled employee rarely becomes eligible for a benefits check. Besides tending to stabilize current employment, S.U.B. tends to slow down technological advances by making the new installations more costly; that is, the cost of benefits for those displaced must be considered in the calculations. As a rule, however, rapid technological advance occurs in periods of high employment as a response to high demand for a firm's products. Thus in times of high business expectations S.U.B. is not much of a deterrent, and appears to work in harmony with the major determinants of technological progress.

On the union side, S.U.B. brought about a change of attitude toward work sharing, which many industrial unions practiced during the depression

---

[3] W. C. Hampton, "Administering an S.U.B. Plan: The Ford Experience," *Personnel*, vol. 34 (July–August 1957), pp. 76–83.

when they got their start. Unions with S.U.B. agreements prefer a reduction in the work force to a reduction in the scheduled work week.

Accidents and Illness, Health and Welfare

The earliest governmental measures aimed at protecting industrial workers came in the form of Workmen's Compensation, a state-by-state system without federal counterpart. Starting at the turn of the century in Massachusetts, New Jersey, and other northeastern industrial states, the system spread until by mid-century laws were in effect in every state of the union. Even today they are not uniform, but follow a general pattern. They make the employer responsible for accidents occurring at the work place and illness or disease traceable to working conditions, and thus financially liable for the consequences. This substitutes statute law for older common law doctrines under which employers often escaped liability for employee injuries. It gives employers a financial stake in safety on the job.

Most of the state programs are noncontributory, with the employer paying all the costs. Some are funded under state administration, some insured, some pay-as-you-go with the employer self-insured; indeed, some states give a company its choice of financing methods. Eligibility arises out of the accident or disease and claims are heard by a board, on medical evidence, or taken to court. Benefits vary greatly between states (remember that severed thumb, "worth more" in Connecticut than in Oregon) and within a state, particularly if appealed to the courts.

Workmen's Compensation is wholly governmental and does not figure in collective bargaining. Any effort unions or employers make to alter its policies or affect its operations consists of lobbying at the state legislature or representations to boards and commissions.

Workmen's Compensation stops far short of providing comprehensive protection against the hazards that threaten a worker's health and physical fitness, and hence earning ability. It does not compensate for accidents that take place off the job, or illness not directly job-connected, yet either of these could be disabling. It does not extend to members of a worker's family. The only other governmental program dealing with health, Medicare, does not become available to a worker until after age 65. Unions have consequently raised the demand for benefits that give protection during a worker's active earning career, that include family, and that arise from sources not directly job-connected.

Collective Bargaining on Health and Welfare.   Health and welfare bargaining deals with contingencies against which people who earn a regular income could protect themselves by buying insurance from a private company; but doing it as a group is cheaper and in many ways better. Because the risks are spread, a group can get protection against a greater range of hazards, at lower cost, with higher benefits. Persons who might be denied insurance, or have to pay dearly for it if they applied as individuals, can get it on equal terms as members of a group. These are the main considerations reinforcing the union drive for health and welfare programs.

Historically, the early American craft unions got their start as providers of health and welfare benefits. Later, some progressive companies instituted health and welfare plans in the as yet nonunion factories of the prosperous 1920s, though the depression of the 1930s wiped out most of these plans. A few industrial unions—notably the Ladies' Garment Workers—set up comprehensive health and welfare programs for members and their families. More recently, however, unions have pretty much gotten out of the business of *directly* providing health and welfare benefits from union funds because contingent benefits have become available from other sources. Collective bargaining on health and welfare benefits began to open up these sources after World War II, and the movement has yearly gathered impetus. The bureau of Labor Statistics estimated that the number of workers covered by collective bargained health and welfare programs skyrocketed from 0.5 million in 1945 to 7 million in 1950 to 14.5 million—about 78 percent of all workers under collective bargaining agreements—in 1960. The figures are naturally higher today.[4]

Issues in Health and Welfare Bargaining.   The issues that unions and management have to resolve in health and welfare bargaining are much the same as for other contingent benefits; but three issues of principle stand out and a complex of substantive issues making up the problem of what may be called *design.* To be discussed are the following four topics: (1) actuarial soundness; (2) the contributory versus noncontributory principle; (3) level of costs versus level of benefits; and (4) design of the program.

Actuarial Soundness.   It would not be unfair to say that only the most restricted and conservative health and welfare programs can be accurately sound. There are so many possible contingencies, of such unpredictable consequence and duration to so wide a potential population, that no program drawn up in advance can be considered settled, adequate, and reliable. Just how to assure payoff on promises—whether by funding, insurance, or self-insurance on the pay-as-you-go principle—becomes controversial.

The needs for health care are so many and diverse that there is always room for pioneering; and the management even of a company which in its business affairs is innovative and progressive tends to be reluctant to pioneer in the benefits field. Getting health care and protection are an end to the union, but to management they are means to other ends. By their benefits they may advance, but by their costs they burden, progress toward those other management ends. Any initial advantage one company gets by pioneering is soon lost as others find themselves compelled to follow suit, while

---

[4] U.S. Department of Labor, *Analysis of Health and Insurance Plans under Collective Bargaining, Late 1955* (BLS Bulletin no. 1221, 1957), p. iii; and *Health and Insurance, and Pension Plan Coverage in Union Contracts, Late 1960* (BLS Report no. 228), p. 1.

gratitude for the effort from its beneficiaries soon gives way to the attitude best expressed in the query: What have you done for us—lately?

Health and welfare bargaining will probably continue to push out into the areas beyond the safe bounds of actuarial soundness. Programs adopted will not necessarily come to grief, but it would be well to remember what the depression of the 1930s did to many well-intentioned plans.

The Contributory Principle. On the ground that individuals should be self-reliant, and responsible in whole or in part for their own welfare, management tends to insist that the programs be contributory. Unions argue against this. A noncontributory plan makes the total wage package look bigger; in addition, it has tax advantages. The tax collector allows an employer's contribution to go tax-free as a business expense, but considers an employee's contribution part of personal income which is taxed. A noncontributory plan also gives better protection and in itself costs less because it assures full coverage of employees and does not require individual solicitation.

Fixed Costs versus Guaranteed Benefits. Unions generally prefer a cents-per-hour method of paying for a benefits program. This fixed contribution makes savings from experience with the plan available to employees. It widens their choice of possible benefits.

The kinds of benefits available from various sources provide a wide and tempting range of choice; the beneficiaries would like a free hand in shopping for the benefits they want, and, if they find a bargain, to be able to spend the money saved on something else. Management tends to want to guarantee benefits and have a free hand in seeking to get them at the least possible cost. This enables a company to recover the savings from favorable experience. A company policy of restricting its guarantee to benefits also permits it to limit the program to the types of benefits generally available from insurance companies and nonprofit service organizations such as Blue Cross and Blue Shield.

In multiemployer bargaining, management usually has to give in to the union's cents-per-hour or percentage-of-payroll demand in order to provide for employees who move from job to job. The larger the group covered, the lower the cost of providing any medical, hospital, or cash indemnity benefit other than life insurance. As the employer enters a larger group, personal influence diminishes over the amount of benefits to be granted.

Design of the Benefits Program. No two companies, even if they stand side by side on the same street, or operate in the same industry, or deal with the same union, are likely to have identical benefits programs. The variety of benefits available from many sources at different prices matches the variety of situations for which managements and their unions design the programs. The ultimate shape of a given company's program usually has to take account of several or all of the following: (*a*) comprehensiveness, (*b*) form of the benefits, (*c*) coverage, (*d*) freedom of choice, (*e*) integration with community services, and (*f*) special problems.

Comprehensiveness. The scope of protection offered or risks and hazards provided against by the plan is its comprehensiveness. This can range from emergency surgery or long-term hospitalization to routine ambulatory care; the group as a whole is not properly protected except by a comprehensive program. Even so, there may have to be limits, with an expectation of pressure to expand the limits. Can a plan include, for instance, extended psychoanalysis?

Form of the Benefits. This is analogous to payment "in cash or kind." Both management and union probably prefer the form of benefit payment to be in kind: actual, direct medical services, rather than cash. Money paid to beneficiaries is all too easily diverted to uses other than those intended by the plan, leaving the needs the plan was devised for unfulfilled.

Coverage. This has to be defined in terms of numbers and of time: who is to be entitled to the benefits, what family members, what other dependents; and for how long in their lives. A plan might cover the employee's active working life. For an employee's spouse, perhaps a good deal younger than the mate, benefits might have to extend for years beyond the date when the worker would have retired; for children, to age 18, or later; and so on.

Freedom of Choice. Giving the beneficiary more or less wide discretion in selecting a doctor, a hospital, or treatment defines freedom of choice. This issue, in a more generalized form, created the greatest controversy over the government's Medicare program. Unions and management have to face it, too, when they design their programs.

Integration with Community Services. Generally this saves costly duplication, avoids waste and lessens friction, and strengthens the community services as well. It may require the negotiation of contracts for services with community agencies. There may be situations, however, in which integration is not possible or may not be desirable.

Special Problems. All sorts of special problems can, of course, arise, but among the most common are provisions against catastrophe, and the inherently "inflationary" nature of health and welfare plans. One benefit gained tends to call for others to be added; all this with the costs of health care steeply on the rise. As with the argument over what is called the "wage-price spiral," there is no agreement over which is cause and which effect: rising medical costs or rising health and welfare benefits.

The most common form of catastrophe insurance is "major medical." Major medical insurance was designed to help meet medical expenses that in some cases might run as high or higher than an employee's annual earnings. Major medical extends basic coverage such as that provided by Blue Cross or Blue Shield to guarantee, with certain reservations, all medical expenses, whether incurred in outpatient care or in a hospital. The reservations are: (1) deductibility, (2) co-insurance, (3) total maximum benefits, and (4) requiring that medical charges must be "reasonable and necessary."

The *deductible* feature (like deductible auto insurance) means that for any year in which benefits are claimed, the insured must pay the first $50 or

$100. The *co-insurance* feature means that even beyond the deductible amount, the insurance company pays only 75 or 80 percent of the bill, the insured paying the rest. The *total maximum benefits* feature sets an absolute limit—which can, however, be very high: $10,000 or $25,000 or even more —on the insurance company's liability. Finally, *reasonable and necessary* medical expenses could be matter for argument, but are usually interpreted broadly as those prescribed by competent physicians in the area where the service is rendered.

Reducing the cost of benefits has become a special problem rather than a purely administrative one because it is a chronic problem in the face of rising medical costs. Management and unions share a common concern in this, and have almost identical interests. One public-minded corporation and the union with which it dealt established and jointly administer a foundation dedicated to research and planning in the field. The corporation is U.S. Industries, Inc., which designs and manufactures automation equipment and systems. The union is the International Association of Machinists. They agreed that savings in labor costs from the corporation's own automation measures should be turned over to a Foundation on Employee Health, Medical Care and Welfare, Inc. This foundation has published the result of studies in benefits and costs, which are available to unions and management engaged in health and welfare bargaining and administration of the collectively bargained plans.

To go into the details of the many arrangements that have been tried, altered, improved, found wanting, reorganized, expanded, stabilized, or cut down again—but almost never abandoned—would open up, as the saying goes, a long subject. Those who have a particular interest in the field, or who face bargaining on specific issues, would be best advised to consult the books and authorities that devote full attention to it. References to sources of detail information may be found in the bibliography.

Death and Disability

This category of hazard follows in close relationship with the preceding one, but the emphasis here falls on *loss of earnings* because of disability or untimely death rather than medical treatment, either as prevention or cure.

In the cosmic scheme of things, death may never be "untimely," but when it comes during a person's active working career it is untimely to dependents and survivors. The federal government's social security program dealing with death and disability also provides old age pensions. A person who lives long enough to draw a pension has escaped the hazards of incapacitating disability and untimely death. This discussion leaves the pensions to be examined later and confines its attention to the provisions for the contingency of having one's life or active working career cut short of normal expectations.

Social Security. The governmental program for survivors and disability insurance is part of the contributory, funded, federal system called by the catch-all title, social security. As part of a total program it provides regular monthly income to eligible workers who become disabled, to widows and dependent children, and may also provide a lump-sum cash payment after a worker's death.

The Social Security Administration, under the Department of Health, Education, and Welfare gives out public information so complete and up-to-date that it would be presumptuous to try to present any of the details here. Standards of eligibility, claims, benefits, policies and procedures are all set by statute or administrative law. In addition to the official documents, the Social Security Administration issues brief, clearly written pamphlets explaining the law and its workings. By reference to one of these, for instance, it is possible for anyone who has a social security number to calculate the benefits he or she is or will be entitled to.

Collective Bargaining on Death and Disability Benefits. Unions and management frequently negotiate supplements to social security death and disability benefits. Such benefits are often linked—as social security is linked —with pensions, since there is an *either-or* character about the twin hazards of untimely death or disability and old age.

A common answer to the either-or dilemma is to combine life insurance (including provisions on dismemberment and disability) with a retirement annuity. The life insurance component starts out at a high figure early in a person's working career, decreasing as the years go by. The annuity component to provide a retirement income starts out low, but increases as the life-and-disability part of the protection diminishes. This corresponds with the needs of the breadwinner and family. When a couple is young with growing children, loss of earned income is the catastrophe to be feared. As children leave home and become independent, what the parents have to fear is loss of income in old age.

Some plans provide for a cash payment to a widow or dependents in case of a worker's death. The arrangements worked out in this area can take many forms. There seem to be no special problems worthy of note in bargaining collectively for death and disability contingent benefits.

Pensions

A folk song of the labor movement in the depression years expresses the predicament of the industrial worker before the days of social security:

> Too old to work, too old to work,
> Too old to work, and too young to die.
> Who will take care of me, how'll I get by?
> When I'm too old to work and too young to die.

The songwriter seems actually to have had in mind the situation of the Detroit auto worker who, according to a cliché of the times was "on the scrap heap at 40." Only a young worker at a vigorous prime could keep up with the implacable, constantly increasing pace of the mechanized conveyor lines. The moment physical efforts began to flag, one was out of a job and not rehired.

Unionization of the automobile industry gave workers some control over the speed of the conveyor, and seniority rights kept them on the job into and through middle age, but only postponed the day of separation. By general agreement a person aged 60 or 65 is getting too old to work, yet with increasing life expectancy, too young to die. To such a person, the question is still pertinent: How'll I get by?

Traditionally, business enterprises granted pensions to executives and to long-service white-collar workers. Some firms—a very few—voluntarily included hourly paid manual workers in their pension plans. Civil service systems, whether federal or state or local, gave pension rights to public employees. Only the hourly paid blue-collar workers in industry, for the most part, lacked comparable protection.

They did not get it until 1938, when the social security system of the federal government came into being. Social security initially provided retirement income after age 65, though later amendments reduced this to age 62 in certain cases. Collective bargaining on pensions followed the lead given by social security. Today, collectively bargained pensions may be said to have in many ways outstripped the model.

Retirement, Survivors, and Disability Insurance. This is a federal program providing cash benefits to retired persons (as well as to totally and permanently disabled persons) who have worked in "covered" employment for certain periods of time. Ever since 1955, RSDI has covered more than 90 percent of all American citizens who were gainfully employed.

Past earnings and marital status determine RSDI benefits. To be eligible, no one needs to work more than 10 years (or 40 quarters) in covered employment, although some who are presently close to retirement age may qualify as "fully insured" in a shorter length of time. Examples of monthly cash benefits now in effect appear in Table 11–1.

In the light of figures shown in Table 11–1 both for average annual earnings and for monthly benefits, it may be interesting to look back and remember that in the early years of the program unions commonly negotiated pensions for long-service employees that would *make up the difference* between social security and a *total retirement income* of as little as $100 a month. Figures are higher today. The use of the government pension as a *complementary* element of a private pension plan has virtually ceased, but it remains the base for pension bargaining to *supplement* social security.

With this in mind, certain characteristics of RSDI as compared with privately financed pension plans need to be noted:

1. RSDI benefits are *vested*. Private plans need not be.
2. RSDI benefit levels reflect a person's *average earnings* rather than dura-

TABLE 11-1
Examples of Monthly Social Security Payments (effective June 1974)

Benefits can be paid to	$923 or less	Average yearly earnings since 1950								
		$3,000	$3,500	$4,000	$5,000	$6,000	$7,000	$8,000	$9,000	$10,000
You, the worker										
Retired at 65	93.80	194.10	210.40	228.50	264.90	299.40	335.50	372.20	393.50	412.40
Under 65 and disabled	93.80	194.10	210.40	228.50	264.90	299.40	335.50	372.20	393.50	412.40
Retired at 62	75.10	155.30	168.40	182.80	212.00	239.60	268.40	297.80	314.80	330.00
Your wife										
At 65	46.90	97.10	105.20	114.30	132.50	149.70	167.80	186.10	196.80	206.20
At 62, with no child	35.20	72.90	78.90	85.80	99.40	112.30	125.90	139.60	147.60	154.70
Under 65 and one child in her care	47.00	102.70	130.90	162.00	224.00	249.90	262.40	279.20	295.20	309.40
Your widow										
At 65 (if worker never received reduced retirement benefits)	93.80	194.10	210.40	228.50	264.90	299.40	335.50	372.20	393.50	412.40
At 60 (if sole survivor)	74.90	138.80	150.50	163.40	189.50	214.10	239.90	266.20	281.40	294.90
At 50 and disabled (if sole survivor)	56.80	97.10	105.30	114.30	132.60	149.80	167.80	186.20	196.80	206.30
Widowed mother and one child in her care	140.80	291.20	315.60	342.80	397.40	449.20	503.40	558.40	590.40	618.60
Maximum family payment	140.80	296.80	341.30	390.50	488.90	549.30	597.90	651.40	688.70	721.80

A word of explanation. Some people think that if they've always earned the maximum amount covered by social security they'll get the highest benefit shown on the chart. This isn't so. Although retirement benefits as high as $412.40 a month are shown, payment this high can't be paid to a worker retiring at 65 now. The maximum retirement benefit for a man who becomes 65 in June 1974 is $304.90 a month, based on average covered yearly earnings of $6,132.

Source: U.S. Dept. of Health, Education & Welfare, *Your Social Security.* (Washington, D.C.: Social Security Administration, February 1974), pp. 16-17.

tion of continuous employment or seniority. Private plans often make the number of years of continuous service, as well as average earnings during all or some portion of that period, a factor in the formula that determines level of benefits.

3. *Marital status* affects RSDI benefits; private plans usually ignore this.
4. RSDI is *contributory*. So are some private plans, but many are not.
5. RSDI is *funded*. So are many private plans, but some are not.

Collective Bargaining on Pensions. As brought out earlier in this chapter, pension plans are promises made today against the future. Pensions became a prominent element in the pay package in collective bargaining during World War II. Not long after the war's end, when the promises began to come due, both management and the unions, started to take a good look at the subject of pensions. In 1950 the executive council of the American Federation of Labor (not yet merged in the AFL–CIO) set up a special committee to study pension trends, while management organizations and consultant firms analyzed existing plans and made recommendations for the future.

The AFL committee took a rather cautious approach, saying:

> Whether or not a pension plan is actually a good idea, and the type of plan that ought to be set up, are questions with no single answer that would apply to all groups alike.[5]

The committee went on to caution against haste, but it would appear that unions—particularly industrial unions, including industrial locals of AFL unions—must have ignored the cautionary advice; for in the same year a management consultant organization had this to say: "To put it rather extremely, very little credit is now given for instituting a pension plan, but vigorous criticism may result from not having such a plan."[6]

Today there can be no question that pensions are more than a trend: They are a firmly fixed part of collective bargaining.

Issues in Pension Bargaining. Management and the unions face the same issues of principle and policy as on other contingent benefits when they bargain collectively on pensions, but standards for determining the substantive arrangements are more readily available. Thus in deciding on the adequacy of a pension, the bargainers do not have to appeal to abstract principle or seek new absolutes, they have concrete reference points: the pensioner's before-retirement earnings as a ceiling, and social security as a floor. The benefit level will fall somewhere between these points. Experience with pension plans exceeds that with any other type of benefit, and in addition, the contingency itself is more predictable.

---

[5] Lane Kirkland, *Pension Plans under Collective Bargaining: A Guide for the Trade Unions*, rev. ed. (Washington, D.C.: American Federation of Labor, December 1954), p. v.

[6] Walter James Couper and Roger Vaughan, *Pension Planning: Experience and Trends* (New York: Industrial Relations Counselors, Inc., 1954), p. 172.

It would be well, however, to glance briefly at certain issues of pension bargaining as they present themselves under the following headings: (*a*) adequacy, or level of benefits; (*b*) eligibility (vesting; and compulsory versus discretionary retirement); (*c*) finances and funding.

Adequate Benefits. A pension always represents a lower income than the recipient earned on the job: To be "on half pay" is almost the accepted figure of speech for retirement. A worker accustomed to living at or near the limit of full income has to adjust to a lower standard of living after retirement, even though there will also be some reductions in the cost of living and reduced personal and family obligations. How much less than full pay will suffice? How little would not be enough, even in retirement, to maintain a "modest and decent" living?

One standard that unions use as a base for bargaining is the elderly couple budget of the Bureau of Labor Statistics. Beyond this, they ask allowances for such things as improved housing, locally higher variations in the Consumer Price Index, and items not included in the BLS budget such as car maintenance, essential to an "American" standard of living. Management tends to take a more cost-conscious view. "About all that can be said," remark Couper and Vaughan, quoted above, "is that benefits must be large enough to enable a company to retire its superannuated employees without any adverse reaction from other employees or the community."[7]

Pensions are notoriously fixed income, which inflation hits hardest. Keeping retirement income in step with rising costs of living is a chronic problem.

Eligibility. Unions assert that pensions are deferred compensation and not (as management spokesmen sometimes imply) a favor from the employer given out of kindness of heart. If the union premise is accepted, the union conclusion logically follows: Pension rights "belong" to the individual and hence should be vested. The contrary premise does not logically preclude vesting, but allows nonvested pensions.

A nonvested pension tends to tie workers to a company by depriving them of benefits if for any reason they leave its employ before reaching retirement age. An employee with vested rights in a pension may or may not want to change employers, but if one does, suffers no penalty. Vesting, however, makes pension plans more expensive, often much more expensive. An employer who declines to agree to a vested plan is not necessarily hardhearted, only cost-conscious; and may have other quite legitimate ends in view. Nonvested pensions tend to cut down turnover of employees and build a stable work force. A trend, nonetheless, seems to be setting in toward vesting of privately financed pensions.

Nonvested plans do tend, indeed, to stabilize a company's work force, but (as they spread through the economy) tend also to decrease labor mobility and reduce job opportunities for younger workers and minority-group workers entering, or seeking to enter, the labor market. In a time of

---

[7] Ibid., p. 53.

rapid technological change, too close an attachment of workers to their enterprises tends to slow down progress and could result in painful dislocations. The rigidity of nonvested plans thus begins to run counter to the public interest. As a consequence, the weight of public policy may come down eventually on the union side in favor of vesting.

In certain industries, moreover, private plans cannot help but be vested. The worker employed in building construction, clothing manufacture, or the maritime occupations rarely works long for any one employer. If such workers are to get their retirement income through collective bargaining, the employers must either offer separate vested plans at prohibitively high cost or join together in multiemployer plans.

Multiemployer Plans. These are either fully integrated programs providing equal benefits and equal employer costs, or special arrangements providing some financial pooling but allowing variations between employers in costs or benefits.

Fully Integrated. Fully integrated plans flow naturally from the logic of multiemployer bargaining. They commit employers to identical pension costs (as they are already committed to identical wage rates). This takes pension bargaining out of competition. Fully integrated plans pool the risks of employing older with younger workers, and so reduce age discrimination; and they pool investment resources and opportunities.

Special Arrangements. These sometimes meet the needs of a number of small companies engaged in single-employer bargaining. As a function of their small size, such companies face higher costs in providing benefits. They find it to their advantage to pool certain risks and to pool funds for investment, without necessarily making either costs or benefits uniform. Here, where employees do not move from job to job, there is no need for vesting, though nothing inherently prevents it.

Multiemployer plans do not attract large firms that bargain with industrial unions, for here they increase rather than reduce the risks. Age and sex distribution of the separate work forces almost inevitably results in the probability that some firms will subsidize the benefits of others. A multiemployer plan of this type would also lessen each firm's control over investment policy and eligibility standards, and weaken the presumed, though nebulous element of employee loyalty to the firm which provides the pension.

Compulsory Retirement. Another issue of eligibility is: Should a person still able and willing to do productive work have to retire? On the other hand, should someone younger, with lesser resources, greater obligations, and smaller benefits entitlement have to stand and wait while another who could draw retirement income continues to hold a job at full pay? There is much to be said on both sides, and the age of the person saying it seems to determine which side is argued.

Two demographic facts of the 70s bring opposite pressures to bear on this issue: (1) life expectancy continues to increase and the number of old people in the population continues to rise; and (2) young people, including minority-group youths hitherto all but excluded from employment opportunity, are pressing for jobs in growing numbers, and with growing militancy. Older workers tend to dread the day when they will be "on the shelf," and even when eligible for a pension prefer to go on working. Every older worker eligible to retire who keeps a job by seniority deprives a younger worker of the opportunity to displace her or him. As a pensioner, on the other hand, this same older worker becomes a drain on the resources available to active participants in the labor force. There seems to be neither a clear-cut and consistent union or management position on this issue. The age of the work force currently active in the enterprise probably gives the bargainers their cue.

Finances and Funding. The actual out-of-pocket costs of operating a pension plan will in the long run be determined by:

1.   The amount of money paid to each retiring worker per month or other benefit period.
2.   The number of workers qualifying for benefits.
3.   How long retirees live to receive benefits.
4.   The rate of return on investment of money held in the pension fund (whether held by a trustee or an insurance company).
5.   The expenses incurred in administering the pension system.

The employer with an older work force will incur higher costs than if the work force were younger; so may the company with a higher percentage of women than of men, because women tend to live longer and so on. Vested pensions cost more than unvested pensions. A benefits formula based on fixed maximum earnings or years of service costs less than a formula allowing unlimited accrual of rights. These few examples illustrate the problem of computing the reserve needed to provide pensions for any specific work force. Making the computation is work for an actuary. The actuary works from data on the number of employees, their age and sex distribution, their seniority, average earnings, rate of turnover, level of benefits to be provided, and a decision on what vesting, if any, is to be provided. Discounting probable employee separations before acquiring eligibility, the actuary estimates the total fund required to pay projected benefits to present employees when they become eligible.

The entire fund need not be established at the time the initial agreement is made; it may take 20 years to accumulate. As money accumulates in the fund, it is invested and begins to earn interest, which is also part of the calculation. The actuary tells the parties what they will have to pay in costs and contributions for different levels of benefits for the work force being considered.

Methods of Financing. The two most common methods of financing pensions are: (1) insured plans, which arrange to purchase benefits from an insurance company, and (2) trusteed plans which employ a bank or trust company to invest the funds and administer them for the union and management under the collective bargaining agreement. Both types of plan subdivided into limitless variations. Each has its peculiar advantages and disadvantages.

As an illustration of how they work, a brief discussion follows on two insured plans (group annuity and deposit administration) and a self-administered trusteed plan.

The *group annuity contract* is the oldest form of insured pension plan. Every year the employer buys an increment of annuity, or retirement income, for each employee covered by the plan; which the insurance company guarantees. A contract can be written for a firm of any size, with no minimum premium requirement; thus the plan eminently suits the employer of fewer than 50 persons, and is easily vested. The insurance company guarantees the benefits, but not the premium rate, which may be adjusted upward or downward after five years of experience under the plan.

The *deposit administration contract* offers flexible funding. The employer contributes yearly, but nothing is set aside for an individual employee until actual retirement. The pension purchased at that time is guaranteed as in a group annuity contract. The advantages are: (1) more flexible funding than in trusteed plans; (2) guaranteed benefits for retired employees; (3) competent handling of investments by the insurance company's experts; (4) guaranteed integrity of the principal, plus fixed earnings; and (5) small companies can write their own benefit plans. The disadvantages are: (1) low earnings on investment reflect conservative practices of insurance companies; (2) insurance company retentions are usually higher than a trustee's management fees; and (3) higher original costs and lower original benefits than in most trusteed plans.

The *self-administered trusteed plan* deposits money with an outside agency other than an insurance company, usually a bank or trust company, which becomes the trustee. The trustee does *not* guarantee the benefits prescribed in the collective bargaining agreement, but assumes legal liability against fraud or gross negligence. The advantages of this plan are: (1) possible higher income from investment because the law does not limit a trustee, as it does insurance companies, on the extent that they can invest in corporation stocks; (2) some flexibility in funding; slower for past service credits which have been earned by older employees brought into the plan, heavier funding in good profit years, with resultant tax savings; (3) lower *initial* costs; (4) greater responsiveness to changes in benefits and eligibility bargaining; and (5) possible avoidance of certain administrative costs included in an insurance company's premiums. The disadvantages are: (1) possible loss from bad investments; (2) unsuitability for small groups of employees because of higher actuarial risk; and (3) possible inadequate funding because of overoptimistic assumptions about mortality, earnings, expenses, and employee turnover.

To sum up on finances and funding: The great diversity in plans and variety in financing methods calls for the services of a full-time expert to advise the negotiators. Probably the best way for the company and union to make financing decisions is to hire a pension consultant and to get competitive bids from several insurance and trust companies. With the consultant's advice, the principals then consider the bids and decide on the basis of long-term cost, quality of services rendered, and the flexibility offered by the various alternatives.

SOCIAL IMPLICATIONS OF CONTINGENT BENEFITS

The impact of today's pension bargaining will be felt 20 to 40 years from now. In a period as long as 20 or more years, both technological change and business mortality can bring about upheavals and dislocations of employment relationships. Only full vesting, a costly policy, truly protects earned pension rights. Small employers in stable or expanding industries can provide partial protection from the risk of business failures by multiemployer plans. No matter what precautions today's bargainers take, however, only control of inflation would give people on fixed incomes real protection. Collective bargaining cannot control inflation; indeed, some hold it to be a factor in inflation. Some workers covered by pension plans today will not retire before the year 2000. If present trends continue, companies and unions will liberalize their pension plans from time to time—but usually for those who are to retire in the future, not those already in retirement. Management usually resists union attempts to negotiate for retired workers, and lengthening life expectancy rates will probably increase this resistance. Yet the absolute and relative number of pensioners continues to grow. The funds to pay the pensions keep accumulating.

With assets running into billions of dollars, pension funds exert weight in the capital market. Unions increasingly insist on participating in the investment decisions. Future government regulation of pension funds may well extend beyond ethical trusteeship to investment policy and question the propriety of certain types of investment.

Medicare has already influenced collectively bargained health and welfare plans, and since many unresolved issues still surround Medicare, will have further impact. The influence can also work the other way: toward a more comprehensive governmental program of medical care, perhaps on a group-practice basis.

The guaranteed annual wage and supplemental unemployment benefits have also made their mark on economic and social life. They involve people who remain attached to the labor force; thus, unlike pensions and disability benefits, they affect personnel utilization and the labor force. Unemployment remains the greatest hazard. It seems to strike when least expected, and affects the largest number of people who work for a living. Because of its scale, complexity, and unpredictability, employers and workers find it hard to cope with. Only the government has power to minimize its severity, but there is still no general agreement on what government should do about it.

Collective bargaining for contingent benefits points out the problems and finds partial solutions. For employed workers it is better—much better—than what they had before, but for society it does no more, at present, than provide experience in dealing with the problems, and perhaps some guidelines for the future.

SUMMARY

Daily and hourly the American economic system creates an abundance of goods and services in which not all Americans share, but which puts within the reach of workers employed in the industry, beyond the wage or salary, a means of gaining through collective bargaining a measure of personal security hitherto unknown. The employed worker no longer has to rely solely on personal and family resources for protection against contingencies arising out of the four main hazards of a working life: unemployment, accident and illness, disability and untimely death, or old age.

Governmental programs put a floor under benefits gained through collective bargaining in each of the categories of hazard: Unemployment Compensation, Workmen's Compensation, and Retirement, Survivors, and Disability Insurance.

Management and the unions hold sometimes conflicting, sometimes identical views on the principles behind contingent benefits, and come to accommodation jointly on costs and the level and scope of worker insurance and income-continuity benefits. Public policy accepts this as a legitimate, and indeed, commendable subject for collective bargaining.

The programs adopted so far have had varying impact on economic and social life and on the life styles of those who participate in them. They do not solve all social ills, but may point the way to more fundamental solutions.

QUESTIONS FOR DISCUSSION

1. The text argues that unions and managements have developed certain principles in bargaining over worker insurance and income-continuity programs. Would you agree that principles exist in this field?
2. Are collectively bargained worker insurance and income-continuity programs compatible with a system of social security?
3. Is it socially desirable to permit the development of worker insurance and income-continuity programs which tie worker to employer, or vice versa? Are the ties different in different worker insurance and income-continuity programs?
4. How do you plan to provide for your needs in old age? What will those needs be? What contribution (if any) do you expect your employer to make toward fulfilling those needs?

5. What are the unique advantages and disadvantages of multiemployer pension plans? Multiemployer health insurance plans?

6. Some authorities have advocated governmental reinsurance of private pensions, i.e., freedom to purchase any amount of benefits desired from the social security system. How do you feel about this idea?

SELECTED ANNOTATED BIBLIOGRAPHY

This bibliography consists of four parts: (1) General, (2) Pensions, (3) Health and Welfare, and (4) Unemployment Benefits.

General

BELCHER, DAVID W. *Compensation Administration*. Englewood Cliffs, N.J.: Prentice-Hall, 1974.
    See chapters 14 and 15 for an examination of different kinds of fringe benefits and how they fit into a total compensation package.

BOOTH, PHILIP with FAURI, FEDELE. *Social Security in America*. Ann Arbor: University of Michigan and Wayne State University, Institute of Labor and Industrial Relations, 1973.
    The authors analyze the development and content of such social insurance programs as unemployment insurance, disability insurance, and workmen's compensation.

BRITTAIN, JOHN A. *The Payroll Tax for Social Security*. Washington, D.C.: Brookings Institution, 1972.
    The author examines the economic effects of the payroll tax as the mechanism to finance our Social Security (OASDHI) system and stresses the inequity of using such a tax.

BURNS, EVELINE M. *Social Security and Public Policy*. New York: McGraw-Hill Book Co., Inc., 1956.
    A penetrating analysis of the major policy questions involved in providing economic security through the instrumentality of government.

BUTLER, ARTHUR. "The Relationship between Public and Private Economic Security Plans," *Proceedings of the Tenth Annual Meeting of the Industrial Relations Research Association*, pp. 139–45. Madison, Wis.: The Association, 1958.
    Discusses possible incompatibility of privately established economic security plans with governmental programs and economic welfare of the society.

GREENE, RICHARD. "Unions Report Slow Rise in Health, Insurance, and Pension Coverage," *Monthly Labor Review*, vol. 98, no. 1 (January 1975).
    A brief look at the growth of collectively bargained health and retirement plans during the postwar era.

LIVERNASH, E. ROBERT. "Wages and Benefits." In *A Review of Industrial Relations Research*, vol. 1. Madison: Industrial Relations Research Association, 1970.
    A review of much of research on wages and benefits which was published in the 1960s.

MABRY, BEVARS. "The Economics of Fringe Benefits," *Industrial Relations*, vol. 12, no. 1 (February 1973).

The author presents a "theory of fringe benefits" which shows that fringes have become more popular because they satisfy employer, employee, and union preferences.

McCAFFERY, ROBERT M. *Managing the Employee Benefits Program.* New York: American Management Association, 1972.

A "how-to" book aimed at practitioners to assist them in administering a wide variety of employee benefit plans.

MILLER, GLENN W. "Appraisal of Collectively Bargained and Governmental Programs for Employee Security." In HAROLD W. DAVEY, HOWARD S. KALTENBORN, and STANLEY H. RUTTENBERG. *New Dimensions in Collective Bargaining.* New York: Harper & Bros., 1959, pp. 117–33.

Analyzes the relationship between public and private employee security programs. Concludes that from the viewpoint of the society as a whole, public programs are preferable to private programs.

MYERS, ROBERT J. "Experience of the UMWA Welfare and Retirement Fund," and "Further Experience of the UMWA Welfare and Retirement Fund," *Industrial and Labor Relations Review*, vol. 10 (October 1956), pp. 93–100, vol. 14 (July 1961), pp. 556–62.

Analyzes the experience of Mine Workers program over time. Plan worthy of special consideration because of financing methods, multiemployer form, and pioneering work in medical treatment of most severe occupational injuries.

RIMLINGER, GASTON V. *Welfare Policy and Industrialization in Europe, America, and Russia.* New York: John Wiley & Sons, 1971.

The author examines the development and content of various social security programs (retirement, unemployment insurance, etc.) in five countries, an examination which offers some interesting comparisons with the U.S. experience.

SLICHTER, SUMNER H.; HEALY, JAMES J.; and LIVERNASH, E. ROBERT. *The Impact of Collective Bargaining on Management.* Washington, D.C.: Brookings Institution, 1960.

Special attention is invited to the following chapters: 13, "Pension Plans"; 14, "Health and Welfare Plans"; 15, "Employee Benefits"; and 16, "Income Security and Severance Pay Plans."

Pensions

ACKERMAN, LAURENCE J. "Financing Pension Benefits," *Harvard Business Review*, vol. 34 (September–October 1956), pp. 63–74.

Outlines the main cost factors involved in pensions and compares the various possibilities under both insured and trusteed funds.

BARTLETT, H. ROBERT, JR. "Patterns of Pensions Funds Investment," *Eighteenth Annual Proceedings of the Industrial Relations Research Association*, pp. 302–11.

Compares fund investment practice of corporate and multiemployer pension funds.

CLAGUE, EWAN; PALLI, BALRAJ; and KRAMER, LEO. *The Aging Worker and the Union.* New York: Praeger Publishers, 1971.

A selective account of what some unions are providing their older and retired members in the form of pensions and social services.

CORSON, JOHN J., and McCONNELL, JOHN W. *Economic Needs of Older People.* New York: Twentieth Century Fund, 1956.

This book deals with the need of older persons for continuing income. Earnings from employment, social insurance and public assistance, private pension plans, and other sources of income are carefully considered. The adequacy of the various income sources to the economic needs of older people and their impact on the national economy are appraised and assessed.

DAVIS, HARRY E. "Multiemployer Pension Plan Provisions in 1973," *Monthly Labor Review,* vol. 97, no. 10 (October 1974).

An examination of the growth and key provisions of multiemployer pension plans.

HARBRECHT, PAUL P. *Pension Funds and Economic Power.* New York: Twentieth Century Fund, 1959.

Pensions are charged with being vast aggregations of wealth upon which many have claims but of which none can call oneself owner. To remove ambiguity of ownership and to restore line of responsibility, it is proposed that pension funds be treated as deferred wages. This would establish certain rights for the worker and would return some of the economic independence the pension system has taken away.

HENLE, PETER, and SCHMIDT, RAYMOND. "Pension Reform: The Long, Hard Road to Enactment," *Monthly Labor Review,* vol. 97, no. 11 (November 1974).

The authors analyze the landmark 1974 pension reform act, including a brief legislative history and some of the implications of the law for employees and employers.

KIRKLAND, LANE. *Pension Plans under Collective Bargaining: A Reference Guide for Trade Unions.* Rev. ed. Washington, D.C.: American Federation of Labor, December, 1954.

The basic union source book on collective bargaining on pensions.

LESSER, LEONARD. "Tax Aspects of Collectively Bargained Pension Plans." In *New York University Seventh Annual Conference on Labor,* EMMANUEL STEIN, ed. pp. 617–26. Albany, N.Y.: Matthew Bender & Co., Inc., 1954.

A legal consultant of the UAW Social Security Department discusses tax aspects of different pension contribution bases, termination of pension plans, and pooled pension plans.

MACKIN, JOHN P. *Protecting Purchasing Power in Retirement: A Study of Public Employee Retirement Systems.* New York: Fleet Academic Editions, 1971.

The author examines the mechanisms used by numerous public employee retirement plans to maintain the real value of retirement benefits during inflationary periods.

MURRAY, ROGER F. "Management Interests in the Investment of Pension Funds," *Eighteenth Annual Proceedings of the Industrial Relations Research Association,* pp. 312–16.

Defines the primary objective of management in the investment of pension funds as that selection of investment opportunities which will maximize future returns and minimize the costs of retirement benefits within the range of acceptable risks.

STEIN, EMMANUEL, ed. *New York University Tenth Annual Conference on Labor*. Albany, N.Y.: Matthew Bender & Co., Inc., 1957.

Most of the volume devoted to pension plans. Partial contents.

HOLLAND, DANIEL M. "The Pension Climate."

COLLINS, ROBERT D. "Economics of Pension Planning."

TILOVE, ROBERT. "The Organization of a Pension Plan."

MEUCHE, A. J. "Past Service Benefits."

MELNIKOFF, MEYER. "Actuarial Bases: The Interest Rate."

WHITE, WILLIAM K. "Actuarial Bases: Mortality Tables."

WILLIS, E. S. "Administration of Single Employer Pension Plans."

VLADECK, STEPHEN C. "Public Regulations of Pension Plans."

SHELDON, HORACE E. "Regulation of Pension Plans."

SERGENT, DWIGHT S. "Planning for Retirement."

HINES, JOHN M. "Split-Funding and Insurance Company Plans."

KEARSHES, ANTHONY J. "Method of Funding in Pension Planning: The Trustee Plan."

GOLDSTEIN, MEYER M. "Inflation and Deflation in Pension Planning."

OLMSTEAD, R. G. "The Variable Annuity."

BERNSTEIN, PETER L. "The Financial Aspects of Pension Funds; Problems of Investments."

HOWELL, PAUL L. "Investment Management of Union Pension Funds; Problems of Administration and Sources of Assistance."

O'BRIAN, JAMES J. "Investment Management of Pension Plans: Selection of Investment."

FARNUM, C. WADSWORTH. "Pension Fund Investment Media: Bond Investments."

BUEK, CHARLES W. "The Investment Media: Equity Investments."

JOHNSON, RALPH B. "The Continuing Supervision of Investments."

TILOVE, ROBERT. "Multi-Employer Pension Plans." In *New York University Seventh Annual Conference on Labor*, edited by EMMANUEL STEIN, pp. 639–58. Albany, N.Y.: Matthew Bender & Co., Inc., 1954.

The Director of the Pension Department of Martin E. Segal & Company outlines the forces which make the establishment of a multi-employer pension plan particularly attractive to small employers and unions whose members have only intermittent employment with a single employer.

Health and Welfare Plans

FOUNDATION ON EMPLOYEE HEALTH, MEDICAL CARE AND WELFARE, INC. *Studies* (of Health and Welfare Problems). 477 Madison Avenue, New York 22, New York.

Jointly sponsored by the International Association of Machinists and U.S. Industries, Inc., the Foundation has conducted a number of studies of problems in providing the best medical care benefits at minimum cost. Studies cover financing methods for various plans, types of coverage, e.g., medical, dental, hospitalization, and efficiency of various kinds of carriers. Specific reference to two studies is made in chapter on Health and Welfare. Future studies by the Foundation are in progress.

GARBARINO, JOSEPH W. *Health Plans and Collective Bargaining.* Berkeley, Calif.: University of California Press, 1960.

Study of the provisions of hospital and medical care through collectively bargained health plans, with emphasis upon the attempt by these plans to meet important social problems largely through voluntary, privately administered action.

"Hospital Insurance, Supplemental Medical Insurance, and Old-Age Survivors and Disability Insurance; Financing Basis under the 1965 Amendments," *Social Security Bulletin,* vol. 28 (October 1965), pp. 17–28.

Discusses the three systems, financed separately, made possible by the 1965 amendments to the Social Security Act.

GLASSER, MELVIN A.; LOREN, EUGENE L.; and SOLENBERGER, WILLARD E. *Survivor Benefits of Blue Collar Workers.* Lexington, Mass.: D. C. Heath, 1970.

Three UAW staffers investigate the impact on the family of the death of the primary breadwinner and the means by which the family copes with the loss.

MYERS, ROBERT J. "The Mine Workers Welfare and Retirement Fund: Fifteen Years' Experience," *Industrial and Labor Relations Review,* vol. 20 (January 1967), pp. 265–74.

The article calls attention to difficulties in designing elaborate welfare and retirement programs, especially the pitfalls present in financing such plans on a nonactuarial basis.

NAGI, SAAD V., and HADLEY, LINDA W. "Disability Behavior: Income Change and Motivation to Work," *Industrial and Labor Relations Review,* vol. 25, no. 2 (January 1972).

The authors examination of the work motivations of disabled employees.

SOMERS, HERMAN MILES, and SOMERS, ANNE RAMSAY. *Doctors, Patients and Health Insurance.* Washington, D.C.: Brookings Institution, 1961.

A study of the organization, distribution, and financing of personal medical care. Considers efficiencies of various methods of health insurance and various methods of organizing the distribution of medical care.

Unemployment Benefits

BACKMAN, JULES. "High Cost of Liberalizing SUB Plans," *Harvard Business Review,* vol. 34 (November–December 1956), pp. 69–75.

Outlines a statistical method for estimating the ultimate cost of reducing eligibility standards for S.U.B., lengthening the duration of eligibility, increasing the weekly benefit amounts and other proposed liberalizations of the pioneer S.U.B. plans.

BECKER, JOSEPH M. "Twenty-Five Years of Unemployment Insurance: An Experiment in Competitive Collectivism," *Political Science Quarterly,* vol. 75 (December 1960), pp. 481–99.

A survey and discussion of the U.S. unemployment insurance program as an amalgam of capitalistic and socialistic elements. Discussion concentrates on "two most distinctively competitive aspects of the American program—the existence of separate state systems and the use of that tax technique called experience rating."

————. *Guaranteed Income for the Unemployed: The Story of SUB* Baltimore: Johns Hopkins Press, 1968.

An intensive analysis of experience with SUB since the Ford agreement of 1955.

BEIER, EMERSON H. "Financing Supplemental Unemployment Benefit Plans," *Monthly Labor Review*, vol. 92, no. 11 (November 1969).

An examination of the coverage and financing of negotiated SUB plans as of 1967.

FOX, HARLAND, and WORTHY, N. BEATRICE. *Severance Pay Patterns in Manufacturing.* New York: National Industrial Conference Board Studies in Personnel Policy no. 174, 1959.

Study gives broad general picture of severance pay practices in manufacturing. It also outlines patterns in several important industries.

LESTER, RICHARD A. *The Economics of Unemployment Compensation.* Princeton, N.J.: Princeton University Industrial Relations Section, Research Report no. 101, 1962.

An analysis of state and federal experience during the period 1948–61. Recommendations for improving the system.

PAPIER, WILLIAM. "Standards for Improving Maximum Unemployment Insurance Benefits," *Industrial and Labor Relations Review*, vol. 27, no. 3 (April 1974).

The author presents evidence which shows that unemployment benefits (at least in Ohio) do not provide recipients with a very large portion of their previous earnings.

STIEGLITZ, HAROLD. "Financing the Ford Plan," *Management Record*, vol. 17 (September 1955), pp. 350–53, 372–74.

Certainly the most comprehensive, and probably the most authentic, explanation of the thinking of Ford Motor Company executives on the problems of financing a supplemental unemployment benefit plan. Emphasis is placed on statistical tools adapted by Ford for testing the funding of the company's proposal and safety factors built into the plan.

UNTERBERGER, HERBERT S. *Guaranteed Wage & Supplementary Unemployment Pay Plans.* Chicago: Commerce Clearing House, Inc., 1956.

An excellent handbook for the study of G.A.W. and S.U.B. plans. Outlines labor's demand for the G.A.W., management opposition to the G.A.W., and the emergence of S.U.B. Deals with major problems in the operation of a S.U.B. plan: estimating the cost, minimizing the cost, financial problems in operating under a G.A.W. or S.U.B. plan. Appendix includes full text of Ford, American, and Continental Can S.U.B. agreements.

WICKERSHAM, EDWARD D. "Controlling Unemployment at the Company Level," *Industrial and Labor Relations Review*, vol. 14 (October 1960), pp. 68–82.

Discusses changes in methods of controlling unemployment at the company level since the Great Depression.

12 Individual Security: Job Rights and Due Process

BESIDES GOOD pay and working conditions, most workers want some kind of a guarantee of continuity of employment and a fair appraisal of their job performance. As we emphasized in Chapter 9, management needs the freedom to lay off workers when business is slack, to transfer workers between jobs, to select good prospects for promotion, and to discipline for just cause. The worker's desire for job rights and fair play roughly coincides with the manager's desire to avoid excessive turnover and to maintain discipline. Workers and unions recognize management's need for flexibility and efficiency. At the same time managers understand the worker's need for security and fair play. These needs of workers and managers are accommodated through the negotiation of rules for job rights and due process under collective bargaining.

Collectively bargained rules protect the types of work usually assigned to union members and establish the individual worker's *relative* claim to available work. Craft unions and industrial unions follow somewhat different methods of establishing job rights.

Collectively bargained rules for due process establish the individual worker's *absolute* claim to fair treatment in the employment relationship. The worker's claim for fair treatment is the *quid pro quo* for acceptance of the obligation to perform a job as specified in the agreement or as directed by management in day-to-day operations. Rules for due process are similar in the domains of craft and industrial unions.

JOB RIGHTS

It is important to note that union jurisdictional claims and union security arrangements may play an important part in establishing the individual worker's job rights. Union security is a major concern of the union *as an institution*, sometimes totally divorced from its members. At the same time, the effectiveness of the union's claim to all available work sets the outside limits of what job rights are available to its members.

Craft unionists obtain job rights through custom and practice, while industrial unionists obtain job rights through the provisions of their collective bargaining agreements. The cornerstones of the craft union's program of job control are exclusive union jurisdiction, the closed shop, and the hiring hall. The industrial union obtains job rights through agreement clauses restricting the assignment of work to nonrepresented employees and a system of seniority. Both systems aim at protecting work for assignment to union employees and establishing the individual worker's *relative* claim to available work.

Job Rights in Craft Unions

The craft union's claim of jurisdiction becomes a device of job control as soon as an employer signs a collective bargaining agreement. Under the terms of a typical agreement with the Carpenters union, the employer assigns all of its work "within the jurisdiction of the Carpenters union" to members of the union. An employer who tries to subcontract carpentry work or to assign it to other craftsmen finds that no carpenters are available to perform duties requiring the skills of a carpenter. Frequently the employer also finds that no plumbers, masons, electricians, or structural steelworkers are available either until carpentry work is reassigned to the carpenters union.

Craft workers establish their *relative* claim to available work through the union. When the closed shop or the "seven-day union shop" is operative, members of the union have exclusive rights to all available work on unionized jobs. Most craft-union collective bargaining agreements make no reference to seniority. This is to be expected because the typical craft unionist has only an intermittent relationship with a single employer. The craft unionist may seek job opportunities or use the union hall as an employment office. If they use the union hall as base of operations, and craft unionists frequently do, they may find that the business agent gives job opportunities first to the unemployed members with the most dues stamps in their union books. If the business agent uses this system of allocating job opportunities, the craft unionist carries seniority in the union. This is a noncontractual seniority system, but it is a seniority system and it works well for workers in industries with intermittent employment relationships. The business agent who distributes job opportunities on the basis of familiarity with the members at the union hall, is following a less formalized seniority system but it probably reflects the relative seniority of unemployed members. Finally, of course it is possible that the business agent does not believe in seniority and distributes jobs to friends regardless of their seniority; or to the highest bidder. The only check on this discriminatory action is the fact that someday the business agent comes up for reelection and an infuriated rank and file can deprive that agent of such abusive power. When jobs are hard to find, the rank and file probably scrutinize the business agent's allocation of jobs with some care.

Job Rights in Industrial Unions

While the craft union's methods of job control are informal, the industrial union obtains job security through a highly formalized contractual agreement. Industrial unions protect their total claim to available work by collective bargaining clauses which restrict the freedom of management to assign work to nonmembers of the bargaining unit. These clauses take the form of limitations on the amount and type of work that may be performed by supervisors and salaried employees, full crew clauses, and restrictions on the freedom of management to subcontract work normally performed in the bargaining unit.[1] In the absence of detailed contractual provisions, industrial unions are sometimes successful in forcing the continuance of management's past practices in the assignment of work through the arbitration process. Almost universally seniority clauses are the method of establishing the individual industrial unionist's *relative* claim to available work.

Seniority Defined. Seniority is a vast and complicated field of claims and counterclaims by individuals. It confers on its possessor only a *relative* claim to available work or other benefits flowing from the enterprise. The collective bargaining agreement tends to be a fine balancing mechanism between the interests of various groups of workers. Seniority grants certain preferential treatment to long-service employees almost at the expense of short-service employees. In times of business distress, the seniority rights of long-service employees may be diluted by work sharing. For example, instead of 80 percent of the employees with high seniority working 40 hours per week, all of the employees might be scheduled for 32 hours per week. Another example of the dilution of seniority rights is the rather common procedure of compulsory retirement under a pension plan. In this case, the high seniority employee is forced to convert seniority rights to pension benefits at the prevailing rate of exchange. Retirement of the high seniority employee, in turn, creates a job opportunity for a lower seniority employee or a new hire.

In the most general terms, seniority is defined as length of service. A worker usually does not acquire seniority until after serving a probationary period. Probationary periods usually range from the first week to the first six months of employment. After the probationary period, the worker is

---

[1] A full crew clause specifies the number of persons who must be assigned to a work group. For example, an airliner must have so many crew in the cockpit before the plane is permitted to operate. Subcontracting clauses have been very important in the garment industries and building trades for many years. In a 1959 BLS study of subcontracting clauses in agreements covering over 1,000 workers each, less than one in four agreements contained a subcontracting clause. See *Subcontracting Clauses in Major Collective Bargaining Agreements* (BLS Bulletin no. 1304, 1961), 33 pp. Some arbitrators have ruled that subcontracting was restricted by other provisions of the agreement even in the absence of a subcontracting clause. Prohibitions on work of nonrepresented employees, full crew rules, and subcontracting clauses are most important to unions in periods of general unemployment.

credited with seniority equal to the probationary period. Seniority usually is broken or eliminated by such events as discharge for cause, layoffs of very long duration (say, over one year), retirement, or unauthorized leaves of absence. The definition of seniority is completed by reference to the "area" of seniority or seniority "unit." The area of seniority may be as broad as the trade in the case of the craft union, where seniority may be defined as years and months of union membership. Or the area of seniority may be as narrow as the time that an employee has spent on a particular job in a particular plant of the General Electric Company. Between these two extreme areas of seniority is a whole spectrum of "occupational group," "departmental," "plant," "company," "company-community," and other variations. A single worker may possess different "seniorities" (in terms of time of service) in different areas concurrently. Figure 12–1 illustrates various areas of seniority taken from different collective bargaining agreements.

FIGURE 12–1
Illustrative "Areas" of Seniority

Occupational Seniority

Noninterchangeable occupational groups will be established on a plant-wide basis. In case of layoff, the Company agrees to give preference to the employee with the greatest seniority in his established noninterchangeable occupational group. Laid-off employees shall be recalled to work within their respective occupational groups in order of their seniority before any new employees are hired by the Company within the same group.

Departmental Seniority

Straight seniority by department for all employees shall be the rule, except as necessarily modified in connection with classification of tasks. If an employee is transferred from one department to another, seniority shall be determined in the following manner: Employee shall be considered a new employee in the new department and should a layoff be necessary in the new department before having worked in the new department a period of time exceeding the amount of time in the previous department, employee shall return to the previous department with accumulated time from both departments. However, should an employee have worked in the new department an amount of time exceeding that of the old department, the entire seniority shall be transferred to the new departmen and employee shall have no more seniority in the old department.

Plant-Wide Seniority

Strict plant seniority shall prevail from the original date of hiring on any job the employee is capable of handling. Employees may be retained or recalled on a temporary basis for special jobs out of line with seniority after consultation with the Shop Committee.

Special Variants of above Types

Plant seniority shall be observed and determined by the last hiring date of each employee. Seniority shall operate as follows: First as to occupation within the department; second on a departmental basis; third on a plant-wide basis.

Seniority lists shall be set up by divisions within the plant. Each intraplant division may include one or more departments. Each employee in the intraplant division shall exercise seniority in the various occupations within such divisions for which employee has been classified by the supervisor of the department included in the divisions. The divisions are listed as follows:

(There follows a detailed listing of company divisions.)

Divergent definitions of the area of seniority take on meaning only when we attempt to apply seniority against the benefits which it bestows on its possessor. We turn now to the problems in the application of seniority.

The Application of Seniority.   In Chapter 8 we referred to seniority of protection, opportunity, and privilege. Protective seniority establishes the relative job rights of employees in layoff and recall. Seniority of opportunity involves job promotions and transfers. Seniority of privilege establishes workers' relative claims to wage supplements and worker insurance and income continuity benefits, such as pensions.

Layoff and Recall.   Seniority is most frequently used as a criterion in worker layoff and recall. The usual arrangement is that workers with the greatest length of service will be the last to be laid off when business is poor and the first to be recalled when business picks up again. This simple rule poses extremely serious problems for management. The major modifications in the application of the general rule are the area of seniority and "bumping" rights. If length of service were not qualified by a statement of area of application, management might find itself in a position where the high seniority employees still on the job were incapable of performing essential tasks. Because of this potential problem, the areas of seniority described in Figure 12–1 become a critical issue in seniority as applied to layoffs. While areas of seniority determine who is available for layoff, bumping rights are the final determinant of which workers are actually laid off.

Areas of seniority are defined by a union-management compromise within the rather rigid limits established by the work flow of a particular group of employees. From the union point of view, the *ideal* area of seniority would provide the maximum possible security for the senior worker. This would be achieved if the area of seniority were defined as any employment within the jurisdiction of the union regardless of employer, job assignment, or geographic area attachment. For the industrial union employer, this broad seniority area would pose frequently insurmountable problems. From the employer's viewpoint, the *ideal* area of seniority would be defined so as to minimize interference with efficient operations. The best method of achieving this goal would be to limit the area of seniority to workers doing identical jobs within a single plant. Under such a system, the worker would have little security in a plant employing only a few workers on each of many different jobs. Most seniority agreements are commonsense compromises of the union's desire for worker security and management's desire for efficiency in production. Industrial unions are able to broaden the area of seniority from the single plant and the single job only in cases where many jobs tend to be interchangeable. In general, industrial unions lack the employment-office type of facilities needed to broaden the geographic area of seniority beyond all the plants of a single corporation. Further, the broadening of the area of seniority to cover more than one employer has generally been vigorously opposed by managements dealing with industrial unions. The area of seniority indicates the order in which employees become available for layoff. The question of whether a particular employee is separated from the payroll remains to be settled.

Workers who are available for layoff within their seniority area are not necessarily actually laid off. Whether they are or not depends upon their bumping rights. "Bumping rights" are the contractual privileges of employees available for layoff within their own area of seniority to displace employees with less seniority on jobs in other areas of seniority. For example, if tool-and-die makers and machine-tool operators were separate areas of seniority, a tool-and-die maker with five years' seniority and available for layoff might possess the bumping right to displace a machine-tool operator with three years' seniority. The machine-tool operator, in turn, might possess the bumping right to displace a sweeper with two years' seniority. It can readily be seen that unlimited bumping rights might cause a chaotic chain reaction of job reassignments. We are reminded of the case of a two-plant company which granted sweeping seniority rights as an inducement to union cooperation in the first contract after an NLRB election. One plant was located in Brooklyn and the other was located in Garden City, Long Island. At the time of negotiating the first contract, the company had very large government contracts and was expanding employment and production. Three years later the unforeseen cancellation of several government contracts necessitated a 20 percent reduction in force. Under the seniority arrangements which had been agreed to, it was necessary to reassign some 800 of the 1,000 employees who survived the first layoff. Many workers were reassigned from Garden City to Brooklyn and vice versa. Needless to say, it required several weeks before these reassigned workers could be integrated into an efficient work team. Eventually the seniority provisions of this union contract were renegotiated so as to provide both a degree of security to the workers and needed flexibility to management. However, the management of this company had paid a very dear price for the fairweather thinking which had dominated in the negotiation of its first union contract. The confusion caused by these transfers may have been partially responsible for further contract cancellations which the company experienced.

If the workers in the Garden City and Brooklyn plants had all been doing *identical* jobs, the bumping experience would have caused no more inconvenience than a longer subway ride or drive for some of the 800 workers who were transferred. But our two-plant company employed its workers on a great variety of different jobs. Most of the jobs were simple, but it required some time for workers to be fitted into a production team. Because of the differences in jobs and the large number of small jobs in most factory situations, bumping rights are usually limited or qualified in the collective bargaining agreement. The exact nature of the restrictions of bumping rights depends upon the individual employment relationship. Usually one or more of the following restrictions on bumping rights are contained in collective bargaining agreements:

1. The area of seniority itself may be narrowly defined. If so, this means that the original impact of reductions-in-force is minimized.
2. Bumping rights may be declared inoperative for short-term (say, less than two-week) layoffs.
3. Before one employee can bump another, the employee may be required to establish proof that he or she is capable of performing the job into which they wish to bump.
4. Employees may be permitted to bump only into jobs which they have previously performed satisfactorily.
5. Bumping rights may be conferred only on workers who satisfy a minimum service requirement greater than the probationary period from the date of original hire.
6. Employees may be permitted to bump only into seniority areas in which they have previous experience.
7. Employees wishing to bump may be required to have a specified amount of longer service than the employee they wish to replace.
8. Displaced employees may be placed in a labor pool where they have seniority claims on new jobs which they are capable of performing as created by turnover.

The foregoing list of possible limitations on bumping rights offers several potential problems in administration. For example, should employees claiming ability to perform jobs claimed by bumping rights be given a trial period on the new job? What is a *reasonable* trial period? If an employee fails in the trial period, is the employee discharged, or laid off, or given another trial period on another job?

Recall rights of seniority workers pose other serious problems in administration. Do recall rights apply only to the specific job from which the worker was separated? or seniority area? or any new jobs of which one might be capable? How much and what kind of recall notice must be given to a laid-off worker? What reasons for failure to return when a recall notice is received are sufficient to preserve the seniority rights of the worker who fails to report back for work?

Before leaving seniority and its application to layoffs and recall, it is important to note that most industrial unions insist upon "superseniority" for local union officers and shop stewards or committeemen. A reasonably typical contract clause reads as follows:

> The President, 1st and 2nd Vice Presidents and Financial Secretary shall be given top seniority in their occupational group during their term of office if they have three (3) years' service with the Company and it is agreed that they shall not perform duties of their office during working hours.
>
> The members of the Executive Shop Committee, Chief Stewards, and Stewards will have top seniority in the Department or occupational groups which they represent. Such representatives, in order to receive seniority as specified, must have one (1) year's service with the Company. If there is no

work in their classification in the departments or occupational groups which they represent, they must, in order to remain employed, be able to qualify for some other job classification within their jurisdiction. Upon such transfer, they will be paid the average hourly rate being paid at the time in the job classification to which they have been transferred.

Such a contract clause preserves union representational rights in the shop even in periods of very high unemployment.

Managements often succeed in trading superseniority for stewards for similar privileges for a group of "key" employees or jobs. Such key employees might include management trainees, setup personnel, or maintenance experts. A key-employee clause which was obtained in trade for the above superseniority concession for union representatives reads as follows:

> Exceptional employees may be retained irrespective of seniority. Exceptional employees are employees whose work in the judgment of the Management and Executive Shop Committee is of exceptional value to the department. The Company agrees to limit the number of such employees to two (2) percent of the total on the payroll. A list of such exceptional employees is to be furnished to the Executive Shop Committee.

The major application of seniority is in the area of layoffs and recall. Seniority provides *substantial* individual security against the uncertainties caused by business fluctuations. The disciplinary factor has pretty much been removed from layoffs caused by poor business conditions. Whatever jobs are available go to the senior workers capable of performing them. Although seniority is also applicable in promotions and transfers, it is generally of less importance here than in layoffs and recall.

Seniority as a Benefit to Management

While managers face certain problems, and seem to lose some discretionary authority when they agree to a seniority program, they also derive certain benefits. When seniority becomes the criterion in a layoff, supervisors lose the power to select by name the workers who are to go and those who are to stay, but at the same time are spared the necessity of making difficult choices and drawing invidious distinctions between individuals. Does it matter, to the manager, after all, who does the work, as long as the work gets done? Anyone kept on a job after the normal probationary period must have been able to perform well enough to meet standards. Under a well-conceived plan, therefore, anyone on the seniority lists should be able to give standard performance. It matters very much to the workers involved who goes and who stays in a layoff: If they are willing to let the impersonal element of seniority decide the question, managers are spared many personal problems. Imagine, for example, trying to make up and justify a list of names arranged in order of comparative merit.

Managers benefit again when workers are recalled from layoff. Without having to spend money for hiring or training new employees, the firm gets experienced people ready to resume their part in operations the first day back on the job. And they are more likely to return on call rather than drift away to other jobs, because they knew their name was on that seniority list. The enterprise thus gains a stable yet flexible work force as a result of a good seniority agreement.

Carried one step further, to seniority of opportunity, managers often find that a bid-and-bump system for promotion and upgrading makes for more versatile employees, hence a more flexible crew.

Promotions and Transfers. Seniority also provides a degree of individual opportunity when business is good. It not only protects its possessor in bad times, it gives some degree of preference when business is improving. Thus seniority may establish certain preferences in the area of job promotions and transfers.

Promotions and transfers are differentiated in many collective bargaining agreements. Generally a "promotion" means a job carrying a higher rate of pay. "Transfer" may be applied to any change in job assignment. In an effort to minimize the interferences to production caused by many shifts in job assignments, management frequently seeks to limit seniority preferences in job assignment to the area of promotions. For the same reasons, management may seek to restrict the application of seniority in such matters as shift preference, leaves of absence for vacations, and overtime allocation.

Seniority is almost universally qualified in its application to promotions. Three examples of promotional arrangements illustrate the variety of possible applications:

1. "When new jobs are created, management shall fill these jobs with the most able and meritorious persons available. Present employees shall be considered before an attempt is made to recruit new employees from outside the plant." (Such an arrangement places a minimum of emphasis on seniority in filling new jobs.)

2. "When new jobs are created, management shall attempt to fill these jobs with the most able and meritorious persons presently in the employ of the company. Notices of new jobs shall be posted and any employee on a lower-graded job may apply for consideration. Such applications shall be carefully considered by management. When two or more employees applying for the new job possess equal merit and ability, management shall award the job to the employee with the greatest seniority. In the event that no person applying for the job possesses the required abilities, the company may seek to fill the job by outside recruitment." (Such an arrangement continues to place primary emphasis on merit and ability, but formalizes the rights to consideration and preference conferred by the possession of seniority.)

3. "When new jobs are created, management shall attempt to fill these jobs with persons presently in the employ of the company. Notices of new jobs shall be posted and any employee on a lower-graded job may apply for consideration. New jobs shall be awarded to the applying employee with the greatest seniority capable of performing the job. Outside recruitment may be used to fill jobs when no capable employee applies." (Such an arrangement places near-maximum emphasis on seniority in filling new jobs. In *very* exceptional cases, even greater emphasis may be placed on seniority by granting the senior applicant preference for whatever training may be necessary to learn the new job. Such arrangements are found almost exclusively in situations where outside recruitment of needed skills is impossible.)

The foregoing arrangements introduce two new terms, "merit" and "ability," which must be defined either by custom and usage or in the contract itself. The meaning of these terms determines the actual value of seniority preference in promotions.

"Ability" may mean many things: Able to learn? Able to produce at full efficiency on the day of assignment to the new job? Able to produce at full efficiency after a break-in period?

Perhaps even more important than the meaning of the term "ability" is the question of whose judgment shall be controlling in the case of the individual applicant. If tests of ability are used, is management the sole judge of the reliability and validity of the tests? If tests are not used, may management insist that the only valid proof of ability is previous successful experience on the exact vacancy to be filled?

Many managements feel that a merit consideration alleviates some of the difficulties inherent in the ability criterion and improves the chances of filling jobs with satisfactory persons. "Ability" normally implies a *prediction* of future performance. "Merit" is the evaluation of past performance. By adding a merit consideration, promotions become a reward *earned* by efficient performance in the past. It seems reasonable to expect that an employee who has a record of good performance will work out better on a new job than an employee with a poor record and possessing the same ability to perform the new job.

The more refined the criteria for promotion, the greater the difficulties in finally determining the person eligible for promotion. Merit, like ability, is an evasive concept. In many factory situations, formal merit rating has been abandoned because of difficulties in administration. Without effective merit rating, an attempt to apply merit to promotional situations boils down to disqualifying persons with many disciplinary actions in their personnel records for promotion. Obviously, under these circumstances merit is being measured only in a negative manner.

Many detailed studies have been made of the difficulties inherent in merit-rating systems.[2] We may briefly summarize these difficulties as follows:

1. Determining and defining the factors to be rated. The major consideration here is that the factors rated should be precisely defined and valid as a measure of efficiency. For example, a vaguely defined "attitude" factor might, in application mean that the employee being rated did or did not have the same political affiliation as the rater. Unless political affiliation were a major determinant of productive efficiency, such interpretation of the factor would grievously thwart the purpose of merit rating.

2. Assuring objectivity in rating. Untrained raters begin the rating process with widely different interpretations of the meaning of the factors and personal standards of excellency. Further, most of us are rather poor observers of human behavior. We tend to put undue emphasis on the *last* thing we have observed or have failed to observe. Finally, we usually fail to analyze people's behavior. We may erroneously attribute observed low production to "poor attitude," or "low intelligence."

To a degree, these difficulties in merit rating may be overcome by improving the definitions of the factor rated and training the raters.

The balancing of merit and ability considerations and seniority considerations in promotional decisions poses a delicate problem for managements, unions, and arbitrators called in to decide grievance cases. The delicacy of this problem is clearly illustrated by the summary of a workshop held by the National Academy of Arbitrators:

> There was no attempt to formulate conclusions or to arrive at a consensus of views, and it would belie the nature and purpose of this all-too-brief discussion to summarize it in such terms. The most that might be done is to note certain comments and viewpoints which, to this reporter, seemed to stand out by virtue of their frequency, firmness, or artistic flair with which they were expressed. They are: (1) it all depends on how the contract is written; (2) the arbitrator is concerned, not only with the correctness of the conclusions of the employer or the union, but whether the answers given by either were addressed to the proper questions; (3) the determination of relative skill and ability should be based on evidence and standards which are reasonable, demonstrable, and objective—but with a suggestion here and there, "let's not carry this objectivity too far"; and (4) in determining questions of skill and ability, the judgments of management should not be set aside where they have not been shown by the evi-

---

[2] For a discussion of these problems, see M. Joseph Dooher, ed. *Rating Employee and Supervisory Performance: A Manual of Merit-Rating Techniques* (New York: American Management Association, 1951), pp. 192, or the merit rating chapter of any standard textbook on personnel management.

dence to be arbitrary, capricious, whimsical, or discriminatory—or different from our own.[3]

Seniority is difficult to apply in the problem of promotional opportunities. At the same time, seniority is the essence of simplicity when applied to the question of eligibility for numerous wage supplements.

Eligibility for Wage Supplements. We have discussed the importance of seniority in determining eligibility for, and the amount of, such wage supplements as pensions, health and welfare benefits, and supplemental unemployment benefits. In addition, vacation benefits are usually related to seniority. In some cases, overtime is distributed on the basis of seniority as are shift assignments. Severance pay is also graduated to reflect the individual's seniority.

Modified though it may be, seniority is almost universally applied as at least a consideration in layoffs, promotions, and fringe benefits. We turn now to several complex and important seniority problems which are of less general application.

Problems in Seniority. In this section we will deal with special problems relating to the individual and seniority status, seniority and automation, and seniority in corporate mergers.

Individual Problems in Seniority. The accumulation or retention of seniority rights is of great importance to a worker who goes on leave of absence, is called into military service, or who accepts employment outside the bargaining unit with the company.

1. Leaves of Absence. Most collective bargaining agreements prescribe conditions requiring the company to grant leaves of absence, upon proper application, to persons for official union business. Other leaves of absence and the accumulation of seniority for their duration are frequently left to management's sole discretion.

A common clause on seniority and leaves of absence is: "Seniority shall accumulate during the period of an approved leave of absence." Sometimes such a clause is qualified by limiting the amount of seniority that may accrue during leaves of absence for various causes, e.g., illness, union business, personal business, etc.

2. Military Service. Since the seniority and reemployment rights of persons in military service are prescribed by law, most collective bargaining agreements contain a clause similar to the following: "Employees now serving in the Armed Forces of the United States or employees who shall hereafter serve in the Armed Forces of the United States shall be entitled to reinstatement upon the completion of such service to the extent and under the

---

[3] James C. Hill, "Summary of Workshop on Seniority and Ability," in Jean T. McKelvey, ed., *Management Rights and the Arbitration Process* (*Proceedings of the Ninth Annual Meeting of the National Academy of Arbitrators, January 26–28, 1956*) (Washington, D.C.: BNA Incorporated, 1956), p. 49.

circumstances that reinstatement may be required by the applicable laws of the United States." Sometimes such a clause is enlarged with a statement that, "provided that any employee whose discharge from service is other than dishonorable, shall be accorded the same reinstatement rights as such laws provide in the case of persons honorably discharged." A generation of young men subject to the draft made clauses of this sort necessary. They may begin to disappear from labor agreements if the all volunteer army proves that conscription is unnecessary.

3. Employment outside the Bargaining Unit. Probably the most troublesome question relating to an individual's seniority rights arises when a worker is promoted to supervision or transferred to a job outside the bargaining unit. Workers are frequently reluctant to risk a new job as supervisor or on other work outside the bargaining unit unless they can retain their security by knowing that they have rights to the old job in the event of failure on the new one. Some managements seek to preserve the seniority rights of workers promoted to supervision as an inducement to accepting the new job. On the other hand, some managements believe that the new supervisor's break with the union-guaranteed right of seniority should be complete, thereby avoiding any possible conflicts in interest or loyalty on the part of supervision. Many unions oppose long accumulations of seniority by former union members promoted to supervision or outside the bargaining unit because they fear that management might seek to weaken the union by transferring seniority-holding supervisors back into the bargaining unit. Other unions feel that allowing former unionists promoted to supervision to accumulate seniority is conducive to better foreman-worker relationships.

The following provisions from an automobile industry collective bargaining agreement illustrate one method of handling the problem:

> A seniority employee in a classification subject to the jurisdiction of the Union, who has been in the past or will be in the future promoted to Assistant Foreman, Foreman, or any other supervisory position, and is thereafter transferred or demoted to a classification subject to the jurisdiction of the Union shall accumulate seniority while working in a supervisory position and when so transferred or demoted shall commence work in a job similar to the one he held at the time of his promotion with the seniority ranking he had at the time of his promotion plus the seniority accumulated while he was working in the supervisory position in conformity with the seniority rules of plants covered by this Agreement.
>
> No temporary demotions in supervisory positions will be made during temporary layoffs.

Seniority and Automation. Unions argue that automation necessitates a substantial revision of seniority practices. For example, an AFL–CIO publication states:

> It may be necessary, for example, substantially to revise seniority provisions in collective bargaining contracts. Unions are giving much thought

to the need for the broadening of seniority areas—company-wide or plant-wide seniority, for example—to assure equitable seniority protection for their members and the right to interdepartment and interplant transfer, based on seniority. Preferential hiring provisions are being considered, which will require all plants under contract with the union to give preference to laid-off workers in the same industry and area.

Also seniority systems should assure senior employees a full opportunity to qualify for new higher-skill jobs. Such employees should not be passed over in favor of new or junior employees simply because of age or an employer unwillingness to provide the training to enable qualification for the job.[4]

The exact form of the new seniority clauses which may develop as a result of automation is hard to predict. However, it seems likely that if automation creates any substantial dislocation of the labor force, unions will intensify their efforts for greater security for seniority workers. A major difficulty in negotiating new types of seniority clauses may be caused by the changes in automated job content. For example, Prof. James Bright of the Harvard Business School states that automation creates an entirely new breed of maintenance technicians. Professors Baldwin and Schultz have suggested that "ability to learn" may replace "ability to perform" as the criterion for selecting workers for promotion to automated jobs.

Seniority in Corporate Mergers.[5]   The relative employment rights conferred by seniority usually vanish when a business fails. Corporation mergers may cause the transferring of work between plants, changes in the products manufactured, or plant closures. Such developments may reduce the number of available jobs or change the nature of jobs available. Mergers always present new problems in allocating whatever jobs may be available. These problems are particularly acute when the number of jobs is substantially reduced, two or more unions are involved, the jobs involve nontransferable skills, the places of employment are geographically remote, and reemployment opportunities elsewhere are scarce. The solution to these problems is never easy and in some instances may do violence to workers' job rights.

Three basic alternative methods of integrating seniority lists have been defined by Prof. Mark L. Kahn. They are: by length of service, by ratio, or by rank. Figure 12–2 is an illustration of these three methods. Length of service integration treats service with either company as equivalent to service with the new corporate entity. Ratio integration preserves the proportionate position held by employees on the premerger seniority lists. Rank integration, which is seldom used, places extreme emphasis on the actual distance that each employee stood from the top of the premerger seniority

---

[4] AFL–CIO, *Labor Looks at Automation* (Washington, D.C.: AFL–CIO Publication no. 21, May 1956), p. 23.

[5] For an excellent discussion of this problem, see Mark L. Kahn, "Seniority Problems in Business Mergers," *Industrial and Labor Relations Review*, vol. 8 (April 1955), pp. 361–78.

FIGURE 12–2
Rank, Ratio, and Length of Service Methods of Integrating Seniority Lists

Given: Company A, 10 employees, length of service from 10 down to 1 year, respectively.

Company B, 5 employees, length of service from 5 down to 1 year, respectively.

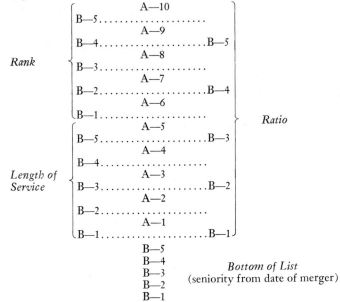

Note: In this example, employees of "A" have been given the advantage of any tie in seniority. In a real situation, this problem is not significant since length of service goes back to a particular date, not a particular year.

Source: Mark L. Kahn, "Seniority in Business Mergers," *Industrial and Labor Relations Review,* vol. 8 (April 1955), p. 374.

lists. Of course, integration may be rejected by placing all of the employees of one of the groups in a subordinate position.

In merging seniority lists, management's primary concern is assuring the position of employees with hard-to-replace skills. In addition, management seeks to minimize the dislocation caused by bumping. After these two goals are achieved, management may just pass the problem along to the union(s) involved. With the union(s) distributing the seniority rights, the interests of a minority group may be roughly overridden.

Seniority and Affirmative Action

It seems unlikely that any union or management ever framed a seniority program with the deliberate intention of discriminating against any category of worker, but wherever *past hiring practices* have been discriminatory, seniority rules perpetuate the injustice. A company that used to hire no blacks, women, chicanos, or other minority-group applicants, does not comply with the new civil rights laws simply by reversing its practices and starting to hire these formerly neglected people. It has to treat them, after they are hired, without discrimination, just like other employees. If now the newcomers go to the bottom of the seniority lists, as the rules would require, they become most vulnerable to layoff and loss of income and so are the ones who must continue to pay for the company's past unfairness. In this situation, a union that would blindly cling to the rules and blame the company, which did the hiring, makes itself an accomplice after the fact. Administrators of the civil rights laws, and judges interpreting and enforcing them with court orders, do not treat seniority rules as if they were sacred. The substantive rule that was legal yesterday may be declared illegal today. Managers and unions are having to devise new rules.

Unions rather than managers are uniquely to blame for discrimination when it takes place in the union hiring hall or in admission to a trade apprenticeship. At present, perhaps, few women *want* to become longshoremen, but many women and blacks and others would like to learn a trade. The craft unions are bound to experience increasing pressure in the years ahead.

DUE PROCESS

A worker's *absolute* claim to fair treatment is analogous to the citizen's constitutional right to due process of law. Under Anglo-Saxon law, the accused is considered innocent until proven guilty. The accused is entitled to representation by counsel. Guilt or innocence is determined by a reference to the law by a judge or jury which is free from any personal bias for or against the accused. *Ex post facto* laws and laws aimed at depriving an individual or group of liberty or property are invalid.

The collective bargaining agreement establishes both the law of employee conduct and the judicial system by which the accused is tried. Unions and managements may negotiate a complex system of rules and penalties. More commonly, the collective bargaining agreement merely states that management has the right to discipline workers for "just cause" or to establish "reasonable" rules of employee conduct. The grievance procedure and arbitration provisions of the agreement create the judicial system of the employment relationship.

The Judicial System under Collective Bargaining

Management is vested with the responsibility for maintaining law and order in the employment relationship under collective bargaining. The initial determination of whether an employee has failed to abide by the rules or obligations to perform duties as directed is made by management. If workers feel that management has acted unfairly, they call in the union to act as defense counsel. In almost all collective bargaining agreements, the worker and the union have final recourse to arbitration in the pursuit of the worker's *absolute* claim to fair treatment.

The Law of Fair Treatment

When the worker's claim finally gets to arbitration, how does the "judge" decide if the worker has been deprived of fair treatment? Like a judge, the arbitrator relies on statutory law (the collective bargaining agreement) or the common law of the employment relationship. If the collective bargaining agreement (statutory law) covers the situation, the arbitrator must weigh the facts and administer justice as defined in the agreement. If the collective bargaining agreement does not cover the situation, the arbitrator must formulate "reasonable and just" laws from the practice of the parties and the mores of the present-day employment relationship. These arbitrator-made rules take on many of the characteristics of a new "common law" of the employment relationship.

The common law of the employment relationship is as difficult to define as the common law of liberty. At the same time, this common law exists and provides very substantial guidance to arbitrators, managers, and unions in providing meaning to the workers' *absolute* claim to fair treatment.

Discharge is frequently called the "capital punishment" of the employment relationship. By examining the common law of just cause for discharge, we obtain an insight on the meaning of due process. Prof. J. Fred Holly has analyzed 1,055 discharge arbitration cases. On the basis of his analysis, Professor Holly has formulated eight principles for handling discharge cases which have wide applicability in the arbitration process:

1. Policies must be both known and reasonable.
2. Violation of policies must be proven, and the burden of proof rests on the employer.
3. The application of rules and policies must be consistent:
    a. Employees cannot be singled out for discipline.
    b. Past practice may be a controlling consideration.
4. Where employees are held to a standard, that standard must be reasonable.
5. The training provided employees must be adequate.
6. The job rights of employees must be protected from arbitrary, capricious, or discriminatory action.
7. Actions must be impersonal and based on fact.
8. Where the contract speaks, it speaks with authority.[6]

---

[6] J. Fred Holly, "The Arbitration of Discharge Cases: A Case Study," in Jean T. McKelvey, ed., *Critical Issues in Labor Arbitration—Proceedings of the Tenth Annual Meeting, National Academy of Arbitrators* (Washington, D.C.: BNA Incorporated, 1957), p. 16.

As Holly states, the application of these principles to the individual case is difficult because of extenuating circumstances which are almost always present. However, the principles do provide a useful guide for unions and management. The principles clearly indicate the need for careful training of supervisors in meting out disciplinary penalties.

SOCIAL IMPLICATIONS OF JOB RIGHTS AND DUE PROCESS

The seniority principle in layoffs probably has worked in the direction of lengthening the average "work life" of employees. Before unionism, discharge for old age was rather common. Seniority means that a worker on the rolls is reasonably free from discrimination because of age up to retirement age. Of course seniority has no influence at all in preventing discrimination against older workers seeking employment.

The substantial rights granted employees under industrial jurisprudence have emphasized the need for the careful selection and training of new employees. After the short probationary period, the burden of proof in discharges tends to shift to management. To a lesser degree, the employee with the greatest seniority also possesses a claim on whatever higher paying jobs may become available. Although seniority isn't the sole criterion in these areas, and frequently isn't the major criterion, the general significance of seniority is widely recognized and has motivated management to carefully select, appraise, and, when necessary, dismiss new employees before the expiration of the probationary period.

Seniority has probably worked in the direction of reducing voluntary worker mobility. The area of seniority rarely extends beyond the plants of a single corporation. Since seniority provides a degree of job security, many workers are reluctant to leave an employer and forfeit their accrued job rights. Unions have indicated some interest in extending the area of seniority to the entire jurisdiction of the union, but little has been done in this respect in any industry with nonintermittent employment relationships. Substantial employer resistance to this union proposal seems likely to continue as long as each employer insists upon establishing qualifications for prospective employees. In the society as a whole, we continue to have substantial worker mobility between employers, especially among the new entrants to the labor market.

Job rights and due process have implications which reach out into the employment relations of nonunion firms. Although workers in nonunion firms do not possess the right to a day in court before an arbitrator, there is little question that many managements have accepted the broad principles of discipline outlined by Professor Holly above. To a lesser degree, many managements also give substantial consideration to an employee's length of service during layoffs or in determining whether the employee should have a chance at an opportunity for promotion.

SUMMARY

In this chapter we have discussed individual security measures. Individual security measures aim at giving the worker some promise of continuity of employment and fair appraisal of job performance. Individual security measures are accommodated to the need of management for efficient operations.

The system of establishing a worker's *relative* claim to available work in craft unions may be highly informal. In industrial unions a highly formalized system of seniority establishes the worker's *relative* claim to available work. Both craft and industrial unionists and their unions as institutions are vitally concerned in establishing firm claims to the largest possible number of work-hours. In industrial unions, the seniority system establishes the relative claims to available work. In craft unions, the union hiring hall may allocate available work among unionists.

The worker's *absolute* claim to fair play is protected by collectively bargained rules of employment, the grievance procedure, and arbitration. When the collective bargaining agreement provides only general guidelines to fair play, the arbitrator must rely on the common law of the employment relationship.

QUESTIONS FOR DISCUSSION

1. Is it proper to distinguish between an *absolute* right to fair treatment and a *relative* claim to available work?
2. How are job rights distributed in craft unions?
3. Explain the process by which a "common law" of fair treatment has emerged under collective bargaining. Why do few collective bargaining agreements reduce this common law to detailed written "statutory law?"
4. Does a worker have a "property right" to his job? What is the significance of your answer?

SELECTED ANNOTATED BIBLIOGRAPHY

CRAWFORD, DONALD A. "The Arbitration of Disputes over Subcontracting." In *Challenges to Arbitration*, JEAN T. McKELVEY, ed. *Proceedings of the Thirteenth Annual Meeting of the National Academy of Arbitrators*. Washington, D.C.: Bureau of National Affairs, 1960, pp. 51–72. Discussion by MARK L. KAHN, pp. 73–77.

Based on an analysis of published arbitration awards, Crawford concludes that: "The doctrine seems to be that the company cannot undermine the status of the collective bargaining agent by contracting out work primarily to beat union prices, nor can the company contract out permanent work without compelling reasons other than a seeming desire to reduce the status of the exclusive agent." Kahn discusses the arbitrability of contracting out disputes and emphasizes the bearing of past practice on the contracting out decision.

DENNIS, BARBARA D. and SOMERS, GERALD G., eds. *Labor Arbitration at the Quarter-Century Mark. Proceedings of the Twenty-Fifth Annual Meeting of the National Academy of Arbitrators.* Washington, D.C.: Bureau of National Affairs, 1973.

In a section entitled "Changing Life Styles and Problems of Authority in the Plant," ROLF VITALIN, THOMAS J. McDERMOTT, and MARTIN A. COHEN discuss the questions posed for arbitrators in grievance cases dealing with such manifestations of changing life styles as long hair, beards, drug use, personal attire, etc.

FISHER, ROBERT W. "When Workers Are Discharged—An Overview," *Monthly Labor Review,* vol. 96, no. 6 (June 1973).

The author reviews the contractual and legal provisions available to employees to fight discharges and shows that unionized and government employees enjoy the most protection.

FLANAGAN, JOHN C., and BURNS, ROBERT K. "Employee Performance Record: A New Appraisal and Development Tool," *Harvard Business Review,* vol. 33 (September–October 1955), pp. 95–102.

The men who developed the "critical-incident" method of performance review tell about its development and operation.

FLEMING, R. W. "Due Process and Fair Procedure in Labor Arbitration." In *Arbitration and Public Policy,* SPENCER D. POLLARD, ed. *Proceedings of the Fourteenth Annual Meeting of the National Academy of Arbitrators.* Washington, D.C.: Bureau of National Affairs, 1961, pp. 69–91. Discussion by DAVID ZISKIND and IRVIN SOBEL, pp. 91–101.

Discusses the reactions of a broad sampling of members of the National Academy of Arbitrators on how they would handle model situations dealing with (1) notice and appearance, (2) surprise, (3) confrontation, and (4) the agreed case. Ziskind urges that further thought be given to laying down guidelines for weighing the fairness of a hearing. Sobel emphasizes that the worst denials of "due process" take place at other points in the collective bargaining process than arbitration.

FRIEDMAN, JOEL W. "Individual Rights in Grievance Arbitration," *Arbitration Journal,* vol. 27, no. 4 (December 1972).

The author examines the balance between the rights of the union and management organizations on the one hand and the individual employee-member on the other.

HEALY, JAMES J. "The Factor of Ability in Labor Relations." In *Arbitration Today,* JEAN T. McKELVEY, ed. *Proceedings of the Eighth Annual Meeting of the National Academy of Arbitrators.* Washington, D.C.: Bureau of National Affairs, 1955, pp. 45–61.

A professor at the Harvard Business School and arbitrator discusses the findings of a research study on seniority and merit as factors in promotion. Details the problems in measuring merit and the approach of arbitrators to disputes over merit and seniority in promotions. Paper is discussed by Professor J. T. McKELVEY of Cornell and GABRIEL N. ALEXANDER, arbitrator and attorney of Detroit.

HILL, JAMES C. "Summary of the Workshop on Seniority and Ability." In *Man-*

agement Rights and the Arbitration Process, JEAN T. McKELVEY, ed. *Proceedings of the Ninth Annual Meeting of the National Academy of Arbitrators.* Washington, D.C.: Bureau of National Affairs, 1956, pp. 44–49.

Outlines major contentions of a number of arbitrators on the consideration of merit and ability in disputed cases in labor relations.

JONES, DALLAS L. *Arbitration and Industrial Discipline.* Ann Arbor: University of Michigan, Bureau of Industrial Relations, 1961.

Based on the intensive study of 19 discharge-reinstatement cases, the monograph investigates each phase of the disciplinary process and considers the impact of arbitration upon future policies and worker performance.

LARROWE, CHARLES P. *Shape-Up and Hiring Hall.* Berkeley, Calif.: University of California Press, 1955.

A study of the International Longshoremen's Association and the International Longshoremen's and Warehousemen's Union in New York and Seattle and their contrasting methods of hiring workers in a casual employment industry.

McDERMOTT, THOMAS J., and NEWHAMS, THOMAS H. "Discharge-Reinstatement: What Happens Thereafter," *Industrial and Labor Relations Review*, vol. 24, no. 4 (July 1971).

The authors examine the work records of employees who were reinstated in their jobs after being discharged, and report generally good performance.

McKELVEY, JEAN T. "Sex and the Single Arbitrator," *Industrial and Labor Relations Review*, vol. 24, no. 2 (April 1971).

The author examines the clash between contractual rights under the collective bargaining agreement and legal rights under Title VII of the Civil Rights Act, and how arbitrators tend to resolve such conflicts.

MEYERS, FREDERICK. "The Analytic Meaning of Seniority," *Eighteenth Annual Proceedings of the Industrial Relations Research Association*, pp. 194–202.

Compares and contrasts seniority and the closed shop as individual security measures.

PHELPS, ORME W. *Discipline and Discharge in the Unionized Firm.* Berkeley and Los Angeles: Institute of Industrial Relations, University of California, 1959.

A discussion of the rulings of arbitrators which have produced a definite pattern, consisting of proper grounds for disciplinary action, required procedures, and acceptable penalties and how these factors are qualified by such tests as the burden of proof, firm and industry practices, quality of the evidence, condonation, consistency, extenuating circumstances, and so on.

SLICHTER, SUMNER H.; HEALY, JAMES J.; and LIVERNASH, E. ROBERT. *The Impact of Collective Bargaining on Management.* Washington, D.C.: Brookings Institution, 1960.

Special attention is invited to the following chapters: 3, "The Control of Hiring"; 4, "Union Policies on Training and Apprenticeship"; 5, "Basic Concepts of Seniority"; 6, "Work Sharing and Layoff Systems"; 7, "Promotion Policies and Procedures"; 8, "Work Scheduling"; 9, "Work Assignment and Jurisdiction"; 10, "Subcontracting"; 11, "Make-Work Rules and Practices"; and 21, "Disciplinary Policies and Procedure."

SMITH, ARTHUR B., JR. "The Impact on Collective Bargaining of Equal Employment Opportunity Remedies," *Industrial and Labor Relations Review*, vol. 28, no. 3 (April 1975).

The author examines the impact of equal employment opportunity pressures upon the formulation and administration of collective bargaining agreements, with special attention to seniority rights and the arbitration process.

SOMERS, GERALD G. and DENNIS, BARBARA D., eds. *Arbitration and Social Change. Proceedings of the Twenty-Second Annual Meeting of the National Academy of Arbitrators.* Washington, D.C.: Bureau of National Affairs, 1970.

In a section titled "Ramifications of Back-Pay Awards in Suspension and Discharge Cases," Dallas L. Jones and Patrick J. Fisher discuss some of the issues involved in cases where the arbitrator rescinds a disciplinary action and orders back pay to the employee involved.

SUMMERS, CLYDE W. "The Individual Employee's Rights under the Collective Agreement: What Constitutes Fair Representation." In *Arbitration–1974*, BARBARA D. DENNIS and GERALD G. SOMERS, eds. *Proceedings of the Twenty-Seventh Annual Meeting of the National Academy of Arbitrators.* Washington, D.C.: Bureau of National Affairs, 1975.

A law professor and arbitrator examines the legal rights an individual employee has to be fairly represented by the union in the grievance procedure and in arbitration. See also the "Comments" by LESTER ASHER, BERNARD DUNAU, ROBERT H. KLEEB, and LEO KOTIN.

TAYLOR, GEORGE W. "Seniority Concepts." In *Arbitration Today*, JEAN T. McKELVEY, ed. *Proceedings of the Eighth Annual Meeting of the National Academy of Arbitrators.* Washington, D.C.: Bureau of National Affairs, 1955, pp. 127–47.

Professor Taylor discusses the variations in the use of seniority as a security measure and as an allocator of opportunities between unions and industries. Professor Taylor's long and distinguished experience as an arbitrator and advisor to government results in the formulation of the fundamentals involved in the problem of seniority. The paper is discussed by Professors JOHN A. HOGAN of the University of New Hampshire and CHARLES C. KILLINGSWORTH of Michigan State University.

13 Agreement Administration

The collective bargaining agreement states the rights and duties of the parties. It is more than a contract; it is a generalized code to govern a myriad of cases which the draftsmen cannot wholly anticipate. . . . It calls into being a new common law—the common law of a particular industry or a particular plant.

The grievance procedure is . . . a part of the continuous collective bargaining process. It, rather than a strike, is the terminal point of a disagreement.

. . . The labor arbitrator is usually chosen because of the parties' confidence in his knowledge of the common law of the shop and their trust in his personal judgment to bring to bear considerations which are not expressed in the contract as criteria for judgment. The parties expect that his judgment of a particular grievance will reflect not only what the contract says but, insofar as the collective bargaining agreement permits, such factors as the effect upon productivity of a particular result, its consequence to the morale of the shop, his judgment whether tensions will be heightened or diminished. For the parties' objective in using the arbitration process is primarily to further their common goal of uninterrupted production under the agreement to make the agreement serve their specialized needs.

—MR. JUSTICE DOUGLAS
United Steelworkers of America v. *Warrior and Gulf Navigation Company*
June 20, 1960

THE QUOTATION at the head of this chapter comes from the majority opinion in a trio of cases decided by the Supreme Court in 1960. As might be expected in a pronouncement from the bench, it reflects the judicial point of view. It regards a collective bargaining agreement as "a generalized code" that spells out rights and duties and sees this code as emerging from amidst a continuing set of customary relations, mutual expectations, and accepted modes of behavior that constitute "a new common law."

There is indeed, as Mr. Justice Douglas points out, an aspect of industrial jurisprudence in the administration of a collective bargaining agreement, but managers and union members know that this is only half—perhaps less than half—the story. The arbitrator and the judge come in on appeal when things go wrong; it is up to the manager and the union official to make things go right, as things are expected to do. An agreement made in good faith is intended to be observed, not violated. Along with the Supreme Court opinion which sanctions the agreement as a "code," it would be well to recall the Dunlop theoretical framework, explained in the first chapter of this book, which calls the terms of the agreement "substantive rules."

In the Dunlop terminology, the two principal actors, management and labor, make the rules and live under them, regulating their relations with each other in accordance with the terms agreed upon. Presumably, they reach an acceptable accommodation that reconciles their separate interests and brings them into a joint relationship conferring mutual advantage. Among the rules they make are rules for implementing and enforcing—in a word, administering—the activities the rules govern. These implementing rules authorize and create a system of on-the-job representation for employees that corresponds to the organization's structure of management and supervision. They also provide for calling in, on occasion, a third actor normally not part of the organization: the arbitrator, one of Dunlop's "regulators." This third actor comes in when the two primary actors find that the machinery for internal administration cannot effectively resolve some problem of application or interpretation of the substantive rules.

AIMS OF AGREEMENT ADMINISTRATION

Ideally, the aim common to both management and the union in administering the agreement is to make the rules work in such ways as to result in mutual benefit. Successful attainment of this joint aim becomes difficult if the rules themselves are one-sided or if either management or the union seeks to take one-sided advantage of them. It may be presumed that when each side acts in its own best interest, both jointly further the common aim, given good rules to begin with and good faith in their administration.

This chapter takes for granted a good agreement—one whose rules are well-conceived and well-formulated—as the norm. Even so, as will be seen, the implementing roles, prescriptions, and procedures make demands on both parties to the agreement and require implementing machinery that is both internal and external to the organization. (Please note, by the way, in the discussion that follows, the use of two words spelled almost alike but with very different meanings: *rules*, and *roles*.)

THE SUBSTANTIVE RULES

By definition, the management of an organization consists of a structure, or (to use a more dynamic metaphor) the working machinery, for administering operations that look toward the attainment of organizational objectives. A manager at any level reaches objectives only when employees, including subordinate managers, behave toward their tasks and toward each other in ways that the manager prescribes or expects. In a nonunion enterprise, management makes the rules of employee behavior (as well as the rules of manager behavior), but these rules cannot deviate very greatly from social norms and accepted standards. Even a nonunion firm could not expect an unchanged employee response if wages were cut in half and the work doubled. Implicit then, even in management-formulated rules, is the need for reciprocal benefits.

In a unionized firm, management and the union jointly make the rules. Both have an interest in fair and uniform observance of the reciprocal rights and obligations. A simple slogan expresses this, albeit in a primitive, traditional way: A fair day's pay for a fair day's work. Unionized enterprises make explicit provision in the agreement for a system of employee on-the-job representatives, usually called shop stewards, or committeemen. The steward system that the rules create becomes a *counterpart* or *control* to the management structure in the administrative machinery of the enterprise.

The steward system, brought into being, differs between craft and industrial unions and between organizations and unions in both categories, but serves essentially the same function in all. The internal administrative machinery of *management* remains primarily responsible for implementing the substantive rules, just as the management organization remains responsible for planning, directing, coordinating, and controlling operations. The shop steward's role does not permit the steward to substitute personal judgment for the supervisor's or exercise supervisory authority. It does give the steward the right to make sure that the supervisor does, in fact, implement the substantive rules that management and the union have agreed to.

If the union's understanding of a rule, or of its application, differs from the supervisor's action in observing or enforcing the rule, the steward still cannot substitute his or her own interpretation for the supervisor's, or countermand the order. What the steward can do is set in motion a process to challenge and test the supervisor's action.

Thus, for example, the substantive rule might be that an employee is to perform work "as directed" by the supervisor, in return for the wages and other material benefits; but there is more to the rule than that. The employee must, indeed, work as directed; may not pick and choose tasks; but does so at a specified wage and at a tempo that has also been specified, or that, unspecified, is the standard or "common law" of the shop. If, now, the supervisor gives the employee tasks that under other substantive rules call for higher pay or requires faster work than the normal pace, the supervisor has broken the rule. The worker can go to the shop steward and lodge a complaint. While waiting for redress of the grievance, the worker must still go on working as directed by the supervisor; but the shop steward, as part of that recognized role, can officially challenge the supervisor's action and set in motion grievance procedures capable of eventually bringing the supervisor's behavior into conformity with the rules.

The administrative provisions of an agreement thus create new roles for policing and enforcing compliance with agreement terms and promoting proper observance, alongside the implementing role that already belongs to managers and supervisors. Chapter 4 has touched on some of these new roles in its account of the activities of shop stewards and grievance committee members. The same set of provisions also gives roles in the administrative procedures to some persons external to the enterprise and independent of it: to arbitrators on occasion, sometimes to mediators; and on a routine or special-occasion basis to certain union officials who are not employees of the organization nor of the local union such as, most commonly, district or international representatives.

If there were no appeal to an external, impartial arbitrator, labor and management would probably find that the machinery for internal administration did not work very well; but neither party would want to have the rules administered entirely by an outsider. "Don't call us, we'll call you" probably expresses (without the snide or contemptuous implication) the attitude of both primary actors to this third actor. They don't need arbitration every day; but when they do, they "need it bad."

Arbitration procedures thus wait at the end of the line in agreement administration. The arbitrator stands outside the enterprise, apart from operations. Most of the labor-management interaction that makes up the ongoing and dynamic content of agreement administration takes place between supervisors and employee representatives directly, at the work place, and goes on from day to day, from hour to hour.

This chapter examines that activity and discusses the roles of the representatives on both sides who carry it out. It then goes on to explain what happens when agreement administration hits a snag or breaks down, bringing the arbitrator on the scene.

CRAFT UNION AGREEMENT ADMINISTRATION

In industries like construction where craft unionism prevails, the norms and standards of behavior on the job are of long standing and are well known to the participants. As a consequence, the substantive rules are either understood or simply stated and simply administered. The implementing structure for agreement administration puts a job steward opposite the supervisor or subcontractor supervising a crew of skilled workers, and the local union business agent opposite the employer or general contractor. Any dispute that this latter pair cannot settle between them is likely to result in a strike or lockout.

One kind of dispute that in the past frequently led to strikes arose out of conflicting jurisdictional claims between unions. Most jurisdictional strikes resulted from changes in technology. Who, for instance, should install a new type of prefabricated metal window, already glassed when brought to the building site? Should it be the carpenters, who always have installed the frames, which have always before been made of wood? Or the glaziers, who traditionally glassed the panes? Or the metal workers, who have never worked with wood or glass, but do work with metal? Today, the building trades unions and the associated contractors jointly participate at the national level in a board for the settlement of jurisdictional disputes. On the board an impartial umpire—an arbitrator—casts a deciding vote; the industry and the unions have bound themselves to abide by the board's decisions. Thus a third actor, one of Dunlop's "regulators," finds a place in the administration of the rules under craft unionism.[1] The jurisdictional strike, once the bane of the construction industry, has all but disappeared. Other disputed issues may, under some present-day agreements, go to an interunion body on the one side and an employer association on the other, and from there to arbitration rather than inevitably to a strike or lockout. Craft unions, nonetheless, resort to arbitration over disputes with the employer much less frequently than industrial unions.

Craft union practice at the level of the local gives the business agent discretion to appoint job stewards. Often the job steward is the first one sent out on a job in response to an employer's requisition for skilled workers. The job steward acts as a control over employer observance of the agreement for the union. Stewards check to see that all hired are union members in good standing or have a valid work permit from the union. They watch to make sure that bosses, apprentices, laborers, and members of other unions do not perform work that belongs to journeymen of a craft. If they should come across a breach of the agreement—any failure either by management or workers to abide by the rules—they notify the business agent.

A craft union job steward rarely argues a grievance with the gang boss; but rarely has to. Craft union members are skilled workers. They know their jobs. They control the rate at which they carry out their tasks. They receive uniform pay—the union scale—and carry their seniority or other job rights not with the employer of the moment or the season, but with the union. They have few interests that depend on the discretion of their boss or supervisor. For that matter, the boss is likely to be a union member—or former member, carrying a withdrawal card entitling him to renew membership if he should cease to be a boss—so that he knows very well the limits to his authority. Bosses plan and lay out the work, tell workers simply what to do, and when; they do it. If the job steward were not there, the rules might not be quite so well enforced, but the important rules are union rules, anyway, and the job steward plays primarily an intra-union role.

The business agent to whom the job steward reports is not an employee

---

[1] Incidentally, for a number of years the umpire for building trades disputes was that same John T. Dunlop, in his role as a practitioner.

of any of the enterprises that employ the union members, but draws pay from and works for the union. The agent may still be considered part of the internal administrative apparatus, representing one of the primary actors, the union, which is a party to the agreement.

INDUSTRIAL UNION AGREEMENT ADMINISTRATION

In any sizeable enterprise where the industrial form of unionism finds appropriate application, agreement administration is not simple, but complex. The wage and salary system, for example, does not consist of a single "union scale" for a single category of skilled workers, but a structure of differentiated rates within a wide and often-changing range. Tasks making up job content also change; tempo of work depends not on the worker alone but may be machine-paced, or may derive from time and motion studies, work sampling, or other techniques not under worker control. Carpenters usually remain carpenters throughout their working career, but factory workers change jobs; move up, down, and sideways in the differentiated job structure of the enterprise; master no single skill but perform many varied tasks. For these and many other reasons administration of the rules requires a rather comprehensive structure or machinery, creates special roles peculiar to industrial union agreements, and relies heavily on arbitration.

The important roles in industrial union agreement administration are those of the *shop steward, grievance committee member* (individually and as a collective body), and *arbitrator*.

The Shop Steward

Shop stewards in the industrial type of union plays a more active and strategic role than their craft union counterparts. While they may carry out some intra-union duties, their primary function is to handle grievances. Arguing grievances with the supervisor is, in fact, the steward's characteristic activity.

There are other differences. Shop stewards are not appointed, but elected. They are chosen by, and serve, a particular constituency consisting, usually, of a department or recognized subdivision of the enterprise headed by a work-group supervisor. The union members in the work group who elect the steward also have the right of recall and replacement; and in any case, a steward comes up for election again at the end of a term of a year or two.

Management has no say in the selection of shop stewards, but binds itself by agreement to deal, through the work-group supervisor, with the steward the employees elect. The agreement thus creates the role. The steward gets authority to act in that role and capacity from the terms of the agreement—hence, ultimately, from management. The rules permit the steward to question and, indeed, to challenge, acts and decisions of the work-group supervisor, as a means of insuring respect for the rules. If complaints or grievances arise that the steward has to handle during working hours, the rules permit the steward, under most agreements, to leave her or his work station in order to carry on investigations, interview employees, and negotiate with the supervisor. Usually the company pays a steward at the regular rate for time spent away from work on steward's duties. Often the agreement gives stewards the special protection of "superseniority," which puts them at the top of the list of the unit, regardless of actual length of service, as long as they hold office as steward. This is to guarantee that the steward will be available to perform the role of on-the-job representation.

The rules providing on-the-job representation thus create a new, non-management role assigned to play a part in the control of management performance. It is a completely internal role: Shop stewards are always enterprise employees.

They are also union members and, in fact, union officials. They are like noncoms in the local union's "army," serving alongside the enlisted members. They give the union a communications net in the enterprise during the working day; a union grapevine; the union's eyes and ears in the shop —and its voice, too, capable of reaching the remotest corner of the working organization.

Unless a union-shop agreement makes membership mandatory and automatic, shop stewards solicit new employees to join the union. When the agreement has no checkoff provision, they collect dues. Meeting together as a steward council, regularly or on call, they become a powerful, compact, functioning auxiliary of the local union. In larger organizations they collectively make up a hierarchy of employee representatives parallel to the management hierarchy: the mirror image of the management structure of the enterprise. Thus opposite a work-group supervisor stands the shop steward, and opposite the supervisor's boss, a chief steward of one sort or another, depending on the structure of the organization. This departmental or divisional chief steward may in turn take part in the election of a chief steward at the next-higher echelon, and so on up the ranks. While the agreement may not explicitly recognize all the intermediate roles, it makes provision invariably for the shop stewards at the bottom of the hierarchy and a chief steward at the top; the others still play a functioning part in administration. The steward *system* may be thought of as a counterstructure to the management organization.

The Grievance Committee

The steward system permeates an organization to provide on-the-job representation for employees throughout the bargaining unit. A *grievance committee*[2] deals with the central personnel department. Jointly and centrally the union and management representatives deal with matters of administration that a shop steward could not settle with the work-group supervisor, or that affect more than one work group, or that concern all employees in the bargaining unit.

The grievance committee represents the local union and is headed by its president or other designated union officer. If the union employs a business agent, he or she is a member and often the chief speaker. As might also be expected, the chief steward is an ex officio member by virtue of heading the steward network.[3]

Additional union officials or elected members may also serve on the grievance committee, depending on the size of the enterprise or as specified in the agreement. Frequently one or more shop stewards may sit in, ad hoc, on sessions of the grievance committee when issues that are to be discussed affect their work groups, and in the same way management may call in the work-group supervisor temporarily.

Neither the grievance committee on the union side nor the personnel department on management's has any policy-making power. They cannot alter the agreement. Their job is to interpret it and apply its terms. Even if they should come to agree that a rule needs changing, they can do no more than recommend the change to the bodies that they represent: higher management or the local union. These higher bodies, having made the agreement in the first place, may agree to change it; but if either one declines, the existing agreement stands. Arbitration, incidentally, cannot change the rules either, but comes in when the two actors disagree about application or interpretation.

The grievance committee meets with management regularly or on call, usually at fixed minimum intervals such as a month or a fortnight. Between these meetings, the business agent may transact purely routine union business with the personnel manager, but any item of on exceptional nature or

---

[2] Nomenclature varies: The union may call its committee a "bargaining" or "negotiating" committee, just as management may call its department an industrial or employee relations department. The agreement may refer to it only as a joint committee with both management and union members; and indeed it transacts business in joint sessions; but the two elements are separable and this chapter's discussion deals with the union element. Whatever its local name, this standing committee must not be confused with the special committee or representation that also meets jointly with management to bargain on terms and negotiate the agreement establishing substantive rules. Calling the standing committee a grievance committee, as this chapter does, emphasizes its administrative function. Neither the grievance committee nor the personnel department makes the rules; both play a part, during the life of the agreement, in enforcing the rules.

[3] Because the chief steward's duties and position in the steward system make the person holding that office an essential member of this union committee, most local unions require that election as chief steward by the stewards be ratified by vote of the members of the local.

FIGURE 13–1

An Industrial Union Grievance Procedure

This diagram represents a four-step grievance procedure in a manufacturing plant with an industrial union steward system. Grievance procedures may have few or many steps. The only essential requirements are at least one policy-*administration* step and at least one policy-*making* step. Almost without exception the first policy-*administration* step in a grievance procedure is a conference between the supervisor and a steward. The top and final policy-*making* step is either arbitration or a strike.

The department, at the bottom of the diagram, consists of workers managed by a supervisor, who have elected a steward. The supervisor and the steward are responsible for policy *administration*. If a grievance is not settled at the first step, it proceeds upward in the grievance procedure until it is settled. Grievances may enter the process initially at the second step, when they affect more than one department, or as in the case of a peremptory discharge, when the department supervisor has taken action that puts the case out of range of the department steward.

If a grievance remains unsettled until it involves the top management of the company and the local (and, sometimes, international) union officers, it becomes a policy-*making* matter because of its company-wide implications. Every grievance ultimately must be settled. Over 90 percent of all American collective bargaining agreements provide for arbitration as the final means of settlement of grievances. However, many of these agreements specify that certain grievances are not arbitrable and, consequently, the strike remains as an alternative final policy-*making* step in the grievance procedure.

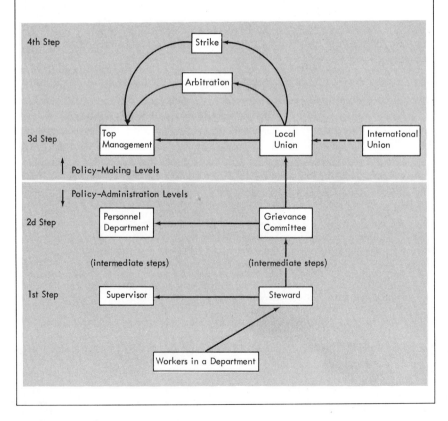

disagreement over routine affairs goes to the committee and a joint session. The joint sessions deal with accumulated grievances unsettled at lower levels in the enterprise and matters affecting the work force as a whole or sizable portions of it or affecting more than one work group. It would be safe to say that the two central administrative organs of management and the union, meeting together and discussing the various issues that arise from day to day manage, with goodwill, to clear up most of the misunderstandings that might affect operations, and deal with most of the instances of misapplication of the rules. As in all human affairs, however, questions do arise from time to time that have no easy administrative answers, and disagreement results. What happens now?

The management decision prevails.

Management is, after all, directly responsible for administration. When management says "No" to the union, and still says "No" after hearing all the arguments, that settles the question—at least for the time being. The grievance committee then has two choices: Take "No" for an answer and drop the issue or take the problem to the local union.

The local union decides whether to take an issue to arbitration or, if there is no arbitration clause in the agreement, to a strike; otherwise, again, the management decision stands. If it should choose either of these alternatives, the issue becomes a matter of *external* administration (arbitration) or renewed bargaining, backed by the strike.

The *arbitrator's* role, which the agreement creates, will be discussed below as part of the external administration of the rules.

EXTERNAL ADMINISTRATION

Before any grievance can be handled, the management and union must agree to a procedure for processing grievances. Regardless of differences in procedures for handling grievances, the methods of investigating grievances and the methods of settlement available to the parties are the same in handicraft and mass-production industry. In this chapter, we will be discussing general methods of grievance settlement. Our hypothetical grievance is drawn from mass-production industry and is handled through a factory grievance procedure.

Given the presence of legitimate and unforeseeable problems, what avenues for settlement are available to unions and management during the life of the contract? The possible methods of settlement here are just the same as the possible methods for settlement in negotiating a new contract. The critical difference between day-to-day problem settlement and contract renegotiation settlement is the different emphasis which the parties place on the alternative methods under the two sets of circumstances. Either type of dispute can be settled by: (1) arbitration—submitting the issues to an outside party who has been given authority to issue a binding decision, (2) mediation—asking a "friend of the family" to cool tempers and suggest methods of settlement which the parties may accept or reject, or (3) a strike, a lockout, or other resort to force.[4] Of course, none of these possibilities should be considered before both parties have done their best to settle their disagreement within the privacy of their own home.

It is very important to note that all three of these possibilities may be envisaged in the wording of a collective bargaining agreement. Nearly 90 percent of all collective bargaining agreements provide for arbitration as a final method of settling *some* disputes over the interpretation of their terms. At the same time, some of these *same* contracts clearly provide that certain disputes will *not* be settled by arbitration. For the items *not* subject to arbitration and *not* finally settled by the terms of the contract, the employer reserves the right to institute changes not agreeable to the union and the union reserves the right to strike. Even in the case of disputes not subject to arbitration because of *planned* loopholes in the arbitration section of the agreement, strikes are infrequent for several reasons. The infrequency of these strikes, the reasons for which will be discussed below, has caused some students to assume incorrectly that *any* strike during the life of an agreement is an unlawful strike or a strike in breach of the agreement. Many strikes during the life of an agreement are breaches of that agreement, but many are *not* breaches of the agreement because the agreement itself is an agreement to *strike* as the final method of settlement of a very few, but extremely important, kinds of disputes.

Dispute Settlement between the Parties by the Parties Themselves

A grievance is almost always an individual or group human problem. The agreement may define grievances in abstract terms as far as arbitrability goes, but in the day-to-day process of living together the grievances are a human problem. Union stewards' manuals on grievance processing usually contain statements such as the following:

> You can usually decide whether a complaint is a genuine grievance by asking yourself two questions:
> 1. Did the company violate the contract?
>   If the answer is "yes," you've got a grievance for sure.
> 2. Has the worker been treated unfairly by the company?
>   If the answer is "yes" to this question, you've probably got a grievance even though you're not sure that the contract has been violated. Sometimes this kind of grievance is hard to win, though, because of a loophole in the contract. When this happens, make a note that this clause in the contract should be improved at the next contract negotiations.[5]

---

[4] In private enterprises, the use of arbitration as a means of settling contract negotiation disputes is so exceptional that it must be noted lest it be overlooked. Strikes and mediation, instead of arbitration, are so infrequently used in agreement interpretation disputes that they must be noted lest they be overlooked as possibilities.

[5] Department of Education and Research, CIO. *The Shop Steward: Key to a Strong Union* (Washington, D.C.: CIO Publication no. 271, 1955), p. 21.

The human aspect of grievances is further borne out by company foremen's manuals. The variety of statements is too wide to present a representative quotation, but almost every manual emphasizes the supervisor's job of resolving grievances at early stages and *preventing* situations from arising which cause grievances. The company's preventive program is closely akin to the union's fairness program.

A worker *feels* the company has violated the contract or treated the worker unfairly. This is the beginning of a grievance. Maybe the company hasn't violated the contract or treated the worker unfairly; if one *feels* one has been treated unfairly we have an embryo grievance which can be run through the dispute-settlement process. Sometimes a union representative will "cook up" grievances for the purpose of embarrassing the company. Sometimes a company will work at creating unfair situations in the hope of provoking the union into a strike that the union can ill afford. But wherever the grievance really came from, its first obvious appearance is usually in a worker protest against some actual or alleged management action or inaction.

Assume, for simplicity of discussion, that Millie, a punch press operator, feels that the supervisor is violating the contract by instructing her to stack finished pieces in a new and time-consuming way on the cart used to take the pieces to the packing department. Millie claims that this is work "outside of my classification" and is a management speed-up. Since this is a grievance against the individual supervisor, Millie will probably take it to Joe, the union steward, as the first step. The worker tells the story to the steward.

The grievance is now in the lap of the steward. What does Joe do with it? The first thing any steward should do it get all the facts. Pertinent facts in this case would include such questions as:

1. When did the supervisor first give you orders to stack the pieces in a certain way?
2. Were similar *new* orders given to the other workers in your department?
3. How long has it been your practice to pile the pieces on the cart without stacking them in a certain way? Has the supervisor ever told you to stack them this new way before? When? Do the other workers stack them this new way?
4. What did you do in the past when you ran off more pieces than you had cart space for? Who picked up and piled this surplus on the next cart that came along?
5. What does the job description for this job say about preparing finished work for transfer? How do other departments with similar jobs handle the stacking problems?
6. Does the production standard or incentive wage rate for this job provide time allowances or money allowances for stacking?

7. What does the contract say about job reevaluations and changes in production standards?
8. By *actual observation*, what additional fatigue or effort does this new order impose on the worker?
9. What effect would the processing of this grievance have on the overall production of workers in the company? If the grievance were aired and we "lost" would the result be a general speed-up throughout the plant?

In processing the grievance, the steward may consider one other important fact: personal political position within the department and the union. If Joe is up for reelection, he may show little restraint in processing questionable grievances from potential political supporters. In a plant without a union-shop agreement, the steward may show a natural reluctance to energetically process grievances originating with "free riders." When the union is trying to soften up management for impending negotiations, a steward may even manufacture grievances. Stewards seldom refuse to process grievances, because the individual worker has the right to process a grievance through exclusively management channels. The steward can ill afford to refuse to process a grievance and have management later grant the individual worker's request for an adjustment. Having noted these possibilities, let us assume that our steward, Joe, has no political problems and judges this grievance to be fully justified by the facts and the collective bargaining agreement. His next move is the conference with Alice the supervisor.

As a general rule, a grievance is not reduced to writing before this conference is held. A steward might very well prepare for the discussion with the supervisor by outlining the grievance as it may ultimately be reduced to writing. This process clarifies the grievance in the steward's mind and may suggest further fruitful avenues for discussion. However, both the supervisor and the steward frequently prefer to talk it out before the formality of writing out the grievance. This talk before writing gives both sides flexibility in their thinking. If the grievance is clear and justified, both the union and the management profit from better feelings by settling it informally and with dispatch. In the conference with the supervisor, the steward requests redress for the alleged injustice.

Alice listens to Joe's request and asks whatever questions she deems necessary to fully understand the nature of the grievance. Both Alice and Joe are well advised to control their tempers. As supervisor, Alice usually postpones an answer to the steward until after reviewing the agreement and gathering facts about the situation. One of the critical facts which she considers is the opinion of higher management or the personnel department on what disposition should be made of this grievance. It is very important that the supervisor do this because any settlement made may be used later as a precedent in other departments.[6] After considering these facts, Alice delivers a decision to Joe. We shall assume that for a good reason she believes this grievance to be invalid and denies the request for an adjustment.

The grievance then moves up through higher echelons of the company and union organizations. We shall assume that our grievance goes through to the top echelon of the company and union organizations without a mutually satisfactory adjustment. What happens next?

Although increased interest has recently been shown in grievance mediation, this method of settling agreement interpretation disputes is still infrequently used. Grievance mediation occurs when the disputants ask an impartial outsider to suggest possible avenues for agreement. The mediator cools tempers, brings a fresh outlook to the dispute, and may propose perfectly acceptable means of agreement which the disputants overlooked. Grievance mediation seems to be uniquely appropriate when the same mediator has played an influential role in the negotiation of the agreement now in dispute. Although either or both of the disputants might for strategic or tactical reasons oppose resort to this method, when it is acceptable to the parties it is probably the *ideal* means of dispute settlement. In questions of agreement interpretation almost anything that the parties will agree to is preferable to a decision made by an outsider or resort to force. Failure in grievance mediation almost always results in a resort to arbitration or the use of force in achieving a settlement.

The final step, beyond company and union organizations, may be established by the terms of the collective bargaining agreement or improvised at the time of the deadlock. When face-to-face agreement proves impossible, what *other means* for grievance settlement are available to the parties?

Grievance Settlement by Means Other than Negotiation

Depending upon whether management or the union is the grievant, the nature of the grievance itself, and the provisions of the applicable collective bargaining agreement, the dispute may be settled by arbitration or the use

---

[6] In the period 1935–45 many managements, confronted with unionism for the first time, centralized all authority for labor relations matters at a high level. This was a natural, and probably necessary, reaction to militant unionism. Dealing with unions was a radical new departure and a few "experts" monopolized this activity in the management hierarchy. The union itself was a new challenge to the supervisor's authority, who was disillusioned when management met this outside challenge by stripping the supervisor's authority in labor relations. Once collective bargaining was established and management became competent in its practice, many managements began training supervisors in contract administration and restoring their authority in labor relations. At the present time, the main current of progressive management practice seems to be flowing in the direction of giving supervisors increased discretion in labor relations matters. Nevertheless, it is quite likely that consultation with higher management on many grievance settlements will remain a necessity because of their potential precedent-making character.

of force. We shall discuss the use of force before the much more commonly used method of arbitration. It must be repeated for emphasis that the vast majority of agreement interpretation disputes are settled by resort to peaceful voluntary arbitration.

Use of Force in Agreement Interpretation Disputes.   Both unions and managements occasionally use force as a means of settling their disputes over agreement interpretation or matters not specifically covered by the agreement. Sometimes, as in the case of strikes over nonarbitrable issues, they have agreed in advance to fight it out when disagreements arise. Other resorts to force, such as injunctions, law suits, and disciplinary actions against workers violating the terms of an agreement, result from inadequate advanced planning for handling certain particularly tough disagreements. It is an encouraging sign that resort to force seems to be a steadily declining practice because of increased responsibility in agreement observance by both unions and managements.

Five different forms of resort to force may be delineated: (1) strikes over nonarbitrable issues, (2) lawsuits by either managements, workers or unions to recover damages suffered as a result of alleged agreement violations, (3) injunctions sought by either managements, workers, or unions to prevent an anticipated breach of the agreement, (4) voiding a contract which has been breached, and (5) disciplinary action against workers who have engaged in strikes, slowdowns, sabotage, or other violations of a collective bargaining agreement. These instruments of force vary in the frequency with which they are used and their utility to each of the disputants.

When an agreement reserves the right to strike for the union over certain nonarbitrable issues during the life of the agreement, management may institute or continue the practice, e.g., higher production standards or a low wage rate on a new job, which the union considers objectionable. The union either "agrees" with the practice by continuing to work under these objectionable conditions or it disagrees by calling a strike. Although the strike power in this situation is a powerful instrument of persuasion, the union is usually extremely reluctant to enforce its claim for "justice." Typically nonarbitrable issues involve only a few workers at a single time. The union leader is frequently confronted with the prospect that hundreds of workers just won't respond to a strike call aimed at obtaining concessions for only a handful of workers. The risks of striking frequently are too great when compared to the possible gains obtainable from winning a strike over contract interpretation.

When workers engage in contract violations such as slowdowns or strikes, management may seek redress through the lockout. Like the strike, this method is seldom used because of the dangers inherent in its use. Although many collective bargaining agreements provide for the right of management to process grievances against the union, such grievances seldom arise except in the case of slowdowns or strikes in breach of the agreement. The infrequency of grievances against the union is due to the fact that management retains the power of initiative in most of the situations unforeseen or not agreed to at the time of negotiations.

Suits for damages and injunctions usually are considered to be the substitute of law for the exercise of force. We have classified them as resorts to force because the initiating party is seeking to enlist the coercive power of government to help it impose its will on the offending party. Enlisting the support of government is perfectly legitimate, but it tends to leave a scar on the collective bargaining relationship just like other resorts to force.

Both unions and managements have the legal right to sue the offending party for breach of contract. From the union viewpoint, there have been a few suits for damages in the case of "runaway" plants, violations of clauses limiting management's right to subcontract or "farm out" work normally performed within the bargaining unit, or for restitution in wage payment cases. From the company viewpoint, suits for damages are possible remedies for such things as boycotts, strikes in violation of the agreement, and slowdowns. Suits for damages are seldom used in present-day collective bargaining because both parties tend to view them as "divorce" actions.[7] Arbitration, strikes, or disciplinary actions against workers are often preferred over suits for damages and injunctions because they leave less severe long-term scars on the company-worker-union relationship.

Injunctions are available, under severely restricted conditions, to either unions or managements as a means of settling disputes over agreement interpretation. The injunction, which stops the threatened misapplication or breach of the agreement, is an *ideal* union remedy against runaway plants. From the management viewpoint, the injunction (if it is obeyed) is the *ideal* remedy for the wildcat strike in violation of a collective bargaining agreement.

When a union or a management misinterprets an agreement to the extent of violating its provisions, the offended party has the legal right to void the entire agreement. There are few recorded cases where this remedy has been used because its application usually results in an immediate strike, suit, or injunction. A hypothetical example may clarify the possible application of this remedy. Assume that a union engages in a strike in violation of the agreement. Management could then reduce wages, discontinue employee benefits, or deny union security on the ground that the whole agreement had been voided by the union's failure to abide by some of its terms.

In wildcat strikes, slowdowns, or sabotage in violation of a collective bargaining agreement, management may discharge or otherwise discipline the workers involved. The value of this remedy depends entirely upon

---

[7] It might be noted that many managements insist that the international union be made a signatory party to the collective bargaining agreement. One advantage of this procedure is that the larger financial resources of the international would be available for the satisfaction of any court-awarded financial damages. It seems likely that international unions' urgings of wildcat strikers to return to work are sometimes motivated by a fear of this consequence.

the individual circumstances. When all the workers are on strike, management's *practical* power to discipline even the strike instigators is severely limited if it wants to resume production promptly. In such cases, the union frequently protects the strike leaders by refusing to return to work until an agreement is worked out on disciplinary action. If the strike has solid support and the management strongly wants to resume production, the disciplinary measures against strike leaders may be bargained down to nothing. Mass disciplinary action against very large numbers of strikers or slowdown participants frequently is a practical impossibility since such managerial action would cause even further interruptions to production.

Before leaving these seldom-used methods, it might be well to note again that all of them involve the infliction of injury on one party by the other, sometimes assisted by government. These methods tend, therefore, to leave more or less enduring scars on the collective bargaining relationship. Arbitration is a process which settles the dispute without the unpleasantness of direct combat. Except where the issues are of vital importance to one or both of the parties, they usually prefer to settle their differences over contract interpretation without direct combat. This peaceful adjudication of disputes is our next topic.

Voluntary Arbitration: Peaceful Adjudication of Grievance Disputes

Our worker's grievance over stacking finished parts on the cart might very well be a strikeable issue under some collective bargaining agreements. However, we shall assume that like the vast majority of grievances it is not. Under the circumstances, the normal last step is voluntary arbitration. Usually the collective bargaining agreement itself establishes the broad outline of the procedure to be followed for arbitrating disputes over its interpretation.

In arbitration, the disputants ask an impartial person for a determination of the dispute on the basis of evidence and argument presented by them. The disputants agree in advance to accept the decision of the arbitrator as final and binding. Before discussing the preparation for, and conduct of, an arbitration hearing, we shall briefly note the procedural decisions which precede the hearing.

Procedural Arrangements for Arbitration. The company and the union must create an arbitration tribunal and submit their dispute to that tribunal before the case can be heard and a decision rendered. In writing their collective baragining agreement or later submitting their dispute to arbitration, they have several choices to make about procedural matters. There are several public and private organizations which will help them in handling these problems.

Creating an Arbitration Tribunal. Should a different tribunal be established for each dispute (ad hoc arbitration) or should a single tribunal be established to decide all disputes between the parties (umpire or permanent chairman system)? Ad hoc arbitration is most commonly used in small companies because of the infrequency of arbitration hearings. It has the important advantage of low procedural costs. Even where companies have only a few arbitrations per year, occasionally they establish an umpire system to give continuity to arbitration procedures and decisions. An umpire, like an ad hoc arbitrator, serves only so long as one is acceptable to both parties. The powers of the ad hoc arbitrator or umpire are detailed and limited by the terms of the collective bargaining agreement or the submission agreement.

Should the arbitration tribunal consist of a single impartial member or should representatives of the disputants also be members of the tribunal? An impartial one-member tribunal offers the advantage of a unanimous decision without compromising the position of either of the disputants or the impartial member. The disputants sometimes favor a tripartite tribunal as an opportunity to educate the impartial member in the full complexities of the dispute and to be certain that he considers all relevant facts and arguments. It may give both disputants a fuller understanding of the award than exists under a one-member tribunal. The tripartite tribunal has the disadvantage of frequently handing down only "majority" decisions. Even here, the impartial member may have to compromise his judgment of the issue in dispute to get a decision from the deadlocked tribunal. A tripartite tribunal may tend to shade off from arbitration into the field of mediation.

How is an impartial person selected as sole arbitrator or as a member of a tripartite tribunal? The disputants are free to select any person as their arbitrator so long as they both agree to his selection. Because labor arbitration is a process requiring complete impartiality, high intelligence, and a knowledge of the issues, unions and managements frequently solicit the assistance of public or private organizations in arranging for an arbitrator's services. The American Arbitration Association, a private nonprofit organization, the Federal Mediation and Conciliation Service, and several state mediation boards maintain rosters of professional arbitrators for selection by the disputants. These organizations supply information about the arbitrator's qualifications to the parties seeking an arbitrator's services.

The collective bargaining agreement itself frequently details the procedures to be followed in selecting an arbitration tribunal. A commonly used method is the standard arbitration clause of the American Arbitration Association:

> Any dispute, claim or grievance arising out of or relating to the interpretation or the application of this agreement shall be submitted to arbitration under the Voluntary Labor Arbitration of the American Arbitration Association. The parties further agree to accept the arbitrator's award as final and binding upon them.

This clause is supplemented by a statement providing for an impartial or tripartite tribunal.

When the American Arbitration Association clause is included in an agreement, either party may initiate arbitration proceedings by filing a Demand for Arbitration with the regional AAA office.

When a dispute arises between parties who are not subject to an arbitration clause, they may bring the matter to arbitration by means of a jointly signed statement setting forth the nature of the dispute and affirming their willingness to abide by the arbitrator's award. This statement is called a submission agreement. Submission agreements may also be used when a collective bargaining agreement terminates and the company and the union are unable to agree to new terms.

Selecting an Arbitrator. Selecting an arbitrator is somewhat like selecting a physician. Just as an ill person needs a physician *now*, the parties with an unresolved grievance need an arbitrator *now*. The minimum qualifications of a physician are reasonably easy to establish, but the selection of the *most* able physician is a tough problem for a medical society let alone an ill person. In selecting an arbitrator, the parties may get some help from government and private agencies as well as their trusted neighbors in management or the labor movement.

The use of the procedures of the Federal Mediation and Conciliation Service, the American Arbitration Association, or a State Mediation Board in selecting an arbitrator assures a timely arbitration hearing. Under these procedures, the management and union usually select their own arbitrator from lists submitted by the agency. If none of the arbitrators listed (on a "panel") is acceptable to one of the parties, the agency may designate an arbitrator to hear the case. Although agency designation of arbitrators is unusual, there must be some final power to appoint an arbitrator in order that neither party may void their arbitration agreement by unreasonable delays.

Arbitrators act in a quasi-judicial capacity. They should possess the judicial qualifications of fairness to both parties in order to render a faithful, honest, and disinterested opinion. They must lay aside all bias and approach the case with a mind open to conviction and without regard to any previously formed opinions as to the merits of the parties or the case. Their conduct must be free from even the inference that either party is the special recipient of favoritism. An arbitrator is expected to disqualify himself from any arbitration if he has any financial or personal interest in the result of the arbitration. Or herself; for there are many women arbitrators.

Any arbitrator on the panels of the American Arbitration Association, Federal Mediation and Conciliation Service, or State Mediation Board meets certain minimum standards of impartiality, acceptability, and professional competence. These agencies review the arbitrator's education, experience, and general reputation with management and unions. These minimum standards cannot be stated with exact precision. Although most arbitrators possess either law or other postgraduate degrees, some prominent arbitrators did not graduate from college. Arbitration experience cannot be an absolute requirement for membership on an arbitration panel since most arbitrators get their *first* cases by selection from panels. Industrial relations experience as a member of management might make an arbitrator unacceptable to unions, just as industrial relations experience as a union representative might make an arbitrator unacceptable to management. A *perfect* neutral, for example, a college professor or lawyer with no business, union, or arbitration experience, would be of little value as an arbitrator because of lack of vital knowledge of union-management practice.

Very frequently both the management and the union enter arbitration with the clear-cut goal of *winning* the case. If you want to win fairly, you are much more interested in how a specific arbitrator is likely to view your case than you are interested in that arbitrator's general reputation for impartiality. This very natural desire to win results in sometimes extensive investigations of arbitrators' backgrounds and awards. Employers' associations and unions frequently keep extensive records of arbitrators' awards which may be used by members in selecting the arbitrators most likely to lean either to the management or the union side.

The records on arbitrators kept by employers' associations and unions have both desirable and undesirable effects on the arbitration process. It is obviously desirable that both parties have access to detailed information on the qualifications of any arbitrator they might select. The best way to evaluate an arbitrator is by a careful review of awards. An undesirable effect of using records developed by either an employer's association or a union is that these records may be incomplete or inaccurate. Because not all arbitration awards are published, anyone building a record on an arbitrator is working with incomplete data. An obvious inaccuracy in interpretation would be a record based on a "box score": Arbitrator X who out of 20 cases decided 18 for management may be considered good or bad. Arbitrators can be judged fairly only on an evaluation of the full circumstances of each case.

It seems likely that the desire to *win* will remain as an important criterion for the selection of arbitrators in many collective bargaining relationships. Fortunately for the arbitration process, this attitude is not totally destructive because both parties must accept the arbitrator. Arbitrators who try to play a promanagement or a prounion game find themselves out of the arbitration business.

Preparing a Case for Arbitration. The American Arbitration Association suggests that companies and unions follow 10 steps in preparing a case for arbitration. These steps are:

1. Study the original statement of the grievance and review its history through every step of the grievance machinery.
2. Examine carefully the initiating papers (Submission or Demand) to determine the authority of the arbitrator. It might be found, for in-

stance, that while the original grievance contains many elements, the arbitrator, under the contract, is restricted to resolving only certain aspects.

3. Review the collective bargaining agreement from beginning to end. Often, clauses which at first glance seem to be unrelated to the grievance will be found to have some bearing on it.

4. Assemble all documents and papers you will need at the hearing. Where feasible, make photostatic copies for the arbitrator and the other party. If some of the documents you need are in the possession of the other party, ask that they be brought to the arbitration. Under some arbitration laws, the arbitrator has authority to subpoena documents and witnesses if they cannot be made available in any other way.

5. If you think it will be necessary for the arbitrator to visit the plant for on-the-spot investigation, make plans in advance. The arbitrator will have to be accompanied by representatives of both parties; it is also preferable that the Tribunal Clerk be present.

6. Interview all witnesses. Make certain they understand the whole case and particularly the importance of their own testimony within it.

7. Make a written summary of what each witness will prove. This will be useful as a checklist at the hearing, to make certain nothing is overlooked.

8. Study the case from the other side's point of view. Be prepared to answer the opposing evidence and arguments.

9. Discuss your outline of the case with others in your organization. A fresh viewpoint will often disclose weak spots or previously overlooked details.

10. Read as many articles and published awards as you can on the general subject matter in dispute. While awards by other arbitrators for other cases have no precedent value, they may help clarify the thinking of parties and arbitrators alike.[8]

If both parties have carefully followed these steps in preparing the case, the arbitration hearing is very likely to run smoothly and provide all the information the arbitrator needs to make a fair decision.

The Hearing.   The arbitrator has substantial latitude in establishing the time, place, and conduct of the hearing. An arbitrator's job is to give both sides full opportunity to introduce relevant evidence and argument and to decide the case upon due consideration of that evidence and argument. The arbitrator may ask whatever questions deemed necessary to the proper consideration of the dispute. All witnesses are subject to cross-examination. Both parties must try to convince the arbitrator of the justice of their positions.

The statements of the American Arbitration Association also provide adequate and concise guidance for the effective presentation of an arbitration case:

Every party approaching arbitration should be prepared with—

---

[8] American Arbitration Association, *Labor Arbitration: Procedures and Techniques* (New York: The Association, 1947), pp. 17–18.

1. An opening statement which clearly but briefly describes the controversy and indicates what must be proved. The opening statement lays the groundwork for witnesses and helps the arbitrator understand the relevance of testimony. For this reason it is frequently advisable that the opening statement be in writing, with a copy given to the arbitrator. This opening statement should also discuss the remedy sought.
2. Names of all witnesses in the order in which they will be called, together with a list of the points they are to cover. Questions should be brief and to the point, and witnesses should be instructed to direct their answers to the arbitrators.
3. A list of exhibits in the order in which they are to be introduced and a notation of what each is to establish. It speeds up proceedings considerably and never fails to make a good impression on the arbitrator when copies are available for distribution to all parties.
4. A closing statement. This should be a summation of evidence and arguments, and a refutation of what the other side has brought out.[9]

The American Arbitration Association also lists 10 common errors in presenting an arbitration case as follows:

1. Overemphasis and exaggeration of the grievance.
2. Reliance on a minimum of facts and a maximum of arguments.
3. Using arguments where witnesses or exhibits would better establish the facts.
4. Concealing essential facts; distorting the truth.
5. Holding back books, records, and other supporting documents.
6. Tying up proceedings with legal technicalities.
7. Introducing witnesses who have not been properly instructed on demeanor and on the place of their testimony in the entire case.
8. Withholding full cooperation from the arbitrator.
9. Disregarding the ordinary rules of courtesy and decorum.
10. Becoming involved in arguments with the other side. The time to try to convince the other party was before arbitration, during grievance processing. At the arbitration hearing, all efforts should be concentrated on convincing the arbitrator.[10]

Before closing the hearing, the arbitrator determines the wishes of the parties concerning posthearing briefs and arranges for their submission through a neutral party. The parties do not communicate directly with the arbitrator except when both sides are present. The hearing is closed and the arbitrator considers the evidence and issues an award.

The Award. In the case of tripartite tribunals there may be some difficulty in preparing an award. If a deadlock seems likely, the union and management members of the Board of Arbitration may authorize the impartial member to write an award without their concurrence. Failing to achieve this sort of an arrangement, the impartial member may have to compromise judgment of the dispute in order to achieve a majority opinion. We shall

---

[9] Ibid., pp. 18–19.
[10] Ibid., pp. 18–19.

assume that our case is heard by a single impartial arbitrator, thereby avoiding this difficulty.

In writing an award, the arbitrator considers the content of the agreement, the practice of the parties, and the evidence and arguments presented at the hearing in exhibits and briefs. The arbitrator usually defers to the wishes of the parties in the form of the award. A simple statement of findings and the action required by the decision is an adequate award. In our hypothetical case, an award might read: "Machine operators are required to stack finished work on carts for movement to the packing department in the way presently directed by supervision. The grievance claiming that such work is 'out of classification' is without merit and is denied." However, at the request of the parties. arbitrators usually will summarize the pertinent evidence and arguments, their findings, and the reasoning used to reach a decision. As a rule, the parties want the arbitrator to give them a reasonably detailed award. Such an award, often running to as many as 20 typewritten pages, may be more useful to the parties in their future relationships.

Once the award is delivered the matter is settled. It is no longer a bone of contention between the parties and they can get back to the business of living together. If the award is unsatisfactory, they usually can negotiate a more satisfactory arrangement in their next agreement. The arbitrator has enabled both sides to talk the matter out and alone is responsible for the results of the award. Either the management or the union or both may be angry about the award, but they should not be angry with each other about it.

Voluntary arbitration deserves much more detailed discussion than it has been given here because it makes a major contribution to harmonious union-management relations.[11] In a few cases, unions and managements have been so satisfied with grievance arbitration that they have adopted voluntary arbitration as a means of settling disputes in contract negotiations. On the other hand, some unions and managements have used arbitration as a means of harassing each other. The act of arbitration may be evidence of good or bad faith. In general, experience with grievance arbitration is a most encouraging sign of increasing trust and mutual respect on the part of American unions and managements. To the authors of this book, an even more encouraging sign is the effort of both parties to avoid arbitration by working hard at settling their disagreements within the grievance procedure. Both of these trends are optimistic signs for the future of collective bargaining.

---

[11] Students are urged to read from the bibliography at the end of this chapter. Three books, Copelof's *Management-Union Arbitration*, Elkouri's *How Arbitration Works*, and Stone's *Labor-Management Contracts at Work*, are especially recommended. Frequent references to the proceedings of the annual meetings of the National Academy of Arbitrators are made throughout this book. These proceedings offer an insight on current issues in labor arbitration and recent research findings.

The Legal Environment of Arbitration.   Although labor arbitration is a quasi-judicial process, it is not governed by a comprehensive code of law. There is no United States Labor Arbitration Act, although such legislation has been advocated by the influential National Academy of Arbitrators. Several states have labor arbitration statutes, but these laws provide only minimal guidance to the conduct of arbitration. In decisions in 1957 and 1960, the U.S. Supreme Court has taken the first steps in fashioning a federal law of labor arbitration from the public policy statements contained in the Labor-Management Relations Act of 1947.

The arbitrator derives power from the agreement of the parties to submit a dispute (or disputes generally) for decision. Arbitrators operate within the specific or general rules established by the parties in their agreement to utilize arbitration services. In several states, they are given the added legal authority to subpoena witnesses if needed to decide the issues. In all cases, the courts will set aside an award if there is evidence that it was influenced by corruption, fraud, or other undue means. In some cases, the courts will set aside an award if it is clear that it exceeds the authority vested in the arbitrator by the parties.

The law of arbitration becomes a vital issue when one of the parties refuses to submit an issue to arbitration on the grounds that the issue is not arbitrable under the terms of the agreement to arbitrate. Although such refusals to arbitrate are indeed rare, either party could emasculate an arbitration agreement if it were allowed to be the sole judge of the meaning of the agreement.

The federal law of arbitration which the Supreme Court is fashioning from the public policy statements of the Labor-Management Relations Act deals with the question of arbitrability. Four Supreme Court decisions must be mentioned in a discussion of labor arbitration. In 1957 in the case of *Textile Workers Union of America* v. *Lincoln Mills,* the Supreme Court ruled that federal courts were empowered by Section 301(a) of the Labor-Management Relations Act of 1947 to order specific performance of an agreement to arbitrate grievance disputes. In the cases of *United Steelworkers of America* v. *American Manufacturing Company, United Steelworkers of America* v. *Warrior and Gulf Navigation Company,* and *United Steelworkers of America* v. *Enterprise Wheel and Car Corporation,* decided in 1960, the Supreme Court dealt in some detail with questions of arbitrability of grievances in different situations.

In the *Lincoln Mills* case, the employer refused to submit to arbitration grievances involving work assignments and work loads under a collective bargaining agreement which provided for abitration as the terminal step in the grievance procedure.[12] The Supreme Court ruled that the Norris–La Guardia Act does not withdraw the jurisdiction of federal courts to require specific performance of an agreement to arbitrate grievance disputes.

---

[12] 353 U.S. 448.

Before the Cout ruled in this case, the employer had ceased to do business so the questions of job assignments and work loads were held to be moot. However, the Court ruled that monetary damages to the employees who grieved were not moot.

In *American Manufacturing*, the union sought to force the arbitration of the claim of one Sparks that he was eligible for recall to his job after an absence due to a work injury. Sparks had accepted a settlement for the work injury based on a permanent partial disability. The District Court held that Sparks, having accepted this settlement on the basis of a disability, was estopped to claim any seniority or employment rights. The Circuit Court of Appeals upheld the District Court on the grounds that Sparks' grievance was "a frivolous, patently baseless one, not subject to arbitration under the collective bargaining agreement." The pertinent provisions of the agreement were: (1) provision for arbitration of all disputes between the parties "as to the meaning, interpretation and application of the provisions of this agreement," (2) managerial authority to suspend or discharge "for cause," and (3) the requirement that the employer employ and promote employees on the principle of seniority "where ability and efficiency are equal." The Supreme Court reversed the lower courts and ordered arbitration of Sparks' grievance. The Supreme Court commented that, "when the judiciary undertakes to determine the merits of a grievance under the guise of interpreting the grievance procedure of collective bargaining agreements, it usurps a function which . . . is entrusted to the arbitration tribunal."

In *Warrior and Gulf Navigation*, the union sought to force the arbitration of a grievance arising from the subcontracting of work. The agreement contained a general abitration clause and a provision that "matters which are strictly a function of management shall not be subject to arbitration." The employer refused arbitration of the grievance, and the union sued in District Court to require arbitration. The District Court dismissed the union's complaint after hearing evidence that the agreement did not "confide in an arbitrator the right to review the defendant's business judgment in contracting out work." The Circuit Court affirmed, finding that contracting out fell within the exception of "matters which are strictly a function of management." The Supreme Court reversed the lower courts and ordered that the dispute be submitted to arbitration. The Supreme Court found: "whether contracting out in the present case violated the agreement is the question. It is a question for the arbitrator, not for the courts."

In *Enterprise Wheel and Car Corporation*, the union sought judicial enforcement of an arbitrator's award of reinstatement and back pay to employees who had engaged in a wildcat strike. The District Court ordered the employer to comply with the arbitrator's award. On appeal, the Court of Appeals held that the award was unenforceable because it included back pay subsequent to the termination of the agreement and that the expiration of the agreement made the order of reinstatement unenforceable. The Supreme Court agreed with the Court of Appeals that the arbitrator's award of back pay was ambiguous. However, the Supreme Court ruled that an ambiguity in the award did not render the award unenforceable. The Supreme Court remanded the case to the District Court for proceedings "so that the amount due to employees may be definitely determined by arbitration."

The brevity of the foregoing summaries of leading Supreme Court decisions in intentional. The meaning of these cases will be argued in law journals and court proceedings for some years to come. Our single conclusion from these cases is that the Supreme Court has given arbitrators very substantial discretion in deciding the question of arbitrability *within the provisions of the agreement to arbitrate*. If the parties wish to reduce this discretion, it is within their power to agree to arbitration procedures which accomplish their mutual objective.

Drawbacks of Arbitration

For all its usefulness, unions and managers have found that there are some disadvantages to conventional arbitration. Mainly, they complain that it is slow, costly, and cumbersome.

It is slow because the arbitrator or arbitration panel have to schedule hearings and other activities that involve busy people with other claims on their time. The case that goes from filing to an award in less than three months is exceptional; delays of all sorts have dragged some cases out, literally, for years. There is an old saying: Justice delayed is justice denied. At any rate, long-delayed decisions tend to lose whatever corrective value they might have had for the people who started the issue.

Conventional arbitration is costly because it usually involves professional people and high-placed officials on both sides, not to mention the arbitrator, who charges a fee. It may cost the parties several thousand dollars just for the record of a hearing; and further expense if one or both sides files a brief.

On top of all this, one or both sides sometimes feels as if they had been trying to swat flies with a baseball bat: all this trouble and expense, and portentous machinery brought to bear on trivialities. Not every arbitration is an important precedent-setter.

These drawbacks of conventional arbitration have given rise to streamlined new procedures called "expedited" arbitration.

Expedited Arbitration

For grievance settlement over lesser issues, unions and the managements with which they deal have begun to turn toward more rapid and less complicated procedures. The postal service and union led the way because of the huge backlog of unadjusted grievances that helped precipitate their historic 1970 strike. In 1971 the steelworker union and steel companies tried the experiment, and other managements and unions have followed.

In essence, expedited arbitration dispenses with cumbersome courtroom procedures. A single special arbitrator hears a number of cases in sequence on the same day. Company and union representatives rather than lawyers make brief statements on the facts in each case, and the arbitrator gives a decision, within 48 hours; often immediately. There is no provision for appeal; and while the proceedings may be put on tape, there is no written record.

Thus far, the parties using expedited arbitration seem to be satisfied with its speed, simplicity, and economy, which help make up for what appears to be its arbitrary nature. None have abandoned the conventional method. They reserve the full-scale procedures for the more important issues, such as precedent-setting contract interpretation, and cases involving discharge.

SUMMARY

In this chapter we have discussed the problems of administering the collective bargaining agreement. Agreement administration is of vital importance to the parties because actions speak louder than words and the word of the agreement frequently must be somewhat imprecise.

The key roles in agreement administration are played by supervisors and stewards in their day-to-day activities. When the parties are unable to agree as to the meaning of their agreement or the proper application of their agreement to a particular set of facts and circumstances, they may use either force or voluntary arbitration to resolve their differences. In some disputes, the parties specifically reserve to themselves the right to resort to economic force. Much more commonly today the parties are placing greater reliance on voluntary arbitration to settle agreement interpretation disputes. Recent court decisions have the effect of encouraging the parties to make use of arbitration.

QUESTIONS FOR DISCUSSION

1. What are the functions of an arbitrator?
2. How can the parties to collective bargaining minimize the use of arbitration?
3. What is the legal status of an arbitrator's award?
4. How would you go about selecting an arbitrator from a panel of five provided by the American Arbitration Association?
5. Discuss the importance of preparation for arbitration on the part of both unions and management.

APPENDIX: SIGNIFICANT COURT DECISIONS ON ARBITRATION[13]

Role of Arbitration

The courts have established a national labor policy in favor of arbitration, the voluntary method of resolving grievances. In a series of cases commonly referred to as the "steelworkers trilogy," the Supreme Court established rules concerning grievance arbitration. The court said that there is a presumption that a matter is within the arbitration clause of a contract. If one party refuses to abide by the agreement to arbitrate, the other party is entitled to seek an order to require arbitration. The arbitrator and not the courts has the major responsibility for determining the scope of the arbitration clause. While the courts will review the decision of the arbitrator, the courts are not entitled to substitute their judgment for the judgment of the arbitrator merely because they disagree. (*United Steelworkers* v. *American Manufacturing Co.*, 363 U.S. 564 (1960); *United Steelworkers* v. *Warrior & Gulf Navigation Co.*, 363 U.S. 574 (1960); *United Steelworkers* v. *Enterprise Wheel and Car Corp.*, 363 U.S. 593 (1960).)

The presumption of arbitrability also applies to safety grievances between miners and coal mine operators when the contract provides for comprehensive arbitration. Neither federal legislation on mine safety nor the unique aspects of safety questions overcome the presumption. (*Gateway Coal Company* v. *United Mine Workers*, 94 Supreme Court 629 (1974).)

In instances of alleged racial discrimination, where the contract contains antidiscrimination provisions, an adequate arbitration clause, and the parties are willing to arbitrate, an individual employee is bound to arbitrate the dispute rather than engage in individual picketing against the employer. If the individual does picket, without arbitration, the employer does not violate the NLRA by disciplining or discharging the employee. (*Emporium Capwell Co.*, v. *Western Addition Community Organization*, 95 Supreme Court 977 (1975).)

In view of the importance given to the processes of arbitration, the NLRB has adopted a rule that defers a complainant's statutory rights in unfair labor practice complaints until after arbitration under the private grievance-arbitration machinery provided in the contract has been invoked. This rule applies when the unfair labor practice alleged revolves mainly around the meaning of the contract wording. Among the conditions necessary to defer the statutory rights are the following; the issue involves the special knowledgeability of the arbitrator; there has been a long and successful collective bargaining relationship; there is no evidence that the employer is trying to undermine the union; the arbitrator's decision will resolve both the unfair labor practice charge and the contractual issue in a manner compatible with the NLRA. The NLRB will retain limited jurisdiction to insure a timely decision, fair and regular procedures, and a result not repugnant to the Act. (*Collyer Insulated Wire*, 192 NLRB No. 150.) Extensive guidelines on the application of *Collyer* have been promulgated.

Section 8-a-1 protects an employee who requests union assistance at an investigative interview before a grievance is filed with the employer where the em-

---

[12] This appendix contributed by Professor Donald W. Brodie of the University of Oregon Law School.

ployee reasonably believes disciplinary action may result. (*NLRB* v. *J. Weingarten, Inc.*, 95 Supreme Court 959 (1975).)

SELECTED ANNOTATED BIBLIOGRAPHY

AHNER, C. W. "Arbitration: A Management Viewpoint." In *The Arbitrator and the Parties*, JEAN T. McKELVEY, ed. *Proceedings of the Eleventh Annual Meeting of the National Academy of Arbitrators*. Washington, D.C.: The Bureau of National Affairs, 1958, pp. 76–87. Discussion by Maurice S. Trotta, pp. 87–92.

Ahner urges the more widespread use of tripartite mediation as a substitute for arbitration, the simplification of awards, and arbitrators making themselves available to the parties to explain their awards and to educate foremen and stewards on the agreement and its operation. Trotta disagrees with the proposition that arbitrators should shift from arbitration to mediation as the situation dictates and that "education" on lost awards is almost hopeless.

ALEXANDER, GABRIEL N. "Impartial Umpireships: The General Motors-UAW Experience." In *Arbitration and the Law*, JEAN T. McKELVEY, ed. *Proceedings of the Twelfth Annual Meeting of the National Academy of Arbitrators*. Washington, D.C.: The Bureau of National Affairs, 1959, pp. 108–51. Discussion by Joseph E. Shister and Sylvester Garrett, pp. 151–60.

Alexander, who served as GM-UAW Umpire from 1948 to 1954, discusses the history of the umpireship, the operation of the system, and appraises its successes and failures. Based on personal experience, previously unavailable information supplied by the parties, and extensive interviews with the umpires, this paper is the first of a series of monographs on umpire systems prepared for the National Academy of Arbitrators. Shister emphasizes the uniqueness of the GM-UAW experience as contrasted with ad hoc arrangements. Garrett emphasizes the importance of ideas and personalities in developing a constructive system of arbitration.

———. "Evaluation of Arbitrators: An Arbitrator's Point of View." In *The Arbitrator and the Parties*, JEAN T. McKELVEY, ed. *Proceedings of the Eleventh Annual Meeting of the National Academy of Arbitrators*. Washington, D.C.: The Bureau of National Affairs, 1958, pp. 93–100. Discussion by James C. Hill, pp. 100–110.

Alexander comments on the failure of labor and management to formulate objective and realistic criteria for the evaluation of arbitrators. Hill discusses the pros and cons of publishing arbitration awards.

BAER, WALTER E. *Practice and Precedent in Labor Relations*. Lexington, Mass.: D.C. Health, 1972.

The author analyzes numerous arbitration cases and negotiating issues which deal with "past practice."

BAMBRICK, JAMES J., JR., and SPEED, JOHN J. *Grievance Procedures in Nonunionized Companies*. New York: National Industrial Conference Board Studies in Personnel Policy no. 109, 1950.

Discusses the problem of grievance handling in nonunion companies.

BRODIE, DONALD W. "Antidiscriminating Clauses and Grievance Processes." Labor Law Journal, June, 1974, pp. 352–379.

Discusses how well traditional arrangements are responding to new issues posed by civil rights laws, as evidenced in arbitration and court cases.

Cox, Archibald. "Rights under a Labor Agreement," *Harvard Law Review,* vol. 69 (February 1956), pp. 601–57.

Suggests that union and employer should be permitted to specify in their agreement whether the union or individual employees should have the authority to settle claims or sue the employer. When no specific intent is specified in the agreement, Professor Cox would have the courts apply presumptions, based on the nature of the agreement, as to whether the union or individuals have the right to sue.

De Vyver, Frank T. "Labor Arbitration after Twenty-Five Years," *Southern Economic Journal,* vol. 28 (January 1962), pp. 235–45.

The author's presidential address to the 1961 conference of the Southern Economic Association considers the position of management under the present system of grievance arbitration; how management decision making is affected by arbitration; and suggests alternatives to arbitration.

Elkouri, Frank, and Elkouri, Edna A. *How Arbitration Works.* 3d ed., Washington, D.C.: Bureau of National Affairs, 1973.

The authors discuss the scope of arbitration, arbitration tribunals, arbitrability, interpretive standards, the burden of proof, precedent, and the issues involved in arbitration cases.

Fairley, Lincoln. "Area Arbitration in the West Coast Longshore Industry," *Labor Law Journal,* vol. 22, no. 9 (September 1971).

A description of how "instant" or on-the-spot arbitration operates in West Coast longshore.

Fischer, Ben. "The Steel Industry's Expedited Arbitration: The Judgment after Two Years," *Arbitration Journal,* vol. 28, no. 3 (September 1973).

The United Steelworkers' Director of Contract Administration examines the steel industry's experience with expedited arbitration, which was implemented to avoid the costs, complexities, and delays of "deluxe" arbitration, and issues a relatively favorable verdict.

Fleming, R. W. "Some Problems of Evidence before the Labor Arbitrator," *Michigan Law Review,* vol. 60 (December, 1961), pp. 133–68.

Considers the procedures and processes that have evolved for the protection of the parties in arbitration. Based on arbitrators' replies to hypothetical case situations.

Fleming, Robben W. *Labor Arbitration Process.* Urbana: University of Illinois Press, 1965.

Reviews the growth and development of grievance arbitration and makes recommendations for some of its current problems: costs, time lag, and formality; predictability; individual rights; and problems of evidence and procedural regularity.

Givens, Richard A. "Responsibility of Individual Employees for Breaches of No-Strike Clauses," *Industrial and Labor Relations Review,* vol. 14 (July, 1961), pp. 595–600.

Considers the following questions: Is it wise for employers to bring damage actions against individual employee conduct in a wildcat strike? Do such suits for damages conflict with national labor policies? And is legislation to bar individual damage suits desirable when employees peacefully participate in a strike?

HAYS, PAUL R. *Labor Arbitration: A Dissenting View.* New Haven: Yale University Press, 1966.

A distinguished arbitrator roundly criticizes arbitration and arbitrators in a book that caused considerable controversy within the arbitration profession.

JENSEN, VERNON H. "Dispute Settlement in the New York Longshore Industry," *Industrial and Labor Relations Review,* vol. 18 (July 1957), pp. 588–608.

Discusses reasons for recent reduction in wildcat strikes on the New York waterfront and the emerging system for grievance settlement.

KAGEL, SAM. *Anatomy of a Labor Arbitration.* Washington, D.C.: Bureau of National Affairs, 1961.

A "how to do it" volume on preparing for and participating in arbitration proceedings. Principles are illustrated through analysis of an actual arbitration.

KUHN, JAMES. *Bargaining in Grievance Settlement.* New York: Columbia University Press, 1961.

Kuhn's thesis is that the grievance procedure is more than a judicial procedure; it is a way of extending collective bargaining to the lowest organizational levels. The contract becomes the rule for rule-making in the grievance arena of bargaining. Conclusions based on study of grievance process in rubber industry.

LYTHGOE, R. F. "On Improving Arbitration: The Transcript Trauma," *Monthly Labor Review,* vol. 97, no. 6 (June 1974).

A union representative decries the length and complexity of grievance arbitration proceedings, with special condemnation aimed at the verbatim transcripts which he sees as one of the prime culprits contributing to excessive legalism.

McPHERSON, WILLIAM H. "Grievance Mediation under Collective Bargaining," *Industrial and Labor Relations Review,* vol. 9 (January 1956), pp. 200–212.

Discusses increasing use of grievance mediation in U.S.

NORTHRUP, HERBERT R., and KAHN, MARK L. "Railroad Grievance Machinery: A Critical Analysis, I and II," *Industrial and Labor Relations Review,* vol. 5 (April, July 1955), pp. 365–82; pp. 540–49.

Discusses and evaluates the unique system of grievance adjustment on U.S. railroads.

PRASOW, PAUL, and PETERS, EDWARD. *Arbitration and Collective Bargaining: Conflict Resolution in Labor Relations.* New York: McGraw Hill, Inc., 1970.

The most comprehensive current analysis of the operation of the grievance-arbitration process in print. Relates the process to contract negotiations, labor, and most importantly the decision-making framework used by American arbitrators.

SEGAL, ROBERT M. "Arbitration: A Union Viewpoint." Chap. 2 in *The Arbitrator and the Parties,* JEAN T. McKELVEY, ed. *Proceedings of the Eleventh Annual Meeting of the National Academy of Arbitrators.* Washington, D.C.: The Bureau of National Affairs, 1958, pp. 47–70. Discussion by Lewis M. Gill, pp. 70–75.

Segal discusses a number of criteria used by unions in evaluating arbitrations and the relationship of arbitration of the courts. Gill comments on Segal's list of reasons for "blacklisting" of arbitrators by unions, i.e., mediating when the parties don't want mediation, excessively long and involved opinions, excessive citation of outside decisions, and slowness in the issuance of decisions.

SLICHTER, SUMNER H.; HEALY, JAMES J.; and LIVERNASH, E. ROBERT. The *Impact of Collective Bargaining on Management*. Washington, D.C.: Brookings Institution, 1960.

Special attention is invited to the following chapters: 23, "The Problem of Grievances"; 24, "Adjustment of Grievance"; 25, "The Grievance Arbitration Process"; and 26, "Arbitration and the Bargaining Relationship."

SMITH, RUSSELL A. "The Question of 'Arbitrability'—The Roles of the Arbitrator, the Court, and the Parties," *Southwestern Law Journal*, vol. 16 (April 1962), pp. 1–42.

A penetrating analysis of the 1960 Supreme Court decisions and their impact on the courts, arbitrators, and the parties to arbitration.

SMITH, RUSSELL A., and JONES, DALLAS L. "Management and Labor Appraisals and Criticisms of the Arbitration Process: A Report with Comments," *Michigan Law Review*, vol. 62 (May 1964).

Two labor law scholars empirically examine the impact of the Supreme Court's *Trilogy* decisions and other cases on a sample of union and management representatives, with a large majority of the respondents favoring arbitration over such alternatives as a labor court and the application of economic muscle.

SMITH, RUSSELL A.; MERRIFIELD, LEROY S.; and ROTHSCHILD, DONALD P. *Collective Bargaining and Labor Arbitration*. Indianapolis: Bobbs-Merrill, 1970.

A very detailed examination of the processes of collective bargaining and arbitration, with emphasis on the subject matter of arbitration cases.

SOMERS, GERALD G. *Grievance Settlement in Coal Mining*. Morgantown: West Virginia University, Business and Economic Studies, vol. 4, no. 4, 1956.

A statistical review of the procedures, subject matter, level of settlement, and disposition of 970 grievance cases heard between 1933 and 1954 in bituminous coal mining.

SOVERN, MICHAEL I. "When Should Arbitrators Follow Federal Law?" In *Arbitration and the Expanding Role of Neutrals*, GERALD G. SOMERS and BARBARA D. DENNIS, eds. *Proceedings of the Twenty-Third Annual Meeting of the National Academy of Arbitrators*. Washington, D.C.: Bureau of National Affairs, 1970.

A discussion of grievance cases in which an arbitrator is asked to base his decision on a statute or other source of law instead of on the collective bargaining agreement.

SPELFOGEL, EVAN J. "Wildcat Strikes and Minority Concerted Activity—Discipline, Damage Suits and Injunctions," *Labor Law Journal*, vol. 24, no. 9 (September 1973).

The author examines the use of wildcat strikes during the life of the agreement and how they are treated by the NLRB and the courts.

U.S. DEPARTMENT OF LABOR, BUREAU OF LABOR STATISTICS. *Monthly Labor Review*, vol. 95, no. 11 (November 1972).

This issue contains a collection of articles under the heading of "New Directions in Grievance Handling and Arbitration," including reports on expedited arbitration, mediation-arbitration, and the training of arbitrators.

Woodcock. Leonard. "Problem Areas in Arbitration." Chap. 4 in *Arbitration and the Law*, Jean T. McKelvey, ed. *Proceedings of the Twelfth Annual Meeting of the National Academy of Arbitrators*. Washington, D.C.: Bureau of National Affairs, 1959, pp. 90–97.

A then UAW vice president discusses the need for a more detailed study of arbitrators and arbitrators' awards, more adequate training of the parties in case preparation and presentation, and the rising costs of arbitration.

14 Unions of Professionals and White Collar Workers

MANUAL WORKERS and their organizations dominated the preceding chapters of this book. In this chapter the professionals and white collar workers take center stage. They differ from manual workers and from each other in the *occupational roles* they take on in an organization. They differ, that is, in their relationship to work place technology.

They differ in other ways that are important perhaps to the sociologist, economist, or political scientist—outlook and ideology, life styles and spending patterns, voting habits, etc.—but in this chapter we're not going to try to define their total social role. Instead we'll analyze (as we did with the manual worker) the roles of white collar workers and professionals in the industrial relations system. We'll use the same analytical tools that served so well to clarify the traditional bargaining system; that is, the Dunlop framework first set forth in Chapter 1 but called into service throughout the book, and the Chapter 8 analysis of the substantive issues dealt with in collective bargaining.

Who are the white collar workers? Broadly speaking, they are the office staff and sales personnel of an organization. In a manufacturing company they are those who do *not* work directly on production or maintenance. In a service organization they may include those who carry out operations (as in a bank) or provide professional services (as in a school). Managers are white collar workers, but differ from nonmanagers by virtue of their role in the organization and by law. Professionals are also white collar workers, but differ from nonprofessionals in ways to be dealt with in some detail later in this chapter. All the rest—a heterogeneous crew—wear that figurative white collar without other adornment. By analogy with manual workers, professionals correspond to skilled craftsmen; nonmanagerial white collar workers, to the semiskilled.

The framers of labor relations law did not exclude professionals or white collar workers from its protection and benefits unless they happened to be managers or supervisors. They were just as free as manual workers to form and join unions and to engage in collective bargaining, and could call on the services of the NLRB. Many white collar workers (like the railway clerks and telephone company employees) did in fact unionize and some have been bargaining for half a century or more. Others (like bank clerks and general office employees) tended to hold back and remain largely unorganized.

Professionals, in contrast, are and have long been very well organized, but not for collective bargaining. Large numbers of them (like doctors and lawyers) are self-employed and so do not—in fact, cannot—bargain collectively, for they would be bargaining with themselves. Others, employed professionals like nurses and teachers, have turned to collective bargaining only recently.

White Collar Roles

White collar workers turn out no tangible product except the words and figures on paper that symbolize an organization's transactions. Unlike professionals, ordinary white collar wokers bring to their jobs only such special skills or knowledge as a person can acquire in a conventional education (with perhaps some business courses) but on the job they develop expertise. Collectively, they learn how to make *that organization* go; individually they become experts (humble or great) in some part of its particular operations. As the saying goes, they "learn the ropes." In this they resemble, by analogy, the nonskilled factory worker who has no trade but learns to perform the tasks demanded by operations and develops expertise in their performance. The main difference is that the white collar tasks are mental rather than manual.

People in white collar roles usually have to use their heads more than their hands. The tasks they are called on to perform are more often transactions with people than with mere things. That is, an organization expects its manual workers to produce uniform results by working upon or with materials—parts machined to close tolerances, processes carried out to standard specifications—but expects its white collar workers to respond differently, with the appropriate behavior, to change and variety. Every letter an executive composes, for example, or a secretary types, is in some way unique; even a form letter goes out to different addresses, and if sent out by computer—well, someone has to program the computer. While it is true that some white collar roles require very little discretion, many demand enterprise, initiative, ingenuity, imagination, and the highest quality of mental effort. People in white collar roles serve an organization by doing its paperwork, but also by doing its thinking and planning, its internal and external communicating, its recording and remembering; they make up two of the three kinds of staff personnel.[1]

----

[1] See Chapter 4.

From all this it might be expected that when nonmanager white collar workers unionize they would follow the industrial union model; and in fact, they do. Having no special skills but practicing a highly differentiated expertise in the operations of a common employer, they organize on the basis of work place or employing organization. They form white collar *industrial* unions. And just as a factory local will take in skilled workers in a maintenance gang, the white collar local may take in the few full-time professionals working for the same employer. White collar locals may also admit manual workers—or vice versa, the manual worker local may admit white collar members working for the same employer—when together they would make an appropriate bargaining unit.

White Collar Organizations

Two kinds of organization have in the past given white collar workers the opportunity to join with their co-workers toward the ends associated with collective bargaining: (1) *unions*, affiliated with organized labor, and (2) unaffiliated *associations*.

Unions. White collar unions seem to be most successful in the service industries, and in manufacturing when there is an allied, or at least friendly manual worker union in the enterprise. One of the powerful railway unions, for instance, was the Brotherhood of Railway Clerks, which today also claims jurisdiction over airline and steamship clerks, freight handlers, express and station employees. The Communications Workers of America, AFL–CIO, takes in the manual and white collar employees of the telephone companies that span the continent. Not so successful have been the white collar unions that tried to organize general office workers, banks and insurance companies, scattered from coast to coast.

The Newspaper Guild, affiliated with the AFL–CIO, bargains for office workers and reporters alongside printer unions bargaining for the back shop. One of these former printer unions, the mailers, has in fact merged with the Guild. Office workers in enterprises organized by the Teamsters often join the local, or set up a Teamster local of their own. In some manufacturing plants organized by the UAW the office workers have their own, separate UAW local; this is a common pattern.

More often, it seems, in manufacturing organizations with a strong manual worker union the white collar workers find it more to their advantage *not* to unionize. Management grants raises and makes other concessions "in tandem" with what they grant the union. In effect, therefore, the union bargains for the white collar workers as well as for themselves.[2] This doesn't give the union a strong motive for trying to organize the office workers. Even though they are in a sense free riders, they pose no such direct threat to union security as would free riders in the factory unit.

---

[2] See Case No. 5.

Associations.   Unaffiliated associations of white collar workers arose early in the public sector, but have always been rare in private industry. If they weren't company unions to begin with, they had a hard time organizing, and remained ineffectual unless and until they affiliated with some bona fide international union, and so changed categories. Unlike public sector organizations, which were permitted to lobby and bring influence to bear at levels above the employing agency, unaffiliated associations had to grapple with a management active and all-powerful at the work place.

Professional Roles

The word "professional" is all too loosely used. In one sense it merely connotes a person's occupation: a professional entertainer, football player, burglar, soldier. The professional entertainer may be a sword swallower in a carnival or the star of a dozen box office hits; the professional soldier a private or a general. What makes them professionals in this sense of the word is their attachment to a particular source of livelihood. This attachment is usually lifelong, or for a goodly stretch of time; longer, for instance, than a single hitch in the army or navy. It is not what people do that makes them professionals—amateurs and rookies do the same things—but the fact that they do it for a living. In this shade of its meaning the word "professional" is always an adjective.

It becomes a noun as soon as we think of such typical figures as the lawyer, the doctor, the engineer, the teacher, the accountant. It would be ludicrous to refer to someone as a "professional surgeon." No one can be a surgeon without being a (noun) professional. An amateur surgeon had better not take the knife to a patient.

This substantive meaning of the word is clear enough, but presents its problems, too. A registered nurse is surely some kind of a professional—not on the same plane as a medical doctor, though still a professional—but how about the licensed practical nurse? And how about a parent nursing a child through an illness with the essential tender loving care no hired professional could provide? The work done is very much the same, but somewhere between the parent and the R.N. runs the line of true professionalism. Where does it put the practical nurse? On the parent's side of the line? Or the R.N.'s? A union of registered nurses would be a professional association: an association of professionals. If the practical nurses insisted on calling their organization a professional association, who would deny them the courtesy of the term? But who would allow them the same authority to set nursing standards?

CHARACTERISTICS OF A PROFESSION

Almost everybody wants to be called a professional and almost every occupation or career field has tried to stake a claim to professional status.

Thus any attempt to lay down a definition of a professional has to be arbitrary. It seems best to start with a very restrictive definition. With this as a base, additional occupations can joint the professional ranks, but each addition dilutes the basic definition.

A professional, then, is someone who measures up to *all* of the following criteria: (1) completes a course of study requiring college education and special postgraduate work; (2) qualifies for a license or certificate sanctioned by the profession and approved by government; (3) makes a primary commitment to the service of humanity; (4) accepts a code of ethics, and (5) supports a professional association dedicated to the enforcement of the ethical code.

Only a handful of professionals qualify under this restrictive definition: doctors, lawyers, some clergy. As you relax requirements under any of the five criteria, more people qualify: engineers, college professors, certified public accountants, high school and elementary teachers, registered nurses, pharmacists, social workers, and others. After this second wave, others come forward to claim professional status, such as chartered life underwriter, certified professional secretary, certified practical nurse; perhaps even to certified shopping center manager.

Figure 14–1 reveals 1975 employment in the major professional occupations. Employment in the basic professions of medicine, law, and the clergy totals barely a million persons. College, secondary, and elementary teaching employs over two million; engineering and technical employment almost as much. Both accounting (not limited to certified public accountants) and registered nursing account for more practitioners than any one of the basic professions.

Clergy, listed as "basic" professionals, provide quite a gamut themselves. Some religious groups lay down no formal educational requirements, others ordain persons who have received various amounts of training in liberal arts colleges, bible colleges, or bible institutes. An increasing number of denominations, however, require a three-year course of professional study in theology after college graduation.

Historically, the professions seem to have started out with practitioners who were self-employed, as many are to this day. Even teachers, for example, once gave lessons to private pupils for tuition fees. A very few still do. Generally speaking, the market for educational services now consists of a number of private universities and a few private secondary schools, with the bulk of students in public school systems from kindergarten through graduate school. The teacher has become an employee: performs professional services for hire, under management.

Where an enterprise, public or private, needs professional services, managers can either contract with a self-employed professional or firm or, if operations justify it, hire full-time professionals. Or, in fact, do both. For example, staff engineers may do routine engineering while a consulting engineering firm comes in for special or unusual work.

FIGURE 14-1
Employment in Selected Professional Occupations and Membership in Related Organizations

Occupation	Employment*	Related Organization(s)†	Membership†
Teachers			
Elementary and secondary	2,275,000	National Education Association‡	1,103,485
		American Federation of Teachers	400,000
College	260,000	American Association of University Professors	86,000
Engineers	1,100,000	American Institute of Electrical and Electronic Engineers§	167,000
		American Society of Mechanical Engineers§	61,194
		American Society of Civil Engineers§	67,000
		American Institute of Aeronautics and Astronautics§	26,000
		American Institute of Chemical Engineers§	38,000
Registered engineers	275,000 (est.)	National Society of Professional Engineers§	70,000
Registered nurses	750,000	American Nursing Association	175,000
Clergymen	320,000	No relevant organization	
Physicians	300,000	American Medical Association	219,000
Lawyers	275,000	American Bar Association	175,000
Dentists	100,000	American Dental Association	119,000
Certified public accountants	100,000	American Institute of Certified Public Accountants	96,000

* U.S. Department of Labor, Bureau of Labor Statistics, *Occupational Outlook Handbook,* 1972–1973 Edition, p. 25. Information on CPAs, p. 30.
† Frederick G. Ruffner, Jr., R. C. Thomas, Ann Underwood, and H. C. Young, eds. *Encyclopedia of Associations,* vol. 1 (Detroit: Gale Research Company, 1975).
‡ NEA membership includes elementary and secondary schoolteachers, college and university professors, administrators, principals, counselors, and others interested in education. Bulk of membership composed of elementary and secondary teachers and administrators.
§ Membership includes students.

In any case, professionals take no direct part in the day to day operations of most enterprises, unless the product or service sold consists at least in part (as it does in a school or hospital) of professional services. Then the professionals *are* the operation.

Professional associations and their members reflect this relationship to work place technology. Full-time employees of a company's legal department, for instance, retain their membership in the American Bar Association, but the ABA does not bargain for them with their employer. Full-time teachers, on the other hand, have come to look to their associations as their bargaining agent as well as the guardian of professional standards and ethics.

Markets for Professional Services

Persons entitled to call themselves professionals command special knowledge, have mastered certain special skills, and provide special professional services no one else is competent to offer except other practitioners of the same profession. A doctor—and only a doctor—can diagnose a patient's complaint, prescribe for it, and carry out the measures necessary for a cure. Only a lawyer can evaluate a client's legal rights, and assert or defend them in a court of law. The lawyer can't set a compound fracture nor the doctor draft a valid deed.

Like everyone else, professionals make a living by selling their services in the market. Three kinds of buyers create market demand for different kinds of professional services: (1) *individuals*, (2) organizations that we shall call *companies*, and (3) organizations that we shall call *institutions*.

Individuals from time to time need medical or dental or psychiatric or legal services, and go directly to a practitioner who provides the service for a fee. Companies need special staff work, such as engineering, and so may hire engineers as full-time employees, but would have to be quite large or engaged in special kinds of work to hire a full-time lawyer. Instead, they retain an outside law firm. Institutions, such as schools and hospitals, hire full-time professionals because the service they provide the public, such as health care and education, *consists of* professional services.

Professionals relate differently to these three kinds of buyers. Some enter the market as self-employed proprietors, selling their services directly to individuals, or on a retainer-and-fee basis to companies—even institutions. A practicing physician, for instance, could serve private patients and also contract to do medical examinations for a company. A lawyer could serve company or institutional clients as well as individuals.

Some professionals, like engineers, accountants, or research scientists, would find little demand for their services from individuals. A consulting engineer, for example, could remain self-employed and independent, serving a clientele consisting of a number of companies. A certified public accountant, similarly, could serve individuals as well as companies or institutions. Most holders of an accounting or engineering degree, however, expect to become full-time employees of a company, where they function as special staff people.

Finally, still other professionals, like college professors, other teachers, nurses, and clergy, *have* to find employment with an institution, since the market as currently organized supplies the demand for their services through institutional channels. The professor has to have a class and classroom; the nurse, patients under a doctor's care, and hospital facilities; the clergy, a church and congregation. In the institution, whatever its nature, these professionals render the actual service the institution was set up to provide. They are its "production workers." Without them, the institution could not survive. Not surprisingly, collective bargaining by unions of professionals occurs most often in the third, or institutional setting.

The two kinds of institution that depend most heavily on professionals are the schools and hospitals or, as the term now goes, health care institutions. Any of these may be public, or private proprietary, or private nonprofit. Public schools and public hospitals fall under the public sector rules for rule-making and will be dealt with in Chapters 15 and 16, the public sector. Here we concern ourselves strictly with the private sector schools and health care institutions, profit and nonprofit. Until 1974 private nonprofit hospitals were exempt from the workings of labor relations law. Private schools and colleges presumably fell under the law, but not until the 1970s did any organizations try seriously for collective bargaining there. In the remainder of this chapter we'll examine the activities of the organizations of professionals in education and health care.

ORGANIZATIONS OF PROFESSIONALS IN EDUCATION

Teacher organizations and educational administrators agree in recognizing two big divisions of the American school system. One they call, in their jargon, K–12; that is, kindergarten through high school; the other is higher education, the colleges and universities.

The K–12 schools are overwhelmingly public and tax-supported. Only the Roman Catholic church with its nationwide system of parochial schools offers, even on a small scale, anything comparable. There are also some private church-connected or secular prep schools, including military schools, mostly attended by the children of the rich; and as a consequence of the busing controversy a certain number of alternate nonpublic schools which may or may not endure; but unions seem not to have penetrated the nonpublic K–12 schools to any significant degree. We therefore leave discussion of the K–12 educational system entirely to the public sector chapters. Higher education has a somewhat different look. Private colleges and universities no longer dominate, as they did a century ago, but they still play a significant part, and some of them have been touched by collective bargaining. It has been held that they engage in "interstate commerce," and so fall under the Labor-Management Relations Act and the administration of the NLRB.

Professionals in Higher Education

The men and women who teach in the nation's colleges and universities come closest of any in education to the restricted definition of professionals: that is: (1) they must have completed at least three years of postgraduate education; (2) while not directly licensed by government, they hold advanced degrees from accredited institutions chartered by the state; (3) implicit in the scholar's commitment to the search for truth, they make a primary commitment to humanity; (4) they subscribe to a code of ethics, implicit in the standards of scholarship; and (5) they have created a professional association to enforce the ethics and advance the interests of the higher education academic teaching community: namely, the American Association of University Professors, or AAUP.

The American Association of University Professors (AAUP)

In one sense, the professional association of teachers in higher education is the learned society of the particular discipline any one of them happens to profess, such as sociology, chemistry, or marketing; that is, their scholarly colleagues. In another sense, it is the faculty of the university in which they do their teaching; that is, their institutional colleagues. Neither quite serves in the way the bar association, for example, serves the legal profession.

University professors earn their professional reputations in the discipline, but draw pay and seek promotion in the institution. The learned society of any single discipline can't exert much influence on a local campus, while the faculty may find itself quite powerless. They may be dependent on administrators—deans and the president—who might have been teachers themselves but now serve a board of regents or trustees. The board represents the interests of those who control the funds that support the school. These supporters may be a religious or secular body not made up primarily of scholars, and while not necessarily unsympathetic to scholarly concerns, with aims and interests that can clash, on occasion, with academic interests.

Very early, the AAUP recognized that a code of ethics for the scholarly pursuits would have to be enforced against the *institutions* employing the scholars. No professor was likely to suppress academic freedom, but administrators and governing boards might, and could, and often did. No professor was likely to ignore the claims of tenure, but again the administration might. No faculty would try to hold down their own salaries, but again. . . . And when a teacher suffered an injustice, to whom could an appeal be made? What sanctions could an organization of professors invoke against administrators and boards of trustees?

Professors might be without power, but not without some influence. While they earn their living from the university, they earn prestige from their standing in the discipline and in public opinion, both of which are beyond the university's control; and the university gains its prestige and public standnig by the renown of its professors. They don't all have to be distinguished, but good ones will attract more. The saying in academic circles is: Good faculty go where good faculty are. Prestige is the coin of academic life; when a university starts to lose its best professors, its academic credit starts to slip.

The AAUP built its policy on this apparently tenuous base. It developed an appeals procedure which consisted of appointing committees to investigate complaints of such things as the violation of academic freedom, improper or unjust dismissal, failure to respect tenure. The AAUP committee had no authority over an offending institution, but a listing on the AAUP list of censured administrations after an objective and careful investigation did not enhance the prestige of any university. As time went on, many administrators preferred to settled a case with the AAUP committee rather than be listed.

Another thing the AAUP did was to compile and publish salary comparisons, listing the universities by name but preserving the privacy of individuals. Regents, trustees, and administrators became subject to pressure not from the faculty directly, but from the fear of losing the people who were its main adornment. Thus the association, without engaging in collective bargaining with any administration, achieved higher pay, and improved individual security through the academic version of job rights (tenure) and due process (appeals channels and procedures for colleague participation in tenure and promotion decisions). Tenure comes usually after a probation period longer than any manual or white collar union would stand for—two to three years, up to as much as five or six—but once gained, gives a professor powerful protection, in two ways. First and most obviously, a tenured professor need no longer fear dismissal or nonrenewal of contract; second and less obviously, he or she gains a strong bargaining position for dealing with job offers. Others still seeking tenure want protection from arbitrary negative decisions and from negligence and delays in making the tenure decision.

The Shift to Collective Bargaining

Over the years, college administrations slowly gave ground to the gentle pressures the AAUP exerted; some, in fact (including state-supported institutions) adopted word for word, as their own policy, the AAUP position on such issues as academic freedom and tenure. Many, of course, did not; but one can always hope to "bring the sinners into the fold." Content with its professional association role and its approach to issues by example and persuasion, the AAUP changed its policy and embraced collective bargaining as one form of activity only reluctantly, and only as late as its convention of 1972. It did so under pressure and in the face of competition.

The pressure came from developments in the public sector, which will be dealt with in the chapters that follow. Put very briefly, the states passed laws that opened up the publicly-supported campuses to collective bargaining. The AAUP had members on these as well as on the private campuses, and standards prevalent on one affect the other. That is because professors are in a nationwide labor market that takes no account of whether the employer institution is public or private. Professors move freely from jobs on state campuses to private campuses, and vice versa. They don't really care who puts up the money for the institution.

The competition came mainly from two organizations that had hitherto concentrated on the K–12 grades and not been much heard from in higher education. They were the National Education Association (NEA) and the American Federation of Teachers (AFT), AFL–CIO. But other possible union competitors loomed over all of them; nothing in the rules for rule-making either on the public or private side could keep the Teamsters, for instance, from moving onto the campus, if the Teamsters felt so inclined, and the campus was willing to accept them. Under the rules for rule-making, new and old, professors have the right to select their own representatives for collective bargaining. Whether the public or the private sector laws applied, the winner in a representation election now had the say in negotiating conditions and standards. The AAUP saw that changes might be in store that could endanger the whole structure of academic relationships it had so painstakingly worked out. Without ceasing to be a professional association, the AAUP turned into a union, and began competing with other unions for bargaining rights on both the public and the private campuses.

Bargaining Issues in Higher Education

Even the absent-minded professor of legend must have had to think about money once in a while. Like everyone else who works for a living in an inflationary period, professors today are concerned about salaries. They can no longer depend on the forces of a rising market to maintain demand for their services, because the market is relatively declining. While pay levels are important, professors feel more acutely what they perceive as threats to their individual security and, some think, to academic freedom. Collective bargaining that gives faculty members a voice in university governance is beginning to look like the best defense of academic freedom and tenure, the very ramparts of the ivory tower.

Academic Tenure

During the campus unrest of the past decade, militant students often cried out against the tenure system. They claimed that it protected old, incompetent, conservative professors and fenced out promising and progressive younger teachers. Off-campus critics at the same time could be heard decrying tenure because it protected what they perceived as bearded, radical, firebrand professors who, if not actually inciting students to riot stood by, permissively, and let riot and chaos erupt. If in the passions of the moment either of these extremist groups had had their way, university campuses today would surely be the poorer: a sterile and one-sided environment. Tenure protects tenured professors, but it also protects the *university* from any one group or faction's belief that theirs is the only and ultimate way to truth. The academic world has come to regard tenure as a mainstay of academic freedom.

Tenure serves the same function as seniority in the conventional labor agreement; it is the academic form of job rights. One tenured professor can never have "more" tenure than another, but anyone with tenure has prior claims over *all* untenured persons teaching in the same discipline or subdiscipline on campus. In this sense tenure is like job seniority except that what might correspond to layoffs only affects the untenured and virtually never touches the tenured faculty. Untenured professors, waiting and working toward that privileged status, don't object to the tenure system—they want tenure themselves—but they often object to the way tenure decisions are made. Collective bargaining on tenure in higher education, therefore, is likely to aim at rules governing the *procedures* for making tenure decisions. The faculty wants a voice in setting the criteria and passing on the qualifications of those being considered for tenure; procedural rather than prescriptive substantive rules.

Teaching Loads

Another sensitive issue is the teaching load. Workers who put in a 40-hour week may well find it hard to swallow the idea that a professor with a six-hour teaching load is pulling full weight; though time spent in the classroom is only the tip of the iceberg. Universities have, in fact, come under attack from legislatures, the press, and the public for schedules not always as low as six classroom hours a week, but rarely more than twice that, or twelve hours, and sometimes even less: a single, three-hour class.

There would be no point in denying that teaching load has become a status symbol between universities or on a given campus. Those critics may be right who claim that some professors take advantage of it. The fact remains that institutions where the teaching load is heavy—and it can't exceed 15 hours, or accreditation lapses—aren't the ones renowned for scholarship and research; quite the contrary; yet the six-hour load is costly, and doesn't guarantee results. Some faculty members use the time outside the classroom to become better teachers and scholars—to do research, or writing, or consulting—but some, once they gain tenure, "retire on the job."

There is probably no ultimate remedy against abuse, but academic people see the teaching load as a professional issue. If an institution has to save costs by increasing the *average* teaching load, professors will want to have a say on how the loads are redistributed. Collective bargaining appears to be the way they can be sure of having some control. Again, procedural arrangements rather than outright, specific substantive rules, would seem to be the form a negotiated solution would take.

UNIONS OF PROFESSIONALS IN HEALTH CARE

Institutions in the private sector offering health care facilities, such as hospitals, clinics, sanatoriums, and nursing homes, are basically hotels or boarding houses with a difference; a big difference. They provide lodging, food, and facilities for medical care. The people who go to them and who in one way or another pay for the services they provide, cannot enter at will, but are admitted at the request or with the approval of doctors who treat them there. The doctors who refer the patients normally don't work for the hospitals; they are self-employed. Such medical attention as the patients otherwise receive they get from another order of professionals, registered nurses (R.N.s). The R.N.s are hospital employees.

Other kinds of professionals work in private hospitals as permanent or temporary employees, such as internes—young M.D.s serving part of their apprenticeship—and X-ray specialists and others. Many paraprofessionals also serve, like practical nurses, nurse's aides, and lab technicians; and, like a hotel, many nonprofessionals such as office workers, kitchen personnel, cleanup people and orderlies. The R.N.s, by their presence and the professional work they do, make the difference between a hotel and a hospital.

Measured against the severe, touchstone definition of professionals we have been using, R.N.s rank well below M.D.s in educational requirements, but are at least equal to a K–12 teacher nowadays. And they rate high—very high—on the commitment to humanity and code of ethics. The Florence Nightingale tradition set the tone for nursing care, and hospital administrators (the hotel keepers) were not backward about exploiting that image. The R.N. professional organization, while devoted to the code of ethics and of service, eventually began questioning whether a commitment to humanity necessarily meant a commitment to low pay, retrictive living conditions, and a 12-hour working day. The nurse organization had to struggle against obstacles peculiar to the health care industry.

The American Nursing Association

The American Nursing Association, or ANA, corresponds, for nurses, to the American Medical Association for doctors, but with a difference: nurses are not self-employed, but are employed professionals. Of all employees in the health care institutions they work for, they are the key professionals, since doctors in the private hospitals are not usually employees.

As early as 1946 the ANA, without ceasing to be a professional association, began acting like a union of professionals and turned to collective bargaining as a way of improving the conditions under which nurses worked, and of raising their pay.

The institutions they worked for were either publicly-owned and tax-supported—and so outside the bounds of this chapter's discussion—or they were private. If privately-owned, they were either nonprofit or proprietary; that is, operated for profit. Only in the last of these three categories could nurses (or for that matter, other employees) theoretically gain recognition through the procedures of the NLRB. Of course they could do this only if the institution was engaged in interstate commerce, and this was rarely proveable; most of them were small, doctor-owned enterprises, clinics or nursing homes. Nothing in the law prevented the other category of private institutions—the nonprofit hospitals—from bargaining with nurses, but nothing in the law obliged them to; and they were often reluctant. A hospital administrator could fire a nurse, or any other hospital employee, for engaging in union activity. Still, the ANA made most of its collective bargaining gains before the late 1960s in the big nonprofit private hospitals, either as a result of successful strike action or by decision of enlightened administrators.

As with the campuses, private hospitals felt the impact of collective bargaining developments in the public sector. The ANA showed increasing militancy in the hospitals, and kept up a lobbying campaign aimed at striking out the Taft-Hartley exclusion of health care institutions from the jurisdiction of the NLRB. They won their legislative victory in 1974 with passage of health care amendments to the LMRA.

THE MOVE FOR PROFESSIONALIZATION

Employed professionals increase their control over both economic status and professional standards when they organize and bargain collectively, particularly when the service the employer sells, as in education and health care, depends directly on their professional knowledge, skills, and activity.

They can do this because there is no substitute for professional knowledge and professional skill. Further, as proof that they possess the knowledge and the skill (otherwise evident only to another professional) they hold certificates and degrees from the appropriate official bodies. Ordinarily they need both the knowledge and the certificate to practice the profession: a disbarred lawyer retains knowledge of the law, but would not be allowed to plead a case in court.

Many people whose current occupational roles don't meet the "touchstone" requirements—course of study, certification, code of ethics, and professional association—would nevertheless like to reap the benefits and enjoy the status that professional recognition confers. They would justify this by adding requirements—natural or artificial—to the role, and getting an official body to issue certificates. This is called "professionalization." It happened in K–12 teaching; it could happen—naturally or artificially—in other fields.

In 19th century America any young man or woman who completed high school was eligible to get a job teaching school. By the turn of the century, a would-be teacher had to complete what was called "normal school," which went two years beyond high school. Nowadays teachers qualify for a certificate only after four years of college. Not every college graduate may teach; only those whose programs included courses in what used to be called "pedagogy." Although it is much more certain that people can learn than that pedagogues can teach, these courses in how to teach (plus supervised practice teaching) make the difference between the teacher as professional and other holders of the bachelor's degree.

Firefighters and police officers are currently seeking professional recognition. They are almost always city employees, and as such will be dealt with in the public sector chapters, but as would-be professionals they call for passing attention here.

Most people would concede that police and firefighters make an essential contribution to public safety; taxpayers and property owners would be willing to cut many other services before touching the police and fire protection budgets. Unions of police and firefighters, consequently, are in a strong bargaining position. At the same time, citizen or "civilian" control of police and other uniformed public employees is as much part of the American credo and tradition as local control of the schools. It seems not unlikely that in public safety, as in public education, conflicts will arise between the interests of citizens in general and the organized public employees, who would see the issue, or present it, as one of professional autonomy; that is, a question that only professionals can resolve. More than a hint of this appeared in the successful ballot-box fight of the New York City police unions to defeat a plan for citizen review boards which were to hear complaints and investigate allegations of police brutality, shakedowns, and other possible abuses.

Police and firefighters are, of course, not the only city employees holding strategic positions that give their unions bargaining power. Transit workers and sanitation employees (garbage handlers) perform equally essential services, and by shutting these services down can bring comparable pressure on a city administration. (Sanitation workers in San Francisco, incidentally, earn as much or more than assistant professors with the Ph.D. in the California state universities.) These others don't always work directly for the city—sometimes for private firms franchised by the city—but their strategic position is the same as if they were public employees.

Any unionized body of workers is bound eventually to discover its relative strength and bargaining power, and to drive the best bargains it can for the members. Unions of police and firefighters will undoubtedly do the same. Now that they are demanding recognition as professionals, city officials dealing with them might do well to bear in mind the touchstone definition of professionals given on all five criteria. Beyond the special pedagogy (or criminology) courses and the certificate there must be a commitment to humanity—not just the welfare of the members—and a code of ethics. And an association just as strong to enforce the ethics as to enforce the law.

SUMMARY

White collar workers and professionals differ from manual workers in occupational role, or relation to work place technology, but fall under the same laws, or rules for rule-making, both in private industry and public employment. Unions composed mainly or exclusively of white collar workers appear mostly in the service industries, often in association with a friendly or allied manual worker union.

Persons practicing a profession possess special skills and knowledge that others do not have, and form associations composed exclusively of members of the same profession, but not for bargaining purposes. In those enterprises whose operations consist of the offering of professional services, as in education and health care, professional associations have begun in recent years to bargain collectively on behalf of the employed professionals. Here the associations have metamorphosed into unions without necessarily giving up their professional interests and preoccupations.

Unions striving to metamorphose into professional associations without relinquishing their union functions are beginning to appear.

QUESTIONS FOR DISCUSSION

1. Management literature used to call white collar workers "nonproducers," even "parasites," while manual workers were called "producers." What's wrong with this way of thinking? Is there a grain of truth in it?
2. Can you make out a case for managers as professionals? How about labor leaders?
3. Doctors today receive a large part of their income from treating patients whose bills are paid by Medicare, Blue Cross, or other agencies. Are doctors on the way to becoming employed professionals?
4. Should colleges adopt the industry practice of setting up seniority lists instead of tenure? Or abolish tenure? Could industry operate effectively under a system patterned on academic tenure?

SELECTED ANNOTATED BIBLIOGRAPHY

BAIN, GEORGE S. *The Growth of White Collar Unionism.* Oxford: Clarendon Press, 1970.
    The author analyzes the growth of white collar unionism and offers a

theory to explain this growth, focussing on employment concentration (or bureaucratization), union recognition, and government action.

KLEINGARTNER, ARCHIE. *Professionalism and Salaried Worker Organization.* Madison: University of Wisconsin, Industrial Relations Research Institute, 1967.

An excellent review of the occupational characteristics of professionals and how these vocational traits relate to the organization of an effective collective bargaining representative.

NATIONAL INDUSTRIAL CONFERENCE BOARD. *White Collar Unionization.* Studies in Personnel Policy No. 220, 1970.

A survey of 140 white collar organizing campaigns reveals both union and management strategy and tactics in approaching the ever-increasing numbers of white collar workers.

SEIDMAN, JOEL, and CAIN, GLEN G. "Unionized Engineers and Chemists: A Case Study of a Professional Union," *Journal of Business* (University of Chicago), vol. 37 (July 1964) pp. 238–57.

Presents a case study of unionism among professional engineers and chemists in a large oil refinery to learn their views of unionism and to compare it with the concept held by blue collar workers.

STRAUSS, GEORGE. "Professionalism and Occupational Associations," *Industrial Relations*, vol. 2, no. 3, (May 1963).

An examination of the concept of professionalism and the role of professional employees' occupational organizations in advancing employee interests, with emphasis on engineers.

part four

Collective Bargaining in the Public Sector

During the last decade, public and professional workers have comprised the two fastest growing segments of the labor force. They also have become avid organizers and bargainers. Part Four chronicles the rapid emergence of bargaining activity among these workers and profiles current practices and problems in public and professional bargaining.

Including the nonprofit health care institutions, one out of every five workers is a public employee. In 1975, over half of these workers were either members of labor organizations or covered by collective agreements as compared to only 10 percent in 1960. In the intervening 15 years, a virtual explosion of worker militancy and collective bargaining has occurred. Ironically, this explosion has been ignited by professional employees—an occupational class that in the past more typically has derided than advocated collective bargaining.

More than one half of the 5.2 million organized white collar workers are professional, technical, and kindred workers—some 40 percent of the workers so classified by the census bureau in 1970. The vast majority of these organized professionals is in the public sector, principally in education and health care. Also in the public sector, established professionals, such as engineers, doctors and lawyers, have shown the greatest interest in bargaining.

Chapter 15 examines the general causes, structure, and consequences of this dramatic spread of bargaining among public and professional employees. Chapter 16 profiles in detail the bargaining practices and problems of various governmental agencies and professional groups. Together the two chapters comprise a study of what has become the most active arena of bargaining in the industrial relations system in the 1970s.

15 The Public Sector

No EMPLOYEE of government is a more familiar figure than the mail carrier shouldering a mail pouch or pushing a cart along the sidewalks of city, town, and village with a faithfulness and regularity that have become legendary. No department of government touches the daily life of more citizens more intimately. Excluding the armed forces, it is the biggest government agency, with employees and a branch post office in every community. Business and industry, education, the public services, private welfare and happiness, all depend on the regular delivery of mail. When the postal workers went out on strike in early 1970 for the first time since—almost—the founding of the Republic, the whole country recognized it as an event of historic importance.

Postal workers (like other federal employees) were forbidden by law to strike; but they did strike. The same law forbade the postmaster general to bargain with strikers; but he did bargain—and so, practically speaking, did the president of the United States. According to law, any postal worker who went on strike became liable to summary discharge from the federal service; but none were fired. The president called out troops. Not many soldiers are trained to handle mail, but many are trained to disperse crowds, including picket lines. These soldiers walked through the lines and did not disperse the pickets. Under the direction of postal supervisors they kept some of the most important mail moving; but the mail bags piled up. The strike did not come to an end until after negotiations with the strikers; and the fact that such negotiations, strictly speaking, were illegal, was overlooked as quite irrelevant. The strikers, reinstated without prejudice, got a raise in pay and subsequently received bargaining rights comparable to those granted public employees under Taft-Hartley along with the quid pro quo for denial of their right to strike, namely, final and binding arbitration of negotiation impasses.

Many of the salient features of the foregoing scenario have been repeated in countless other bargaining situations involving public and professional

449

employees. Militant job actions—actual or threatened—have led to positive outcomes with virtually no retribution against the workers involved. This has been the key to the rapid organization and use of collective bargaining by public and professional employees: Success breeds success. As teachers, police, nurses, firefighters and, finally in 1975, even physicians challenged traditional prerogatives with collective militancy the results were on balance quite positive. Police and firefighters became pattern setters in terms of wages, fringe benefits and due process rights in municipalities across America. Teachers and nurses gained increased economic benefits and professional autonomy through bargaining. Even less skilled and traditionally less powerful employee groups such as secretaries and clerical employees in cities like New York and San Francisco found that through collective bargaining activity they could achieve as good, or better conditions of employment than their private sector counterparts. Such examples were not wasted on other public and professional employees.

The public sector, long considered to be outside the bounds of conventional collective bargaining, today seems to be taking the center of the stage. The numbers of people involved would be enough to make this new activity significant, but in addition, the nature of the essential services public employees render and their relation to the sources of political power magnify and multiply the impact of everything that happens in public sector bargaining.

Professionals typically have been apathetic—if not often downright disdainful—toward unions and collective bargaining. Therefore, the president of the American Medical Association (AMA) speaking sympathetically in 1975 of a strike by New York interns and residents is an historical event. Increasing accountability pressures on professionals coupled with continued economic uncertainty has caused both established professionals, like doctors, and aspiring professionals, like police officers, to use collective and militant measures to maintain or enhance their occupational autonomy, integrity, prestige, and economic welfare. Such developments are doubly important to both individual citizens and public policy makers since the services provided by professionals touch the lives of their clients in a profoundly personal way.

THE SPREAD OF COLLECTIVE BARGAINING IN THE PUBLIC SECTOR

While recent years have witnessed a declining proportion of the nonagricultural civilian labor force in the private sector organized into unions for purposes of collective bargaining, the opposite is the case in public employment.

In 1955 less than one million government employees were members of labor organizations; by 1965 this figure had reached 1½ million. However, by 1975 this figure had jumped to close to 6 million—a 4-fold increase in just 10 years. Proportionally the number of public workers organized is virtually double that of their private sector counterparts—45 percent versus 22 percent. In terms of numbers, government employees today reflect almost one out of three organized American workers, though comprising only one sixth of the noninstitutional labor force.

Membership in public employee labor organizations is split between two types of organizations: the union and the association. The union type is dominant in the federal government and the association type is dominant in state and local governments. The five biggest unions, the American Federation of Government Employees (AFGE) and National Postal Workers Union at the federal level; and the American Federation of State, County, and Municipal Employees (AFSCME), American Federation of Teachers (AFT), and the International Association of Fire Fighters (IAFF) at the state and local level, account for approximately one third of the total organized. They are all affiliated with the AFL–CIO. The growing importance of public employees to the labor movement was recognized with the establishment in 1974 of the Public Employee Department within the AFL–CIO on a par with such old line departments as the Industrial Union and Maritime Trades Departments.

The largest Association, the National Educational Association (NEA), alone accounts for over one fourth of all organized public employees and well over one half of the organized professionals in the United States. Thirty-six independent state government employee associations account for one out of ten organized public employees. The three largest single associations, the International Conference of Police Associations (ICPA), the Fraternal Order of Police (FOP), and the American Nurses Association account for another 5 percent of organized public employees. The remaining organized employees are scattered among hundreds of local, state, and national unions and associations, many of which are employer-specific such as the National Labor Relations Board Union.

The major differences between the Union and association organization types lies in the scope of activities and businesslike attitude with which they pursue their respective representational activities. Unions, on the whole, tend to have significantly higher dues, more paid staff, and a single purpose of negotiating and administering contracts. Associations, on the other hand, historically were formed for purposes other than bargaining such as professional training, lobbying, low-cost group insurance programs, and credit unions. Today most associations continue to perform these functions and also provide bargaining representation; many were spurred into a bargaining role by competition from unions, such as the competition between the AFT and NEA in organizing teachers. Outside of education, however, the policies and practices of unions generally tend to be more militant than those of associations.

The number of organized public employees would be even greater were it not for the typical absence of union or agency shop clauses from public sector contracts. These clauses are still banned in federal contracts, prohibited in many states by law and vigorously opposed by many public employers who were not prohibited by the rules for rulemaking. Hence, many employees remain outside the relevant labor organization but are affected by its activities. In the federal service, for example, labor organizations have enrolled one third of all employees, but gained exclusive recognition in bargaining units employing about one half. If the rules had permitted these organizations to bargain for union or agency shop clauses, they might well have been able to enroll one half of all employees eligible for membership. Comprehensive figures for state and local government are not available, but would undoubtedly reveal a similar situation. AFSCME estimates it could probably double its 500,000 plus membership if it had union or agency shop clauses in all the contracts it has negotiated with state and local agencies. We normally associate collective bargaining with labor-management relations in private industry. The foregoing figures and proportions show that it is just as much a part of the public sector; perhaps more so. This does not imply that collective bargaining arrangements and procedures have penetrated as deeply into the prerogatives of public as of private management. The institutional framework in the public sector puts obstacles in the way of bilateral decision making on a comparable scale.

How are we to account for the dramatic spread of collective bargaining in the public service in recent years? Undoubtedly, public sector bargaining gets much of its impetus from the example and the impact of unionization and collective bargaining in private industry. The example provided direct guidance, after the impact had transformed the economic, social, and political environment. Not until New Deal days had industrial unions in the private sector come at all strongly on the scene. They spread explosively thereafter throughout the country's basic industries. The wage bargains they drove, the working conditions they imposed, brought change not just to the work place, but to the whole society. Accumulation of these changes over a generation prepared the ground for a comparable sudden upsurge in the public sector.

The Union Example

Before widespread unionization, public employees enjoyed many advantages over their private industry counterparts. At a time when an office clerk or factory hand could be laid off or discharged at will, many of the men and women who worked for the city, state, or federal government had the security of job tenure under civil service regulations and a system of due process for presenting complaints. While they might earn only a modest income, they received fringe benefits in the form of pay for time not worked—vacations and paid holidays—and contingent benefits, such as paid sick leave, and a pension after retirement. Some white collar workers in private industry got the same privileges as a matter of company benevolence, but without a protective guarantee; and factory workers got none at all. The government set itself up as a model employer. A person with a government job often became the envy of the neighbors.

Earlier chapters of this book tell how the industrial unions, year by year, succeeded at the bargaining table and on the picket line in winning for factory workers one after another of these benefits plus higher and higher wages. The comparative advantages of public employment began to disappear. Even in the area of job rights, where civil service had provided appeals procedures (better than no procedures at all, but still employer-dominated), the unions established grievance-handling systems that culminated in binding arbitration by a neutral third party.

Union-negotiated wages and benefits, furthermore, improved at an increasingly faster rate than pay in the public sector, where adjustments came slowly and through cumbersome procedures. Inflation, especially in recent years, put the public employee, who had already dropped below the income levels of private industry, even behind the steady increase in the cost of living, to which the union raises had contributed. In both absolute and relative terms, the government workers saw themselves slipping. They still had job security through tenure, but several decades of nearly full employment made tenure almost irrelevant; and the industrial worker had achieved its counterpart, first in the form of seniority, then Supplemental Unemployment Benefits, and finally, a guaranteed annual wage. As for the various forms of "psychic" pay that go with some jobs—such as prestige—the government employee in America has never been much of an idol to the public.

It is hardly surprising that the deteriorating economic position of public service employees became an inducement to action. The once favored—now underpaid, once docile—now militant government worker set out on a drive to catch up with the times and with his private industry counterpart; and by the same means: collective bargaining.

Civil Rights and Social Unrest

Another environmental factor that fostered public employee militancy (and may hold the key to its timing) was the changing social mood of the last third of the century. Americans in significant numbers began to question, openly, the legitimacy of the social system. The civil and women's rights movements and the antiwar movement, challenged the tenets of the conventional wisdom. The civil rights movement in particular gave dramatic witness to the way organized militant protest could influence governmental decision making. The example was not lost on public employees; indeed, they were sometimes participants. One of the most dramatic events in the decade directly linked public-sector collective bargaining with the civil rights upsurge: the assassination of the Rev. Dr. Martin Luther King, civil rights leader and Nobel Prize winner. King went to Memphis, Tennessee, to support the 9-week strike of sanitation workers against the city administration. After his murder the city signed a labor agreement with AFSCME Local 1733.

In this atmosphere of questioned legitimacy and authority, public employees found the nerve to challenge the prerogatives of their supposedly sovereign employers. The concept of sovereignty had bolstered the traditional objections of those who argued against the propriety of government's bargaining collectively with employees. The argument was simple: Sovereign power, by definition, cannot be shared. In a time of social change and challenge, public employees found themselves in no mood any longer to accept such simplistic logic.

Political Developments

Political developments in the 1960s reinforced the kind of mass activity and direct action that led public employees to seek bargaining rights. Supreme Court decisions upholding individual and civil rights drew attention to the disparity between the rights of workers in private industry, and the lack of them in public employment. Perhaps even more fundamentally, the court's "one man, one vote" reapportionment decisions in 1962 and 1964 strengthened the position of the public employee. Reapportionment resulted in the election of state legislatures more sympathetic to labor. Laws authorizing collective bargaining for state and local government employees began to come out of these legislatures with increasing frequency after 1965.

Even before these developments in the states, the ball had started rolling in the federal government. John Fitzgerald Kennedy won the presidency with heavy labor backing, and within a year of his inauguration issued a presidential decree, Executive Order 10988, which made collective bargaining on a limited scale the policy of the federal government in its relations with its own employees. As limited as were its provisions, the Kennedy order signaled that times were changing in public sector labor relations.

None of these developments could have made much difference if employees themselves had not taken the initiative. A few vanguard public employee groups such as teachers and registered nurses had already provided successful models for others to follow. Both groups broke long-established taboos by going out, when forced to that extreme, on strike. Instead of universal outrage, they received a good deal of sympathy; and both returned to render their professional services as soon as the strikes were settled, without having brought about the catastrophes their employers predicted. The status of teachers and nurses as professionals undoubtedly helped make collective bargaining respectable in the eyes of other public employees. Besides, it escaped no one's notice that typically no legal retribution followed the successful use of the strike weapon, even by employees forbidden by law to strike.

CONTEXTS OF PUBLIC EMPLOYEE BARGAINING

Collective bargaining in the public sector differs from its counterpart activity in private industry because of variations in the underlying market and power relations contexts. It resembles the private sector only in the range of technology on which it draws. Thus, for example, a branch office of the Social Security Administration uses the same kind of procedures and equipment as the branch office of a big insurance company, but serves a different market and must conform to different laws and regulations. Or, for another example, a naval machine shop uses the same technology as a privately owned machine shop, and employs workers with the same skills; but market and power relations differ.

In certain instances the similarities as well as the differences were starkly contrasted, as for instance, between publicly and privately owned electrical utilities in two adjoining communities. Employees in the private utility had bargaining rights and could strike while their counterparts in the neighboring public utility had none and could not legally strike. Public employee groups often used such examples to point up their second class status.

It is these market and power relations differences that set off the public from the private sector. Although it is often hard to draw a sharp line between economic and political power, political influence and sanctions tend to dominate the public sector; economic forces, the private. Public-sector participants in the volatile activities of labor-management relations feel the constraints of political forces more directly than their private-sector counterparts, who operate in a comparatively simpler and more stable institutional setting.

The Market Context

According to Dunlop's theoretical framework (see Chapter 1), the budget is the market in the public sector, but the market as normally understood in the private sector is absent. For many reasons, government provides services which private industry is unable or unwilling to offer: a military force, for instance; police and fire protection; education and welfare services; street lights and sewers; highways; and mail deliveries. Government takes on the burden of providing these essential services; and, as a consequence, they become a government monopoly. Monopoly removes the restraints of product competition and substitution that put downward pressure on wages and prices and thereby temper the bargaining strategies of both unions and management in private industry. Competitive pressures in the public sector come, instead, from rival organized publics exerting not buying power but political influence. From different directions these groups place demands on a relatively fixed budget administered by vote-conscious politicians.

Some of these organized publics, like taxpayer's leagues, simply try to reduce the size of the budget. Others, including public employee labor organizations, seek a bigger share of the budget for their constituents. In a sense, therefore, the market in public employment is not so much a market as a political tug-of-war between various organized publics and pressure groups. Each tries to get what it wants for itself from what is available for all from the politicians who control the appropriations. The relative political strength of the rival groups, and not competing enterprises, tempers the behavior of the participants in collective bargaining.

In this free-for-all, strategies and tactics commonly resorted to in private-sector bargaining find no place or work with different effect. An example is the traditional strike and its counterweapon—the lockout. Given the character of public service—that is, the expectations people have of their government and their dependence on it—lockouts are viewed as impossible. By contrast, strikes, while they are illegal in almost every political jursdiction, are often particularly effective. They succeed almost in direct proportion to the essentiality of the service strikes deny the public, for they quickly generate pressure for settlement of the strike from affected citizens on their public officials.

This is particularly true in the larger political jurisdictions. The average citizen does not see a direct connection between a high-wage settlement and eventual tax increases. Thus in the post office strike of 1970 public outcry for a quick settlement helped bring pressure to get the mails moving again, with little concern for a rise in postage rates. When the price of a 6-cent stamp went up to 8 cents—a one-third increase—there was only minor grumbling.

Many people see the strike as giving organized public employees an unfair advantage over other groups of citizens. Some regard it as a distortion of democratic political processes.[1] The labor organization's special leverage becomes most noticeable and particularly noxious to many when collective bargaining deals with public policy issues, such as school decentralization, welfare policies, or law enforcement practices. In 1970 the New York City teachers' union, for example, went on strike and defeated a citizens' plan for decentralized control of schools in the black ghetto area of Brownsville. The issue was not money but job rights—tenure and transfer privileges of teachers—as opposed to the rights that Brownsville parents and citizens were to be granted by a Board of Education plan to bring policy control of education closer to the needs of the community. Further experimentation along these lines had to be abandoned in view of the effective union opposition.

Lobbying. Because the market in public employment depends more on political than on economic factors, employee organizations have historically

---

[1] Harry H. Wellington and Ralph K. Winter, Jr., "The Limits of Collective Bargaining in Public Employment," *The Yale Law Journal*, vol. 78, no. 7, June 1969.

resorted to lobbying rather than bargaining to attain their goals. Lobbying is preeminently a form of political activity. A group derives lobbying power from the influence it can ultimately bring to bear on getting a politician elected or reelected. Some organizations of public employees have fared very well by lobbying.

In many jurisdictions, for example, skilled workers have won agreements granting pay scales equal to, or very near, the prevailing wage in their trades in private industry such as construction. Although skilled tradesmen constitute only a small proportion of all public employees, they draw on the political influence of their craft unions in the state and city AFL–CIO councils. No politician up for election typically wants to be known as antilabor.

Other, unaffiliated employee groups have not done as well. One reason the powerful building trades lobbies have not pushed hard for formalized collective bargaining in the public sector is perhaps a shrewd calculation that they might thereby lose their lobbying advantage. A public employer required by law to bargain in good faith with employees other than skilled workers might not be willing, or find it possible, to continue this favored treatment of the skilled.

Behavioral patterns like lobbying and political action are slow to change, and organizations cling to them. This often retards meaningful negotiations at administrative levels, as the same groups gain formal collective bargaining rights in an increasing number of political jurisdictions. Employee spokespersons who are accustomed to getting their answers from the city council or state legislature decline to take as final the decision of an agency administrator or the city manager. They know the ultimate decision-making power remains in the hands of elected officials and legislators, even though not directly involved in bargaining procedures. The fear that employee representatives will appeal administrative decisions and take the final resolution out of their hands acts as a damper on the administrator's willingness to bargain in good faith. Many public employee organizations have done nothing to allay those fears. Formal bargaining thus comes close to having bad faith built into it when it becomes just a preliminary to a lobbying appeal or escalation of demands by political activity.

The Power Relations Context

Interwoven therefore with the market context is the context of power relations in the industrial relations system of the public sector. The most conspicuous feature of the power relations context is that the government exercises *sovereignty*. Sovereign power is ultimate power, beyond which there is no human appeal.

In any society, government makes the rules regulating the relationships between its citizens, and arbitrates private arrangements they work out between themselves. Government also arbitrates its own rules; it rules others and also rules itself. Previous chapters of this book have shown how government exercises rule-making power to regulate labor-management relations in the private sector, over which it has sovereignty. As an employer, it also exercises sovereignty over its own labor-management relations.

Sovereignty. The fact of sovereignty has given rise to an ideology deep-rooted in tradition. It is the ideology, quite as much as the fact, that animated government policy, and so shaped power relations in the public sector. Those who believed in the ideology long regarded sovereignty as an insurmountable obstacle to collective bargaining in the government service. Those who opposed collective bargaining appealed to the ideology. And those who favor collective bargaining in the public sector found the ideological argument hard to overcome.

Here is how it goes. Under the American democratic system, government exercises its sovereign power in trust for all the people. To share this power with a segment of the people violates the trust. Therefore, to bargain collectively with organized public employees—a segment of the people, and a small segment at that—not only violates the trust but is a surrender of sovereignty and abdication of responsibility.

This thinking lay behind early legal and administrative prohibitions on *bargaining* in public employment and the laws still on the books forbidding strikes. Proponents of the sovereignty argument declared that organized public employees, at best, could petition the government in the same way as any other group of citizens. It was, they held, a matter of solemn principle.

Principles often set hard and get harder with the years, but practical affairs can sometimes undermine the ideological foundations. As the complexities of operating the vast network of public enterprise multiplied, government turned increasingly to contracting with private persons and corporations for goods and services needed to carry out the governmental mission. Contracts involve at least a modicum of joint decision making. At a pragmatic level, the government found it harder to justify the difference between the negotiation of contracts and collective bargaining agreements. Besides, some labor advocates pointed out: If government really has sovereign power and can do anything it wants, it can bargain with its employees.

Behind the arguments and counterarguments, it seems clear that managers in public enterprises were just as reluctant, as managers, to divest themselves of what they regarded as their prerogatives as any of their counterparts in private industry. The sovereignty argument merely gave them a convenient shield for fending off demands for union recognition and collective bargaining. It let them picture themselves as champions of the public interest, responsible to all the people.

Even that argument began to lose its force with the accumulation of economic, social, and political change dealt with earlier in this chapter. The ever increasing militancy of public employees and their organizations forced the issue. Administrators had to face the question: Is it more logical to permit chaos in the provision of public services by refusing to bargain, or to lay the sovereignty argument quietly to rest? A growing body of public policy clearly favors the second as the more responsible alternative.

Government as Rule Maker. Disposing of sovereignty as an ideology and rationale for the refusal to bargain does not annul sovereignty as a fact. Above the government or beyond it, no human power holds sway that can step in, as government does in the relations between its citizens, either to make the rules, or interpret and arbitrate. Government is still the rule maker in bargaining with its employees, and at the same time a party to proceedings under those rules. This is particularly true at federal and state levels; less so at the local level, where rules for rule making come down as a mandate from state legislatures. The state does not identify its interests completely with the interests of local government officials; in fact, it has sovereignty over them.

It would appear then that the number of actors in Dunlop's theoretical framework shrink from the three he identifies in the private sector to only two in the public sector industrial relations system. Public employees and their labor organizations tend to regard this as a disadvantage. It gives them no ultimate appeal from management decisions. The current limited scope of collective bargaining in the federal service reveals how government can so set up the rules of the game as to preclude effective bargaining on many substantive issues.

At the local level, in contrast, a rule maker (the state) stands above local public management. As a consequence, meaningful collective bargaining relations have developed much faster.

Managers in public enterprises may not feel as keenly as the employee representative with whom they bargain about the lack of a third actor; but managers are not unaware of the problem nor have they proved entirely unsympathetic. Impasse procedures including binding arbitration by impartial third parties has, therefore, received special attention in the public sector. In Dunlop's scheme the arbitrator is a third actor, a "regulator," called into being by action and agreement of the two main actors.

The Right to Strike. Organized public employees would perhaps not feel so keenly the lack of a genuine third actor if the law allowed them the right to strike. When government denies this right to its employees, as it does in most jurisdictions, it tips the balance strongly in its own favor. Unions in private industry have the right to strike. Their freedom to use the strike weapon as an ultimate argument gives weight to the verbal arguments they offer at the bargaining table. No comparable weight of countervailing power backs up the bargaining-table arguments of public employee representatives.

Public employee labor organizations sometimes have the *power* to strike, as has been shown already, but for the most part they still lack the legal *right*. It makes a difference. It limits the bargaining effectiveness of the organization by increasing the risk an employee faces by going on strike, and so inhibits willingness to back up bargaining-table demands. A strike is never without risk for strikers, but workers in private industry do not break the law merely by taking the strike decision. Losing a strike usually means no more to them than getting a smaller raise than they had hoped for. To the public employee a lost strike could mean a lost job and permanent ineligibility for further government employment.

While strikes may have special significance to public employees, the challenge they present to public policy makers is a serious one. To date public employees have violated no-strike laws with relative impunity. Faced with growing disregard for its laws, government must either move to uniformly and vigorously enforce strike prohibitions, remove such prohibitions, or provide an acceptable alternative for resolving bargaining impasses.

To date experience suggests vigorous enforcement is not feasible. First, amnesty for strikers is often a condition for settlement of the strike. Second, the sheer numbers or critical skills of employees often make their replacement quite difficult. Third, the punishment of strikers, especially strike leaders, only serves to stimulate union solidarity and militancy, compounding rather than solving the problem. Also public employers, like private employers, shy away from aggravating the long-term bargaining relationship by invoking negative sanctions in response to illegal strike activity. On occasion too, such punitive action only arouses public sympathy for strikers, especially if sanctions are applied against weaker unions while stronger ones go unpunished. For these reasons, public policy makers are currently looking closely at the other alternatives of relaxing strike prohibitions and providing impasse procedures to reduce the number of strikes.

A recent study of strikes in public employment suggests that a more selective strike ban, to apply only where immediate danger exists to public health and safety, is both more pragmatic and equitable than a blanket prohibition against all strikes.[2] Of course the major problem of such a proposal is establishing criteria used to decide when such danger actually exists. The problem is similar to that experienced in determining when a "national emergency" exists in the private sector. But despite these difficulties a few states have begun to experiment with relaxing strike prohibitions.

Separation and Diffusion of Powers.   Other uncertainties becloud labor-management relations and hold back meaningful collective bargaining because of the diffusion of decision-making power within the institutions of a democratic government designed with a system of checks and balances.

Ideally, the legislative branch forges public policy and appropriates money from taxes to carry it out. The executive branch implements policy and carries it into action. The judicial branch stands aside, using its powers only to ensure that the executive does not overstep its policy mandates and that acts of both the executive and legislative branches are consistent with the constitution.

---

[2] John F. Burton, Jr. and Charles Krider, "The Role and Consequences of Strikes by Public Employees," *The Yale Law Journal*, vol. 79, no. 3, January 1970.

The legislative branch customarily determines general pay levels and other economic benefits for government employees. Administrators in the executive branch exercise varying degrees of discretion on other matters affecting personnel policies and practices. A civil service system in most jurisdictions further limits the discretionary authority of government administrators by prescribing standards and regulations. Collective bargaining thus takes place within three sets of limitations, any or all of which, through lack of coordination, could confuse or frustrate the negotiations.

Civil Service.   The civil service system first entered into government late in the last century. Under the spoils system then prevalent, elected officials made party or personal loyalty rather than ability in the duties of the job, their criterion for appointing backers and followers to positions on the public payroll. When a new administration won election on a pledge to "turn the rascals out," they would carry out that campaign promise, by appointing their own rascals instead.

Reformers offered the novel idea that government employees ought to serve, primarily, the public interest. Instead of favoritism as the standard for getting and holding a government job, they proposed the idea of merit. Congress eventually accepted the reform principles and established the U.S. Civil Service Commission to put them into practice. A few states had already instituted the reforms; others followed, along with cities and other units of local government. Most of them did this by legislative action, but some by constitutional provisions or amendments.

Civil service administration unifies and coordinates personnel policies and practices between various branches of the political jurisdiction it serves. Regulations emphasize job tenure, merit promotion, equity in compensation, and due process procedures for hearing employee complaints. The civil service administration may be likened to a benevolent personnel department of the government. The standards and procedures introduced made government, indeed, for many years the model employer.

Given these protections, many public employees saw no necessity for unions or collective bargaining. In fact, some independent associations of public employees, have opposed legislation that would authorize collective bargaining, on the ground that it would be incompatible with the privileges that civil service has accorded personnel in government service. It is noteworthy, however, that once the bills they opposed turned into law, most of these same associations quickly reversed their position and sought bargaining recognition for the members they represented.

With all the acknowledged improvements that it brought, civil service performance fell short of promises in many instances. Politicians with power of appointment sometimes found ways of frustrating the intent of the merit system. Even when civil service operated almost ideally, as planned, employees began to look on it as a form of bureaucratic paternalism; for in the last analysis, it gave them little to say in setting the rules and regulations. Its standards dealt with the important issues in their relation to the government as their employer, but could do little to shield them, in the work group, from the autocracy of a supervisor who might happen to be a petty bureaucrat. Work-group relations, after all, give tone and set the values in a person's daily life. The more general conditions, over which civil service did hold sway, lost their attraction as compared to private industry when, as noted earlier, conditions in the private sector improved. Large numbers of government employees became disillusioned.

As they turned now to collective bargaining for improvements in their lot, they often found themselves bumping head-on against the civil service regulations. These regulations, they were told, were not negotiable, because they carried out a legislative mandate. Administrators too found civil service regulations hamstringing their honest efforts to bargain with employees. When both sides turned to the boards and administrators of the civil service system, they encountered frustration. The guardians of the system all too frequently interpreted requests for change as attacks on the merit principle. In upholding principle, some of them perhaps—humanly enough—were actually springing to the defense of their own personal prerogative.

The policy of public employee unions like AFSCME and many public employee associations is to eventually replace the protective features of civil service with negotiated agreements. As this occurs civil service systems will come more to resemble the personnel system of unionized private employers. Moreover, the demise of the paternal role of civil service systems will cause a corresponding ascendency of the authority of line administrators in determining personnel policy and practices—albeit often on a shared basis with the employee organization.

Who Speaks for the Public Employer? Private industry experience clearly indicates that bargaining is most effective when labor and management speak, from their respective sides of the bargaining table, with a single voice. Achieving comparable unity on the employee side in the public sector appears to be no problem; but as the preceding section showed, the same cannot be said for the management side. This raises a critical question for collective bargaining: Who speaks for the public employer? And, on what issues?

The answer to this double-barrelled question varies from one jurisdiction to another. But at present, and probably for some time to come, the response to the question, who speaks for the public employee, would have to be in the plural; and to the question, on what issues, complex and confusing. It becomes more confusing when employee organizations deliberately—or even reluctantly, as a result of the plurality of employer spokesmen—play one decision-making level of government against another.

A firefighter union, for example, may first try to bargain with city executives for a reduction in the work week from 56 hours to 48. Failing to get this concession, they carry their case to the city council, where they may exercise sufficient political influence over enough of the council members to win their point. Failing here, however, they carry the issue to the state legislature through their state-wide organization and its labor union allies. They try to lobby through a bill that would make mandatory on the cities the 48-hour week for firefighters. Often, they succeed.

Little wonder that executives in local government hesitate to make concessions. They can be almost certain the employee organization will make the concessions they grant a floor from which to escalate demands, and then go on to better them at higher levels. It seems more responsible—though less popular—to say no to the union at the very start. This nay-saying attitude, carried over a range of issues, can frustrate even reasonable demands. It is hard to convince public employee labor organizations to refrain from such tactics, and probably just as hard to keep the higher-level bodies from going along with them.

Imagine a similar arrangement in private industry. Suppose the private employer should delegate some bargaining authority to production-oriented line managers, some to a professionally oriented personnel director, while reserving ultimate authority to a fiscal-minded board of directors far removed from the workplace. Imagine further the union's having substantial influence with the board by the possession of proxy voting power. Then let any one of the three attempt to write out with the union a collective bargaining agreement satisfactory to the needs and interests of all.

What the public sector situation amounts to is a breakdown—or at least a common defect—in the delegation of management authority. This weakness may be inherent in democratic government. Until government speaks with a single voice in collective bargaining, it is likely to continue.

Winston Churchill (or some other statesman to whom it is customary to attribute wise sayings) is supposed to have remarked: "Democracy is not a very good system of government; it just happens to be the best we have been able to devise." Perhaps the diffusion of decision-making power, which applies to many aspects of government and not just to collective bargaining, is as much a strength as a weakness of the system, but it makes bargaining more difficult and confusing to the participants.

Professional Authority

Through education and training, professionals acquire expert power; by social convention and sometimes liscensure they acquire, to varying degrees, authority over their occupation and work lives. Emerging professionals such as police officers seek such power and authority so they may claim full professional status.

The inherent conflict between professional and bureaucratic authority is well-documented in the organizational behavior literature. Elected officials and bureaucrats believe their positions entitle them alone to make policy decisions. In contrast, professionals believe that their knowledge better qualifies them to make decisions when policy decisions relate to their professional area of expertise. This conflict is intensified in the public sector because of the principles of representative democracy and governmental sovereignty. Thus, decisions like those about educational curriculum, nurses' control over patient care, and the kind of ammunition police officers use, have become hotly contested bargaining issues in public sector negotiations. However, it also should be remembered that concerns about pay, fringe benefits, and job security—traditional trade union issues—also have been the cause of heated negotiations and strikes by professionals. Often it is difficult to distinguish whether an item in contention is a professional or bread-and-butter issue. For instance, is a teacher organization's demand for reduced class size a reflection of a concern for educational quality or a move to strike a better wage and effort bargain? In reality, elements of both professional and pecuniary concerns are present in many demands made in professional negotiations. Regardless, it is clear that professional expertise gives these individuals a different perspective on bargaining as well as more bargaining power.

Professionals make demands for bilateral decision making in areas traditionally thought to be the private reserve of public as well as private sector management, such as agency mission, staffing levels, budget priorities, and job assignments. Sorting out the various rights and responsibilities of professional employees, public administrators, and elected officials will remain a perennial problem in public sector bargaining.

The Public.   A final element in the power relations context is the people. In a democracy it is the people—however indirectly, however feebly —who exercise the ultimate decision-making power. The people enter the processes of collective bargaining infrequently, but when they do, they become the court of last appeal. A striking example of public intervention over a noneconomic bargaining issue came in New York City in 1968.

The Patrolmen's Benevolent Association (PBA) demanded an end to the use of a public review board in the police department's disciplinary system. Having failed to get city executives to remove it by administrative action or the board of aldermen to dissolve it by legislative action, the PBA took the issue to the people of the city by initiative referendum. They won an easy victory.

The tactic of going to the people has also worked on bread-and-butter issues such as pay. In 1968 the San Francisco firefighters' union, unable to convince city officials that firefighters should get parity pay with police, took the issue to the people. They won their point.

While public intervention of so direct a nature is infrequent, public opinion remains a constant and pervasive element of the power relations context. Labor and management in the private sector do not have to reckon with it to the same extent. More often than not, when they work out arrangements they find satisfactory, they can ignore public opinion, but not so either public management or public employee labor organizations.

Both sides often appeal directly to the public. Since wages and benefits have fallen behind in recent years, employees feel they have a convincing case, which they do not hesitate to lay before the public. As the gap narrows and discrepancies begin to disappear, they will probably be less inclined to do this. A day may come when public opinion could conceivably shift in favor of management. Wry tribute to the power of public opinion came in the action of New York City firefighters to improve their public image. The leaders of the union launched a quiet campaign to discourage members from such practices as sitting out in front of fire stations in captain's chairs apparently doing nothing while they drew their pay. This undercut the professional firefighter image the leaders were trying to impress on the public mind.

Multilateral Bargaining

Many variations in the context of public and private sector bargaining can be summarized by a discussion of the concept of multilateralism. Multilateral bargaining occurs when either or both parties directly involved in bargaining are influenced by one or more other parties able to impose costs on the negotiators. To some extent, multilateralism is endemic to the concept of collective bargaining, i.e., the public at large always has some impact on negotiations whether public or private. However, in the public sector we find situations and interrelationships that often encourage, if not require, multilateral bargaining.

The concerns and influence that established interest groups, such as PTAs, Chambers of Commerce, and similar community organizations, have been brought to bear directly on the parties to public sector negotiations. For instance, a local chamber may see that if a costly work rule demanded by a firefighters' union is acceded to by the city that it would result in drastically reduced fire insurance rates for business. The pressure they bring to bear on public administrators and elected officials may be sufficient to result in the desired outcome, despite the fact that the city administration sees such a concession as imposing overall inefficiencies in department operations.

Moreover, many public sector negotiations involve professionals whose clients often can be an effective influence on public management. For instance, in the late 1960s the organized professional social workers in Los Angeles successfully rallied their welfare clients to bring additional pressure on city and county negotiators. Teachers also have been able to do likewise on numerous occasions.

The system of checks and balances built into American government at all levels promotes multilateralism. In addition, the increasingly complex web of intergovernmental programs and grants and contracts result in another form of multilateralism. For instance, the federal government requires in many instances that recipients of federal grants and contracts, such as cities and states, adhere to rigorous fair employment and merit principle standards. It was just such "strings" that were involved in the 1975 confrontation between the Detroit Police Officers Association (DPOA), the

City of Detroit, and the federal government about whether impending lay-offs of police officers would be based on the seniority principle or on the principles of equal employment and affirmative action. A federal court eventually ruled that the fair employment provisions of federal regulations overrode the seniority principle negotiated by the parties in their collective agreement.

In summary, multilateral bargaining is endemic to public sector negotiations. While present to some degree in all negotiations, it is less so in the private sector negotiations where the parties can hammer out their contract largely unrestrained by the influences of third parties. Multilateral bargaining compounds the problem of carrying on good faith negotiations since it increases the chances that negotiators may have to backtrack when and if some interested third parties take an interest in the negotiations.

Strikes

Strikes by public employees rose alarmingly during the 1960s and early 1970s. In 1960 there were 36 strikes involving 28,600 workers; by 1970 the totals were 412 and 333,500, respectively—approximately one third of both totals was the result of job actions by teachers. In 1970 one out of ten strikes in the United States involved public employees—a rate fast approaching the proportion of public to private sector workers. Clearly by 1970 the strike was no longer an exceptional event in public sector labor relations. Excluding the 1970 postal strike and major slowdown by federal air traffic controllers there have been only a handful of other minor walkouts by federal employees. State and local employees, particularly teachers, have been the most prone to use the strike weapon as shown in Table 15–1.

TABLE 15–1
Strike Activity by Service and Level of Government Involved, 1972*

Public Service Involved	Number of Strikes		Workers Involved		Work Days Idle	
	State	Local	State	Local	State	Local
Education	15	178	9,283	81,243	81,807	806,220
Teachers	2	144	5,125	66,591	5,125	639,437
Others	13	82	4,158	14,652	76,682	166,783
Highways and streets	4	54	663	2,673	663	22,047
Public welfare	1	10	53	2,473	106	15,081
Hospitals	7	9	8,588	2,466	30,876	9,073
Police protection	—	22	—	611	—	2,561
Fire protection	—	11	—	572	—	3,606
Sanitation	—	65	—	4,080	—	27,465
Totals†	34	347	20,758	110,113	119,809	1,004,198

* October 1971 through October 1972.
† Detail of data in all columns, except for "Workers Involved" may not add to state and local totals because of strikes involving more than one of the services shown.
Source: U.S. Bureau of the Census, Census of Governments, 1972, *Public Employment,* vol. 3, *Management-Labor Relations,* no. 3, 1974.

The table discloses that public employees in a variety of occupational categories have continued to find the strike a viable bargaining tactic. In terms of frequency, duration, and number of employees involved, there is no sign of public employee militancy tapering off significantly in the 1970s.

No wonder then that public policy makers have been concerned with formulating rules for rule-making that would reverse or at least stabilize the amount of strike activity by public and professional employees. For this reason a number of state and local governments have enacted legislation establishing the rights of such employees to organize and negotiate with their employers. As with the passage of the Wagner Act in 1935, this drastically has reduced the number of strikes involving the issue of the employer refusing to recognize or bargain with the employee organization. In addition, a growing number of jurisdictions are requiring the parties to utilize impasse procedures such as mediation, fact finding, and arbitration.

Impasse Procedures

By 1975 over half the states, the federal government and the nonprofit health care industry required that the parties avail themselves of impasse procedures when negotiations reached a deadlock. Most of these prescribed procedures involve only mediation and fact finding steps. However, some of these regulations require that the parties be prepared to submit their bargaining disputes to final and binding arbitration—most notably in disputes involving police officers, fire fighters, and postal workers.

Mediation as a process in which a neutral third party assists the disputing parties in a search for compromise and agreement has been a significant force in public sector bargaining, primarily because of the newness of the participants. Mediators typically play an important educational role in introducing the parties to the bargaining process. The technical expertise and data they bring to the disputants often is sufficient to permit, after realistic reappraisal, voluntary settlement. Mediators also perform their time-honored roles of listener, issue definer, and communicator between the parties. As a catalyst and leader performing these and other activities, mediators have facilitated agreement in the public as they have likewise done in the private sector.

For example, in Wisconsin, mediators successfully promoted settlement in 75 percent of the cases where impasses were declared in police and fire disputes in 1973 under new legislative impasse procedures.[3] In part this success is due to the risks associated with binding arbitration—the final step in these procedures. This fact highlights a typical difference between public and private mediation: In the private sector the strike deadline poses real incentives to make mediation work. Comparable risks often are missing in

---

[3] James Stern, "Final Offer Arbitration—Initial Experience in Wisconsin," *Monthly Labor Review*, vol. 97 (1974), p. 39.

the public sector where no such deadline exists—unless set by a militant employee group or a requirement to arbitrate.

Fact-finding proceedings may be conducted by a tripartite panel or a single neutral party. Most public bargaining relationships experience fact finding as the terminal impasse step. Fact finding is a multifaceted process combining features of both mediation and arbitration. Like mediators, fact finders typically attempt through the infusion of new information, fresh perspectives, and expert persuasion to move the parties toward voluntary settlements. Failing this they exercise their best judgment to recommend a settlement to the parties in light of generally accepted standards and their findings of fact.

As with mediation, fact finding often has been successful in resolving contract disputes in direct proportion to the inexperience of the parties involved. Fact-finding often serves as a crash course in the bargaining process, particularly in the factors normally and traditionally utilized in collective bargaining for determining wages and working conditions. To do so requires that fact finders take an active role in striving for consensus on disputed items rather than assuming a passive, quasijudicial posture of simply acting as an umpire between two opponents in a contest.

Another major reason for the success of fact finding is that while the negotiators are knowledgeable about patterns, principles, and power relations dictating the settlement, their constituents are not. The fact-finding process provides another opportunity, this time through a disinterested third party, for negotiators to communicate to these constituents the realities dictating the settlement range in the negotiations. In this same vein, fact-finders' recommendations often permit one or both negotiators to "get off the hook" when they are not secure enough politically to recommend a settlement they know is about the best their side could hope to achieve under the circumstances.

Final and binding arbitration is the terminal point in an increasing number of bargaining relationships—most noticeably in those dealing with vital services such as police and fire protection. In 1975 many of the most populous states provide for arbitration as the terminal point of impasse procedures in bargaining disputes involving public safety employees. Arbitration can serve some of the same functions as fact finding; i.e., providing a scapegoat for one or both parties faced with an unsatisfactory settlement. In addition, arbitration has the added advantage of serving as a point of finality in negotiations that might otherwise necessitate a strike or inhibit bargaining in the absence of a deadline.

However, fears exist that granting the right by either party to demand arbitration of disputed contract terms will undercut the motivation to negotiate in good faith. The rationale for this apprehension is that it always will be to the advantage of either party to go to arbitration—typically the one whose demands are within recognized industry patterns. Therefore, that party simply will go through the motions prior to arbitration—including mediation and fact finding if required. The other party, frustrated by this strategy, typically will not make its best offers for fear an arbitrator might eventually sweeten this final offer by adding something more in a spirit of compromise. Therefore, arbitration retards the good faith making of proposals and counterproposals, and thereby, frustrates or chills the bargaining process.

However, the record to date does not substantiate these fears. A recent study of the experience with binding arbitration in Pennsylvania, Michigan, and Wisconsin concluded that the existence of a statutory requirement to arbitrate had a salutory rather than chilling effect on bargaining—while, at the same time, virtually eliminating strikes by police officers and firefighters covered by the laws.[4] A major reason for the positive impacts on bargaining is identified to be the tendency of such laws to provide a better balance of power between police and fire employee organizations and their municipal employers. The greater potential risks in terms of contract outcomes, coupled with the direct costs of arbitration itself, apparently is strong stimulus for the parties to reach voluntary settlements. Another cited reason is the tendency of interest arbitrators to wear a "mediator's hat" until a decision is necessary. This has resulted in many arbitration proceedings being concluded short of the issuance of an award.

The "last best offer" variant of binding arbitration introduced in Wisconsin and Michigan in 1972 appears to provide a particularly strong stimulus to bargain. Under this form of interest arbitration each party, after exhausting the potentials for voluntary settlement, submits its final and best offer on all disputed items. The arbitrators then are required to pick one or the other's final offer as being most reasonable and equitable. By eliminating any possibility of compromise or difference-splitting by the arbitrators, this form of arbitration obviously decreases a party's motivation to not make its best offer in negotiation and increases the potentially negative contract outcomes of going to an arbitrator rather than settling the issues through give and take at the bargaining table. The "winner take all" psychology underlying the last offer form of arbitration generally results in the parties opening negotiations with more realistic positions. It also tempers their final offers should the dispute reach the arbitration step. In either case the chances are better for a voluntary settlement occurring.

The procedures of interest arbitration parallel those of fact finding. After hearing testimony and receiving data and exhibits the arbitrators assess the positions of the parties using a test of reasonableness. Is one or the other party's position—or some middle position—reasonable in light of past negotiations between the parties; employment practices in comparable situations; prevailing patterns of wages, hours, and working conditions in the

---

[4] Charles M. Rehmus, "Legislated Interest Arbitration," *Proceedings of the Twenty-Seventh Annual Winter Meetings,* Industrial Relations Research Association, 1974, pp. 307–314.

community, area, state, region, and industry as well as consistent with the realities of the labor market. The critical question asked most often by interest arbitrators in assessing reasonableness is: In regard to the disputed issues, what have parties similarly situated found reasonable to agree to? Because of this fact and the typical emphasis on comparability and prevailing practice, interest arbitration tends to be a status quo-oriented process. It seldom produces innovative contract terms or above-average economic packages.

It is precisely because interest arbitration tends to be status quo-oriented that it has been shunned traditionally by the labor movement which has viewed its primary goal as making breakthroughs for its members in wages, benefits, and working conditions. Such breakthroughs are difficult, if not impossible, to achieve through arbitration. Despite these drawbacks some public employee organizations prefer to justify needed contractual changes before an arbitrator rather than strike to achieve improvements. In part interest arbitration has been successful in the public sector because of this willingness and a corresponding acceptance by public employers that the results of arbitration may well be less costly to its constituents than the costs of strikes and the potentially more expensive settlements that might result from strike induced bargaining. It is noteworthy that currently neither union or management representatives in Pennsylvania, Michigan, or Wisconsin are pushing to have arbitration statutes repealed.

In summary, binding arbitration has stimulated rather than retarded bargaining in light of experience to date. However, this success has been largely confined to the protective services where strong sentiments exist on both sides to accept the process even if acceptance is reluctant. Moreover, the last offer form of arbitration shows significant promise of building enough risk into the arbitration step to make it a viable alternative to the strike particularly in other situations where strong ethical or practical reasons exist on the part of both parties to avoid strikes.

SUMMARY

Proportionally more public than private workers are involved directly in collective bargaining activities. Only a decade ago the situation was reversed dramatically. Variations in the market and power relations contexts of their industrial relations systems make for differences in bargaining practices between the public and private sectors. The absence of true markets for most public services coupled with democratic political institutions causes a deemphasis of economic forces and highlights political considerations in public sector bargaining. Governmental sovereignty, civil service systems, restrictions on strike activity, professional authority and greater use of interest arbitration are major power relation features that alter practices in the public sector.

Market forces, as commonly understood, are absent; instead, there is competition over claims to shares in a relatively fixed budget between rival segments of the public, including organized public employees. Power relations consequently provide the context of greatest significance for the practice of collective bargaining.

Unique to public sector power relations is the nature of the government's sovereign power. Because there is no neutral third actor standing above government (except, perhaps, indirectly and remotely the people), there appear to be only two actors in the public sector industrial relations system, one with sovereignty over the other. Most public employees cannot legally resort to a form of sanction, the strike, that is an institutionalized part of the private sector. When they do strike they utilize a weapon unavailable to the competing organized rival publics.

The separation and diffusion of powers in a democratic system of government inject confusion into collective bargaining procedures. This along with a complex set of interrelations among levels of government and organized political pressure groups results in multilateralism being far more characteristic of public than private sector bargaining.

Most organized professionals are found in the public sector—notably teachers and nurses. The oft-noted conflict between bureaucratic authority and professional expertise becomes a focal point of professional bargaining, along with traditional trade union issues of pay and job security. The clash between principles of representative democracy and professional expertise as the basis for public decisions forms a frequent and dramatic backdrop for public sector bargaining.

QUESTIONS FOR DISCUSSION

1. In what sense can it be said that there is no "market" in the public sector? What implications does this have for the practice of collective bargaining?
2. Why have public employees been almost 25 years behind private sector employees in making widespread use of collective bargaining?
3. Why is the question "Who speaks for the public employer?" particularly perplexing? What implications does the answer have for the character of the bargaining relationship?
4. What role has the concept of sovereignty played in the evolution of the public sector industrial relations system?
5. What special problems are often involved when professional employees bargain with governmental employers?
6. How does compulsory and binding arbitration impact the practice of bargaining? As contrasted with mediation?
7. What are some examples of multilateral bargaining that you are familiar with?

SELECTED ANNOTATED BIBLIOGRAPHY

Barrett, Jerome T., and Lobel, Ira B. "Public Sector Strikes—Legislative and Court Treatment," *Monthly Labor Review*, September 1974, pp. 19–23.

Study shows increasing experimentation with allowing employees a limited right to strike and reluctance of courts to issue injunctions to stop walkouts.

BLAU, PETER, and SCOTT, W. RICHARD. *Formal Organizations: A Comparative Approach.* New York: Chandler Publishing, 1962.

A classic text in organizational behavior that focuses closely on the dynamics of professional-bureaucratic conflict in organizations.

BLUM, ALBERT A.; ESTEY, MARTEN; KUHN, JAMES; and WILDMAN, WESLEY. *White Collar Workers.* New York: Random House, 1971.

Engineers, teachers and government professional employees among others are comprehensively surveyed with particular attention to their use of collective bargaining.

BUREAU OF NATIONAL AFFAIRS. *Government Employees Relations Reporter,* and *White Collar Report.* Washington, D.C.: U.S. Government Printing Office.

These two series of reports are continuing publications of the Bureau that report and index relevant bargaining developments among public and professional employees.

BUREAU OF THE CENSUS, CENSUS OF GOVERNMENTS, 1972. *Public Employment,* vol. 3, *Management-Labor Relations in State and Local Governments,* no. 3. Washington, D.C.: U.S. Government Printing Office, 1974.

Done every five years, this volume gives detailed statistical data on the extent of bargaining in the 50 states.

CLARK, R. THEODORE, JR. *Coping with Mediation, Fact Finding and Forms of Arbitration.* Chicago: International Personnel Management Association, 1974.

A brief review by a noted labor attorney of practices typically encountered during impasse procedures. Special emphasis on how to participate in a fact finding and arbitration proceedings.

ELKOURI, FRANK, and ELKOURI, EDNA A. *How Arbitration Works.* 3rd ed. Washington, D.C.: Bureau of National Affairs, 1973.

A comprehensive treatise on the arbitration process. Chapter 18 contains a detailed analysis of standards arbitrators use in deciding interest disputes.

GILROY, THOMAS, and RUSSO, ANTHONY. *Bargaining Unit Issues: Problems, Criteria, Tactics.* Public Employee Relations Library Series No. 43.

A discussion of the factors such as community of interest that go into determinations by the parties and/or administrative agencies of federal, state, and local governments in determining appropriate bargaining units. Discusses pros and cons of large versus small units.

KLEINGARTNER, ARCHIE. "Collective Bargaining between Salaried Professionals and Public Sector Management," *Public Administration Review,* vol. 33, no. 2 (March–April, 1973), pp. 165–72.

A concise overview of dynamics of professional-public agency bargaining with particular attention to bureaucratic-professional conflict over agency mission.

KLEINGARTNER, ARCHIE. *Professional and Quasi-Union Organization and Bargaining Behavior: A Bibliography.* Los Angeles: University of California, Institute of Industrial Relations, 1972.

A good source for beginning a literature search on the problems of specific professional groups such as librarians, engineers, scientists, and doctors. Also covers behavioral science literature on professionalism. Most citations are prior to 1970.

KOCHAN, THOMAS A. *Resolving Internal Management Conflicts for Labor Negotiations.* Chicago: International Personnel Management Association, 1974.

A brief discussion of the roles of elected civil service and administrative officials in bargaining and techniques for building internal cohesion in the management team.

LOWENBERG, J. JOSEPH. "Multilateral Bargaining: Variations on a Theme," *Labor Law Journal,* February 1975, pp. 107–118.

Discussion of how requirements of federal personnel programs and grants such as CETA add a new dimension to multilateral bargaining.

LOWENBERG, J. JOSEPH, and MOSKOW, MICHAEL M. *Collective Bargaining in Government: Readings and Cases.* Englewood Cliffs, N.J.: Prentice-Hall, 1972.

An excellent compilation of articles and case studies that provide both a wide and deep perspective on public sector bargaining.

NEWLAND, CHESTER, ed. *MBO and Productivity Bargaining in the Public Sector.* Chicago: International Personnel Management Association, 1974.

A series of articles on the promises and pitfalls of using a management by objectives approach to labor relations problems, including bargaining.

REHMUS, CHARLES M. "Legislated Interest Arbitration." *Proceedings of the Twenty-Seventh Annual Winter Meeting, Industrial Relations Research Association, 1974,* pp. 307–14.

Excellent summary article of recent experience under compulsory and binding interest arbitration with particular attention to the experience in Michigan, Wisconsin, and Pennsylvania.

SMITH, RUSSELL A., ET AL. *Labor Relations Law in the Public Sector.* New York: Bobbs-Merrill Company, 1974.

A comprehensive volume of source material on public sector bargaining. Includes brief analysis with case material on major areas from unit determination to the legality of arbitration.

STANLEY, DAVID. *Managing Local Governments under Union Pressure.* Washington, D.C.: The Brookings Institution, 1972.

After an analysis of bargaining relations in a representative set of U.S. cities concludes that the major impact of bargaining will be the displacement of civil service protections with collective agreements. Otherwise, public management is not seen as being seriously hamstrung by the advent of bargaining.

STERN, JAMES L., ET AL. *Final Offer Arbitration.* Lexington, Mass.: D. C. Heath Co., 1975.

The published results of a study of such laws discloses both the promise and pitfalls of the process. Study does suggest that "last best offer" arbitration holds promise of being a viable substitute for strikes under certain conditions.

STERN, JAMES L. "Final Offer Arbitration—Initial Experience in Wisconsin," *Monthly Labor Review,* vol. 97 (1974), p. 39.

Analyzes experience under new "last best offer" arbitration statute passed in 1972. Concludes that impact has on the whole been positive, in large part because of a heavy emphasis on mediation prior to arbitration.

STIEBER, JACK. *Public Employee Unionism: Structure, Growth, Policy.* Washington, D.C.: The Brookings Institution, 1973.

A detailed account of the development of public sector unions and associations, their internal operation and bargaining objectives.

WELLINGTON, HARRY H., and WINTER, RALPH K., JR. *The Unions and the Cities.* Washington, D.C.: The Brookings Institution, 1973.

The authors contend through analysis of the impact of bargaining on cities that the private sector bargaining model is inappropriate in the public sector principally because militant public unions gain an inordinate share of political power.

ZAGORIA, SAM, ed. *Public Workers and Public Unions.* New York: Prentice-Hall, 1972.

A collection of provocative essays by noted authorities such as A. H. Raskin, labor editor of the *New York Times,* whose article "Politics Up-Ends the Bargaining Table," gives classical examples of both two-step bargaining and multilateralism.

16 Patterns of Bargaining among Public Agencies

THE PRECEDING chapter drew attention to the diffusion of decision-making power in American government. This traces back to the Constitution which, besides creating a system of checks and balances, divided power between the 13 previously independent states and the federal government they established. Each of the 50 states now making up the federal union differs internally in some respects from every other, but all contain many political jurisdictions with local constituencies and special powers: cities, counties, school districts, port authorities, and so on.

This democratic structure brings governmental actions and decisions close to the people they affect, but does create diversity and sometimes confusion. In France, for instance, a central ministry of education directs, finances, and controls the entire public school system down to the smallest primary school in the remotest village—and, incidentally, bargains collectively with a national union of teachers. By contrast, in the United States the states set general educational standards and license the teachers, but leave the school districts largely autonomous. If teachers unionize, they bargain with the district school board and superintendent.

Moreover, public agencies are increasingly dependent on the "knowledge worker"—their professional and quasi-professional employees that supply the critical expertise needed to deliver many public services. As noted in the previous chapter such workers pose special problems for management control—and ultimately democratic control—of governmental agencies at the federal, state and local levels.

This chapter examines the patterns of bargaining that have emerged among the wide diversity of governmental agencies in the United States as well as the quasi-public, nonprofit health care industry. Particular attention is paid to the involvement of professional employees in these patterns and to other bargaining pacesetters in the public sector such as fire fighters and police officers. We begin by looking at the largest single public employer— if one may call it a single employer—the federal government.

THE FEDERAL SERVICE

The practice of bargaining in the federal government is difficult to generalize about since it occurs in a wide variety of different contexts. Some agencies, like the Postal Service, Tennessee Valley Authority, and Federal Reserve System, are semiautonomous public corporations, each with different rules for rule-making. Other agencies, like the Treasury and Labor Departments, are tied closely to the White House. Contrasting two of the largest federal agencies, bargaining in the Department of Health, Education and Welfare (HEW) is quite different than in the Department of Defense (DOD). In HEW, bargaining often involves professional employees who seek to bargain on matters of the agency's mission as well as work scheduling. Bargaining in DOD typically involves blue collar workers and relates to traditional "bread and butter" issues, such as hours of work.

Background of Labor Relations in the Federal Service

Large bureaucracies, almost by definition, are rigid and conservative. With few exceptions, federal administrators have run their agencies autocratically under the paternalistic eye of the U.S. Civil Service Commission. Employee attempts to get some say in their working conditions by union organization and activity called forth from the administrations of Presidents Theodore Roosevelt and William Howard Taft what were called at the time "gag orders." In 1912 Congress nullified the gag orders by passing the Lloyd–La Follette Act that gave federal employees the right to join labor organizations and to petition Congress without fear of reprisal. This focused the activities of labor organizations on the legislative branch of government. It encouraged lobbying tactics rather than collective bargaining. The Wagner Act of 1935, while it encouraged bargaining in the private sector, specifically excluded government employees from its benefits.

In the years that followed, government apologists found it increasingly difficult to justify one policy for governmental and another for private employers. The civil rights movement of the 1960s intensified concern for equal treatment. In January 1962 President Kennedy issued an Executive Order, E.O. 10988, which for the first time granted restricted bargaining rights to federal employees. After several years of experience with Kennedy's order, President Nixon reaffirmed its basic principles and amplified its provisions in E.O. 11491.

Presidential action thus shifted somewhat the initiative for labor relations policy formulation in the federal service from the legislative to the executive branch. Lobbying in the halls of Congress still goes on—but so does collective bargaining in the operating agencies.

Executive Order 10988

Executive Order 10988 and two later implementing directives affirmed the right of federal employees to join or refrain from joining labor organizations. It set up procedures for bargaining unit determination and for recognition. It required agency heads to bargain in good faith with labor organizations that succeeded in gaining exclusive recognition through these procedures; this was probably the most important provision of the order. It specified unfair labor practices forbidden both to unions and management and contained a code of conduct to be adhered to by labor organizations. Many of these provisions were similar in content to those enacted for the private sector in the Labor-Management Relations Act (LMRA) or Taft-Hartley law.

Differences from Private Sector Labor Relations Law. With all these similarities, E.O. 10988 deviated in several important ways from principles and policies laid down in the LMRA. It continued an absolute ban on strikes by federal employees. It prohibited the union shop, in effect, but provided for exclusive recognition and added two lesser forms: formal and informal recognition, which gave unions consulting (but not bargaining) rights in units without an exclusive bargaining agent.

It left implementation to the agency heads, with staff help from the Secretary of Labor and the U.S. Civil Service Commission. It did not establish a separate agency comparable to the NLRB to conduct representation elections and safeguard employee rights. It limited the scope of bargaining by requiring that agreements must conform to existing laws and civil service regulations; and finally, it dictated a strong management rights clause to be included as part of every agreement as follows:

> Management officials of the agency retain the right, in accordance with applicable laws and regulations, (*a*) to direct employees of the agency, (*b*) to hire, promote, transfer, assign, and retain employees in positions within the agency, and to suspend, demote, discharge, or take other disciplinary action against employees, (*c*) to relieve employees from duties because of lack of work or for other legitimate reasons, (*d*) to maintain the efficiency of the Government operations entrusted to them, (*e*) to determine the methods, means, and personnel by which such operations are to be conducted; and (*f*) to take whatever actions may be necessary to carry out the mission of the agency in situations of emergency.

Even with these exceptions and limitations, E.O. 10988 brought governmental labor relations policy more in line with previously affirmed public policy in the private sector.

Response to E.O. 10988. Federal employees responded dramatically to the promulgation of E.O. 10988. Before its issuance in 1962, unions represented only 19,000 employees in 26 units of exclusive recognition. By 1968 they had negotiated written agreements for 1,175,542 employees and represented a total of 1,416,073 in 2,305 units; and consultation rights under formal or informal recognition in more than 2,000 additional units.[1] These figures had added significance in view of the lack of experience of agency heads with the mechanics of collective bargaining and their quite frequent lack of sympathy with the idea of bargaining.

Difficulties were anticipated, since the order had been intended as a transitional policy instrument. In 1967 President Johnson appointed a panel to review experience under E.O. 10988 and to recommend improvements. The major recommendations of the panel dealt with four substantive areas: (1) the establishment of a workable third-party procedure for resolving negotiation impasses because of the ban on strikes; (2) the establishment of a central authority to coordinate administration of the order and issue definitive interpretations of its provisions; (3) simplification of the kinds of recognition accorded unions; and (4) widening the scope of negotiations at all levels, primarily through greater decentralization of bargaining authority.

No action was taken on the panel's findings until the new Nixon administration took office in 1969 and issued Executive Order 11491.

Executive Order 11491

On October 29, 1969, the Nixon administration superseded E.O. 10988 with E.O. 11491. The stated purpose was to bring federal labor relations closer to the private sector model and to standardize procedures among the federal agencies. The text of this order as amended appears in the Appendix to this volume.

Nixon's order gives the Assistant Secretary of Labor authority to determine appropriate bargaining units, supervise recognition procedures, rule on unfair labor practices, and promulgate and enforce standards of conduct for labor organizations. There is no mistaking here the analogy to the powers and functions of the NLRB and General Counsel. Under the old order, agency heads had exercised all but the last of the above listed functions. E.O. 11491 also creates the central agency that had been lacking before: a Federal Labor Relations Council (FLRC).

The Council is composed of the Chairman of the Civil Service Commission, who serves as Council chairman, the Secretary of Labor, and the Director of the Office of Management and Budget. The Council has the final word on: (1) appeals from decisions of the Assistant Secretary of Labor; (2) negotiability of issues; (3) exceptions to arbitration awards; and (4) other matters pertaining to implementation.

While resembling the NLRB, the Council lacks independent agency

---

[1] Report of the President's Review Committee on Employee-Management Relations in the Federal Service, *Government Employee Relations Report*, Bureau of National Affairs, January 20, 1969.

status but supervises a wider range of responsibilities. The most notable of these is impasse resolution in the establishment of a Federal Service Impasse Panel.

Federal Service Impasse Panel. The impasse panel consists of seven impartial members appointed by the President from among neutrals outside the federal service. They have authority to take any action necessary to settle a dispute.

The panel has wide discretion. It may recommend procedures to the parties or issue orders. Without the panel's permission, the parties to a dispute may not resort either to fact-finding with recommendations or binding arbitration which would sidestep the panel. This latitude in the choice of methods open to the panel encourages both sides in negotiation to work out their problems jointly, since neither knows for sure how the panel will act.

Recognition and the Bargaining Unit. E.O. 11491 dropped "formal" and "informal" recognition as defined in the old order. Experience showed that these forms had promoted factionalism and inhibited meaningful relations. With a single exception, exclusive recognition became the only form attainable under the new order. To get exclusive bargaining rights a union had only to win a simple majority of voting employees rather than 60 percent as before. The one exception gives consultation rights, similar to the old formal recognition, but only at the national level. This permits unions with a substantial following at regional or lower levels, but not enough to win agency-wide exclusive recognition, the right to be heard (but not to bargain) at the agency's national headquarters on matters that would affect their members.

The new order added specific criteria for bargaining unit determination and recognition. These criteria follow the NLRB lead in trying to reconcile the needs and interests of the employees in a unit with the agency's need for efficiency in operations. The new order also made an important break with E.O. 10988 by excluding units of supervisors from achieving exclusive recognition except where historical precedence had been established. Supervisors are similarly denied these prerogatives under the NLRA.

The 1975 Amendments to E.O. 11491

In 1974 the FLRC carefully reviewed the positions of E.O. 11491 along with proposals for change from the parties. This led to a series of recommended changes, almost all of which were effectuated by E.O. 11838. The major thrust of the amendments, effective May 1975, was to broaden the scope of negotiations. All agency regulations were deemed negotiable unless the agency could show a "compelling need" not to negotiate. Likewise, all major changes in an agency's personnel policy and practices were made mandatory subjects of bargaining even when a contract is already in force. The FLRC is designated as the final arbiter as to what constitutes com-

TABLE 16–1
Total Employees in Exclusive Units and Covered by Agreement 1963–1974

| | Total Employees | | Employees in Exclusive Units | | | | Employees Covered by Agreement | |
| | | | Wage System Employees (blue collar) | | General Schedule Employees (white collar / professional) | | | |
Year	Total	Percent	Number	Percent	Number	Percent	Number	Percent
1963	180,000						110,573	6
1964	230,543	12					241,850	12
1965	319,724	16					291,532	14
1966	434,890*	21	226,150	40	179,293	15	423,052	20
1967	629,915	29	338,660	54	291,255	21	556,962	28
1968	797,511	40	400,669	67	396,842	28	559,415	28
1969	842,823	42	426,111	72	416,712	29	601,505	31
1970	916,381	48	429,136	81	487,245	35	707,067	36
1971	1,038,288	53	437,586	84	600,702	42	753,247	39
1972	1,082,587	55	427,089	83	655,498	46	837,410	43
1973	1,086,361	56	404,955	84	681,406	47	984,553	49
1974	1,142,419	57	406,000	82	736,419	48		

Note: 1963–66 statistics are based on figures as of mid-year; 1967–74 figures are as of November.
* Wage system and general schedule combined do not equal total due to unavailability of information on status of some employees.

pelling need or major personnel changes. Changes were also made in procedures for determining bargaining units that would encourage agency-wide bargaining.

A final major change made by E.O. 11838 was to give more vigor to negotiated grievance procedures by permitting them to deal with the interpretation and application of agency regulations as well as negotiated agreements. However, there was no change from the historic exclusion from negotiated grievance/arbitration procedures of matters subject to statutory appeals such as discharge, demotion, or discrimination based on race, sex, etc. Neither did the new amendments to E.O. 11491 repeal its ban on union or agency shops or the requirement that the management rights clause quoted above be part of all negotiated agreements.

Patterns of Organization and Bargaining

Since the issuance of E.O. 10988 there has been a steady increase in the number of federal employees involved in collective bargaining. Table 16–1 contains trend data on recognition and bargaining activity by employees of the executive branch.

The data disclose that in 1974 virtually all eligible blue collar employees and well over half the eligible white collar workers were in exclusive bargaining units in 1974. It also discloses a steady rise in the negotiation of contracts in the last few years as the scope of bargainable issues has begun to open up under recent amendments to E.O. 11491.

However, while over half of the eligible federal employees were covered by collective agreements, a significantly smaller proportion are dues-paying members of the 72 unions and associations representing federal employees in 1974. For instance, the largest single labor organization in the federal service, the American Federation of Government Employees (AFGE), AFL-CIO, in 1973 had representation of rights of 642,322 federal employees but only had 292,809 dues-paying members. This experience, while not typical, exemplifies the impact of the continuing ban on union security provision in federal contracts.

The vast majority of organized federal employees are members of AFL-CIO unions, which dominate in the organization of postal and wage board employees. However, in the classified service independent associations like the National Treasury Employees Union with 50,392 members and the National Federation of Federal Employees with 118,139 members in 1973 compete well with AFL-CIO unions for representation rights. Most all of the approximately 100,000 professional employees that are organized in the federal service are members of these associations as are many other classified white collar employees. All told, nearly one and three quarter millon federal employees were represented in 1975 for the purposes of collective bargaining.

Categories of Federal Employees

For the most part federal employees fall into one of three general categories: (1) wage board (hourly); (2) classified, or general schedule (salaried); and (3) postal (hourly and salaried, in a special program).

Wage Board Employees. Wage board employees are blue-collar workers in the trades, crafts, and manual occupations. In 1970, 81 percent of wage board employees were covered by exclusive recognition. They earn hourly wages comparable to private sector rates prevalent in the area where they work. Because the various agencies used different methods of wage comparison, inequities developed. So, in 1968 the U.S. Civil Service Commission set up a coordinated federal wage system. The aim was to make sure that no two employees working in the same job class for different agencies would be paid unequally—a chronic complaint of labor organizations representing wage board employees.

Some agencies had negotiated their wage comparisons with unions. The new program permits this practice to continue, but prohibits its spread. Instead, it provides representation for labor organizations on wage board committees at local and national levels. Of the 11-member National Wage Policy Committee, 5 are labor representatives, and 4 of these are appointed by the president of the AFL-CIO. For the first time this gives labor an official voice in wage board deliberations.

It is noteworthy that the Civil Service Commission did not move to establish this program until it seemed likely that union lobbying pressure in Congress would produce legislation threatening the commission's prerogatives.[2]

Classified Employees. More than half of all federal employees—about one and one-third million—are classified or general schedule employees: white-collar workers in clerical, technical, and professional occupations. They are classified in 18 grades for which, until recently, Congress directly set the pay levels. In 1970 the Federal Pay Comparability Act gave the President authority to adjust salaries of classified employees to make them comparable to private sector rates for similar jobs. The act also established a Federal Employee Pay Council to advise the President on the adjustments. This corresponds to the system for wage board employees, except that the salary schedules are uniform nationally and pay level comparisons national in scope. The President appoints five members of the council from labor organizations representing substantial numbers of federal employees.

Classified employees at 50 percent are the least organized category of federal employees. About one of seven of the 736,419 represented federal white collar workers is a professional. The majority of these professionals work for the Treasury, Army, Labor Departments, and Veterans Admin-

---

[2] Robert F. Repas, *Collective Bargaining in Federal Employment* (Honolulu: University of Hawaii, Industrial Relations Center, 1970).

istration, and include accountants, engineers, nurses, statisticians, and lawyers. Other federal departments with more than 1,000 represented professionals include: Navy, Transportation, Interior, Agriculture, Commerce, Health, Education and Welfare, National Aeronautics and Space Administration, Equal Employment Opportunity Commission, and the Tennessee Valley Authority.

As in private industry white collar employees in the federal service have been less inclined to organize or bargain than their blue collar counterparts —yet not nearly as strongly as in the private sectors. Only about 10 percent of private sector white collar workers are organized as compared with 50 percent in the federal service.

The Postal Service. As a result of the 1970 reorganization, the postal service is the most distinctive of the three groups. The post office employs over 700,000 workers. Unionism has always been strongest among postal workers and they have spearheaded the drive for collective bargaining rights in federal employment. They showed their strength in the week-long strike in March 1970 when more than 200,000 walked off the job. The postal reform bill that followed this impressive demonstration grants their union rights almost identical to those of unions in the private sector.

Congress acted speedily in the wake of the strike. On August 12, 1970, the Postal Reorganization Act became law. Article 12 of the act deals with labor-management relations. In essence, Article 12 brings postal workers under the provisions of the LMRA and within the jurisdiction of the NLRB. It authorizes collective bargaining on wages and other conditions of employment.

The act still bans strikes, but sets up impasse procedures that culminate in binding arbitration over terms of an agreement that are in dispute. It also bans the union shop, but appears to permit the agency shop.

Postal employees are more thoroughly unionized than either wage board or classified employees, with 87 percent in units of exclusive recognition. Almost all of these are in AFL–CIO unions. The traditional form of organization has been by what the postal workers called "crafts"—clerks, carriers, mail handlers, motor vehicle employees, and maintenance employees—but these separate unions amalgamated into a single union in May 1971 when 4 of the former crafts and 1 rival industrial union, the National Postal Union, merged to form the American Postal Workers Union (APWU) which reported a membership of 238,763 in 1973. At that same time it represented approximately 400,000 postal workers. If the National Association of Letter Carriers ever amalgamates with the APWU, the resulting organization will represent virtually all postal employees.

Since the 1970 reorganization three two-year national agreements have been negotiated in the postal service—without resort to either a strike or final and binding arbitration. Supplemental local agreements to the national pact are also negotiated. A significant feature of recent postal bargaining has been the utilization of expedited arbitration procedures to take care of many grievances such as those dealing with discipline and discharge. The system is analogous to one in the basic steel industry. Under its provision there is only an informal hearing on the grievance with an award within 48 hours. There are no briefs, no transcript, no opinion. Simply a hearing and a quick decision. The system succeeded and it was continued at the end of its trial period in early 1975.

Bargaining Structure

Community of interest was originally the only criteria for determining appropriate bargaining units under federal executive orders. This encouraged fragmentation in the bargaining structure. Along with the three levels of recognition permitted under E.O. 10988, this unit determination policy facilitated the creation of numerous small bargaining units.

Executive Order 11491 attempted to stimulate larger units by balancing the community of interest of the employees with two more criteria in the determination of appropriate bargaining units, namely, agency operating efficiency and stability of labor relations. It also made exclusive recognition the only kind available to employee organizations. In part these changes account for the recent trend toward larger bargaining units and the decreasing success of organizing attempts over larger more heterogenous bargaining units. However, the residual effect of the early policy still finds a highly fragmented bargaining structure that hampers both contract negotiation and administration. National employee organizations do not have the resources to service numerous small units and the local leadership typically lacks the expertise to do an adequate job of either bargaining or handling grievances. The most recent amendments to E.O. 11491 are designed to encourage consolidation of bargaining units to stimulate the development of a more efficient bargaining structure in the future.

Extent of Bargaining in the Non-Postal Service

Except in a few agencies (most notably the postal service) collective bargaining is currently decentralized. Most agreements cover only a local installation or activity, and deal mainly with working conditions because of the narrow scope permitted as subjects of negotiation prior to 1975. Items include hours of work, rest periods, parking, work clothing, safety, discipline, grievance procedures, union prerogatives—that is, the rights to union representatives in agreement administration—and provisions for impasse resolution.

Local level bargaining previously had to steer clear of agency-wide policy and regulations; hence it could not alter agency personnel practices. Wages and nonwage economic benefits furthermore (except in the postal service) are outside the bounds of collective bargaining. In addition, civil service rules that regulate the most important conditions of employment also lay outside the scope of bargaining. However, under the new 1975 rules the commission will be "deregulating" except in areas it finds there is "compelling need" to retain control.

Somewhat in recompense, wage board and classified employees have gained representation on the council that set pay levels; and the executive branch has gained greater freedom to establish the basic scales as well as to adjust inequities. Here "bargaining" occurs over the comparability of private and federal jobs, timing and sampling procedures in doing compensation surveys, changes in cost of living after surveys are completed and related matters.

Grievance Procedures.   A great deal of federal service bargaining has focused on trying to get satisfactory grievance procedures. Most agreements provide grievance systems separate from civil service procedures, but give grievants the right to choose either channel. They specify the grounds for grievances and the steps for adjusting them and most are now providing for arbitration as the final step. Like bargaining itself, however, the grievance procedures are limited in scope—they cannot deal with matters of statutory appeal under federal civil service statutes such as discharge and demotion even under the 1975 vintage executive orders.

Negotiability

Since 1962 then, the scope of negotiations—the assortment of issues over which both parties agree that bilateral decisions are required or desirable—has been the major bone of contention in federal sector bargaining. The vast majority of the hundred or so substantive decisions made by the FLRC through 1974 have dealt with the issue of negotiability. The 1975 changes to E.O. 11491 make it likely that negotiability will continue to expand yet to be a frequent and hotly contested issue before the FLRC as federal administrators claim "compelling need" to retain unilateral control in an area of agency policy. How the FLRC handles these cases will determine the future scope of federal sector bargaining.

Needless to say, the restrictions on the scope of negotiations have impeded the development of meaningful bargaining and true bilateral decision making about major conditions of employment in the federal service. An "a priori" limited bargaining agenda impacts the process of bargaining. It limits tradeoff possibilities, for instance, in the private sector it is typical practice to tradeoff contract language items for economic benefits. Such maneuvers are virtually unavailable to federal sector negotiators. Moreover, with a limited scope of bargaining there is little incentive for unions and associations to prefer the practice of bargaining over the time-honored political route of congressional lobbying.

Impasse Procedures.   Because federal employees are forbidden to strike, their unions have tried hard to get satisfactory impasse procedures for deadlocked contract talks. All of the presidential orders permit the negotiation of such procedures, as long as they stop short of arbitration. Most early agreements consequently contained impasse provisions which referred disputed issues to higher authority for binding decision. Another popular agreement was fact-finding without public disclosure or recommendations. A few specified only mediation.

Regardless of the procedure adopted in a particular agreement, none provide for appeal to a neutral third party. Widespread and growing dissatisfaction with this situation under E.O. 10988 led to the creation in E.O. 11491 of the Federal Service Impasse Panel (FSIP).

Between 1970 and 1974, approximately one in six federal sector negotiations came to impasse. The Federal Mediation and Conciliation Service (FMCS) mediated most of these successfully; the remainder were referred to the Federal Service Impasse Panel (FSIP). None resulted in a major walkout by federal employees.

In the over 100 requests for assistance it has received since 1970, the FSIP has been able to handle the majority informally. As of June 1974 it had issued formal recommendations as part of a fact-finding procedure in only 18 instances. These recommendations always have been the basis for agreement between the parties, though one wonders on what basis they could disagree since the FSIP is the court of last resort for the parties.

The new postal legislation, on the other hand, gives both sides access to final and binding arbitration, if they wish it, within 180 days of a declared deadlock. Mediation and fact-finding must precede. Arbitration is tripartite, with the Federal Mediation and Conciliation Service supplying a roster of arbitrators from which each party selects one member. These two then select a third. If they cannot agree, the conciliation service makes the selection.

Strikes.   Strikes have been rare in the federal service. The BLS records only 8 work stoppages, involving 5,870 federal employees, in the 10 years, 1958–68.

The postal strike of 1970 was the first major walkout. The same year, air traffic controllers carried out a job action that was only technically not a strike. They "called in sick" in large numbers. Their union, the Professional Air Traffic Controllers Association (PATCO), demanded higher wages and the hiring of more personnel. They carried their case to the public and to Congress by publishing a report alleging that insufficient personnel in traffic control towers at the airports had made flying unsafe. This PATCO appeal illustrates the indirect political pressure tactics that unions in the public sector sometimes adopt. The Hatch Act of 1939 prohibits public employees from direct involvement in political party activities and political campaigns.

Summary on Federal Bargaining

The federal government clearly has pursued a policy of gradualism regarding collective bargaining. In part because of a more than ceremonial deference on the part of the executive branch to the sovereignty principle and insistence by the U.S. Civil Service Commission on adherence to the merit principle as embodied in its regulations. In large part, however, it is the general resistance of agency bureaucrats and the general inertia of the federal bureaucracy that has impeded the development of bargaining. A federal manager whose discretion already is circumscribed by reason of agency and civil service regulations is not too enthusiastic about negotiating contracts that will further delimit the scope of authority. Ironically, the sheer size, complexity, and inertia of federal bureaucracies appears to be a major reason for federal employees' organizing and desire to bargain. For in terms of salary, benefits, and due process rights federal employees have comparatively little to gain through negotiated contracts. Their prime motivation to organize and bargain appears to be a need to influence and determine working conditions and which for professional employees may involve matters related to the agency's mission.

The new 1975 rules for rule-making offer some substantive promise of stimulating the practice of bargaining in the federal sector. Unit consolidation, deregulation of personnel practices by the Civil Service Commission, and the expanded scope of grievance procedures all point to an expansion of bargaining throughout the 1970s. Moreover, the upholding in 1974 by the U.S. Supreme Court of the Hatch Act, which prohibits direct partisan political activity by federal employees, will underscore the motivation to utilize bargaining as opposed to direct political action to achieve the collective goals of federal employees. Finally, if Congress adopts legislation before it to put all federal employees on a comparable footing with postal workers then the practice of bargaining in the federal sector would become more vigorous.

STATE AND LOCAL AGENCIES

Two out of every three public employees work for agencies of state and local governments, totaling some 8.6 million. Of that number three quarters work for local jurisdictions—over 2 million of which work for local school districts as classroom teachers. Table 16–2 highlights major features of state and local employment and bargaining activity.

The table discloses that employees in all major public service areas are highly organized with fire fighters and teachers leading the way at 77 and 70 percent, respectively. Almost half the total number of organized workers are involved in public education which is clearly the most strike-prone of public services.

These organized employees negotiated and on occasion struck in the process of obtaining some 20,000 written agreements that were in force in 1972 with some 17,000 state and local government agencies. Though this is only about one of seven state or local governmental agencies, it includes most of the larger ones, particularly those in the East, Midwest, and West; the South is the least active area for local and state bargaining just as it is in

TABLE 16–2
Bargaining Activity in State and Local Governments, 1972

Public Service	Number of Full-Time Employees (thousands)	Percent Organized	Number of Strikes	Number of Work Days Idle (thousands)
Education	4,114	56.6	193	888
Teachers	2,719	69.5	146	645
Other	1,395	31.4	95	243
Highway/streets	551	46.0	58	23
Public welfare	283	45.1	11	15
Hospitals	856	41.7	16	40
Police protection	473	55.6	22	3
Fire protection	194	76.5	11	4
Sanitation	117	50.1	65	—
Total	8,568	50.4	381	1,124

Source: *Public Employment,* vol. 3, no. 3, U.S. Department of Commerce.

private sector bargaining activity. Only 15,454 jurisdictions employ more than 50 persons.

In addition an estimated 1.25 million workers are employed by over 3,500 nonprofit community hospitals and related health care institutions. For the sake of discussion we treat them as local public agencies. In 1970 over 12 percent of these workers had collective bargaining agreements with their employees. If we look at those institutions with 500 or more beds, almost 4 out of 10 had negotiated labor agreements. With the inclusion of these institutions under the LMRA in August 1974, rapid expansion of bargaining activity undoubtedly will occur in the last half of the 70s.

The Rules for Rulemaking

A patchwork of rules exists in the conduct of bargaining in nonfederal public agencies. In approximately 12 states, there is virtually no legislation that addresses the issue, yet in another 20 states fairly comprehensive legislative and administrative rules exist for bargaining. In some states a limited right to strike is granted, but in most, strikes remain illegal. Municipalities like New York and counties like Los Angeles have passed their own bargaining legislation. Legislation currently pending in the Congress would set up a national policy which would provide uniform rules across the fifty states and be largely reflective of current national labor policy for the private sector. This legislation received extensive hearings in 1975, but its final fate is far from clear.

Recent years have witnessed a gradual loosening on the strictures against the strike. By 1975 Vermont, Hawaii, Pennsylvania, Montana, Oregon, and Minnesota had granted limited rights to strike. Most states require that mediation or fact finding occur prior to strike action and that the strike pose no clear and present danger to public welfare. Even where laws prohibit or are silent as to the strike issue, courts generally have been reluctant to grant injunction without a showing of a threat to public welfare. This is particularly true where the record shows the public employer has refused to negotiate in good faith. In addition a number of states now require final and binding arbitration of contract disputes involving public safety employees and a few more for other groups of public employees such as teachers and hospital employees.

In 1969 a U.S. court of appeals in effect said that the right of public employees to organize was a constitutionally protected right under the first and fourteenth amendments.[3] But while the right to organize appears to be mandated by the U.S. Constitution, the obligation to recognize and bargain by a public employer is not. Until the 1974 amendments to Taft-Hartley, nonprofit hospitals did not have a duty to bargain. Most state and local agencies still do not have a duty to bargain. However, experience has shown that legislation is not always a prerequisite for good faith bargaining to occur. Ohio has no bargaining legislation yet contracts are almost as common with local governments as they are in states with legislation. Some states permit, while others ban, union or agency shops. Most legislation does not speak to the issue of union security. On the average it is the more populous, industrialized states that have passed comprehensive bargaining legislation setting up rules for recognition, unit determination, adjudication of unfair labor practices and the like. California is a notable exception in this regard. In 1975 it still only required employers to "meet and confer" with employee organizations.

In addition, several states have different bargaining rules for different groups of public employees. Teachers are often singled out for special legislative treatment as are firefighters and police officers—owing in large part to the typically stronger lobbying pressure their organizations exert in state legislatures.

An examination of the patterns of bargaining in state and local public agencies reveals that three service areas not only account for the bulk of bargaining activity but also profusely illustrate the special problems involved in bargaining by public and professional employees discussed in the previous chapter. They are: education, health care and the protective services—police and fire.

EDUCATION

Teacher bargaining and militancy began in earnest with the strike against the New York public schools by the United Federation of Teachers, AFL–CIO in 1962. The results of the strike were impressive: a written contract and a good economic package for 50,000 teachers. This event heralded a

---

[3] *AFSCME* v. *Woodward*, 406 F.(2d) 137, 1969.

new day in education. As more teachers walked out and won sustantial concession, a wave of militancy swept the ranks of classroom teachers that crested in the period 1968–70 when there were 312 teacher strikes involving over 4 million lost work days. The level of militancy has remained relatively constant in recent years. There were 154 strikes by teachers reported during the 1973–74 school year. This militancy has produced a dramatic rise in the number of teachers under collective bargaining agreements. In 1975 over one million teachers were covered by contracts. About nine out of ten agreements have been negotiated by NEA affiliates. However, due to its greater presence in the larger urban systems, AFT contracts cover two out of every ten teachers currently under contract.

New York, New Jersey, Michigan, Illinois, Ohio, Pennsylvania, Maryland, and Wisconsin account for most of the bargaining activity in education. It is interesting to note that Ohio and Illinois have no legislation governing teacher bargaining but are also states that have experienced a disproportionate share of teacher strikes—many of which have been over demands for recognition and written agreements.

The number of contracts negotiated with local school districts is impressive given the general reluctance of most school boards—particularly those outside of metropolitan areas—to bargain away any of the responsibility and authority as representatives of patrons and taxpayers in their districts.

Many of the bitterest disputes in public education have not been over bread and butter issues but, rather, over professional autonomy and control as in the 1970 New York teacher strike. In response to pressure of school patrons—most notably its black patrons—the school administration had decided to "decentralize" control of the schools. Teachers feared that such neighborhood control not only would threaten their job security but also would result in an inferior education for children in many neighborhoods, particularly for the black neighborhoods. The strike over this issue made abundantly clear the problem of democratic control versus professional expertise—and job security—in setting school policy. Similar tensions have underscored numerous negotiations in school districts across the country in recent years.

For the most part state and local teacher organizations are affiliated with one of two national organizations: the largest is the National Education Association (NEA) which in 1974 reported 1,824,376 members in 9,728 locals of its state affiliates. In contrast the American Federation of Teachers (AFT), AFL–CIO reported only 414,153 members in 1,900 locals in 1973.

Fifteen years ago the policies and practices of the two organizations were poles apart. The AFT openly advocated collective bargaining and strikes when necessary. It excluded school administrators from its membership and unabashedly saw its job as being the advocate of the interests—both pecuniary and professional—of the classroom teacher.

In contrast the NEA saw itself as primarily a professional organization of educators. It shunned the adversary relation it saw implicit in bargaining and denounced the use of the strike. In this posture it resembled the professional associations of professional engineers. It stressed the oneness of all educators, and administrators were not only members but traditionally dominated the leadership of the NEA.

However, as the AFT and some of the NEA's own state affiliates, such as in Michigan and New York, began to show teachers what they would achieve through bargaining, the NEA began a rapid metamorphosis. By 1975 few in the public could distinguish between the NEA and AFT affiliates, particularly in terms of their activities as bargaining agents. Merger talks between the two organizations have continued since the late 1960s. As of 1975, the only publicly declared stumbing block preventing merger was the insistence by the AFT that the merged organization still retain its affiliation with the AFL–CIO.

Collective bargaining activity in education is not restricted to elementary and secondary schools. Some higher education faculties have begun to practice bargaining in earnest in the face of the increasingly bleak prospects faced by many institutions of higher education. In part the growing interest of college professors in collective bargaining has been spurned by the shrinking differential between the pay and prerogatives of K–12 and college faculties. But in larger part it is due to declining public support for higher education. This is both a legacy of the antiwar protest era of the late 1960s and early 1970s, and because a college degree has lost much of its appeal in an era when a greater percentage of people have one but also have a more difficult time in cashing it in for a good job. Public funding for higher education under this pragmatic cost/benefit approach has been easier to cut in recent inflationary years than other public services, particularly those that benefit more active lobbying groups such as the highway interests.

Academics protest such crude evaluations of the worth of higher education and often interpret public concern for accountability as an assault on professional autonomy. Moreover, requests for reviews of tenure systems are viewed by some academics as a threat to academic freedom. Against this backdrop of concerns over their status, prestige, and prerogatives, a number of faculties of higher education have voted for bargaining representation while others have not. Often the campaigns are spearheaded by younger, untenured, or liberal arts faculty members who view the academic establishment as being biased against their interest—particularly in a recessionary academic market.

In 1968 less than a handful of college professors were organized for bargaining. By 1973 some 80,000, or roughly 1 in 10, academics were covered by collective bargaining contracts. Ninety percent of these professors were employed by public institutions—though over one half were in the New York and New Jersey public systems. NEA and AFT affiliates account for more than three fourths of the bargaining activity in higher education— most of which is at two-year colleges. The traditional professional organization of college professors, the American Association of University Professors (AAUP), has been more successful at the university level. The AAUP appears to be currently going through a change as regards bargaining similar to that of the NEA in the 1960s. In 1972 the AAUP voted in convention to pursue collective bargaining as another way of achieving its goals. However, the AAUP currently has only about 90,000 members nationwide and lacks the widespread support on campuses that the NEA enjoyed in the K–12 systems.

Nonprofessional employees of public school systems also have been active and militant as the data in Table 16–2 show. These employees are represented most frequently by AFL–CIO unions such as AFSCME and the Service Employee International Union (SEIU). The total number of employees engaged in bargaining activity in education is more than in the basic steel, auto, and construction industries combined. The health care industry has the potential of reaching like stature.

HEALTH CARE

In 1974 roughly 2.6 million workers were employed in America's 7,000 plus hospitals. Over half of these worked in nonprofit community hospitals; approximately another third worked in hospitals run by federal, state, and local governments; and the remainder worked in proprietary hospitals. Registered Nurses (R.N.s) comprise the largest single occupational group in these hospitals and also have comprised the vanguard group in collective bargaining by health care professionals.

To date, however, nurses have not been able to match the bargaining success of teachers despite the fact that the American Nurses Association in 1946 was the first major professional organization to openly endorse collective bargaining. By 1967 ANA affiliates had representational rights and contracts covering nurses at only about 3 percent of the nation's hospitals. In 1968 the ANA adopted a more militant bargaining posture by removing a self-imposed ban on strikes from its constitution. By 1974 when the health care amendments to the Taft-Hartley were passed by Congress—in large part through ANA lobbying efforts—state affiliates of the ANA had bargaining agreements covering almost one in five hospitals—most of which were run by federal, state, or local governments.

Despite the continuous efforts by the ANA to promote the economic as well as professional interests of nurses, it has not been as successful as the NEA or AFT in improving working conditions for its members. In part this is because they lack the organizational resources of the NEA or AFT, both of which charge more than twice as much in membership dues and which together have well over 2 million members. In contrast only about one fourth of the roughly 900,000 R.N.s in the country are members of ANA state affiliates. ANA state affiliates in California, New York, Washington, and Michigan traditionally have been better organized and more militant and have been pacesetters in nurse bargaining. Today they account for the bulk of bargaining activity by R.N.s in not-for-profit and proprietary hospitals.

As with teachers, professional issues of occupational integrity, identification, and autonomy often have been of great importance in nurse bargaining. It generally was recognized that a fundamental issue underlying the 1974 strike of nurses against San Francisco area hospitals was the rights and responsibilities of nurses vis-à-vis doctors in patient care decisions. Leaders of the striking nurses said that in the absence of the patient care issue there would not have been sufficient motivation to strike among rank and file nurses. Similar concerns have surrounded negotiations and job actions by nurses in recent years.

Yet such dramatic shows of militancy as occurred in San Francisco are the exception rather than the rule, as are collective bargaining contracts by ANA affiliates. Some nurses, in frustration at the inability of the ANA to function well as a bargaining agent, have turned to established unions like the Teamsters to get a good contract. However, comparatively low salaries and professional concerns with patient care, equal rights issues, and newly acquired LMRA bargaining rights all combine to make it certain that bargaining by nurses will continue to be an expanding activity in America's hospitals. Many of these same factors inicate a similar future for other health care professionals, such as X-ray technicians, physical therapists, and laboratory workers.

The 1974 health care amendments to the LMRA give nurses and other hospital employees and their organizations fundamentally the same rights enjoyed by other employees and labor organizations covered by the Act with several exceptions. The parties must give each other 90 days' notice and the FMCS 60 days' notice of contract termination or intent to modify. Strikes or lockouts are prohibited in this period. Strikes or picketing are prohibited without a prior 10-day notice being given the FMCS. Mediation is required and fact finding with recommendations may be required at the discretion of the director of the FMCS. However, once all the notice requirements are met and the impasse procedures completed employees are free to picket and strike.

The future structure of bargaining in the health care industry was indicated in May 1975 when the NLRB issued its guidelines on unit determination. The board held that in the absence of mitigating circumstances, such as bargaining history, that five board units generally would be deemed appropriate: (1) all registered nurses; (2) licensed practical nurses and all other technical employees; (3) all other professional employees; (4) business office employees; and (5) service and maintenance employees. The board did not address the status of physicians.

Dramatic changes have recently occurred in the attitude of doctors toward collective bargaining and strikes. On March 17, 1975 the committee of Interns and Residents—an organization representing doctors in New

York City hospitals—called the first major strike by physicians in the history of this country. Over half of its 3,000 members walked off their jobs protesting low pay and 100-hour work week—the latter which they claimed also endangered patients who had tired interns tending them.

Similar organizations of doctors, mostly salaried employees of public hospitals, recently have emerged. The largest of these is the Physicians National Housestaffs Association (PNHA). The PNHA was founded in 1972 and claims members at more than 100 hospitals across the country. It is ironic that interns and residents in some Chicago area hospitals are affiliated with a local union of the Amalgamated Meatcutters and Butcher Workmen of North America, AFL–CIO. Local 756 of the SEIU (Service Employees International Union) currently represents approximately 65 of the 450 physicians practicing in Nevada.

There are several independent unions, guilds, and federations seeking to represent self-employed doctors nationally such as the American Physicians Union and the American Federation of Physicians and Dentists which in 1973 had about 8,000 member doctors. However, these organizations seek primarily to represent the self-employed physician in dealings with insurance companies and government agencies—who together pay over two thirds of the nation's medical bills. Promoters of these organizations claim that this fact makes physicians "de facto" employees of the government and insurance companies.

It would indeed be a dramatic development in collective bargaining if the over 300,000 doctors in this country are able to organize effectively and negotiate collective agreements with these third-party intermediaries to achieve protection of professional autonomy and enhance their economic rewards—the same ends their salaried colleagues and other professionals seek to achieve through negotiations with their employers. If agencies like HEW continue to expand their "oversight" of medical practice as they did again in 1975, and if insurance companies continue to hike malpractice insurance which prompted a "wildcat strike" by physicians in California, then the future may well see a metamorphosis of the AMA comparable to that of the NEA.

Regardless of the course physicians take it is almost certain that nonprofessional health care employees will organize more rapidly given the new protections of the NLRA. AFSCME and the SEIU are two AFL–CIO unions that have currently organized the great bulk of these employees. It appears that they will continue to be the dominant labor organizations in organizing nonprofessional health care employees.

While physicians are just beginning to do battle in their struggle to maintain their occupational autonomy and privileges, the less prestigious health care professionals, like R.N.s, appear poised for a vigorous attempt to gain through bargaining with their employers some of what doctors have enjoyed for years. At the same time, nonprofessional health care employees are going to seek to increase their portion of the pie. An interesting aspect of all these developments will be the multilateral bargaining that will inevitably occur between R.N.s, hospital administrators, physicians, and interested third parties such as government agencies, insurance companies, and other employers and labor unions who are increasingly faced with rising health care costs as a major item in their negotiations.

PUBLIC SAFETY

Police and fire protection services together make up more than half the budgets of most American cities. Not only are these critical services costly, but also they are of the greatest concern to the average taxpayer—particularly in recent years as crime, including arson, have soared. The danger, irregular hours, and paramilitary character of the work inspire a strong occupational cohesion among fire fighters and police officers. This cohesion, in part, accounts for their high level of organization; nearly all the full-time firefighters and police officers employed by cities in metropolitan areas are organized.

In most cities and states, police and fire employees' organizations have traditionally been effective lobbying agents on behalf of their members' employment concerns. Many of them have used the advent of public sector bargaining in the 1960s to augment this traditional lobbying strategy.

Of the two occupations firefighters are the best organized. The International Association of Fire Fighters (IAFF) currently has membership of over 75 percent of the full-time paid firefighters in the United States. The IAFF has been an international union of the AFL–CIO since 1914 and has a field staff that assists its state and local affiliates in bargaining activities. Also, the IAFF has no serious competition in organizing.

In contrast, several organizations compete to represent police officers. The International Conference of Police Associations (ICPA) is a federation of independent local and state police employee organizations and claims upward of 200,000 police officers are represented through its affiliates. The Fraternal Order of Police (FOP) claims approximately 90,000 members. Both of these organizations are loose federations with few staff resources to assist affiliates. Several other unions, and independent associations also represent police officers such as the International Brotherhood of Police Officers, AFSCME and the Teamsters.

Police and fire organizations sometimes work together in achieving their goals, particularly legislative goals such as state pension systems or binding arbitration laws. The effectiveness of the protective service lobby is attested to by the large amount of special interest laws they get passed as compared to other municipal employee groups. More often, though, each goes its own way at the local, state, and national levels.

Organized firefighters and police officers are typically pattern setters in municipal bargaining. Several factors account for this, not the least of which is their strong occupational cohesion and identification. Another is the fact that police officers and firefighters have limited alternative for plying their trade elsewhere. They are typically tied to a single municipal employer. Hence their motivation to organize for lobbying and bargaining are greater. Firefighters especially are known for the willingness to engage in grass roots political activity to gain a sympathetic ear for their problems. This traditional leverage has been augmented by an increased willingness of protective service workers to strike in recent years. In lieu of the right to strike many protective service workers now enjoy the right to demand binding arbitration. All told, these factors combine to give firefighters and police officers typically more clout than other municipal employee groups. This clout is reflected in the better than average rise in the real compensation levels of protective service workers in the last decade.

A key and sometimes devisive issue in public safety bargaining has been pay parity between police officers and firefighters. While firefighters traditionally have been on duty more hours per week than police officers, the annual salaries of these two groups typically have been equal. In recent years police organizations—armed with reports of presidential commissions documenting the need for higher police salaries—have made a concerted drive in many cities to break pay parity. Pay parity is still the rule in America but has been upset in both directions in several cities, some as a result of arbitration awards. In 1969 the Connecticut Public Employee Relations Board ruled that a parity clause in a firefighter's contract calling for equal pay with police officers must be removed on the principle that it violated the principle of exclusive recognition under which separate police and fire bargaining units were established. In essence, the commission ruled it to be bad faith bargaining on the part of the city to acede to and the union to demand a "me too" salary clause since to do so deprived the police organization—an AFSCME local—of its rights to act as the sole and exclusive bargaining agent for police officers.

Police bargaining often touches on matters of law enforcement policy. When should an officer use a weapon? How many officers in a patrol car? How vigorously should vice laws be enforced? Such questions have been raised in formal and informal bargaining between police officers and their employers. Many police officers believe that, like teachers, they have expert knowledge that entitles them to a voice in setting police policies since these policies impact their safety and welfare as well as those of their "clients."

A related and a very heated issue in the social protest era of the late 1960s was public review and civilian control of police internal affairs—specifically the disciplining of officers for alleged brutality and misconduct. Police organizations fought hard, and usually successfully, in both the bargaining and political arenas to keep disciplinary matters within the department. Having done so, they have bargained and lobbied hard to get the same due process rights they daily must give suspects they arrest, namely, the right to remain silent and to representation in disciplinary hearings. Even some unrecognized police organizations have managed to gain such rights through the courts, such as Chicago's Confederation of Police which successfully challenged the department's Rule 51 which required an officer to give evidence which might be self-incriminating or be dismissed.[4] COP is still working on city recognition, collective bargaining, and a bill of rights. Such "bill-of-rights" provisions continue to be a prime bargaining objective of many police organizations. Despite highly publicized confrontation on these kinds of sensitive issues, the overall impact of negotiated settlements on police management in most instances has been no worse than comparable impacts on management prerogatives in the private sector.

For firefighters major bargaining issues involve increases in pay commensurate increased workloads and increased exposure to hazard caused by more fires, false alarms, and often decreasing personnel levels on equipment. Moreover, the fire service has begun to evolve into an emergency service; firefighters increasingly are demanding that their specialized, required medical training be recognized and compensated.

The protective services promise to remain the most active and volatile areas of municipal bargaining in the years to come. Given the tremendous fiscal impact of negotiated settlements, the immediate future holds some long and tough negotiations for city and union officials in light of the current fiscal crisis of American cities. New York City in 1975 is but the first of several large cities to face insolvency. It appears that collective bargaining by public safety and other municipal employees has, at least, hastened this crisis.

OTHER STATE AND LOCAL AGENCIES

Independent state employee associations currently represent over 600,000 public employees, 100,000 plus of which are employed by local agencies. Most of these associations were formed years ago to champion the establishment of civil service or pension systems, or simply to provide low cost group insurance plans.

The associations differ widely in activities, and attitudes towards collective bargaining. Where they face union competition, they engage in it; elsewhere, they tend to rely on their traditional practice of lobbying at the state capitol. They give unions tough competition for bargaining rights. In 1969 the New York Civil Service Association beat the AFSCME in four out of five statewide bargaining unit elections. In Hawaii, rivalry between AFSCME and the Hawaiian Government Employees Association ended in 1970 with a merger of the two organizations.

Local independent associations represent over 300,000 additional employees of local governments. Like the state associations, they take varying positions towards collective bargaining, and often reverse former policy to

---

[4] *Confederation of Police v. James B. Conlisk, individually and as Superintendent, Chicago Police Dept.* 487 F.2d 563 (7th Cir. 1973).

engage in it when faced with union competition. In 1968, for instance, the Los Angeles County Employees Association opposed the passage of a comprehensive collective bargaining law by the county board. Upon passage of the law, the association fired its old director and hired a new one to lead a fight to gain bargaining rights. The presence of a rival local of the SEIU, which also had a substantial number of county employee members, undoubtedly hastened the transformation. There is currently no national federation of these local employee associations.

In contrast, in AFSCME locals the association's chief union competition at both the state and local level are more homogeneous in their militant advocacy of collective bargaining. They are also closely allied with well staffed state and national organizations. AFSCME is by far the largest union in state and local government. It is currently growing faster than any other union in the United States, having more than tripled its membership in the past 10 years. It represents well over a half a million workers in a wide range of occupations from garbage collectors to psychiatrists. Its industrial union organizing policy often brings it into conflict with other AFL–CIO unions, usually those of craftsmen which have recently tried to organize public employees.

The organizational vigor of AFSCME stems in large part from the leadership of Jerry Wurf, elected president in 1964. The previous administration had operated more in the traditional way by lobbying and trying to reform civil service procedures.

Under Wurf's presidency, AFSCME shifted its policy to demand bargaining rights equal to those that unions enjoy in the private sector including the right to strike. The 1970 union conventions removed a constitutional ban on strikes by police members. Locals of AFSCME have, in fact, conducted many strikes in recent years.

The almost half-million AFSCME members are distributed in some 2,200 local and 72 district councils. Current policy calls for two councils in each state, one for local and another for state employees. District councils exercise certain authority over the constituent locals. In some instances, as in Milwaukee, locals bargain jointly through the district council, often over the protest of some locals which would prefer to bargain separately.

The AFSCME takes a progressive stand on civil rights. Blacks and other minorities make up more than a third of the membership. The union practices what it preaches: Jerry Wurf marched arm in arm with civil rights leader Martin Luther King in support of the striking garbage workers, black members of an AFSCME local in Memphis, on the occasion already noted. This strong civil rights tie has often made it harder for the union to organize some of the more conservative public employees.

Several other major unions have been active in organizing state and local government employees. Over 100,000 public employees make up roughly one fourth of the membership of the Service Employees International Union

(SEIU)—the bulk of them are low-skilled workers in the health and education fields. This large, industrially organized union is most active in public employment in California where it has organized professional social workers. Next most active is the Laborers International Union (LIU), also affiliated with the AFL–CIO. It has about one fourth as many public employee members as the SEIU, mostly unskilled blue collar workers in public works departments. Both SEIU and LIU occasionally compete with AFCSME for members.

The Teamsters union is the largest union which also organizes public employees. They represent well over 50,000. The core of the union's public employee membership consists of truck drivers and helpers in highway, streets, and sanitation departments, but the Teamsters cross occupational lines and may be found bargaining for such diverse groups as nurses and police.

Bargaining Characteristics

Great diversity prevails in bargaining practice and procedures at state and local levels because of the diversity of the specific contexts. These are quite different, for instance, in a city like Chicago, dominated by the Democratic party machine of Mayor Richard J. Daley, and in an affluent, Republic, north-shore suburb. They differ between charter city with wide discretion in personnel matters and a state agency whose head may have little such discretionary authority.

State and local governments also show the same diffusion of authority noted in the federal service, reduced in scale, perhaps, and mitigated by closer proximity. A mayor or city manager normally has greater latitude in personnel matters than the head of a federal agency. One or the other of these administrators may also have influence over the local legislative body. Civil service systems, where they exist, usually exercise more restricted authority than the federal system. Special district boards usually exercise broad authority in matters affecting personnel.

Two-Step Bargaining. Collective bargaining in state and local governments typically takes place in two steps. First, the employee organization hammers out an agreement with an administrator. Second, they take their agreement to the appropriate legislative body for validation of its economic portions. Occasionally, they lobby jointly for validation. More often, the employee organization "renegotiates" for better terms at the legislative level by partisan lobbying.

The ideal arrangement would centralize management bargaining authority in a single person or administrative body, but legislatures seem to hate giving up power, particularly over the purse-strings; hence the governmental structure tends to encourage the two-step procedure. This discourages meaningful bargaining at the first step.

Agreements and Negotiations. Written agreements are becoming more prevalent every day, but their number is no measure of the extent of real negotiations. Many public employee labor organizations—particularly associations—content themselves with getting the results of their negotiations codified in a city ordinance, administrative order, or change in civil service regulations. Written agreements, however, usually indicate a greater degree of bilateral decision making than a code or ordinance.

Wage Issues in Collective Bargaining. The core activity in both private and public sectors is wage and effort bargaining. One reason true collective bargaining is more prevalent in the public sector than at state and federal levels is that labor organizations bargain more directly with those who have authority to set the wages. Bargaining at local levels tends to focus on two key issues: pay comparability and the ability to pay.

Pay Comparability. Firefighters want parity pay with police; both want comparability with the skilled trades. Skilled workers want parity with the construction union scale and are not impressed with the retort that they get better pension benefits and no slack-season layoffs. Teachers in central cities want parity with the suburbs. Similar arguments in other job classifications stress the reasonableness of the comparisons made.

The Budget. Even when public employers accept the comparative argument, they often plead inability to pay. Fiscal restraints are tightening in more and more local jurisdictions. The employer's line, "We'd like to, but . . ." meets the response, "You could if you'd slow down urban renewal, or don't build a domed stadium, or. . . ." This illustrates the point made earlier that budget constraints, priorities, and taxing limits, rather than market forces, tend to set the wage bargain in public employment.

The problems are real enough. Public employees often go to bat for their employers to try to boost revenues. The Houston fire fighters, for example, helped get additional taxing authority for the city from the Texas legislature. They got a handsome pay raise in reward. In education, the tie-in between pay and taxing level has made teacher organizations tireless campaigners for millage levies to support the schools.

Grievance Handling. State and local civil service usually provides appeals procedures. Employees typically look on civil service as an arm of management; they would prefer grievance procedures ending in neutral third-party binding arbitration. Unions of public employees are more insistent than associations in pressing for grievance procedures separate from civil service. They oppose having a board that formulates the rules and then adjudicates them.

Union Security. Union security is an important issue at the state and local levels. Most states do not insist on the federal ban against the union shop, but most public employers have resisted it as a threat to the merit principle: They say they do not want to have to fire a good employee who does not want to join the union. The AFSCME estimates it could double its membership by getting union or agency shop agreements in political jurisdictions where they are not yet authorized. Associations, on the other hand, generally do not make as big an issue of union security.

Political Action. State and local employees also exert pressure in the political arena. They lobby, and take political action under the traditional slogan, "Elect our friends and defeat our enemies." Laws patterned on the Hatch Act, designed to dampen such activities, have proved easy to evade and generally ineffective.

Unions and associations appear equally adroit at politics. The AFL–CIO tie gives unions a great deal of leverage, of which the fire fighters, conspicuously, have taken notable advantage. Police unions, too, often wield strong political influence. By pulling the political levers, both groups have made gains over workers in jobs that require no more education or training. Political action remains an element of strategy in collective bargaining not just for them, but all employees at state and local government levels.

This is probably unavoidable. Bargaining power on one side seeks out the sources of power on the other and will not be put off with underlings. And politicians will probably never shut their ears when an organized body of constituents asks: "What have you done for us . . . lately?"

SUMMARY

The diversity of bargaining practices in the public sector is greater than in the private sector due to wide differences in the rules for rule-making, historic patterns of lobbying and political action, civil service bureaucracies largely separated from operating line agencies and the fact that roughly a third of the public employees currently organized and bargaining are professionals. The scope of bargaining is steadily increasing at all levels of government and in the future comprehensive contracts may well eclipse civil service systems. The quest by nurses and other health care employees for full fledged professional status threatens to upset traditional power relations within health care institutions. Moreover, the growing organizational militancy of doctors may well cause the future writing of a new chapter in this book as we see the process of collective bargaining used to establish some important working conditions for self-employed professionals.

Education is the most active arena of public and professional bargaining. Declining student enrollments, an overabundance of educators and shrinking tax resources point toward a turbulent bargaining period in the late 1970s.

Should pending legislation in Congress be passed then the public policy differences between the private and public sectors would largely evaporate —with the exception of the strike issue. Yet even if public policy for both sectors becomes indistinguishable, the practice of collective bargaining will not. Differences in the market and power relations contexts will continue to set them apart. The political activity of organized public employees is bound to continue as long as democratic forms of government prevail in America.

QUESTIONS FOR DISCUSSION

1. Discuss the differences in the pattern of bargaining found in the postal service and the classified service.
2. What features distinguish the practice of collective bargaining in the federal service from that in local political jurisdictions?
3. How comparable will collective bargaining in the public and private sectors be in 10 years?
4. What kind of contracts can you envision between organized, self-employed physicians and third parties such as insurance and government agencies?
5. Is it possible to draw a line between matters suitable for bargaining and those suitable only for determination by elected representatives of the people?
6. What is the difference between "bread and butter" and professional issues?

SELECTED ANNOTATED BIBLIOGRAPHY

ADVISORY COMMISSION ON INTERGOVERNMENTAL RELATIONS. *Labor-Management Policies for State and Local Governments*. Washington, D.C.: U.S. Government Printing Office (September 1969).

A comprehensive analysis of the early public policy toward bargaining in state and local government. The volume also includes analysis of membership data for public employee unions, strikes and recommendations of the commission, and position papers by management and labor representatives.

AUSSIEKER, BILL, and GARBARINO, J. W. "Faculty Unionism in Institutions of Higher Education," *Monthly Labor Review*, April 1974.

A good review of major developments through 1974. Professor Garbarino has written extensively in this area.

BOWERS, MOLLIE H. *Labor Relations in the Public Safety Services*. Chicago: International Personnel Management Association, 1974.

A brief survey of the development of unionism and bargaining among police officers and firefighters with an emphasis on experience with impasse procedures.

BUNKER, CHARLES S. *Collective Bargaining: Non-Profit Sector*. Columbus, Ohio: Grid, Inc., 1973.

Readings and texts on bargaining practices and issues in government, education and health care.

CRAVEN, JOHN V. "Strike of Self-Employed Professionals: Belgian Doctors in 1964," *Industrial and Labor Relations Review*, October 1967.

Gives a good perspective on the causes of doctor militancy in another society and provides a basis for looking into possible development in the United States.

DELAWARE MEDICAL SOCIETY. "Special Report on Physicians Union," *Delaware Medical Journal*, February 1973.

Provides a brief overview of some important developments in physician organization, particularly among self-employed doctors.

DEPARTMENT OF LABOR. *Directory of National and International Unions and*

Employee Associations: 1973. Washington, D.C.: U.S. Government Printing Office, 1974.

Published every two years the directory gives a periodic updating of the affairs and membership of both unions and associations in both the public and private sectors.

DEPARTMENT OF LABOR. *Summary of State Policy Regulations for Public Sector Labor Relations: Statutes, Attorney General's Opinions and Selected Court Decisions.* Washington, D.C.: U.S. Government Printing Office, 1973.

ELAM, M.; LIEBERMAN, M.; and MOSKOW, MICHAEL H., eds. *Readings onCollective Negotiations in Public Education.* Chicago: Rand McNally, 1967.

FIBISH, NANCY C. "A Mediator's View of Federal Sector Labor Relations," *Public Personnel Administration, Labor Management Relations.* Prentice-Hall Labor Services, February 5, 1974, at 3153.

An excellent perspective on the dynamics of federal bargaining by an FMCS mediator who has been involved in numerous federal disputes.

GERHART, PAUL F. "The Scope of Bargaining in Local Government Labor Relations," *Labor Law Journal,* August 1969.

A good conceptualization of the multilateral bargaining process in local government over items stated and unstated in written agreements concludes that the real scope of bargaining is far wider than contracts would indicate because of political avenue open to public employees.

JURIS, HARVEY A., and FEUILLE, PETER. *Police Unionism: Power and Impact in Public Sector Bargaining.* Lexington, Mass.: D. C. Heath Co.

A comprehensive analysis of police bargaining with particular attention on its impact on managerial prerogatives.

KIENAST, PHILIP, and PETERSON, RICHARD. "Bargaining Alternatives for University Faculties," *Journal of Collective Negotiations in the Public Sector,* Fall 1973.

The article analyzes the different alternatives available to faculties at two year community colleges as contrasted with large public universities.

KLEINGARTNER, ARCHIE. *Professionalism and Salaried Worker Organization.* Madison: University of Wisconsin, Industrial Relations Research Institute, 1967.

One of the earliest detailed analysis of the interface between professional values and the requirements of collective bargaining. Provides an excellent conceptual framework for analysis.

KRAWLEWSKI, JOHN. "Collective Bargaining among Professional Employees," *Hospital Administration,* Summer 1974.

Provides a brief but up-to-date review of developments in bargaining among health care professionals.

LIEBERMAN, MYRON, and MOSKOW, MICHAEL H. *Collective Negotiations for Teachers.* Chicago: Rand McNally, 1966.

An excellent book to provide an analytic framework for integrating material from the book of readings by ELAM et al., cited above.

LOEWENBERG, J. JOSEPH, and MOSKOW, MICHAEL H. *Collective Bargaining in Government.* Englewood Cliffs, N.J.: Prentice-Hall, 1972.

This book offers an excellent selection of articles on the developing patterns of bargaining in federal, state, and local government agencies. Of particular interest are articles comparing and contrasting private and public bargaining.

LUDD, EVERETT CARLL, JR., and LIPSET, SEYMOUR MARTIN. *Professors, Unions and American Higher Education.* Washington, D.C.
    A report on the experiences with and attitudes toward collective bargaining by American professors. Prepared for the Carnegie Commission on Higher Education it presents a detailed analysis of why and how bargaining is spreading.

METZGER, N., and POINTER, D. D. *Labor-Management Relations in the Health Service Industry: Theory and Practice.* Washington, D.C.: Science and Health Publications, Inc., 1972.
    The first comprehensive treatment of the subject occurs in this volume. An excellent sourcebook in the field.

MEYERS, FREDRIC. "Public Employee Unions: The French Experience," *Industrial Relations,* February 1973.
    The author draws many illuminating comparisons between public sector labor relations in the United States and France.

MOSKOW, MICHAEL H.; LOEWENBERG, J. JOSEPH; and KOZIARA, EDWARD CLIFFORD. *Collective Bargaining in Public Employment.* New York: Random House, 1970.
    This volume integrates conceptual models with data analysis of developments in the federal service, state, and local governments. It is an excellent companion volume for the book of readings just cited.

POINTER, DENNIS D. "How the 1974 Taft-Hartley Amendments Will Affect Health Care Facilities," *Hospital Progress,* October–November 1974.
    A detailed two-part examination of the laws impact by one of the acknowledged experts in the field.

PRENSSEL, WILLARD G. "The Short-Term Outlook for Unionization of Federal Engineers," *Personnel Administration and Public Personnel Review,* September–October 1972.

SEIDMAN, JOEL. "Nurses and Collective Bargaining," *Industrial and Labor Relations Review,* April 1970.
    A good article to get an overview of nurse bargaining through 1970.

SPERO, STERLING D. *Government as Employer.* New York: Remsen Press, 1948.
    This book is a good starting point for gaining a historical perspective on collective bargaining in the public sector.

TRICE, TERRENCE N., ed. *Faculty Bargaining.* Ann Arbor, Michigan: Institute of Continuing Legal Education, 1973.
    A legally oriented book of readings with an introduction by a noted labor arbitrator and resident of the University of Michigan, ROBBEN W. FLEMING. The case materials in the appendices are good original source material.

USERY, WILLIAM J., JR. "An Interview," *Hospitals JAHA,* September 16, 1974.
    A candid discussion by the head of the FMCS of how he thinks labor-management relations will develop in the health care industry and how LMRA impasse procedures will impact that development.

WARNER, KENNETH O., ed. *Collective Bargaining in the Public Service: Theory and Practice.* Chicago: Public Personnel Association, 1967.

A book of readings primarily aimed at assisting public managers in dealing with unions and negotiating contracts.

Weber, Arnold. "Paradise Lost: Or Whatever Happened to the Chicago Social Workers?" *Industrial and Labor Relations Review*, April 1969.

Describes how the diffuse decision making authority in public management and political undercuttings frustrate the establishment of good faith bargaining relationships. Also discusses relations between the emerging professional social union and the Chicago union establishment.

Woodworth, Robert T., and Peterson, Richard B. *Collective Negotiations for Public and Professional Employees, Text and Readings.* Glenview, Illinois: Scott, Foresman and Company, 1969.

A fine selection of readings and comments on the problems of professionals, especially those employed in public agencies, utilizing collective bargaining to deal with their work problems.

Wheeler, Hoyt N. "An Analysis of Fire Fighter Strikes," *Labor Law Journal*, January 1975.

A review of recent firefighter bargaining militancy. One conclusion reached is that where binding arbitration laws exist strikes cease.

Zizkind, David. *One Thousand Strikes of Government Employees.* New York: Columbia University Press, 1940.

Another good volume to assist in getting a historical perspective on the development of public sector bargaining.

part five

Cases in Collective Bargaining

Cases

INTRODUCTION

PART FIVE of this book contains 22 cases, all of them true, but with the names of individuals, companies, and unions disguised in a few instances. Questions about the issues the cases raise or illustrate accompany the presentation of the facts. Many of the cases come from arbitration records and appear here by courtesy of the Bureau of National Affairs, or of Commerce Clearing House, which first published them and have kindly permitted their reproduction for student use. Other cases have been contributed directly by the arbitrators.

Now, why study cases?

Arbitration and legal proceedings account for no more than a small part of the sum total of collective bargaining activities, yet for several reasons the study of arbitration cases, like law cases, is unusually rewarding.

To begin with, the arbitration and legal processes leave a written record. This is not true of all aspects of collective bargaining. Where such a record is not kept, cases have to be written up in narrative form (like a few of those in this section) and lack the authority of official record. The decision of an arbitrator or court usually concentrates on a single, seemingly narrow point, but the record of the hearing often preserves for scrutiny a range of facts and testimony that illuminates a much broader field of view. Furthermore, an issue that has gone all the way to arbitration or to court usually embodies some aspect of the relationship between the contending parties that is unique, with important implications that touch on fundamental principles.

The cases in this book present concrete issues that have arisen between bargaining partners in spite of their best efforts to settle differences in advance by written agreement. Practical problems rising out of the living process of collective bargaining appear here in all the confusion and fragmentation of the forms in which they confront actual participants.

It will be the student's task to analyze the problems as they appear in raw form, applying the principles learned from the text, from collateral reading opened up by the text, and from classroom instruction and discussion. The cases, therefore, help the student develop powers of reasoning, ability to move from the general to the particular, and, perhaps, back from the particular to strengthen understanding of the general. They demand logical organization of ideas and clarity of oral and written expression. (This they demand all the more because in their raw state they are themselves not models of clarity or logic.)

Finally, cases permit the student to express and test value judgments based on personal moral and ethical codes. So far as possible, value judgments have been kept out of the text, because the aim there was to present only the facts. Where any value judgments have been made, the authors have taken care to label them as only their personal opinion and have not tried to pass them off as gospel. Here, in handling cases, students can—and should—give thought to what they believe is right and wrong, what should and should not be. They will undoubtedly find some who disagree with them; they may sway them, or be swayed. Collective bargaining surely cannot stand exempt from ethics and morality, any more than from economic law or any other influence at work in society, and it is only by free exchange of views and values that understanding (if not full agreement) can be reached.

Like almost everything in this book, the cases here presented do not pretend to be exhaustive, but suggestive. There is no limit to the number of true-life cases students could collect and subject to the process of analysis these cases demonstrate. Having started with these cases, let students bring in their own experiences and observations, either in oral or written form, for presentation to the class and for class discussion.

HOW TO USE THE CASES

Chapter 13 contains the valuable advice of the American Arbitration Association on how to prepare for arbitration. This is worth reviewing before tackling a case problem. After that, two ways of using the cases stand open to the instructor and the class.

One way is to take the case as the starting point for a written exercise. The student writes what he or she considers should be the arbitrator's award, or in the cases not drawn from arbitration records, directly answers the questions. In either event, the student should justify the solution.

Another way, and probably better, is the role-playing method. A team of two or three students can take the union side, a similar team the management side, with a student (or the instructor) to sit as arbitrator and act as chairman. The two sides then act out their roles before the class.

Oral presentation in this manner should not neglect the value—perhaps it might be said, the necessity—of written support in the form of a brief of the argument, and perhaps also "exhibits" in lieu of testimony where "evidence" consists of facts drawn from the printed case. After the class has heard the arguments, each member may then write an example of an "award.'" Other variations will undoubtedly suggest themselves.

A word about briefs and a hint on their preparation.

Most college students will have last encountered brief-writing in their freshman English course, or perhaps in high school. Here is chance to review an important subject and develop a useful skill.

The hint is this: study the *questions* that follow the cases for clues that will lead to the most logically developed argument, along lines indicated by the interest to be defended, or the value judgment to be upheld. Merely to summarize the arguments already put forward in the "union position," or "management position" of the printed case will fail to develop the full strength of either side's position.

This cases section of the book calls for active student participation, and brings the practice of collective bargaining into play in a form as realistic as it is possible to get in the classroom. A mock arbitration hearing or role-playing session should not be allowed to degenerate into clowning or farce, but need not exclude humor and good spirits. This part of the course can be, and ought to be, good fun as well as good instruction.

CASE 1
Who Speaks for the Union?

Company: Midwest Manufacturing Corporation
             Galesburg, Illinois
Union: International Association of Machinists
             Midwest Lodge No. 2063
Arbitrator: Charles N. Anrod

This case involves the authority of representatives and the procedures for amending an agreement during its term.

The following discussion of the issue and the facts in this case was prepared by Charles W. Anrod, the arbitrator.

The Corporation, a wholly owned subsidiary of Admiral Corporation, is engaged in the manufacture of refrigerators, freezers, air conditioners, and electric ranges at Galesburg, Illinois. It employs about 1,750 persons of whom approximately 1,400 are in the bargaining unit represented by the Union.

For many years, the employees in said bargaining unit were represented by Federal Labor Union No. 22278 which entered into successive collective bargaining agreements with the Corporation. In February 1956, the employees decided, however, to affiliate with the International Association of Machinists (AFL–CIO) and received a charter therefrom for the Union. Since the transfer occurred during the period of the 1955–56 collective bargaining agreement between the Federal Labor Union and the Corporation, the Union became a party to that agreement in lieu of the Federal Labor

Union until it expired at about the end of October 1956. Thereafter, the Union negotiated with the Corporation a collective bargaining agreement which was signed on November 26, 1956, and which became effective for the period from November 1956, to November 1957 (hereinafter referred to as the "1956–57 Agreement"). It was signed on behalf of the Corporation by L. H. Moos, vice president and general manager, and on behalf of the Union by the members of a committee consisting of five Union representatives, among them William E. Boen, its president. The signature of William Hammond, special representative of the International Association of Machinists, AFL–CIO, was also affixed to it.

The grievances of three employees in the press room, namely, Virgil F. Odean, Ira D. Luallen, and Howard Hook, which are the subject of this arbitration arose out of the following facts:

The 1955–56 collective bargaining agreement provided initially for strict departmental seniority in the event of temporary layoffs. The application of that rule had, however, caused some dissatisfaction among the employees. As a result, the Federal Labor Union and the Corporation entered into a written agreement, dated June 16, 1955, which modified the pertinent provision of the 1955–56 collective bargaining agreement as follows:

> It is agreed between the Company and the Union that when it is necessary to reduce the working force the least senior employee in the classification in the department and on the shift in which the reduction is necessary shall be laid off (Company Exh. No. 4).

This agreement was signed by Harley Morss, then president of the Federal Labor Union, and by Don E. Johnson, director of personnel of the Corporation.

During the negotiations preceding the 1956–57 Agreement, the matter of a satisfactory seniority rule in case of temporary layoff was again discussed between the parties. The Corporation pointed out that, if strict departmental seniority should be applied (as was originally provided in the 1955–56 collective bargaining agreement), it could happen that the youngest employees in a department who had to be laid off temporarily were on the night shift and that their positions had then to be filled by employees from the day shift. This, the Corporation stated, had, in the past, created certain difficulties because some employees so transferred had contended they had been on specific shifts by their choice and felt that they should stay there. Accordingly, the Corporation proposed the following provision for the 1956–57 Agreement:

> In applying departmental seniority in temporary layoffs, the least senior employees in the classification and on the shift in which the surplus occurs shall be the first to be laid off . . . (Company Exh. No. 5).

The Union rejected, however, the Corporation's proposal. Its spokesman asserted that, if classification and shift were determining in applying departmental seniority, employees with greater seniority could conceivably be laid off while employees with less seniority remained at work.

The parties finally agreed to restore strict departmental seniority in case of temporary layoffs (as was originally provided in the 1955–56 collective bargaining agreement) and, thereby, rescinded the agreement, dated June 16, 1955 (quoted above).

Their understanding was incorporated into Article VI, Section 6, of the 1956–57 Agreement which provides, so far as pertinent, the following:

> In case of a temporary layoff departmental seniority shall prevail (joint Exh. No. 1, P. 8).

Yet, the matter did not come to rest. Shortly after the signing of the 1956–57 Agreement, a temporary layoff occurred. In accordance with the departmental seniority rule as stipulated in said Article VI, Section 6, some employees who happened to be on the night shift were laid off and other employees were then transferred from the day shift to the night shift. This procedure caused unrest among the transferees. They did not want to go on the night shift and also raised the question of overtime premium contending they were working outside their regularly scheduled shifts.

In an effort to find a satisfactory solution, the parties again discussed the question as to which seniority rule should be applied in case of temporary layoffs. They reached a tentative agreement under which seniority in the department and on the shift should govern in such instances. This understanding was submitted to a regular meeting of the Union by William Boen, its president, and approved in said meeting. The parties then entered into the following written agreement:

> It is agreed by the parties hereto that the provisions of Article VI Section 6 shall be amended as follows: In case of a temporary layoff the least senior employee in the department and on the shift where such surplus exist shall be first laid off.
>
> (*signed*)   Don E. Johnson
>   Director of Personnel
> (*signed*)   William Boen, President
>   Midwest Lodge #2063
>
> January 31st, 1957 (Union Exh. No. 1)

Thereafter, the Corporation followed the seniority rule as agreed upon in the above agreement of January 31, 1957. About three months later, the membership of the Union voted, however, to rescind said agreement and sent the following letter dated April 23, 1957, to the Company:

> Re: Agreement signed 1–31–57
> This will inform you that the membership of Lodge 2063, at their last regular meeting, voted to return to the provisions of the current contract, and to declare the agreement made and signed by the Management and the Union Representatives on the 31st day of the first month in 1957 void. This

agreement will have to do with Article VI, Section 6, . . . on the subject of Seniority.

(*signed*)   Roy E. Routt, Rec. Sec'y.
Midwest Lodge #2063

The Corporation took the position that the Union could not unilaterally rescind the written agreement of January 31, 1957. It disregarded, therefore, the Union's letter of April 23, 1957, and continued to make temporary layoffs in accordance with the January 31, 1957, agreement.

On May 16 or 17, 1957, the three grievants were temporarily laid off in conformity with the seniority rule stipulated in said agreement. They then filed the instant grievances (Union Exh. Nos. 3, 4 and 5). The Corporation denied the grievances which are now before the Board of Arbitration for decision.

At the same time these layoffs occurred, John R. Healey, an employee in the inspection department, was also temporarily laid off. His supervisor made that layoff in accordance with the original wording of Article VI, Section 6, of the 1956–57 Agreement, i.e., on the basis of strict departmental seniority. Healey filed a grievance which was submitted to the Corporation by John J. Cox, a Union steward. On or about June 4, 1957, the Corporation paid an amount equal to 16 hours' straight time to Healey in settlement of his grievance.

UNION'S POSITION

The Union does not dispute the above-related facts. But it contends that the agreement of January 31, 1957, which amended Article VI, Section 6, of the 1956–57 Agreement regarding the seniority rule in case of temporary layoffs was void.

In support of such contention, the Union asserts the correct procedures as prescribed by the constitution and bylaws of the International Association of Machinists (IAM) were not followed. It particularly states that the agreements of January 31, 1957, was not signed by an international representative of the IAM and, therefore, did not become effective.

It also states that, while said agreement was approved in a regular union meeting, the subject was not posted in advance on the bulletin board as required under the rules of the IAM.

The Union concedes that the letter of April 23, 1957, was afflicted with the same defects and, therefore, regards it void, too.

As a result, the Union concludes that the strict departmental seniority rule as originally contained in Article VI, Section 6, of the 1956–57 Agreement was still in effect when the three grievants were laid off. Since the Corporation followed the terms of the agreement of January 31, 1957, the Union argues that the Corporation violated said Article VI, Section 6.

With respect to the grievance filed by John R. Healey, the Union claims that the Corporation made the payment to Healey for the sole reason that it (the Corporation) was in default of the time limits prescribed for the handling of grievances in the 1956–57 Agreement but not in recognition of the substantive merits of that grievance.

For the above mentioned reasons, the Union seeks an award which would require the Corporation to reimburse the three grievants for the time lost on May 16 and/or 17, 1957.

CORPORATION'S POSITION

The Corporation points out that, while the immediate issue before the Board of Arbitration is whether or not the grievants were properly laid off, there is implicitly a broader question of considerable interest to it involved in this case, namely, whether the Union must live up to and be bound by an agreement made by its duly authorized officers.

The Corporation submits that it had in the past entered into a number of supplementary agreements with the president of the Federal Labor Union during the period of a collective bargaining agreement and that such supplementary agreements had always been carried out by both parties.

Moreover, the Corporation states that, prior to the grievances under consideration, it had no knowledge or notice of any restrictions on the authority of the Union's president to enter into such a supplementary agreement. It specifically emphasizes that it was not aware of any rules or regulations of the IAM requiring the signature of an international representative or the posting of a subject on the bulletin board prior to its discussion in a Union meeting.

The Corporation argues that it acted in good faith when it entered into the January 31, 1957, agreement with the Union and is of the opinion that both parties were bound thereby.

It asserts that, when it was informed of the proper steps as outlined in the rules and regulations of the IAM after the instant grievances had arisen, it readily agreed to respect the requirement of a signature or approval of an international representative in the future and also to adhere no longer to the January 31, 1957, agreement. At the same time, the Corporation contends, it was, however, made clear to the representative of the Union that its (the Corporation's) concessions would not apply retroactively to actions taken in accordance with said agreement in the past.

As to the grievance of John R. Healey, the Corporation contends that it immediately recognized the foreman had made a mistake and informed the Union's representative over the telephone on or about the day of the filing of the grievance that payment would be made.

For the above-mentioned reasons, the Corporation asks that the three grievances here involved be denied.

QUESTIONS

1. Precisely state the issue to be decided by the Board of Arbitration.
2. What "lessons" does this kind of situation contain for both union and management about (*a*) the nature of the agreement, (*b*) the credentials and authority of representatives, and (*c*) seniority provisions.

CASE 2
Management's Right to Close the Plant

Company: Texas Rebuilders, Inc.
Union: International Brotherhood of Boilermakers, Iron Shipbuilders, Blacksmiths, Forgers and Helpers, Local 96.
Arbitrator: Clyde Emery

The following presentation of facts in this case, which call in question the assertion of management rights, was prepared by Clyde Emery, the arbitrator.

Facts of the Case

The Company is one of six subsidiary corporations, the parent corporation's plant being in Illinois; all are engaged in rebuilding automobile parts. During the first quarter of 1974, sales declined; April, May and June were the worst sales quarter in Company history. It became imperative to reduce inventory and the expense of maintaining it,—while avoiding layoff if possible.

In June the parent office directed the subsidiary plants to sound out the Union on the possibility of a shorter workweek; during the week of June 17 the Plant Manager and Director of Personnel involved here talked with the Union Committee about a four-day week. A one-day shutdown on July 5 (to continue the closing on July 4) was also probably considered. The Plant Manager so recalled and testified; so did the Director of Personnel; and the Warehouse Foreman, who had been Chief Steward at the time of the meeting, after several efforts to remember what was said, recalled that a woman on the Union Committee had insisted that the employees should be paid if the plant closed down on July 5.

On June 25, 1974, the following notice was posted:

> To: All Employees—Subject: July 4th Holiday
> Thursday, July 4 will be a paid holiday for all eligible employees. The Plant will also be closed Friday, July 5th. This will *not* be a paid holiday; however, all employees desiring to take one day of their vacation will be allowed to do so. The determining dates for eligibility for holiday pay (7 hours on last day before and 7 hours on first day following) will be Wednesday, July 3rd and Monday, July 8th.

I want to wish everyone a safe and enjoyable holiday.
[W.]—Personnel

On July 10 all probationary employees were terminated. The next day, July 11, approximately 50 employees were laid off from the bargaining unit of 325 or 350. (The laid-off employees were recalled about August 1, but only 75 percent returned; some new employees were hired. Then Company and employees proceeded to have in August a record month for the plant.)

The Union had filed a grievance on July 8 alleging that the July 5 shutdown violated the Agreement and seeking one day's pay for the employees. This was the only grievance filed throughout the Company-wide system. (All the plants are organized.)

QUESTIONS

1. Would it have made a difference if July 4th had fallen on a Wednesday instead of a Thursday in 1974? Could the union in that case have demanded two days' pay? Or four days', if the holiday had fallen on a Monday, followed by a shutdown to the following week?
2. The company failed to get union agreement to a 4-day week, but apparently laid off 50 employees without consulting the union. Could the company have gone to a 4-day week without union agreement?
3. Are there any limitations on management's right to close down the plant?

CASE 3
Prefabrication of Materials

Company: Safeway Stores, Incorporated
San Diego, California
Union: Amalgamated Meat Cutters and Butcher Workmen of North America Local No. 229
Arbitrator: Thomas T. Roberts

Does an employer undermine the union when he introduces prefabricated materials which change the customary work of union members in a retail store?

Thomas T. Roberts, arbitrator in this case, prepared the following discussion of the issues and facts involved.

ISSUE

The stipulated issues are:

a. Did the employer breach the contract by introducing packaged ground beef in one- and two-pound packages in visking casings for direct sale to consumers in the San Diego markets covered by the Contract?
b. If so, what shall the remedy be?

STATEMENT OF FACTS

This grievance arose under, and is controlled by, the agreement between the parties entered into on November 5, 1962, and by its terms in full force and effect until the first Monday of November, 1964.

The Company operates a national chain of food supermarkets. The Union is the exclusive collective bargaining representative for employees working in the meat departments of the Company's markets located in San Diego, California, and surrounding communities. A collective bargaining relationship has existed between the parties since 1937.

This dispute involves the introduction by the Company, in September of 1963, of prepackaged ground beef sold directly to customers in the San Diego area in one- and two-pound quantities encased within visking wrapping. For many years prior to that time, it was the practice of the Company to prepackage ground beef in visking casings of 15- or 20-pound sizes (known as "catch weights") at a central cutting plant located in Los Angeles, California. Two types of ground beef prepackaged in this manner were then supplied to the retail stores in the San Diego area. The first was a coarse ground product which had to be reground before being offered for sale in the markets. The second was a fine grind which did not have to be reground at the store level, except that if it had been placed on display it was sometimes necessary that it be reground prior to being offered for sale on the succeeding day.

The coarse grind ground beef, after its receipt at the market, was removed from its visking casing, reground, packaged, priced, and displayed for sale. The fine grind ground beef, with the exception noted above, required no regrinding at the store. It was simply sliced, packaged, priced, and then displayed for sale. As to both the coarse and fine grinds, all of the above operations conducted at the store level were performed by employees within the jurisdiction of the Union.

In September of 1963, the Company discontinued the shipment to the San Diego area of fine grind beef in the larger catch-weight quantities. In its stead, one- and two-pound "chubs" of prepackaged ground beef in visking casings were introduced. Upon their receipt at the markets, the chubs are simply priced and then displayed for sale in their original package. As was formerly the case with catch-weight quantities, the grinding and packaging of the chubs is accomplished in Los Angeles.

The Union learned of the pending introduction of these chubs and on August 30, 1963, sent the Company two telegrams and a letter protesting that the use of chubs would be a violation of that portion of the collective bargaining agreement which is set forth hereinafter. The Company has nevertheless continued the sale of chubs in the San Diego area and the parties, being unable to resolve their differences, have submitted the matter to arbitration.

CONTROLLING CONTRACT PROVISIONS

Section III
Jurisdiction of Merchandise
Displayed and Sold

(*a*) All fish, poultry, rabbits, meat and/or kindred products, fresh or frozen, cooked or uncooked except as hereinafter provided shall be displayed, handled, and sold under the jurisdiction of Local #229 by journeymen meat cutters under the terms and conditions contained in this Agreement. Wherever any of the above described products and merchandise is being offered for sale at least one (1) employee classified as a head meat cutter or journeyman meat cutter, an employee covered by this Contract, shall be on duty, except during the lunch hour in markets manned by one employee. All sales of products enumerated immediately above shall be credited to the meat department and/or division of the undersigned Employer. All meat products enumerated immediately above shall be cut, prepared, and fabricated on the Employer's premises or immediately adjacent thereto so as to enable said Employer to effectively supervise such operation and conduct the same under sanitary conditions. With regard to beef, veal, lamb and/or pork in carcass form, it is agreed that an exception will be made and the same may be broken down into primal cuts such as rounds, ribs, chucks, plates and loins off the premises, but said primal cuts shall be fabricated on the premises by employees covered by this Contract, and all sales shall be credited to the meat department and/or division of the undersigned Employer. With regard to luncheon meats, presliced bacon, dissected and prefabricated fowls, ground beef and pork sausage in visking casings, fish, rabbits and/or frozen packaged meat, which pursuant to current custom and practices are presently prefabricated, predissected and precut, said products not be cut on the premises, but all of the above products will likewise be handled and sold by employees covered by this Contract, and the sales thereof shall likewise be credited to the meat department and/or the division of the undersigned Employer.

POSITION OF THE UNION

It is the position of the Union that the introduction of chubs to the San Diego area was a violation of Section III of the agreement between the parties. It asks that the sale of such chubs be prohibited in those markets within the jurisdiction.

The Union argues that Section III prohibits the handling, displaying, and selling of ground beef by its members unless such meat is cut, prepared, and fabricated at the markets. It is contended that the new chubs do not qualify as an exception to this mandate because the merchandising of such items is not pursuant to the custom and practice existing at the time the present Agreement was executed in November 1962.

The Union points out that prior to the introduction of the chubs, the sole use of visking casing as a method of packaging ground beef was the transportation of catchweight quantities from Los Angeles to the San Diego markets. Ground beef was never sold directly to the customer in its original visking casing.

At the hearing, the Union introduced an interoffice memo directed to the Company's store managers in San Diego and announcing the pending introduction of the chubs. It is argued that the statements contained therein acknowledge that the new product dispenses with the cutting, packaging, and weighing of fine grind ground beef, all of which were formerly done in the markets.

The alleged failure of the Company to respond to the letter and telegrams from the Union protesting the chubs is cited as an admission on the part of management that the introduction of the new items did in fact involve a violation of the agreement.

The Union draws the attention of the arbitrator to the fact that the agreement does not contain a so-called Management Prerogatives clause and states that the unilateral introduction of the chubs by the Company amounts to "contracting out" bargaining unit work to the derogation of the rights of members of the Union. It is contended that the reduction of work operations here involved constitutes a threat to job security of affected employees and has resulted in layoffs within the meat departments.

POSITION OF THE COMPANY

It is the position of the Company that the introduction of chubs to the San Diego area was not a violation of Section III of the agreement because that provision expressly recites that ground beef in visking casings need not be fabricated in the markets.

The Company contends that in any event Section III restricts the fabrication of meat products only to the "employer's premises" and asserts that the preparation of chubs at its Los Angeles facility falls within the purview of that language. In this regard, it is noted that the employees in the Los Angeles central cutting plant of the Company are represented by the Amalgamated Meat Cutters and Butcher Workmen of North America.

Finally, the Company states that the "existing practice and custom" referred to in the agreement means the packaging of prefabricated ground beef in visking casings of whatever form or weight and the chubs are therefore in conformance with the language of Section III.

QUESTIONS

1. Is the Los Angeles cutting plant part of "the employer's premises" as contemplated by Section III of the agreement?
2. To what does the "current custom and practices" phrase of Section III re-

fer? cutting? grinding? visking casings? or the quantities encased in visking casings?

3.   Why is the union grieving in this case?

CASE 4
Assignment of an Employee to Work Outside His Job Classification

Company: Phillips Petroleum Company
               Kansas City, Missouri
Union: Oil Chemical and Atomic Workers International Union
               Local 5–64
Arbitrator: Marion Beatty

This case involves the performance of work outside of an employee's job description.

The following discussion of the issue and facts in this case was prepared by Marion Beatty, the arbitrator.

The issue is "whether or not the work assignment given to S. Hachinsky on December 25, 1956, pertaining to lineups to tanks on vacuum flasher stream and lube asphalt stream was a violation of the working agreement, particularly Exhibit A thereof."

The Union seeks an award ordering the Company to cease such assignments and allowing the low man in the "asphalt blender loader/senior loader group" on December 25, 1956, to work four hours at overtime rate to correct the alleged violation.

The Company denies that the work assignment in question violated any part of the contract and takes the further position that the arbitrator has no authority to issue any injunctive type of relief applying to the future conduct of the Company.

CONTRACT PROVISIONS

Contract provisions cited by the parties as relevant to the issues in dispute include the Management Prerogatives clause, the Arbitration clause defining the authority and jurisdiction of the arbitrator, a provision for four hours' call-in pay, Article VII, Section 6, entitled "Procedure for Filling Temporary Shift Vacancies," and an Appendix A to the contract which is a chart entitled "Employment, Progression, Regression and Classification Chart." This chart shows three job classifications in the asphalt and loading section and they are, from high to low, "Asphalt blender loader/senior loader," "Loader A," and "Loader-operating helper." It also shows three pumper classifications in a separate section known as the transfer section or pumper section. They are from high to low, "senior pumper," "special pumper," and "pumper."

All of these were considered.

STATEMENT OF FACTS

On December 25, 1956, when many employees in the refinery were off with a paid holiday, S. Hachinsky was employed as a pumper on the 8 A.M. to 4 P.M. shift. His job is in the transfer section. Ordinarily he does not work in the asphalt plant. The asphalt plant was down for the holiday, but several valves had to be turned to make changes in lineups and tanks on the vacuum flasher stream and lube asphalt stream. A supervisor requested Hachinsky to come a short distance from his regular station in the pumping section to the asphalt plant to turn the necessary valves as directed by the supervisor. The turning of such valves is a type of work regularly performed by Hachinsky, but he does not work at the asphalt plant. The work involved required approximately 10 minutes. Hachinsky had ample leisure time to perform the work and did perform the work promptly as directed, but under protest.

These duties ordinarily are performed and are the responsibility of the "asphalt blender loader/senior loader," the title given to the employee who is stationed at the asphalt plant and whose duties embrace, among other things, the turning of such valves for making lineups of charge and yield streams to and from the vacuum flasher and lineups for loading of trucks and tank cars with asphalt.

The Company knew in advance of December 25 that these valves would have to be turned. It could have called in a regular employee in the asphalt plant and paid for four hours at premium rate. It chose to use Hachinsky, a pumper who ordinarily did the same kind of valve turning at a nearby section.

POSITION OF THE UNION

The Union contends that the above-described assignment to Hachinsky violated the working agreement and particularly Article VII, Section 6c and Appendices A and B. The Union states that this work was the duty and responsibility of an "asphalt blender loader/senior loader" and that in the absence of such it should have been assigned to another employee in the asphalt and loading section in accordance with Article VII, Section 6c of Appendix A, the "Employment Progression, Regression and Classification Chart." It maintained that Hachinsky was regularly employed in the pumper section, not a part of the asphalt and loading section, and that even though he might have known how to turn valves under supervision, he was not familiar with these valves in the asphalt loading section and should not have been called to do any work in another section either permanent or temporary and that an employee in the asphalt section was entitled to the work.

The Union maintains that one of the purposes of the "Progression, Regression and Classification Chart" is to give "organizational status" to the many job classifications shown thereon, not only for the purpose of progression and regression, but also for the filling of vacancies, both temporary and permanent, and for the assignment of work in each basic classification, and that the Company could not cross the definite classification, and for the assignment of work from one to another.

It maintains that the Company violated the contract for the purpose of saving four hours of premium pay which otherwise would have gone to an employee in the asphalt loader section.

POSITION OF THE COMPANY

The Company states that the turning of these valves in making these line-ups is the sort of work normally done by pumpers, that all Hachinsky had to do was to turn several valves as directed by the supervisor, the same kind of work which he did normally and regularly, and that it was no violation of any part of the contract, and was proper and reasonable under the circumstances. It states that the work in question is identical in job content and skill required to that work which is performed by him and other pumpers every day.

The Company admits that if it had called an employee especially for this assignment it would have called someone regularly employed within the asphalt and loading section, but points out that it was not necessary to call one for 10 minutes on a Christmas holiday, and that therefore Article VII, Section 6c, and Appendix A do not apply for they provide a procedure for filling temporary shift vacancy and that no shift vacancy was involved.

The Company contends that there is nothing in the contract which prohibits it from assigning the work in question to pumper Hachinsky who was on duty, qualified and available, doing the same kind of work elsewhere, and in the absence of restriction has the right to exercise its managerial prerogatives.

The Company further contends that the Union is attempting to read jurisdictional lines into the contract where none are provided, and that the contract as well as the progression chart attached thereto is not an outline of job jurisdiction and that jurisdictional lines were never discussed in negotiation.

Lastly the Company points out that it has on 14 previous occasions made similar assignments of pumpers to perform jobs in the asphalt plant when the regular staff was off on holidays.

QUESTIONS

1. The contract and exhibits do not clearly prohibit the company from assigning Hachinsky to this fill-in job. What sorts of inferential material could be introduced by the union to support its claim?

2. If the arbitrator upheld this grievance, what effect would the ruling have on plant operations?
3. This dispute appears to be over a very minor issue: "ten minutes" versus "four hours' pay." What are its deeper implications for workers, the company, and the union?

CASE 5
"Tandem" Compensation Adjustments for Nonunion Personnel

Names and places in this case are fictitious. The case involves the deter-mination of a policy on salary adjustments for both nonunion and unionized employees. "Mr. Allen" employed one of the authors of this book as a con-sultant on this problem.

BACKGROUND

The Ralta Company is engaged in the manufacture and distribution of products in an expanding industry. At the present time, it is about midway in a 15-year program of product and process diversification. Profits of both Ralta and its principal competitors reflect the general prosperity and ex-pansion of the industry. In this industry labor costs equal between 15 per-cent and 20 percent of total costs of production. Ralta sells its products in a somewhat restricted geographic area and could be seriously hurt by geo-graphic price wars which sometimes plague the industry.

In his annual report to stockholders, the president of Ralta said, "With regard to the outlook for next year, we anticipate that demand for our products will average 4 percent to 5 percent higher than this year. Ordi-narily we would expect such an increase to result in moderate gain in profits. While management seeks this result, it cannot now be assumed with any assurance because our industry faces more than the usual number of uncertainties." Over the past 5 years, industry estimates of increased vol-ume have leveled off at the 4 percent to 5 percent figure from a higher esti-mate of progress in the previous decade. Actual progress in the industry has fallen somewhat short of these estimates. However, Ralta has expanded each year approximately at the 4 percent to 5 percent industry estimated rate.

The Ralta Company employs 12,000 wage and salary workers. They are engaged in diverse operations geographically spread over the eastern sea-board and southeastern states. Five thousand hourly employees are concen-trated in two plants: one in Pennsylvania employing 4,500 and one in Texas employing 500. Hourly employees are represented by one union in Pennsyl-vania and by a rival union in Texas. Another 5,000 employees work for a commission or in isolated locations and are not related to the present prob-lem. The direct concern of this case is with 2,310 salaried employees, about 700 of whom are represented by the Pennsylvania union.

The salaried employees of the Ralta Company can be classified into three groups:

A.   Earning between $25,000 and $100,000 per year—55 employees—not represented by a union.
B.   Earning between $15,000 and $25,000 per year—155 employees—not represented by a union.
C.   Earning less than $15,000 per year—2,100 employees—this group includes middle-management people, production supervisors, engineers, and staff personnel (about 1,400 people) earning more than the top rate paid to union represented workers and about 700 employees earning less than the top rate paid to union represented workers. The latter 700 employees include secretarial, clerical, and custodial personnel, some of whom are represented by the union.

Union-negotiated wage increases over the last 15 years have been substantial and frequent (almost annually). The Company and Union have never agreed on basic principles which should be uniformly applied in wage determination. However, changes in the cost of living, Company profitability, wage increases and wage levels paid by the Company's competitors, and changes in productivity have been discussed in negotiations and probably exerted an influence on what was finally agreed to.

For the last 15 years, the Ralta Company has followed the practice of granting salary increases approximately equal to the negotiated wage increases immediately upon the conclusion of negotiations with the union. On several occasions the Company bypassed the A Group positions or gave a fixed dollar increase which was less than the full percentage increase to Group A positions. All employees in Groups A, B, and C may receive annual *merit* increases until they reach the maximum of their salary classification. These merit increases have been awarded apart from and *in addition to* the general "tandem" adjustments for salaried employees.

THE PROBLEM

Members of the top management of the Ralta Company became concerned over the prospect that salaried employees might feel that the unions were negotiating for the salaried people. Management did not want the salaried people to have this sympathetic interest in the success of the unions. When this matter was discussed in the operating executives' meeting, the president of Ralta directed Mr. Allen, the industrial relations director, to look into the situation and recommend a solution.

GATHERING THE FACTS

Mr. Allen started his analysis by stating the following Company objectives:

1. To provide fair and equitable compensation for salaried employees.
2. To retain and attract competent salaried employees at all salary levels.
3. To build management morale and loyalty to the company.
4. To pay salaries which have an incentive value.
5. To provide flexibility in salary administration.
6. Not to prejudice the company's position in collective bargaining.
7. To minimize the belief among salaried employees that their pay is determined by union negotiations.

This listing of objectives by Mr. Allen represented his beliefs concerning the relative priority of each goal. He realized that the goals were not mutually exclusive. He recognized that salary increases had closely paralleled wage increases negotiated with the unions. However, he insisted that this is "natural" since the same economic forces which generated wage increases are responsible for salary increases. Announcement of general salary increases before reaching agreements with rival unions would seriously prejudice the company's position in collective bargaining.

In wage negotiations, Ralta had openly accepted only two criteria for wage increases: (a) practice of industry competitors—"meeting the average" and (b) rapid and substantial increases in the cost of living. However, it was obvious that competitors' concessions and Ralta's willingness to "meet the average" were strongly influenced by the high profits of the industry and the firm. This in turn could be related to rapid technological progress and increasing man-hour productivity.

Mr. Allen wrote to other companies in his industry about how they handled this problem. The responses indicated that every major company in the industry followed Ralta's practice and that they were equally disturbed about its bad psychological effect. No one in the industry proposed a more satisfactory way of handling the problem.

Not satisfied with these responses, Mr. Allen broadened his inquiry to other industries. Some dozen industrial relations directors responded to Allen's inquiry. They added the following possibilities as methods for handling the salary problem:

1. Grant a percentage increase equal to the union-negotiated increase but announce it at times so that it will not be associated with collective bargaining negotiations. "When adjustments were made considerably after union negotiations, it usually became a question in management personnel's minds whether the adjustments granted were related to the last increase given to the union or were a forecast of the next increase to be negotiated. We are not sure that all of the confusion so generated has been to the advantage of the Company."
2. Award all salary increases exclusively on a "merit" basis. Prepare an annual forecast of total salary adjustments and budget funds to each department on the basis of this forecast. Allow each department head to award salary increases to approximately one twelfth of the employees each month. Each meritorious employee receives the salary increase on a strictly personal and confidential basis. "We have encountered two problems with this system. First, if we overestimate or

underestimate the forecast in one year, we try to compensate for this error the next year. Although we have been generally successful in providing equity *over a number of years,* inequities have arisen in some individual years. The other problem is the timing of the increases. An employee receiving an increase in January may receive a greater annual increase than a more meritorious employee who receives an increase in November."

3. Announce general adjustments at a predetermined annual date. The amount of the annual adjustment will be determined by an analysis of economic conditions at the time of the announcement.

4. Adopt a fixed formula for general adjustments to be made at a predetermined annual date. One such formula might consider changes in the Consumers' Price Index plus a fixed percentage increase to reflect increases in general "productivity."

5. Provide for salaried employees to participate in a stock-purchase or profit-sharing plan.

RECOMMENDATIONS

You are Mr. Allen. Next week you must present your recommendations to the operating executive's committee.

Prepare your recommendations on the basis of the alternatives developed in your research. Weigh each of the alternatives against the objectives outlined above.

Precisely state the problems surrounding the application of your recommendations.

CASE 6
Arbitrability and Management Rights in
Job Classification and Assignment

Employer: Sea-Land Services, Inc.
Union: Office and Professional Employees Union,
Local No. 8
Arbitrator: Philip K. Kienast

What happens when management believes that the union is trying to get at arbitration more than the company agreed to in negotiations, namely, the right to grieve and arbitrate job classification and job assignment decisions?

The following discussion of the issues and facts in this case was prepared by Philip K. Kienast, the arbitrator.

OPINION

Background

Sea-Land Services, Inc. is a water carrier headquartered in Elizabeth, New Jersey. Its business is transportation of cargo to and from various ports. The Company has expanded rapidly in recent years. White collar employment at the various ports has risen from 450 in 1963 to 9,000 in 1975. The Seattle bargaining unit is comprised of approximately 120 office and clerical workers.

The Company and the Office and Professional Employees International Union at the national level entered their first agreement in 1960. After a card count of the office and clerical employees at the Seattle facility they were brought under the agreement in 1970. The current agreement is a two year contract that terminates in November of this year.

The grievant was hired 22 November 1972 as a "Transmittal Clerk" (Pay Grade 2). In August 1973 he bid on and was awarded a "OS&D Clerk" (Pay Grade 4) position. His main function in this job was that of "plucking." Plucking consists of the employee periodically checking bills of lading against manifests, checking for proper destination, hazardous cargo and similar related tasks for each van being loaded for shipment. This typically involves some 20 vans during an 8 hour day shift. As soon as a van is completely packed the bills are plucked and taken to the billing department so as to expedite their arrival before the cargo itself at Alaska destinations. The grievant's other duties included checking on shortages, damaged cargo and expediting shipments, etc. These other duties took up between one half to one fourth of his average work day.

In June of 1974 the Company decided the plucking function would be better performed if integrated into the overall warehouse operation rather than being part of the OS&D (Overage, Short and Damaged) department. It subsequently assigned the grievant to the position "warehouse clerk" (Pay Grade 4) on the Alaska dock where he continued to perform the plucking function.

Early in 1975 the Company decided it was necessary to reduce from 48 to 24 hours the time in which it took to close out all billing for vans on a ship and get them forwarded to Alaska. As a result of this decision it became necessary to pluck on a continuous (free flow system) rather than a periodic basis (van pack system). The company determined that it would need one clerk plucking full time on both the day and swing shifts to implement this change.

Therefore, early in 1975 the Company assigned the plucking function to two newly hired "general clerks" (Pay Grade 2). It had determined through its job evaluation system that plucking alone warranted only grade 2 pay. The grievant was subsequently informed that he would be transferred from the Alaskan dock to the yard office—still as a "warehouse clerk" (Pay Grade 4). The two assignments involve the same essential job elements, namely, checking in cargo and keeping the necessary proper work in an orderly manner. As of the date of the hearing the Company had not actually effectuated the transfer owing in part to a management change at the Seattle facility.

On 28 January 1975 Mr. Farrington filed the grievance which has become the issue in this proceeding. The grievance alleged that the Company was violating the agreement by unilaterally assigning the plucking function to lower grade positions and reassigning him from the Alaskan dock to the yard office.

The pertinent contract language in the instant case has not been subject to major alteration since the first agreement was signed and includes the following:

Article IX—Promotions, Assignments, and Transfers.

7. An employee shall follow his regular position of work when it is transferred substantially in whole from one location or department to another location or department. The Employer agrees to notify the Union of a change of an employee's location or department prior to such change. No employee shall be transferred permanently to a lower rated position, or permanently to work for which the employee was not hired, except in the case where the transfer results from application for such transfer by the employee, transfer in lieu of layoff, or by agreement between the Employer and the Union.

Article XIII—Maintenance of Standards.

(*a*) The Employer will continue to provide benefits which have not been superseded by this Agreement and which were enjoyed generally by all employees. Any question relating to these benefits shall be referred immediately to Step 3 of the Grievance Procedure.

*   *   *   *   *

Article XV—Grievance Machinery—Arbitration.

1. Any complaint or dispute arising between the parties to this Agreement involving the interpretation, application, or claimed breach of this Agreement may be considered a grievance. Any employee having a grievance which has not been settled by him with his supervisor shall waive the same unless he pursues the following procedure:

Step 1: The matter shall be taken up by the employee affected and his steward with the employee's supervisor. This step shall be taken within five (5) working days from the date when the grievance arose. If not satisfactorily settled, the grievance shall be reduced to writing and submitted to the Employer, then

Step 2: The matter of the grievance shall be taken up by the Chief Steward with a representative of the Employer within three (3) working days after Step 1 has failed to settle the matter. If not here satisfactorily settled, then

Step 3: The matter shall be taken up between a representative of the Union and an executive of the Employer within five (5) working days after Step 2 has failed to settle the matter. If not here satisfactorily settled, then the matter may be taken to arbitration by either party as hereinafter provided in Section 3.

2. If the Employer or the Union has a grievance hereunder, it shall be presented within three (3) working days from the time when it arose to a representative of the other party of this contract. Should the grievance not be settled by the parties, then either party may invoke the procedure pro-

vided for in Section 3 hereof in accordance with the time limits therein stated.

3. Any grievance as herein defined which is not settled under the grievance procedure above outlined may be submitted, upon notice to the other party, to arbitration within one (1) week after the last applicable step of the grievance procedure has failed to produce a settlement thereof, before an arbitrator appointed pursuant to the rules of, and from the panel of arbitrators of American Arbitration Association, unless the parties agree upon a mutually acceptable arbitrator within five (5) working days after delivery of the notice of intention to arbitrate. In the event the parties do not agree upon an arbitrator from the panel furnished by the American Arbitration Association, an arbitrator shall be designated by the American Arbitration Association and such designation shall be final and binding upon the parties hereto. Where arbitration is not demanded within the time limit herein fixed, the grievance in question is deemed waived.

4. The cost of any arbitration hereunder shall be borne equally by the parties, and the arbitrator's decision shall be final and binding on all parties and shall be fully enforceable in any appropriate court of law. It is understood that the arbitrator shall not have the power to amend, modify, alter or subtract from this Agreement or any provision thereof.

Article XIX—Salaries.

1. Employees shall be classified pursuant to the skills and responsibilities required in the performance of their duties. A table of job classifications and rates of pay marked Exhibit "E" covering the various positions included within the bargaining unit is attached hereto and made a part of this Agreement. Job classifications are not intended to restrict work assignment. They are intended to provide an approximate gauge of the skill and responsibility required, so that employees can be compensated equitably. The Employer agrees, when reasonably requested, to review job classifications. If a review of a job results in an upgrading, the change must be made effective within one month of the time the review was formally requested.

*   *   *   *   *

Article XX—Rights of Management.

All the usual inherent and fundamental rights of Management that the Employer had prior to the execution of this Agreement shall continue to be vested in the Employer except those specifically abridged herein.

Procedural Issues

This proceeding was conducted pursuant to Article XV of the parties' collective bargaining agreement. The arbitrator was appointed by the American Arbitration Association per the provisions of that Article on 20 February 1975. A hearing was held 1 May 1975 in Sea-Land Services' conference room located at 2805 26th Avenue S.W. The hearing was closed on 19 May 1975 when briefs containing the parties' final arguments were received by the arbitrator.

At the hearing the Company raised the issue of arbitrability and noted that it was not waiving its challenge by participating in the proceeding. This fact was made a point of record, and it was mutually agreed to take testimony at that time both as to arbitrability and the merits of grievance itself.

Inasmuch as the parties were unable to agree on a framing of the issue to be resolved it has fallen within the province of the arbitrator to do so. After reviewing the record the arbitrator believes the issue to be properly framed by the following questions:

1. Did the Company violate the Agreement by hiring two employees as "General Clerks" (Pay Grade 2) to perform the task of "plucking" which traditionally has been performed by "Warehouse Clerks" (Pay Grade 4)? If yes, what shall the remedy be?
2. Did the Company violate the Agreement when it decided to assign the grievant from the Alaskan dock to the yard? If yes, what shall the remedy be?

Substantive Issues

Underlying the Union's position in the instant case is the assertion that the Company does not have the unilateral right to abolish and create jobs during the term of the agreement when such actions result in a situation as in the instant case, namely, where an abolished job "reappears" in a job posting but reduced two pay grades, a difference of over $30 per month in pay at the top of each grade.

The Union maintains that were the Company permitted to proceed as it has in the instant case then bargaining unit employees could, at the discretion of the Company, be deprived of the fruits of the agreement. The Union contends that its members have a right to expect the Company's job structure to remain relatively stable in terms of task assignments and pay levels unless reasonable cause exists for change. The Union contends no reasonable cause exists in the instant case. It argues, rather, that the changes that precipitated the grievance is only one of a series of unwarranted job changes at the Seattle facility that has resulted in a general downgrading of jobs and hence unilateral changes in pay levels during the term of the current agreement. It points to the testimony of both the grievant and steward Burton in support of this contention.

As regards the reassignment of the grievant from the dock to the yard the Union contends that Article IX, Section 7 prohibits such reassignment without the express consent of the grievant and bases its contention on what it construes as clear and specific contract language on the point at issue.

In contrast the Company contends that clear contract language, the history of negotiations between itself and the international union as well as firmly established practice give it the right to assign both work and employees as it determines is necessary for the conduct of its business. It points specifically to the language in Article XIX that delineates the right of employees or the Union to request classification reviews and notes that no such review was requested in the instant case. It also points to language in Article XIX that states that: "Job classifications are not intended to restrict work assignments."

The company argues that at least a couple of dozen classification reviews per Article XX have been conducted in the past with some leading to subsequent upgrading (Mr. McIntyre and Ms. Morris). The Company vigorously contends that the review procedure in Article XX is the only agreed upon channel for handling the classification issues involved in the instant case and, therefore, that the grievance should be denied on that ground alone. By implication the Company has also argued that the grievance is defective until the review process has been implemented and completed. Moreover, the Company notes that in none of its contractual negotiations with the Union has the Union requested to become involved in the job evaluation or classification process. It contends, therefore, that the Union has been satisfied with the review procedures under Article XX and that if it is now dissatisfied that the proper place to deal with the issue is at the bargaining table and not in the grievance procedure.

As regards the second contested issue of the grievant's assignment to the yard the Company contends the jobs are the same, i.e. "warehouse clerk" (Pay Grade 4) and hence the grievant has not been transferred to a new or different job. Therefore, it argues that Article IX, Section 7 does not come into play. Moreover, the Company notes that there is a clearly established practice of the Company assigning personnel within job classification that does not substantiate the Union's narrow construction of the language in question.

Arbitrability

The Company staunchly maintains that the grievance is not arbitrable inasmuch as both the grievant and the Union have failed to follow the only contractually proscribed procedures for dealing with classification disputes as specifically provided for in Article XIX which reads in part that: "The Employer agrees when reasonably requested, to review job classifications." It argues that such review is the only contractually agreed upon appeal procedure in classification disputes. It asserts that past practices in similar disputes underscores this point. It maintains that the arbitrator who finds otherwise would be exceeding given authority by in effect "adding" a second and different appeal procedure to that agreed upon by the parties.

In direct contrast the Union contends that if it could not arbitrate classification disputes that management could frustrate the agreement by making unilateral changes in rates of pay through its classification process. In fact, the Union intimates that this is precisely what appears to be happening at the Seattle facility.

Moreover, the Union points to the grievance/arbitration clause in the contract which it maintains clearly gives it the right to demand arbitration when it can show reasonable cause for claiming a violation of the agreement.

CASE 7
Seniority versus Affirmative Action

Company: Bethlehem Steel Corporation, Sparrows Point Plant
Union: United Steelworkers of America, Local 2609
Arbitrator: Seymour Strongin

This case involves a conflict between seniority rights as provided in the labor agreement and a directive of the Secretary of Labor aimed at correcting past discrimination, as this directive was interpreted by the company.

The following discussion of the issues and the facts in this case was prepared by Seymour Strongin, the arbitrator.

These are "pilot cases", typical of a large number of pending grievances which arise out of the Company's compliance with a decision of the Secretary of Labor, issued January 15, 1973, after proceedings involving this Plant before the Office of Contract Compliance under Executive Order 11246. In that Decision the Secretary held, with respect to a certain class of "affected employees" (black employees at the Plant who were hired prior to March 31, 1968, and who were initially assigned to all-black or predominately black units), that their seniority rights in certain situations should thereafter be determined by their plant seniority, rather than by their unit seniority, as provided in Article X of the Agreement. The particular grievances here before the Umpire arose in October, 1973, when the Company, in the course of reductions in force in the Continuous Anneal seniority unit and the Tandem Mill seniority unit, followed the "plant seniority" rule laid down in the Secretary's Decision. The grievants in these cases suffered demotions and loss of wages (and, in one case, an eventual layoff) when they lost positions they would have retained under the "unit seniority" provisions of Article X, and these positions were filled, applying the Secretary's Decision, by "affected employees" with plant seniority over the grievants. In this proceeding the grievants assert their alleged right under the Agreement to be compensated in accordance with its terms for work to which they were entitled under the "unit seniority" provisions of Article X. The Company contends that the case is without merit, and indeed is not even arbitrable, because the Company was compelled to observe and apply the "plant seniority" rule set forth in the Secretary's Decision.

In the Umpire's judgment, the Company's defense has not been altogether responsive to the Union's contentions. The Union admits that the Company was bound to follow "plant seniority" as prescribed in the Secretary's Decision. The Union does not question the validity of the Executive Order or of the Secretary's decision, or of the Secretary's authority to issue it and to implement it. Insofar as certain employees benefitted from the Decision and achieved positions or rates of pay which they would not have achieved under the Agreement, the Union has no quarrel with the Company's action. What the Union does contend here is that, while those employees are entitled to be assigned to certain jobs and paid for that work in accordance with the Secretary's Decision, the grievants here are entitled to be paid under the Agreement for the work which they were ready to perform and to which they were entitled under the terms of Article X. The Union does not, therefore, complain over the Company's action in protecting the "plant seniority" employees, but only over its not protecting the "unit seniority" employees. The Union argues that if the former group is entitled to benefits under the Secretary's Decision, the latter group is no less entitled to benefits under the Agreement. To be sure, adopting this contention would require the Company to pay the same wages to two employees where only one was doing the work for which that wage is contractually payable. But this, says the Union, is simply the result of the Company's own earlier conduct which gave rise to the Department of Labor proceeding. That proceeding vindicated the rights of employees with plant seniority who had been the victims of earlier discriminations. The Union contends that the employees with unit seniority, however, still have their rights as prescribed in the Agreement, and, further, that the Umpire, whose power is limited to applying the Agreement, is bound by its terms.

The foregoing statement of the issues establishes, the Umpire believes, that the grievances are "arbitrable", and he therefore must reject the Company's threshold challenge to arbitrability. The Company supports its "non-arbitrability" argument with a number of court decisions holding that where an employer has taken action in compliance with requirements of federal law, he cannot be subjected to an arbitration procedure which would result, if the grievant were successful, in obstructing or thwarting such compliance. But the Union is not seeking to overturn any action taken by the Company in compliance with federal law. If the Union were to prevail in this arbitration, there would be no thwarting or obstructing of the Company's compliance with the Secretary's Decision. The employees who benefitted from that Decision and from the Company's compliance therewith would continue to benefit precisely as if these grievances had never been brought. What the Union presents here is a claim arising under the Agreement, and it seeks to have the Agreement applied and effectuated for the benefit of these grievants. Such a claim is arbitrable.

Having held the grievances to be arbitrable, the Umpire must now turn to a consideration of the merits of the grievances. On the merits, the Union's claim rests on its theory that the Secretary's Decision while creating rights in "affected employees" did not correspondingly affect adversely the rights of other employees set forth in the Agreement. In the umpire's view, however, the Union has misconceived the force of the Secretary's Decision. That decision, issued after a proceeding in which both this Company and this Union were represented, does not merely lay down a program of plant seniority. On the contrary, it expressly bars the application of Article X, in this plant, where such application could be inconsistent with the Secretary's directives. The Secretary's Decision is not merely, as the Union would have it, a directive to grant "affected employees" promotional rights. It is, in addition, a specific declaration of the invalidity of the provisions of Article X at this plant insofar as those provisions would give rights to employees inconsistent with those which the decision gives to "affected employees". This is the inescapable impact of the language of the Secretary's Decision that the remedy he adopted "will result in some disruption on the expectations of white employees". In so stating the Secretary recognized that in this industry (with a few exceptions not relevant here, such as employees paid "red circle" rates) employees who are relieved of job assignments in the course of a reduction in force of similar seniority event do not continue to be compensated at the rate of pay which was attached to the job from which they were demoted, and are entitled to compensation only at the rate applicable to the job which they actually perform.

It is not material that the Company at one time proposed, and the Union rejected, a proposal which would have expressly recognized that the Secretary's Decision superseded the Agreement. The legal impact of the Secretary's Decision on the agreement is not dependent on the consent or the construction of the parties. In this connection, the Umpire emphasizes that he is not relying on his own construction or interpretation of a statute or court decision or executive order or administrative decision which is generally applicable, but rather on the administrative decision which by its terms is specifically directed to this Agreement and to this plant. The result here might be otherwise if the Company had simply proceeded, based on its own interpretation of legal requirements, to ignore the provisions of Article X, and then asked the umpire to confirm its interpretation of the law. On the contrary, in this case there has been an express and authoritative determination directed at this particular plant which has barred the application of Article X in the situation presented by these grievances. The umpire cannot he believes, give effect to the Agreement in a situation where it has been barred by a federal order. This is particularly true in a case such as this where, as the umpire understands it, the grievants do not challenge the government's authority, and the government acted only after according full notice and hearing to the interested parties.

Finally, the Union suggests that the grievants are entitled to recover under the "Company convenience" provision of Article IV, Section 5. It goes without saying that the assignments made during the reductions in force in question were not temporary assignments for the Company's convenience, hence, the assignments fall outside both the language and purpose of Article IV, Section 5.

DECISION

The grievances are denied.

CASE 8
Improperly Acquired Job Qualifications for Promotion

Company: South Pittsburgh Water Company
Union: Utility Workers of America, Local 174
Arbitrator: David C. Altrock

Does a person with qualifying experience have prior claim to a promotion when that experience was gained as a result of discriminatory practices engaged in by both union and company in the past?

The following discussion of facts and issues was prepared by the arbitrator, David C. Altrock.

Background

ALTROCK, Arbitrator:—This grievance was filed by employee Patricia C. Szarell on August 10, 1970. It reads:

> The company has unlawfully and wilfully violated the terms of Sec. 6 of the present Contract Agreement, as well as the applicable Federal and State laws forbidding discrimination on the basis of sex inasmuch as the company displayed and posted for a job classification requesting a MALE WORK ORDER CLERK. I submitted my name and believe the only reason I was not given the job was because of the fact that I am a female. To substantiate this claim, I submit that the job which was posted required the exact same skills as the job I am presently doing. Furthermore, I am in a Grade II job, which is the same class as a *Work Order Clerk*. The individual appointed was in a Class I job. Since a Grade II job requires more skills than a Grade I job, it is rather obvious that I possess more skills than the appointed individual. It is readily obvious that I possess the requisite skills without further training, but the individual who got the job did not. In light of this and the company's posting the job for *Male Work Order Clerk*, I am led to the inescapable conclusion that the only reason I was not given the job was because I am a female. This is grossly prejudice, contrary to our Labor Management Agreement, as well as Federal and State laws. I demand that I be given the job effective the date it was awarded.

Many of the facts are virtually stipulated to by the parties. On July 3, 1970, the Company posted notices stating that there was a vacancy in the Work Order Department for the job of Male Work Order Clerk. On July 15 the Company notified the Union that Mrs. Szarell and one E. J. Olkosky had filed bids. The job was awarded to Mr. Olkosky on the basis of claimed ability to perform the job. On advice from the Union that the Contract and the law had been violated by advertising for a Male Work Order Clerk, the Company reposted and simply asked for bids for a Work Order Clerk. There were the same two bidders and Olkosky again prevailed.

The Union points out that Olkosky was first employed by this Company as a Grade I Office Boy (the job title has since been changed to Office Boy or Girl) on March 19, 1969. He remained on this job for one year and four months before being promoted to the job in question. The grievant possessed eight months more seniority than Olkosky; her ability was equal to or better than Olkosky's; and it is believed she was passed over on the basis of her female sex.

The current labor agreement specifically provides that "In all cases of promotion . . . or transfer of employees within the scope of this contract, the length of continuous service and ability to perform the work to be done, shall be considered. Where ability to perform work is equal, length of continuous service shall govern." Section 6 of the agreement states that the "Company agrees there shall be no discrimination by the company or its agents against any employee because of his membership in the union, or race, color, creed, sex or national origin."

It is claimed that the Company "has made a sham of Section 11 of the contract inasmuch as they never properly considered the ability of the grievant vis-a-vis the ability of the individual awarded the job." The impropriety of this is recognized in another arbitration opinion:—"In determining the propriety of an employer's promotion of a junior employee to a vacant job where contract provides that seniority shall be controlling if employee's qualifications are relatively equal, arbitrator must decide whether employer made reasonable efforts to ascertain relative qualifications of competing employees and whether preference of junior employee was reasonable under the circumstances."

It is said that the Company never made an adequate investigation or tried to discover whether the grievant could read maps, which ability is claimed to be an important segment of the Work Order Clerk job. Nor did it ask the grievant about operating a two-way radio; about sketching; or about possessing a driver's license essential to the desired job.

As the Union views the case, Olkosky received the job because he had 793½ hours at filling in on the Work Order Clerk job. This is not sufficient reason, since relative qualifications were not compared.

According to the Union, the Work Order Clerk job has "constantly and continually served as a stepping stone to a managerial position." The sequence has been Office Boy-Work Order Clerk-Management, and no woman has ever taken that route. The original posting said "Male Work Order Clerk" and this, although corrected later, revealed the true state of thinking. So did the change of job title from Office Boy to Office Boy or Girl. And all of this is in a framework of an office employing about 22 women and 5 men.

Mrs. Szarell has asked on several occasions for exposure to the Work Order Clerk job so that she could broaden her experience. It seems that she was told that "women should take care of babies and not try so hard to get ahead."

Mrs. Szarell has made two job changes—one lateral and one promotional —and they were granted on the basis of seniority. The move presently sought is lateral—from Grade II to Grade II.

The Company agrees that Olkosky did indeed receive 793½ hours of exposure to or training on the Work Order Clerk job while classified as an Office Boy. He was filling in when incumbents were absent for one reason or another. This has been the practice for years and occurs, for one reason, because the parties have written job descriptions that provide, in a sense, for lines of progression through the job structure. The Company estimates that it takes six months to a year to become proficient as a Work Order Clerk. The complexities of the job were explained at the hearing in great detail.

The grievant did not fill in on the Work Order Clerk job because her own job was a "pretty full-time job." Moreover, she did not even ask to fill in until after the job was awarded to Olkosky.

The Company urges strenuously that "Seniority is controlling only where ability to perform the work in question is equal." It is all very simple. Mrs. Szarell started as a Mail Teller and progressed to Billing Clerk and then to Meter Book Clerk. Nothing in her education or previous working experience had exposed her to the qualities looked for in a Work Order Clerk. There was no discrimination based on sex. Sex is not a factor in reading maps, calculating water pressures, sketching water lines, preparing work orders, etc. Furthermore, there have never been any other cases filed accusing the Company of discrimination for reasons of sex.

QUESTIONS

1. Do you agree with Ms. Szarell that the only reason she didn't get the job posted as Male Work Order Clerk was that she was female?

2. Do you doubt that the successful male candidate was better qualified for the duties of the position *at the time?*

3. Why do you suppose that the union, which condoned discrimination based on sex in the past, is pressing this grievance now?

4. If the company had given the promotion to Ms. Szarell at her request, do you think the union would have (or could have) filed a grievance on behalf of Mr. Olkosky?

CASE 9
Reverse Discrimination in Favor of Female Ushers

Company: Cincinnati Reds, Inc.
Union: Office & Professional Employees International Union, Local 375
Arbitrator: Samuel S. Kates

Was the company justified in favoring junior female ushers over senior males in assigning preferential work locations in the stadium during the baseball season?

The following discussion of the facts and issues was prepared by Samuel S. Kates, the arbitrator.

ISSUES

Did the Company violate the collective bargaining agreement in its method of assigning ushers at the time of the grievance here in arbitration?

The grievance, signed by a number of Company ushers reads as follows:

> We protest the companies' assignment of working positions, in that, seniority is not observed as it has been in the past.

In the instant case, the contractual provision for a board of arbitration was waived and the issue submitted to the undersigned as sole arbitrator.

CONTRACTUAL HISTORY

Article VIII—Seniority, of the 1964 contract, provided in Section 2 for "preferential employment status", and further provided in Section 3 as follows:

> Seniority grants the right to first call for work, but the placement of Ushers as to their capabilities is still the right of management.

The "preferential employment status" became "preferential call-in status" in Section 2 of Article VIII in the 1967 and subsequent agreements.

The quoted language of Section 3 was completely dropped in the 1967 and subsequent contracts. However, the reference to "capabilities" was transferred to VIII-2 in the 1967 contract by use of the words "ability to perform the work".

In the 1968 contract, a new section (Section 7 of Article VIII) was added to the Seniority article, which section has been retained in the current 1969–1972 contract reading as follows:

> No usher to be permanently removed from their normal assignment unless for just cause. This shall not restrict right of the Company to make temporary transfers.

Although Section 1 of Article VIII calls for a "seniority list based upon continuous seasonal service in the classifications covered hereby,"[1] Section 2 provides for seniority based upon "service points", which in practice has served as the basis of seniority application with respect to Ushers. Section 2 of Article VIII ever since 1967 has read as follows:

> Preferential call-in status will be applied and enforced by the Employer based upon the seniority list. That is, the Employees having the greatest amount of service points and the ability to perform the work assigned them shall be called in first, and all other Employees shall follow thereafter according to their respective seniority.

---

[1] Article VII establishes three job classifications, namely, Assistant Chief Usher, Ushers, Directors (Main Gate).

Section 14 of Article X came into the contract in 1968 and was carried into the current 1969–1972 contract, reading as follows:

> Neither the Union nor the Employer in carrying out their obligations under this contract shall discriminate in matters of hiring, training, promotion, transfer, layoff, discharge or otherwise because of race, color, creed, national origin, sex, or employee's activity as a member of the Union.

Section 2 of Article I recognizes that the management of the ball park "and the direction of the Employees covered hereby is an exclusive prerogative of the Management of the Company. The Employees agree to perform the work properly assigned to them in a satisfactory manner. . . ."

THE EVIDENCE

In preparation for the opening of the new Riverfront Stadium, the Company hired a number of women and a smaller number of men to serve as additional ushers. These newly employed persons were treated as a separate seniority unit in 1970, including the date of the grievance. They were subsequently blended into a single seniority roster of all the ushers in 1971.

At and prior to the date of the grievance, the women were assigned to various desirable levels and aisles at the Stadium contrary to the past practice of usher assignment.

The previous practice had long been to maintain a single seniority list of the ushers based upon their accumulated "service points". As I understand the evidence of the previous practice, the chief usher before each game would call the role of the ushers who had indicated to the caller that they would serve at that game. The roll call would start with the name of the most senior usher and descend according to relative service point seniority. As each name would be called, the chief usher would inform the named usher as to the "level" (Blue, Green, Gold, Red) to work during that game and as to the aisle which would be his responsibility in that game. If an usher had regularly ("normally") worked a particular level, the chief usher would assign him to the same level at roll call. If, as was true as to a portion of the ushers in certain levels, a particular usher had regularly worked in a certain aisle of that level, the chief usher would customarily assign such usher to that aisle at roll call, provided that an usher were needed in that aisle.

Very few variations from assignments to a particular regular level or aisle had occurred when need for an usher at that location had existed. The few variations which did occur, on occasions when need to provide an usher in that level or aisle arose, resulted from the chief usher's judgment that particular senior ushers, because of age or appearance or lack of capability to control the crowd, lacked the "ability to perform the work assigned them".

Nevertheless, it was not the practice at roll call to pemit each usher to specify a choice of assignment as his name was called.

In general, seniority (subject to "ability" including age, appearance and crowd control competency) was the controlling element in regular work assignments.

As special need would arise, temporary transfers from one aisle to another and from one level to another would be made by the chief usher from time to time notwithstanding any particular usher's customary assignment to a particular level or aisle.

Those, who had not in the course of time acquied a regular level or aisle as their normal assignments, would ordinarily be assigned to the other open locations in descending order of desirability, based upon their relative seniority according to the chief usher's good faith judgment of the relative desirability of location and of the usher's ability to perform in that location.

The relative desirability of levels and aisles seems to have become reasonably well recognized by the ushers and chief usher.

Prior to the present grievance, this system seems to have worked satisfactorily to all concerned, in view of the fact that the instant grievance seems to be the first known to those who testified at the arbitration hearing in which complaint has been made as to the assignment method followed by the chief usher. It was not shown that the chief usher's judgment as to the propriety of any assignments had previously been questioned during or after roll call.

The instant grievance arose from a departure by the chief usher in 1970 from the previous practice, in that he assigned certain of the more desirable locations to the women from a separate seniority list comprising only the women and the newly hired male ushers, in disregard of their seniority in relation to that of the pre-existing corps of ushers, and without permitting the more senior previously employed ushers to serve in the desirable locations so assigned to the women.

QUESTIONS

1. The company's treatment of junior female ushers seems to be in the spirit of Title VII of the Civil Rights Law of 1964 and to exhibit Affirmative Action. Why do you suppose the union objects?

2. Who gains and who loses if the company is found in violation of the collective bargaining agreement? If upheld? What do they gain or lose? How could the losers (if any) be "made whole?"

CASE 10
Arbitration of a General Wage Adjustment

Company: Remco Industries
Union: International Brotherhood of Teamsters
Teamsters Industrial and Allied Workers, Local No. 97
Arbitrator: Daniel House

Cases of this type are rarities. Only in very exceptional cases will a management and a union entrust to an arbitrator the question of general wage adjustments which is vital to both management and the union.

What criteria should an arbitrator use in making or refusing to make a general wage adjustment?

The following discussion of the issue and facts in this case was prepared by Daniel House, the arbitrator.

ISSUE

"Should an increase be granted under Article XXI, Section 2, of the Agreement between the parties; if the answer is in the affirmative, how much shall the increase be?"

The parties agreed that if an increase was granted, it was to be made retroactive to December 23, 1963, and paid to all employees with seniority on that date.

CONTRACT PROVISIONS

Article XXI, Section 2, of the agreement is as follows:

> Effective thirty (30) days before December 23, 1963, the Company and the Union shall negotiate wages; failure to agree, the matter shall be submitted to arbitration in accordance with Article VIII, Section 1(d) of this Agreement.

Article VII, Section 1(d), provides for the selection of an arbitrator by the New Jersey State Board of Mediation.

THE CONTROVERSY

Following a strike by the Union, the parties entered into a three-year agreement, effective December 23, 1962, providing, among other things, a general increase of seven cents per hour effective December 23, 1962, and wage negotiations in each of the following two years, subject to arbitration in the event of failure to come to agreement. The parties failed to agree on the wage question in the December, 1963, negotiations. The Union requested a general wage increase of fifteen cents per hour; the Company refused to concede any wage increase.

The Company's Argument

The Company is engaged in the manufacture and sale of toys. The industry is a highly competitive and volatile one, differences of a fraction of a cent an item often making the difference between a sale and no sale, a "fad item" catching on (but with an indeterminate life) suddenly lifting employment in the manufacturing end and, as suddenly, dropping it. Employment in this Company ranges from 200 to 2,000 employees in production during a year.

The Company argues that its business has been off since 1961; that from an annual net profit ranging, for all the years up to 1961, from 7 to 9 percent, it has reduced each year since, and for the calendar year 1963 was just over 4 percent; that its stock, as a result, is now reduced to about one-half its 1959 value; that it entered into the agreement with the Union in 1962 with misgivings about the wisdom of the seven-cent general increase provided therein but agreed to it as "a token of confidence," hoping that a new item it was about to introduce would go well; that the new item was a disappointment and 1963 a worse year even than 1962; that the Company had ceased to pay cash dividends in 1962 as a result of the declining profit picture; that the financial problems of the successive poor seasons had been compounded by the costs of financing of the new plant they had built to try to keep competitive in manufacturing operations; and that the wage rates paid were in line with those of the major competitors in the area.

The Company stated that the average base rate (before piecework earnings) is about $1.40 per hour. A Union witness thought that the average would be closer to $1.30 per hour. By agreement of the parties, the arbitrator examined payrolls at the Company plant; the data was duplicated and copies submitted to the arbitrator and to the Union by mail. The arbitrator's examination of the records showed that the average base hourly rate for the "basic crew" is $1.38 per hour. The parties agreed that the "basic crew" consisted of about 400 employees who were laid off for only brief periods between seasons; they further agreed that the crew employed at the time of the hearing would be representative of the "basic crew."

In summary, the Company took the position that since its pay rates were not out of line with the competition in the area, since its profit picture was poor, and since the seven-cent wage increase in 1962 had been unwarranted, and the anticipated good season to justify it had not materialized, the 1962 error should not be repeated; the Company urged, therefore, that no wage increase be awarded.

The Union's Argument

The Union did not contest that the industry is highly competitive and volatile, nor that the Company's wage rates were in line with the area competition. However, the Union argued that the Company was not losing money; that the reduction in profits for the last few years had been more than offset by the continued adequate rate of profits for all the many years prior to 1962; that the Company should have had the foresight to set aside from the profits of the fat years enough to take care of the employees' legitimate desires for improvements in the lean years; further, the Union claimed that the effect of the seven-cent increase in 1962 was in part negated by the operation of the federal law establishing $1.25 minimum wage rate in 1963. For these reasons the Union requested an award of 15 cents per hour general increase.

QUESTIONS

1. If you disregard the actual wage levels in effect at the time this case reached arbitration, what *criteria* for general wage adjustments are argued by the parties? Do the criteria argued by the parties exhaust a list of conceivably valid criteria? As an arbitrator would you feel obligated to consider only the criteria argued by the parties?
2. As representative of the union, how would you justify your demand for a 15 cents per hour general wage increase?
3. Why did the parties in this case sign a reasonably common three-year agreement with annual reopeners? Why did the parties sign an agreement with the *very unusual* provision for arbitration of the general wage adjustment disputes arising at reopening dates?

CASE 11
Discontinuance of Free Meals

Company: Lutheran Medical Center
Union: Retail, Wholesale and Department Store Union, Drug and Hospital Employees Union
            Local 1199
Arbitrator: Benjamin H. Wolf

Can an employer practice of providing free meals be discontinued without bargaining with the union? Does the fact that the employer "bought back" the free meals from the union in previous negotiations justify the discontinuance of the meals a long time after the employer bargained the meals away?

The following discussion of the issues and facts in this case was prepared by Benjamin H. Wolf, the arbitrator.

BACKGROUND

This arbitration is concerned with a protest made by the Union against the decision by the Employer to discontinue the practice of supplying meals to its employees in the dietary department.

The parties are in substantial agreement on the facts. Prior to 1951, the employees ate their meals family style at a big table and received their meals without charge. That year a change was made. A cafeteria was established and the hospital announced that employees eating in the cafeteria would be required to pay for whatever food they ate. To compensate for the loss of three meals a day, the employees were given wage increases ranging from $10 to $20 per month.

In 1953 Mrs. Fevang became personnel director of the hospital. At that time all the employees were paying for their meals. Some time between 1953 and 1956 the employees of the dietary department stopped paying for their food. No one seems to know when and how this happened but there is no denial that some of the lower echelon supervisory employees knew about it. When the administrator learned of it, he issued a memorandum directing that dietary employees should no longer receive their meals free and again, in order to compensate them, he announced that they would be paid $10 a month in addition to their regular wage. Sometime between July, 1956, when the memorandum was issued and June, 1963, when the Union agreement was signed, the dietary employees again began eating their meals without paying for them.

Mr. Johnson, the present administrator, came to the hospital in August, 1962. It is conceded by the Employer that Mr. Johnson, who headed the management team in the negotiation of the Union agreement, was aware that the employees in the dietary department were eating meals in the cafeteria and not paying for them. He was not aware, however, of the history of this problem, and that on two occasions the Employer had "bought back" the practice of furnishing free meals to the employees for substantial wage increases.

In November, 1963, the hospital engaged an independent contractor to manage the dietary department. He informed Mr. Johnson that the dietary employees were not paying for their meals. On July 1, 1964, the hospital notified the dietary employees that from July 15, 1964, on they would have to pay for their meals.

It was stipulated that Marshall Dubin telephoned Mrs. Fevang shortly after July 1, 1964, and told her that the employees were dissatisfied with the notice. He requested a meeting, which was held on July 22.

POSITIONS OF THE PARTIES

On the merits of the controversy, the Union argued that a practice which had existed for a long period of time and which had not been changed by the contract should be left undisturbed by the parties until they jointly agreed to alter it. The Union urged that the granting of a meal to an employee is not only a condition of employment but a method of compensation and that by taking the meal away the Employer reduced the wages of these employees. Thus, it was a basic change not only in the working conditions which existed at the time the bargain was entered into but also in the compensation they had received for more than a year since the contract was signed.

Although there is no provision in the contract which covers the granting of free meals to these employees, the Union urged that the myriad of conditions which exist outside of the contract are part of the collective bargaining relationship and hence, part of the agreement between the parties.

The position of the Employer is that the free meals were not an existing benefit or a past practice in the conventional sense of the word. It urged that the Employer, having already twice bought itself out of this practice, should not be required to negotiate itself out a third time. It stated that the hospital never deemed the free meals as compensation to the employees and, therefore, never reported them on the W-2 tax forms. Under the Internal Revenue Code, therefore, the meals were deemed to have been furnished as a convenience to the hospital, not as compensation to the employees.

The Employer argued that the problem was analogous to the discontinuance of a Christmas bonus when parties made no reference to the bonus and cited two New York Supreme Court cases in support of its position.

QUESTIONS

1. Were the meals for dietary employees "wages" or a "bonus"?
2. What weight should be given to a practice that apparently arose by mistake?
3. How many times must the hospital "buy back" the meals?
4. How would you rule in this case?

CASE 12
Company Practice versus Agreement Language
in Recall from Layoff

Company: Seymour Manufacturing Company
Union: United Automobile, Aircraft and Agricultural Implement Workers of America
Local 1827
Arbitrator: Sidney L. Cahn

Does the long continuance of a practice clearly contrary to the wording of the agreement take precedence over the agreement?

The following discussion of the issue and facts in this case was prepared by Sidney L. Cahn, the arbitrator.

THE ISSUE

"Did the Company violate the Collective Bargaining Agreement, Article VIII, Sections 1, 2(a), 2(c), 5, 6, and 15, governing seniority for the purposes of recall when it recalled employees L and M instead of employees X, Y, and Z? If so what should be the remedy?

THE FACTS

In June 1963, the Company laid off a number of its employees predicated upon its shutdown of the rolling mills. Among the employees laid off at that time were the three grievants, X, Y, and Z. X was then a roller in the rolling mill with a plantwide seniority date of November 7, 1949; Y was then a jitney driver in the rolling mill with a plantwide seniority date of October 26, 1949; and Z was then a pickler in the wire mill with a plantwide seniority date of February 14, 1950. Other employees laid off included L and M, fine wire drawers in the wire mill, with plantwide seniority dates of July 31, 1961, and August 4, 1961, respectively.

In the Spring of 1964 two jobs of fine wire drawer in the wire mill became open, one on April 20 and the other on April 27. The Company recalled L and M to the jobs. None of the grievants (all of whom had greater plantwide seniority than L or M, but none of whom had ever worked the jobs in question) were recalled to work until a later date.

The Union filed the instant grievance claiming that plantwide length of service should have been the sole criterion employed in determining which employees should be first recalled. Under this criterion, concededly all of the grievants would have been entitled to have been recalled prior to either L or M.

OPINION

Article VIII of the parties' collective bargaining agreement dated November 15, 1961, deals with the question of seniority. This article *inter alia* sets forth general policy in Section 1 (i.e., "to provide maximum job security and opportunity based upon—continuous service"); it defines "seniority" as "total length of unbroken service" in (Section 2); it provides for departmental seniority to govern in the case of layoff from a department (Section 3) with the right of a laid-off employee to exercise plant seniority to replace an employee in another department with less plant seniority (Section 5); and it considers the questions, among others, of recalls to work (Section 6); bidding for open jobs (Section 7); promotions (Section 8); and retention of certain employees by the Company regardless of seniority (Section 15).

Section 6 of this article is the section dealing with the immediate problem before me. This section provides as follows:

> Rehiring in all mills except the Laboratory Department shall be on the basis of plantwide seniority, *governed by the nature of the job to be filled, with due consideration being given to the necessary skill and ability to do the required work.* (emphasis supplied).

This section then goes on to deal with the exception pertaining to the laboratory department, not here relevant.

The grievants in the instant case all had greater plantwide seniority than both L and M. Although Section 15 of this article gives the Company the right with certain limitations "to retain seven employees, irrespective of seniority, who possess value to the operation of the Company" it is conceded that neither L nor M were recalled pursuant to this section, and accordingly it need not concern me any further. The sole question, therefore, is whether the above-emphasized language found in Section 6 applies to the instant case and justifies the Company's recall of L and M.

The Union has not attempted to show that at the time L and M were recalled any of the grievants possessed "the necessary skill and ability to do the required work" as contemplated by the emphasized language. It argues instead that the Company has at least, since 1946, totally disregarded contractual references in this and prior agreements as to skill and ability in recalling employees; that it has been solely governed by length of continuous service in recalling employees whether employees were recalled to jobs previously held or to jobs never held by them; and that by reason of this fact the Company has in effect waived any rights it may have had to rely upon the emphasized language and to question a senior employee's skill and ability in recalling him from layoff.

The testimony introduced was impressive and convincing on this score. It appears without contradiction and in fact was admitted that since at least 1946, until the instant situation, the Company consistently recalled its employees based solely upon plantwide seniority, and without reference to skill and ability. Only three alleged "exceptions" to this practice were shown.

a. One alleged exception dealt with employees recalled to jobs in the laboratory department; this, however, is clearly made an exception to Section 6 by the express language of that section and accordingly is not a relevant exception to the practice claimed by the Union;

b. Another exception occurred in 1949 when the Company recalled a junior employee to a wire drawer job in preference to a utility man on layoff; this exception resulted in a grievance which was settled to the satisfaction of the Union by calling in additional help;

c. The third and only relevant exception involved the recall in October, 1963, without objection by the Union, of a junior employee to the job of machinist third class. However, even as to this exception the Union took the position that this was consistent with the practice, claiming that this recall was made pursuant to Section 15 referred to above, and was not made pursuant to Section 6; the Company took issue with this claim and this is the only factual matter in dispute.

Under Article X, Section 5, of the collective bargaining agreement, the arbitrator has no authority to "add to, subtract from or in any way modify" the terms of the parties' collective bargaining agreement.

QUESTIONS

1. The arbitrator here is confronted with a choice between agreement language and the existence of a well-established practice. What factors should the arbitrator consider in making his choice?
2. How would you rule in this case? Why?

CASE 13
Tests as Measures of Ability in Job Bidding

Company: National Seal Company
                 Van Wert, Ohio
Union: United Rubber Workers of America
                 Local 426
Arbitrator: Harry J. Dworkin

Can the employer eliminate a senior employee from consideration for a new job on the basis of test scores? This case involves the interpretation of an agreement on promotion and transfers.

The following discussion of the issue and facts in this case was prepared by Harry J. Dworkin, the arbitrator.

The issue submitted for arbitration and developed during the course of the hearing concerns itself with the application of the contract provisions pertaining to seniority and the qualifications and "job requirements" of employees who bid for a job opening in a particular classification.

The grievant, Frances Brotherwood, bid for the job of packer and machine operator which had been duly posted by management. In accordance with the established procedure, the company gave a test to the job applicants in order to determine whether they met the job requirements with particular reference to aptitude for simple mathematics. On the basis of the results of the examination, the grievant was given a failing score and was adjudged by the company to lack the job requirements insofar as they concerned proficiency in simple mathematics. The grievant, although having greater seniority, was bypassed and the job was given to an applicant who was successful in the examination, even though she had less seniority than the grievant.

The union thereupon processed a grievance on behalf of Frances Brotherwood, claiming that she was entitled to the job vacancy. The grievance is as follows:

STATEMENT OF GRIEVANCE

I signed a job posting for the job of packer in the packing department on the 2nd shift. The job was given to a employee who has less seniority than I do. The Co. made a mistake in giving the job to the less senior employee. I am asking to be given the job & back pay up to the time the less senior employee was transferred to that job.

P.S. I have done the job several times before the job posting was put up.

(Signed) Frances Brotherwood
Signature of Employee

COMPANY RESPONSE

The company's answer was based on the fact that she failed to attain the minimum requirements necessary to qualify:

> Performance on numbers test fell considerably below the minimum requirements necessary to qualify for the job. The position was filled by a person meeting minimum qualifications.

The company further explained its position in a subsequent step of the grievance procedure:

> The contract provides that selection of employees to fill this job will be made on the basis of seniority and job requirements.
>
> Because employees performing this job are required to calculate, from the number of shipping cases and seals per case, the seals packed, and are responsible for making the final report of transfer to the shipping department, the requirements of this job include reasonable proficiency at simple arithmetic.
>
> The aggrieved states that she has done this job. It is true that she has done *a part* of this job. But obviously she is not qualified to do *all* the job.
>
> The job was given to the most senior employee who met the minimum job requirements.

In an explanatory letter to the union dated December 21, 1956, the company pointed out that this is the only female job in the plant except department clerks on which written tests are used to determine whether or not the employee meets the job requirements. Since this job involves the computation of seals packed for delivery to the customer, this requirement along with legibility of writing is critical on the job. The math requirements can be determined objectively by tests which have been standardized for industry and such tests have been used for at least the past four years for that purpose.

The test that was used for the purpose of determining mathematical proficiency is prepared by the Industrial Psychology Corporation and its use is explained by the company as follows:

> The test used is standardized on a percentile basis. The lowest 1 percent of scores are in the 1st percentile group and the highest 1 percent in the 100th percentile group, etc. The minimum acceptable on the job is a score in the 25th percentile group. (Far below average but acceptable as a minimum.) This is consistent with the requirement for successful bidding on the job for at least the past 4 years, and has been required of other employees bidding on this job. Frances' score was in the 8th percentile group. To award her the job when in the past other bidders who came closer to meeting the job requirement were denied the job would not only be hazardous as far as computing seals packed is concerned but would also be discriminatory. There were no grievances filed in the other cases.
>
> As was previously suggested, if Frances believes there were any circum-

stances at the time she took the test which did not permit her to work on it effectively, we were and are willing for her to take another form of the same test.

The examination paper itself was introduced in evidence and the following portion is indicative of the nature of the test given:

	1	2	3	4	Answer
4 plus 7 plus 3 equals:	12	13	14	15	( )
24 divided by 6 plus 3 equals:	7	8	6	10	( )
5 times 9 plus 4 equals:	45	49	51	54	( )

The job description for the packer and machine operator (female) includes the following duties:

> What duties does the incumbent personally perform in the usual course of work?
> Duties include operations related to packaging of seals and preparation of cartons and cases. These operations involve packing finished seals in rolls, cartons, or envelopes; operating equipment such as multigraph, printing press, box opener, box closer, and stapler; and preparing shipping cases for packing.
> Must be able to read and interpret Production Orders, count production, make out stock receipts, etc.
> Performs other duties as directed.
> Specific education requirements: High school graduation or equivalent.

The job of packer and machine operator was created in November 1954, resulting from an amalgamation of two then existing separate jobs, and since that time the posting of the job indicated a requirement of proficiency in simple arithmetic and "all of the employees have taken the test." The company has consistently utilized the test as a means for determining whether the employee met the job requirements with reference to proficiency in simple mathematics, and the union has consistently opposed the use of the test, and has refused during the course of prior contract negotiations to acknowledge the propriety of the test by way of contract language. However, no prior grievance has been filed by any employee although successful applicants for jobs have been rated in part by the results of the examination.

In accordance with the terms of the current contract, the issue was developed by the parties during the course of the oral hearing, at which time the parties submitted oral testimony and documentary evidence in support of their respective positions. An opportunity was given the parties to file a brief by way of summation, the union indicating that it preferred to submit the case on basis of the evidence adduced, whereas the company has filed a post-hearing brief. In addition, all of the proceedings before the arbitrator were embodied in transcript of the evidence which has been considered in the preparation of this opinion and award.

PROVISIONS OF CONTRACT

The collective bargaining agreement between the company and the union, effective November 1, 1956, provides as follows with reference to the filling of vacancies:

> *Section 3. Job Bidding and Shift Preference.*
> ... Selection of employees to fill such jobs shall be made on the basis of seniority and job requirements for all jobs except machine set up classifications. ...

A trial period is given to employees who have successfully bid for a job opening:

> *Section 4. General Provisions.*
> B. An employee transferred to a job as a result of job bidding will have a reasonable trial period not exceeding thirty (30) calendar days. If he fails to qualify for the job during this period he will return to the job from which he transferred and all other employees affected by the return of this employee will be moved back to their former jobs also.

The contract further contains the customary management prerogative clause:

> *Article I. Statement of Policy.*
> The right to hire, promote, discharge or discipline for just cause and to maintain discipline and efficiency of employees is solely the responsibility of the Company, subject to the terms of this Agreement.

POSITION OF THE UNION

The Union bases its grievance upon the charge that the Company violated the collective bargaining agreement and the provisions relating to the filling of vacancies, and contends that the grievant had greater seniority than the employee who was assigned to the job. Accordingly, the Union claims that the grievant was bypassed in violation of her rights under the contract.

It is the Union's position that on the basis of seniority, prior job experience, and familiarity with the duties required, the grievant was entitled to the opportunity to bid for the job and that she should have been permitted to fill the job on a trial basis since she, in fact, possessed the job requirements and had the ability to do the work required. The Union points to her background and experience, including the fact that she had performed the job on a temporary basis for a total period of thirty-three (33) days, and that her work generally was satisfactory.

The Union contends that the examination used by the company in determining an employee's aptitude is unjust and beyond the scope of the contract. The Union states that the examination is "an added burden on the part of an employee who bids on a job."

The Union further points out that in the contract negotiations it informed the Company that it would not accept or recognize written tests on job bidding, and that the language in the present contract governing selection of employees to fill job vacancies omits any reference to written examinations and requires that selection be made on the basis of "seniority and job requirements."

In the course of the contract negotiations, the Union represents that the Company had consistently endeavored to phrase the contract in such a manner as to put job requirements ahead of seniority, while the Union has maintained the position that seniority should be the determining factor in job promotion with the ability to meet the job requirements a matter of secondary significance. In any event, written tests were at no time agreed to by the Union as the means for determining whether an employee was possessed of the required aptitude and qualifications.

Furthermore, as evidence that the grievant had the qualifications for the job, the Union established that previously she had been assigned to this classification on a temporary basis and had performed the work satisfactorily and without complaint.

The Union reasons that under Section 3 of the contract seniority is the determining factor in the designation of the applicant for an available position where such applicant has the ability to perform the work and is possessed of the necessary physical qualifications: that in the event there is any question or doubt concerning such applicant's ability or fitness she should be accorded a qualifying trial period of thirty (30) days; that in this instance the grievant was denied the right to qualify for the job as specified in Section 4(B) of Article VIII of the agreement. While the Union acknowledges that the contract language requires that vacancies be filled on the basis of both seniority and job requirements, it points out that the contract language does not include the testing procedure adopted by the Company, and that this is, therefore, an "added burden" not within the scope of the contract.

With reference to the uncontroverted evidence on behalf of the Company that the Company had consistently since November 1, 1956, when the job as presently described came into existence, required that all of the employees who bid on the job vacancies in the classification take the test, and that no prior grievances had been filed in similar situations, the Union representative states as follows:

> I might say this, that some of the tests that the company referred to that they had been denied jobs, the Union was aware of some of those. They were protected. Because of individual circumstances or feelings, the employees did not wish to protest and file a grievance and process it on through. We do not consider, because one employee does not consider it important enough to process a grievance—that it does not relinquish the rights of another employee to protest and file a grievance.

The Union asserts that it has never orally or in writing acknowledged the validity or propriety of the tests used by the Company, and that, in fact, it has orally protested their use on a number of occasions. The Union therefore states that although the contract required that when a vacancy occurred in a classification, the employee with the highest seniority was entitled to first preference provided he met the job requirements, this pocedure was not followed or adhered to by the Company.

The employee who was awarded the position had less seniority than the grievant, and, in the event there remained any doubt or question as to the ability of the grievant to do the job required, she should have been given a thirty (30) day qualifying trial. Accordingly, the Union states that the Company violated the contract with reference to seniorty and requests that the arbitrator rule that she be assigned to the job, together with an award of compensation of any lost wages.

POSITION OF THE COMPANY

The Company contends that the Union's claims are unfounded and that its action with respect to the assignment of an employee to the classification of packer and machine operator was fully justified and warranted by the evidence and was consistent with the terms of the collective bargaining agreement, and in accordance with established past practice. The Company's position is that its action was not the result of any arbitrary, capricious, or discriminatory conduct or bias toward the grievant, and points out that the contract does not provide for filling a vacancy on the basis of seniority alone; that the express language of the contract requires that the employee's rights to the job in question must be determined on whether the applicant can fulfill the job requirements.

Furthermore, the procedure which was followed in this instance has been consistently adhered to since November 1, 1954, in the filling of approximately eighteen (18) vacancies in which each applicant was required to take a test to determine mathematical proficiency, and that no prior grievance has been filed. The Company vigorously contends that the testing method is the only known means for objectively determining the proficiency of the applicant for the job, and whether she is possessed of the job requirements involved in the job description.

The examination which the grievant failed to pass by the required minimum grade is prepared by the Industrial Psychology Corporation and is a type of test used widely in industry. The test is standardized on a percentile basis and, to determine average proficiency in simple arithmetic, anyone whose score is twenty-five (25) percentile or above meets the requirements and is considered as having demonstrated the minimum mathematical proficiency required. On the basis of the results of the examination, the Company gave the job to the employee who met the minimum posted job requirements in preference to the grievant who claimed the job on the basis of her seniority plus job experience.

Since the time this job was classified, all persons who have made application for existing vacancies have been required to meet the job requirements, one of which being "average proficiency in simple arithmetic." The Company has uniformly insisted that all applicants for these jobs pass a test to establish the necessary knowledge and has consistently refused the job to senior applicants who did not meet the requirements. At least eighteen (18) employees were denied jobs during 1955 and 1956 for failure to pass the same test which was given to the grievant without any formal grievance having been filed. The test itself is reasonable and was properly administered.

The Company points out that it is a standard test, widely used and accepted in industry generally. There is no recognized means for objectively and fairly determining an employee's proficiency in simple arithmetic except through a test in the subject matter. Since the job description and evaluation plan require that the applicant be either a high school graduate or have the equivalent educational background, and since the applicant was not a high school graduate, the test was a reasonable requirement in order to determine whether she had the "equivalent" requirement.

In the interpretation of the contract language pertaining to job bidding, the Company points out that under the express language of the agreement, the job must be given to the senior employee who meets the job requirements "not to some employee who has temporarily worked on the job or who claims to be qualified by ability or who thinks he can learn the job in a reasonable time. *The employee must meet the job requirements.*"

Thus, the Company urges that there is an apparent difference between the phrases, "meeting job requirements" and "ability to qualify or perform a job." The successful bidder for a vacancy must *first* meet the job requirements and *then* qualify on the job within a reasonable time. To grant the grievance in this case would have the effect of leaving the Company completely without any objective standard to apply in filling job vacancies and would result in interminable grievances on the part of senior employees whose claims to the vacancies would be based solely upon their length of service in disregard of their lack of ability to meet the requirements of the job.

Furthermore, the Company represents that the practice of requiring the job applicants to submit to a reasonable examination has been followed for almost three years and it would be unfair to both the Company and the employees to upset the established procedure, and would render the contract terms meaningless; this would be tantamount to reading into the contract language limitations that are not therein expressed.

By way of summary of its position, the Company states that the test and the manner in which it is given are both fair and reasonable and is within the inherent right of the Company in light of the pertinent contract language referred to:

> This right rests not only upon past practice, but upon the contractual power to fix job requirements and require some proof that they are met. Without objective means of measuring the meeting of job requirements, they are meaningless. A requirement of a certain height is nonsense if the man's height cannot be measured. A job requirement of average proficiency in simple arithmetic is nonsense if the employee's proficiency cannot be measured. There is absolutely no way to measure objectively and impartially the physical or mental attainments of an applicant other than by a test. The Union has not and cannot suggest any alternative.

Accordingly, the Company alleges that it has faithfully followed the clear language of the contract in the awarding of the job; that the test was voluntarily taken by the applicant and was fairly administered; that she failed to demonstrate the minimum requirement of mathematical proficiency; and that, therefore, the job was properly assigned to the employee with less seniority who qualified under the testing procedure. The Company urges that, for the aforesaid reasons, the union's grievance be denied.

QUESTIONS

1. Does the union's repeated refusal to accept tests or an agreement upgrading the ability criterion in negotiations deny management the right to use non-discriminatory testing methods in determining ability?
2. Does the wording of the agreement clearly define the relative emphasis which will be given to ability and seniority?
3. On what basis did the company justify its promotion of a junior employee?
4. Under this agreement, who is the final judge of ability? Who determines the criteria for this judgment?
5. The union argues that the grievant's past temporary placement on the job is substantiation for her ability. The company later attempted to rebut this argument by introducing evidence of errors in the grievant's work. What is the relevancy of the union's contention and the company's rebuttal to the issue in this case?

CASE 14
Conflict of Loyalty to the Company and the Union

Company: Contra Costa Readymix and Building Materials, Inc.
Union: International Brotherhood of Teamsters
Local No. 70
Arbitrator: Adolph M. Koven

This case involves the dual loyalty of a worker to his employer and to his union.

The following discussion of the issue and facts in this case was prepared by Adolph M. Koven, the arbitrator.

THE ISSUE

Was J.P. discharged for just cause under Article X of the Contract? If not, what is the appropriate remedy under Article X?

RELEVANT SECTIONS OF THE CONTRACT

Article X. Union Activity

No employee shall suffer discharge without just cause. In the event of discharge without just cause the employee may be reinstated with payment for time lost. In the event of a dispute, the existence of "just cause" shall be determined as provided in Article IX, "Adjustment of Grievances."

Article IX. Adjustment of Grievances

The Umpire shall have only that limited jurisdiction and authority necessary to interpret, apply, or ascertain compliance with the provisions of this Agreement, insofar as shall be necessary for the determination of grievances appealed to the Umpire. Among those subjects the Umpire shall have neither jurisdiction nor authority to consider or decide shall be those subjects although not limited thereto, involving . . . the assignment of work duties . . . the scheduling of work, and working conditions not otherwise agreed to within the Agreement. The Umpire shall not have jurisdiction or authority to add to, detract from, or alter in any way, the provisions of this Agreement.

Article XVII. Prior Agreements and/or Practices

All written and/or oral agreements, all past practices, including agreements resulting from grievance settlements nor specifically contained or referred to in this Contract shall become null and void as of the effective date of this Agreement.

On December 21, 1961, the grievant was directed to make piers. When asked by the dispatcher to do this work, the grievant replied, "I can't," and stated that the Union had told him he was not to do yard work. After the dispatcher had pointed out the consequences of a refusal, the grievant was directed to get his timecard and report to the general manager. To the general manager, the grievant still insisted, "I can't," when asked to give his reason for refusing to pour piers. The grievant was thereupon discharged.

Two sister locals of the Teamsters, Warehouse Local No. 853 and Auto Truck Drivers Local No. 70, each have contracts with the Company. Though making piers is covered in its contract by Local No. 853, there is no jurisdictional dispute between the two sister locals. Prior to two years ago when Local No. 853 signed its first contract with the Company, Local No. 70 performed yard work. Currently Local 70 also performs similar work in other plants in the industry.

The problem of doing such work was first raised when employees returned to work on December 1, right after their four-month strike ended. On December 4, the dispatcher was approached by two employees who raised the question of making piers and stated they had been instructed by the Union not to do such work. The dispatcher told them they would be well off to follow work orders until the matter was straightened out between the parties. During that day following that discussion, one of these two employees was assigned to make piers and did the work without refusal.

On December 6, two employees refused to set up screens because they had been told not to do this work by their Union. They are still in the employ of the Company despite this refusal. As a result of this incident, the president of the Company directed his management staff to warn the employees that any refusal from then on would result in disciplinary consequences.

Accordingly, on the next day, December 7, the employees were put on notice by both the general manager and the dispatcher, who each contacted different employees. The general manager stated he personally warned the grievant on this day, which the grievant denies.

A major incident next occurred on December 15. Edwards, a Local No. 70 member, when asked to do yard work stated that "I am sorry but I can't" because he could not afford a $50 fine. Edwards was then sent to see the general manager and while discussing his dilemma, the work in the meantime was completed by a Local 853 man, so that the issue of refusing to do the work was never sharply joined. The Company views the difference between the Edwards's incident and the grievant's situation as a matter of lucky circumstances for Edwards and in the difference of attitude of both men. Earlier that day, another Local No. 70 employee had been asked to do yard work and followed the order without refusal.

The next and last incident, of course, occurred on December 21, and involved the grievant's refusal to pour piers and his subsequent discharge.

On the grievant's background and the facts of his discharge, there was considerable testimony. He had been an employee since June 1955, and was characterized by the Company as an average driver with a fair work history. The grievant described himself as one who had always tried to do a good job. The Company stated that he had never before refused to do work assigned to him and that his discharge was related only to this one event of December 21, and not to any previous history.

The general manager, president of the Company, and dispatcher each testified that on December 7, 14, and 21, respectively, they personally either warned the grievant of the consequences of a refusal or put him on notice that he would have to carry out any order given him by a supervisor. The grievant denies that management ever talked with him until the day of discharge about the problem of not doing the work.

In his testimony, the general manager stated that the grievant refused to disclose his reason to him for refusing to make piers, and it was his feeling that the grievant was daring the Company to do something about his refusal. Yet, he would not characterize the grievant's manner as belligerent and stated that the grievant would not, in his opinion, have refused to do any other work in Local No. 70's jurisdiction if given such an assignment. Perhaps if there had been a long discussion of the problem, as there had been with Edwards, the Company might have relented in its decision to discharge.

According to the grievant, on December 21, when the dispatcher told him he was supposed to do the work and if he had any objections to file a grievance afterward, he replied that if he would do that, he would be "scabbing" on the warehouse Union. When the dispatcher insisted, the grievant stated he wasn't refusing, but he just couldn't make piers. Furthemore when he was called into the general manager's office he wasn't testing the Company, but was just "scared" because he didn't want to get fired.

There have been a considerable number of times when the grievant was instructed by the Union that he should not do Local No. 853 work, and that he would be "scabbing" on the warehouse Union if he did. The reason he did not tell the general manager the basis for his refusal is that he was directed by the Union not to give the reason. He has also been directed by the Union not to file a grievance, first, because he was not supposed to do such work in the first instance, and second, because filing a grievance would be a useless act since the umpire under the contract does not have the authority to decide grievances involving questions of work assignments. Apparently the Company also holds the same view that an arbitrator would not have such authority.

Both parties stated for the record that they have not submitted the issue of deciding work jurisdiction to this arbitrator in the instant case and that he is precluded from making an award which affects the work jurisdiction of the two Unions with whom the Company has collective bargaining agreements.

POSITION OF THE COMPANY

The grievant was discharged for refusing to do work under a proper work order. He had ample warning of the consequences of any refusal, for he was warned in some fashion on December 4, and specifically on December 7, 14, and 21, by the general manager, president of the Company, and dispatcher, respectively.

If it is correct to say that the blame for generating the situation falls upon the Union, then the equities may suggest that the Union has been unfair to the grievant. However, this was a situation where the Company had to act, and if the grievant willingly or unwillingly became the foil of the Union, then it also became the grievant's problem and not the Company's. The Company could do nothing other than what it did do. It had no other alternative.

But the grievant had a choice. He could have done the work, he could have discussed his situation with management, and he could have resorted to the grievance procedure. The grievant had the time from December 4 until December 21, a period of 17 days, to think through his situation. Instead he made a deliberate intentional attack upon the authority of the Company.

The only question before the arbitrator is not whether disciplinary action was proper but only whether discharge was the proper penalty for this industrial offense. Discharge was a proper penalty because the question of work jurisdiction never serves as a ground for mitigation. The grievant cannot look to misunderstanding as a mitigating factor, for he knew exactly where he stood, and instead of taking on the Union and the $50 fine, he chose to take on the Company. He did so at his peril.

The only other possible point in the grievant's favor is the alleged discrimination in favor of Edwards. But the cases differ on the facts. Edwards was never faced with the ultimate order to do the work and so did not have the opportunity to refuse. The grievant, however, was given an order. He refused to carry it out. It was for this refusal that he was discharged.

Since this is the type of offense which warrants discharge and one which has been consistently upheld by arbitrators, the discharge of this grievant should be sustained.

POSITION OF THE UNION

This is a case involving the broad terms of just cause and involves a claim by the Company against the grievant of insubordination where he declines to perform certain work.

No one has claimed that the grievant was defiant or recalcitrant, but rather that his attitude was one of peaceful resistance to an order. The compliance with that order would have subjected him to sanctions from another source. And since his attitude cannot be said to have been malicious, certainly the Company should not have innsisted on being so retaliatory and so bent on recrimination as to treat this grievant, an employee of seven years' standing, as if it were dealing with a man who had repeatedly refused to perform work.

A discharge must be examined in the light of the sociological questions involved, because discharge is a punishment. More and more in our modern time, punishment is exacted only where it serves some valuable social or industrial purpose. The Union believes that retaliation, although that might be the momentary instinct which all of us sometimes give in to and which could have been involved in the case, cannot be advanced as a justification for the discharge.

At the time of the discharge, the grievant did not have the full opportunity to consult with someone with a little more expert knowledge on such a complicated question of resolving the dilemma of a choice between loyalties. Subsequent to his discharge he has had time to think it over and has come to a different conclusion. The grievant has now come to a clearer understanding as to what he must now do and that is to follow Company orders as given until the parties resolve their difficulties on the larger issue.

What purpose is served by holding that the grievant cannot go back to work where the only complaint the Company has is that on one day he declined to do work which he now says he will do? It cannot serve any valuable purpose at all. And this is particularly true because there is no damage to the Company resulting from that paticular incident on that one day.

Thus, the Union urges that the grievant be reinstated and that he be compensated for time lost, with restoration of seniority and other rights.

QUESTIONS

1. What rights on the part of J. P., the company, and the union are involved here?
2. Both the company and the union reminded the arbitrator that he is *not* authorized to settle the jurisdictional dispute involved in this case. How would the arbitrator's ruling on J. P.'s discharge influence the outcome of the jurisdictional dispute?
3. Both the company and the union admit that J. P. is the unfortunate victim of circumstances beyond his control. Is this a fair conclusion or did J. P. have control over his own fate?
4. How would you rule in this case? Why?

CASE 15
An Accident Record as a Basis for Discharge

Company: Our Own Bakeries, Inc.
Union:　　Retail, Wholesale and Department Store Union
　　　　　　Local No. 655
Arbitrator: Robert S. Thompson

This case involves the discharge of a truck driver for a second serious accident in six months. This case requires not only a definition of just cause but also consideration of the standards of discipline which are appropriate to employees who work without direct supervision and have individual responsibility for very expensive equipment.

The following discussion of the issue and facts in the case was prepared by Robert S. Thompson, the arbitrator.

Our Own Bakeries is a large and well-known wholesale bakery which distributes its products throughout the Upper Peninsula of Michigan and parts of Wisconsin. Robert Carlton, the grievant, was a transport driver, one of six such who drove large tractor-trailer equipment. The route covered by Mr. Carlton was from Marquette to Ironwood, a round distance of about 310 miles. His schedule called for leaving Marquette about 1 A.M. and returning about 11 A.M. He had been employed with the Company about nine years, the last four years as a transport driver. On October 29, 1960, he had an accident which resulted in the total loss of his tractor-trailer and merchandise. The next day, October 30, he was discharged because of a poor driving and accident record.

ACCIDENT RECORD

From testimony at the hearing and various accident reports entered into evidence by the Company, a summary of Mr. Carlton's record is presented below:

> October 29, 1960, 5. A.M. heavy fog, poor visibility, vehicle left the road on the left side of highway. Tractor-trailer and merchandise nearly a total loss. Mr. Carlton had cut on temple and a bruised leg, but walked mile to phone police. Officer did not reach scene until about two and a half hours later. Sales manager, Mr. Roberts, in charge of transport drivers, came out from Marquette. Accident report stated: "It is the opinion of the officer that the driver fell asleep causing him to drive to the left side of the road." Mr. Carlton stated he did not know what happened. Testified that it had taken him from 30–45 minutes to drive 18 miles; that poor visibility made it impossible to follow the center line; also suggested that trailer might have turned over because of imbalance in loading. Estimated damages about $4,100. Not ticketed.
>
> March 22, 1960, 12:45 A.M. Struck private automobile parked or stalled on highway. Impact pushed car into driver who was standing near. Severe blizzard conditions with low visibility. No police report in evidence. Not ticketed. Insurance carrier paid claims in amount of $937.60.
>
> November 6, 1959, 1:30 A.M. Mr. Carlton's trailer was struck from behind by tractor-trailer driven by Mr. Bengry, another transport driver employed by the Company. Heavy snow storm. Grievant was to make left turn from Highway 41 into Highway 95. Snow plow at the intersection and to left of grievant's truck. Grievant stopped when hit. Company alleged that grievant was in conversation with snow plow operator. Grievant claims snow plow was blocking intersection. Snow so thick rear lights probably obscured. Extensive damage to both units. Tractor of other truck was total loss. Not ticketed.
>
> April 17, 1956, 9:10 A.M. Slippery conditions. Grievant started to slow down as a private automobile approached from other direction. Double tracks slipped off right side of pavement; his truck started to skid; touched brake and went into a jackknife to the left side of road. Approaching car hit grievant's truck toward right rear. Driver of car seriously injured and passenger (wife) killed. State trooper who investigated checked these items on report: Vision *not* obscured; excessive speed; snowing; no improper driving by second driver. Not ticketed. Insurance carrier paid in total of $12,969 in claims.

In addition to the accidents listed above, the record of Mr. Carlton on file with Michigan Secretary of State shows the following:

November 21, 1956. Closed without action.
January 21, 1959. Drove left of center line. Improper left turn.
July 13, 1960. Driving 80 miles in 65 mph zone.

Before his employment by the Company, when 17 years old, Mr. Carlton was involved in a fatal accident. This was in 1945. In a suit for $25,000 damages the judge directed a verdict in favor of the defendant, Mr. Carlton.

Complete data as to the accident records of the other transport drivers was not available. Ray Trevillion, driver with highest seniority, has had one accident in the last five or six years (due to falling asleep). John Stone, sales route driver for four years, and transport driver for last six months, has had two nonticketed accidents in that period.

PUBLISHED AWARDS

An examination of a number of published arbitration awards (several cited by Mr. Kirkwood plus others) turns up little of assistance in the instant matter. In contrast to the law, precedent is generally considered to have little weight in arbitration. The situation in each arbitration tends to be unique, and part of the usefulness and vitality of arbitration inheres in its rejection of legalisms. However, published awards are sometimes helpful in being suggestive. With respect to discharge of truck and bus drivers for highway accidents, the decisions show wide diversity.

In Hudson County Bus Owners Association, 3 LA 786, the discharge of a bus driver was upheld on the ground of a bad record of minor accidents and one serious accident; in Schreiber Trucking Company, 5 LA 430, a discharge following a third accident was sustained, mainly on the basis that the "driver habitually drove at excessive speed"; in Ward Baking Co., 8 LA 837, discharge of a driver-salesman was affirmed after his sixth accident within three years (average rate of other company drivers within same three-year period was one accident); in Chestnut Farms, Chevy Chase Dairy, 8 LA 897, a driver with five accidents within a period of less than a year was held to be properly discharged. In Kroger Co., 24 LA 48, a seventh accident within five years, with the last four of the seven occurring within a three-month period, plus a warning that the next accident would bring discharge, was considered to justify discharge.

On the other hand, discharges were voided and reinstatements directed in the following: In Boston & Maine Transportation Co., 5 LA 3, a driver involved in an accident resulting in several deaths was reinstated even though there was evidence of violation of safety rules; in Mason & Dixon Lines, 9 LA 775, trailer truck driver who lost control and collided with a gasoline truck causing a loss of $30,000 was reinstated even though he had failed to take action which might have kept his truck on the road; in Safe Bus Co., 21 LA 456, a bus driver who had had two accidents within six months and who was at fault in the second was reinstated even though the damages exceeded $1,000; in Pacific Greyhound Lines, 30 LA 830, reinstatement without back pay was ordered of a driver responsible for a serious accident in which his bus struck a truck in the rear on a highway.

. . .

This arbitration is based upon a contractual agreement between the parties. Article VII acknowledges the power to discharge, but it also requires that "this power be exercised with justice with regard for the reasonable rights of the Employees."

QUESTIONS

1.   Do the cited cases suggest standards for an award in this dispute?
2.   In assessing Carlton's accident record, what weight should be given to negligence, extent of damage resulting, driving conditions, the obligation to meet a delivery schedule, the elapsed time between accidents?
3.   How would you rule in this case? Why?

CASE 16
Discharge of a Senior Employee for "Failure to Perform Work as Required"

Company: Hawaiian Telephone Company
Union: International Brotherhood of Electrical Workers
              Local 1260
Arbitrator: Ted T. Tsukiyama

What obligation does an employer have to an employee 48 years old with 26 years of seniority who appears to be incapable of doing the job she has filled for this long time?

The following discussion of the issue and facts in this case was prepared by Ted T. Tsukiyama, the arbitrator.

ISSUE

Was the Company's action on July 20, 1964, in discharging the grievant on ground of "failure to perform work as required" undertaken with just cause in accordance with the terms of the collective bargaining agreement in effect between the parties?

CONTRACT CLAUSE

Section 6 of the agreement covering discipline applicable in this grievance is quoted in part as follows:

> Supervision and Discipline
> 6.1 The supervision and control of all operations and the direction of

all working forces, which shall include, but not be limited to, the right to hire, to establish work schedules, to suspend or discharge for proper cause, to promote or transfer employees, to relieve employees from duty because of lack of work, or for other legitimate reasons, shall be vested exclusively in the Company, except as otherwise covered in this Agreement.

6.2 Proper causes for suspension or discharges shall include, but not be limited to, insubordination, pilferage, use of intoxicants during working hours, incompetence, failure to perform work as required, falsification of reports, violation of the terms of this Agreement, violation of the secrecy of communications, failure to observe safety rules and regulations, failure to observe the Company's House Rules, which shall be conspicuously posted.

BACKGROUND FACTS

Up to the time of her discharge, grievant was employed as a toll operator in the traffic department of the Company. Grievant is 48 years old and had started working with the Company on another island in 1936. After nine years she began working for the Company in its Honolulu office where, after a maternity leave in 1947, she worked up to the date of discharge—a total period of 26 years' employment with the Company. The toll operator's job duties generally involve the placing and maintaining of long-distance calls for customers on the switchboard, servicing such calls to the extent necessary, and registering certain pertinent information concerning each call on an IBM mark sense card to be used by the Company for billing purposes.

About August 5, 1963, it came to the attention of the general traffic manager that the grievant was committing a significant number of "ticket errors" and "irregularities" in the performance of her duties as toll operator. Grievant's work record was reviewed by the manager at that time upon discovery of an erasure on one of her ticket entries, which is considered a serious "irregularity" on the toll board operations. The "irregularities" noted on her record included tardiness, talking at the switchboard, monitoring (listening) of calls, dozing off at the board, failure to give notifications, and low board loads and failure to collect on toll calls. The Company found grievant particularly weak in "ticket errors'" which consisted of errors made on the mark sense cards, which were rejected by the IBM machines or which were otherwise not acceptable for billing purposes. Such errors included failure to mark certain capsules (spaces), marking the wrong capsule, or failing to note necessary data on the cards. The chief operator recommended dismissal of grievant but the traffic manager, considering grievant's long seniority with the Company, sent grievant a written reprimand and warning on August 26, 1963 (Company's Exhibit "A"), which listed all of her job weaknesses, required at least average job performance in the future, and exhorted her to do better.

On or about April 19, 1964, grievant failed to collect a $109.75 charge from a coin station call. Another review of her work record subsequent to August, 1963, revealed a high average of ticket errors committed by grievant, which convinced her superiors that the warning had not been effective, and grievant was consequently suspended for two weeks following this incident. The evidence shows that from the August, 1963, warning letter to the suspension in April, 1964, grievant's work record indicated at least seven failures to notify, four late notifications, several failures to collect, poor timing (failure to record correct time on each call), and numerous ticket errors (e.g., 156 errors for December, January, February, 1964). When notified of her suspension, grievant requested her chief operator to be transferred to the auxiliary operators' group in the department, but this was denied on the basis of a department policy prohibiting transfers between the toll and auxiliary work groups. The letter of suspension (Company's Exhibit "B") sent to her on April 23, 1964, listed all of her recent failures and insisted that her future performance (1) must abide by all work rules, (2) must show a 65 percent improvement in ticket errors, failure to notify, etc., (3) must not fail to collect on pay station calls, and (4) show good attendance and punctuality. Otherwise discipline, including dismissal, would follow.

Although the chief operator again recommended discharge on April 23, 1964, the traffic manager recommended against grievant's dismissal at this point because of her long years of service and because he thought the Company should make further attempts to rehabilitate grievant's work performance. Thus when grievant returned from her suspension, two service assistants were assigned to give special supervision, attention, and training to the grievant on her mark sensing work at the switchboard. During the remainder of the month of May, 1964, grievant received special supervision from Pauline Nakamori up to 1½ hours per day and about six 15–20 minute special training sessions fom Irene Iseri until the first part of June, when the special assignments were terminated. Both service assistants testified that grievant showed improvement in her mark sensing work during the limited periods they supervised grievant.

During May, June, and July of 1964, an unexpected heavy load of long-distance traffic calls occurred, resulting in a six-day workweek with considerable overtime for the toll operators group. In the middle of July, 1964, a compilation sheet of operators' ticket errors revealed that grievant had committed 121 ticket errors during the month of June, which called for another review of her record by the traffic manager. The traffic manager and chief operator found that grievant had the highest number of ticket errors among the operators (29.38 error average) for that month and concluded that she had made no improvement in failures to notify, timing, and mark sensing; thus they found no alternative but to dismiss the grievant. Grievant was dismissed on July 20, 1964, on grounds of "failure to perform work as required" under Section 6 of the agreement.

DISCUSSION

There is no evidence in the record that grievant consciously or knowingly or deliberately committed the shortcomings and errors noted in her performance record. There is not even a suggestion of any evidence that she willfully "laid down" on the job or wantonly committed irregularities and errors to spite the Company or her superiors. The evidence does reveal that grievant often tried to alibi or offer excuses, such as personal or domestic problems, when confronted with her poor performance, that she has a crusty temperament and is probably not easy to work with or over, that she felt the Company should be more tolerant of the job weaknesses of "old-timers" like herself. It is also easily inferable from her statements that she chaffed at finding herself, a veteran of many years' service, taking direction from employees much younger than herself who had ascended into "supervisory" positions over her. On one occasion, she argued with a service assistant about the length of a coffee break and signing out (7/11/64—charged with "uncooperative attitude").

She may have been unfit, unable, or incapable of meeting certain job standards, but this is not to say she was unwilling or refused to do what she was physically and mentally able to perform. There was no instance shown where she balked at carrying out any order or instruction of her superiors or was otherwise guilty of insubordination. When her superiors asked her to try to improve her work, the evidence shows that she did make a genuine and bona fide attempt (albeit the results were not satisfactory to the Company).

WORK RECORD

Grievant regularly committed a high, if not one of the highest, number of mark sense ticket errors compared to the other toll operators. In addition there were at least four failures to collect on toll calls involving sums of $55 and $25.30 besides the 4/19/64 incident, customer complaints for eight failures to give three-minute notification and for four late notifications, and poor timing and overlapping operations, contributing to her ticket and billing errors. She was also tardy to work a dozen times. In view of this type of performance record, I find the Company's action in reprimanding grievant on her 7/18/63 ticket erasure and suspending her for two weeks on her 4/19/64 failure to collect to be fully warranted. And the Company's efforts toward corrective discipline in lieu of discharge on these occasions, as reflected by the traffic manager's recommendation that she be given another chance and more rehabilitation was most considerate and commendable.

In the 2½-month period following her return from suspension on May 5, 1964, the evidence shows that grievant had three complaints for failure to notify and one late notification, two failures to collect, 26 ticket errors for April (3 weeks), 42 ticket errors for May (27 days) and 121 ticket errors for June. Bearing in mind the four minimum conditions set forth in the Company's suspension letter of 4/19/64, grievant fell down in two areas (ticket errors and failure to collect) and the promised disciplinary action was forthcoming.

Against this record several counterconsiderations should be weighed. The two service assistants who gave grievant direct and personal supervision testified that grievant's mark sensing and board work was improving during the limited time they were assigned to her. (Note that grievant's ticket error average for May (27 days) while under special training was roughly 70 percent of her monthly average up to that time.) Why, then, should grievant's ticket errors suddenly jump more than 200 percent over her usual average in the very next month? There is no indication that the Company attempted to look into the reasons for this unusual phenomenon, an astoundingly dramatic and high error level even for this subject. Nothing in the record explains why those working around and over grievant had not been aware that her ticket errors during June had become alarmingly frequent and high, a fact not discovered until two weeks passed in July. It was made clear that neither the traffic manager nor the chief operator interviewed or obtained an evaluation report from the two employees who were specially assigned to help grievant and upgrade her work, which raises another question as to the seriousness or bona fides of the attempted rehabilitation. In explaining why the two service assistants were not consulted, the traffic manager stated they were not supervisory employees and were not in a position to judge "over-all-performance" of an operator, but further went on to state that errors were the heavyweight item in over-all job performance—the very item these two employees were instucted to correct and improve. Further, the traffic manager repeatedly emphasized grievant failed to improve in "over-all performance," yet it is clear that it must have been only the 121 ticket errors in June that precipitated her downfall, since other aspects of her performance did not appear noticeably bad in comparison with her prior record. Also, there was no evidence to show how the Company determined that grievant had failed to make a 65 percent improvement in her performance as laid down in the April 23, 1964, "ultimatum.'" Finally, consideration must be given to the unexpected peak traffic that hit the Company during this exact period from May to July, which caught it short staffed, required a heavier workweek and overtime schedule for all operators, and which, incidentally, raised the ticket error average for all operators during this period. In short, this exact period when grievant's job was put at stake was a highly abnormal period for all concerned. Suffice it to surmise that grievant probably "got lost in the shuffle" during this rush period and was forgotten until those 121 errors came to light.

QUESTIONS

1. Is there a difference between "incompetence," "failure to perform work as

required," and "falsification of records"? Is the grievant guilty of each of these offenses?

2. Evaluate the company's efforts at constructive discipline as applied to the grievant.

3. What weight should be given to the grievant's "attitude" and long service record in this discharge proceeding?

CASE 17
Sex Discrimination in a Layoff

Company: International Paper Company, Southern Craft Division
(Springhill, La.)
Union: United Papermakers and Paper Workers
Local 398
Arbitrator: Ralph Roger Williams

Under a contract providing that no opportunity could be closed to any employee because of sex, was the company justified in laying off five senior female employees rather than five male employees with less seniority when the jobs in questions required physical ability and "muscle power?"

The following discussion of the issue and facts in this case was prepared by Ralph Roger Williams, the arbitrator.

This case requires an interpretation of the antidiscrimination clause of the Agreement, on the basis of sex. It involves the layoff of five female grievants who were senior to five male employees who were retained. All the employees involved worked in the Company's Finishing Department, but regularly performed different jobs. While the five grievants and the five junior male employees all performed base-rated jobs, they did not regularly perform the same jobs. The issue may be stated to be:

"Did the Company violate the Agreement, and Section V(C) thereof, by laying off senior female employees and retaining junior male employees in base-rated jobs?"

"Base-rated jobs" are jobs for which no lines of progression are established.

The hearing was duly held at Springhill, Louisiana, on October 21, 1966, and the parties filed post-hearing briefs with the arbitrator on November 30, 1966.

The grievants are five female employees classified as "Finishing Room Girls," their names and Company seniority dates being:

Ruth Thomas—July 8, 1953
Dorothy Dennis—August 6, 1951
Vera Riggs—July 13, 1948
Hettie Dean—August 8, 1947
Modie Crye—October 23, 1946.

On September 27, 1965 (the date here involved), all the above-named grievants were working on base-rated jobs. They were laid off for lack of work for a period of more than seven days, and five male employees (all of whom also worked on base-rated jobs) were retained. Each of the retained male employees had less seniority than the least senior of the laid-off female employees.

The Agreement provides:

"The parties signatory to this Agreement shall not discriminate against any Employee because of race, color, sex, religion, or national origin."
(Section V-C)
"Base-rated Employees will be laid off according to Paragraph (E) (6) below."
(Section VI-2 E-2)
"For layoffs of seven days or more, base-rated Employees will be laid off according to Company seniority."
(Section V-E-6)

Prior to 1963, female work in the Finishing Department had always been confined to sorting and counting cut sheets. In 1963, when a grievance was filed on the matter, it was suggested by the Union that the Company try females on three base-rated jobs where they had not previously worked. The Company subsequently made a study to determine whether or not three jobs suggested by the Union (carton filling, carton stitching, and unstacker) could be performed by women. After the study, the Company placed these jobs—as well as the job of "Stenciller"—in the category which it considered women could perform. Women were placed in these jobs, and have performed satisfactorily in them.

Prior to the 1963 grievance and subsequent study, the jobs referred to had traditionally not been considered female jobs, and the parties had apparently recognized that women had been hired to do only counting and sorting.

The Company now contends that its 1963 study revealed that the nature of the other Finishing Room jobs contained required tasks which involved physical demands "that would put an unfair physical burden on women, and even contained physical lifting in tasks that women could not do." It contends that, in assigning women to the additional four jobs in 1963, "the Company proved to the Union that the other jobs could not be performed by women."

During the hearing on the instant grievance, the Company contended that the jobs now being performed by men could not be performed completely by women. Certain jobs were suggested by the Union at the hearing as being within the physical capabilities of women. Job summaries were placed in evidence.

CONTENTIONS

The Union contends the Company violated the Agreement and discriminated against the female grievants because of their sex, by laying them off while retaining junior male employees. It alleges that the Company failed to consider each female employee based on her ability and capacity to perform a specific job, with respect to layoffs and promotions, and contends the Company only considers its female employees as a group rather than as individuals.

The Company contends that the female grievants were laid off because there were no jobs which they could physically perform, and that therefore they were not discriminated against because of their sex. It contends the grievants were denied the assignments because of their lack of qualifications, and that physical ability to perform all aspects of a job falls within the category of qualifications. It also contends that no requirements were added to the existing jobs. The Company contends that Section VI(E)6, (a) of the Agreement must be interpreted within the conditions that exist in a specific case and under the actual circumstances, and that the judgment which the Company made was fair, reasonable, and based upon sufficient data and job information, and that the Agreement was not violated.

QUESTIONS

1. Title VII, Section 703, of the 1963 Civil Rights Act contains an exception allowing the limitation of equal employment opportunities on the basis of sex, when sex is a bona-fide qualification reasonably necessary to the normal operation of the business. Although the company did not cite this law to justify its position, would its provisions apply in this case?
2. When the company opened four base-rated jobs to women in 1963 that were previously performed by men, and the union accepted the changes, did this exclude women from other base-rated jobs that had not been opened up?
3. Who is to determine whether a job cannot be performed by a woman? How would such a determination be made?

CASE 18
Elimination of a Job by the Company

Company: Potter and Brumfield, Inc.
　　　　　　Princeton, Indiana
Union: International Association of Machinists
　　　　　　Local Lodge No. 1459
Arbitrator: Carl A. Warns, Jr.

The case involves the right of the Company to eliminate a job.

The following discussion of the issue and the facts in this case was prepared by Carl A. Warns, Jr., the arbitrator.

The question before the arbitrator is whether or not the Company has violated the contract by eliminating the job of group leader in Department 41.

The Company manufactures electrical relays. Actual production takes place on production lines of varying sizes dependent upon the type of work of each line. Prior to the strike, Line 41, in addition to the usual complement of employees actually servicing the line, contained a "group leader" whose duties are set forth in a job description and whose job title and rate are listed in Appendix A ("a part" of the contract). The group leader on Line 41 did not return to the employ of the Company after the strike and the Company did not replace him. The Union asserts in this grievance that this failure to assign another group leader to the line violates the collective agreement between the parties. The Company explains that time did not justify the training of a new group leader since the line would be moved to another plant within a short time. The group leader's supervisory duties were assigned to the foreman and the remainder of his work to a material handler. The Company states in their post-hearing brief that subsequent to the hearing on this case the line has been in fact moved and that the relays previously produced on Line 41 are manufactured elsewhere. Regardless of this factor, however, it is the position of the Company that they retain the right under the current agreement to eliminate jobs and that there is no contractual basis for this grievance challenging the failure to fill the job of group leader on Line 41 after the strike.

CONTRACT PROVISIONS INVOLVED

Article X—Wages

Section 1: Effective the first pay period after this contract is signed, the Company will grant a general wage increase of five (5) cents per hour and include such increase in Exhibit "A" attached hereto and made a part hereof. On February 4, 1957 all employees shall receive a wage increase of five (5) cents per hour which increase shall be added to the then present rates as shown in Exhibit "A" attached.

. . .

Section 3: Production rates, which serve as the basis of this plan, shall be established by the Company through time study wherein proper allowances are made for unavoidable delays and incentive earnings. These production rates are guaranteed by the Company to remain unchanged except as agreed upon in this contract.

Article XIV—Full Agreement Clause

This Contract represents complete Collective Bargaining and full agreement by the parties in respect to rates of pay, wages, hours of employment or other conditions of employment which shall prevail during the term hereof and neither party may hereafter negotiate on any other matters during the life of this agreement.

POSITION OF THE UNION

The breach of contract by the Company in failing to assign a group leader to Line 41 not only adversely affects the earnings of the employees on that line but establishes a precedent whereby larger lines and more employees are reduced in earning capacity. The employees on Line 41 are compensated on a group incentive basis; the group leader on a full average plant incentive. It is obvious from a reading of the job description of the group leader that he is an essential element in the ability of the individual employee to maintain the rate. It is no answer for the Company to say that the instructional responsibilities of the group leader can be transferred to a foreman; the latter is responsible for several lines and may frequently be absent while the employees are sitting idle on base wages due to lack of parts and instruction. The group leader, on the other hand, is assigned to one line and is therefore constantly available to maintain the flow of materials and to give needed instruction; his importance to the efficient teamwork of the line as reflected in earnings is clear. Nor is it for new classifications such as "material handlers," whose basis of compensation is unknown to the Union, or instructors, to do the work of group leaders at considerably lesser pay. If these "instructors" or "material handlers" are compensated at a straight hourly rate, they lack the incentive of the group leader who had a direct and immediate interest in high production on the line.

This contract contains no management prerogative clause. During the last negotiation the Company wished to have such a provision added but the Union would not agree. Since the contract does not expressly authorize the Company to eliminate the job classification of group leader and in the absence of a management clause which might be argued as permitting this by implication the Company lacks the contractual right to take the action challenged in this grievance. The Union requests the arbitrator to find that the Company violated the contract and the principles of good collective bargaining and to compensate the group leader for all or part of any earnings lost while foremen, material handlers, instructors, or other persons are performing group leader work while such individuals are on layoff and subject to recall.

POSITION OF THE COMPANY

It is well established in industrial relations and confirmed in numerous published arbitration cases that in the absence of a restriction in the collective agreement management has the inherent right to eliminate jobs, classifications, and to combine duties in interest of production. The only limitation is that the admitted right not be exercised in an arbitrary or discriminatory manner. In this case there is no reference to either job descriptions or group leaders in the body of the contract. The only reference to group leaders is in Exhibit "A" which is for the sole purpose of classifying the employees and to designate the rates of pay for each classification. Such classification and rate of pay simply set forth the rate that must be paid to job-holders in particular jobs and does not mean that there must be an employee or employees in each classification at all times. The incumbent group leader on Line 41 resigned from the Company and was not replaced because it was determined that a group leader for so small a group would not make for an efficient operation. In addition, there were no group leaders available with experience on this line. Since it was anticipated that the line would be moved to another plant, it would have been poor management to spend from eight weeks to three months training a group leader for a nonexistent job. Furthermore, group leaders are used as an adjunct in assisting foremen in the operation of the department. Where the department is so small, as here, such a classification is a surplus one. The foreman is fully capable of taking care of all supervisory duties. There is no instructor on Line 41 and the use of a material handler is proper. There is such a classification listed in Appendix A called Material Handler (Machine Shop). The duties of the material handler here are comparable and therefore it was not deemed necessary to add a new job classification or description to be filed with the others.

The Union's position that the absence of a management prerogative clause prevents the Company from exercising traditional prerogatives is untenable. Management has an inherent right to make all essential decisions designed to make the Company competitive. The elimination of jobs and the combination of job duties is one of them. Limitations on this basic right can be granted only at the bargaining table by the Company. Since this contract contains no such limitations, it follows that the Company's decision in this case must be confirmed and the grievance denied.

QUESTIONS

1. The union argues here that the signing of an agreement without a management's rights clause after negotiations on the inclusion of such a clause means that management has only those rights explicitly stated in the contract. What influence should an unsuccessful management argument for a management's rights clause in negotiations have on this case?

2. What is the significance of company motivation in a case of this type? The company here claims that it couldn't fill the job from present employees and that the job was going to be moved to another plant in the near future. Without these special circumstances, could the company eliminate the job for such a reason as saving money?

3. What kinds of evidence should the union and company supply in the controversy over loss of incentive earnings resulting from the elimination of the group leader job? How would you judge the validity of the evidence that might be supplied?

CASE 19
Learning to Live with a Union of Police Officers

Agency: The City of Port Huron, Mich.
Union: American Federation of State, County and Municipal Employees, AFL–CIO, Local No. 1518, Council No. 55
Arbitrator: M. David Keefe

Adjusting to the presence of a union in day-to-day work relations is not easy for public administrators used to having their own way and dealing directly with individual employees. This adjustment is all the more difficult for police patrol officers accustomed to the procedures of a paramilitary type of organization. This case deals with the problems of both parties in disciplinary cases for which the collective agreement provides due process through a grievance procedure.

Mr. David Keefe, the arbitrator, prepared the statement of facts and issues in the case that follows.

The hearing took place on July 29, 1968, in conference quarters of the City-County Building located in Port Huron, Michigan. The parties stipulated that the single grievance scheduled for hearing was free from procedural defects under the Agreement between the parties dated July 1, 1967 (Joint Ex. #1) and was properly before the arbitrator for final and binding decision.

STATEMENT OF THE CASE

On January 5, 1968, the grievant, Patrolman N., reported as scheduled on the second shift. He immediately approached Lt. Lewis (who at the time was Sergeant on the desk) to straighten out an overtime pay problem which affected the Grievant. After a short discussion, Lt. C. (who was in charge of the shift) entered the conversation but was rudely rebuffed by Patrolman N. Lt. C. invited the Grievant into the Captain's office for a private talk. Patrolman N. demanded Union representation. Lt. C. thereupon asked Lt. Cole (then Sergeant Cole) to be present as his witness. At the time, no Union representative was there. Lt. C. demanded that the Grievant come into the office. Patrolman N. refused to do so unrepresented. The Lieutenant then ordered him to comply or go home. The Grievant persisted in his refusal. He was thereupon suspended, with the penalty being later fixed at thirty (30) days off without pay.

PERTINENT CONTRACT PROVISIONS CITED BY THE PARTIES

Item 1: Section 1–3. Management Clause.

> The Union recognizes fully all rights and prerogatives of the Employer to operate and manage its affairs in all respects in accordance with the Employer's responsibilities, and all rights, powers, and authority which the Employer has not officially abridged, delegated or modified by the agreement are retained by the Employer.

Item 2: Section 3–13. Use of Past Records.

> The employer agrees that for the purposes of promotion and in matters of discipline, the employees' performance records covering incidents of minor infractions shall not be used beyond the time period of four (4) years. This is in no way to be interpreted that the Employer does not have

the right to retain on file the complete personnel records of the employees
from the initial hire date.

Item 3: Section 4–1.1. Notice of Discharge or Discipline.

The Employer agrees promptly upon the discharge or discipline of an
employee to notify in writing the Steward of the discharge or discipline.

Item 4: Section 4–1.2.

The discharged or disciplined employee will be allowed to discuss his discharge or discipline with the Steward of the shift. Upon request, the Employer or his designated representative will discuss the discharge or discipline with the employee and the Steward.

STIPULATIONS BY THE PARTIES

The parties stipulated that the grievant's past performance record, as submitted to the arbitrator, was accurate. These documents consist of both
commendations and disciplinary notices, which latter include three (3)
time-off suspensions. The most recent of these occurred more than four (4)
years prior to the incident in this case. The parties, having failed to establish criteria for differentiating between minor and major offenses, empowered the arbitrator to evaluate each of these previous infractions for purposes of making such a determination. Finally, inasmuch as the current
contract is the initial Agreement and AFSCME did not previously enjoy
representation rights, protests against these disciplinary actions could not
follow contract grievance procedure but, rather, were restricted to the civil
service appeals system which was not utilized.

SUMMARY OF THE GRIEVANT'S PAST PERFORMANCE RECORD

Patrolman N. has been a member of the Port Huron Police Department
for a period in excess of twelve years. His record, compiled during that
span, shows the following:

Item 1	4–18–56:	Police Chief's Commendation; job well done, alert to duty
Item 2	8–10–56:	Police Chief's Commendation; job well done—citation
Item 3	2–14–57:	Police Chief's Commendation; job well done—splendid
Item 4	7– 2–57:	Police Chief's Commendation; polite, courteous, considerate
Item 5	8–20–57:	Reassignment from patrol car; near accident
Item 6	2– 4–58:	Police Chief's Commendation; alert, attentive to duty
Item 7	4–20–59:	Employee Performance Report—rated satisfactory
Item 8	8– 3–61:	15 day Suspension—"conduct unbecoming officer"
Item 9	6– 2–62:	Police Chief's Commendation; diligence and follow-up
Item 10	10–31–62:	10 day Suspension—"conduct unbecoming officer"

Item 11   11–15–62:   County Sheriff's Commendation; assistance and co-operation

Item 12   1– 3–64:   20 day Suspension—"conduct unbecoming officer"

Item 13   10– 8–64:   U.S. Immigration Service Commendation—efficient, prompt action

Item 14   3–29–65:   Record Notation: attended FBI classes on own time

Item 15   7–22–65:   Police Captain Notation: keen observation, quick action

Item 16   8–27–65:   Citizen's Commendation; credit to force

Item 17   3–10–67:   Police Captain Commendation; keen observation, fine police work

Item 18   8– 8–67:   Record Notation; failure to respond to direct order

Item 19   5–12–68:   Citizen's Commendation; prompt action saved 2 fingers

THE CITY OF PORT HURON'S POSITION

The City pointed out that a police force is a semimilitary organization which functions through compliance with orders. Unless self-discipline is ingrained as an employee attitude toward his vocation, it must be imposed by the Employer or the effectiveness of and purpose for the oganization's existence will be undermined from within itself. It is not only the City's inherent right to maintain discipline among and require respect from the members of this employee group; it is, in fact, an absolute responsibility. In this case, the City contends that the Grievant was guilty of flagrant public insubordination to a superior officer.

Lieutenant C., who had overheard the overtime pay discussion between the Grievant and then Sergeant Lewis, testified that, with constructive intent, he interposed with a remark that the payroll records were unavailable at that hour. The Grievant turned to him and, in substance, retorted that the witness should keep his nose out of the matter; that it was none of his business and that he (the Grievant) was tired of "this shit." The witness, who averred that he had not been antagonistic, described Patrolman N.'s attitude as hostile, in the manner of an offended person. His comments had been expressed quite loudly. The witness, who considered the matter trivial at that stage, felt that he should talk privately on the matter with the grievant and asked him into the Captain's office, which was vacant. Patrolman N. thereupon declared that he wanted Union representation. Lt. C. countered that, in such case, he, in turn, wanted then Sergeant Cole with him as a witness. The Grievant, continuing to demand representation, went to the Squad Room and talked to Officer Bowns, Unit President. The witness followed-up with Patolman N. and told him to come into the office. The Grievant said he wanted Officer Klaus, the Union Steward, to be present. Patrolman Klaus was out on call. Lt. C. then ordered the Grievant to come into the office or put his gear away and go home. Officer N. persisted in his refusal, putting his gear away—but not leaving. He never went to the Captain's office.

Steward Klaus returned within five minutes of the Grievant's suspension and asked Lt. C. about the incident. The witness told him that he would have discussed the matter before Patrolman N. was suspended but refused to meet on the matter at that point. The Lieutenant told the Steward that the Grievant was dismissed to return at the pleasure of the Chief of Police. There was no further discussion until a later grievance meeting was called by the Union.

Lt. C. admitted, under cross examination, that he had raised his voice during the development of the difference. He was loud but hesitated to describe his tone as "yelling." At any rate, neither man used out-and-out profanity in their exchange, according to the witness.

Lieutenants Lewis and Cole (then Sergeants) confirmed the general account given by Lt. C. They both testified that the Grievant and Lieutenant were loud—but not yelling or screaming. The altercation was overheard by other officers (the shifts were just changing and many were in the vicinity) and, also, by certain prisoners who were in the process of being booked.

Police Chief Falk testified that he was told of the incident on the following day. He asked Lt. C. for a written report. Personnel Director Provost was then informed and, together with the Chief, investigated the incident through interviews with Lts. C. and Cole. Lt. Lewis was talked to on the phone. The Grievant was unavailable. However, Steward Klaus asked for a meeting which took place on January 6, 1968. This meeting was followed by a further session in which the incident was fully explored. At that time, the penalty had not been fixed. The grievant was asked if he had made the initial remark about "none of your business, etc." and admitted that he might have used words to that effect. He was also asked if he had refused to go into the Captain's office and affirmed that he had refused unless and until he had representation. As far as the Lieutenant's alleged abuse of him, the Grievant reported that it was not what was said that was improper but rather how it was said, with sarcasm. At the end of the session, the Chief felt that he had the facts and, based on the seriousness of the insubordination, the aggravating circumstances of the public display and the past record of three (3) suspensions, recommended a thirty (30) day suspension as the penalty in this case.

Personnel Director Provost corroborated the account given by Chief Falk as to the meetings and method for evaluation of the penalty.

The City argued that the image, public acceptance of and respect for the Police Department was damaged to the extent that citizens, in the process of being booked, overheard what transpired. Internally, organizational morale and decorum was dealt a blow due to the presence during the incident of many officers in the building because of shift change. These aggravating circumstances, when considered as the background to the outright and persistent refusal of the Grievant to comply with a direct order, added up to a most serious infraction. When considered in the light of the three (3) previous suspensions, discharge was deemed merited but was not imposed out of recognition of the commendations in the Grievant's record.

The City asked that the grievance be denied.

THE UNION'S POSITION

Grievant N. related that, when he approached Lt. Lewis on his overtime pay problem, he observed Lt. C. nearby, who seemed upset. At any rate, in the course of his conversation with Lt. Lewis, Lt. C. rudely interrupted and was very sarcastic in giving his advice. The Grievant told him to keep his nose out of the conversation. The Lieutenant then began to yell, calling for Lt. Cole and telling the Grievant to get his ass into the Captain's office for a talk. The witness felt that he was in a tenuous position, with Lt. C. acting extremely excited. He stated that he wanted Union representation in any projected interviews. Lt. C. reminded him that he was, actually, the Union President and asked why he needed representation. The Grievant went to the Squad Room, looking for Steward Klaus. There, he met Unit President Bowns who was about to leave and who advised him Officer Klaus was working the shift. He could not be found at the time. It developed that he was out on a call right then. Lt. C., meanwhile, continued yelling. He threatened to send the Grievant home. Patrolman N. explained that he was waiting for the return of Steward Klaus before entering into the interview. At that point, Lt. C. ordered him to go home. The Steward came in almost immediately after that. The Grievant informed him of the incident. When the pair approached the Lieutenant to discuss the problem, Lt. C. refused and "ranted" at the Grievant that: "Ever since this God damned Union came in you've been pretty cocky and stuck your nose into everything around here. You think this is your Union and the word is out that it's N.'s Union." The grievant added that, in the January 6 meeting, he had been cut short from presenting his side in full.

Officer Klaus was absent on vacation and, therefore, did not testify. However, *Officer Everitt* appeared in behalf of the grievant. He stated that, as the incident began, he was in the hall, outside the office where the altercation first took place. He heard Lt. C. speaking in a loud voice, although he could not make out what was said. The Grievant came out of the office. Lt. C. followed, calling for Lt. Cole. He called to the Grievant to go to the Captain's office. Patrolman N. said he wanted a Union representative before he went in. Lt. C. then loudly told him to go to the office or put his gear away and go home. At that stage, Patrolman Everitt, who was finishing his shift, went home. He added that the exchange which he witnessed was marked by yelling on the part of Lt. C. but not by the Grievant.

The Union argued that Lt. C. was motivated by bias against the Grievant due to his Union activity and that this incited him to lay down the ultimatum which precipitated the suspension. When Steward Klaus appeared, almost on the heels of this overt decision, he was rebuffed, in spite of his contract right to meet with the Lieutenant on the matter. Furthermore, the required written notice to the Steward was not rendered until some days later. All this, in the Union's view, adds up to intemperate and improper management action. The initial exchange had been described by Lt. C. as trivial. Obviously, then, it was blown up to federal-case proportions by the Lieutenant, inspired by his animosity against the Grievant.

The Union asked that the grievance be upheld.

QUESTIONS

1. What allowance, if any, should an arbitrator make for the inexperience of career police officers in the new relationship with subordinates brought on by a first collective bargaining agreement? Does this apply both ways: to the union and its members as well as management?

2. Under the terms of the agreement, what weight would you give to Patrolman N.'s past performance record? Would you count it in his favor or against him? Does it apply at all? Do you think his superiors gave it proper consideration in coming to their disciplinary decision? Why, or why not?

3. Should Patrolman N.'s past performance record count at all in the disposition of this case?

4. Did the police lieutenant and the Department follow the grievance procedures set down in the agreement? Did the grievant? The union? What weight should this have in the arbitrator's award? Does the stipulation that the grievance was "free from procedural defects" prevent the arbitrator from considering this?

CASE 20
Arbitrability of a Tenure Claim

Agency: Hoboken Board of Education
Union: Hoboken Teachers Association
Arbitrator: Lawrence I. Hammer

Does a high school teacher's claim of tenure extend to an assignment as Year Book Advisor; and is the issue arbitrable?

Lawrence I. Hammer, the arbitrator, discusses the issues and the facts as follows:

THE ISSUES

1. Is the alleged grievance arbitrable? If so . . .
2. Did the Board of Education violate the Contract when it failed to continue the Grievant as the Year Book Advisor?

REMEDY SOUGHT

Reinstatement of the Grievant to the position of Year Book Advisor for the 1974–75 school year with full pay retroactive to September, 1974.

BACKGROUND

The Grievant, an English Teacher in the High School, had been the Year Book Advisor for the School Years 1970–71, 1971–72, 1972–73 and 1973–74, and received a $125.00 annual stipend for such position.

When given his original 1974–75 Schedule, the Grievant was listed as Year Book Advisor. Later that same day, the Grievant was advised of an error in his Schedule and was informed that he would not be the 1974–75 Year Book Advisor.

CONTRACT PROVISIONS ON ARBITRABILITY

Article 14—Promotions

14.1 All vacancies in permanent promotional positions as defined in paragraph 14.2 of this article shall be adequately publicized by the Superintendent.

14.2 Promotional positions are defined as follows: Positions paying a salary differential and/or positions on the Administrative-Supervisory levels of responsibility.

14.3 All above-mentioned appointments to the aforesaid vacancies and openings shall be made at the discretion of the Superintendent and Board, and the following factors shall enter into promotions:

a. Certification for position

b. Seniority of employment

c. Experience in area of promotion

d. Nature of promotions as to duties

14.5 Any person assigned by the Superintendent and approved by the Board to an acting position for three months or more shall be compensated at the rate of pay normally paid at his proper step in the existing Salary Guide for that position.

SCHEDULE "B"
Salary Guide of Athletic Program Personnel

Athletic Program Personnel	*Special Services Personnel*
Athletic director	Evening school rate
Treasurer	Guidance counsellors
Head coach—Football	Director of career & college services
Assistant football coaches	Department chairmen
Head coach—Basketball	Special education teachers
Assistant basketball coaches	Reading specialists
Baseball coach	Learning disability consultant
Soccer coach	Social worker
Swim coach	Speech therapist
Track coach	Psychometrician
Band director	
Majorette coach	
Cheerleader coach	

The monetary sums set forth for each position under both the "Athletic Program Personnel" and the "Special Services Personnel" are immaterial and thus, not set forth.

The Board agrees that other special personnel not listed under this Article shall continue to receive their present additional compensation.

POSITIONS AND ARGUMENTS ON ARBITRABILITY

The Board of Education argued that the alleged grievance is not Arbitrable for the following reasons:

1. That the position of Year Book Advisor is neither a permanent nor promotional position, same not being subject to tenure.
2. That extra-curricular activities and compensation thereof is not a part of the negotiated contract.
3. That appointment and compensation for the position is solely at the discretion of the Principal, and not subject to Board of Education approval.
4. That the grievance involves the assignment of personnel to a position, a right which is exclusive to the Board of Education.

The Grievant, seeking to overcome the Arbitrability question raised by the Board of Education, relied upon Sections 14.2 of Article 14, on the basis that Department Chairman and other nontenured positions are considered promotions and are posted; and on Sections 14.5 of Article 14, in that the $125.00 annual stipend paid for the position of Year Book Advisor resulted in a "position paying a salary differential."

The Grievant also argued, most forcefully, that the "Catch-All" paragraph under "Special Services Personnel" of Schedule B, guaranteed his continued appointment and continuation of his receiving the additional ($125.00) compensation.

QUESTIONS

1. What, if anything, casts doubt on the arbitrability of the issue in this case?
2. Can the "catch-all" paragraph under "Special Services Personnel" of Schedule B of the agreement be construed to include the position of Year Book Advisor? If not, why not? If so, how could you justify it?
3. Do you see any contradiction between the Board of Education's points 3 and 4?

CASE 21
Maternity Leaves

Agency: Middletown Board of Education
Union: Middletown Education Association
Arbitrator: John A. Hogan

Does an agreement provision making maternity leave mandatory at the end of the fifth month of pregnancy violate Title VII of the Civil Rights Act of 1964?

The following discussion of facts and issues in this case were prepared by John A. Hogan, the arbitrator.

THE ISSUE

HOGAN, Arbitrator: The Association's Demand for Arbitration contains the following statement of the nature of the dispute:

> In the contract under Maternity Leave, the following statement precedes and addresses itself to all the items included under Maternity Leave. "Teachers in the Middletown School System *may* become eligible for a maternity leave subject to the following conditions . . ." This implies that a choice can be exercised, since the word *may* indicates the possibility of or opportunity for a maternity leave if the conditions that follow are met. The teacher involved elected not to be eligible for a maternity leave and thus is of the opinion that she is not subject to the conditions required of a teacher who elects to be considered for a maternity leave. The Board of Education has ruled that all teachers are subject to the conditions of the Maternity Leave.

The issue before the Arbitrator, therefore, is whether the Board of Education may require all teachers to vacate their positions at the end of the fifth month of pregnancy under the Collective Bargaining Agreement.

STATEMENT OF THE CASE

M, nontenured, teacher and grievant, conceived in October, 1970. She and her husband had planned this first child with the hope and objective of birth subsequent to the end of the school year in June. They say they were not aware of any five-month rule although this is contained in the Contract effective July 1, 1970 under Article XII, Section H, 5. This clause was agreed upon several months prior to the effective date of the Contract.

The Association submits two letters from the grievant's doctor as proof that she was physically able to work beyond the fifth month of pregnancy without risk to herself. These letters dated January 13, 1971 and March 3, 1971 read as follows:

> Mrs. M has been a patient in this office since 1964. She is currently pregnant in her first pregnancy. Her conceptual date has been thought to be October 1, 1970 which would give the patient an expected due date of late June. In my opinion, based on my knowledge of Mrs. M's health, she should be able to carry out her duties through the completion of the school term. In the case of a healthy woman such as Mrs. M, I feel is no contraindication for her working even up to the onset of labor, providing that she does not become unduly fatigued. I think that most of the policies in regard to length of time which a woman may work during pregnancy are arbitrary and artificial. Each case warrants individual consideration.
>
> Very truly yours,
> Virginia M. Stuermer, M.D.

March 3, 1971....

> Mrs. M is a patient under my care. Mrs. M's health has not changed since my letter of January 13th and she is still in excellent physical condition with a due date of late June.

The Board of Education allowed M to continue working pending the arbitration decision in the case. She was working at the time of the hearing on April 2, 1971, in her seventh month of pregnancy.

The five-month clause appears in Article XII, Leaves of Absence, under Section H, Maternity Leave, Paragraph 5. An introductory sentence prior to Paragraph 1 reads as follows:

> "Teachers in the Middletown School System may become eligible for a maternity leave, subject to the following conditions."

(Thereupon follow provisions for maternity leave.)
Paragraph 5 reads as follows:

> "Teachers shall be required to vacate their positions at the end of the fifth month of pregnancy."

The Association argues that the word "may" in the introductory sentence gives an option and the grievant chose not to be eligible for maternity leave and therefore is not subject to the conditions that apply to teachers who elect to be considered for maternity leave—including the condition of the five month termination (Section H, 5).

In the event the Association argues that the five-month rule is void since it contravenes other clauses in the Contract that prohibit discrimination on the basis of sex (Article IV, H; Article V, D) and is void under Article I, H.

These clauses read as follows:

IV, H.

> H. Teacher assignments and transfers shall be made without regard to age, race, creed, religion, nationality, sex, or marital status.

V, D.

> D. All appointments to the aforesaid vacancies and openings shall be made without regard to age, race, creed, color, religion, nationality, sex, or marital status.

I, H.

> H. Nothing in this Agreement shall in any way limit or contravene the authority of any Municipal, State or Federal board, commission, agency, or other governmental body or authority.

The Association contends further that the five-month rule contravenes Connecticut General Statutes 31–26 which establish a four-week-before-confinement and four-week-after-birth rule for not working in mills, factories or mercantile establishments.

At the federal level, the Association argues that XII, H, 5, contravenes Title VII of the Civil Rights Act, as interpreted under the interpretive regulations of the E.E.O.C.; that it contravenes Article XIV of the U.S. Constitution (equal protection of the laws) and Article IX (Right of Privacy) and that the Courts have upheld the Association's position (Mary Shattman v. Texas Employment Commission, 3 FEP Cases 311, 468, 1971, DC WTex).

The Board of Education sees the issue as confined to XII, H, 5 of the Contract. The Board points out that the grievant had no choice under the first sentence of XII, H since she was not on tenure. She had no rights to maternity benefits and therefore no "option" and the Association's claim here is off the mark. The Board says that the intent of XII, H, 5 was that it apply to all teachers. It was carefully negotiated into the Contract for the purpose of giving the Board sufficient notice in pregnancy cases so that it could arrange for a satisfactory substitute for the teacher, and for the purpose of protecting the teacher's health. The Board distinguishes between the Shattman case and this case since here the parties freely negotiated a clause that constitutes a joint agreement whereas in the Texas case the decision was unilaterally made by a Commission.

QUESTIONS

1. Since only females can become pregnant, is it discriminatory to make special rules for pregnant female employees?
2. Supposing that female employees will need some time off at the birth of a child, is it reasonable to make them take unpaid leave at the end of the fifth month of pregnancy? If not, when should they be required to take the leave, if at all? Can it be left to their own discretion? Why or why not?
3. In this case, does it matter that the grievant is nontenured?

CASE 22
Factfinding: An Illustrative Example

Agency: School District 24J, Marion County, Oregon
Union: Salem Education Association
Factfinder: Paul J. Kleinsorge

When negotiations reach an impasse public employees either cannot legally strike, or may not strike without first having exhausted other procedures. In Oregon, public employees may legally strike, so long as they do not endanger public safety and health, provided they make use of mediation, and if that is unsuccessful, submit to factfinding. If that fails, they may resort to binding arbitration, but this is not mandatory; both sides have to agree to it.

Factfinding is like interest arbitration except that there is no binding award; but the factfinder makes recommendations. Like mediation, factfinding often clears the air and helps the parties reach agreement without the confrontation of binding arbitration or a strike.

This example of factfinding in a public employee dispute was prepared by the factfinder, Paul J. Kleinsorge. His recommendations are withheld in order not to prejudice the reader's decisions on the various issues.

REPORT OF FACTFINDER CASE INVOLVING
SCHOOL DISTRICT 24 J, MARION COUNTY, OREGON
AND SALEM EDUCATION ASSOCIATION

Oregon Laws 1971, Chapter 755, amends ORS 342.460 to provide that certificated school personnel "shall have the right to confer, consult and discuss in good faith with the district school board by which they are employed on matters of salaries and related economic policies affecting professional services, grievance procedures and compensation beyond the normal duties for which the teacher or administrator is employed." Chapter 755 also provides for mediation and factfinding in the event that the school board and the representatives of the teachers and administrators cannot reach agreement. The chapter states that "if the mediation does not result in agreement within 10 days of appointment of the mediator, the mediator shall so report and a factfinder shall be appointed by the Superintendent of Public Instruction. Within 15 days of the time of his appointment, the factfinder shall submit in writing to the board and to the employees' representatives his report, including a recommendation for a reasonable basis for the settlement of the disagreement."

Since the school board for School District 24J, Marion County, and the representatives of the certificated personnel could not reach agreement, a mediator was appointed. Again agreement could not be reached, and in accordance with the statute, the factfinder in the present case was appointed as of January 18, 1973, to serve through February 1.

THE ISSUES

Salaries

The Salem Education Association (SEA), representing the teachers, asks that the teachers be granted an increment based salary schedule for 1973–74 with a starting salary of $7,500 for a beginning teacher with a B.A. degree. The schedule, as worked out by the SEA, would provide for a maximum salary increase of $800 over present salary, and a minimum of $400 or 4%, which ever is larger. The overall average increase would be about $650. The top salary would occur at the eighteenth step for a teacher with an M.A. degree plus 45 additional hours of college credit, and would be $13,869. The SEA considers this proposal to be only the first move toward an increment based salary schedule with considerably fewer steps from the beginning salary to the maxima of the various categories, B.A., B.A. + 45, M.A. (or B.A. + 69), M.A. + 24 (or B.A. + 93), and M.A. + 45 (or B.A.

M.A. (or B.A. + 69), M.A. + 24(or B.A. + 93), and M.A. + 45 (or B.A. + 115).

The SEA supports its request with numerous arguments, the chief of which are:

1. The current system offers no advancement opportunities. That is, teachers are locked in relatively the same step. Except for those who already have reached the top, they never can reach the maximum of the schedule.

2. The current system is internally inequitable in that too many of the budget dollars are going to teachers occupying the top of the schedule in the B.A. and B.A. + 24 columns. Also, the settlement made with the administrative officers of the District is for far more than the SEA is asking. The settlement made with the administrators (whole salary schedule is on an incremental basis) is for a $750 increment plus $500. This means that those administrators who are not already at the top salary will receive a salary increase of $1,250. Those at the top will receive an increase of $500.

3. Except for some maximum salaries, Salem teachers' salaries do not rank well with salaries paid in other districts in the state. This is particularly true of the middle areas of the steps. A study of thirty-seven districts indicates that Salem frequently occupies positions below twenty-fifth place. Also, comparisons of Salem teachers' salaries with salaries paid in other professions indicate that the teachers' salaries are very low.

4. The Board states that the average settlement in sixteen fairly comparable districts so far this year is $510, but the SEA disputes this statement. The SEA points out that the $510 figure is an average of the first step increases, which are likely to be considerably lower than the average overall increases. Some of the maximum increases are over $1,000. According to the SEA figures, the overall average increase is between $650 and $700. The SEA also indicates that there are reporting errors in the figures quoted by the Board, and that for this additional reason the $510 figure is not reliable.

5. The Salem School Board's offer is not adequate. It will not cover increases for the average teacher in taxes, retirement and F.I.C.A. contributions, and cost of living.

6. Salem has enjoyed business prosperity in 1972 and is expected to be a prosperous community in 1973. The SEA maintains that the Salem School District is well able to pay the increased salaries requested.

The Salem School Board offers a $500 across-the-board salary increase with the maintenance of the present system. The Board is not opposed to an increment based salary schedule, but believes that such a system should take into account performance criteria which the SEA proposal does not do. The Board feels that its offer is adequate for the following reasons:

1. Salaries have increased more rapidly than cost-of-living. The board presented statistics to show that in 1971–72 the cost-of-living rose 2.72 percent while the improvement factor averaged approximately 3.3 percent. In addition, Salem teachers' salaries have been rising at a more rapid rate than the national average.
2. The $500 offered by the Board is close to the average of the settlements reported in fairly comparable districts. The average increase for sixteen districts was $510. The Board answers the SEA's criticisms of this figure by pointing out that the SEA's figures include districts which are on increment based schedules. The teachers in those districts received incremental as well as general increases. The Board admits that the increases received by teachers being paid at the middle of those schedules would be considerably higher than the $510, but the Board claims they would not be higher at the top or at the bottom.
3. The Salem School District is maintaining its competitive position. There are many more applicants for teaching positions in Salem than there are vacancies. Teacher turnover is very low. Salem teachers' salaries appear to be above the state wide averages.
4. The Board has gone on record that it will attempt to operate the Salem schools during 1973–74 without an increase in the school portion of the tax levy. Therefore, large increases in teachers' salaries would have to be at the expense of District program budgets which already have been reduced.

Insurance

The SEA asks that the Salem teachers be granted the Choice Health Plan, a plan which already has been adopted by a number of school districts in the State through the greater Oregon Health Service. The plan permits the individual covered to make several options as to the type of coverage he desires. The Salem teachers apparently are very anxious to have the plan adopted. If the SEA's request is granted, the employer contribution of $123 per year per employee for health insurance benefits ($10.25 per month) would be increased to $251.16 per year per employee $20.93 per month). The SEA presents the following arguments in favor of the adoption of the plan:

1. The Salem School District ranks very low with regard to insurance benefits for employees. Of the thirty-seven largest districts in the State, Salem ranks thirty-second. The average contribution of the thirty-seven for insurance is $171.00 per year per employee ($14.25 per month). A number of districts make contributions of well over $200.00. Recent settlements indicate very large increases in fringe benefits which would bring the average for employer insurance contributions well above $171.00

2. It is the moral obligation of the school district to provide for the health and welfare of its employees, and the Choice Plan provides the best coverage for the money.

The Salem School Board offers to increase the District's contribution to insurance benefits by $36 per year per employee ($3 per month). This would bring the total per employee per year to $159 ($13.25 per month). The Board feels that this increase brings the Salem District's contribution in line with contributions made by other districts. The Board insists that whatever plan is adopted, specifications must be developed and put out to bid. The Board will not operate through the Greater Oregon Health Service unless that organization submits the most acceptable bid.

Personal Leave

The SEA proposes that Clause 6.671 concerning personal emergency leave be eliminated from the rules and regulations, and that in its place a new system be adopted. The new system would allow teachers having 10 to 25 days of accumulated sick leave at the beginning of the contract year to take 1 day of personal leave for that contract year; those having 26 to 50 days of accumulated sick leave, 2 days of personal leave; and those having in excess of 50 days of accumulated sick leave, 3 days of personal leave. Notification of such absence would have to be made by the teacher to the building principal as soon as possible in advance of the leave. Other personal leave would be granted at the discretion of the Superintendent. It is understood that personal leave would be requested by teachers only in situations involving emergencies, such as required appearance in court or urgent business problems, and would not be used to extend vacations or holiday periods.

The SEA argues that the present emergency leave policy is too restrictive. It allows leave only under the most dire circumstances. It does not recognize the fact that teachers, like other human beings, encounter various problems which require immediate attention to be solved. The SEA also points out that the concept of personal leave is recognized throughout Oregon. Many school districts have adopted personal leave systems.

The Board wishes to continue the present emergency leave policy which provides that the Superintendent may grant personal leave up to three days a year "for only obvious unpredictable and hardship reasons." The Board offers to liberalize the interpretation of the present policy by allowing emergency leave to be used to attend to important matters that the teacher cannot control and that could not be taken care of except during school hours. The Board points out that personal leave is a cost item. If a teacher is granted personal leave, a substitute must be hired. If an average of two days personal leave are granted per year, the estimated cost would be equivalent to an increase of $100 in average salary.

Grievance Procedure

The SEA asks for a three-step grievance procedure with the third step ending in the submission of the grievance to the school board or to binding arbitration. Apparently the grievant and/or the SEA would have the right to decide whether the final appeal would be to the Board or to an arbitrator. The SEA recalls that binding arbitration was recommended by the impasse panel in March 1971, as the final step in the grievance procedure. The SEA also points out that the Oregon Board of Education has recommended binding arbitration and that a number of school districts have adopted it. The SEA emphasizes that binding arbitration would be used only for grievances and not for general adjustments.

The Board is willing to make minor changes in the grievance procedure, but is not willing to submit policy decisions to compulsory binding arbitration. The Board states that every aspect of the District Code, except those related to teacher compensation, deals with policy matters, and that, therefore, the power of final decision should be left with the policy making body as is the case in the existing grievance procedure, adopted in 1971. The Board points out that since the adoption of the existing procedure, no grievance has progressed beyond the first step of the procedure. The Board maintains, therefore, that there is no evidence to indicate that the existing procedure is not workable.

Transfer Policy

The SEA proposes that Code Number 6.315 on transfers and vacancies be revised to include the consideration of certain criteria in the transfer of personnel, such as the well being of the program of instruction, the equitable treatment and desire of personnel, and seniority when qualifications are substantially equal. A list of open positions in the school system is to be made available to all teachers. Since transfers may be involuntary as well as voluntary, the SEA wishes to be sure that if a teacher objects to an involuntary transfer, he will have an opportunity (with an SEA representative) to discuss the matter with the superintendent. The SEA also wishes to be sure that transfers will not be used by any administrator as a punitive or disciplinary action.

The Board has no strong objection to the SEA proposal on transfer policy. The Board has agreed to work with the SEA to find ways to create a more favorable image of intra-district transfers. However, the Board feels that it is held accountable for the overall educational program, and must retain its authority to assign personnel in the best interests of the District. The Board is not willing to share this responsibility with the teachers or the SEA, and is not willing to allow teachers or the SEA an equal voice in judgments or transfers. The Board points out that objections to transfers could be processed through the grievance procedure.

Preparation Time

The SEA asks that all Salem teachers be granted preparation time. The SEA proposes that the Board and the SEA appoint a committee to devise a system under which each teacher would be provided with daily preparation time. The committee should report by May 1, 1973, so that the system could be implemented during the 1973–74 school year. The SEA notes that Salem is the only district of the thirty-seven of its size which does not provide guaranteed preparation time for all elementary, junior high, and senior high teachers. Also, there are inequities within the Salem district, since three junior highs and one senior high have managed to provide some preparation time. The SEA contends that with new and diversified programs, it is essential to give teachers preparation time to maintain and improve the quality of education in Salem.

The Board concedes that the arguments for preparation time have merit, and states that the Superintendent is presently developing some alternatives for discussion with teacher representatives. However, the Board maintains that it is the Superintendent who must decide on the most effective distribution of the District's resources in order to achieve the optimum results consistent with Board policies. The Board is not willing to negotiate how teachers are to spend their time during classroom hours.

Early Dismissal

Salem has a teacher-parent conference program which involves the holding of one-half hour conferences during a three week period twice each year. The time spent preparing and conducting these conferences adds to the teacher's burden. In 1969–70 and in 1970–71 elementary classes were dismissed one hour early for one week prior to a full conference day, but in 1971–72 this practice was discontinued. The SEA proposes that the 1969–70 and 1970–71 system be reinstituted to the extent that classes be dismissed one hour early for three days prior to the full day of conferencing for grades 3 to 6.

Again the Board feels that it must retain final authority in establishing class hours. The Board on its own motion could initiate an early dismissal system, but the Board is not willing to negotiate the matter with the SEA. In addition, the Board states that parents are greatly interested in the hours during which their children are in school. The Board feels that it must be free to act in the parents interest in determining when students are to be in school.

Calendar

The SEA asks that a longer Christmas vacation be adopted. Actually this has been done for the 1973–74 school year, but the teachers want the longer

Christmas vacation as a permanent feature. Apparently in the past, the Christmas vacation was as short as ten days instead of the two weeks the SEA requests. Since the teachers' contracts require that they be on duty a certain number of days (190), the longer Christmas vacation might mean that the schools would be open later into June, but the teachers are willing to accept this possibility.

The Board is not willing to negotiate the length of the Christmas vacation. The Board has previously indicated its willingness to negotiate the total number of days a teacher is expected to be on duty, but within that period, the Board feels that it must retain the right to schedule the instructional program to obtain the best results. There are many factors aside from teacher convenience to consider. Whether a two-week Christmas vacation is acceptable will depend partially on the day of the week upon which the holiday falls.

QUESTION

1. Given the facts as presented here by the factfinder, what would you recommend?

appendixes

Federal Statutory and Administrative Laws on Collective Bargaining

APPENDIX I

Norris–La Guardia Act
Taft-Hartley Act as Amended
Landrum-Griffin Act as Amended

APPENDIX II

Executive Order 11491 as Amended

Appendix I

THE MAJOR FEDERAL laws on collective bargaining in effect at the close of 1975 were the Railway Labor Act of 1926 as amended; the Norris–La Guardia Act of 1932; the Labor-Management Relations Act of 1947 (Taft-Hartley Act) as amended by Public Law 86–257, 1959 (Landrum-Griffin Act); and the Labor-Management Reporting and Disclosure Act of 1959 (Landrum-Griffin Act) as amended. The Railway Labor Act of 1926 will not be covered in this appendix because of its limited application.

This appendix is designed as a ready reference to the *major* elements of national labor relations law. This appendix excludes the rich interpretations of the statutes cited which have been developed by the National Labor Relations Board and the courts.

THE NORRIS–LA GUARDIA ANTI-INJUNCTION ACT OF MARCH 23, 1932

This law was passed for the purpose of eliminating certain abuses of the injunction in labor disputes. It severely restricts the authority of federal courts to issue injunctions in labor disputes. The full text of the original law is reproduced below. The Norris–La Guardia Act was amended by the Labor Management Relations Act of 1947 (the Taft-Hartley law).

NORRIS–LA GUARDIA ANTI-INJUNCTION ACT
OF MARCH 23, 1932

(PUBLIC—No. 65—72D CONGRESS)
(H.R. 5315)

AN ACT

To amend the Judicial Code and to define and limit the jurisdiction of courts sitting in equity, and for other purposes.

Be it enacted by the Senate and House of Representatives of the United States of America in Congress assembled, that no court of the United States, as herein defined shall have jurisdiction to issue any restraining order or temporary or permanent injunction in a case involving or growing out of a labor dispute, except in a strict conformity with the provisions of this Act; nor shall any such restraining order or temporary or permanent injunction be issued contrary to the public policy declared in this Act.

SEC. 2. In the interpretation of this Act and in determining the jurisdiction and authority of the courts of the United States, as such jurisdiction and authority are herein defined and limited, the public policy of the United States is hereby declared as follows:

Whereas under prevailing economic conditions, developed with the aid of governmental authority for owners of property to organize in the corporate and other form of ownership association, the individual unorganized worker is commonly helpless to exercise actual liberty of contract and to protect his freedom of labor, and thereby to obtain acceptable terms and conditions of employment, therefore, though he should be free to decline to associate with his fellows, it is necessary that he have full freedom of association, self-organization, and designation of representatives of his own choosing, to negotiate the terms and conditions of his employment, and that he shall be free from the interference, resraint, or coercion of employers of labor, or their agents, in the designation of such representatives or in self-organization or in other concerted activities for the purpose of collective bargaining or other mutual aid or protection; therefore, the following definitions of, and limitations upon, the jurisdiction and authority of the courts of the United States are hereby enacted.

SEC. 3. Any undertaking or promise, such as is described in this section, or any other undertaking or promise in conflict with the public policy declared in section 2 of this Act, is hereby declared to be contrary to the public policy of the United States, shall not be enforceable in any court of the United States and shall not afford any basis for the granting of legal or equitable relief by any such court, including specifically the following:

Every undertaking or promise hereafter made, whether written or oral, express or implied, constituting or contained in any contract or agreement of hiring or employment between any individual, firm, company, association, or corporation, and any employee or prospective employee of the same, whereby

(a) Either party to such contract or agreement undertakes or promises not to join, become, or remain a member of any labor organization or of any employer organization; or

(b) Either party to such contract or agreement undertakes or promises that he will withdraw from any employment relation in the event that he joins, becomes, or remains a member of any labor organization or of any employer organization.

SEC. 4. No court of the United States shall have jurisdiction to issue any restraining order or temporary or permanent injunction in any case involving or growing out of any labor dispute to prohibit any person or persons participating or interested in such dispute (as these terms are herein defined) from doing, whether singly or in concert, any of the following acts:

(a) Ceasing or refusing to perform any work or to remain in any relation of employment;

(b) Becoming or remaining a member of any labor organization or of any employer organization, regardless of any such undertaking or promise as is described in section 3 of this Act;

(c) Paying or giving to, or withholding from, any person participating or interested in such labor dispute, any strike or unemployment benefits or insurance, or other moneys or things of value;

(d) By all lawful means aiding any person participating or interested in any labor dispute who is being proceeded against in, or it prosecuting, any action or suit in any court of the United States or of any State;

(e) Giving publicity to the existence of, or the facts involved in, any labor dispute, whether by advertising, speaking, patrolling, or by any other method not involving fraud or violence;

(f) Assembling peaceably to act or to organize to act in promotion of their interests in a labor dispute;

(g) Advising or notifying any person of an intention to do any of the acts heretofore specified;

(h) Agreeing with other persons to do or not to do any of the acts heretofore specified; and

(i) Advising, urging, or otherwise causing or inducing without fraud or violence the acts heretofore specified, regardless of any such undertaking or promise as is described in section 3 of this Act.

SEC. 5. No court of the United States shall have jurisdiction to issue a restraining order or temporary or permanent injunction upon the ground that any of the persons participating or interested in a labor dispute constitute or are engaged in an unlawful combination or conspiracy because of the doing in concert of the acts enumerated in section 4 of this Act.

SEC. 6. No officer or member of any association or organization, and no association or organization participating or interested in a labor dispute, shall be held responsible or liable in any court of the United States for the unlawful acts of individual officers, members, or agents, except upon clear proof of actual participation in, or actual authorization of, such acts, or of ratification of such acts after actual knowledge thereof.

SEC. 7. No court of the United States shall have jurisdiction to issue a temporary or permanent injunction in any case involving or growing out of a labor dispute as herein defined, except after hearing the testimony of witnesses in open court (with opportunity for cross-examination) in support of the allegations of a complaint made under oath, and testimony in opposition thereto, if offered, and except after findings of fact by the court, to the effect—

(a) That unlawful acts have been threatened and will be committed unless restrained or have been committed and will be continued unless restrained, but no injunction or temporary restraining order shall be issued on account of any threat or unlawful act excepting against the person or persons, association, or organization making the threat or committing the unlawful act or actually authorizing or ratifying the same after actual knowledge thereof;

(b) That substantial and irreparable injury to complainant's property will follow;

(c) That as to each item of relief granted greater injury will be inflicted upon complainant by the denial of relief than will be inflicted upon defendants by the granting of relief;

(d) That complainant has no adequate remedy at law; and

(e) That the public officers charged with the duty to protect complainant's property are unable or unwilling to furnish adequate protection.

Such hearing shall be held after due and personal notice thereof has been given, in such manner as the court shall direct, to all known persons against whom relief is sought, and also to the chief of those public officials of the county and city within which the unlawful acts have been threatened or committed charged with the duty to protect complainant's property: *Provided, however,* That if a complainant shall also allege that, unless a temporary restraining order shall be issued without notice, a substantial and irreparable injury to complainant's property will be unavoidable, such a temporary restraining order may be issued upon testimony under oath, sufficient, if sustained, to justify the court in issuing a temporary injunction upon a hearing after notice. Such a temporary restraining order shall be effective for no longer than five days and shall become void at the expiration of said five days. No temporary restraining order or temporary injunction shall be issued except on condition that complainant shall first file an undertaking with adequate security in an amount to be fixed by the court sufficient to recompense those enjoined for any loss, expense, or damage caused by the improvident or erroneous issuance of such order or injunction, including all reasonable costs (together with a reasonable attorney's fee) and expense of defense against the order or against the granting of any injunctive relief sought in the same proceeding and subsequently denied by the court.

The undertaking herein mentioned shall be understood to signify an agreement entered into by the complainant and the surety upon which a decree may be rendered in the same suit or proceeding against said complainant and surety, upon a hearing to assess damages of which hearing complainant and surety shall have reasonable notice, the said complainant and surety submitting themselves to the jurisdiction of the court for that purpose. But nothing herein contained shall deprive any party having a claim or cause of action under or upon such undertaking from electing to pursue his ordinary remedy by suit at law or in equity.

Sec. 8. No restraining order or injunctive relief shall be granted to any complainant who has failed to comply with any obligation imposed by law which is involved in the labor dispute in question, or who has failed to make every reasonable effort to settle such dispute either by negotiation or with the aid of any available governmental machinery of mediation or voluntary arbitration.

Sec. 9. No restraining order or temporary or permanent injunction shall be granted in a case involving or growing out of a labor dispute, except on the basis of findings of fact made and filed by the court in the record of the case prior to the issuance of such restraining order or injunction; and every restraining order or injunction granted in a case involving or growing out of a labor dispute shall include only a prohibition of such specific act or acts as may be expressly complained of in the bill of complaint or petition filed in such case and as shall be expressly included in said findings of fact made and filed by the court as provided herein.

Sec. 10. Whenever any court of the United States shall issue or deny any temporary injunction in a case involving or growing out of a labor dispute, the court shall, upon the request of any party to the proceedings and on his filing the usual bond for costs, forthwith certify as in ordinary cases the record of the case to the circuit court of appeals for its review. Upon the filing of such record in the circuit court of appeals, the appeal shall be heard and the temporary injunctive order affirmed, modified, or set aside with the greatest possible expedition, giving the proceedings precedence over all other matters except older matters of the same character.

SEC. 11. In all cases arising under this Act in which a person shall be charged with contempt in a court of the United States (as herein defined), the accused shall enjoy the right to a speedy and public trial by an impartial jury of the State and district wherein the contempt shall have been committed: *Provided,* That this right shall not apply to contempts committed in the presence of the court or so near thereto as to interfere directly with the administration of justice or to apply to the misbehavior, misconduct, or disobedience of any officer of the court in respect to the writs, orders, or process of the court.

SEC. 12. The defendant in any proceeding for contempt of court may file with the court a demand for the retirement of the judge sitting in the proceeding, if the contempt arises from an attack upon the character or conduct of such judge and if the attack occurred elsewhere than in the presence of the court or so near thereto as to interfere directly with the administration of justice. Upon the filing of any such demand the judge shall thereupon proceed no further, but another judge shall be designated in the same manner as is provided by law. The demand shall be filed prior to the hearing in the contempt proceeding.

SEC. 13. When used in this Act, and for the purposes of this Act—

(a) A case shall be held to involve or to grow out of a labor dispute when the case involves persons who are engaged in the same industry, trade, craft, or occupation; or have direct or indirect interests therein; or who are employees of the same employer; or who are members of the same or an affiliated organization of employers or employees; whether such dispute is (1) between one or more employers or associations of employers and one or more employees or associations of employees; (2) between one or more employers or associations of employers and one or more employers or associations of employers; or (3) between one or more employees or associations of employees and one or more employees or associations of employees; or when the case involves any conflicting or competing interests in a "labor dispute" (as hereinafter defined) of "persons participating or interested" (as hereinafter defined).

(b) A person or association shall be held to be a person participating or interested in a labor dispute if relief is sought against him or it, and if he or it is engaged in the same industry, trade, craft, or occupation in which such dispute occurs, or has a direct or indirect interest therein, or is a member, officer, or agent of any association composed in whole or in part of employers or employees engaged in such industry, trade, craft, or occupation.

(c) The term "labor dispute" includes any controversy concerning terms or conditions of employment, or concerning the association or representation of persons in negotiating, fixing, maintaining, changing, or seeking to arrange terms or conditions of employment, regardless of whether or not the disputants stand in the proximate relation of employer and employee.

(d) The term "court of the United States" means any court of the United States whose jurisdiction has been or may be conferred or defined or limited by Act of Congress, including the courts of the District of Columbia.

SEC. 14. If any provision of this Act or the application thereof to any person or circumstance is held unconstitutional or otherwise invalid, the remaining provisions of the Act and the application of such provisions to other persons or circumstances shall not be affected thereby.

Sec. 15. All Acts and parts of Acts in conflict with the provisions of this Act are hereby repealed.

Approved, March 23, 1932.

The National Labor Relations Act of 1935 (Wagner Act)

From 1935 to 1947, the Wagner Act was the major federal law regulating collective bargaining. This law provided for the establishment of the National Labor Relations Board to certify employee representatives for collective bargaining and to prevent five "unfair labor practices" *by management*. These management unfair labor practices were essentially unchanged by the Labor Management Relations Act of 1947.

THE LABOR MANAGEMENT RELATIONS ACT OF 1947 (TAFT-HARTLEY LAW AS AMENDED)

Title I of the Labor Management Relations Act was entitled Amendments to the National Labor Relations Act. The major change was the addition of Section 8(b), unfair labor practices by labor organizations. The Taft-Hartley law also made major procedural changes in National Labor Relations Board operations and added four entirely new titles to collective bargaining law. The Taft-Hartley law has been amended by Public Law 189, 82d Congress, and the Landrum-Griffin law (the Labor Management Reporting and Disclosure Law of 1959). The Taft-Hartley law and its amendments are shown in the text below:

TEXT OF LABOR MANAGEMENT RELATIONS ACT, 1947, AS AMENDED BY PUBLIC LAW 86–257, 1959*

[Public Law 101—80th Congress]

AN ACT

To amend the National Labor Relations Act, to provide additional facilities for the mediation of labor disputes affecting commerce, to equalize legal responsibilities of labor organizations and employers, and for other purposes.

Be it enacted by the Senate and House of Representatives of the United States of America in Congress assembled,

---

* Section 201(d) and (e) of the Labor-Management Reporting and Disclosure Act of 1959 which repealed Section 9(f), (g), and (h) of the Labor Management Relations Act, 1947, and Section 505 amending Section 302(a), (b), and (c) of the Labor Management Relations Act, 1947, took effect upon enactment of Public Law 86–257, September 14, 1959. As to the other amendments of the Labor Management Relations Act, 1947, Section 707 of the Labor-Management Reporting and Disclosure Act provides:

The amendments made by this title shall take effect sixty days after the date of the enactment of this Act and no provision of this title shall be deemed to make an unfair labor practice, any act which is performed prior to such effective date which did not constitute an unfair labor practice prior thereto.

SECTION 1. (a) This Act may be cited as the "Labor Management Relations Act, 1947."

(b) Industrial strife which interferes with the normal flow of commerce and with the full production of articles and commodities for commerce, can be avoided or substantially minimized if employers, employees, and labor organizations each recognize under law one another's legitimate rights in their relations with each other, and above all recognize under law that neither party has any right in its relations with any other to engage in acts or practices which jeopardize the public health, safety, or interest.

It is the purpose and policy of this Act, in order to promote the full flow of commerce, to prescribe the legitimate rights of both employees and employers in their relations affecting commerce, to provide orderly and peaceful procedures for preventing the interference by either with the legitimate rights of the other, to protect the rights of individual employees in their relations with labor organizations whose activities affect commerce, to define and proscribe practices on the part of labor and management which affect commerce and are inimical to the general welfare, and to protect the rights of the public in connection with labor disputes affecting commerce.

TITLE I—AMENDMENT OF NATIONAL LABOR RELATIONS ACT

SEC. 101. The National Labor Relations Act is hereby amended to read as follows:

FINDINGS AND POLICIES

SECTION 1. The denial by some employers of the right of employees to organize and the refusal by some employers to accept the procedure of collective bargaining lead to strikes and other forms of industrial strife or unrest, which have the intent or the necessary effect of burdening or obstructing commerce by (a) impairing the efficiency, safety, or operation of the instrumentalities of commerce; (b) occurring in the current of commerce; (c) materially affecting, restraining, or controlling the flow of raw materials or manufactured or processed goods from or into the channels of commerce, or the prices of such materials or goods in commerce; or (d) causing diminution of employment and wages in such volume as substantially to impair or disrupt the market for goods flowing from or into the channels of commerce.

The inequality of bargaining power between employees who do not possess full freedom of association or actual liberty of contract, and employers who are organized in the corporate or other forms of ownership association substantially burdens and affects the flow of commerce, and tends to aggravate recurrent business depressions, by depressing wage rates and the purchasing power of wage earners in industry and by preventing the stabilization of competitive wage rates and working conditions within and between industries.

Experience has proved that protection by law of the right of employees to organize and bargain collectively safeguards commerce from injury, impairment, or interruption, and promotes the flow of commerce by removing certain recognized sources of industrial strife and unrest, by encouraging practices fundamental to the friendly adjustment of industrial disputes arising out of differences as to wages, hours, or other working conditions, and by restoring equality of bargaining power between employers and employees.

Experience has further demonstrated that certain practices by some labor organizations, their officers, and members have the intent or the necessary effect of burdening or obstructing commerce by preventing the free flow of goods in such commerce through strikes and other forms of industrial unrest or through concerted activities which impair the interest of the public in the free flow of such commerce. The elimination of such practices is a necessary condition to the assurance of the rights herein guaranteed.

It is hereby declared to be the policy of the United States to eliminate the causes of certain substantial obstructions to the free flow of commerce and to mitigate and eliminate these obstructions when they have occurred by encouraging the practice and procedure of collective bargaining and by protecting the exercise by workers of full freedom of association, self-organization, and designation of representatives of their own choosing, for the purpose of negotiating the terms and conditions of their employment or other mutual aid or protection.

DEFINITIONS

SEC. 2. When used in this Act—

(1) The term "person" includes one or more individuals, labor organizations, partnerships, associations, corporations, legal representatives, trustees, trustees in bankruptcy, or receivers.

(2) The term "employer" includes any person acting as an agent of an employer, directly or indirectly, but shall not include the United States or any wholly owned Government corporation, or any Federal Reserve Bank, or any State or political subdivision thereof, or any corporation or association operating a hospital, if no part of the net earnings inures to the benefit of any private shareholder or individual, or any person subject to the Railway Labor Act, as amended from time to time, or any labor organization (other than when acting as an employer), or anyone acting in the capacity of officer or agent of such labor organization.

(3) The term "employee" shall include any employee, and shall not be limited to the employees of a particular employer, unless the Act explicitly states otherwise, and shall include any individual whose work has ceased as a consequence of, or in connection with, any current labor dispute or because of any unfair labor practice, and who has not obtained any other regular and substantially equivalent employment, but shall not include any individual employed as an agricultural laborer, or in the domestic service of any family or person at his home, or any individual employed by his parent or spouse, or any individual having the status of an independent contractor, or any individual employed as a supervisor, or any individual employed by an employer subject to the Railway Labor Act, as amended from time to time, or by any other person who is not an employer as herein defined.

(4) The term "representatives" includes any individual or labor organization.

(5) The term "labor organization" means any organization of any kind, or any agency or employee representation committee or plan, in which employees participate and which exists for the purpose, in whole or in part, of deal-

ing with employers concerning grievances, labor disputes, wages, rates of pay, hours of employment, or conditions of work.

(6) The term "commerce" means trade, traffic, commerce, transportation, or communication among the several States, or between the District of Columbia or any Territory of the United States and any State or other Territory, or between any foreign country and any State, Territory, or the District of Columbia, or within the District of Columbia or any Territory, or between points in the same State but through any other State or any Territory or the District of Columbia or any foreign country.

(7) The term "affecting commerce" means in commerce, or burdening or obstructing commerce or the free flow of commerce, or having led or tending to lead to a labor dispute burdening or obstructing commerce or the free flow of commerce.

(8) The term "unfair labor practice" means any unfair labor practice listed in section 8.

(9) The term "labor dispute" includes any controversy concerning terms, tenure or conditions of employment, or concerning the association or representation of persons in negotiating, fixing, maintaining, changing, or seeking to arrange terms or conditions of employment, regardless of whether the disputants stand in the proximate relation of employer and employee.

(10) The term "National Labor Relations Board" means the National Labor Relations Board provided for in section 3 of this Act.

(11) The term "supervisor" means any individual having authority, in the interest of the employer, to hire, transfer, suspend, lay off, recall, promote, discharge, assign, reward, or discipline other employees, or responsibly to direct them, or to adjust their grievances, or effectively to recommend such action, if in connection with the foregoing the exercise of such authority is not of a merely routine or clerical nature, but requires the use of independent judgment.

(12) The term "professional employee" means—

(a) any employee engaged in work (i) predominantly intellectual and varied in character as opposed to routine mental, manual, mechanical, or physical work; (ii) involving the consistent exercise of discretion and judgment in its performance; (iii) of such a character that the output produced or the result accomplished cannot be standardized in relation to a given period of time; (iv) requiring knowledge of an advanced type in a field of science or learning customarily acquired by a prolonged course of specialized intellectual instruction and study in an institution of higher learning or a hospital, as distinguished from a general academic education or from an apprenticeship or from training in the performance of routine mental, manual, or physical processes; or

(b) any employee, who (i) has completed the courses of specialized intellectual instruction and study described in clause (iv) of paragraph (a), and (ii) is performing related work under the supervision of a professional person to qualify himself to become a professional employee as defined in paragraph (a).

(13) In determining whether any person is acting as an "agent" of another person so as to make such other person responsible for his acts, the question of whether the specific acts performed were actually authorized or subsequently ratified shall not be controlling.

NATIONAL LABOR RELATIONS BOARD

SEC. 3. (a) The National Labor Relations Board (hereinafter called the "Board") created by this Act prior to its amendment by the Labor Management Relations Act, 1947, is hereby continued as an agency of the United States, except that the Board shall consist of five instead of three members, appointed by the President by and with the advice and consent of the Senate. Of the two additional members so provided for, one shall be appointed for a term of five years and the other for a term of two years. Their successors, and the successors of the other members, shall be appointed for terms of five years each, excepting that any individual chosen to fill a vacancy shall be appointed only for the unexpired term of the member whom he shall succeed. The President shall designate one member to serve as Chairman of the Board. Any member of the Board may be removed by the President, upon notice and hearing, for neglect of duty or malfeasance in office, but for no other cause.

(b) The Board is authorized to delegate to any group of three of more members any or all of the powers which it may itself exercise. The Board is also authorized to delegate to its regional directors its powers under section 9 to determine the unit appropriate for the purpose of collective bargaining, to investigate and provide for hearings, and determine whether a question of representation exists, and to direct an election or take a secret ballot under subsection (c) or (e) of section 9 and certify the results thereof, except that upon the filing of a request therefor with the Board by any interested person, the Board may review any action of a regional director delegated to him under this paragraph, but such a review shall not, unless specifically ordered by the Board, operate as a stay of any action taken by the regional director. A vacancy in the Board shall not impair the right of the remaining members to exercise all of the powers of the Board, and three members of the Board shall, at all times, constitute a quorum of the Board, except that two members shall constitute a quorum of any group designated pursuant to the first sentence hereof. The Board shall have an official seal which shall be judicially noticed.

(c) The Board shall at the close of each fiscal year make a report in writing to Congress and to the President stating in detail the cases it has heard, the decisions it has rendered, the names, salaries, and duties of all employees and officers in the employ or under the supervision of the Board, and an account of all moneys it has disbursed.

(d) There shall be a General Counsel of the Board who shall be appointed by the President, by and with the advice and consent of the Senate, for a term of four years. The General Counsel of the Board shall exercise general supervision over all attorneys employed by the Board (other than trial examiners and legal assistants to Board members) and over the officers and employees in the regional offices. He shall have final authority, on behalf of the Board, in respect of the investigation of charges and issuance of complaints under section 10, and in respect of the prosecution of such complaints before the Board, and shall have such other duties as the Board may prescribe or as may be provided by law. In case of a vacancy in the office of the General Counsel the President is authorized to designate the officer or employee who shall act as General Counsel during such vacancy, but no person or persons so designated shall so act (1) for more than forty days when the Congress is in session unless a nomination to fill such vacancy shall have been submitted to the Senate, or (2) after the adjournment *sine die* of the session of the Senate in which such nomination was submitted.

Sec. 4. (a) Each member of the Board and the General Counsel of the Board shall receive a salary of $12,000* a year, shall be eligible for reappointment, and shall not engage in any other business, vocation, or employment. The Board shall appoint an executive secretary, and such attorneys, examiners, and regional directors, and such other employees as it may from time to time find necessary for the proper performance of its duties. The Board may not employ any attorneys for the purpose of reviewing transcripts of hearings or preparing drafts of opinions except that any attorney employed for assignment as a legal assistant to any Board member may for such Board member review such transcripts and prepare such drafts. No trial examiner's report shall be reviewed, either before or after its publication, by any person other than a member of the Board or his legal assistant, and no trial examiner shall advise or consult with the Board with respect to exceptions taken to his findings, rulings, or recommendations. The Board may establish or utilize such regional, local, or other agencies, and utilize such voluntary and uncompensated services, as may from time to time be needed. Attorneys appointed under this section may, at the direction of the Board, appear for and represent the Board in any case in court. Nothing in this Act shall be construed to authorize the Board to appoint individuals for the purpose of conciliation or mediation, or for economic analysis.

(b) All of the expenses of the Board, including all necessary traveling and subsistence expenses outside the District of Columbia incurred by the members or employees of the Board under its orders, shall be allowed and paid on the presentation of itemized vouchers therefor approved by the Board or by any individual it designates for that purpose.

Sec. 5. The principal office of the Board shall be in the District of Columbia, but it may meet and exercise any or all of its powers at any other place. The Board may, by one or more of its members or by such agents or agencies as it may designate, prosecute any inquiry necessary to its functions in any part of the United States. A member who participates in such an inquiry shall not be disqualified from subsequently participating in a decision of the Board in the same case.

Sec. 6. The Board shall have authority from time to time to make, amend, and rescind, in the manner prescribed by the Administrative Procedure Act, such rules and regulations as may be necessary to carry out the provisions of this Act.

RIGHTS OF EMPLOYEES

Sec. 7. Employees shall have the right to self-organization, to form, join, or assist labor organizations, to bargain collectively through representatives of their own choosing, and to engage in other concerted activities for the purpose of collective bargaining or other mutual aid or protection, and shall also have the right to refrain from any or all of such activities except to the extent that such right may be affected by an agreement requiring membership in a labor organization as a condition of employment as authorized in section 8(a) (3).

---

* Pursuant to Public Law 88-426, 88th Congress, 2d Session, Title III, approved August 14, 1964, the salary of the Chairman of the Board shall be $28,500 per year and the salaries of the General Counsel and each Board member shall be $27,000 per year.

UNFAIR LABOR PRACTICES

Sec. 8. (a) It shall be an unfair labor practice for an employer—

(1) to interfere with, restrain, or coerce employees in the exercise of the rights guaranteed in section 7;

(2) to dominate or interfere with the formation or administration of any labor organization or contribute financial or other support to it: *Provided*, That subject to rules and regulations made and published by the Board pursuant to section 6, an employer shall not be prohibited from permitting employees to confer with him during working hours without loss of time or pay;

(3) by discrimination in regard to hire or tenure of employment or any term or condition of employment to encourage or discourage membership in any labor organization: *Provided*, That nothing in this Act, or in any other statute of the United States, shall preclude an employer from making an agreement with a labor organization (not established, maintained, or assisted by any action defined in section 8(a) of this Act as an unfair labor practice) to require as a condition of employment membership therein on or after the thirtieth day following the beginning of such employment or the effective date of such agreement, whichever is the later, (i) if such labor organization is the representative of the employees as provided in section 9(a), in the appropriate collective-bargaining unit covered by such agreement when made, and (ii) unless following an election held as provided in section 9(e) within one year preceding the effective date of such agreement, the Board shall have certified that at least a majority of the employees eligible to vote in such election have voted to rescind the authority of such labor organization to make such an agreement: *Provided further*, That no employer shall justify any discrimination against an employee for nonmembership in a labor organization (A) if he has reasonable grounds for believing that such membership was not available to the employee on the same terms and conditions generally applicable to other members, or (B) if he has reasonable grounds for believing that membership was denied or terminated for reasons other than the failure of the employee to tender the periodic dues and the initiation fees uniformly required as a condition of acquiring or retaining membership;

(4) to discharge or otherwise discriminate against an employee because he has filed charges or given testimony under this Act;

(5) to refuse to bargain collectively with the representatives of his employees, subject to the provisions of section 9(a).

(b) It shall be an unfair labor practice for a labor organization or its agents—

(1) to restrain or coerce (A) employees in the exercise of the rights guaranteed in section 7: *Provided*, That this paragraph shall not impair the right of a labor organization to prescribe its own rules with respect to the acquisition or retention of membership therein; or (B) an employer in the selection of his representatives for the purposes of collective bargaining or the adjustment of grievances;

(2) to cause or attempt to cause an employer to discriminate against an employee in violation of subsection (a)(3) or to discriminate against an employee with respect to whom membership in such organization has been

denied or terminated on some ground other than his failure to tender the periodic dues and the initiation fees uniformly required as a condition of acquiring or retaining membership;

(3) to refuse to bargain collectively with an employer, provided it is the representative of his employees subject to the provisions of section 9(a);

(4) (i) to engage in, or to induce or encourage any individual employed by any person engaged in commerce or in an industry affecting commerce to engage in, a strike or a refusal in the course of his employment to use, manufacture, process, transport, or otherwise handle or work on any goods, articles, materials, or commodities or to perform any services; or (ii) to threaten, coerce, or restrain any person engaged in commerce or in an industry affecting commerce, where in either case an object thereof is:

(A) forcing or requiring any employer or self-employed person to join any labor or employer organization or to enter into an agreement which is prohibited by section 8(e);

(B) forcing or requiring any person to cease using, selling, handling, transporting, or otherwise dealing in the products of any other producer, processor, or manufacturer, or to cease doing business with any other person, or forcing or requiring any other employer to recognize or bargain with a labor organization as the representative of his employees unless such labor organization has been certified as the representative of such employees under the provisions of section 9: *Provided,* That nothing contained in this clause (B) shall be construed to make unlawful, where not otherwise unlawful, any primary strike or primary picketing;

(C) forcing or requiring any employer to recognize or bargain with a particular labor organization as the representative of his employees if another labor organization has been certified as the representative of such employees under the provisions of section 9;

(D) forcing or requiring any employer to assign particular work to employees in a particular labor organization or in a particular trade, craft, or class rather than to employees in another labor organization or in another trade, craft, or class, unless such employer is failing to conform to an order or certification of the Board determining the bargaining representative for employees performing such work:

Provided, That nothing contained in this subsection (b) shall be construed to make unlawful a refusal by any person to enter upon the premises of any employer (other than his own employer), if the employees of such employer are engaged in a strike ratified or approved by a representative of such employees whom such employer is required to recognize under this Act: *Provided further,* That for the purposes of this paragraph (4) only, nothing contained in such paragraph shall be construed to prohibit publicity, other than picketing, for the purpose of truthfully advising the public, including consumers and members of a labor organization, that a product or products are produced by an employer with whom the labor organization has a primary dispute and are distributed by another employer, as long as such publicity does not have an effect of inducing any individual employed by any person other than the primary employer in the course of his employment to refuse to pick up, deliver, or transport any goods, or not to perform any services, at the establishment of the employer engaged in such distribution;

(5) to require of employees covered by an agreement authorized under subsection (a)(3) the payment, as a condition precedent to becoming a member of such organization, of a fee in an amount which the Board finds excessive or discriminatory under all the circumstances. In making such a finding, the Board shall consider, among other relevant factors, the practices and customs of labor organizations in the particular industry, and the wages currently paid to the employees affected;

(6) to cause or attempt to cause an employer to pay or deliver or agree to pay or deliver any money or other thing of value, in the nature of an exaction, for services which are not performed or not to be performed; and

(7) to picket or cause to be picketed, or threaten to picket or cause to be picketed, any employer where an object thereof is forcing or requiring an employer to recognize or bargain with a labor organization as the representative of his employees, or forcing or requiring the employees of an employer to accept or select such labor organization as their collective bargaining representative, unless such labor organization is currently certified as the representative of such employees:

(A) where the employer has lawfully recognized in accordance with this Act any other labor organization and a question concerning representation may not appropriately be raised under section 9(c) of this Act,

(B) where within the preceding twelve months a valid election under section 9(c) of this Act has been conducted, or

(C) where such picketing has been conducted without a petition under section 9(c) being filed within a reasonable period of time not to exceed thirty days from the commencement of such picketing: *Provided,* That when such a petition has been filed the Board shall forthwith, without regard to the provisions of section 9(c)(1) or the absence of a showing of a substantial interest on the part of the labor organization, direct an election in such unit as the Board finds to be appropriate and shall certify the results thereof: *Provided further,* That nothing in this subparagraph (C) shall be construed to prohibit any picketing or other publicity for the purpose of truthfully advising the public (including consumers) that an employer does not employ members of, or have a contract with, a labor organization, unless an effect of such picketing is to induce any individual employed by any other person in the course of his employment, not to pick up, deliver or transport any goods or not to perform any services.
Nothing in this paragraph (7) shall be construed to permit any act which would otherwise be an unfair labor practice under this section 8(b).

(c) The expressing of any views, argument, or opinion, or the dissemination thereof, whether in written, printed, graphic, or visual form, shall not constitute or be evidence of an unfair labor practice under any of the provisions of this Act, if such expression contains no threat of reprisal or force or promise of benefit.

(d) For the purposes of this section, to bargain collectively is the performance of the mutual obligation of the employer and the representative of the employees to meet at reasonable times and confer in good faith with respect to wages, hours, and other terms and conditions of employment, or the negotiation of an agreement, or any question arising thereunder, and the execution of a written contract incorporating any agreement reached if requested by either party, but such obligation does not compel either party to agree to a proposal or require the making of a concession: *Provided,* That where there is in effect a collective-bargaining contract covering employees in an industry affecting commerce, the duty to bargain collectively shall also mean that no party to such contract shall terminate or modify such contract, unless the party desiring such termination or modification—

(1) serves a written notice upon the other party to the contract of the proposed termination or modification sixty days prior to the expiration date thereof, or in the event such contract contains no expiration date, sixty days prior to the time it is proposed to make such termination or modification;

(2) offers to meet and confer with the other party for the purpose of negotiating a new contract or a contract containing the proposed modifications;

(3) notifies the Federal Mediation and Conciliation Service within thirty days after such notice of the existence of a dispute, and simultaneously therewith notifies any State or Territorial agency established to mediate and conciliate disputes within the State or Territory where the dispute occurred, provided no agreement has been reached by that time; and

(4) continues in full force and effect, without resorting to strike or lockout, all the terms and conditions o fthe existing contract for a period of sixty days after such notice is given or until the expiration date of such contract, whichever occurs later:

The duties imposed upon employers, employees, and labor organizations by paragraphs (2), (3), and (4) shall become inapplicable upon an intervening certification of the Board, under which the labor organization or individual, which is a party to the contract, has been superseded as or ceased to be the representative of the employees subject to the provisions of section 9(a), and the duties so imposed shall not be construed as requiring either party to discuss or agree to any modification of the terms and conditions contained in a contract for a fixed period, if such modification is to become effective before such terms and conditions can be reopened under the provisions of the contract. Any employee who engages in a strike within the sixty-day period specified in this subsection shall lose his status as an employee of the employer engaged in the particular labor dispute, for the purposes of section 8, 9, and 10 of this Act, as amended, but such loss of status for such employee shall terminate if and when he is reemployed by such employer.

(e) It shall be an unfair labor practice for any labor organization and any employer to enter into any contract or agreement, express or implied, whereby such employer ceases or refrains or agrees to cease or refrain from handling, using, selling, transporting or otherwise dealing in any of the products of any other employer, or to cease doing business with any other person, and any contract or agreement entered into heretofore or hereafter containing such an agreement shall be to such extent unenforceable and void: *Provided,* That nothing in this subsection (e) shall apply to an agreement between a labor organization and an employer in the construction industry relating to the contracting or subcontracting of work to be done at the site of the construction, alteration, painting, or repair of a building, structure, or other work: *Provided further,* That for the purposes of this subsection (e) and section 8(b)(4)(B) the terms "any employer," "any person engaged in commerce or in industry affecting commerce," and "any person" when used in relation to the terms "any other producer, processor, or manufacturer," "any other employer," or "any other person" shall not include persons in the relation of a jobber, manufacturer, contractor, or subcontractor working on the goods or premises of the jobber or manufacturer or performing parts of an integrated process of production in the apparel and clothing industry: *Provided further,* That nothing in this Act shall prohibit the enforcement of any agreement which is within the foregoing exception.

(f) It shall not be an unfair labor practice under subsections (a) and (b) of this section for an employer engaged primarily in the building and construction industry to make an agreement covering employees engaged (or who, upon their employment, will be engaged) in the building and construction industry with a labor organization of which building and construction employees are members (not established, maintained, or assisted by any action defined in section 8(a) of this Act as an unfair labor practice) because (1) the majority status of such labor organization has not been established under the provisions of section 9 of this Act prior to the making of such agreement, or (2) such agreement requires as a condition of employment, membership in such labor organization after the seventh day following the beginning of such employment or the effective date of the agreement, whichever is later, or (3) such agreement requires the employer to notify such labor organization of opportunities for employment with such employer, or gives such labor organization an opportunity to refer qualified applicants for such employment, or (4) such agreement specifies minimum training or experience qualifications for employment or provides for priority in opportunities for employment based upon length of service with such employer, in the industry or in the particular geographical area: *Provided,* That nothing in this subsection shall set aside the final proviso to section 8(a)(3) of this Act: *Provided further,* That any agreement which would be invalid, but for clause (1) of this subsection, shall not be a bar to a petition filed pursuant to section 9(c) or 9(e).*

REPRESENTATIVES AND ELECTIONS

SEC. 9. (a) Representatives designated or selected for the purposes of collective bargaining by the majority of the employees in a unit appropriate for such purposes, shall be the exclusive representatives of all the employees in such unit for the purposes of collective bargaining in respect to rates of pay, wages, hours of employment, or other conditions of employment: *Provided,* That any individual employee or a group of employees shall have the right at any time to present grievances to their employer and to have such grievances

---

*Section 8(f) is inserted in the Act by subsection (a) of Section 705 of Public Law 86–257. Section 705(b) provides:

Nothing contained in the amendment made by subsection (a) shall be construed as authorizing the execution or application of agreements requiring membership in a labor organization as a condition of employment in any State or Territory in which such execution or application is prohibited by State or Territorial law.

adjusted, without the intervention of the bargaining representative, as long as the adjustment is not inconsistent with the terms of a collective-bargaining contract or agreement then in effect: *Provided further,* That the bargaining representative has been given opportunity to be present at such adjustment.

(b) The Board shall decide in each case whether, in order to assure to employees the fullest freedom in exercising the rights guaranteed by this Act, the unit appropriate for the purposes of collective bargaining shall be the employer unit, craft unit, plant unit, or subdivision thereof: *Provided,* That the Board shall not (1) decide that any unit is appropriate for such purposes if such unit includes both professional employees and employees who are not professional employees unless a majority of such professional employees vote for inclusion in such unit; or (2) decide that any craft unit is inappropriate for such purposes on the ground that a different unit has been established by a prior Board determination, unless a majority of the employees in the proposed craft unit vote against separate representations or (3) decide that any unit is appropriate for such purposes if it includes, together with other employees, any individual employed as a guard to enforce against employees and other persons rules to protect property of the employer or to protect the safety of persons on the employer's premises; but no labor organization shall be certified as the representative of employees in a bargaining unit of guards if such organization admits to membership, or is affiliated directly or indirectly with an organization which admits to membership, employees other than guards.

(c)(1) Wherever a petition shall have been filed, in accordance with such regulations as may be prescribed by the Board—

(A) by an employee or group of employees or any individual or labor organization acting in their behalf alleging that a substantial number of employees (i) wish to be represented for collective bargaining and that their employer declines to recognize their representative as the representative defined in section 9(a), or (ii) assert that the individual or labor organization, which has been certified or is being currently recognized by their employer as the bargaining representative, is no longer a representative as defined in section 9(a); or

(B) by an employer, alleging that one or more individuals or labor organizations have presented to him a claim to be recognized as the representative defined in section 9(a);

the Board shall investigate such petition and if it has reasonable cause to believe that a question of representation affecting commerce exists shall provide for an appropriate hearing upon due notice. Such hearing may be conducted by an officer or employee of the regional office, who shall not make any recommendations with respect thereto. If the Board finds upon the record of such hearing that such a question of representation exists, it shall direct an election by secret ballot and shall certify the results thereof.

(2) In determining whether or not a question of representation affecting commerce exists, the same regulations and rules of decision shall apply irrespective of the identity of the persons filing the petition or the kind of relief sought and in no case shall the Board deny a labor organization a place on the ballot by reason of an order with respect to such labor organization or its predecessor not issued in conformity with section 10(c).

(3) No election shall be directed in any bargaining unit or any subdivision within which, in the preceding twelve-month period, a valid election shall have been held. Employees engaged in an economic strike who are not entitled to reinstatement shall be eligible to vote under such regulations as the Board shall find are consistent with the purposes and provisions of this Act in any election conducted within twelve months after the commencement of the strike. In any election where none of the choices on the ballot receives a majority, a run-off shall be conducted, the ballot providing for a selection between the two choices receiving the largest and second largest number of valid votes cast in the election.

(4) Nothing in this section shall be construed to prohibit the waiving of hearings by stipulation for the purpose of a consent election in conformity with regulations and rules of decision of the Board.

(5) In determining whether a unit is appropriate for the purposes specified in subsection (b) the extent to which the employees have organized shall not be controlling.

(d) Whenever an order of the Board made pursuant to section 10(c) is based in whole or in part upon facts certified following an investigation pursuant to subsection (c) of this section and there is a petition for the enforcement or review of such order, such certification and the record of such investigation shall be included in the transcript of the entire record required to be filed under section 10(e) or 10(f), and thereupon the decree of the court enforcing, modifying, or setting aside in whole or in part the order of the Board shall be made and entered upon the pleadings, testimony, and proceedings set forth in such transcript.

(e)(1) Upon the filing with the Board, by 30 per centum or more of the employees in a bargaining unit covered by an agreement between their employer and a labor organization made pursuant to section 8(a)(3), of a petition alleging they desire that such authority be rescinded, the Board shall take a secret ballot of the employees in such unit and certify the results thereof to such labor organization and to the employer.

(2) No election shall be conducted pursuant to this subsection in any bargaining unit or any subdivision within which, in the preceding twelve-month period, a valid election shall have been held.

PREVENTION OF UNFAIR LABOR PRACTICES

SEC. 10. (a) The Board is empowered, as hereinafter provided, to prevent any person from engaging in any unfair labor practice (listed in section 8) affecting commerce. This power shall not be affected by any other means of adjustment or prevention that has been or may be established by agreement, law, or otherwise: *Provided,* That the Board is empowered by agreement with any agency of any State or Territory to cede to such agency jurisdiction over any cases in any industry (other than mining, manufacturing, communications, and transportation except where predominantly local in character) even though such cases may involve labor disputes affecting commerce, unless the provision of the State or Territorial statute applicable to the determination oi such cases by such agency is inconsistent with the corresponding provision of this Act or has received a construction inconsistent therewith.

(b) Whenever it is charged that any person has engaged in or is engaging in any such unfair labor practice, the Board, or any agent or agency designated by the Board for such purposes, shall have power to issue and cause to be served upon such person a complaint stating the charges in that respect, and containing a notice of hearing before the Board or a member thereof, or before a designated agent or agency, at a place therein fixed, not less than five days after the serving of said complaint: *Provided,* That no complaint shall issue based upon any unfair labor practice occurring more than six months prior to the filing of the charge with the Board and the service of a copy thereof upon the person against whom such charge is made, unless the person aggrieved thereby was prevented from filing such charge by reason of service in the armed forces, in which event the six-month period shall be computed from the day of his discharge. Any such complaint may be amended by the member, agent, or agency conducting the hearing or the Board in its discretion at any time prior to the issuance of an order based thereon. The person so complained of shall have the right to file an answer to the original or amended complaint and to appear in person or otherwise and give testimony at the place and time fixed in the complaint. In the discretion of the member, agent, or agency conducting the hearing or the Board, any other person may be allowed to intervene in the said proceeding and to present testimony. Any such proceeding shall, so far as practicable, be conducted in accordance with the rules of evidence applicable in the district courts of the United States under the rules of civil procedure for the district courts of the United States, adopted by the Supreme Court of the United States pursuant to the Act of June 19, 1934 (U.S.C., title 28, secs. 723-B, 723-C).

(c) The testimony taken by such member, agent, or agency or the Board shall be reduced to writing and filed with the Board. Thereafter, in its discretion, the Board upon notice may take further testimony or hear argument. If upon the preponderance of the testimony taken the Board shall be of the opinion that any person named in the complaint has engaged in or is engaging in any such unfair labor practice, then the Board shall state its findings of fact and shall issue and cause to be served on such person an order requiring such person to cease and desist from such unfair labor practice, and to take such affirmative action including reinstatement of employees with or without back pay, as will effectuate the policies of this Act: *Provided,* That where an order directs reinstatement of an employee, back pay may be required of the employer or labor organization, as the case may be, responsible for the discrimination suffered by him: *And provided further,* That in determining whether a complaint shall issue alleging a violation of section 8(a)(1) or section 8(a)(2), and in deciding such cases, the same regulations and rules of decision shall apply irrespective of whether or not the labor organization affected is affiliated with a labor organization national or international in scope. Such order may further require such person to make reports from time to time showing the extent to which it has complied with the order. If upon the preponderance of the testimony taken the Board shall not be of the opinion that the person named in the complaint has engaged in or is engaging in any such unfair labor practice, then the Board shall state its findings of fact and shall issue an order dismissing the said complaint. No order of the Board shall require the reinstatement of any individual as an employee who has been suspended or discharged, or the payment to him of any back pay, if such individual was suspended or discharged for cause. In case the evidence is presented before a member of the Board, or before an examiner or examiners thereof, such member, or such examiner or examiners, as the case may be, shall issue and cause to be served on the parties to the proceeding a proposed report, together with a recommended order, which shall be filed with the Board, and if no exceptions are filed within twenty days after service thereof upon such parties, or within such further period as the Board may authorize, such recommended order shall become the order of the Board and become effective as therein prescribed.

(d) Until the record in a case shall have been filed in a court, as hereinafter provided, the Board may at any time, upon reasonable notice and in such manner as it shall deem proper, modify or set aside, in whole or in part, and finding or order made or issued by it.

(e) The Board shall have power to petition any court of appeals of the United States, or if all the courts of appeals to which application may be made are in vacation, any district court of the United States, within any circuit or district, respectively, wherein the unfair labor practice in question occurred or wherein such person resides or transacts business, for the enforcement of such order and for appropriate temporary relief or restraining order, and shall file in the court the record in the proceedings, as provided in section 2112 of title 28, United States Code. Upon the filing of such petition, the court shall cause notice thereof to be served upon such person, and thereupon shall have jurisdiction of the proceeding and of the question determined therein, and shall have power to grant such temporary relief or restraining order as it deems just and proper, and to make and enter a decree enforcing, modifying, and enforcing as so modified, or setting aside in whole or in part the order of the Board. No objection that has not been urged before the Board, its member, agent, or agency, shall be considered by the court, unless the failure or neglect to urge such objection shall be excused because of extraordinary circumstances. The findings of the Board with respect to questions of fact if supported by substantial evidence on the record considered as a whole shall be conclusive. If either party shall apply to the court for leave to adduce additional evidence and shall show to the satisfaction of the court that such additional evidence is material and that there were reasonable grounds for the failure to adduce such evidence in the hearing before the Board, its member, agent, or agency, the court may order such additional evidence to be taken before the Board, its member, agent, or agency, and to be made a part of the record. The Board may modify its findings as to the facts, or make new findings, by reason of additional evidence so taken and filed, and it shall file such modified or new findings, which findings with respect to questions of fact if supported by substantial evidence on the record considered as a whole shall be conclusive, and shall file its recommendations, if any, for the modification or setting aside of its original order. Upon the filing of the record with it the jurisdiction of the court shall be exclusive and its judgment and decree shall be final, except that the same shall be subject to review by the appropriate United States court of appeals if application was made to the district court as hereinabove provided, and by the Supreme Court of the United States upon writ of certiorari or certification as provided in section 1254 of title 28.

(f) Any person aggrieved by a final order of the Board granting or denying in whole or in part the relief sought may obtain a review of such order in any circuit court of appeals of the United States in the circuit wherein the unfair labor practice in question was alleged to have been engaged in or wherein such person resides or transacts business, or in the United States Court of Appeals for the District of Columbia, by filing in such court a written petition praying that the order of the Board be modified or set aside. A copy of such petition shall be forthwith transmitted by the clerk of the court to the Board, and thereupon the aggrieved party shall file in the court the record in the proceeding, certified by the Board, as provided in section 2112 of title 28, United States Code. Upon the filing of such petition, the court shall proceed in the same manner as in the case of an application by the Board under subsection (e) of this section, and shall have the same jurisdiction to grant to the Board such temporary relief or restraining order as it deems just and proper, and in like manner to make and enter a decree enforcing, modifying, and enforcing as so modified, or setting aside in whole or in part the order of the Board; the findings of the Board with respect to questions of fact if supported by substantial evidence on the record considered as a whole shall in like manner be conclusive.

(g) The commencement of proceedings under section (e) or (f) of this section shall not, unless specifically ordered by the court, operate as a stay of the Board's order.

(h) When granting appropriate temporary relief or a restraining order, or making and entering a decree enforcing, modifying, and enforcing as so modified, or setting aside in whole or in part an order of the Board, as provided in this section, the jurisdiction of courts sitting in equity shall not be limited by the Act entitled "An Act to amend the Judicial Code and to define and limit the jurisdiction of courts sitting in equity, and for other purposes," approved March 23, 1932 (U.S.C., Supp. VII, title 29, secs. 101–115).

(i) Petitions filed under this Act shall be heard expeditiously, and if possible within ten days after they have been docketed.

(j) The Board shall have power, upon issuance of a complaint as provided in subsection (b) charging that any person has engaged in or is engaging in an unfair labor practice, to petition any district court of the United States (including the District Court of the United States for the District of Columbia), within any district wherein the unfair labor practice in question is alleged to have occurred or wherein such person resides or transacts business, for appropriate temporary relief or restraining order. Upon the filing of any such petition the court shall cause notice thereof to be served upon such person, and thereupon shall have jurisdiction to grant to the Board such temporary relief or restraining order as it deems just and proper.

(k) Whenever it is charged that any person has engaged in an unfair labor practice within the meaning of paragraph (4)(D) of section 8(b), the Board is empowered and directed to hear and determine the dispute out of which such unfair labor practice shall have arisen, unless, within ten days after notice that such charge has been filed, the parties to such dispute submit to the Board satisfactory evidence that they have adjusted, or agreed upon methods for the voluntary adjustment of, the dispute. Upon compliance by the parties to the dispute with the decision of the Board or upon such voluntary adjustment of the dispute, such charge shall be dismissed.

(l) Whenever it is charged that any person has engaged in an unfair labor practice within the meaning of paragraph (4) (A), (B), or (C) of section

8(b), or section 8(e) or section 8(b)(7), the preliminary investigation of such charge shall be made forthwith and given priority over all other cases except cases of like character in the office where it is filed or to which it is referred. If, after such investigation, the officer or regional attorney to whom the matter may be referred has reasonable cause to believe such charge is true and that a complaint should issue, he shall, on behalf of the Board, petition any district court of the United States (including the District Court of the United States for the District of Columbia) within any district where the unfair labor practice in question has occurred, is alleged to have occurred, or wherein such person resides or transacts business, for appropriate injunctive relief pending the final adjudication of the Board with respect to such matter. Upon the filing of any such petition the district court shall have jurisdiction to grant such injunctive relief or temporary restraining order as it deems just and proper, notwithstanding any other provision of law: *Provided further,* That no temporary restraining order shall be issued without notice unless a petition alleges that substantial and irreparable injury to the charging party will be unavoidable and such temporary restraining order shall be effective for no longer than five days and will become void at the expiration of such period: *Provided further,* That such officer or regional attorney shall not apply for any restraining order under section 8(b)(7) if a charge against the employer under section 8(a)(2) has been filed and after the preliminary investigation, he has reasonable cause to believe that such charge is true and that a complaint should issue. Upon filing of any such petition the courts shall cause notice thereof to be served upon any person involved in the charge and such person, including the charging party, shall be given an opportunity to appear by counsel and present any relevant testimony: *Provided further,* That for the purposes of this subsection district courts shall be deemed to have jurisdiction of a labor organization (1) in the district in which such organization maintains its principal office, or (2) in any district in which its duly authorized officers or agents are engaged in promoting or protecting the interests of employee members. The service of legal process upon such officer or agent shall constitute service upon the labor organization and make such organizations a party to the suit. In situations where such relief is appropriate the procedure specified herein shall apply to charges with respect to section 8(b)(4)(D).

(m) Whenever it is charged that any person has engaged in an unfair labor practice within the meaning of subsection (a)(3) or (b)(2) of section 8, such charge shall be given priority over all other cases except cases of like character in the office where it is filed or to which it is referred and cases given priority under subsection (1).

INVESTIGATORY POWERS

SEC. 11. For the purpose of all hearings and investigations, which, in the opinion of the Board, are necessary and proper for the exercise of the powers vested in it by section 9 and section 10—

(1) The Board, or its duly authorized agents or agencies, shall at all reasonable times have access to, for the purpose of examination, and the right to copy any evidence of any person being investigated or proceeded against that relates to any matter under investigation or in question. The Board, or any member thereof, shall upon application of any party to such proceedings, forthwith issue to such party subpenas requiring the attendance and testimony of

witnesses or the production of any evidence in such proceeding or investigation requested in such application. Within five days after the service of a subpena on any person requiring the production of any evidence in his possession or under his control, such person may petition the Board to revoke, and the Board shall revoke, such subpena if in its opinion the evidence whose production is required does not relate to any matter under investigation, or any matter in question in such proceedings, or if in its opinion such subpena does not describe with sufficient particularity the evidence whose production is required. Any member of the Board, or any agent or agency designated by the Board for such purposes, may administer oaths and affirmations, examine witnesses, and receive evidence. Such attendance of witnesses and the production of such evidence may be required from any place in the United States or any Territory or possession thereof, at any designated place of hearing.

(2) In case of contumacy or refusal to obey a subpena issued to any person, any district court of the United States or the United States courts of any Territory or possession, or the District Court of the United States for the District of Columbia, within the jurisdiction of which the inquiry is carried on or within the jurisdiction of which said person guilty of contumacy or refusal to obey is found or resides or transacts business, upon application by the Board shall have jurisdiction to issue to such person an order requiring such person to appear before the Board, its member, agent, or agency, there to produce evidence if so ordered, or there to give testimony touching the matter under investigation or in question; and any failure to obey such order of the court may be punished by said court as a contempt thereof.

(3) No person shall be excused from attending and testifying or from producing books, records, correspondence, documents, or other evidence in obedience to the subpena of the Board, on the ground that the testimony or evidence required of him may tend to incriminate him or subject him to a penalty or forfeiture; but no individual shall be prosecuted or subjected to any penalty or forfeiture for or on account of any transaction, matter, or thing concerning which he is compelled, after having claimed his privilege against self-incrimination, to testify or produce evidence, except that such individual so testifying shall not be exempt from prosecution and punishment for perjury committed in so testifying.

(4) Complaints, orders, and other process and papers of the Board, its member, agent, or agency, may be served either personally or by registered mail or by telegraph or by leaving a copy thereof at the principal office or place of business of the person required to be served. The verified return by the individual so serving the same setting forth the manner of such service shall be proof of the same, and the return post office receipt or telegraph receipt therefor when registered and mailed or telegraphed as aforesaid shall be proof of service of the same. Witnesses summoned before the Board, its member, agent, or agency, shall be paid the same fees and mileage that are paid witnesses in the courts of the United States, and witnesses whose depositions are taken and the persons taking the same shall severally be entitled to the same fees as are paid for like services in the courts of the United States.

(5) All process of any court to which application may be made under this Act may be served in the judicial district wherein the defendant or other person required to be served resides or may be found.

(6) The several departments and agencies of the Government, when

directed by the President, shall furnish the Board, upon its request, all records, papers, and information in their possession relating to any matter before the Board.

SEC. 12. Any person who shall willfully resist, prevent, impede, or interfere with any member of the Board or any of its agents or agencies in the performance of duties pursuant to this Act shall be punished by a fine of not more than $5,000 or by imprisonment for not more than one year, or both.

LIMITATIONS

SEC. 13. Nothing in this Act, except as specifically provided for herein, shall be construed so as either to interfere with or impede or diminish in any way the right to strike, or to affect the limitations or qualifications on that right.

SEC. 14. (a) Nothing herein shall prohibit any individual employed as a supervisor from becoming or remaining a member of a labor organization, but no employer subject to this Act shall be compelled to deem individuals defined herein as supervisors as employees for the purpose of any law, either national or local, relating to collective bargaining.

(b) Nothing in this Act shall be construed as authorizing the execution or application of agreements requiring membership in a labor organization as a condition of employment in any State or Territory in which such execution or application is prohibited by State or Territorial law.

(c)(1) The Board, in its discretion, may, by rule of decision or by published rules adopted pursuant to the Administrative Procedure Act, decline to assert jurisdiction over any labor dispute involving any class or category of employees, where, in the opinion of the Board, the effect of such labor dispute on commerce is not sufficiently substantial to warrant the exercise of its jurisdiction: *Provided*, That the Board shall not decline to assert jurisdiction over any labor dispute over which it would assert jurisdiction under the standards prevailing upon August 1, 1959.

(2) Nothing in this Act shall be deemed to prevent or bar any agency or the courts of any State or Territory (including the Commonwealth of Puerto Rico, Guam, and the Virgin Islands), from assuming and asserting jurisdiction over labor disputes over which the Board declines, pursuant to paragraph (1) of this subsection, to assert jurisdiction.

SEC. 15. Whenever the application of the provisions of section 272 of chapter 10 of the Act entitled "An Act to establish a uniform system of bankruptcy throughout the United States," approved July 1, 1898, and Acts amendatory thereof and supplementary thereto (U.S.C., title 11, sec. 672), conflicts with the application of the provisions of this Act, this Act shall prevail: *Provided*, That in any situation where the provisions of this Act cannot be validly enforced, the provisions of such other Acts shall remain in full force and effect.

SEC. 16. If any provision of this Act, or the application of such provision to any person or circumstances, shall be held invalid, the remainder of this Act, or the application of such provision to persons or circumstances other than those as to which it is held invalid, shall not be affected thereby.

SEC. 17. This Act may be cited as the "National Labor Relations Act."

SEC. 18. No petition entertained, no investigation made, no election held, and no certification issued by the National Labor Relations Board, under any of the provisions of section 9 of the National Labor Relations Act, as amended, shall be invalid by reason of the failure of the Congress of Industrial Organizations to have complied with the requirements of section 9(f), (g), or (h) of the aforesaid Act prior to December 22, 1949, or by reason of the failure of the American Federation of Labor to have complied with the provisions of section 9(f), (g), or (h) of the aforesaid Act prior to November 7, 1947: *Provided,* That no liability shall be imposed under any provision of this Act upon any person for failure to honor any election or certificate referred to above, prior to the effective date of this amendment: *Provided, however,* That this proviso shall not have the effect of setting aside or in any way affecting judgments or decrees heretofore entered under section 10(e) or (f) and which have become final.

EFFECTIVE DATE OF CERTAIN CHANGES*

Sec. 102. No provision of this title shall be deemed to make an unfair labor practice any act which was performed prior to the date of the enactment of this Act which did not constitute an unfair labor practice prior thereto, and the provisions of section 8(a)(3) and section 8(b)(2) of the National Labor Relations Act as amended by this title shall not make an unfair labor practice the performance of any obligation under a collective-bargaining agreement entered into prior to the date of the enactment of this Act, or (in the case of an agreement for a period of not more than one year) entered into on or after such date of enactment, but prior to the effective date of this title, if the performance of such obligation would not have constituted an unfair labor practice under section 8(3) of the National Labor Relations Act prior to the effective date of this title, unless such agreement was renewed or extended subsequent thereto.

Sec. 103. No provisions of this title shall affect any certification of representatives or any determination as to the appropriate collective-bargaining unit, which was made under section 9 of the National Labor Relations Act prior to the effective date of this title until one year after the date of such certification or if, in respect of any such certification, a collective-bargaining contract was entered into prior to the effective date of this title, until the end of the contract period or until one year after such date, whichever first occurs.

Sec. 104. The amendments made by this title shall take effect sixty days after the date of the enactment of this Act, except that the authority of the President to appoint certain officers conferred upon him by section 3 of the National Labor Relations Act as amended by this title may be exercised forthwith.

TITLE II—
CONCILIATION OF LABOR DISPUTES IN INDUSTRIES AFFECTING COMMERCE; NATIONAL EMERGENCIES

Sec. 201. That it is the policy of the United States that—

(a) sound and stable industrial peace and the advancement of the general welfare, health, and safety of the Nation and of the best interest

---

* The effective date referred to in Sections 102, 103, and 104 is August 22, 1947. For effective dates of 1959 amendments, see footnote on first page of this text.

of employers and employees can most satisfactorily be secured by the settlement of issues between employers and employees through the processes of conference and collective bargaining between employers and the representatives of their employees;

(b) the settlement of issues between employers and employees through collective bargaining may be advanced by making available full and adequate governmental facilities for conciliation, mediation, and voluntary arbitration to aid and encourage employers and the representatives of their employees to reach and maintain agreements concerning rates of pay, hours, and working conditions, and to make all reasonable efforts to settle their differences by mutual agreement reached through conferences and collective bargaining or by such methods as may be provided for in any applicable agreement for the settlement of disputes; and

(c) certain controversies which arise between parties to collective-bargaining agreements may be avoided or minimized by making available full and adequate governmental facilities for furnishing assistance to employers and the representatives of their employees in formulating for inclusion within such agreements provision for adequate notice of any proposed changes in the terms of such agreements, for the final adjustment of grievances or questions regarding the application or interpretation of such agreements, and other provisions designed to prevent the subsequent arising of such controversies.

SEC. 202. (a) There is hereby created an independent agency to be known as the Federal Mediation and Conciliation Service (herein referred to as the "service," except that for sixty days after the date of the enactment of this Act such term shall refer to the Conciliation Service of the Department of Labor). The Service shall be under the direction of a Federal Mediation and Conciliation Director (hereinafter referred to as the "Director"), who shall be appointed by the President by and with the advice and consent of the Senate. The Director shall receive compensation at the rate of $12,000* per annum. The Director shall not engage in any other business, vocation, or employment.

(b) The Director is authorized, subject to the civil-service laws, to appoint such clerical and other personnel as may be necessary for the execution of the functions of the Service, and shall fix their compensation in accordance with the Classification Act of 1923, as amended, and may, without regard to the provisions of the civil-service laws and the Classification Act of 1923, as amended, appoint and fix the compensation of such conciliators and mediators as may be necessary to carry out the functions of the Service. The Director is authorized to make such expenditures for supplies, facilities, and services as he deems necessary. Such expenditures shall be allowed and paid upon presentation of itemized vouchers therefor approved by the Director or by any employee designated by him for that purpose.

(c) The principal office of the Service shall be in the District of Columbia, but the Director may establish regional offices convenient to localities in

---

* Pursuant to Public Law 88–426, 88th Congress, 2d Session, Title III, approved August 14, 1964, the salary of the Director shall be $27,000 per year.

which labor controversies are likely to arise. The Director may by order, subject to revocation at any time, delegate any authority and discretion conferred upon him by this Act to any regional director, or other officer or employee of the Service. The Director may establish suitable procedures for cooperation with State and local mediation agencies. The Director shall make an annual report in writing to Congress at the end of the fiscal year.

(d) All mediation and conciliation functions of the Secretary of Labor or the United States Conciliation Service under section 8 of the Act entitled "An Act to create a Department of Labor," approved March 4, 1913 (U.S.C., title 29, sec. 51), and all functions of the United States Conciliation Service under any other law are hereby transferred to the Federal Mediation and Conciliation Service, together with the personnel and records of the United States Conciliation Service. Such transfer shall take effect upon the sixtieth day after the date of enactment of this Act. Such transfer shall not affect any proceedings pending before the United States Conciliation Service or any certification, order, rule, or regulation theretofore made by it or by the Secretary of Labor. The Director and the Service shall not be subject in any way to the jurisdiction or authority of the Secretary of Labor or any official or division of the Department of Labor.

FUNCTIONS OF THE SERVICE

SEC. 203. (a) It shall be the duty of the Service, in order to prevent or minimize interruptions of the free flow of commerce growing out of labor disputes, to assist parties to labor disputes in industries affecting commerce to settle such disputes through conciliation and mediation.

(b) The Service may proffer its services in any labor dispute in any industry affecting commerce, either upon its own motion or upon the request of one or more of the parties to the dispute, whenever in its judgment such dispute threatens to cause a substantial interruption of commerce. The Director and the Service are directed to avoid attempting to mediate disputes which would have only a minor effect on interstate commerce if State or other conciliation services are available to the parties. Whenever the Service does proffer its services in any dispute, it shall be the duty of the Service promptly to put itself in communication with the parties and to use its best efforts, by mediation and conciliation, to bring them to agreement.

(c) If the Director is not able to bring the parties to agreement by conciliation within a reasonable time, he shall seek to induce the parties voluntarily to seek other means of settling the dispute without resort to strike, lockout, or other coercion, including submission to the employees in the bargaining unit of the employer's last offer of settlement for approval or rejection in a secret ballot. The failure or refusal of either party to agree to any procedure suggested by the Director shall not be deemed a violation of any duty or obligation imposed by this Act.

(d) Final adjustment by a method agreed upon by the parties is hereby declared to be the desirable method for settlement of grievance disputes arising over the application or interpretation of an existing collective-bargaining agreement. The Service is directed to make its conciliation and mediation services available in the settlement of such grievance disputes only as a last resort and in exceptional cases.

Sec. 204. (a) In order to prevent or minimize interruptions of the free flow of commerce growing out of labor disputes, employers and employees and their representatives, in any industry affecting commerce, shall—

(1) exert every reasonable effort to make and maintain agreements concerning rates of pay, hours, and working conditions, including provision for adequate notice of any proposed change in the terms of such agreements;

(2) whenever a dispute arises over the terms or application of a collective-bargaining agreement and a conference is requested by a party or prospective party thereto, arrange promptly for such a conference to be held and endeavor in such conference to settle such dispute expeditiously; and

(3) in case such dispute is not settled by conference, participate fully and promptly in such meetings as may be undertaken by the Service under this Act for the purpose of aiding in a settlement of the dispute.

Sec. 205. (a) There is hereby created a National Labor-Management Panel which shall be composed of twelve members appointed by the President, six of whom shall be selected from among persons outstanding in the field of management and six of whom shall be selected from among persons outstanding in the field of labor. Each member shall hold office for a term of three years, except that any member appointed to fill a vacancy occurring prior to the expiration of the term for which his predecessor was appointed shall be appointed for the remainder of such term, and the terms of office of the members first taking office shall expire, as designated by the President at the time of appointment, four at the end of the first year, four at the end of the second year, and four at the end of the third year after the date of appointment. Members of the panel, when serving on business of the panel, shall be paid compensation at the rate of $25 per day, and shall also be entitled to receive an allowance for actual and necessary travel and subsistence expenses while so serving away from their places of residence.

(b) It shall be the duty of the panel, at the request of the Director, to advise in the avoidance of industrial controversies and the manner in which mediation and voluntary adjustment shall be administered, particularly with reference to controversies affecting the general welfare of the country.

NATIONAL EMERGENCIES

Sec. 206. Whenever in the opinion of the President of the United States, a threatened or actual strike or lock-out affecting an entire industry or a substantial part thereof engaged in trade, commerce, transportation, transmission, or communication among the several States or with foreign nations, or engaged in the production of goods for commerce, will, if permitted to occur or to continue, imperil the national health or safety, he may appoint a board of inquiry to inquire into the issues involved in the dispute and to make a written report to him within such time as he shall prescribe. Such report shall include a statement of the facts with respect to the dispute, including each party's statement of its position but shall not contain any recommendations. The President shall file a copy of such report with the Service and shall make its contents available to the public.

Sec. 207. (a) A board of inquiry shall be composed of a chairman and such other members as the President shall determine, and shall have power to sit and act in any place within the United States and to conduct such hearings either in public or in private, as it may deem necessary or proper, to ascertain the facts with respect to the causes and circumstances of the dispute.

(b) Members of a board of inquiry shall receive compensation at the rate of $50 for each day actually spent by them in the work of the board, together with necessary travel and subsistence expenses.

(c) For the purpose of any hearing or inquiry conducted by any board appointed under this title, the provisions of sections 9 and 10 (relating to the attendance of witnesses and the production of books, papers, and documents) of the Federal Trade Commission Act of September 16, 1914, as amended (U.S.C. 19, title 15, secs. 49 and 50, as amended), are hereby made applicable to the powers and duties of such board.

Sec. 208.(a) Upon receiving a report from a board of inquiry the President may direct the Attorney General to petition any district court of the United States having jurisdiction of the parties to enjoin such strike or lock-out or the continuing thereof, and if the court finds that such threatened or actual strike or lock-out—

(i) affects an entire industry or a substantial part thereof engaged in trade, commerce, transportation, transmission, or communication among the several States or with foreign nations, or engaged in the production of goods for commerce; and

(ii) if permitted to occur or to continue, will imperil the national health or safety, it shall have jurisdiction to enjoin any such strike or lock-out, or the continuing thereof, and to make such other orders as may be appropriate.

(b) In any case, the provisions of the Act of March 23, 1932, entitled "An Act to amend the Judicial Code and to define and limit the jurisdiction of courts sitting in equity, and for other purposes," shall not be applicable.

(c) The order or orders of the court shall be subject to review by the appropriate circuit court of appeals and by the Supreme Court upon writ of certiorari or certification as provided in sections 239 and 240 of the Judicial Code, as amended (U.S.C., title 29, secs. 346 and 347).

Sec. 209. (a) Whenever a district court has issued an order under section 208 enjoining acts or practices which imperil or threaten to imperil the national health or safety, it shall be the duty of the parties to the labor dispute giving rise to such order to make every effort to adjust and settle their differences, with the assistance of the Service created by this Act. Neither party shall be under any duty to accept, in whole or in part, any proposal of settlement made by the Service.

(b) Upon the issuance of such order, the President shall reconvene the board of inquiry which has previously reported with respect to the dispute. At the end of a sixty-day period (unless the dispute has been settled by that time), the board of inquiry shall report to the President the current position of the parties and the efforts which have been made for settlement, and shall include a statement by each party of its position and a statement of the employer's last offer of settlement. The President shall make such report available to the public.

The National Labor Relations Board, within the succeeding fifteen days, shall take a secret ballot of the employees of each employer involved in the dispute on the question of whether they wish to accept the final offer of settlement made by their employer as stated by him and shall certify the results thereof to the Attorney General within five days thereafter.

SEC. 210. Upon the certification of the results of such ballot or upon a settlement being reached, whichever happens sooner, the Attorney General shall move the court to discharge the injunction, which motion shall then be granted and the injunction discharged. When such motion is granted, the President shall submit to the Congress a full and comprehensive report of the proceedings, including the findings of the board of inquiry and the ballot taken by the National Labor Relations Board, together with such recommendations as he may see fit to make for consideration and appropriate action.

COMPILATION OF COLLECTIVE-BARGAINING AGREEMENTS, ETC.

SEC. 211. (a) For the guidance and information of interested representatives of employers, employees, and the general public, the Bureau of Labor Statistics of the Department of Labor shall maintain a file of copies of all available collective-bargaining agreements and other available agreements and actions thereunder settling or adjusting labor disputes. Such file shall be open to inspection under appropriate conditions prescribed by the Secretary of Labor, except that no specific information submitted in confidence shall be disclosed.

(b) The Bureau of Labor Statistics in the Department of Labor is authorized to furnish upon request of the Service, or employers, employees, or their representatives, all available data and factual information which may aid in the settlement of any labor dispute, except that no specific information submitted in confidence shall be disclosed.

EXEMPTION OF RAILWAY LABOR ACT

SEC. 212. The provisions of this title shall not be applicable with respect to any matter which is subject to the provisions of the Railway Labor Act, as amended from time to time.

TITLE III

SUITS BY AND AGAINST LABOR ORGANIZATIONS

SEC. 301. (a) Suits for violation of contracts between an employer and a labor organization representing employees in an industry affecting commerce as defined in this Act, or between any such labor organizations, may be brought in any district court of the United States having jurisdiction of the parties, without respect to the amount in controversy or without regard to the citizenship of the parties.

(b) Any labor organization which represents employees in an industry affecting commerce as defined in this Act and any employer whose activities affect commerce as defined in this Act shall be bound by the acts of its agents. Any such labor organization may sue or be sued as an entity and in behalf of the employees whom it represents in the courts of the United States. Any money judgment against a labor organization in a district court of the United States shall be enforceable only against the organization as an entity and against its assets, and shall not be enforceable against any individual member or his assets.

(c) For the purposes of actions and proceedings by or against labor organizations in the district courts of the United States, district courts shall be deemed to have jurisdiction of a labor organization (1) in the district in which such organization maintains its principal offices, or (2) in any district in which its duly authorized officers or agents are engaged in representing or acting for employee members.

(d) The service of summons, subpena, or other legal process of any court of the United States upon an officer or agent of a labor organization, in his capacity as such, shall constitute service upon the labor organization.

(e) For the purposes of this section, in determining whether any person is acting as an "agent" of another person so as to make such other person responsible for his acts, the question of whether the specific acts performed were actually authorized or subsequently ratified shall not be controlling.

RESTRICTIONS ON PAYMENTS TO EMPLOYEE REPRESENTATIVES

SEC. 302. (a) It shall be unlawful for any employer or association of employers or any person who acts as a labor relations expert, adviser, or consultant to an employer or who acts in the interest of an employer to pay, lend, or deliver, or agree to pay, lend, or deliver, any money or other thing of value—

(1) to any representative of any of his employees who are employed in an industry affecting commerce; or

(2) to any labor organization, or any officer or employee thereof, which represents, seeks to represent, or would admit to membership, any of the employees of such employer who are employed in an industry affecting commerce; or

(3) to any employee or group or committee of employees of such employer employed in an industry affecting commerce in excess of their normal compensation for the purpose of causing such employee or group or committee directly or indirectly to influence any other employees in the exercise of the right to organize and bargain collectively through representatives of their own choosing; or

(4) to any officer or employee of a labor organization engaged in an industry affecting commerce with intent to influence him in respect to any of his actions, decisions, or duties as a representative of employees or as such officer or employee of such labor organization.

(b)(1) It shall be unlawful for any person to request, demand, receive, or accept, or agree to receive or accept, any payment, loan, or delivery of any money or other thing of value prohibited by subsection (a).

(2) It shall be unlawful for any labor organization, or for any person acting as an officer, agent, representative, or employee of such labor organization, to demand or accept from the operator of any motor vehicle (as defined in part II of the Interstate Commerce Act) employed in the transportation of property in commerce, or the employer of any such operator, any money or other thing of value payable to such organization or to an officer, agent, representative or employee thereof as a fee or charge for the unloading, or the connection with the unloading, of the cargo of such vehicle: *Provided,* That noth-

ing in this paragraph shall be construed to make unlawful any payment by an employer to any of his employees as compensation for their services as employees.

(c) The provisions of this section shall not be applicable (1) in respect to any money or other thing of value payable by an employer to any of his employees whose established duties include acting openly for such employer in matters of labor relations or personnel administration or to any representative of his employees, or to any officer or employee of a labor organization, who is also an employee or former employee of such employer, as compensation for, or by reason of, his service as an employee of such employer; (2) with respect to the payment or delivery of any money or other thing of value in satisfaction of a judgment of any court or a decision or award of an arbitrator or impartial chairman or in compromise, adjustment, or release of any claim, complaint, grievance, or dispute in the absence of fraud or duress; (3) with respect to the sale or purchase of an article or commodity at the prevailing market price in the regular course of business; (4) with respect to money deducted from the wages of employees in payment of membership dues in a labor organization: *Provided*, That the employer has received from each employee, on whose account such deductions are made, a written assignment which shall not be irrevocable for a period of more than one year, or beyond the termination date of the applicable collective agreement, whichever occurs sooner; (5) with respect to money or other thing of value paid to a trust fund established by such representative, for the sole and exclusive benefit of the employees of such employer, and their families and dependents (or of such employees, families, and dependents jointly with the employees of other employers making similar payments, and their families and dependents): *Provided*, That (A) such payments are held in trust for the purpose of paying, either from principal or income or both, for the benefit of employees, their families and dependents, for medical or hospital care, pensions on retirement or death of employees, compensation for injuries or illness resulting from occupational activity or insurance to provide any of the foregoing, or unemployment benefits or life insurance, disability and sickness insurance, or accident insurance; (B) the detailed basis on which such payments are to be made is specified in a written agreement with the employer, and employees and employers are equally represented in the administration of such fund, together with such neutral persons as the representatives of the employers and the representatives of employees may agree upon and in the event the employer and employee groups deadlock on the administration of such fund and there are no neutral persons empowered to break such deadlock, such agreement provides that the two groups shall agree on an impartial umpire to decide such dispute, or in event of their failure to agree within a reasonable length of time, an impartial umpire to decide such dispute shall, on petition of either group, be appointed by the district court of the United States for the district where the trust fund has its principal office, and shall also contain provisions for an annual audit of the trust fund, a statement of the results of which shall be available for inspection by interested persons at the principal office of the trust fund and at such other places as may be designated in such written agreement; and (C) such payments as are intended to be used for the purpose of providing pension or annuities for employees are made to a separate trust which provides that the funds held therein cannot be used for any purpose other than paying such pensions or annuities; or (6) with respect to money or other thing of value paid by any employer to a trust fund established by such representative for the purpose of pooled vacation, holiday, severance or similar benefits, or defraying costs of apprenticeship or other training program: *Provided*, That the requirements of clause (B) of the proviso to clause (5) of this subsection shall apply to such trust funds.

(d) Any person who willfully violates any of the provisions of this section shall, upon conviction thereof, be guilty of a misdemeanor and be subject to a fine of not more than $10,000 or to imprisonment for not more than one year, or both.

(e) The district courts of the United States and the United States courts of the Territories and possessions shall have jurisdiction, for cause shown, and subject to the provisions of section 17 (relating to notice to opposite party) of the Act entitled "An Act to supplement existing laws against unlawful restraints and monopolies, and for other purposes," approved October 15, 1914, as amended (U.S.C., title 28, sec. 381), to restrain violations of this section, without regard to the provisions of sections 6 and 20 of such Act of October 15, 1914, as amended (U.S.C., title 15, sec. 17, and title 29, sec. 52), and the provisions of the Act entitled "An Act to amend the Judicial Code and to define and limit the jurisdiction of courts sitting in equity, and for other purposes," approved March 23, 1932 (U.S.C., title 29, secs. 101–115).

(f) This section shall not apply to any contract in force on the date of enactment of this Act, until the expiration of such contract, or until July 1, 1948, whichever first occurs.

(g) Compliance with the restrictions contained in subsection (c)(5)(B) upon contributions to trust funds, otherwise lawful, shall not be applicable to contributions to such trust funds established by collective agreement prior to January 1, 1946, nor shall subsection (c)(5)(A) be construed as prohibiting contributions to such trust funds if prior to January 1, 1947, such funds contained provisions for pooled vacation benefits.

BOYCOTTS AND OTHER UNLAWFUL COMBINATIONS

SEC. 303. (a) It shall be unlawful, for the purpose of this section only, in an industry or activity affecting commerce, for any labor organization to engage in any activity or conduct defined as an unfair labor practice in section 8(b)(4) of the National Labor Relations Act, as amended.

(b) Whoever shall be injured in his business or property by reason of any violation of subsection (a) may sue therefor in any district court of the United States subject to the limitations and provisions of section 301 hereof without respect to the amount in controversy, or in any other court having jurisdiction of the parties, and shall recover the damages by him sustained and the cost of the suit.

RESTRICTION ON POLITICAL CONTRIBUTIONS

SEC. 304. Section 313 of the Federal Corrupt Practices Act, 1925 (U.S.C., 1940 edition, title 2, section 251; Supp. V, title 50, App., sec. 1509), as amended, is amended to read as follows:

SEC. 313. It is unlawful for any national bank, or any corporation organized by authority of any law of Congress to make a contribution or expenditure in connection with any election to any political office, or in connection with any primary election or political convention or caucus held to select candidates for any political office, or for any corporation whatever, or any labor organization to make a contribution or expenditure in connection with any election at which Presidential and Vice Presidential electors or a Senator or Representative in, or a Delegate or Resident Commissioner to Congress are to be voted for, or in connection with any primary election or political convention or caucus held to select candidates for any of the foregoing offices, or for any candidate, political committee, or other person to accept or receive any contribution prohibited by this section. Every corporation or labor organization which makes any contribution or expenditure in violation of this section shall be fined not more than $5,000; and every officer or director of any corporation, or officer of any labor organization, who consents to any contribution or expenditure by the corporation or labor organization, as the case may be, in violation of this section shall be fined not more than $1,000 or imprisoned for not more than one year, or both. For the purposes of this section "labor organization" means any organization of any kind, or any agency or employee representation committee or plan, in which employees participate and which exists for the purpose, in whole or in part, of dealing with employers concerning grievances, labor disputes, wages, rates of pay, hours of employment, or conditions of work.

TITLE IV

CREATION OF JOINT COMMITTEE TO STUDY AND REPORT ON BASIC PROBLEMS
AFFECTING FRIENDLY LABOR RELATIONS AND PRODUCTIVITY

*   *   *   *   *

TITLE V

DEFINITIONS

SEC. 501. When used in this Act—

(1) The term "industry affecting commerce" means any industry or activity in commerce or in which a labor dispute would burden or obstruct commerce or tend to burden or obstruct commerce or the free flow of commerce.

(2) The term "strike" includes any strike or other concerted stoppage of work by employees (including a stoppage by reason of the expiration of a collective-bargaining agreement) and any concerted slow-down or other concerted interruption of operations by employees.

(3) The terms "commerce," "labor disputes," "employer," "employee," "labor organization," "representative," "person," and "supervisor" shall have the same meaning as when used in the National Labor Relations Act as amended by this Act.

SAVING PROVISION

SEC. 502. Nothing in this Act shall be construed to require an individual employee to render labor or service without his consent, nor shall anything in this Act be construed to make the quitting of his labor by an individual employee an illegal act; nor shall any court issue any process to compel the performance by an individual employee of such labor or service, without his consent; nor shall the quitting of labor by an employee or employees in good faith because of abnormally dangerous conditions for work at the place of employment of such employee or employees be deemed a strike under this Act.

SEPARABILITY

SEC. 503. If any provision of this Act, or the application of such provision to any person or circumstance, shall be held invalid, the remainder of this Act, or the application of such provision to persons or circumstances other than those as to which it is held invalid, shall not be affected thereby.

THE LANDRUM-GRIFFIN ACT OF 1959 AS AMENDED

Popularly known as the "union reform law," the Landrum-Griffin Act contains seven titles, the first six regulating the internal affairs of unions and employers and the seventh amending the Taft-Hartley Act. Landrum-Griffin Title VII amendments to the Taft-Hartley Act are shown in that act above. What follows is the first six titles of the Landrum-Griffin Act.

LABOR-MANAGEMENT REPORTING AND
DISCLOSURE ACT OF 1959, AS AMENDED[1]

[Revised text showing in bold face new or amended language provided by Public Law 89–216, as enacted September 29, 1965, 79 Stat. 888]

AN ACT

To provide for the reporting and disclosure of certain financial transactions and administrative practices of labor organizations and employers, to prevent abuses in the administration of trusteeships by labor organizations, to provide standards with respect to the election of officers of labor organizations, and for other purposes.

Be it enacted by the Senate and House of Representatives of the United States of America in Congress assembled, That this Act may be cited as the "Labor-Management Reporting and Disclosure Act of 1959."

Declaration of Findings, Purposes, and Policy
(29 U.S.C. 401)

SEC. 2. (a) The Congress finds that, in the public interest, it continues to be the responsibility of the Federal Government to protect employees' rights to organize, choose their own representatives, bargain collectively, and otherwise engage in concerted activities for their mutual aid or protection; that the relations between employers and labor organizations and the millions of workers they represent have a substantial impact on the commerce of the Nation; and that in order to accomplish the objective of a free flow of commerce it is essential that labor organizations, employers, and their officials adhere to the highest standards of responsibility and ethical conduct in administering the

---

[1] Public Law 257, 86th Congress (73 Stat. 519–546), as amended by Public Law 216, 89th Congress (79 Stat. 888). This revised text has been prepared by the U.S. Department of Labor.

affairs of their organizations, particularly as they affect labor-management relations.

(b) The Congress further finds, from recent investigations in the labor and management fields, that there have been a number of instances of breach of trust, corruption, disregard of the rights of individual employees, and other failures to observe high standards of responsibility and ethical conduct which require further and supplementary legislation that will afford necessary protection of the rights and interests of employees and the public generally as they relate to the activities of labor organizations, employers, labor relations consultants, and their officers and representatives.

(c) The Congress, therefore, further finds and declares that the enactment of this Act is necessary to eliminate or prevent improper practices on the part of labor organizations, employers, labor relations consultants, and their officers and representatives which distort and defeat the policies of the Labor Management Relations Act, 1947, as amended, and the Railway Labor Act, as amended, and have the tendency or necessary effect of burdening or obstructing commerce by (1) impairing the efficiency, safety, or operation of the instrumentalities of commerce; (2) occurring in the current of commerce; (3) materially affecting, restraining, or controlling the flow of raw materials or manufactured or processed goods into or from the channels of commerce, or the prices of such materials or goods in commerce; or (4) causing diminution of employment and wages in such volume as substantially to impair or disrupt the market for goods flowing into or from the channels of commerce.

Definitions

(29 U.S.C. 402)

SEC. 3. For the purposes of titles I, II, III, IV, V, (except section 505), and VI of this Act—

(a) "Commerce" means trade, traffic, commerce, transportation, transmission, or communication among the several States or between any State and any place outside thereof.

(b) "State" includes any State of the United States, the District of Columbia, Puerto Rico, the Virgin Islands, American Samoa, Guam, Wake Island, the Canal Zone, and Outer Continental Shelf lands defined in the Outer Continental Shelf Lands Act (43 U.S.C. 1331–1343).

(c) "Industry affecting commerce" means any activity, business, or industry in commerce or in which a labor dispute would hinder or obstruct commerce or the free flow of commerce and includes any activity or industry "affecting commerce" within the meaning of the Labor Management Relations Act, 1947, as amended, or the Railway Labor Act, as amended.

(d) "Person" includes one or more individuals, labor organizations, partnerships, associations, corporations, legal representatives, mutual companies, joint-stock companies, trusts, unincorporated organizations, trustees, trustees in bankruptcy, or receivers.

(e) "Employer" means any employer or any group or association of employers engaged in an industry affecting commerce (1) which is, with respect to employees engaged in an industry affecting commerce, an employer within the meaning of any law of the United States relating to the employment of any employees or (2) which may deal with any labor organization concerning grievances, labor disputes, wages, rates of pay, hours of employment, or conditions of work, and includes any person acting directly or indirectly as an employer or as an agent of an employer in relation to an employee but does not include the United States or any corporation wholly owned by the Government of the United States or any State or political subdivision thereof.

(f) "Employee" means any individual employed by an employer, and includes any individual whose work has ceased as a consequence of, or in connection with, any current labor dispute or because of any unfair labor practice or because of exclusion or expulsion from a labor organization in any manner or for any reason inconsistent with the requirements of this Act.

(g) "Labor dispute" includes any controversy concerning terms, tenure, or conditions of employment, or concerning the association or representation of persons in negotiating, fixing, maintaining, changing, or seeking to arrange terms or conditions of employment, regardless of whether the disputants stand in the proximate relation of employer and employee.

(h) "Trusteeship" means any receivership, trusteeship, or other method of supervision or control whereby a labor organization suspends the autonomy otherwise available to a subordinate body under its constitution or bylaws.

(i) "Labor organization" means a labor organization engaged in an industry affecting commerce and includes any organization of any kind, any agency, or employee representation committee, group, association, or plan so engaged in which employees participate and which exists for the purpose, in whole or in part, of dealing with employers concerning grievances, labor disputes, wages, rates of pay, hours, or other terms or conditions of employment, and any conference, general committee, joint or system board, or joint council so engaged which is subordinate to a national or international labor organization, other than a State or local central body.

(j) A labor organization shall be deemed to be engaged in an industry affecting commerce if it—

(1) is the certified representative of employees under the provisions of the National Labor Relations Act, as amended, or the Railway Labor Act, as amended; or

(2) although not certified, is a national or international labor organization or a local labor organization recognized or acting as the representative of employees or an employer or employers engaged in an industry affecting commerce; or

(3) has chartered a local labor organization or subsidiary body which is representing or actively seeking to represent employees of employers within the meaning of paragraph (1) or (2); or

(4) has been chartered by a labor organization representing or actively seeking to represent employees within the meaning of paragraph (1) or (2) as the local or subordinate body through which such employees may enjoy membership or become affiliated with such labor organization; or

(5) is a conference, general committee, joint or system board, or joint council, subordinate to a national or international labor organization, which includes a labor organization engaged in an industry affecting commerce within the meaning of any of the preceding paragraphs of this subsection, other than a State or local central body.

(k) "Secret ballot" means the expression by ballot, voting machine, or otherwise, but in no event by proxy, of a choice with respect to any election or vote taken upon any matter, which is cast in such a manner that the person expressing such choice cannot be identified with the choice expressed.

(l) "Trust in which a labor organization is interested" means a trust or other fund or organization (1) which was created or established by a labor organization, or one or more of the trustees or one or more members of the governing body of which is selected or appointed by a labor organization, and (2) a primary purpose of which is to provide benefits for the members of such labor organization or their beneficiaries.

(m) "Labor relations consultant" means any person who, for compensation, advises or represents an employer, employer organization, or labor organization concerning employee organizing, concerted activities, or collective bargaining activities.

(n) "Officer" means any constitutional officer, any person authorized to perform the functions of president, vice president, secretary, treasurer, or other executive functions of a labor organization, and any member of its executive board or similar governing body.

(o) "Member" or "member in good standing" when used in reference to a labor organization, includes any person who has fulfilled the requirements for membership in such organization, and who neither has voluntarily withdrawn from membership nor has been expelled or suspended from membership after appropriate proceedings consistent with lawful provisions of the constitution and bylaws of such organization.

(p) "Secretary" means the Secretary of Labor.

(q) "Officer, agent, shop steward, or other representative," when used with respect to a labor organization, includes elected officials and key administrative personnel, whether elected or appointed (such as business agents, heads of departments or major units, and organizers who exercise substantial independent authority), but does not include salaried nonsupervisory professional staff, stenographic, and service personnel.

(r) "District court of the United States" means a United States district court and a United States court of any place subject to the jurisdiction of the United States.

TITLE I—BILL OF RIGHTS OF MEMBERS OF LABOR ORGANIZATIONS

Bill of Rights

(29 U.S.C. 411)

SEC. 101. (a)(1) EQUAL RIGHTS.—Every member of a labor organization shall have equal rights and privileges within such organization to nominate candidates, to vote in elections or referendums of the labor organization, to attend membership meetings and to participate in the deliberations and voting upon the business of such meetings, subjects to reasonable rules and regulations in such organization's constitution and bylaws.

(2) FREEDOM OF SPEECH AND ASSEMBLY.—Every member of any labor organization shall have the right to meet and assemble freely with other members; and to express any views, arguments, or opinions; and to express at meetings of the labor organization his views, upon candidates in an election of the labor organization or upon any business properly before the meeting, subject

to the organization's established and reasonable rules pertaining to the conduct of meetings: *Provided*, That nothing herein shall be construed to impair the right of a labor organization to adopt and enforce reasonable rules as to the responsibility of every member toward the organization as an institution and to his refraining from conduct that would interfere with its performance of its legal or contractual obligations.

(3) DUES, INITIATION FEES AND ASSESSMENTS.—Except in the case of a federation of national or international labor organizations, the rates of dues and initiation fees payable by members of any labor organization in effect on the date of enactment of this Act shall not be increased, and no general or special assessment shall be levied upon such members, except—

(A) in the case of a local organization, (i) by majority vote by secret ballot of the members in good standing voting at a general or special membership meeting, after reasonable notice of the intention to vote upon such question, or (ii) by majority vote of the members in good standing voting in a membership referendum conducted by secret ballot; or

(B) in the case of a labor organization, other than a local labor organization or a federation of national or international labor organizations, (i) by majority vote of the delegates voting at a regular convention, or at a special convention of such labor organization held upon not less than thirty days' written notice to the principal office of each local or constituent labor organization entitled to such notice, or (ii) by majority vote of the members in good standing of such labor organization voting in a membership referendum conducted by secret ballot, or (iii) by majority vote of the members of the executive board or similar governing body of such labor organization, pursuant to express authority contained in the constitution and bylaws of such labor organization: *Provided*, That such action on the part of the executive board or similar governing body shall be effective only until the next regular convention of such labor organization.

(4) PROTECTION OF THE RIGHT TO SUE.—No labor organization shall limit the right of any member thereof to institute an action in any court or in a proceeding before any administrative agency irrespective of whether or not the labor organization or its officers are named as defendants or respondents in such action or proceeding, or the right of any member of a labor organization to appear as a witness in any judicial administrative or legislative proceeding, or to petition any legislature or to communicate with any legislator: *Provided*, That any such member may be required to exhaust reasonable hearing procedures (but not to exceed a four-month lapse of time) within such organization, before instituting legal or administrative proceedings against such organizations or any officer thereof: *And provided further*, That no interested employer or employer association shall directly or indirectly finance, encourage, or participate in, except as a party, any such action, proceeding, appearance, or petition.

(5) SAFEGUARDS AGAINST IMPROPER DISCIPLINARY ACTION.—No member of any labor organization may be fined, suspended, expelled, or otherwise disciplined except for nonpayment of dues by such organization or by any officer thereof unless such member has been (A) served with written specific charges; (B) given a reasonable time to prepare his defense; (C) afforded a full and fair hearing.

(b) Any provision of the constitution and bylaws of any labor organization which is inconsistent with the provisions of this section shall be of no force or effect.

Civil Enforcement
(29 U.S.C. 412)

SEC. 102. Any person whose rights secured by the provisions of this title have been infringed by any violation of this title may bring a civil action in a district court of the United States for such relief (including injunctions) as may be appropriate. Any such action against a labor organization shall be brought in the district court of the United States for the district where the alleged violation occurred, or where the principal office of such labor organization is located.

Retention of Existing Rights
(20 U.S.C. 413)

SEC. 103. Nothing contained in this title shall limit the rights and remedies of any member of a labor organization under any State or Federal law before any court or other tribunal, or under the constitution and bylaws of any labor organization.

Right to Copies of Collective Bargaining Agreements
(29 U.S.C. 414)

SEC. 104. It shall be the duty of the secretary or corresponding principal officer of each labor organization, in the case of a local labor organization, to forward a copy of each collective bargaining agreement made by such labor organization with any employer to any employee who requests such a copy and whose rights as such employee are directly affected by such agreement, and in the case of a labor organization other than a local labor organization, to forward a copy of any such agreement to each constituent unit which has members directly affected by such agreement; and such officer shall maintain at the principal office of the labor organization of which he is an officer copies of any such agreement made or received by such labor organization, which copies shall be available for inspection by any member or by any employee whose rights are affected by such agreement. The provisions of section 210 shall be applicable in the enforcement of this section.

Information as to Act
(29 U.S.C. 415)

SEC. 105. Every labor organization shall inform its members concerning the provisions of this Act.

TITLE II—REPORTING BY LABOR ORGANIZATIONS, OFFICERS AND EMPLOYEES OF LABOR ORGANIZATIONS, AND EMPLOYERS

Report of Labor Organizations
(29 U.S.C. 431)

SEC. 201. (a) Every labor organization shall adopt a constitution and bylaws and shall file a copy thereof with the Secretary, together with a report, signed by its president and secretary or corresponding principal officers, containing the following information—

(1) the name of the labor organization, its mailing address, and any other address at which it maintains its principal office or at which it keeps the records referred to in this title;

(2) the name and title of each of its officers;

(3) the initiation fee or fees required from a new or transferred member and fees for work permits required by the reporting labor organization;

(4) the regular dues or fees of other periodic payments required to remain a member of the reporting labor organization; and

(5) detailed statements, or references to specific provisions of documents filed under this subsection which contain such statements, showing the provisions made and procedures followed with respect to each of the following: (A) qualifications for or restrictions on membership, (B) levying of assessments, (C) participation in insurance or other benefit plans, (D) authorization for disbursement of funds of the labor organization, (E) audit of financial transactions of the labor organization, (F) the calling of regular and special meetings, (G) the selection of officers and stewards and of any representatives to other bodies composed of labor organizations' representatives, with a specific statement of the manner in which each officer was elected, appointed, or otherwise selected, (H) discipline or removal of officers or agents for breaches of their trust, (I) imposition of fines, suspensions, and expulsions of members, including the grounds for such action and any provision made for notice, hearing, judgment on the evidence, and appeal procedures, (J) authorization for bargaining demands, (K) ratification of contract terms, (L) authorization for strikes, and (M) issuance of work permits. Any change in the information required by this subsection shall be reported to the Secretary at the time the reporting labor organization files with the Secretary the annual financial report required by subsection (b).

(b) Every labor organization shall file annually with the Secretary a financial report signed by its president and treasurer or corresponding principal officers containing the following information in such detail as may be necessary accurately to disclose its financial condition and operations for its preceding fiscal year—

(1) assets and liabilities at the beginning and end of the fiscal year;

(2) receipts of any kind and the sources thereof;

(3) salary, allowances, and other direct or indirect disbursements (including reimbursed expenses) to each officer and also to each employee who, during such fiscal year, received more than $10,000 in the aggregate from such labor organization and any other labor organization affiliated with it or with which it is affiliated, or which is affiliated with the same national or international labor organization;

(4) direct and indirect loans made to any officer, employee, or member, which aggregated more than $250 during the fiscal year, together with a statement of the purpose, security, if any, and arrangements for repayment;

(5) direct and indirect loans to any business enterprise, together with a statement of the purpose, security, if any, and arrangements for repayment; and

(6) other disbursements made by it including the purposes thereof; all in such categories as the Secretary may prescribe.

(c) Every labor organization required to submit a report under this title shall make available the information required to be contained in such report to all of its members, and every such labor organization and its officers shall be under a duty enforceable at the suit of any member of such organization in any State court of competent jurisdiction or in the district court of the United States for the district in which such labor organization maintains its principal office, to permit such member for just cause to examine any books, records, and accounts necessary to verify such report. The court in such action may, in its discretion, in addition to any judgment awarded to the plaintiff or plaintiffs, allow a reasonable attorney's fee to be paid by the defendant, and costs of the action.

(d) Subsections (f), (g), and (h) of section 9 of the National Labor Relations Act, as amended, are hereby repealed.

(e) Clause (i) of section 8(a) (3) of the National Labor Relations Act, as amended, is amended by striking out the following: "and has at the time the agreement was made or within the preceding twelve months received from the Board a notice of compliance with sections 9(f), (g), (h)."

Report of Officers and Employees of Labor Organizations
(29 U.S.C. 432)

SEC. 202. (a) Every officer of a labor organization and every employee of a labor organization (other than an employee performing exclusively clerical or custodial services) shall file with the Secretary a signed report listing and describing for his preceding fiscal year—

(1) any stock, bond, security, or other interest, legal or equitable, which he or his spouse or minor child directly or indirectly held in, and any income or any other benefit with monetary value (including reimbursed expenses) which he or his spouse or minor child derived directly or indirectly from, an employer whose employees such labor organization represents or is actively seeking to represent, except payments and other benefits received as a bona fide employee of such employer;

(2) any transaction in which he or his spouse or minor child engaged, directly or indirectly, involving any stock, bond, security, or loan to or from other legal or equitable interest in the business of an employer whose employees such labor organization represents or is actively seeking to represent;

(3) any stock, bond, security, or other interest, legal or equitable, which he or his spouse or minor child directly or indirectly held in, and any income or any other benefit with monetary value (including reimbursed expenses) which he or his spouse or minor child directly or indirectly derived from, any business a substantial part of which consists of buying from, selling or leasing to, or otherwise dealing with, the business of an employer whose employees such labor organization represents or is actively seeking to represent;

(4) any stock, bond, security, or other interest, legal or equitable, which he or his spouse or minor child directly or indirectly held in, and any income or any other benefit with monetary value (including reimbursed

expenses) which he or his spouse or minor child directly or indirectly derived from, a business any part of which consists of buying from, or selling
or leasing directly or indirectly to, or otherwise dealing with such labor
organization;

(5) any direct or indirect business transaction or arrangement between
him or his spouse or minor child and any employer whose employees his
organization represents or is actively seeking to represent, except work performed and payments and benefits received as a bona fide employee of such
employer and except purchases and sales of goods or services in the regular
course of business at prices generally available to any employee of such
employer; and

(6) any payment of money or other thing of value (including reimbursed expenses) which he or his spouse or minor child received directly or
indirectly from any employer or any person who acts as a labor relations
consultant to an employer, except payments of the kinds referred to in section 302(c) of the Labor Management Relations Act, 1947, as amended.

(b) The provisions of paragraphs (1), (2), (3), (4), and (5) of subsection (a) shall not be construed to require any such officer or employee to report his bona fide investments in securities traded on a securities exchange
registered as a national securities exchange under the Securities Exchange Act
of 1934, in shares in an investment company registered under the Investment
Company Act of 1940, or in securities of a public utility holding company
registered under the Public Utility Holding Company Act of 1935, or to report
any income derived therefrom.

(c) Nothing contained in this section shall be construed to require any
officer or employee of a labor organization to file a report under subsection (a)
unless he or his spouse or minor child holds or has held an interest, has received
income or any other benefit with monetary value or a loan, or has engaged in a
transaction described therein.

Report of Employers
(29 U.S.C. 433)

Sec. 203. (a) Every employer who in any fiscal year made—

(1) any payment or loan, direct or indirect, of money or other thing
of value (including reimbursed expenses), or any promise or agreement therefor, to any labor organization or officer, agent, shop steward, or other representative of a labor organization, or employee of any labor organization, except
(A) payments or loans made by any national or State bank, credit union, insurance company, savings and loan association or other credit institution and
(B) payments of the kind referred to in section 302(c) of the Labor Management Relations Act, 1947, as amended;

(2) any payment (including reimbursed expenses) to any of his employees, or any group or committee of such employees, for the purpose of
causing such employee or group or committee of employees to persuade other
employees to exercise or not to exercise, or as to the manner of exercising, the
right to organize and bargain collectively through representatives of their own
choosing unless such payments were contemporaneously or previously disclosed to such other employees;

(3) any expenditure, during the fiscal year, where an object thereof,

directly or indirectly, is to interfere with, restrain, or coerce employees in the exercise of the right to organize and bargain collectively through representatives of their own choosing, or is to obtain information concerning the activities of employees or a labor organization in connection with a labor dispute involving such employer, except for use solely in conjunction with an administrative or arbitral proceeding or a criminal or civil judicial proceeding;

(4) any agreement or arrangement with a labor relations consultant or other independent contractor or organization pursuant to which such person undertakes activities where an object thereof, directly or indirectly, is to persuade employees to exercise or not to exercise, or persuade employees as to the manner of exercising, the right to organize and bargain collectively through representatives of their own choosing, or undertakes to supply such employer with information concerning the activities of employees or a labor organization in connection with a labor dispute involving such employer, except information for use solely in conjunction with an administrative or arbitral proceeding or a criminal or civil judicial proceeding; or

(5) any payment (including reimbursed expenses) pursuant to an agreement or arrangement described in subdivision (4);

shall file with the Secretary a report, in a form prescribed by him, signed by its president and treasurer or corresponding principal officers showing in detail the date and amount of each such payment, loan, promise, agreement, or arrangement and the name, address, and position, if any, in any firm or labor organization of the person to whom it was made and a full explanation of the circumstances of all such payments, including the terms of any agreement or understanding pursuant to which they were made.

(b) Every person who pursuant to any agreement or arrangement with an employer undertakes activities where an object thereof is, directly or indirectly—

(1) to persuade employees to exercise or not to exercise, or persuade employees as to the manner of exercising, the right to organize and bargain collectively through representatives of their own choosing; or

(2) to supply an employer with information concerning the activities of employees or a labor organization in connection with a labor dispute involving such employer, except information for use solely in conjunction with an administrative or arbitral proceeding or a criminal or civil judicial proceeding;

shall file within thirty days after entering into such agreement or arrangement a report with the Secretary, signed by its president and treasurer or corresponding principal officers, containing the name under which such person is engaged in doing business and the address of its principal office, and a detailed statement of the terms and conditions of such agreement or arrangement. Every such person shall file annually, with respect to each fiscal year during which payments were made as a result of such an agreement or arrangement, a report with the Secretary, signed by its president and treatsurer or corresponding principal officers, containing a statement (A) of its receipts of any kind from employers on account of labor relations advice or services, designating the sources thereof, and (B) of its disbursements of any kind, in connection with such services and the purposes thereof. In each such case such information shall be set forth in such categories as the Secretary may prescribe.

(c) Nothing in this section shall be construed to require any employer or other person to file a report covering the services of such person by reason of his giving or agreeing to give advice to such employer or representing or agreeing to represent such employer before any court, administrative agency, or tribunal of arbitration or engaging or agreeing to engage in collective bargaining on behalf of such employer with respect to wages, hours, or other terms or conditions of employment or the negotiation of an agreement or any question arising thereunder.

(d) Nothing contained in this section shall be construed to require an employer to file a report under subsection (a) unless he has made an expenditure, payment, loan, agreement, or arrangement of the kind described therein. Nothing contained in this section shall be construed to require any other person to file a report under subsection (b) unless he was a party to an agreement or arrangement of the kind described therein.

(e) Nothing contained in this section shall be construed to require any regular officer, supervisor, or employee of an employer to file a report in connection with services rendered to such employer nor shall any employer be required to file a report covering expenditures made to any regular officer, supervisor, or employee of an employer as compensation for service as a regular officer, supervisor, or employee of such employer.

(f) Nothing contained in this section shall be construed as an amendment to, or modification of the rights protected by, section 8(c) of the National Labor Relations Act, as amended.

(g) The term "interfere with, restrain, or coerce" as used in this section means interference, restraint, and coercion which, if done with respect to the exercise of rights guaranteed in section 7 of the National Labor Relations Act, as amended, would, under section 8(a) of such Act, constitute an unfair labor practice.

Attorney-Client Communications Exempted
(29 U.S.C. 434)

Sec. 204. Nothing contained in this Act shall be construed to require an attorney who is a member in good standing of the bar of any State, to include in any report required to be filed pursuant to the provisions of this Act any information which was lawfully communicated to such attorney by any of his clients in the course of a legitimate attorney-client relationship.

Reports Made Public Information
(29 U.S.C. 435)

Sec. 205. (a)[2] The contents of the reports and documents filed with the Secretary pursuant to sections 201, 202, **203, and 211** shall be public information, and the Secretary may publish any information and data which he obtains pur-

---

[2] Prior to amendment by section 2(a) of Public Law 89–216, the first sentence of section 205(a) read as follows: "Sec. 205. (a) The contents of the reports and documents filed with the Secretary pursuant to sections 201, 202, and 203 shall be public information, and the Secretary may publish any information and data which he obtains pursuant to the provisions of this title."

suant to the provisions of this title. The Secretary may use the information and data for statistical and research purposes, and compile and publish such studies, analyses, reports, and surveys based thereon as he may deem appropriate.

(b)[3] The Secretary shall by regulation make reasonable provision for the inspection and examination, on the request of any person, of the information and data contained in any report or other document filed with him pursuant to section 201, 202, **203, or 211.**

(c)[4] The Secretary shall by regulation provide for the furnishing by the Department of Labor of copies of reports or other documents filed with the Secretary pursuant to this title, upon payment of a charge based upon the cost of the service. The Secretary shall make available without payment of a charge, or require any person to furnish, to such State agency as is designated by law or by the Governor of the State in which such person has his principal place of business or headquarters, upon request of the Governor of such State, copies of any reports and documents filed by such person with the Secretary pursuant to section 201, 202, **203, or 211,** or of information and data contained therein. No person shall be required by reason of any law of any State to furnish to any officer or agency of such State any information included in a report filed by such person with the Secretary pursuant to the provisions of this title, if a copy of such report, or of the portion thereof containing such information, is furnished to such officer or agency. All moneys received in payment of such charges fixed by the Secretary pursuant to this subsection shall be deposited in the general fund of the Treasury.

Retention of Records
(29 U.S.C. 436)

SEC. 206. Every person required to file any report under this title shall maintain records on the matters required to be reported which will provide in sufficient detail the necessary basic information and data from which the documents filed with the Secretary may be verified, explained or clarified, and checked for accuracy and completeness, and shall include vouchers, worksheets, receipts, and applicable resolutions, and shall keep such records available for examination for a period of not less than five years after the filing of the documents based on the information which they contain.

Effective Date
(29 U.S.C. 437)

SEC. 207. (a) Each labor organization shall file the initial report required

---

[3] Prior to amendment by section 2(b) of Public Law 89–216, section 205(b) read as follows: "(b) The Secretary shall by regulation make reasonable provision for the inspection and examination, on the request of any person, of the information and data contained in any report or other document filed with him pursuant to section 201, 202, or 203."

[4] Prior to amendment by section 2(c) of Public Law 89–216, the second sentence of section 205(c) read as follows: "The Secretary shall make available without payment of a charge, or require any person to furnish, to such State agency as is designated by law or by the Governor of the State in which such person has his principal place of business or headquarters, upon request of the Governor of such State, copies of any reports and documents filed by such person with the Secretary pursuant to section 201, 202, or 203, or of information and data contained therein."

under section 201(a) within ninety days after the date on which it first becomes subject to this Act.

(b)[5] Each person required to file a report under section 201(b), 202, 203(a), **the second sentence of section 203(b), or section 211** shall file such report within ninety days after the end of each of its fiscal years; except that where such person is subject to section 201(b), 202, 203(a), **the second sentence of section 203(b), or section 211,** as the case may be, for only a portion of such a fiscal year (because the date of enactment of this Act occurs during such person's fiscal year or such person becomes subject to this Act during its fiscal year) such person may consider that portion as the entire fiscal year in making such report.

Rules and Regulations
(29 U.S.C. 438)

SEC. 208. The Secretary shall have authority to issue, amend, and rescind rules and regulations prescribing the form and publication of reports required to be filed under this title and such other reasonable rules and regulations (including rules prescribing reports concerning trusts in which a labor organization is interested) as he may find necessary to prevent the circumvention or evasion of such reporting requirements. In exercising his power under this section the Secretary shall prescribe by general rule simplified reports for labor organizations or employers for whom he finds that by virtue of their size a detailed report would be unduly burdensome, but the Secretary may revoke such provision for simplified forms of any labor organization or employer if he determines, after such investigation as he deems proper and due notice and opportunity for a hearing, that the purposes of this section would be served thereby.

Criminal Provisions
(29 U.S.C. 439)

SEC. 209. (a) Any person who willfully violates this title shall be fined not more than $10,000 or imprisoned for not more than one year, or both.

(b) Any person who makes a false statement or representation of a material fact, knowing it to be false, or who knowingly fails to disclose a material fact, in any document, report, or other information required under the provisions of this title shall be fined not more than $10,000 or imprisoned for not more than one year, or both.

(c) Any person who willfully makes a false entry in or willfully conceals, withholds, or destroys any books, records, reports, or statements required to be kept by any provision of this title shall be fined not more than $10,000 or imprisoned for not more than one year, or both.

(d) Each individual required to sign reports under sections 201 and 203

---

[5] Prior to amendment by section 2(d) of Public Law 89–216, section 207(b) read as follows: "(b) Each person required to file a report under section 201(b), 202, 203(a), or the second sentence of 203(b) shall file such report within ninety days after the end of each of its fiscal years; except that where such person is subject to section 201(b), 202, 203(a), or the second sentence of 203(b), as the case may be, for only a portion of such a fiscal year (because the date of enactment of this Act occurs during such person's fiscal year or such person becomes subject to this Act during its fiscal year) such person may consider that portion as the entire fiscal year in making such report."

shall be personally responsible for the filing of such reports and for any statement contained therein which he knows to be false.

Civil Enforcement
(29 U.S.C. 440)

Sec. 210. Whenever it shall appear that any person has violated or is about to violate any of the provisions of this title, the Secretary may bring a civil action for such relief (including injunctions) as may be appropriate. Any such action may be brought in the district court of the United States where the violation occurred or, at the option of the parties, in the United States District Court for the District of Columbia.

Surety Company Reports[6]
(29 U.S.C. 441)

Sec. 211. Each surety company which issues any bond required by this Act or the Welfare and Pension Plans Disclosure Act shall file annually with the Secretary, with respect to each fiscal year during which any such bond was in force, a report, in such form and detail as he may prescribe by regulation, filed by the president and treasurer or corresponding principal officers of the surety company, describing its bond experience under each such Act, including information as to the premiums received, total claims paid, amounts recovered by way of subrogation, administrative and legal expenses and such related data and information as the Secretary shall determine to be necessary in the public interest and to carry out the policy of the Act. Notwithstanding the foregoing, if the Secretary finds that any such information cannot be practicably ascertained or would be uninformative, the Secretary may modify or waive the requirement for such information.

TITLE III—TRUSTEESHIPS

Reports
(29 U.S.C. 461)

Sec. 301. (a) Every labor organization which has or assumes trusteeship over any subordinate labor organization shall file with the Secretary within thirty days after the date of the enactment of this Act or the imposition of any such trusteeship, and semiannually therafter, a report, signed by its president and treasurer or corresponding principal officers, as well as by the trustees of such subordinate labor organization, containing the following information: (1) the name and address of the subordinate organization; (2) the date of establishing the trusteeship; (3) a detailed statement of the reason or reasons for establishing or continuing the trusteeship; and (4) the nature and extent of participation by the membership of the subordinate organization in the selection of delegates to represent such organization in regular or special conventions or other policy-determining bodies and in the election of officers of the labor organization which has assumed trusteeship over such subordinate organization. The initial report shall also include a full and complete account of the financial condition of such subordinate organization as of the time trusteeship was assumed over it. During the continuance of a trusteeship the labor organization

---

[6] Section 211 was added by section 3 of Public Law 89–216 (79 Stat. 888).

which has assumed trusteeship over a subordinate labor organization shall file on behalf of the subordinate labor organization the annual financial report required by section 201(b) signed by the president and treasurer or corresponding principal officers of the labor organization which has assumed such trusteeship and the trustees of the subordinate labor organization.

(b) The provisions of section 201(c), 205, 206, 208, and 210 shall be applicable to reports filed under this title.

(c) Any person who willfully violates this section shall be fined not more than $10,000 or imprisoned for not more than one year, or both.

(d) Any person who makes a false statement or representation of a material fact, knowing it to be false, or who knowingly fails to disclose a material fact, in any report required under the provisions of this section or willfully makes any false entry in or willfully withholds, conceals, or destroys any documents, books, records, reports, or statements upon which such report is based, shall be fined not more than $10,000 or imprisoned for not more than one year, or both.

(e) Each individual required to sign a report under this section shall be personally responsible for the filing of such report and for any statement contained therein which he knows to be false.

Purposes for Which a Trusteeship May Be Established
(29 U.S.C. 462)

SEC. 302. Trusteeships shall be established and administered by a labor organization over a subordinate body only in accordance with the constitution and bylaws of the organization which has assumed trusteeship over the subordinate body and for the purpose of correcting corruption or financial malpractice, assuring the performance of collective bargaining agreements or other duties of a bargaining representative, restoring democratic procedures, or otherwise carrying out the legitimate objects of such labor organization.

Unlawful Acts Relating to Labor Organization Under Trusteeship
(29 U.S.C. 463)

SEC. 303. (a) During any period when a subordinate body of a labor organization is in trusteeship, it shall be unlawful (1) to count the vote of delegates from such body in any convention or election of officers of the labor organization unless the delegates have been chosen by secret ballot in an election in which all the members in good standing of such subordinate body were eligible to participate or (2) to transfer to such organization any current receipts or other funds of the subordinate body except the normal per capita tax and assessments payable by subordinate bodies not in trusteeship: *Provided,* That nothing herein contained shall prevent the distribution of the assets of a labor organization in accordance with its constitution and bylaws upon the bona fide dissolution thereof.

(b) Any person who willfully violates this section shall be fined not more than $10,000 or imprisoned for not more than one year, or both.

Enforcement
(29 U.S.C. 464)

SEC. 304. (a) Upon the written complaint of any member or subordinate body of a labor organization alleging that such organization has violated the provisions of this title (except section 301) the Secretary shall investigate the complaint and if the Secretary finds probable cause to believe that such violation has occurred and has not been remedied he shall, without disclosing the identity of the complainant, bring a civil action in any district court of the United States having jurisdiction of the labor organization for such relief (including injunctions) as may be appropriate. Any member or subordinate body of a labor organization affected by any violation of this title (except section 301) may bring a civil action in any district court of the United States having jurisdiction of the labor organization for such relief (including injunctions) as may be appropriate.

(b) For the purpose of actions under this section, district courts of the United States shall be deemed to have jurisdiction of a labor organization (1) in the district in which the principal office of such labor organization is located, or (2) in any district in which its duly authorized officers or agents are engaged in conducting the affairs of the trusteeship.

(c) In any proceeding pursuant to this section a trusteeship established by a labor organization in conformity with the procedural requirements of its constitution and bylaws and authorized or ratified after a fair hearing either before the executive board or before such other body as may be provided in accordance with its constitution or bylaws shall be presumed valid for a period of eighteen months from the date of its establishment and shall not be subject to attack during such period except upon clear and convincing proof that the trusteeship was not established or maintained in good faith for a purpose allowable under section 302. After the expiration of eighteen months the trusteeship shall be presumed invalid in any such proceeding and its discontinuance shall be decreed unless the labor organization shall show by clear and convincing proof that the continuation of the trusteeship is necessary for a purpose allowable under section 302. In the latter event the court may dismiss the complaint or retain jurisdiction of the cause on such conditions and for such period as it deems appropriate.

Report to Congress
(29 U.S.C. 465)
Sec. 305. The Secretary shall submit to the Congress at the expiration of three years from the date of enactment of this Act a report upon the operation of this title.

Complaint by Secretary
(29 U.S.C. 466)
Sec. 306. The rights and remedies provided by this title shall be in addition to any and all other rights and remedies at law or in equity: *Provided,* That upon the filing of a complaint by the Secretary the jurisdiction of the district court over such trusteeship shall be exclusive and the final judgment shall be res judicata.

TITLE IV—ELECTIONS

Terms of Office; Election Procedures
(29 U.S.C. 481)
Sec. 401. (a) Every national or international labor organization, except a federation of national or international labor organizations, shall elect its officers

not less often than once every five years either by secret ballot among the members in good standing or at a convention of delegates chosen by secret ballot.

(b) Every local labor organization shall elect its officers not less often than once every three years by secret ballot among the members in good standing.

(c) Every national or international labor organization, except a federation of national or international labor organizations, and every local labor organization, and its officers, shall be under a duty, enforceable at the suit of any bona fide candidate for office in such labor organization in the district court of the United States in which such labor organization maintains its principal office, to comply with all reasonable requests of any candidate to distribute by mail or otherwise at the candidate's expense campaign literature in aid of such person's candidacy to all members in good standing of such labor organization and to refrain from discrimination in favor of or against any candidate with respect to the use of lists of members, and whenever such labor organizations or its officers authorize the distribution by mail or otherwise to members of campaign literature on behalf of any candidate or of the labor organization itself with reference to such election, similar distribution at the request of any other bona fide candidate shall be made by such labor organization and its officers, with equal treatment as to the expense of such distribution. Every bona fide candidate shall have the right, once within 30 days prior to an election of a labor organization in which he is a candidate, to inspect a list containing the names and last known addresses of all members of the labor organization who are subject to a collective bargaining agreement requiring membership therein as a condition of employment, which list shall be maintained and kept at the principal office of such labor organization by a designated official thereof. Adequate safeguards to insure a fair election shall be provided, including the right of any candidate to have an observer at the polls and at the counting of the ballots.

(d) Officers of intermediate bodies, such as general committees, system boards, joint boards, or joint councils, shall be elected not less often than once every four years by secret ballot among the members in good standing or by labor organization officers representative of such members who have been elected by secret ballot.

(e) In any election required by this section which is to be held by secret ballot a reasonable opportunity shall be given for the nomination of candidates and every member in good standing shall be eligible to be a candidate and to hold office (subject to section 504 and to reasonable qualifications uniformly imposed) and shall have the right to vote for or otherwise support the candidate or candidates of his choice, without being subject to penalty, discipline, or improper interference or reprisal of any kind by such organization or any member thereof. Not less than fifteen days prior to the election notice thereof shall be mailed to each member at his last known home address. Each member in good standing shall be entitled to one vote. No member whose dues have been withheld by his employer for payment to such organization pursuant to his voluntary authorization provided for in a collective bargaining agreement shall be declared ineligible to vote or be a candidate for office in such organization by reason of alleged delay or default in the payment of dues. The votes cast by members of each local labor organization shall be counted, and the results published, separately. The election officials designated in the constitution and bylaws or the secretary, if no other official is designated, shall preserve for one year the ballots and all other records pertaining to the election. The election shall be conducted in accordance with the constitution and bylaws of such organization insofar as they are not inconsistent with the provisions of this title.

(f) When officers are chosen by a convention of delegates elected by secret ballot, the convention shall be conducted in accordance with the constitution and bylaws of the labor organization insofar as they are not inconsistent with the provisions of this title. The officials designated in the constitution and bylaws or the secretary, if no other is designated, shall preserve for one year the credentials of the delegates and all minutes and other records of the convention pertaining to the election of officers.

(g) No moneys received by any labor organization by way of dues, assessment, or similar levy, and no moneys of an employer shall be contributed or applied to promote the candidacy of any person in an election subject to the provisions of this title. Such moneys of a labor organization may be utilized for notices, factual statements of issues not involving candidates, and other expenses necessary for the holding of an election.

(h) If the Secretary, upon application of any member of a local labor organization, finds after hearing in accordance with the Administrative Procedure Act that the constitution and bylaws of such labor organization do not provide an adequate procedure for the removal of an elected officer guilty of serious misconduct, such officer may be removed, for cause shown and after notice and hearing, by the members in good standing voting in a secret ballot conducted by the officers of such labor organization in accordance with its constitution and bylaws insofar as they are not inconsistent with the provisions of this title.

(i) The Secretary shall promulgate rules and regulations prescribing minimum standards and procedures for determining the adequacy of the removal procedures to which reference is made in subsection (h).

Enforcement

(29 U.S.C. 482)

SEC. 402. (a) A member of a labor organization—

(1) who has exhausted the remedies available under the constitution and bylaws of such organization and of any parent body, or

(2) who has invoked such available remedies without obtaining a final decision within three calendar months after their invocation,

may file a complaint with the Secretary within one calendar month thereafter alleging the violation of any provision of section 401 (including violation of the constitution and bylaws of the labor organization pertaining to the election and removal of officers). The challenged election shall be presumed valid pending a final decision thereon (as hereinafter provided) and in the interim the affairs of the organization shall be conducted by the officers elected or in other manner as its constitution and bylaws may provide.

(b) The Secretary shall investigate such complaint and, if he finds probable cause to believe that a violation of this title has occurred and has not been remedied, he shall, within sixty days after the filing of such complaint, bring a civil action against the labor organization as an entity in the district court of the United States in which such labor organization maintains its principal office to set aside the invalid election, if any, and to direct the conduct of an election or hearing and vote upon the removal of officers under the supervision of the Secretary and in accordance with the provisions of this title and such rules and regulations as the Secretary may prescribe. The court shall have power to take such action as it deems proper to preserve the assets of the labor organization.

(c) If, upon a preponderance of the evidence after a trial upon the merits, the court finds—

(1) that an election has not been held within the time prescribed by section 401, or

(2) that the violation of section 401 may have affected the outcome of an election,

the court shall declare the election, if any, to be void and direct the conduct of a new election under supervision of the Secretary and, so far as lawful and practicable, in conformity with the constitution and bylaws of the labor organization. The Secretary shall promptly certify to the court the names of the persons elected, and the court shall thereupon enter a decree declaring such persons to be the officers of the labor organization. If the proceeding is for the removal of officers pursuant to subsection (h) of section 401, the Secretary shall certify the results of the vote and the court shall enter a decree declaring whether such persons have been removed as officers of the labor organization.

(d) An order directing an election, dismissing a complaint, or designating elected officers of a labor organization shall be appealable in the same manner as the final judgment in a civil action, but an order directing an election shall not be stayed pending appeal.

Application of Other Laws

(29 U.S.C. 483)

Sec. 403. No labor organization shall be required by law to conduct elections of officers with greater frequency or in a different form or manner than is required by its own constitution or bylaws, except as otherwise provided by this title. Existing rights and remedies to enforce the constitution and bylaws of a labor organization with respect to elections prior to the conduct thereof shall not be affected by the provisions of this title. The remedy provided by this title for challenging an election already conducted shall be exclusive.

Effective Date

(29 U.S.C. 484)

Sec. 404. The provisions of this title shall become applicable—

(1) ninety days after the date of enactment of this Act in the case of a labor organization whose constitution and bylaws can lawfully be modified or amended by action of its constitutional officers or governing body, or

(2) where such modification can only be made by a constitutional convention of the labor organization, not later than the next constitutional convention of such labor organization after the date of enactment of this Act, or one year after such date, whichever is sooner. If no such convention is held within such one-year period, the executive board or similar governing

body empowered to act for such labor organization between conventions is empowered to make such interim constitutional changes as are necessary to carry out the provisions of this title.

TITLE V—SAFEGUARDS FOR LABOR ORGANIZATIONS

Fiduciary Responsibility of Officers of Labor Organizations
(29 U.S.C. 501)

SEC. 501. (a) The officers, agents, shop stewards, and other representatives of a labor organization occupy positions of trust in relation to such organization and its members as a group. It is, therefore, the duty of each such person, taking into account the special problems and functions of a labor organization, to hold its money and property solely for the benefit of the organization and its members and to manage, invest, and expend the same in accordance with its constitution and bylaws and any resolutions of the governing bodies adopted thereunder, to refrain from dealing with such organization as an adverse party or in behalf of an adverse party in any matter connected with his duties and from holding or acquiring any pecuniary or personal interest which conflicts with the interests of such organization, and to account to the organization for any profit received by him in whatever capacity in connection with transactions conducted by him or under his direction on behalf of the organization. A general exculpatory provision in the constitution and bylaws of such a labor organization or a general exculpatory resolution of a governing body purporting to relieve any such person of liability for breach of the duties declared by this section shall be void as against public policy.

(b) When any officer, agent, shop steward, or representative of any labor organization is alleged to have violated the duties declared in subsection (a) and the labor organization or its governing board or officers refuse or fail to sue or recover damages or secure an accounting or other appropriate relief within a reasonable time after being requested to do so by any member of the labor organization, such member may sue such officer, agent, shop steward, or representative in any district court of the United States or in any State court of competent jurisdiction to recover damages or secure an accounting or other appropriate relief for the benefit of the labor organization. No such proceeding shall be brought except upon leave of the court obtained upon verified application and for good cause shown which application may be made ex parte. The trial judge may allot a reasonable part of the recovery in any action under this subsection to pay the fees of counsel prosecuting the suit at the instance of the member of the labor organization and to compensate such member for any expenses necessarily paid or incurred by him in connection with the litigation.

(c) Any person who embezzles, steals, or unlawfully and willfully abstracts or converts to his own use, or the use of another, any of the moneys, funds, securities, property, or other assets of a labor organization of which he is an officer, or by which he is employed, directly or indirectly, shall be fined not more than $10,000 or imprisoned for not more than five years, or both.

Bonding
(29 U.S.C. 502)

SEC. 502. (a)[7] Every officer, agent, shop steward, or other representative

---

[7] Prior to amendment by section 1 of Public Law 89–216, the first sentence of section 502(a) read as follows: "Sec. 502.(a) Every officer, agent, shop steward, or other

or employee of any labor organization (other than a labor organization whose property and annual financial receipts do not exceed $5,000 in value), or of a trust in which a labor organization is interested, who handles funds or other property thereof shall be bonded **to provide protection against loss by reason of acts of fraud or dishonesty on his part directly or through connivance with others.** The bond of each such person shall be fixed at the beginning of the organization's fiscal year and shall be in an amount not less than 10 per centum of the funds handled by him and his predecessor or predecessors, if any, during the preceding final year, but in no case more than $500,000. If the labor organization or the trust in which a labor organization is interested does not have a preceding fiscal year, the amount of the bond shall be, in the case of a local labor organization, not less than $1,000, and in the case of any other labor organization or of a trust in which a labor organization is interested, not less than $10,000. Such bonds shall be individual or schedule in form, and shall have a corporate surety company as surety thereon. Any person who is not covered by such bonds shall not be permitted to receive, handle, disburse, or otherwise exercise custody or control of the funds or other property of a labor organization or of a trust in which a labor organization is interested. No such bond shall be placed through an agent or broker or with a surety company in which any labor organization or any officer, agent, shop steward, or other representative of a labor organization has any direct or indirect interest. Such surety company shall be a corporate surety which holds a grant of authority from the Secretary of the Treasury under the Act of July 30, 1947 (6 U.S.C. 6–13), as an acceptable surety on Federal bonds: *Provided,* **That when in the opinion of the Secretary a labor organization has made other bonding arrangements which would provide the protection required by this section at comparable cost or less, he may exempt such labor organization from placing a bond through a surety company holding such grant of authority.**

(b) Any person who willfully violates this section shall be fined not more than $10,000 or imprisoned for not more than one year, or both.

Making of Loans; Payment of Fines
(29 U.S.C. 503)

SEC. 503. (a) No labor organization shall make directly or indirectly any loan or loans to any officer or employee of such organization which results in a total indebtedness on the part of such officer or employee to the labor organization in excess of $2,000.

(b) No labor organization or employer shall directly or indirectly pay the fine of any officer or employee convicted of any willful violation of this Act.

(c) Any person who willfully violates this section shall be fined not more than $5,000 or imprisoned for not more than one year, or both.

Prohibition Against Certain Persons Holding Office
(29 U.S.C. 504)

SEC. 504. (a) No person who is or has been a member of the Communist

---

representative or employee of any labor organization (other than a labor organization whose property and annual financial receipts do not exceed $5,000 in value), or of a trust in which a labor organization is interested, who handles funds or other property thereof shall be bonded for the faithful discharge of his duties." Section 1 of Public Law 89–216 also added the proviso at the end of section 502(a).

Party[8] or who has been convicted of, or served any part of a prison term resulting from his conviction of, robbery, bribery, extortion, embezzlement, grand larceny, burglary, arson, violation of narcotics laws, murder, rape, assault with intent to kill, assault which inflicts grievous bodily injury, or a violation of title II or III of this Act, or conspiracy to commit any such crimes shall serve–

(1) as an officer, director, trustee, member of any executive board or similar governing body, business agent, manager, organizer, or other employee (other than as an employee performing exclusively clerical or custodial duties) or any labor organization, or

(2) as a labor relations consultant to a person engaged in an industry or activity affecting commerce, or as an officer, director, agent, or employee (other than as an employee performing exclusively clerical or custodial duties) of any group or association of employees dealing with any labor organization,

during or for five years after the termination of his membership in the Communist Party, or for five years after such conviction or after the end of such imprisonment, unless prior to the end of such five-year period, in the case of a person so convicted or imprisoned, (A) his citizenship rights, having been revoked as a result of such conviction, have been fully restored, or (B) the Board of Parole of the United States Department of Justice determines that such person's service in any capacity referred to in clause (1) or (2) would not be contrary to the purposes of this Act. Prior to making any such determination the Board shall hold an administrative hearing and shall give notice of such proceeding by certified mail to the State, county, and Federal prosecuting officials in the jurisdiction or jurisdictions in which such person was convicted. The Board's determination in any such proceeding shall be final. No labor organization or officer thereof shall knowingly permit any person to assume or hold any office or paid position in violation of this subsection.

(b) Any person who willfully violates this section shall be fined not more than $10,000 or imprisoned for not more than one year, or both.

(c) For the purposes of this section, any person shall be deemed to have been "convicted" and under the disability of "conviction" from the date of the judgment of the trial court or the date of the final sustaining of such judgment on appeal, whichever is the later event, regardless of whether such conviction occurred before or after the date of enactment of this Act.

Amendment to Section 302, Labor Management Relations Act, 1947

SEC. 505. Subsections (a), (b), and (c) of section 302 of the Labor Management Relations Act, 1947, as amended, are amended to read as follows:

"SEC. 302. (a) It shall be unlawful for any employer or association of employers or any person who acts as a labor relations expert, adviser, or consultant to an employer or who acts in the interest of an employer to pay, lend, or deliver, or agree to pay, lend, or deliver, any money or other thing of value—

"(1) to any representative of any of his employees who are employed in an industry affecting commerce; or

---

[8] The U.S. Supreme Court, on June 7, 1965, held unconstitutional as a bill of attainder the section 504 provision which imposes criminal sanctions on Communist party members for holding union office (*U.S.* v. *Brown,* 381 U.S. 437, 85 S. Ct. 1707).

"(2) to any labor organization, or any officer or employee thereof, which represents, seeks to represent, or would admit to membership, any of the employees of such employer who are employed in an industry affecting commerce; or

"(3) to any employee or group or committee of employees of such employer employed in an industry affecting commerce in excess of their normal compensation for the purpose of causing such employee or group or committee directly or indirectly to influence any other employees in the exercise of the right to organize and bargain collectively through representatives of their own choosing; or

"(4) to any officer or employee of a labor organization engaged in an industry affecting commerce with intent to influence him in respect to any of his actions, decisions, or duties as a representative of employees or as such officer or employee of such labor organization.

"(b)(1) It shall be unlawful for any person to request, demand, receive, or accept, or agree to receive or accept, any payment, loan, or delivery of any money or other thing of value prohibited by subsection (a).

"(2) It shall be unlawful for any labor organization, or for any person acting as an officer, agent, representative, or employee of such labor organization, to demand or accept from the operator of any motor vehicle (as defined in part II of the Interstate Commerce Act) employed in the transportation of property in commerce, or the employer of any such operator, any money or other thing of value payable to such organization or to an officer, agent, representative or employee thereof as a fee or charge for the unloading; or in connection with the unloading, of the cargo of such vehicle: *Provided*, That nothing in this paragraph shall be construed to make unlawful any payment by an employer to any of his employees as compensation for their services as employees.

"(c) The provisions of this section shall not be applicable (1) in respect to any money or other thing of value payable by an employer to any of his employees whose established duties include acting openly for such employer in matters of labor relations or personnel administration or to any representative of his employees, or to any officer or employee of a labor organization, who is also an employee or former employee of such employer, as compensation for, or by reason of, his service as an employee of such employer; (2) with respect to the payment or delivery of any money or other thing of value in satisfaction of a judgment of any court or a decision or award of an arbitrator or impartial chairman or in compromise, adjustment, settlement, or release of any claim, complaint, grievance, or dispute in the absence of fraud or duress; (3) with respect to the sale or purchase of an article or commodity at the prevailing market price in the regular course of business; (4) with respect to money deducted from the wages of employees in payment of membership dues in a labor organization: *Provided*, That the employer has received from each employee, on whose account such deductions are made, a written assignment which shall not be irrevocable for a period of more than one year, or beyond the termination date of the applicable collective agreement, whichever occurs sooner; (5) with respect to money or other thing of value paid to a trust fund established by such representative, for the sole and exclusive benefit of the employees of such employer, and their families and dependents (or of such employees, families, and dependents jointly with the employees of other employers making similar payments, and their families and dependents): *Provided,* That (A) such payments are held in trust for the purpose of paying, either from principal or income or both, for the benefit of employees, their families and dependents, for medical or hospital care, pensions on retirement or death of employees, compensation for injuries or illness resulting from occupational activity or insurance to provide any of the foregoing, or unemployment benefits or life insurance, disability and sickness insurance, or accident insurance; (B) the detailed basis on which such payments are to be made is specified in a written agreement with the employer, and employees and employers are equally represented in the administration of such fund together with such neutral persons as the representatives of the employers and the representatives of employees may agree upon and in the event of the employer and employee groups deadlock on the administration of such fund and there are no neutral persons empowered to break such deadlock, such agreement provides that the two groups shall agree on an impartial umpire to decide such dispute, or in event of their failure to agree within a reasonable length of time, an impartial umpire to decide such dispute shall, on petition of either group, be appointed by the district court of the United States for the district where the trust fund has its principal office, and shall also contain provisions for an annual audit of the trust fund, a statement of the results of which shall be available for inspection by interested persons at the principal office of the trust fund and at such other places as may be designated in such written agreement; and (C) such payments as are intended to be used for the purpose of providing pensions or annuities for employees are made to a separate trust which provides that the funds held therein cannot be used for any purpose other than paying such pensions or annuities; or (6) with respect to money or other thing of value paid by any employer to a trust fund established by such representative for the purpose of pooled vacation, holiday, severance or similar benefits, or defraying costs of apprenticeship or other training programs: *Provided,* That the requirements of clause (B) of the proviso to clause (5) of this subsection shall apply to such trust funds."

TITLE VI—MISCELLANEOUS PROVISIONS

Investigations
(29 U.S.C. 521)

Sec. 601. (a) The Secretary shall have power when he believes it necessary in order to determine whether any person has violated or is about to violate any provision of this Act (except title I or amendments made by this Act to other statutes) to make an investigation and in connection therewith he may enter such places and inspect such records and accounts and question such persons as he may deem necessary to enable him to determine the facts relative thereto. The Secretary may report to interested persons or officials concerning the facts required to be shown in any report required by this Act and concerning the reasons for failure or refusal to file such a report or any other matter which he deems to be appropriate as a result of such an investigation.

(b) For the purpose of any investigation provided for in this Act, the provisions of sections 9 and 10 (relating to the attendance of witnesses and the production of books, papers, and documents) of the Federal Trade Commission Act of September 16, 1914, as amended (15 U.S.C. 49, 50), are hereby made applicable to the jurisdiction, powers, and duties of the Secretary or any officers designated by him.

Extortionate Picketing
(29 U.S.C. 522)

SEC. 602. (a) It shall be unlawful to carry on picketing on or about the premises of any employer for the purpose of, or as part of any conspiracy or in furtherance of any plan or purpose for, the personal profit or enrichment of any individual (except a bona fide increase in wages or other employee benefits) by taking or obtaining any money or other thing of value from such employer against his will or with his consent.

(b) Any person who willfully violates this section shall be fined not more than $10,000 or imprisoned not more than twenty years, or both.

Retention of Rights Under Other Federal and State Laws
(29 U.S.C. 523)

SEC. 603. (a) Except as explicitly provided to the contrary, nothing in this Act shall reduce or limit the responsibilities of any labor organization or any officer, agent, shop steward, or other representative of a labor organization, or of any trust in which a labor organization is interested, under any other Federal law or under the laws of any State, and, except as explicitly provided to the contrary, nothing in this Act shall take away any right or bar any remedy to which members of a labor organization are entitled under such other Federal law or law of any State.

(b) Nothing contained in titles I, II, III, IV, V, or VI of this Act shall be construed to supersede or impair or otherwise affect the provisions of the Railway Labor Act, as amended, or any of the obligations, rights, benefits, privileges, or immunities of any carrier, employee, organization, representative, or person subject thereto; nor shall anything contained in said titles (except section 505) of this Act be construed to confer any rights, privileges, immunities, or defenses upon employers, or to impair or otherwise affect the rights of any person under the National Labor Relations Act, as amended.

Effect on State Laws
(29 U.S.C. 524)

SEC. 604. Nothing in this Act shall be construed to impair or diminish the authority of any State to enact and enforce general criminal laws with respect to robbery, bribery, extortion, embezzlement, grand larceny, burglary, arson, violation of narcotics laws, murder, rape, assault with intent to kill, or assault which inflicts grievous bodily injury, or conspiracy to commit any of such crimes.

Service of Process
(29 U.S.C. 525)

SEC. 605. For the purposes of this Act, service of summons, subpena, or other legal process of a court of the United States upon an officer or agent of a labor organization in his capacity as such shall constitute service upon the labor organization.

Administrative Procedure Act
(29 U.S.C. 526)

SEC. 606. The provisions of the Administrative Procedure Act shall be applicable to the issuance, amendment, or rescission of any rules or regulations, or any adjudication, authorized or required pursuant to the provisions of this Act.

Other Agencies and Departments
(29 U.S.C. 527)

SEC. 607. In order to avoid unnecessary expense and duplication of functions among Government agencies, the Secretary may make such arrangements or agreements for cooperation or mutual assistance in the performance of his functions under this Act and the functions of any such agency as he may find to be practicable and consistent with law. The Secretary may utilize the facilities or services of any department, agency, or establishment of the United States or of any State or political subdivision of a State, including the services of any of its employees, with the lawful consent of such department, agency, or establishment; and each department, agency, or establishment of the United States is authorized and directed to cooperate with the Secretary and, to the extent permitted by law, to provide such information and facilities as he may request for his assistance in the performance of his functions under this Act. The Attorney General or his representative shall receive from the Secretary for appropriate action such evidence developed in the performance of his functions under this Act as may be found to warrant consideration for criminal prosecution under the provisions of this Act or other Federal law.

Criminal Contempt
(29 U.S.C. 528)

SEC. 608. No person shall be punished for any criminal contempt allegedly committed outside the immediate presence of the court in connection with any civil action prosecuted by the Secretary or any other person in any court of the United States under the provisions of this Act unless the facts constituting such criminal contempt are established by the verdict of the jury in a proceeding in the district court of the United States, which jury shall be chosen and empaneled in the manner prescribed by the law governing trial juries in criminal prosecutions in the district courts of the United States.

Prohibition on Certain Discipline by Labor Organization
(29 U.S.C. 529)

SEC. 609. It shall be unlawful for any labor organization, or any officer, agent, shop steward, or other representative of a labor organization, or any employee thereof to fine, suspend, expel, or otherwise discipline any of its members for exercising any right to which he is entitled under the provisions of this Act. The provisions of section 102 shall be applicable in the enforcement of this section.

Deprivation of Rights Under Act by Violence
(29 U.S.C. 530)

SEC. 610. It shall be unlawful for any person through the use of force or violence, or threat of the use of force or violence, to restrain, coerce, or intimidate, or attempt to restrain, coerce, or intimidate any member of a labor organization for the purpose of interfering with or preventing the exercise of any right to which he is entitled under the provisions of this Act. Any person who willfully violates this section shall be fined not more than $1,000 or imprisoned for not more than one year, or both.

Separability Provisions

(29 U.S.C. 531)

SEC. 611. If any provision of this Act, or the application of such provision to any person or circumstances, shall be held invalid, the remainder of this Act or the application of such provision to persons or circumstances other than those as to which it is held invalid, shall not be affected thereby.

TITLE VII—AMENDMENTS TO THE LABOR MANAGEMENT RELATIONS ACT, 1947, AS AMENDED

(The Title VII amendments to the Labor Management Relations Act, 1947, as amended, have been incorporated into the text of the latter act as presented above.)

Appendix II
Executive Order 11491

This presidential executive order sets out the rules for rulemaking for almost all non-postal federal employees. Originally issued in 1969, it was subsequently amended in 1971 and 1975 as described in Chapter 16.

EXECUTIVE ORDER 11491
AS AMENDED
Labor-Management Relations in the Federal Service

whereas the public interest requires high standards of employee performance and the continual development and implementation of modern and progressive work practices to facilitate improved employee performance and efficiency; and

whereas the well-being of employees and efficient administration of the Government are benefited by providing employees an opportunity to participate in the formulation and implementation of personnel policies and practices affecting the conditions of their employment; and

whereas the participation of employees should be improved through the maintenance of constructive and cooperative relationships between labor organizations and management officials; and

whereas subject to law and the paramount requirements of public service, effective labor-management relations within the Federal service require a clear statement of the respective rights and obligations of labor organizations and agency management:

now, therefore, by virtue of the authority vested in me by the Constitution and statutes of the United States, including sections 3301 and 7301 of title 5 of the United States Code, and as President of the United States, I hereby direct that the following policies shall govern officers and agencies of the executive branch of the Government in all dealings with Federal employees and organizations representing such employees.

General Provisions

Sec. 1. *Policy.* (a)   Each employee of the executive branch of the Federal Government has the right, freely and without fear of penalty or reprisal, to form, join, and assist a labor organization or to refrain from any such activity, and each employee shall be protected in the exercise of this right. Except as otherwise expressly provided in this Order, the right to assist a labor organization extends to participation in the management of the organization and acting for the organization in the capacity of an organization representative, including presentation of its views to officials of the executive branch, the Congress, or other appropriate authority. The head of each agency shall take the action required to assure that employees in the agency are apprised of their rights under this section, and that no interference, restraint, coercion, or discrimination is practiced within his agency to encourage or discourage membership in a labor organization.

(b)   Paragraph (a) of this section does not authorize participation in the management of a labor organization or acting as a representative of such an organization by a supervisor, except as provided in section 24 of this Order, or by an employee when the participation or activity would result in a conflict or apparent conflict of interest or otherwise be incompatible with law or with the official duties of the employee.

Sec. 2. *Definitions.* When used in this Order, the term—

(a)   "Agency" means an executive department, a Government corporation, and an independent establishment as defined in section 104 of title 5, United States Code, except the General Accounting Office;

(b)   "Employee" means an employee of an agency and an employee of a nonappropriated fund instrumentality of the United States but does not include, for the purpose of exclusive recognition or national consultation rights, a supervisor, except as provided in section 24 of this Order;

(c)   "Supervisor" means an employee having authority, in the interest of an agency, to hire, transfer, suspend, lay off, recall, promote, discharge, assign, reward, or discipline other employees, or responsibility to direct them, or to evaluate their performance, or to adjust their grievances, or effectively to recommend such action, if in connection with the foregoing the exercise of authority is not of a merely routine or clerical nature, but requires the use of independent judgment,

(d)   "Guard" means an employee assigned to enforce against employees and other persons rules to protect agency property or the safety of persons on agency premises, or to maintain law and order in areas or facilities under Government control;

(e)   "Labor organization" means a lawful organization of any kind in which employees participate and which exists for the purpose, in whole or in part, of dealing with agencies concerning grievances, personnel policies and practices, or other matters affecting the working conditions of their employees; but does not include an organization which—

(1)   consists of management officials or supervisors, except as provided in section 24 of this Order;

(2)   assists or participates in a strike against the Government of the United States or any agency thereof or imposes a duty or obligation to conduct, assist, or participate in such a strike;

(3)   advocates the overthrow of the constitutional form of government in the United States; or

(4)   discriminates with regard to the terms or conditions of membership because of race, color, creed, sex, age, or national origin;

(f)   "Agency management" means the agency head and all management officials, supervisors, and other representatives of management having authority to act for the agency on any matters relating to the implementation of the agency labor-management relations program established under this Order;

(g)   "Council" means the Federal Labor Relations Council established by this Order;

(h)   "Panel" means the Federal Service Impasses Panel established by this Order; and

(i)   "Assistant Secretary" means the Assistant Secretary of Labor for Labor-Management Relations.

SEC. 3.   *Application.*   (a)   This Order applies to all employees and agencies in the executive branch, except as provided in paragraphs (b), (c) and (d) of this section.

(b)   This Order (except section 22) does not apply to—

(1)   the Federal Bureau of Investigation;

(2)   the Central Intelligence Agency;

(3)   any other agency, or office, bureau, or entity within an agency, which has as a primary function intelligence, investigative, or security work, when the head of the agency determines, in his sole judgment, that the Order cannot be applied in a manner consistent with national security requirements and considerations; or

(4)   any office, bureau or entity within an agency which has as a primary function investigation or audit of the conduct or work of officials or employees of the agency for the purpose of ensuring honesty and integrity in the discharge of their official duties, when the head of the agency determines, in his sole judgment, that the Order cannot be applied in a manner consistent with the internal security of the agency.

(5)   the Foreign Service of the United States: Department of State, United States Information Agency and Agency for International Development and its successor agency or agencies.

(c)   The head of an agency may, in his sole judgment, suspend any provision of this Order (except section 22) with respect to any agency installation or activity located outside the United States, when he determines that this is necessary in the national interest, subject to the conditions he prescribes.

(d)   Employees engaged in administering a labor-management relations law or this Order shall not be represented by a labor organization which also represents other groups of employees under the law or this Order, or which is affiliated directly or indirectly with an organization which represents such a group of employees.

Administration

SEC. 4.   *Federal Labor Relations Council.*   (a)   There is hereby established the Federal Labor Relations Council, which consists of the Chairman of the Civil Service Commission, who shall be chairman of the Council, the Secretary of Labor, the Director of the Office of Management and Budget, and such other officials of the executive branch as the President may designate from time to time. The Civil Service Commission shall provide administrative support and services to the Council to the extent authorized by law.

(b)   The Council shall administer and interpret this Order, decide major policy issues, prescribe regulations, and from time to time, report and make recommendations to the President.

(c)   The Council may consider, subject to its regulations—

(1)   appeals from decisions of the Assistant Secretary issued pursuant to section 6 of this Order, *except where, in carrying out his authority under section 11(d), he makes a negotiability determination, in which instance the party adversely affected shall have a right of appeal:*

(2)   appeals on negotiability issues as provided in section 11(c) of this Order;

(3)   exceptions to arbitration awards; and

(4)   other matters it deems appropriate to assure the effectuation of the purposes of this Order.

SEC. 5.   *Federal Service Impasses Panel.*   (a)   There is hereby established the Federal Service Impasses Panel as an agency within the Council. The Panel consists of at least three members appointed by the President, one of whom he designates as chairman. The Council shall provide the services and staff assistance needed by the Panel.

(b)   The Panel may consider negotiation impasses as provided in section 17 of this Order and may take any action it considers necessary to settle an impasse.

(c)   The Panel shall prescribe regulations needed to administer its function under this Order.

SEC. 6.   *Assistant Secretary of Labor for Labor-Management Relations.*
(a)   The Assistant Secretary shall—

(1)   decide questions as to the appropriate unit for the purpose of exclusive recognition and related issues submitted for his consideration;

(2)   supervise elections to determine where a labor organization is the choice of a majority of the employees in an appropriate unit as their exclusive representative, and certify the results;

(3)   decide questions as to the eligibility of labor organizations for national consultation rights under criteria prescribed by the Council;

(4)   decide unfair labor practice complaints (*including those where an alleged unilateral act by one of the parties requires an initial negotiability determination*) and alleged violations of the standards of conduct for labor organizations; and

(5)   decide questions as to whether a grievance is subject to a negotiated grievance procedure or subject to arbitration under an agreement *as provided in section 13(d) of this Order.*

(b)   In any matters arising under paragraph (a) of this section, the Assistant Secretary may require an agency or a labor organization to cease and desist from violations of this Order and require it to take such affirmative action as he considers appropriate to effectuate the policies of this Order.

(c)   In performing the duties imposed on him by this section, the Assistant Secretary may request and use the services and assistance of employees of other agencies in accordance with section 1 of the Act of March 4, 1915 (38 Stat. 1084, as amended; 31 U.S.C. § 686).

(d)   The Assistant Secretary shall prescribe regulations needed to administer his functions under this Order.

(e)   If any matters arising under paragraph (a) of this section involve the Department of Labor, the duties of the Assistant Secretary described in paragraphs (a) and (b) of this section shall be performed by a member of the Civil Service Commission designated by the Chairman of the Commission.

Recognition

Sec. 7.   *Recognition in general.*   (a)   An agency shall accord exclusive recognition or national consultation rights at the request of a labor organization which meets the requirements for the recognition or consultation rights under this Order.

(b)   A labor organization seeking recognition shall submit to the agency a roster of its officers and representatives, a copy of its constitution and by-laws, and a statement of its objectives.

(c)   When recognition of a labor organization has been accorded, the recognition continues as long as the organization continues to meet the requirements of this Order applicable to that recognition, except that this section does not require an election to determine whether an organization should become, or continue to be recognized as, exclusive representative of the employees in any unit or subdivision thereof within 12 months after a prior valid election with respect to such unit.

(d)   Recognition of a labor organization does not—

(1)   preclude an employee, regardless of whether he is in a unit of exclusive recognition, from exercising grievance or appellate rights estab-

lished by law or regulations, or from choosing his own representative in a grievance or appellate action, except when *the grievance is covered* under a negotiated procedure as provided in section 13;

(2)   preclude or restrict consultations and dealings between an agency and a veterans organization with respect to matters of particular interest to employees with veterans preference; or

(3)   preclude an agency from consulting or dealing with a religious, social, fraternal, professional or other lawful association, not qualified as a labor organization, with respect to matters or policies which involve individual members of the association or are of particular applicability to it or its members. Consultations and dealings under subparagraph (3) of this paragraph shall be so limited that they do not assume the character of formal consultation on matters of general employee-management policy *covering employees in that unit* or extend to areas where recognition of the interests of one employee group may result in discrimination against or injury to the interests of other employees.

(e)   ~~An agency shall establish a system for intra management communication and consultation with its supervisors or associations of supervisors. These communications and consultations shall have as their purposes the improvement of agency operations, the improvement of working conditions of supervisors, the exchange of information, the improvement of managerial effectiveness, and the establishment of policies that best serve the public interest in accomplishing the mission of the agency.~~

(f)   Informal recognition or formal recognition shall not be accorded.

SEC. 8.   [Revoked.]

SEC. 9.   *National consultation rights.*   (a)   An agency shall accord national consultation rights to a labor organization which qualifies under criteria established by the Federal Labor Relations Council as the representative of a substantial number of employees of the agency. National consultation rights shall not be accorded for any unit where a labor organization already holds exclusive recognition at the national level for that unit. The granting of national consultation rights does not preclude an agency from appropriate dealings at the national level with other organizations on matters affecting their members. An agency shall terminate national consultation rights when the labor organization ceases to qualify under the established criteria.

(b)   When a labor organization has been accorded national consultation rights, the agency, through appropriate officials, shall notify representatives of the organization of proposed substantive changes in personnel policies that affect employees it represents and provide an opportunity for the organization to comment on the proposed changes. The labor organization may suggest changes in the agency's personnel policies and have its views carefully considered. It may ~~confer~~ *consult* in person at reasonable times, on request, with appropriate officials on personnel policy matters, and at all times present its views thereon in writing. An agency is not required to consult with a labor organization on any matter on which it would not be required to meet and confer if the organization were entitled to exclusive recognition.

(c)   Questions as to the eligibility of labor organizations for national consultation rights may be referred to the Assistant Secretary for decision.

SEC. 10.   *Exclusive recognition.*   (a)   An agency shall accord exclusive recognition to a labor organization when the organization has been selected, in a secret ballot election, by a majority of the employees in an appropriate unit as their representative; *provided that this section shall not preclude an agency from according exclusive recognition to a labor organization, without an election, where the appropriate unit is established through the consolidation of existing exclusively recognized units represented by that organization.*

(b)   A unit may be established on a plant or installation, craft, functional, or other basis which will ensure a clear and identifiable community of interest among the employees concerned and will promote effective dealings and efficiency of agency operations. A unit shall not be established solely on the basis of the extent to which employees in the proposed unit have organized, nor shall a unit be established if it includes—

(1)   any management official or supervisor, except as provided in section 24;

(2)   an employee engaged in Federal personnel work in other than a purely clerical capacity; *or*

(3)   ~~any guard together with other employees; or~~

(4)   both professional and nonprofessional employees, unless a majority of the professional employees vote for inclusion in the unit. Questions as to the appropriate unit and related issues may be referred to the Assistant Secretary for decision.

(c)   ~~An agency shall not accord exclusive recognition to a labor organization as the representative of employees in a unit of guards if the organization admits to membership, or is affiliated directly or indirectly with an organization which admits to membership, employees other than guards.~~

(d)   All elections shall be conducted under the supervision of the Assistant Secretary, or persons designated by him, and shall be by secret ballot. Each employee eligible to vote shall be provided the opportunity to choose the labor organization he wishes to represent him, from among those on the ballot, or "no union", *except as provided in subparagraph (4) of this paragraph.* Elections may be held to determine whether—

(1)   a labor organization should be recognized as the exclusive representative of employees in a unit;

(2)   a labor organization should replace another labor organization as the exclusive representative; ~~or~~

(3)   a labor organization should cease to be the exclusive representative; *or*

(4)   *a labor organization should be recognized as the exclusive representative of employees in a unit composed of employees in units currently represented by that labor organization or continue to be recognized in the existing separate units.*

(e)   When a labor organization has been accorded exclusive recognition, it is the exclusive representative of employees in the unit and is entitled to act for and to negotiate agreements covering all employees in the unit. It is responsible for representing the interests of all employees in the unit without discrimination and without regard to labor organization membership. The labor organization shall be given the opportunity to be represented at formal discussions between management and employees or employee representatives concerning grievances, personnel policies and practices, or other matters affecting general working conditions of employees in the unit.

Agreements

SEC. 11.   *Negotiation of agreements.*   (a)   An agency and a labor organization that has been accorded exclusive recognition, through appropriate representatives, shall meet at reasonable times and confer in good faith with respect to personnel policies and practices and matters affecting working conditions, so far as may be appropriate under applicable laws and regulations, including policies set forth in the Federal Personnel Manual[,]; published agency policies and regulations *for which a compelling need exists under criteria established by the Federal Labor Relations Council and which are issued at the agency headquarters level or at the level of a primary national subdivision*[,]; a national or other controlling agreement at a higher level in the agency[,]; and this Order. They may negotiate an agreement, or any question arising thereunder; determine appropriate techniques, consistent with section 17 of this Order, to assist in such negotiation; and execute a written agreement or memorandum of understanding.

(b)   In prescribing regulations relating to personnel policies and practices and working conditions, an agency shall have due regard for the obligation imposed by paragraph (a) of this section. However, the obligation to meet and confer does not include matters with respect to the mission of an agency; its budget; its organization; the number of employees; and the numbers, types, and grades of positions or employees assigned to an organizational unit, work project or tour of duty; the technology of performing its work; or its internal security practices. This does not preclude the parties from negotiating agreements providing appropriate arrangements for employees adversely affected by the impact of realignment of work forces or technological change.

(c)   If, in connection with negotiations, an issue develops as to whether a proposal is contrary to law, regulation, controlling agreement, or this Order and therefore not negotiable, it shall be resolved as follows:

(1)   An issue which involves interpretation of a controlling agree-

ment at a higher agency level is resolved under the procedures of the controlling agreement, or, if none, under agency regulations;

(2)   An issue other than as described in subparagraph (1) of this paragraph which arises at a local level may be referred by either party to the head of the agency for determination;

(3)   An agency head's determination as to the interpretation of the agency's regulations with respect to a proposal is final;

(4)   A labor organization may appeal to the Council for a decision when—

(i)   it disagrees with an agency head's determination that a proposal would violate applicable law, regulation of appropriate authority outside the agency, or this Order, or

(ii)   it believes that an agency's regulations, as interpreted by the agency head, violate applicable law, regulation of appropriate authority outside the agency, or this Order[.], *or are not otherwise applicable to bar negotiations under paragraph (a) of this section.*

(d)   *If, as the result of an alleged unilateral change in, or addition to, personnel policies and practices or matters affecting working conditions, the acting party is charged with a refusal to consult, confer or negotiate as required under this Order, the Assistant Secretary may, in the exercise of his authority under section 6(a)(4) of the Order, make those determinations of negotiability as may be necessary to resolve the merits of the alleged unfair labor practice. In such cases the party subject to an adverse ruling may appeal the Assistant Secretary's negotiability determination to the Council.*

SEC. 12.   *Basic provisions of agreements.*   Each agreement between an agency and a labor organization is subject to the following requirements—

(a)   in the administration of all matters covered by the agreement, officials and employees are governed by existing or future laws and the regulations of appropriate authorities, including policies set forth in the Federal Personnel Manual; by published agency policies and regulations in existence at the time the agreement was approved; and by subsequently published agency policies and regulations required by law or by the regulations of appropriate authorities, or authorized by the terms of a controlling agreement at a higher agency level.

(b)   management officials of the agency retain the right, in accordance with applicable laws and regulations—

(1)   to direct employees of the agency;

(2)   to hire, promote, transfer, assign, and retain employees in positions within the agency, and to suspend, demote, discharge, or take other disciplinary action against employees;

(3)   to relieve employees from duties because of lack of work or for other legitimate reasons;

(4)   to maintain the efficiency of the Government operations entrusted to them;

(5) to determine the methods, means, and personnel by which such operations are to be conducted; and

(6) to take whatever actions may be necessary to carry out the mission of the agency in situations of emergency; and

(c) nothing in the agreement shall require an employee to become or to remain a member of a labor organization, or to pay money to the organization except pursuant to a voluntary, written authorization by a member for the payment of dues through payroll deductions.

The requirements of this section shall be expressly stated in the initial or basic agreement and apply to all supplemental, implementing, subsidiary, or informal agreements between the agency and the organization.

Sec. 13. *Grievance and arbitration procedures.* (a) An agreement between an agency and a labor organization shall provide a procedure, applicable only to the unit, for the consideration of grievances. ~~over the interpretation or application of the agreement. A negotiated grievance procedure may not cover any other matters, including matters for which statutory appeals procedures exist, and shall be the exclusive procedure available to the parties and the employees in the unit for resolving such grievances.~~ *The coverage and scope of the procedure shall be negotiated by the parties to the agreement with the exception that it may not cover matters for which a statutory appeal procedure exists and so long as it does not otherwise conflict with statute or this Order. It shall be the exclusive procedure available to the parties and the employees in the unit for resolving grievances which fall within its coverage.* However, any employee or group of employees in the unit may present such grievances to the agency and have them adjusted, without the intervention of the exclusive representative, as long as the adjustment is not inconsistent with the terms of the agreement and the exclusive representative has been given opportunity to be present at the adjustment.

(b) A negotiated procedure may provide for the arbitration of grievances. ~~over the interpretation or application of the agreement, but not over any other matters.~~ Arbitration may be invoked only by the agency or the exclusive representative. Either party may file exceptions to an arbitrator's award with the Council, under regulations prescribed by the Council.

~~(c) Grievances initiated by an employee or group of employees in the unit on matters other than the interpretation or application of an existing agreement may be presented under any procedure available for the purpose.~~

(d) Questions that cannot be resolved by the parties as to whether or not a grievance is on a matter ~~subject to the grievance procedure in an existing agreement, or is subject to arbitration under that agreement, may be referred to the Assistant Secretary for decision~~ *for which a statutory appeal procedure exists, shall be referred to the Assistant Secretary for decision. Other questions as to whether or not a grievance is on a matter subject to the grievance procedure in an existing agreement, or is subject to arbitration under that agreement, may by agreement of the parties be submitted to arbitration or may be referred to the Assistant Secretary for decision.*

(e) ~~No agreement may be established, extended or renewed after the effective date of this Order which does not conform to this section. However, this section is not applicable to agreements entered into before the effective date of this Order.~~

SEC. 14.   [Revoked.]

SEC. 15.   *Approval of agreements.*   An agreement with a labor organization as the exclusive representative of employees in a unit is subject to the approval of the head of the agency or an official designated by him. An agreement shall be approved *within forty-five days from the date of its execution* if it conforms to applicable laws, *the Order,* existing published agency policies and regulations (unless the agency has granted an exception to a policy or regulation) and regulations of other appropriate authorities. *An agreement which has not been approved or disapproved within forty-five days from the date of its execution shall go into effect without the required approval of the agency head and shall be binding on the parties subject to the provisions of law, the Order and the regulations of appropriate authorities outside the agency.* A local agreement subject to a national or other controlling agreement at a higher level shall be approved under the procedures of the controlling agreement, or, if none, under agency regulations.

Negotiation Disputes and Impasses

SEC. 16.   *Negotiation disputes.*   The Federal Mediation and Conciliation Service shall provide services and assistance to Federal agencies and labor organizations in the resolution of negotiation disputes. The Service shall determine under what circumstances and in what manner it shall proffer its services.

SEC. 17.   *Negotiation impasses.*   When voluntary arrangements, including the services of the Federal Mediation and Conciliation Service or other third-party mediation, fail to resolve a negotiation impasse, either party may request the Federal Service Impasses Panel to consider the matter. The Panel, in its discretion and under the regulations it prescribes, may consider the matter and may recommend procedures to the parties for the resolution of the impasse or may settle the impasse by appropriate action. Arbitration or third-party fact finding with recommendations to assist in the resolution of an impasse may be used by the parties only when authorized or directed by the Panel.

Conduct of Labor Organizations and Management

SEC. 18. *Standards of conduct for labor organizations.* (a) An agency shall accord recognition only to a labor organization that is free from corrupt influences and influences opposed to basic democratic principles. Except as provided in paragraph (b) of this section, an organization is not required to prove that it has the required freedom when it is subject to governing requirements adopted by the organization or by a national or international labor organization or federation of labor organizations with which it is affiliated or in which it participates, containing explicit and detailed provisions to which it subscribes calling for—

(1) the maintenance of democratic procedures and practices, including provisions for periodic elections to be conducted subject to recognized safeguards and provisions defining and securing the right of individual members to participation in the affairs of the organization, to fair and equal treatment under the governing rules of the organization, and to fair process in disciplinary proceedings;

(2) the exclusion from office in the organization of persons affiliated with Communist or other totalitarian movements and persons identified with corrupt influences;

(3) the prohibition of business or financial interests on the part of organization officers and agents which conflict with their duty to the organization and its members; and

(4) the maintenance of fiscal integrity in the conduct of the affairs of the organization, including provision for accounting and financial controls and regular financial reports or summaries to be made available to members.

(b) Notwithstanding the fact that a labor organization has adopted or subscribed to standards of conduct as provided in paragraph (a) of this section, the organization is required to furnish evidence of its freedom from corrupt influences or influences opposed to basic democratic principles when there is reasonable cause to believe that—

(1) the organization has been suspended or expelled from or is subject to other sanction by a parent labor organization or federation of organizations with which it had been affiliated because it has demonstrated an unwillingness or inability to comply with governing requirements comparable in purpose to those required by paragraph (a) of this section; or

(2) the organization is in fact subject to influences that would preclude recognition under this Order.

(c) A labor organization which has or seeks recognition as a representative of employees under this Order shall file financial and other reports, provide for bonding of officials and employees of the organization, and comply with trusteeship and election standards.

(d) The Assistant Secretary shall prescribe the regulations needed to effectuate this section. These regulations shall conform generally to the principles applied to unions in the private sector. Complaints of violations of this section shall be filed with the Assistant Secretary.

SEC. 19.   *Unfair labor practices.*   (a)   Agency management shall not—

(1)   interfere with, restrain, or coerce an employee in the exercise of the rights assured by this Order;

(2)   encourage or discourage membership in a labor organization by discrimination in regard to hiring, tenure, promotion, or other conditions of employment;

(3)   sponsor, control, or otherwise assist a labor organization, except that an agency may furnish customary and routine services and facilities under section 23 of this Order when consistent with the best interests of the agency, its employees, and the organization, and when the services and facilities are furnished, if requested, on an impartial basis to organizations having equivalent status;

(4)   discipline or otherwise discriminate against an employee because he has filed a complaint or given testimony under this Order;

(5)   refuse to accord appropriate recognition to a labor organization qualified for such recognition; or

(6)   refuse to consult, confer, or negotiate with a labor organization as required by this Order.

(b)   A labor organization shall not—

(1)   interfere with, restrain, or coerce an employee in the exercise of his rights assured by this Order;

(2)   attempt to induce agency management to coerce an employee in the exercise of his rights under this Order;

(3)   coerce, attempt to coerce, or discipline, fine, or take other economic sanction against a member of the organization as punishment or reprisal for, or for the purpose of hindering or impeding his work performance, his productivity, or the discharge of his duties owed as an officer or employee of the United States;

(4)   call or engage in a strike, work stoppage, or slowdown; picket an agency in a labor-management dispute; or condone any such activity by failing to take affirmative action to prevent or stop it;

(5)   discriminate against an employee with regard to the terms or conditions of membership because of race, color, creed, sex, age, or national origin; or

(6)   refuse to consult, confer, or negotiate with an agency as required by this Order.

(c)   A labor organization which is accorded exclusive recognition shall not deny membership to any employee in the appropriate unit except for failure to meet reasonable occupational standards uniformly required for admission, or for failure to tender initiation fees and dues uniformly required as a condition of acquiring and retaining membership. This paragraph does not preclude a labor organization from enforcing discipline in accordance with procedures under its constitution or by-laws which conform to the requirements of this Order.

(d) Issues which can properly be raised under an appeals procedure may not be raised under this section. Issues which can be raised under a grievance procedure may, in the discretion of the aggrieved party, be raised under that procedure or the complaint procedure under this section, but not under both procedures. Appeals or grievance decisions shall not be construed as unfair labor practice decisions under this Order nor as precedent for such decisions. All complaints under this section that cannot be resolved by the parties shall be filed with the Assistant Secretary.

Miscellaneous Provisions

SEC. 20. *Use of official time.* Solicitation of membership or dues, and other internal business of a labor organization, shall be conducted during the non-duty hours of the employees concerned. Employees who represent a recognized labor organization shall not be on official time when negotiating an agreement with agency management, except to the extent that the negotiating parties agree to other arrangements which may provide that the agency will either authorize official time for up to 40 hours or authorize up to one-half the time spent in negotiations during regular working hours, for a reasonable number of employees, which number normally shall not exceed the number of management representatives.

SEC. 21. *Allotment of dues.* (a) When a labor organization holds exclusive recognition, and the agency and the organization agree in writing to this course of action, an agency may deduct the regular and periodic dues of the organization from the pay of members of the organization in the unit of recognition who make a voluntary allotment for that purpose. Such an allotment is subject to the regulations of the Civil Service Commission, which shall include provision for the employee to revoke his authorization at stated six-month intervals. Such an allotment terminates when—

(1) the dues withholding agreement between the agency and the labor organization is terminated or ceases to be applicable to the employee: or

(2) the employee has been suspended or expelled from the labor organization.

~~(b) An agency may deduct the regular and periodic dues of an association of management officials or supervisors from the pay of members of the association who make a voluntary allotment for that purpose, when the agency and the association agree in writing to this course of action. Such an allotment is subject to the regulations of the Civil Service Commission.~~

SEC. 22. *Adverse action appeals.* The head of each agency, in accordance with the provisions of this Order and regulations prescribed by the

Civil Service Commission, shall extend to all employees in the competitive civil service rights identical in adverse action cases to those provided preference eligibles under section 7511–7512 of title 5 of the United States Code. Each employee in the competitive service shall have the right to appeal to the Civil Service Commission from an adverse decision of the administrative officer so acting, such appeal to be processed in an identical manner to that provided for appeals under section 7701 of title 5 of the United States Code. Any recommendation by the Civil Service Commission submitted to the head of an agency on the basis of an appeal by an employee in the competitive service shall be complied with by the head of the agency.

SEC. 23. *Agency implementation.* No later than April 1, 1970, each agency shall issue appropriate policies and regulations consistent with this Order for its implementation. This includes but is not limited to a clear statement of the rights of its employees under this Order; procedures with respect to recognition of labor organizations, determination of appropriate units, consultation and negotiation with labor organizations, approval of agreements, mediation, and impasse resolution; policies with respect to the use of agency facilities by labor organizations; and policies and practices regarding consultation with other organizations and associations and individual employees. Insofar as practicable, agencies shall consult with representatives of labor organizations in the formulation of these policies and regulations. other than those for the implementation of section 7(e) of this Order.

SEC. 24. *Savings clauses.* This Order does not preclude—

(1) the renewal or continuation of a lawful agreement between an agency and a representative of its employees entered into before the effective date of Executive Order No. 10988 (January 17, 1962); or

(2) the renewal, continuation, or initial according of recognition for units of management officials or supervisors represented by labor organizations which historically or traditionally represent the management officials or supervisors in private industry and which hold exclusive recognition for units of such officials or supervisors in any agency on the date of this Order.

SEC. 25. *Guidance, training, review and information.* (a) The Civil Service Commission, in conjunction with the Office of Management and Budget, shall establish and maintain a program for the policy guidance of agencies on labor-management relations in the Federal service and periodically review the implementation of these policies. The Civil Service Commission shall continuously review the operation of the Federal labor-management relations program to assist in assuring adherence to its provisions and merit system requirements; implement technical advice and information programs for the agencies; assist in the development of programs for training agency personnel and management officials in labor-management relations; and, from time to time, report to the Council on the state of the program with any recommendations for its improvement.

(b)   The Department of Labor and the Civil Service Commission shall develop programs for the collection and dissemination of information appropriate to the needs of agencies, organizations and the public.

SEC. 26.   *Effective date.*   This Order is effective on January 1, 1970, except sections 7(f) and 8 which are effective immediately. Effective January 1, 1970, Executive Order No. 10988 and the President's Memorandum of May 21, 1963, entitled Standards of Conduct for Employee Organizations and Code of Fair Labor Practices are revoked.

RICHARD NIXON

THE WHITE HOUSE
October 29, 1969

Indexes

Index of Authorities Cited

Subject Index

This book has been set in 10 and 9 point Janson, leaded 2 points. Part numbers are 24 point (large) Helvetica and part titles are 24 point (small) Helvetica Semibold. Chapter numbers are 30 point Helvetica Semibold and chapter titles are 18 point Helvetica. The size of the type page is 27 x 46½ picas.